Microsoft BackOffice 2.5:
The Complete Solution

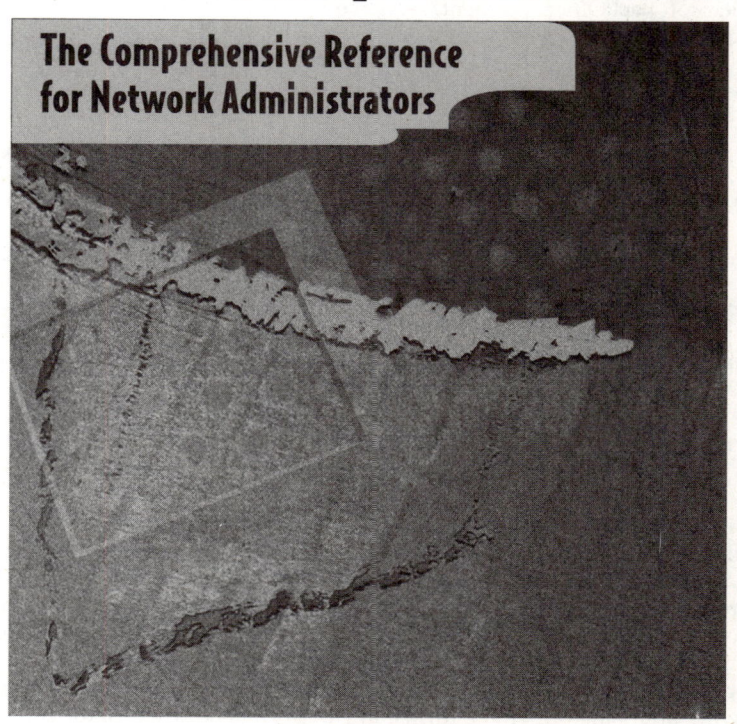

The Comprehensive Reference
for Network Administrators

Windows NT

Peter D. Hipson

VENTANA

Microsoft BackOffice 2.5: The Complete Solution
Copyright © 1997 by Peter D. Hipson

Library of Congress Cataloging-in-Publication Data
    Hipson, Peter D.
        Microsoft BackOffice 2.5 / Peter D. Hipson. — 1st ed.
            p. cm.
        Includes index.
        ISBN 1-56604-296-8
        1. Microsoft BackOffice. 2. Client/server computing. 3. Computer
    networks. I. Title
    QA76.9.C55W37 1997
    005.7'13—dc20   96-33467

                        CIP

First Edition 9 8 7 6 5 4 3 2 1

Printed in the United States of America

Ventana Communications Group, Inc.
P.O. Box 13964
Research Triangle Park, NC 27709-3964
919.544.9404
FAX 919.544.9472
http://www.vmedia.com

Limits of Liability & Disclaimer of Warranty

Trademarks

Vice President of Content Development
Karen A. Bluestein

Director of Acquisitions and Development
Robert B. Kern

Managing Editor
Lois J. Principe

Production Manager
John Cotterman

Technology Operations Manager
Kerry L. B. Foster

Brand Manager
Jamie Jaeger Fiocco

Creative Services Manager
Diane Lennox

Art Director
Marcia Webb

Acquisitions Editor
Neweleen A. Trebnik

Project Editor
Judith F. Wilson

Development Editor
Michelle Corbin Nichols

Copy Editors
Judy Flynn
Susan Christophersen

CD-ROM Specialists
Patrick Bragg
Ginny Phelps

Technical Director
Dan Brown

Technical Reviewer
Russ Mullen

Desktop Publisher
Kristin Miller

Proofreader
Tom Collins

Indexer
Richard T. Evans, Infodex

Cover Illustrator
Alice Whicker Heitchue
Laura Stalzer

About the Author

Peter D. Hipson is a developer, consultant, and author. His work is mostly in the Microsoft Windows arena, both at the programming and user levels. Peter has tested a variety of Microsoft products as a member of the beta-test teams for QuickC for Windows; Visual C++ 1.0, 1.5, 2.0, and 4.0; Windows 3.0 and 3.1; Windows for Workgroups 3.1 and 3.11; Windows 95; and Windows NT 3.5, 3.51, and 4.0 Workgroup and Server.

Peter is the author of *The Windows NT 4 Server Book* (Ventana), as well as *Advanced C*, *What Every Visual C++ 2 Programmer Should Know*, *Database Developer's Guide with Visual C++*, *Visual C++ Developer's Guide*, and *Using QuickC for Windows*. He has also contributed to *Programming Windows 95 Unleashed*, and other titles as an uncredited contract author. Peter often speaks at conferences and user groups including Boston University's WinDev Windows developer's conference, held each year in Boston, Massachusetts and in Santa Clara, California.

Peter is a member of the Board of Directors of ClubWin, a peer-level support group that provides technical support and advocacy for Windows, based on experience in beta testing and broad industry knowledge. He is also a team leader for ClubIE, where he heads Team-9.

When not banging on the keyboard or doing other difficult work, Peter can usually be found cn his road bicycle, or perhaps sailing his catamaran.

Please feel free to contact Peter via e-mail phipson@acm.org.

Acknowledgments

This book is not just the product of the author—far from it! A fine team effort on the part of Ventana, the author, and a few people who just happened to be in the wrong place at the right time are what made this book possible.

Ventana has one of the world's best editing and management teams. Neweleen Trebnik (who worked with me on my very first book, some years back) did wonderfully as my acquisitions editor.

Judy Wilson kept me on track, jumping in as the book's project editor. Without Judy's hard work, this book would not have been nearly as good as it is.

Michelle Nichols' work as development editor was invaluable in making this book a quality product. Never one to give up, Michelle would keep after me to make sure that everything was just right.

Judy Flynn and Susan Christophersen served well as the copy editors. Russ Mullen made sure the book was accurate. Not much escaped his sharp eyes.

A special thanks to Lisa Bucki, who worked as development editor at the beginning of this book and gave me good direction. Maybe someday Lisa and I will finish a book together, too! As with my last book, Lisa's work was greatly appreciated—more than she realizes.

Thanks to Patrick Bragg and Ginny Phelps, CD-ROM Specialists, for their work on the CD. They rounded up products to make the CD interesting.

Away from Ventana, many friends helped. Some of these people don't even realize their assistance. If nothing else, they are leaders in their fields, and their help, no matter what the circumstances, was greatly appreciated!

Bryan Waters' help with this book was immeasurable. Bryan provided the incentive to get the book done, so thanks, Bryan!

Pedro P. Pokaloff III's assistance in the use of Windows NT 4 Server as an ISP made the chapters on using Windows NT with the Internet a reality. Felix Kasza provided a lot of valuable information. Barry Wadman provided good advice and encouragement. Thanks also to Microsoft for their help and support.

Special thanks to Lisa Swayne, my agent. Without Lisa I would never have written this book.

Last and certainly not least, my thanks to Nang, my wife, for forgiving me for another book's worth of understanding. Though I never leave home, Nang certainly doesn't see much of me when I am writing a book.

Thank you all!

Dedication

This book is dedicated to my sister, Kathleen Mary Hipson.

Contents

SECTION II: Microsoft SQL Server 6.5

SECTION VII: Microsoft SNA Server

Introduction

As Windows NT 4 Server becomes the de facto standard for network servers, add-on products become more and more important. Microsoft has produced a suite of server products, called Microsoft BackOffice, that has become one of the most common tools for implementing comprehensive server installations.

Microsoft BackOffice 2.5 is Microsoft's newest release of BackOffice. Microsoft included Proxy Server and updated many of the individual servers, making Microsoft BackOffice 2.5 a new and somewhat different product.

Improved user interfaces and new capabilities and functionalities all make this, the newest version of Microsoft BackOffice, both interesting and better. Though existing users of Microsoft BackOffice will find many differences, experience gained with earlier versions will prove to be valuable in understanding this new release of the product.

Is This Book for You?

Most of us read a book's introduction standing in a bookstore. By doing so, we are trying to determine if the book is what we are looking for. Is the author's coverage of the topic sufficient? Is the book too advanced, or is it too basic? And the basic question: Should I buy this book? These are difficult questions to answer by just reading a book's introduction and maybe scanning a chapter or two.

I've written this book to meet a specific requirement—that a reader who has some experience with both networking and Microsoft Windows will be able to install the Microsoft BackOffice products and make them usable with a minimum amount of effort. This book covers a lot of ground. In addition to a section on Windows NT 4 Server, there is coverage of the six major components that make up BackOffice.

If you are planning to install and configure one or more of the BackOffice components, then this book is for you. If you don't have any Microsoft Windows experience, you will have to work harder (you might consider reading a more basic, introductory Windows book in *addition* to this book). The same is true for networking. There is only a small amount of introductory networking information in this book—I have assumed that the reader will have networking experience. If you have substantial experience with both Windows NT and networking in general, but are just learning about Microsoft BackOffice, then again this book is for you!

Generally each section of this book stands on its own. You don't need to read it from cover to cover. You will, however, want to read all the sections about the components of BackOffice that are interrelated. For instance, Microsoft Systems Management Server (SMS) uses Microsoft SQL Server to manage data. Users of SMS will need to study the section on Microsoft SQL Server as well.

The Internet is the "in" thing today. Both this book, and Microsoft BackOffice reflect this viewpoint. Windows NT 4 Server and Internet Information Server make interacting with the Internet easy. Microsoft Proxy Server serves as a powerful software solution to the need for a firewall to isolate an organization's internal network from the hazards of the Internet.

Hardware & Software Requirements

Microsoft BackOffice has a few basic hardware requirements. A computer capable of running Windows NT 4 Server will be necessary. A typical lower-end platform would be an Intel-based system with a Pentium 100 or better and at least 32MB of RAM. A better lower-end platform would be a Pentium 166 with about 64MB of RAM. A middle-of-the-line system for Windows NT 4 Server would be a Pentium 200, or a Pentium Pro uniprocessor, with between 64MB and 128MB of RAM. A high-end system would easily be a multiprocessor system with between 128MB and 1GB of RAM.

Disk space requirements vary greatly. The author's system has about 10GB of hard disk space. I would not be honest if I didn't mention that things get tight when installing some of the BackOffice components! Were I to have had a larger organization, I would probably want to have between 7GB and 30GB of high-speed (SCSI) hard disk space available on my system.

A CD-ROM drive is also necessary. There is no reason not to choose one of the inexpensive IDE interface CD-ROM drives for local use (to install the BackOffice components, for example). Resist the urge to share, to a significant number of users, a CD-ROM drive. CD-ROMs were never intended for a multiuser environment and only specially designed CD-ROM drives will have sufficient performance to support more than a few (that's usually one or two) users.

Everything else on the Windows NT 4 Server computer is what you would expect for a high-end computer: fast video (such as the Matrox MGA video adapter) with a monitor to match, a modem (if connections to a dial-up computer are necessary), and of course, a sound card.

What's Inside

This book shows you how easy it is to use the Microsoft BackOffice suite of server products. The book has seven sections.

Section I, "Windows NT 4 Server," introduces you to Windows NT 4 Server. Use Section I as a tutorial for installing the Windows NT 4 Server components you need.

Section II, "Microsoft SQL Server 6.5," gets you acquainted with SQL Server, Microsoft's premier client/server database system. Use Section II to familiarize yourself with Microsoft SQL Server, which is used with several of the other Microsoft BackOffice products.

Section III, "Microsoft Systems Management Server (SMS)," describes Microsoft SMS. This server is used to help manage large networks with clients running Microsoft operating systems and environments.

Section IV, "Microsoft Proxy Server," introduces the new Microsoft Proxy Server. The Proxy Server provides necessary isolation between an organization's internal network and the Internet. Microsoft Proxy Server is a valuable tool for managing and securing Internet connections.

Section V, "Microsoft Exchange Server," provides information to help get Microsoft Exchange Server up and running. One of Microsoft's larger (and somewhat intimidating) products, Microsoft Exchange Server is actually not difficult to configure and make operational. Microsoft Exchange Server provides connections to many other mail systems, including an Internet connector, and connections to commonly used corporate e-mail systems.

Section VI, "Microsoft Internet Information Server (IIS)," introduces Microsoft's suite of Internet servers: Web, FTP, and Gopher. Many organizations establishing an Internet presence will want to investigate Microsoft IIS closely.

Section VII, "Microsoft SNA Server," introduces the newest version of Microsoft's SNA Server. The SNA Server is used to connect microcomputer networks and workstations to IBM-compatible mainframe and minicomputers.

The CD-ROM's Contents

This book's Companion CD-ROM contains a number of items, including a number of programs both from Microsoft and from other software suppliers. For more information about the CD-ROM, please refer to Appendix A.

Online Updates

As we all know, the Internet and its related technologies are constantly changing. As hard as we've tried to make the information in this book current, the truth is that some of it may need updating soon after the book goes to press. Ventana provides an easy way to meet this challenge, with the Online Updates for *Microsoft BackOffice 2.5: The Complete Solution*. You can access this valuable resource via Ventana's World Wide Web site at http://www.vmedia.com/updates. Once there, you'll find updated material relevant to this book.

Before You Go On

If possible, find a spare computer on which to install a test copy of Windows NT 4 Server and Microsoft BackOffice. By creating a test installation of these products, you can test your processing and security requirements, experiment with the new features and functionality of Microsoft BackOffice, and start designing and building your intranet or Internet infrastructures.

Consider how your organization will be using BackOffice. BackOffice and Windows NT 4 Server are becoming the products of choice to create connectivity to other networks. Internet connections are being moved from more-difficult-to-manage UNIX systems to Windows NT-based servers at a surprising rate. Microcomputer networks, once the sole domain of Novell, are more and more becoming Windows networks— with a Windows NT Server emulating the Novell NetWare server. With only a very few exceptions, a single Windows NT 4 Server will run both the network operating system and all the ancillary products such as the database server, e-mail servers, and the ever-present Internet connectivity.

If you have already purchased this book, excellent. If you're still browsing in the bookstore, drop this one in your shopping basket! I would like to take this opportunity to express my thanks for your confidence in this book. There is one thing that *does* make a book better, and that's feedback from you, the reader. Please always feel free to contact me at my e-mail address should you have any questions, comments, or especially criticisms of this book. My e-mail address is phipson@acm.org, and I make it a point to respond to all e-mail.

Many thanks, and good luck with your BackOffice experience!

Peter

Windows NT Server

Overview of Microsoft BackOffice 2.5

Microsoft BackOffice 2.5 is a collection of servers, all of which run under Windows NT 4 Server, which is itself a component of BackOffice. Every other component in BackOffice relies on Windows NT 4 Server; that is, Windows NT 4 Server must be installed to use the other components found in Microsoft BackOffice.

This chapter will introduce Microsoft BackOffice and Windows NT 4 Server.

Microsoft BackOffice is available in several configurations:

- An ISP version (the Microsoft project, code-named Normandy), which is intended to be used (primarily) by organizations who are offering ISP services or organizations who have a substantial presence on the Internet.

- A package aimed at small to medium-sized businesses. This version of Microsoft BackOffice offers general functionality with both Internet- and LAN-based products.

- As individual servers, which consist of any of the servers that are components of the other versions of Microsoft BackOffice.

Tip

The EUL (End User License) included with the Microsoft BackOffice package allows you to install BackOffice components on a single machine. If you purchase the BackOffice package that includes Windows NT 4 Server, Systems Management Server (SMS), and Exchange Server, you must install each of these components on the same system.

What Is Microsoft BackOffice?

Microsoft BackOffice consists of collections of Microsoft's Windows NT servers and services (such as Microsoft SQL Server). Because they are placed in a single package, purchasing Microsoft BackOffice 2.5 will typically provide more product for less expenditure. Microsoft BackOffice has been oriented toward general businesses.

In 1997, Microsoft is creating a new family of Microsoft BackOffice products oriented toward organizations providing ISP services; however, this new version will not be covered in this book.

In addition to Windows NT 4 Server, the Microsoft BackOffice family of servers includes the following components:

- **Microsoft Conference Server**—a high-performance system that allows users to interactively conference (chat). Features include a locator to find other users while online, the ability to launch conferencing applications (such as Microsoft NetMeeting), and support for shared applications and Internet-telephone-type voice applications.

- **Microsoft Content Replication System**—used by Web sites to replicate content between two or more Web servers. Multiple Web servers are used to share loading for Web sites that are very popular.

- **Microsoft Exchange Server**—a high-performance, flexible, e-mail server for Windows NT 4 Server. Meeting Internet standards, and extensibility, make Microsoft Exchange Server a logical choice for most electronic messaging systems.

- **Microsoft Merchant Server**—a commerce product used to promote and sell products over the Internet. Substantial security features and a powerful interface with Microsoft SQL Server make the Microsoft Merchant Server a very effective solution to selling products over the Internet.

- **Microsoft Personalization System**—allows a user to customize Web pages (when using Microsoft Internet Information Server) to allow custom user interaction.

- **Microsoft Proxy Server**—provides Internet access to directly connected in-house users and to dial-up Internet users. Powerful security features make the Microsoft Proxy Server an effective firewall, isolating in-house networks, and users, from the hazards of the Internet.

- **Microsoft System Network Architecture (SNA) Server**—a server that allows easy communications between IBM mainframe and AS/400 computers.

- **Microsoft SQL Server**—a client/server database system used by many other Microsoft BackOffice components, including (but not limited to) both SMS and Merchant Server.

- **Microsoft Systems Management Server (SMS)**—provides a tool to manage software, applications, and hardware for users on an in-house network. Includes both client and server components.

Microsoft BackOffice for Non-ISPs

The version of Microsoft BackOffice that is intended for small to medium-sized companies (the non-ISP version) includes a number of different server products. Each may be used with Windows NT 4 Server, on a single server. Windows NT 4 Server comes with the non-ISP version of BackOffice and includes the current versions of:

- **Microsoft Internet Information Server (IIS)**—provides Web, FTP, and Gopher servers, allowing creation of reliable Internet and intranet sites. Typical IIS sites are configured in a few hours.

- **Microsoft Index Server**—adds search capabilities, allowing access to documents and objects stored on the Windows NT 4 Server. Index Server was complete after Windows NT 4 Server and is downloadable without charge to Windows NT 4 Server users.

- **Microsoft FrontPage**—a fast, WYSIWYG (What You See Is What You Get) HTML editor and Web site manager. Attractive and complex Web sites are easily created, without the tedious design and authoring requirements of previous systems.

The non-ISP version of BackOffice also includes the following standard BackOffice components:

- Systems Management Server (SMS)
- System Network Architecture (SNA) Server
- Microsoft SQL Server
- Microsoft Exchange Server
- Microsoft Proxy Server

BackOffice for ISPs

Microsoft Commercial Internet System (previously code-named Normandy) is a collection of servers and systems that support ISPs. These systems provide solutions to publishing, sales and merchandising, and interactive interaction using the Internet. Consisting of primarily four services—chat, news, personalization, and information retrieval—the Microsoft Commercial Internet System also includes other major systems such as content replication and merchant services.

Windows NT 4 Server includes current versions of the following Microsoft products:

- Microsoft Internet Information Server (IIS).
- Microsoft Index Server.
- Microsoft FrontPage.

The ISP version of BackOffice also includes the following standard BackOffice components:

- Microsoft Merchant Server (version 1.0).
- Microsoft Personalization System.
- Microsoft Content Replication System.
- Microsoft Content Replication System SDK—an SDK (Software Development Kit) for developing applications used with the Microsoft Content Replication System.
- Microsoft Commercial Internet System News Server—a high-performance newsgroup server that allows users to enter into noninteractive discussion groups and to post objects (such as files and images) that can be retrieved by other users.

- Microsoft Internet Chat Server SDK—an SDK for developing applications used with the Microsoft Internet Chat Server.

- Microsoft Internet Chat Server—a server that allows users to enter into interactive discussions with other online Internet and intranet users.

- Microsoft Membership System—provides a scalable, distributed authentication and access control system that enables commercial service providers on the Internet to manage their customer relationships. Microsoft Membership System integrates with a range of Microsoft Internet application servers, providing the foundation needed to build a commercial Internet service.

- Microsoft Commercial Internet Mail Server—an Internet-standards-based (POP-3 and SMTP), commercial-grade server that provides the basic mail functionality, scalability, and performance that ISPs and network operators require to provide communications services to thousands or millions of customers. (POP-3 stands for Post Office Protocol, version 3, and SMTP stands for Simple Mail Transfer Protocol.)

Windows NT 4 Server

Because Windows NT 4 Server is such an integral part of Microsoft BackOffice, the rest of this chapter will focus on describing the components and services of Windows NT 4 Server.

Windows NT 4 Server is Microsoft's premier server, a 32-bit Windows-based operating system that has gained considerable acceptance as an NOS (network operating system). Windows NT 4 Server, as a basic NOS, provides both file and printer services and a number of network-related services, including DNS (Domain Name Server), DHCP (Dynamic Host Configuration Protocol), and others.

The Features of Windows NT

The remainder of this chapter lists and explains the features of Windows NT at a very high level. It is meant to familiarize you with the features and their specific benefits. Each of the discussions and explanations around each feature set also points you to the appropriate location in the chapters that follow for using and implementing the particular feature:

- Domain-based security services
- Fault tolerance
- Interoperability with multiple network operating systems
- Wizards for common administrative tasks
- File and printer sharing services
- Enhanced support for network routing
- Network and system diagnostics
- Sophisticated administration tools
- Software license management
- Remote access, both dial-in and dial-out
- Communication services
- Advanced security

Domain-based Security Services

Domain-based security services means one login, one point of administration, no duplication of network information or administrative effort. Those of you who have had to maintain large network and e-mail systems where the two were not integrated will immediately understand the impact of this statement. Windows NT provides a solid core user-account management system that can be used by an administrator from any Windows NT system on the domain using Windows NT's User Manager for Domains.

Note: There is no requirement that a network must be configured as a domain. Windows NT Servers may be configured to manage their own security using the workgroup model (Windows 95 uses the workgroup model as its default network configuration).

When installing Windows NT 4 Server, you may choose to install it as a PDC, BDC, or as a stand-alone server. Note, however, that once Windows NT 4 Server has been installed, the security model (domain versus workgroup) may not be changed without reinstalling Windows NT 4 Server. Changing a domain server to be either a PDC or a BDC is a straightforward task, called promotion and demotion of domain servers.

Just What Is a Domain?

With Windows NT Server, domains are a unit of security and administration. A domain controller is "in charge" of security and authenticates logons for the entire domain. There is typically (though not always) more than one domain controller. The primary domain controller (PDC) maintains the master copy of the security database, and each backup domain controller (BDC) in the domain will receive a copy of the security database from the PDC.

All of the domain controllers become an administrative unit, sharing security policies and all account information with the PDC. Because the master copy of the security database is maintained on the PDC, systems administrators must manage users only at a single location. Once the master security database has been updated, the PDC will then share the master security database with the other BDCs. The User Manager for Domains is used to create and administrate user and group accounts and to administer security policies for the domain.

Using User Manager for Domains (Figure 1-1), an administrator can easily add new users and configure security and user profiles on an individual basis or by user groups. This is useful when users change responsibilities in an organization, because changing computer rights is a simple matter of moving the account from one group to another.

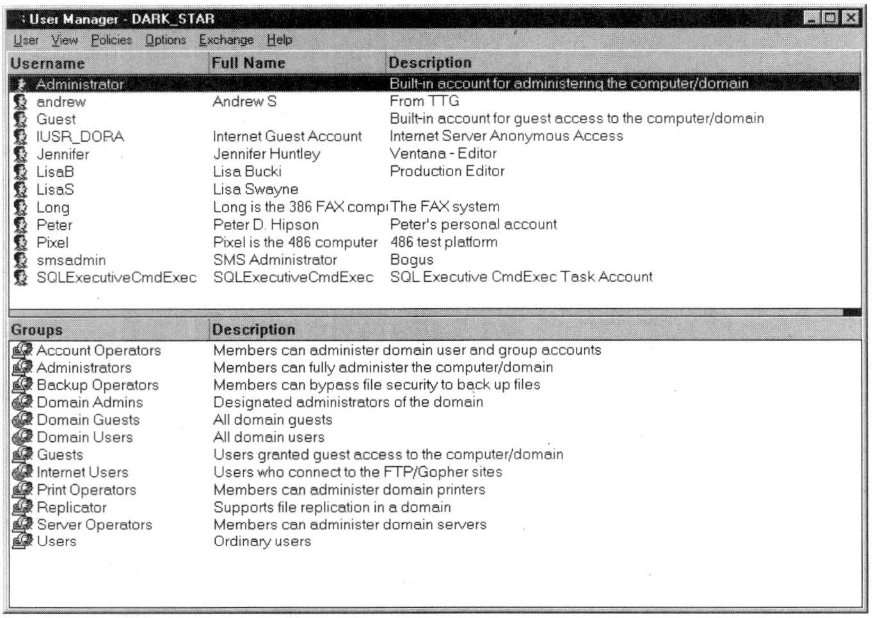

Figure 1-1: The User Manager for Domains dialog box.

For multiserver domains, the user accounts, profiles, and security settings are replicated automatically throughout the network so that even in large networks this information does not cause a synchronization headache for the network administrator.

Tip

When Windows NT 4 Server is configured for workgroup-level security, the user manager is actually very similar to the User Manager for Domains. Networks with two or more servers, however, must manually duplicate user information on each server.

The Browse Service included with Windows NT keeps track of the computers and printers that are available for the entire Windows NT network, even across domains and workgroups. The Windows NT Browse Service makes it possible to create a network environment that makes sense to your organization while still allowing complete communication between groups.

Products in the BackOffice suite (such as Exchange Server and SQL Server) are designed to integrate Windows NT's security manager. This makes ongoing maintenance of these products, and their users, a much simpler task.

User management and printer and file sharing is covered in Chapter 2, while the Browse Service is discussed in Chapter 4. Support for the Internet DNS protocol and server service is covered in detail in Chapter 8.

Fault Tolerance

Probably the single most important task that any network administrator performs is to ensure that the user's information can be recovered in event of a system failure. Depending on your location, you may experience power failures or brownouts. Communications lines fail for intranet and Internet connections. More commonly, hard drives fail, network cards go bad, cables short or open, or they have been run through the ceiling across a light or electrical cable introducing intermittent faults or failures.

Fault tolerance is the ability to recover gracefully from a failure of hardware or software. At the most basic level, Windows NT's core file system, NTFS, is a transaction-based, fully recoverable file system. This means that Windows NT is constantly keeping track of the previous states for any given file so that if, for some reason, the system is interrupted in the middle of making significant changes to a file, NTFS (Windows NT File System) will automatically "roll" the file back to the previous version.

NTFS also supports hot fixes, which allow the system to immediately adapt the file system to work around any bad sectors that are found on hard drives. However, hot fixes won't recover data that were stored on the bad sectors!

Tip

Sure, NTFS is transaction based and supports hot fixes, but NTFS cannot always recover from all failures. For example, a drive may develop a defective sector that can no longer be read. The sector may be repairable (SCSI drives allow for mapping out defective sectors). However, if the defective sector is located in a file or in the NTFS file management areas, data may be lost. A prime example happened on the author's DORA server; a bad sector on the C: drive resulted in four Windows NT 4 Server system files being lost. These files had to be restored from backup, as there was no transaction information to use to recover the files.

Also, Windows NT has support for disk mirroring and disk striping with parity. Disk mirroring allows you to have the system perform simultaneous writes to multiple hard drives to always maintain a hard drive that is an exact duplicate of another.

The Disk Striping With Parity feature of Windows NT is a software implementation of RAID level 5. This feature uses multiple hard drives to write file system data across several hard drives at once in a stripe pattern. By writing data across multiple drives and by writing a little extra information, Windows NT can automatically recover data in case of disk failure. The data is distributed across the disks in such a fashion as to ensure 100 percent data recovery in case of hardware failure for one of the drives.

Figure 1-2 shows the Windows NT 4 Server Disk Administrator program. Management of all types of disk media (except for floppy disks) is done using the disk administrator. Unlike with Windows 95, all drives under Windows NT may have their drive letters changed.

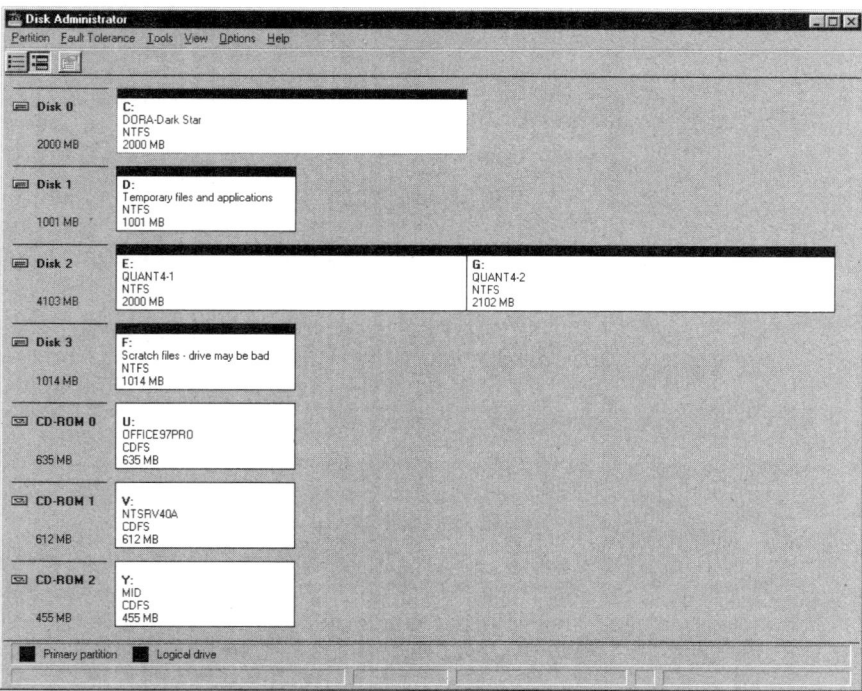

Figure 1-2: The Windows NT 4 Server Disk Administrator program.

Integration With Multiple Networks

One of the major benefits of Windows NT is its ability to support hybrid networks and multiple host operating systems. Windows NT has built-in support for the following desktop networks:

- Windows 3.1 and Windows 3.11 (Windows for Workgroups)
- Windows 95
- Macintosh AppleTalk Networks (including Appleshare)
- LAN Manager (OS/2. DOS, and LAN Manager for UNIX)
- DEC Pathworks
- 3Com 3+Open
- NetWare Networks
- Basic mainframe connectivity (with DLC)
- Internet connectivity (using TCP/IP protocol, both dial-in and direct connections)

The levels of connectivity for each of the various networks is completely dependent upon the network. That is, Windows NT 4 Server may not offer all the functionality that the network offers from the original supplier.

Chapter 4 discusses networking in general in terms of concepts, configuring the networking protocols, and services, as well as basic diagnostics and tips.

Chapter 5 covers the built-in support for NetWare using the NWLink protocol.

Chapter 6 shows you how to create a hybrid PC and Mac network where Windows NT can act as a file and print server for the Mac. Also, the topic of connecting a Macintosh workstation to a PC-based e-mail system is covered in Chapter 28.

Chapter 7 discusses the basic support for interoperability between Windows NT and UNIX and also discusses third-party options for even tighter integration.

Wizards

The concept of wizards is relatively new. It involves a series of dialog boxes that ask questions about how you want to use a certain feature. Once you have answered the questions, the wizard then performs the task for you, eliminating the need for arcane knowledge or keeping a reference manual handy.

Windows NT has built-in wizards, all controlled by the Administrative Wizards dialog box (see Figure 1-3), for common administrative tasks such as adding user accounts, managing files and folders, or installing new programs. The screen shown in Figure 1-3 is the default Getting Started screen. The Windows NT 4 Server Administrative Wizards may be configured to display the Administrative Wizards screen the next time you log on by clicking the check box in the upper section of the Administrative Wizards window.

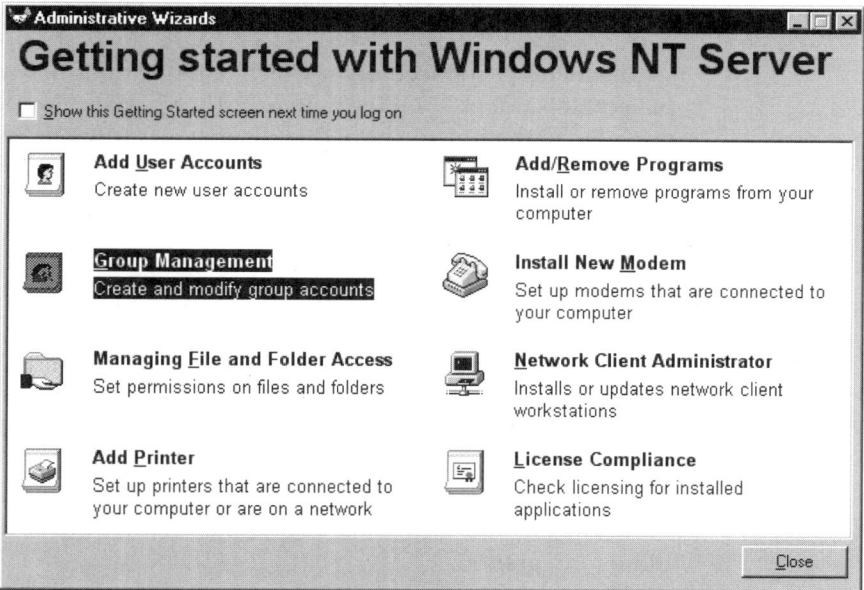

Figure 1-3: The Windows NT 4 Server Administrative Wizards dialog box.

There are eight wizards available to Windows NT 4 Server users. Some wizards simply launch the applicable application (for example, Add/Remove Programs launches the Control Panel's Add/Remove Programs Properties applet). The eight Windows NT 4 Server wizards are:

- **Add User Accounts.** The Add User Account Wizard allows the administrator to add a new user account quickly by simply answering a few prompts.

- **Group Management.** Groups are logical "groupings" of users. For example, you could create a group that has all the users in one department, such as accounting or R&D. The Group Management Wizard allows new groups to be created and existing groups to be modified.

- **Managing File and Folder Access.** With drives that use the NTFS file system, you can manage access to specific files and folders. The Managing Folder and File Access wizard allows a step-by-step modification of file and folder permissions.

- **Add Printer.** The Add Printer Wizard selection lets you add printer drivers for printers attached to the local server or any other server that is sharing printers.

- **Add/Remove Programs.** With the Add/Remove Program Properties applet, you can install any Windows NT 4 Server application that complies with the Windows NT installation standards. Any installed application that supports the Windows NT uninstall feature may be uninstalled by selecting the application in the list and clicking the Uninstall button.

- **Install New Modem.** With the Install New Modem applet, you can install any modem that is compatible with Windows NT 4 Server.

- **Network Client Administrator.** You can use the Network Client Administrator to make startup diskettes and installation disk sets, copy client-based network administration tools, and view remote boot client information.

- **License Compliance.** The License Compliance Wizard lets you check license compliance on either the local domain or a remote domain. The License Compliance Wizard will check for unlicensed products and will warn you if any unlicensed products are discovered.

File & Printer Sharing

While file and printer sharing have always been a core part of Windows NT, sharing support is becoming easier to use and manage than ever before. With a user interface similar to that of Windows 95, any object, such as printers, disk-drives, or files, may be quickly and easily shared.

Sharing Drives, Folders & Files

The tool to manage sharing of drives, folders, and files is the Windows NT 4 Explorer program. Explorer is the replacement for the File Manager and Program Manager found in earlier versions of Windows NT.

There are several ways to start Explorer. First, you can click on the My Computer icon on the Windows NT desktop. Or if you are using a Windows 95-compatible keyboard (such as Microsoft's Natural Keyboard), which has a Windows key, you can press the Windows key and the E key at the same time. Finally, you can use the Start Menu (Start Menu | Programs | Windows Explorer).

Tip

Explorer has two views: a single pane and a double pane. My Computer on the desktop is a single-pane view. Choosing Explorer from the Start Menu, or pressing the Windows and E keys at the same time, will display Explorer in the two-pane mode.

Figure 1-4 shows Explorer with the DarkStar server DORA's desktop displayed. This display shows all drives (both local drives and those drives and shares located on other servers and connected through DORA).

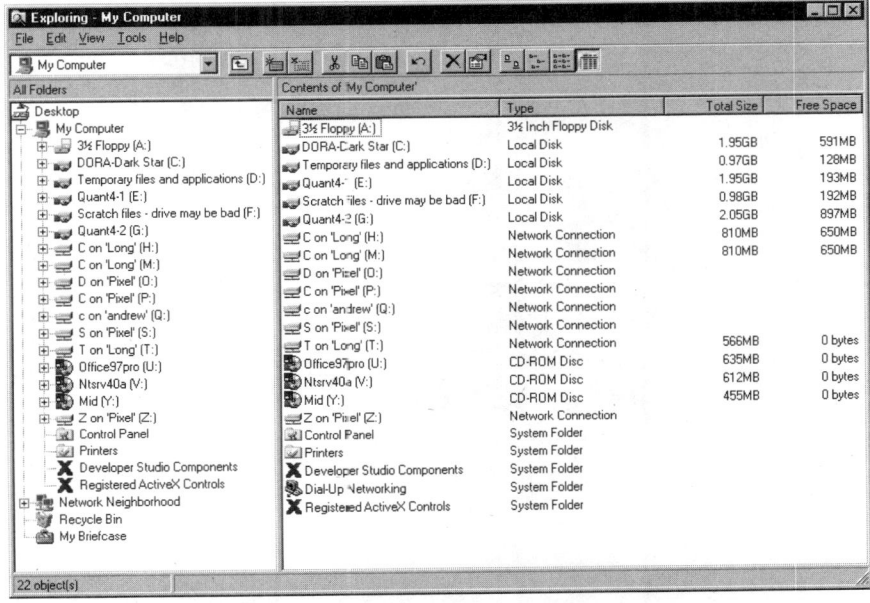

Figure 1-4: The Windows NT 4 Explorer.

Tip

Desktop, shown as a level above My Computer, is actually a folder found on the root drive. Desktop is found in the %systemroot%\profiles\ username where username *is the name of the currently logged on user.*

To share drives or folders, it is necessary to select the object to be shared (in either the left or right Explorer pane) and then choose File | Properties from Explorer's menu bar. The Properties dialog will be displayed for the selected object, as the example in Figure 1-5 shows.

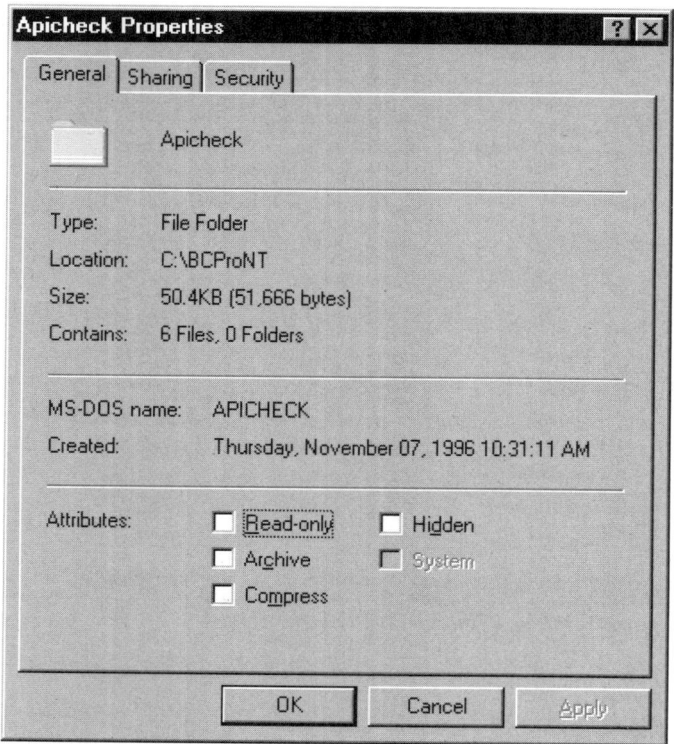

Figure 1-5: Explorer's Properties dialog box for DORA's Apicheck folder.

The Properties dialog box has three tabs for folders and four tabs for drives. The Drives Properties dialog box has an additional tab, Tools, which lets you check the drive for errors (running CHKDSK), backup (which executes the Windows NT Backup program), and defragmentation (which, for Windows NT 4 Server, is not provided). For both drives and folders, the Sharing tab (Figure 1-6) is identical; the New Share and the Remove Share buttons are added and removed by Explorer as needed, so you may not see them when you display your Sharing tab.

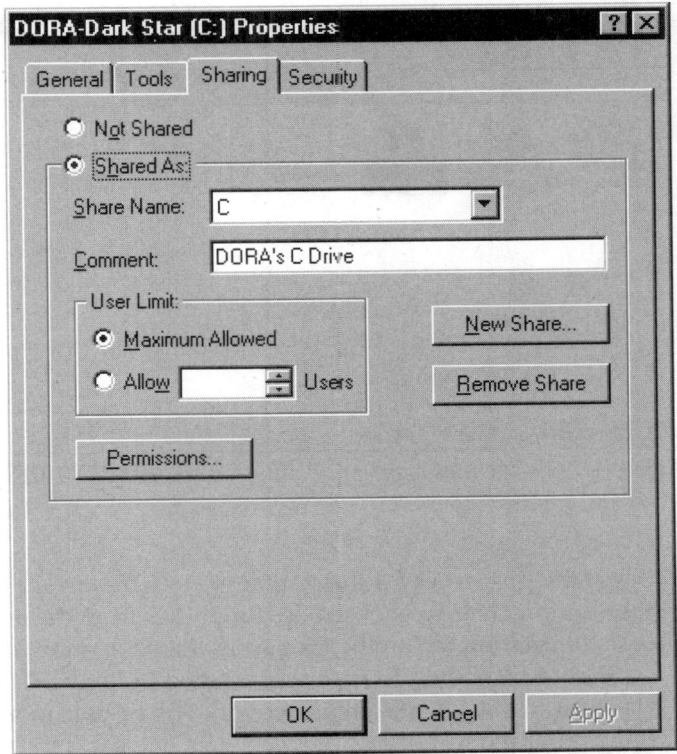

Figure 1-6: Explorer's Properties dialog box Sharing tab for C: on DORA.

When sharing a drive or folder, the access may be limited to specific users or groups as desired.

Windows NT 4 Server has no provisions for sharing individual files. If an individual file must be shared, the folder in which it is located must be shared, and then security for other files in the folder must be used to limit access to only the file being shared.

Sharing Printers

Windows NT 4 Server shares printers from the printer manager. Start the printer manager by choosing Start Menu I Settings I Printers. The application that manages printers is called Printers, as shown in Figure 1-7.

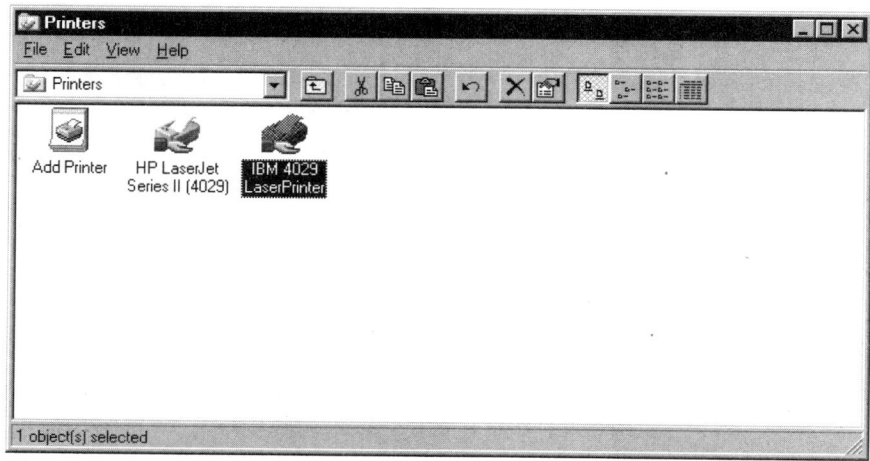

Figure 1-7: The printer manager, Printers, with the IBM 4029 LaserPrinter selected.

Select the properties for the printer to be shared (use either a right-mouse-button-click, or choose File | Properties from the menu), and choose the Sharing tab on the Properties dialog as shown in Figure 1-8.

As Figure 1-8 shows, the printer is shared (with the share name of IBM4029L) so that clients on the network will be able to print documents to this printer if desired.

Tip

Unlike drives and folders, printers are shared without passwords; any client user may use the printer. To limit access to a printer, use the Security tab, and set Permissions for those users who are to be allowed access to the printer.

Windows NT also includes more basic support for printing from mainframes and UNIX-oriented systems using DLC (Data Link Control), for IP file sharing and IP printer sharing, and for printer sharing with mainframes using DLC and TCP/IP printing support.

Chapter 2 covers, in depth, the Windows Explorer, which replaces the Windows File Manager and Program Manager with a cleaner interface that is more integrated with the operating system.

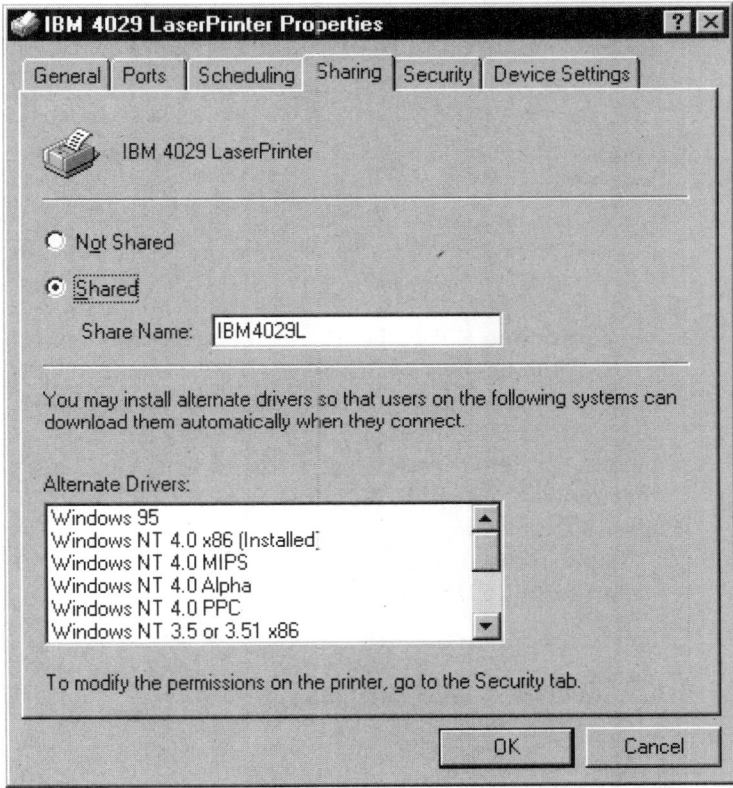

Figure 1-8: The IBM 4029 LaserPrinter Properties dialog box.

Chapter 7 will show you how to configure a printer for use with UNIX workstations.

Chapter 9 covers the security aspects of file management and file sharing with Windows NT file servers.

Multi-Protocol Router (MPR)

MPR (Multi-Protocol Router) is part of Windows NT 4 Server and consists of:

- RIP (Routing Information Protocol) for TCP/IP
- BOOTP relay agent for DHCP
- RIP for IPX

RIP is a protocol that routers use to exchange routing information. RIP supports both IPX and TCP/IP protocols, allowing Windows NT 4 Server to route both protocols dynamically.

Tip

Riproute.wri, which is found in the Windows NT 3.51 service pack CD, contains more information about Multi-Protocol Routing.

In addition to RIP, PPTP (Point-to-Point Tunneling Protocol) may be used to route packets securely. With PPTP, remote client users with Microsoft Windows 95 and Windows NT, and any other PPP-enabled client system (PPP stands for Point-to-Point Protocol), may connect to a corporate system that is connected to the Internet. These remote client users may dial into their ISPs and be securely connected to the Internet-connected corporate network.

Chapter 8 discusses the TCP/IP-based support for routing and support for the RIP and PPTP protocols.

System & Network Diagnostics

The Task Manager, Performance Monitor, and Network Monitor utilities provide the ability to more accurately monitor and manage activity on the server and on the network.

Task Manager

The Task Manager (see Figure 1-9) provides the ability to monitor CPU and memory usage along with other system resources such as paging and VM size. Start the Task Manager by either pressing Ctrl+Alt+Del while logged on (click the Task Manager button) or by right-clicking any blank area on the taskbar and choosing Task Manager from the context menu that Windows NT displays.

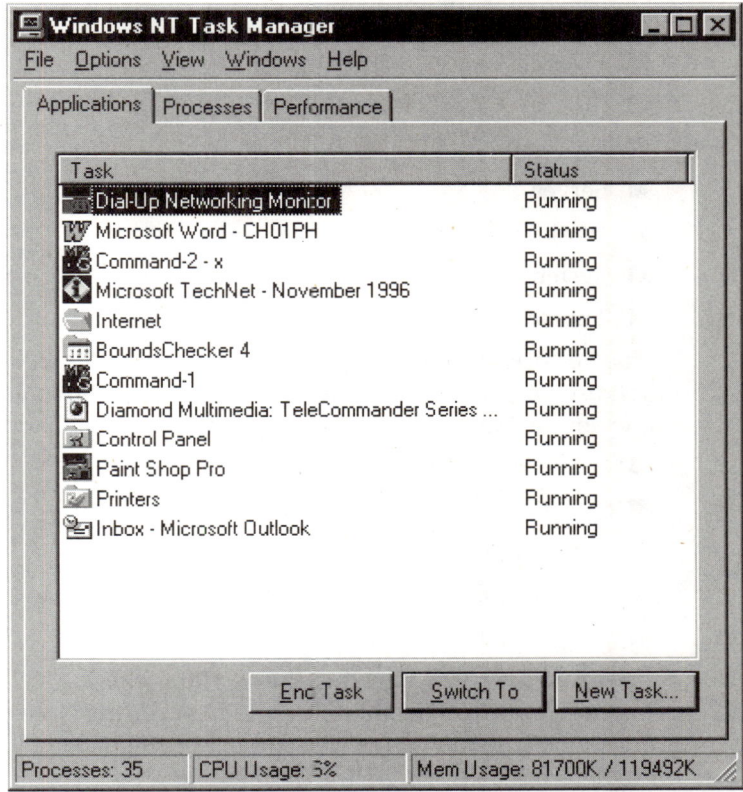

Figure 1-9: The Windows NT Task Manager's Applications tab. I'm running all that?

Performance Monitor

The Windows NT 4 Server Performance Monitor (see Figure 1-10) provides the ability to monitor CPU, memory, hardware, and other resources in the areas listed below:

- Browser
- Cache
- Logical Disk
- Memory

- Paging File
- Physical Disk
- Process
- Processor
- Server
- Work Queues
- System
- Threads

The Performance Monitor has several different modes of display. The graph used most often is a time-related chart, as shown in Figure 1-10. In this example, I have chosen to display the following counters:

- % Processor Time
- % Total User Time
- % Committed Bytes in Use
- Available Bytes
- Avg. Disk Bytes/Transferred

There are over 100 different aspects of the Windows NT 4 Server's performance that can be monitored. Whenever the system performance is questioned, it would be a wise move to check the Performance Monitor to determine just where the problem lies.

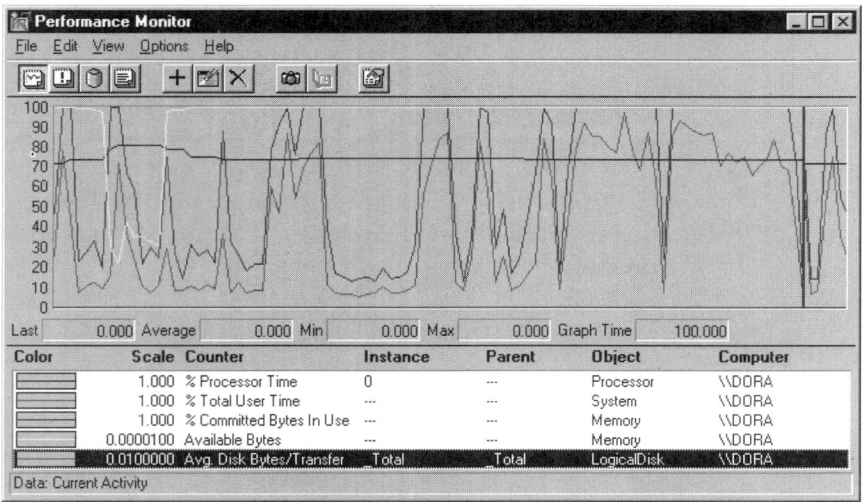

Figure 1-10: The Windows NT Performance Monitor.

Network Manager

The Windows NT 4 Server Network Manager program lets you monitor the performance of the network component of Windows NT 4 Server. Though the Performance Monitor (described in the preceding section) is able to monitor the network component, the Network Monitor is better suited for this task, having been designed for it. The Network Manager allows you to monitor and examine network traffic and even capture network packets for offline analysis.

Figure 1-11 shows the Network Monitor monitoring the DarkStar network. This figure shows that there were two workstations connected to the server DORA, each somewhat active in that each workstation was receiving (reading from the shared drives) information from DORA, but not sending (writing to the shared drives) much information. Server utilization will vary with each network; some networks will have high levels of writes, while other networks may have equal levels or higher levels of reads. Regardless of whether the network traffic is traveling to or from the server, it still will have an impact on the network's performance.

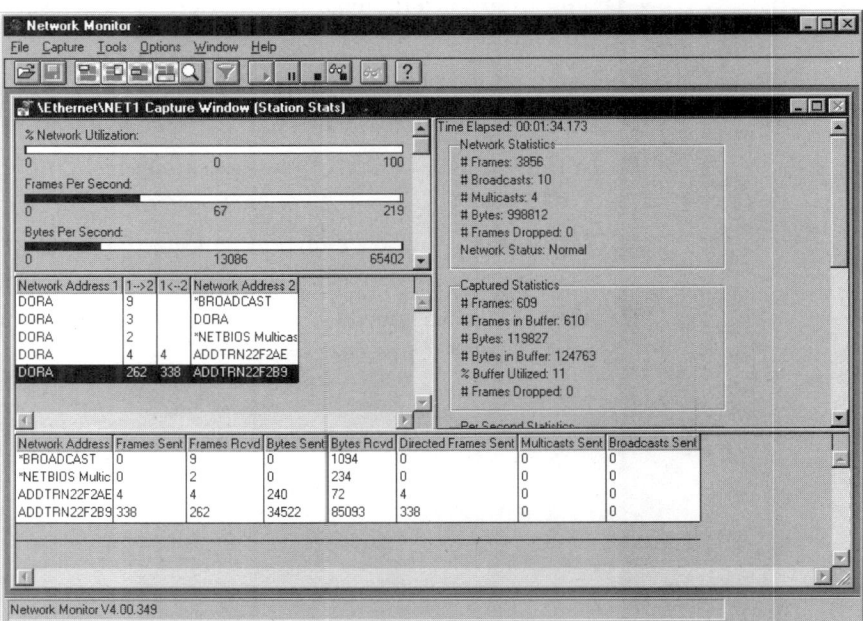

Figure 1-11: The Windows NT 4 Server Network Monitor, with two active workstations.

All the Windows NT 4 Server monitoring tools are not as obviously useful until you actually need them. For example, you will probably never run the Network Monitor right up until the moment you need it; but then the Network Monitor becomes indispensable!

Administrative Tools

The core administrative tools provided with Windows NT are:

- The Server Manager, which allows management and support of the servers that a Windows NT network comprises.

- The User Manager, which allows maintenance of individual and group user accounts for an individual server or for the entire domain.

Server Manager

Server Manager (see Figure 1-12) is used to manage servers that have been configured for remote administration. For each server, it is possible to view the following:

- **Users**—a list of all currently connected users.

- **Shares**—a list of all shares and each share's status.

- **In Use**—a list of all resources that are currently in use by client workstations.

- **Replication**—allows management of directory replication between servers.

- **Alerts**—allows specification of recipients of alert messages (sent when there is a problem).

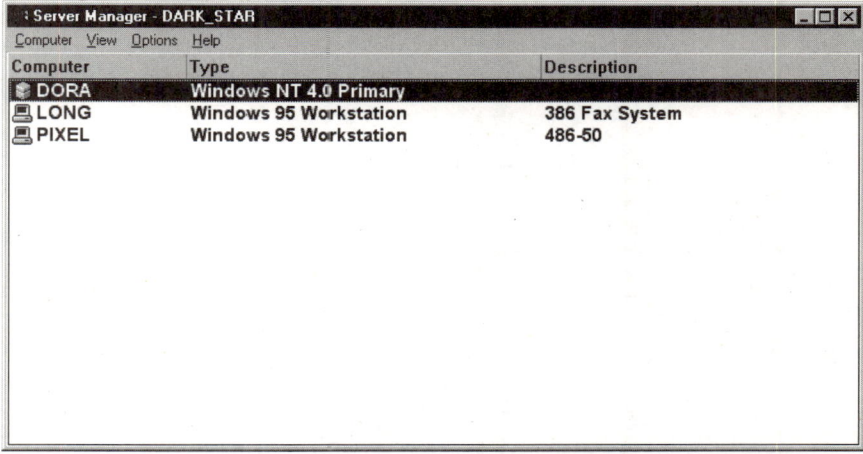

Figure 1-12: The Windows NT 4 Server Manager, showing a server and two workstations.

User Manager for Domains

The User Manager for Domains (see Figure 1-1) allows you to easily manage individual accounts as well as groups. The ability to create and manage groups is one of the key features that makes domain management possible. To manage a large number of users with Windows NT, you should create groups that define the various levels of security required by each group and assign new users to the appropriate groups as accounts are created.

Chapter 2 covers the use of both the Server Manager and the User Manager.

License Management

The License Manager in Windows NT plays an important, but probably not all that popular, role. In a large networking environment, tracking licenses for software is becoming a more monumental task than ever. The Windows NT License Manager (Figure 1-13) is a step in the right direction for getting control over this problem. Start the License Manager by choosing Start Menu | Programs | Administrative Tools (Common).

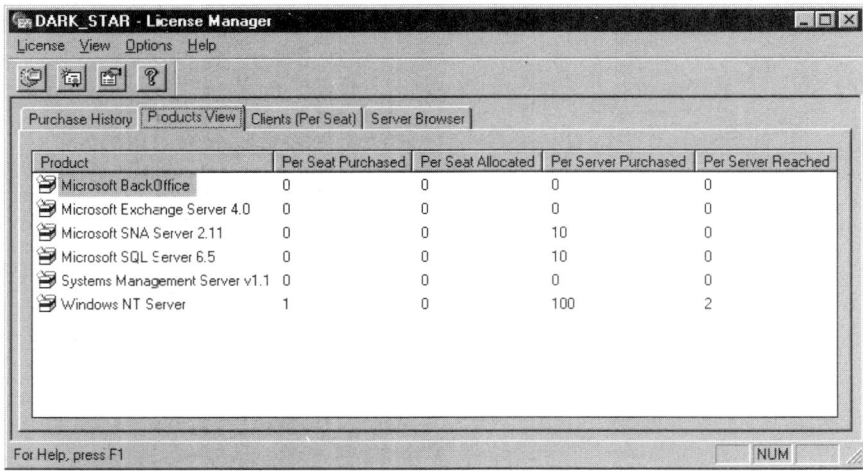

Figure 1-13: The License Manager in use.

License Manager works by integrating tightly with server software packages. The best example of how this product works is with Windows NT itself. When you install Windows NT, it requests that you enter the information for the license you purchased for your product. It then keeps track of the usage of Windows NT and compares it to the information that you provided, alerting you if there is a violation of the license.

Note that this system is still bound to the honor system and requires you to enter correct information. Since it is against the law not to have adequate usage licenses for any software package, the License Manager can be extremely useful.

To go beyond the service provided by the License Manager, you should examine Section III to learn how Systems Management Server helps in keeping track of software inventory networkwide.

Remote Access

Remote access is divided into two parts:

■ RAS (Remote Access Server) is used to allow users to connect to the server using telephone dial-up connections.

■ DUN (Dial-Up Networking) is used to allow a locally logged-on user to connect to a remote network using a dial-up connection.

RAS

Remote Access Server is another one of those indispensable and core features of Windows NT. With the Remote Access Server installed and running on your server, users can dial in using dial-up networking on Windows 95 or NT Workstation 4 and connect to the network as if they were locally connected.

While performance over standard telephone lines is not going to be great (though ISDN may improve performance somewhat), it should be passable for most remote networking requirements such as checking e-mail.

DUN

DUN is used to allow a user to connect to a remote computer. DUN allows connection to most ISPs and to other servers that support the Windows NT 4 Server protocols. It is even possible to connect to a Windows NT 4 Server and access the Internet through the remote computer's Internet connection.

As with RAS, performance over standard telephone lines is not going to be sufficient to access large amounts of data. However, for Web browsing, e-mail, and other non-I/O-intensive tasks, DUN will perform adequately.

Windows NT Security

The Windows NT security system provides the ability to set and manage Windows NT access control lists, which control access to both files and directories. In addition, the Windows NT 4 Server security system controls the ability to log on to the network.

Tip

Windows NT 4 Server security, even at the domain level, will not prevent users of systems that are not secure (such as Windows 95 computers) from accessing resources at the local (workstation) level—Windows NT 4 Server cannot improve the security of insecure systems. If local security is necessary, then a secure operating system such as Windows NT 4 Workstation must be used.

Figure 1-14 shows the Security page for a drive with the Permissions, Auditing, and Ownership buttons.

Chapter 9 covers the basics of security.

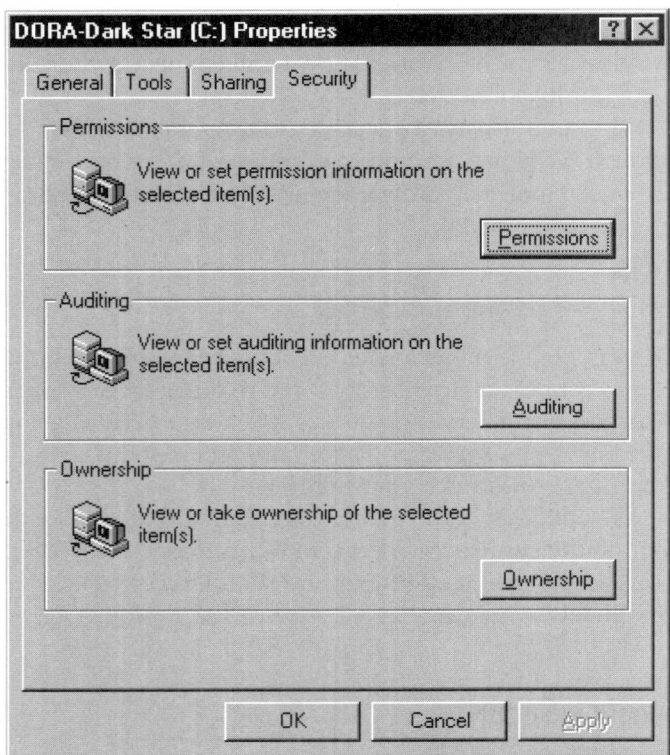

Figure 1-14: A drive's Properties page with the Security tab shown.

Tip

The author does not in any way condone the use of these features to violate a user's privacy.

Moving On

The fact that you are reading this book at all indicates that you realize that a network operating system (NOS) is only one part of a complete networking solution. The NOS supplies the basic management and tends to be the core of the solution, but today's network is heavily supplemented by application servers and special server utilities and services.

Because this book concentrates on a total network solution, Windows NT is presented with the features and components that support this perspective. And for this reason, the following chapters concentrate on the networking aspects of Windows NT combined with the appropriate utilities and support tools.

Chapter 2 covers the basics of setting up and working with the Windows NT security system for both access control lists and user account security.

2

Installing & Configuring Windows NT 4 Server

W hen you install Windows NT 4 Server, many of Windows NT 4 Server's components must be configured. With only a few exceptions, however, these components may be reconfigured after Windows NT 4 Server has been installed.

The actual process of configuration is a continuing one. As Windows NT 4 Server is used, the server should be configured to optimize performance. Not only does the software component of the server need to be configured, but often the hardware must also be changed. For example, the DarkStar server, DORA, had 32MB of RAM when Windows NT 4 Server was first installed. When several Microsoft BackOffice components were also installed, however, system performance became unacceptable. Upgrading DORA to 64MB of RAM improved DORA's performance. How did I know that I needed more RAM? I used the Windows NT 4 Server Performance Monitor program, and the Windows NT 4 Server Task Manager.

What Can't Be Changed After Installing?

Two things come to mind right away:

First, you cannot change a stand-alone server to a domain server. This change would require reinstallation of Windows NT 4 Server.

Second, it may not be possible to change licensing modes from per-server to per-seat. Make sure that you understand the implications of selecting the license mode when you install Windows NT 4 Server.

This chapter covers the main components that must be configured when you install Windows NT 4 Server. Though this chapter cannot cover every possible configuration or option, I describe the more commonly used configurations.

Getting Started

Installation of Windows NT 4 Server can be either a new installation, an upgrade of an existing Windows NT Server installation, or an installation over another operating system such as NetWare, OS/2, Windows 95, or even MS-DOS.

Generally, conversions between disparate operating systems present the most difficult problems. Neither Novell's NetWare disk format nor OS/2's HPFS are compatible with Windows NT 4 Server. Upgrading these systems can be a daunting task and may require considerable work: creating a compatible backup, reformatting the drive, and restoring the user files.

In this section of the chapter, I take a quick look at what you need to do before you begin a typical new installation.

Installing Windows NT 4 Server can be as simple as placing the Windows NT 4 Server distribution CD in the drive and running the installation program. A few preliminary steps are in order before doing this, however:

1. Check the hardware compatibility list (HCL) to make sure that your hardware is compatible. Though Windows NT 4 Server may well install on hardware that is not on the HCL (which is supplied with the Windows NT 4 Server documentation), there is no guarantee that it will work correctly.

2. Make sure that you have sufficient resources to install Windows NT 4 Server. Check RAM (though 16MB is the listed minimum, a working Windows NT 4 Server installation needs an absolute minimum of 32MB and will work better in a 64MB machine). Check the hard drive free space; installation requires a few hundred MB of free space. Check your video card to make sure that you have drivers for it; otherwise, you may end up using that new user interface in 640/480 16-color mode—ugh.

3. Check to make absolutely sure that you have a current backup. Better yet, if there is any critical data on the system, make sure that you have two current backups. A flawed backup pretty much guarantees that you will have serious problems with your installation of the operating system. Do make sure that your backup is complete and current. Make sure that applications and systems (such as BackOffice, Office 95, compilers, and the like) disks are available to allow reinstallation with a minimum of problems.

4. Make sure that you have enough time to do the installation. Anticipate problems and exceptions. Getting halfway through the installation doesn't give you half of the server! Plan ahead . . . Consider what may go wrong, and know that these items probably won't be a problem. Things that you don't take into consideration are the things that will go wrong and halt the installation. Murphy's Law understands installations and strikes constantly at this stage!

Throughout this chapter, I refer to a person called the systems administrator. This is typically you, the reader—the person who is responsible for the Windows NT Server and its administration. Throughout the documentation and help files, Microsoft tells you "if you don't know this item, ask your systems administrator." This can be a difficult task! (I get really funny looks when talking to myself.) When the systems administrator logs onto Windows NT 4 Server, the "administrator" login (or user) ID is used. The Windows NT 4 Server's installation program creates only one login ID automatically, the "administrator" login ID.

Note: There is nothing that prevents you from having multiple installations of Windows NT Server. For example, you can have a working copy of Windows NT 4 Server, a working copy of Windows NT 3.51 Server, and a test version of Windows NT 4 Server on the same machine. In fact, you can have as many "versions" of Windows NT Server as disk space and licensing allow.

If the currently installed version of Windows NT Server is 3.5x, then having a working copy of Windows NT 3.51 Server gives you a "fall back" system in the event that unexpected problems make the new installation of Windows NT 4 Server unstable.

Some of the questions covered in this chapter include:

- How is Windows NT 4 Server installed?

- Do I install Windows NT 4 Server as a clean, new installation, or can Windows NT 4 Server upgrade Windows NT 3.5x Server?

- Is this a good time to change our networking model or configuration?

- How can I minimize the impact of installing Windows NT 4 Server?

- How do I configure networking, users, groups, and services?

You need to address each of these critical questions (and many more that are unvoiced!) when you install a new network operating system. In this chapter, I discuss the answers to these questions, and much more.

Installation Options

A primary question is: How is Windows NT 4 Server installed? There are a number of installation situations, depending on whether the installation is an upgrade of an existing system, a new server being placed online, or, perhaps, a new network or organization. The types of installations arising from these situations include:

- **Clean Installation.** Starting from scratch with nothing on the hard drive that you want to keep.

- **Upgrading from another operating system.** In this situation, you have several options. First, Windows NT 4 Server won't upgrade Windows 3.x or Windows 95. You can either replace the existing version of Windows, or create a dual-boot installation. When you create a dual-boot machine, you must not convert the boot drive's file system to NTFS (NT File System): DOS and Windows 95 cannot be booted from an NTFS partition. Generally, there is no advantage to replacing an existing copy of Windows 95—simply create a dual-boot system, and delete the Windows 95 installation at a convenient time in the future.

- **Upgrading from a previous version of Windows NT.** Typically, this will be Windows NT 3.5x, though you may be upgrading over Windows NT 3.x. You can upgrade over Windows NT 3.5x successfully. You may find it advantageous to do a clean installation, however, rather than upgrade an existing installation: A clean installation creates a known starting point for debugging when problems develop.

- **Upgrading from a previous beta version of Windows NT Server.** In this case, I strongly recommend that a clean installation be made. It may be acceptable to create a dual-boot system to allow items to be transferred to the new version of Windows NT 4 Server, but upgrading a beta version of Windows is not recommended even by Microsoft!

- **Upgrading either OS/2 (with HPFS partitions) or Novell NetWare servers can be problematic.** The safest method to upgrade either of the above is to do the following:

  1. Install a second server, using a different computer (you could rent, for a short period of time, a computer to host the new server if you do not have hardware available).

  2. Install Windows NT 4 Server on the second computer.

  3. Get the Windows NT 4 Server (the new server) system running correctly. Make sure that client users are able to access the second Windows NT 4 Server.

  4. Migrate the data from your OS/2 or NetWare server to the new Windows NT 4 server.

  5. After all data has been migrated, ensure that all client user needs are being met, then shut down the original OS/2 or NetWare server.

  6. If all hell doesn't break loose after a few days, back up the original server, low-level format the drive, and install a second copy of Windows NT 4 Server.

  7. Restoring your server's data from the temporary server completes the installation. If you have only one license for Windows NT 4 Server, don't leave both servers installed.

You can install Windows NT 4 Server on Intel (486, Pentium, or Pentium Pro), PPC (PowerPC), MIPS, or Alpha platforms. Regardless of the platform, the basic installation steps are identical.

Throughout this chapter, the installation examples are for the Intel platform (which is the most commonly used platform). Whenever the CD folder I386 is referred to in this book, and you are using a non-Intel platform, substitute PPC, MIPS, or ALPHA for the folder on the CD where the Windows NT 4 Server installation files are found.

Folder or Directory?

Microsoft, with the introduction of Windows 95, has changed the name of directories to folders. With the arrival of the Windows 95 interface into Windows NT 4 Server, the change in naming of directories as folders has arrived, too!

Throughout this book, I generally use the term folder; however, in those places where Microsoft has not yet updated its application or help to use the new terminology, I generally use the terminology used by Microsoft.

Regardless of which installation option is chosen, you can install Windows NT 4 Server by booting the Windows NT 4 Server distribution CD-ROM, booting the boot diskettes, or running the WINNT32.EXE (or WINNT.EXE for Windows 95 users) setup program. When you run the setup program, you can choose to do one of the following:

- Install without using boot diskettes (the easiest and fastest option).
- Create, then install, using boot diskettes (the safest but slowest option).
- Install using a previously created set of boot diskettes (safer and faster than creating the boot diskettes).

Whenever possible, install without using boot diskettes; the installation will be faster and easier.

The Windows NT 4 Server Setup Program

Existing Windows NT users install Windows NT 4 Server using the setup program: WINNT32.EXE. Existing Windows 95 (or Windows 3.x) system users install Windows NT 4 Server using the WINNT.EXE program. No difference exists between these two programs, other than the fact that

WINNT.EXE is a 16-bit version of WINNT32.EXE. Both setup programs install the same version of Windows NT 4 Server; the difference is that the 16-bit version is designed to run under Windows 95 and Windows 3.x.

The options, and functionality, of WINNT32.EXE and WINNT.EXE are identical, therefore I refer to both of these programs generically as WINNT32.EXE. Simply use the correct version for whichever operating system you are using to install Windows NT 4 Server.

Note: The installation program's output and flow may change with each option, selection, and feature that you select. Generally, things may be added or missing from your installation as compared to the installation described in this chapter. However the general flow of installation will be similar.

(There is a murmuring out there . . . and questions . . . Do I hear questions?)

Why doesn't Windows 95, a 32-bit operating system, use the 32-bit version of the setup program?

I don't know. For reasons that only Microsoft knows, the 32-bit version of the setup program works only under Windows NT. To install from Windows 95, you must use the 16-bit version. Because the results of the installation are identical in either case, this is not a problem.

Can I upgrade my Windows 95 installation to Windows NT 4 Server?

No, there is no upgrade path between Windows 95 and Windows NT 4 Server. You probably will want to install Windows NT 4 Server as a second operating system, and use the dual boot feature.

If I do a clean installation of Windows NT 4 Server, do I have to reinstall all my applications?

Generally speaking, yes. Some applications are able to repair their own installations (Visual C++ is one example) so that they run correctly even if not installed under the current operating system.

If I have Microsoft Office installed under Windows 95, and install dual boot Windows NT 4 Server, do I have to have two copies of Microsoft Office installed?

No, install Microsoft Office under Windows 95, into the MSOffice folder; then, in Windows NT 4 Server, install Microsoft Office into the same folder a second time. This works for Microsoft Office and most other applications.

Do I need to use the bootable diskettes if I am upgrading from an earlier version of Windows NT or installing a dual boot system from Windows 95?

No, probably not. Use the WINNT32.EXE's /B option to disable the creation and use of boot diskettes.

I installed Windows NT 4 Server with dual boot to retain my Windows 95 installation. Later I may want to delete both Windows 95 and dual boot. Can I do so?

Sure: Use DELTREE (or Explorer) to delete the Windows 95 folder, then edit the BOOT.INI file in the root folder to remove the reference to the other operating system. Finally, in the Control Panel's System applet, set the time delay on boot to one second.

Will my Windows 95 (and Windows 3.x) applications work under Windows NT 4 Server?

Generally. The great majority do, though from time to time, we see applications (mostly older ones) that don't behave the way we expected.

(No more questions? Okay, then.)

Options for the setup program are shown in Table 2-1. You can enter these options when you start the setup program, and modify some after you have begun the installation.

Option	Description
/?	Tells the setup program to display the options screen.
/S:*sourcefile*	Specifies the source path to the Windows NT 4 Server setup files. The default is the current path. You can run the setup program from a folder other than the one on the distribution CD.
/I:*inffile*	Specifies the file name and/or path to the Windows NT 4 Server setup INF file. The default is the current path, DOSNET.INF. Some installations may use customized setup INF files. The setup program will attempt to use the drive with the most free space—if this drive is formatted with the FAT-32 file system then the setup program will fail when it attempts to read these files.

Option	Description
/T:*tempDrive*	Specifies the drive to which the Windows NT 4 Server installation temporary files are written. The default is the C drive. This option is very useful when your C drive has limited free space.
/X	Tells the setup program to not create installation boot diskettes. You must have a set of the boot diskettes (either from the distribution package or a set that you create using the /O option).
/B	Tells the setup program to not use installation boot diskettes. The installation is done by reading the necessary files from the CD directly to the temporary file location. Typically, this is the fastest way to install Windows NT 4 Server, but requires that you have an operating system that supports your CD-ROM drive already installed.
/O	Tells the setup program to create the boot diskettes only. Diskettes created with the /O option are used only when installing Windows NT 4 Server using the setup program. These diskettes should not be booted except when prompted by setup program. Windows NT 4 Server is not installed with this option. You use this option to create boot diskettes for a system unable to create the boot diskettes (perhaps because the target system does not yet have any operating system installed). Note: The diskettes you supply must be formatted and blank.
/OX	Tells the setup program to create the boot diskettes for a CD-ROM or diskette-based installation. Windows NT 4 Server is not installed with this option. You use this option to create boot diskettes for a system that is unable to create the boot diskettes (perhaps because the target system does not yet have any operating system installed). Note: The diskettes you supply must be formatted and blank. You use boot diskettes created with the /OX option to booted from power-up to install Windows NT 4 Server/.

Table 2-1: The WINNT32.EXE upgrade/setup program options.

To modify options, such as whether to create boot diskettes, and to specify the name and location of the INF setup file, use the first dialog box of the setup program.

A Clean Windows NT 4 Server Installation

A clean Windows NT 4 Server installation, on a computer that does not already have an operating system, can be the easiest installation to do. However, you must have properly planned your server and network, and have all the necessary information about your system and network at hand (including user names, network topography, and so on).

With systems having bootable CD-ROM drives, an installation of Windows NT 4 Server can be as simple as placing the Windows NT 4 Server distribution CD into the CD-ROM drive and booting the computer. Only some newer Intel-based systems (equipped with SCSI CD-ROM drives) and most non-Intel platforms have bootable CD-ROM drives.

For systems that do not allow booting from the CD-ROM, you must boot the diskettes that accompany the Windows NT 4 Server distribution package. If you do not have the distribution boot diskettes, you can create boot diskettes using a computer that has the same architecture (Intel, MIPS, Alpha, or PPC) and a CD-ROM drive. (Creating boot diskettes is described later in this chapter.)

To begin the installation, you need to boot the system. Regardless of which method is used (diskette or CD-ROM booting), the setup program runs, tests the hardware, and installs the necessary drivers to access the CD-ROM drive and drivers for other necessary system hardware (such as your mouse). After this part of the setup program is complete, the installation is virtually identical to an installation that is done as an upgrade from an earlier version of Windows NT.

Upgrading MS-DOS or Windows 95

Doing an installation over either MS-DOS or Windows 95 is a simple task. Because neither of these operating systems may be upgraded to Windows NT 4 Server, you can treat each situation as a new installation.

One nice factor about Windows NT 4 Server is that it automatically supports dual-booting. This allows you to retain your existing MS-DOS or Windows 95 installation if necessary.

Note: If you're doing an installation over MS-DOS or Windows 95, and you wish to retain your existing DOS or Windows 95 installation, do not change the drive's format to NTFS. Neither DOS nor Windows 95 can directly read an NTFS-formatted drive.

If you are a Windows 95 user with a FAT-32 file system installed, convert back to FAT-16 before you install Windows NT 4 Server. Microsoft plans to support FAT-32 in later releases of Windows NT 4 Server, so check the release notes for more on FAT-32 support.

Note: When this book was written, no support was planned for FAT-32, Microsoft's new high-capacity FAT file system. Microsoft has made it clear that it is working on a FAT-32 enhancement for Windows NT 4 Server that should be released shortly after the initial release of Windows NT 4 Server.

You are not prompted to create a dual-boot system; the Windows NT 4 Server setup program automatically creates a dual-boot system for you. If you later delete the MS-DOS or Windows 95 system from your computer, you can manually edit the boot.ini file (found in the boot drive's root folder, as a system, read-only file) to remove the DOS or Windows 95 boot option.

Tip

To add an MS-DOS/Windows 95 dual boot option after doing a clean installation of Windows NT 4 Server, simply install DOS or Windows 95. Then, use the Emergency Repair Disk (ERD) to restore the Windows NT 4 Server boot. The ERD fixes the boot options for the system.

Plug-and-Play

For those of us who are using PCI bus machines, with Plug-and-Play (PnP) active, it is important to realize that PnP and PCI create situations that are not what most systems administrators expect—Windows NT 4 Server does not support PnP.

PCI, when used with PnP, is slot dependent. For example, say that you have three PCI slots, numbered one through three. In slot one, you have your video card; in slot two, your network card; and in slot three, your SCSI controller card. PnP assigns each card an IRQ. You install Windows 95, and it checks each time it is booted to see what PCI PnP cards are installed and what resources these cards are using.

Fine, and next you install Windows NT 4 Server. During installation, Windows NT 4 Server looks at the PCI cards, determines the resources used by each card, and never checks again. All would still be fine, but you later find that, for some reason (perhaps a cable is too short), you must move your PCI cards to different slots. When the PCI cards are moved, Windows 95 and PnP reassign resources to the cards. Windows 95 automatically detects changes each time it is booted, notes these changes, and works correctly. Windows NT 4 Server, however, is not PnP compatible, and cannot detect when resources have changed; thus, Windows NT 4 Server fails the next time it is restarted.

To solve this problem, if you receive a message that a device (or service) cannot be started, check the system error log. Note which device failed. Then, make sure that the correct resources are assigned to that device.

Note: Unlike Windows 95, Windows NT 4 Server does not have a single unified location for reviewing and setting device resources. For Windows NT 4 Server, you must use the Control Panel and select the applet for the device in question. For example, to set the resources for your sound card, you would select the Multimedia applet, Devices tab, and select properties for the Audio device that match your sound card.

Upgrading Windows NT 3.5x Server

Upgrading to Windows NT 4 Server from Windows NT 3.5x Server is a relatively simple process. The installation can be done from a Windows NT 3.51 Server command prompt, the File Manager's Run menu selection, or by booting the bootable Windows NT 4 Server installation disks.

Note: It is not an option to upgrade a Windows NT Workstation installation to Windows NT Server. You must create a clean installation of Windows NT 4 Server if you are currently using Windows NT Workstation on the target computer.

If the target machine has a local CD-ROM drive, and you wish to perform the simplest installation, then from a command prompt, or File Manager, simply execute the WINNT32.EXE program with the /B option. This installs Windows NT 4 Server in a multiple-step process, copying the necessary files from the CD-ROM to a local drive and then performing the installation.

Tip

Good reasons to install Windows NT 4 Server as a new installation are as follows:

- *Any components that are not fully compatible are excluded from the installation.*
- *You can preserve your existing Windows NT Server installation and use it to keep the server running if you encounter difficulties.*
- *The size of the installation is smaller: The Windows NT 4 Server installation program doesn't remove old, no longer used, files from the Windows NT system directories when upgrading.*

Upgrading Windows NT 4 Server Beta Versions

Neither Microsoft nor I recommend that a final release version of a product be installed as an upgrade over a previous beta version of the product. If you have already installed one of the beta versions of Windows NT 4 Server, then we most strongly recommend that you make your final installation clean and delete the beta installation folder.

The best method to remove an existing Windows NT installation is to back up your data and reformat the drive. Although a clean installation requires that you reinstall your applications, this task is not quite as radical as it seems!

A second method that is almost as good, for drives using the FAT file system, is to reinstall the system boot files to the drive using the SYS command (using an MS-DOS or Windows 95 boot diskette). This action disables the Windows NT 4 Server boot code. Then you can boot to DOS (or Windows 95), use DELTREE to remove the Windows NT folder, and reinstall Windows NT 4 Server.

Creating Boot Diskettes

You create boot diskettes by running the Windows NT 4 Server setup program. You would use the option /O, which tells WINNT32.EXE to create the boot diskettes and not do an installation. Specifying /OX creates boot diskettes for either a CD-ROM or diskette installation.

Whenever you create boot diskettes (as a separate step), no files are written to the system that creates the boot diskettes. This way, you don't make any changes nor require any resources (such as disk space) on the machine that creates the boot diskettes.

Getting Down to Business: Installing Windows NT 4 Server

All installations of Windows NT 4 Server are unique. You may encounter other steps from the ones that are documented in this section. Don't panic: Follow the prompts, use common sense, and use the help features when in doubt.

In the following installation example, a primary domain controller (PDC) Windows NT 4 Server is created. Note that the computer system in the example consists of the following components:

- An Intel Pentium 90 (PCI bus) with 64MB of RAM.

- An Adaptec 2940 SCSI adapter (PCI bus) with four hard drives (a 2GB Quantum, a 1GB Micropolis, a 1GB Toshiba, and a 4GB Quantum), and a Toshiba CD-ROM drive.

- A Matrox Millennium adapter (PCI bus) with 4MB of video RAM.

- A 3Com 3c590 combo network adapter (PCI bus).

- Two Panasonic IDE CD-ROM drives, connected to an internal PCI bus IDE adapter. Yes, I have three CD-ROM drives on this server: The next CD-ROM drive will probably be a changer, however.

All the other hardware on this system is common: Microsoft mouse, standard SVGA monitor, 3.5-inch diskette drive, and so on. The installation CD drive is one of the IDE CD-ROM drives.

The computer system in this example has several versions of Windows NT Server already installed. I wanted to keep these earlier versions of Windows NT Server, so I decided to do a clean install of Windows NT 4 Server, with dual-boot capabilities.

Now, on to the installation!

Before You Begin

Here are a few details that require your attention before you begin:

- **Make sure that your hardware is operating correctly.** If the system has been unstable lately, don't install a new operating system hoping that things will get better. A new operating system will not correct hardware flaws or failures.

- **Ensure that you have enough space on your target drive to hold Windows NT 4 Server.** The setup program tests to make sure that enough space exists to install, but why put up with a failed installation? If installing on your C drive, 120MB to 200MB of free space is sufficient.

- **Make sure that you have a current and complete backup of all drives!** Mr. Murphy has personally assured me that he is watching and will take the necessary steps if your backup is lacking.

- **Make sure that you have the user list with names, groups, passwords, and such to allow restoring, from scratch, the user database.**

- **Make sure that you have all the necessary hardware configuration information.** If you have Windows 95 installed on the target machine, print the equipment summary report (Control Panel, System applet) and save this. If necessary, write down the cards, drives, IRQs, DMA channels, and I/O addresses used on your system. Understand the implications of installing Windows NT 4 Server on a PCI machine that is dual-booted with Windows 95.

- **Make sure that you have a hard copy of any other significant information that you may need.** Computer names, domain names, passwords, and telephone numbers may all be critical to a successful installation. You probably won't be able to stop your installation to look up a name or number!

Tip

If you have Windows 95 installed, you can use the Windows 95 Control Panel's System applet to print an extensive report on the system. To do so, select the Device Manager tab, click on Computer at the top of the tree view, and then click on the Print button.

Now I want to show you how to do a "typical" installation. In this installation, I am installing a clean installation on a machine that has Windows NT 3.51 Server already installed. In this situation, I use File Manager's File | Run option to execute the startup command.

Before installing, advise your client users that the system will be down, or that performance (if you have multiple servers) may be degraded, as the operating system is being upgraded. If you have backup servers, great—they can take the load while you are installing Windows NT 4 Server. If no backup server is available, then you probably will have to upgrade either at night or on a weekend so as to minimize the impact on users.

Beginning the Installation

Put the Windows NT 4 Server CD in the CD-ROM drive. More than one CD-ROM drive? (I have three on my server.) Use the fastest CD-ROM drive that you have; the installation process moves a large number of files from the CD to the hard drive.

The installation process is simple to start:

1. Start a command window running.

2. Change to the CD-ROM drive with the CHDIR command.

3. Use the DIR /s command to make sure that the Windows NT 4 Server distribution CD can be read properly. It can be painful to get part of the way through the installation and find a read error on the CD. If the CD has a read error, the setup program aborts the installation; you do not risk losing anything if this happens.

Note: It's not the end of the world if there is a read error on the CD. The Windows NT 4 Server setup program reads all required files from the CD and copies them to a temporary folder before performing the actual installation. You may successfully cancel an installation at virtually any step!

4. You need to change to the folder that matches your system's architecture (for example, the folder I386 if you are using an Intel 486, Pentium, or Pentium Pro). In this chapter, I am installing Windows NT 4 Server on a Pentium-based system.

5. To install, start the setup program (WINNT32.EXE or WINNT.EXE). Generally, you don't need to use boot diskettes to install Windows NT 4 Server as an upgrade, so try installing with the /B option.

When the setup program starts, it checks the hard drive free space on all local drives.

After the program has checked the drives for free space, a dialog box prompts you for the location of the Windows NT 4 Server files. The default is the path from which the setup program was started. For most installations, that path is the correct location. Additionally, the dialog box, as shown in Figure 2-1, has an Options button that displays the Options dialog box (see Figure 2-2).

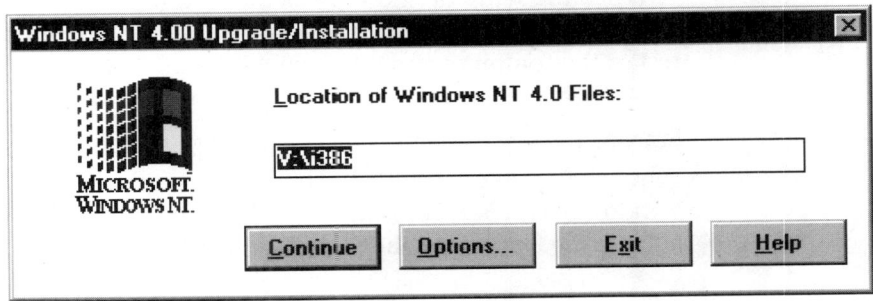

Figure 2-1: The Windows NT 4 Upgrade/Installation dialog box.

With the Options dialog, you may change several options, including the creation of boot diskettes, the creation of local source, and the name of the installation script file.

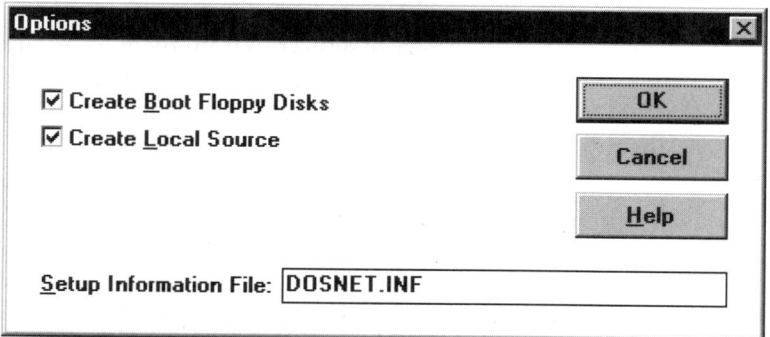

Figure 2-2: The Options dialog box for installation.

After setting any options desired, click on OK on the Options dialog box.

Copying Files to the Temporary Folder

The next stage of the installation is copying files from the CD-ROM to the local temporary folder. The file copy process can be lengthy. Spending the time checking that you have all the information needed to install Windows NT 4 Server may be best. A double-speed CD-ROM drive gives you enough time to grab a quick lunch.

When the setup program has completed the copying of the installation files from the CD to the local hard drive, the system prompts you to restart the computer and continue the installation.

Starting the Installation

When the setup program reboots the system, the boot manager starts the Windows NT 4 Server installation procedure. After the computer has booted, the text screen shown in Figure 2-3 displays.

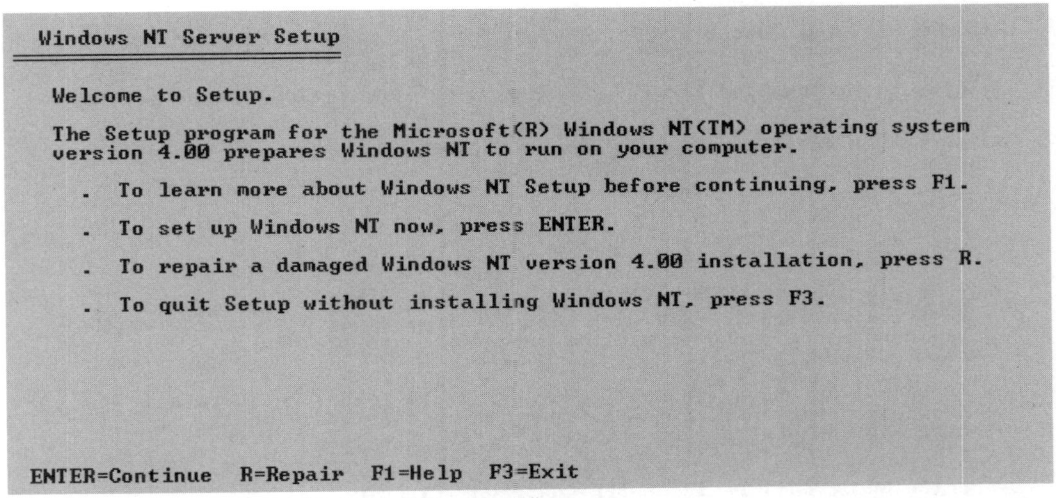

```
Windows NT Server Setup
━━━━━━━━━━━━━━━━━━━━━━━━

Welcome to Setup.

The Setup program for the Microsoft(R) Windows NT(TM) operating system
version 4.00 prepares Windows NT to run on your computer.

    .  To learn more about Windows NT Setup before continuing, press F1.

    .  To set up Windows NT now, press ENTER.

    .  To repair a damaged Windows NT version 4.00 installation, press R.

    .  To quit Setup without installing Windows NT, press F3.




ENTER=Continue   R=Repair   F1=Help   F3=Exit
```

Figure 2-3: The Windows NT Server Setup welcome screen.

Using the setup program, you can continue with the installation, repair an existing installation, get help, or exit the installation process. For a clean installation, press Enter to continue.

Tip

If you had already installed Windows NT 4 Server, but are having problems (perhaps system files were either damaged or deleted in error), you could choose to repair the existing installation. Repair is useful as a complete reinstallation of supporting applications, and the operating system is not needed.

Scanning for Mass Storage

The next stage of the installation process is to scan for mass storage (hard disks and CD-ROM drives) installed on the computer. Generally, the setup program automatically detects both SCSI and IDE drives.

For some devices, you may need to specify the adapter. Figure 2-4 shows the results of the scan for mass storage devices on my computer; your devices will be different, though the screen will be similar. If for some reason the setup program does not find a mass storage device to install Windows NT 4 Server to, the installation cannot continue.

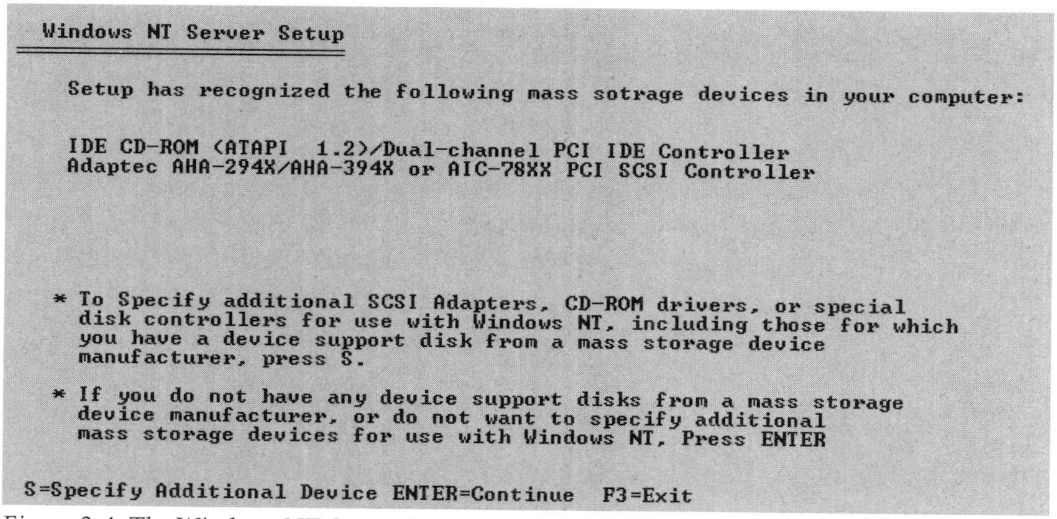

```
Windows NT Server Setup
========================

    Setup has recognized the following mass sotrage devices in your computer:

    IDE CD-ROM (ATAPI  1.2)/Dual-channel PCI IDE Controller
    Adaptec AHA-294X/AHA-394X or AIC-78XX PCI SCSI Controller




  * To Specify additional SCSI Adapters, CD-ROM drivers, or special
    disk controllers for use with Windows NT, including those for which
    you have a device support disk from a mass storage device
    manufacturer, press S.

  * If you do not have any device support disks from a mass storage
    device manufacturer, or do not want to specify additional
    mass storage devices for use with Windows NT, Press ENTER

S=Specify Additional Device ENTER=Continue   F3=Exit
```

Figure 2-4: The Windows NT Server Setup mass storage detection screen lists the storage (disk) devices.

Generally, if most of your mass storage (including your CD-ROM, boot, and installation drives) are detected, you can perform a successful installation. At this stage, you can add any devices that were installed but not detected to the list of devices. Table 2-2 lists some of the supported adapters that are detected or that you can add manually.

After the setup program has detected the mass storage adapters, it will then check to see whether a copy of Windows NT Server is already installed on the system. If setup finds an existing copy of Windows NT, the existing copy of Windows NT may be upgraded or left untouched.

Adaptec AHA-151X/AHA-152X or AIC-6260/AIC-6360 SCSI Host Adapter

Adaptec AHA-154X/AHA-164X SCSI Host Adapter

Adaptec AHA-174X EISA SCSI Host Adapter

Adaptec AHA-274X/AHA-284X/AIC-777X SCSI Host Adapter

Adaptec AHA-294X/AHA-394X or AIC-78XX PCI SCSI Controller

AMD PCI SCSI Controller/Ethernet Adapter

AMIscsi SCSI Host Adapter

BusLogic SCSI Host Adapter

Compaq Drive Array

Dell Drive Array

DPT SCSI Host Adapter

Future Domain TMC-7000EX EISA SCSI Host Adapter

Future Domain 8XX SCSI Host Adapter

Adaptec AHA-2920 or Future Domain 16XX/PCI/SCSI2Go SCSI Host
        Adapter

IBM MCA SCSI Host Adapter

IDE CD-ROM (ATAPI 1.2)/Dual-channel PCI IDE Controller

Mitsumi CD-ROM Controller

Mylex DAC960/Digital SWXCR-Ex RAID Controller

NCR 53C9X SCSI Host Adapter

NCR C700 MCA SCSI Host Adapter

NCR 53C710 MCA SCSI Host Adapter

Symbios Logic C810 PCI SCSI Host Adapter

Olivetti ESC-1/ESC-2 SCSI Host Adapter

QLogic PCI SCSI Host Adapter

MKEPanasonic CD-ROM Controller

Sony Proprietary CD-ROM Controller

UltraStor 14F/14FB/34F/34FA/34FB SCSI Host Adapter

UltraStor 24F/24FA SCSI Host Adapter

Table 2-2: Mass storage adapters supported by the Windows NT 4 Server Setup program.

Choosing the Type of Installation

This is the first critical point in the installation: You must make a choice either to upgrade the existing Windows NT installation (the existing installation will be lost, and there will be nothing to go back to if you have problems) or install a clean copy of Windows NT 4 Server (you'll have to reinstall all existing systems, applications, and networking information). Figure 2-5 shows the list of previous installations. In my example, there were previous installations for both Windows NT 3.51 Server and Windows NT 3.5 Server.

A clean installation is usually more reliable in most situations. Nothing is inherent to Windows NT 4 Server that prevents you from having more than one copy of Windows NT 4 Server installed on the same computer. The DORA server, which was the example for this chapter, has several copies of Windows NT 3.5x Server and Windows 95 installed and managed with Windows NT 4 Server's dual-boot manager.

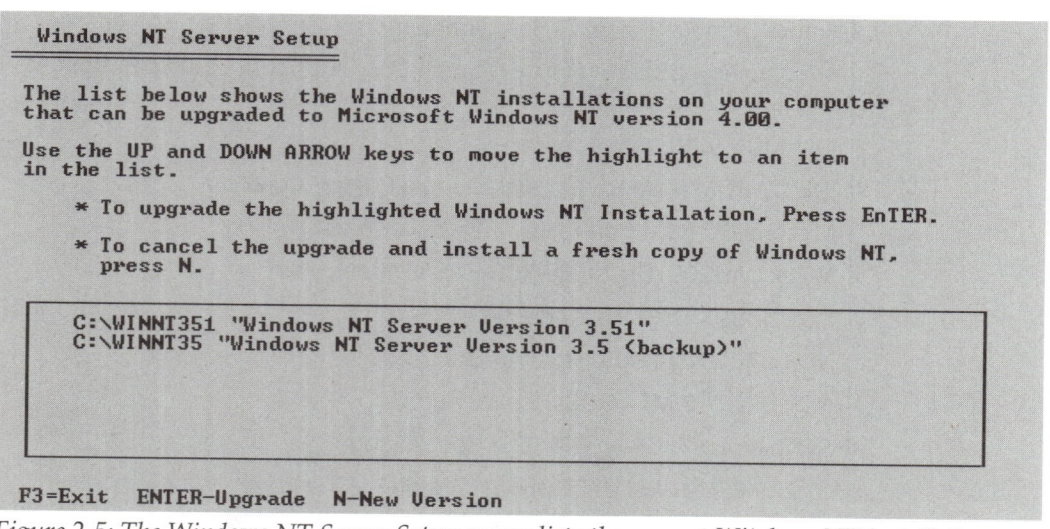

Figure 2-5: The Windows NT Server Setup screen lists the current Windows NT installations.

For this installation, I pressed the N key (for New Version) to perform a new installation.

Updating the List of Standard Devices

When performing a clean installation, the setup program lists the "standard devices" for the target system. For these devices (video, system, keyboard, mouse, and so on), the default selections (as shown in Figure 2-6) are generally satisfactory.

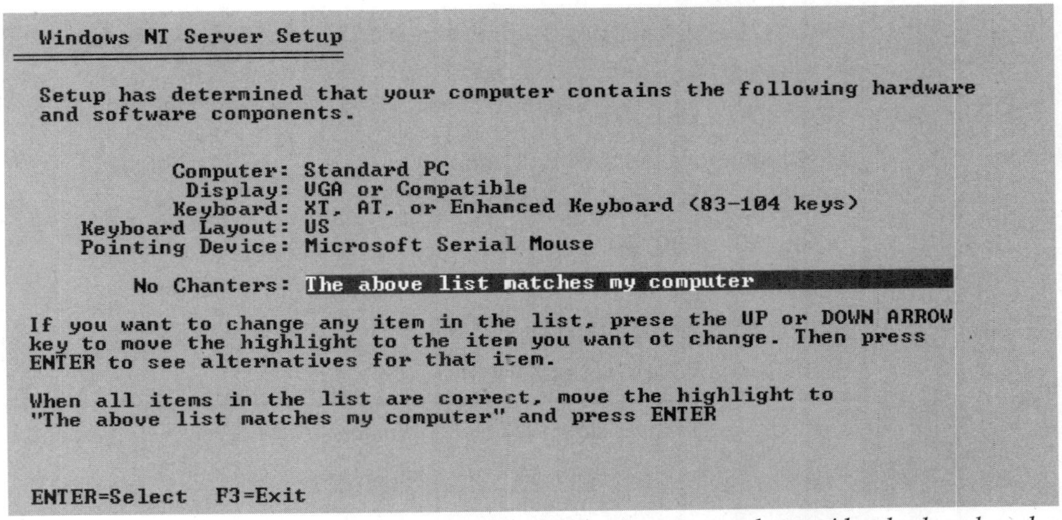

```
Windows NT Server Setup

Setup has determined that your computer contains the following hardware
and software components.

             Computer: Standard PC
              Display: UGA or Compatible
             Keyboard: XT, AT, or Enhanced Keyboard (83-104 keys)
      Keyboard Layout: US
       Pointing Device: Microsoft Serial Mouse

          No Chanters: The above list matches my computer

If you want to change any item in the list, prese the UP or DOWN ARROW
key to move the highlight to the item you want ot change. Then press
ENTER to see alternatives for that item.

When all items in the list are correct, move the highlight to
"The above list matches my computer" and press ENTER


ENTER=Select   F3=Exit
```

Figure 2-6: The Windows NT Server Setup default selections screen shows video, keyboard, and system types.

If you have a higher performance video adapter (such as DORA's Matrox Millennium) use the "standard VGA" selection for video adapter on this screen. Later, Windows NT 4 Server will detect the correct video adapter and install the correct drivers. Check the list of nonstandard computers to make sure that you are not installing Windows NT 4 Server on one of these systems. If you are installing Windows NT 4 Server on one of the nonstandard systems, you must tell the setup program. The nonstandard systems are listed in Table 2-3.

AST Manhattan SMP

Compaq SystemPro Multiprocessor or 100% Compatible

Corollary C-bus Architecture

Corollary C-bus Micro Channel Architecture

IBM PS/2 or other Micro Channel-based PC

MPS Uniprocessor PC

MPS Multiprocessor PC

MPS Multiprocessor Micro Channel PC

NCR System 3000 Model 3360/3450/3550

Olivetti LSX5030/40

Standard PC

Standard PC with C-Step i486

Wyse Series 7000i Model 740MP/760MP

Table 2-3: System types supported by the Windows NT 4 Server Setup program.

Selecting an Installation Drive

The Windows NT 4 Server setup program lists the drives available on which you can install the Windows NT 4 Server. You do not have to install Windows NT 4 Server on the C drive; you can use any drive with sufficient free space for installation. Figure 2-7 shows the D drive selected, which is an NTFS-formatted drive.

If the partition to which you are installing Windows NT 4 Server is currently FAT-based, the setup program prompts you with a message similar to the one shown in Figure 2-8, to convert the partition to the NTFS file system. The drive selected for my installation example is already formatted with the NTFS file system; therefore, the setup program allows only one choice: Leave the current file system intact.

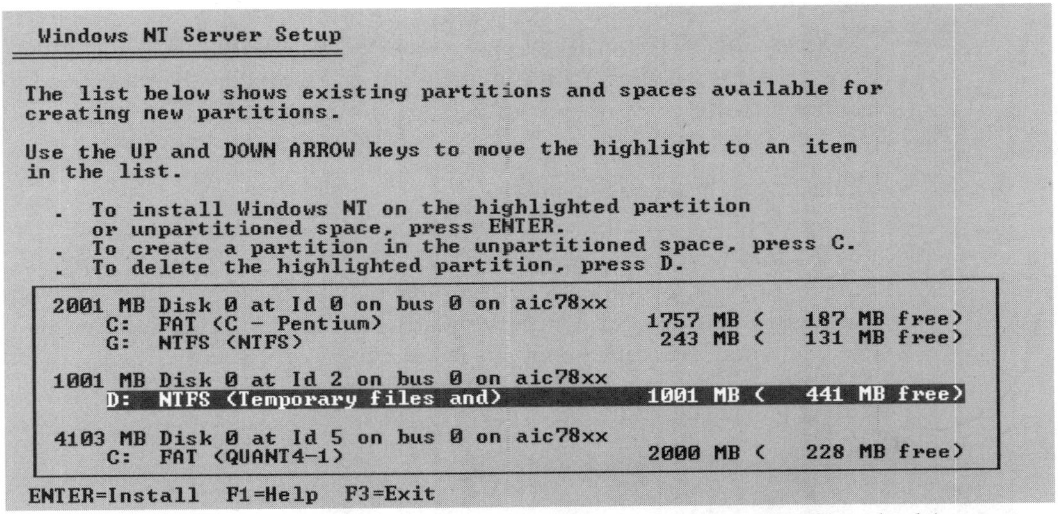

```
Windows NT Server Setup

The list below shows existing partitions and spaces available for
creating new partitions.

Use the UP and DOWN ARROW keys to move the highlight to an item
in the list.

    .   To install Windows NT on the highlighted partition
        or unpartitioned space, press ENTER.
    .   To create a partition in the unpartitioned space, press C.
    .   To delete the highlighted partition, press D.

┌─────────────────────────────────────────────────────────────────────┐
│ 2001 MB Disk 0 at Id 0 on bus 0 on aic78xx                          │
│      C:   FAT <C - Pentium>              1757 MB <   187 MB free>    │
│      G:   NTFS <NTFS>                     243 MB <   131 MB free>    │
│                                                                       │
│ 1001 MB Disk 0 at Id 2 on bus 0 on aic78xx                          │
│      D:   NTFS <Temporary files and>     1001 MB <   441 MB free>   │
│                                                                       │
│ 4103 MB Disk 0 at Id 5 on bus 0 on aic78xx                          │
│      C:   FAT <QUANT4-1>                  2000 MB <   228 MB free>   │
└─────────────────────────────────────────────────────────────────────┘

ENTER=Install   F1=Help   F3=Exit
```

Figure 2-7: The Windows NT Server Setup screen shows the D drive selected as the drive on which to install the Windows NT 4 Server.

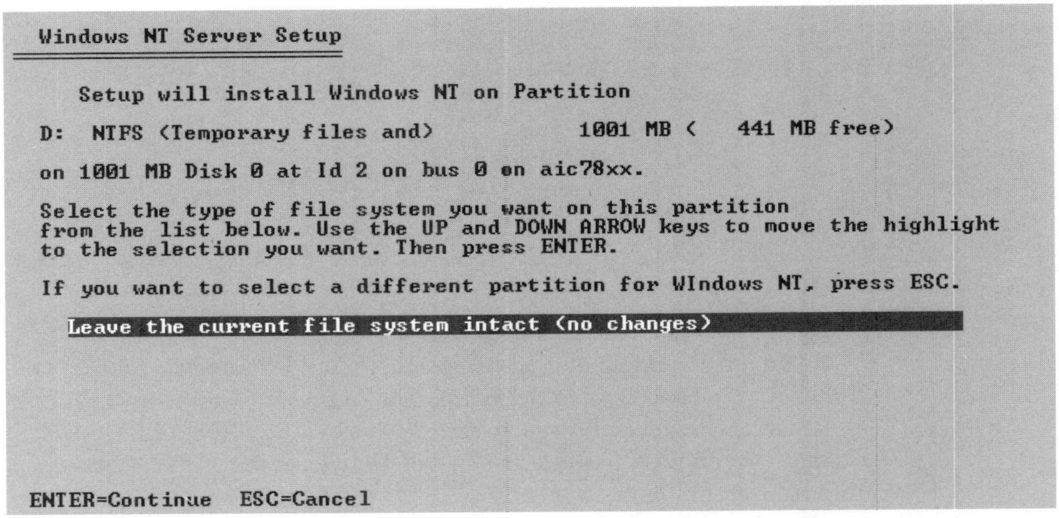

```
Windows NT Server Setup

    Setup will install Windows NT on Partition

D:  NTFS <Temporary files and>             1001 MB <   441 MB free>

on 1001 MB Disk 0 at Id 2 on bus 0 on aic78xx.

Select the type of file system you want on this partition
from the list below. Use the UP and DOWN ARROW keys to move the highlight
to the selection you want. Then press ENTER.

If you want to select a different partition for WIndows NT, press ESC.

    Leave the current file system intact (no changes)

ENTER=Continue   ESC=Cancel
```

Figure 2-8: The Windows NT Server Setup screen is where you select the type of file system that you want on the installation drive/partition.

Do not convert the C partition to NTFS if the computer is being dual-booted to an operating system other than Windows NT (for example, Windows 95 or MS-DOS), because the other operating system is unable to access the NTFS partition(s). If you install only Windows NT 4 Server on the target machine, then converting to NTFS can be advantageous for either security, compression, or performance reasons.

Selecting an Installation Folder

After you have selected your installation drive, you must select the folder into which you'll install Windows NT 4 Server. If you are upgrading an existing Windows NT Server installation, then the folder is the one in which Windows NT Server is already installed. Figure 2-9 shows the screen where you can change the installation folder's name.

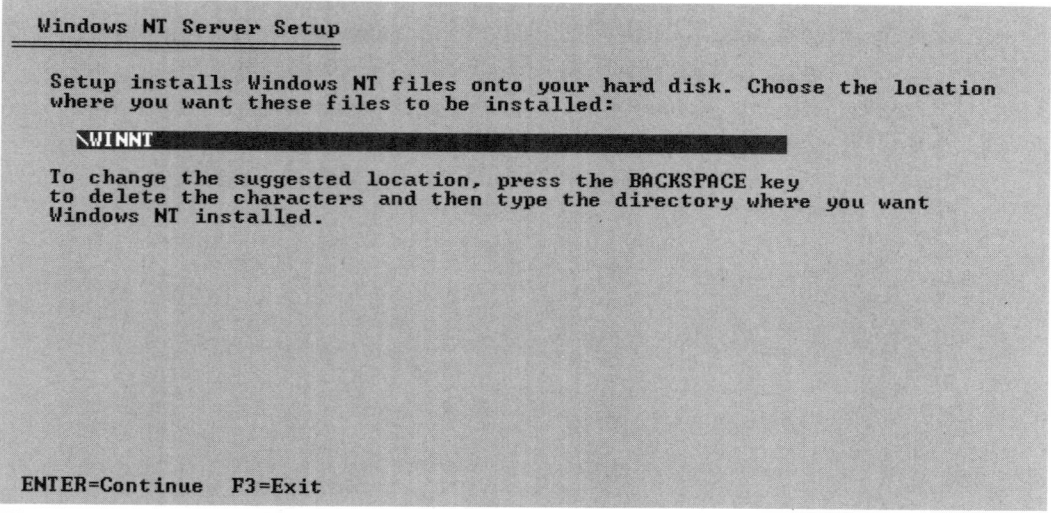

Figure 2-9: Use the Windows NT Server Setup screen to specify the installation folder name.

If you are creating a new, clean installation of Windows NT 4 Server, then you must specify a folder name. The suggested name for this folder is \WINNT; however, you can override this default if the folder exists already or you wish to place this installation of Windows NT 4 Server into a different folder.

Examining Hard Disks

The next step in the installation of Windows NT 4 Server is for the install program to prompt you to do a thorough inspection of your drive, as shown in Figure 2-10. I highly recommend that you allow the setup program to perform this inspection; your drive may have defects, errors, or problems of which you are unaware.

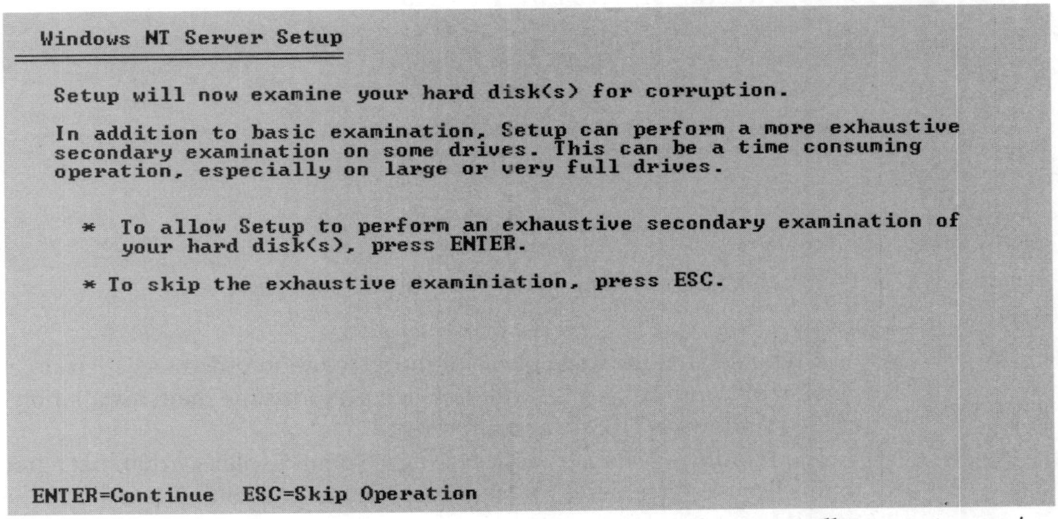

```
Windows NT Server Setup

    Setup will now examine your hard disk(s) for corruption.

    In addition to basic examination, Setup can perform a more exhaustive
    secondary examination on some drives. This can be a time consuming
    operation, especially on large or very full drives.

        *  To allow Setup to perform an exhaustive secondary examination of
           your hard disk(s), press ENTER.

        * To skip the exhaustive examiniation, press ESC.




    ENTER=Continue   ESC=Skip Operation
```

Figure 2-10: The Windows NT Server Setup hard disk examination screen allows you to examine the drive prior to installation.

If you skip this test, the setup program does a simple test of the drive. However, this simple test is not exhaustive enough to detect any serious problems. Skip this inspection only if you are absolutely certain that your drive has no problems or errors.

Copying Files

After checking the drive for errors, the setup program copies files from the temporary folder created previously. This file copy process doesn't take as much time as did copying the files from the CD-ROM; this is a hard drive–to–hard drive copy operation. After all the files are copied to their final location, the setup program displays a reboot screen, as shown in Figure 2-11.

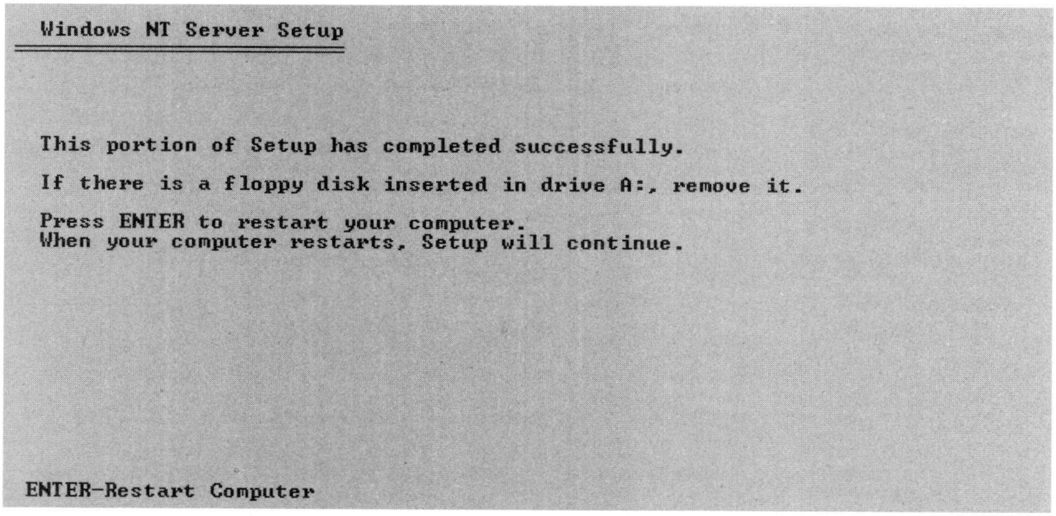

```
Windows NT Server Setup


  This portion of Setup has completed successfully.

  If there is a floppy disk inserted in drive A:, remove it.

  Press ENTER to restart your computer.
  When your computer restarts, Setup will continue.









  ENTER-Restart Computer
```

Figure 2-11: The Windows NT Server Setup screen with the reboot message.

A reboot starts the third phase of the installation process. A special version of Windows NT is started, which performs the main installation of the Windows NT 4 Server components.

The Windows NT 4 Server license agreement displays. You must agree to this license agreement (please read it) before you complete the installation. If for some reason you cannot agree to the license agreement, you must not install Windows NT 4 Server.

Additional Systems Administrator Installation Tasks

After agreeing to the license agreement, the welcome window for the installation appears as shown in Figure 2-12. Read the message describing the next three parts of the setup program and click on the Next button.

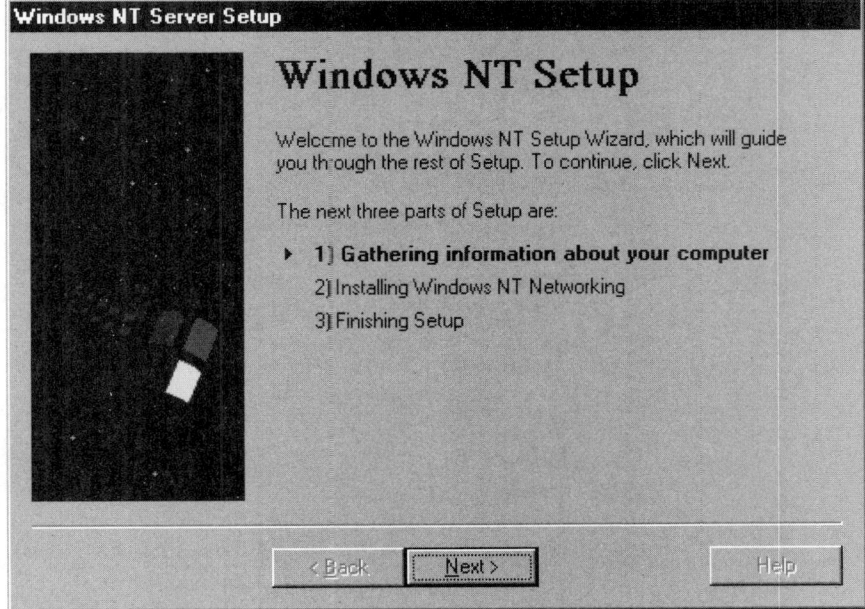

Figure 2-12: The Windows NT Server Setup Wizard welcome window.

Giving Background Information

The next information required by the setup program is your name and organization. This information is placed in the Windows NT 4 Server Registry for registration purposes. Figure 2-13 shows the Name and Organization window. To complete this window, enter your name and organization in the text boxes and then click on the Next button.

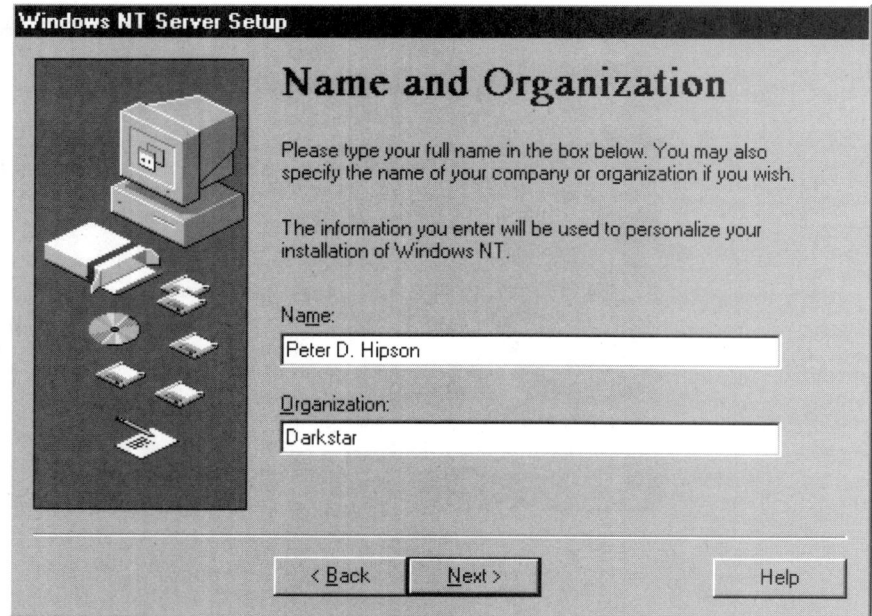

Figure 2-13: Use the Windows NT Server Setup window to enter your name and organization.

Most installations of Windows NT 4 Server prompt for a product ID code, which is found on the back of the Windows NT 4 Server CD case. Enter this number when prompted, and click on the Next button.

The Windows NT 4 Server licensing mode must be determined by the user. The window shown in Figure 2-14 allows you to choose either Per Server or Per Seat licensing modes.

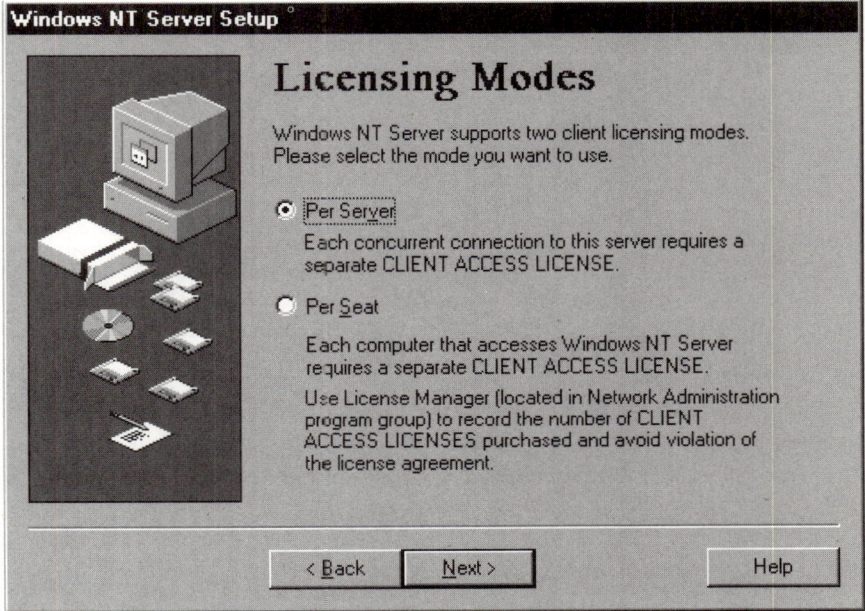

Figure 2-14: Use the Windows NT Server Setup Licensing Modes window to select one of the two licensing modes supported: Per Seat or Per Server.

Windows NT Server supports two client licensing modes: Per Server or Per Seat. Some simple hints for selecting which licensing mode are as follows:

- If you have only one server, Microsoft recommends that you choose the Per Server option. With the Per Server mode, Microsoft allows you to change once to the Per Seat mode. You can make this change any time after selecting the Per Server option.

- However, if you have more than one server and the total number of Client Access Licenses for all servers to support the Per Server mode is equal to or greater than the number of computers or workstations, you should choose (or later convert) to the Per Seat option license option.

After selecting your licensing mode, click on the Next button.

The Setup Wizard prompts you for a computer name, as shown in Figure 2-15. In my case, the computer name is DORA, so other client computers will access shares on DORA in the format of \\DORA\share name. After entering the computer name, click on the Next button.

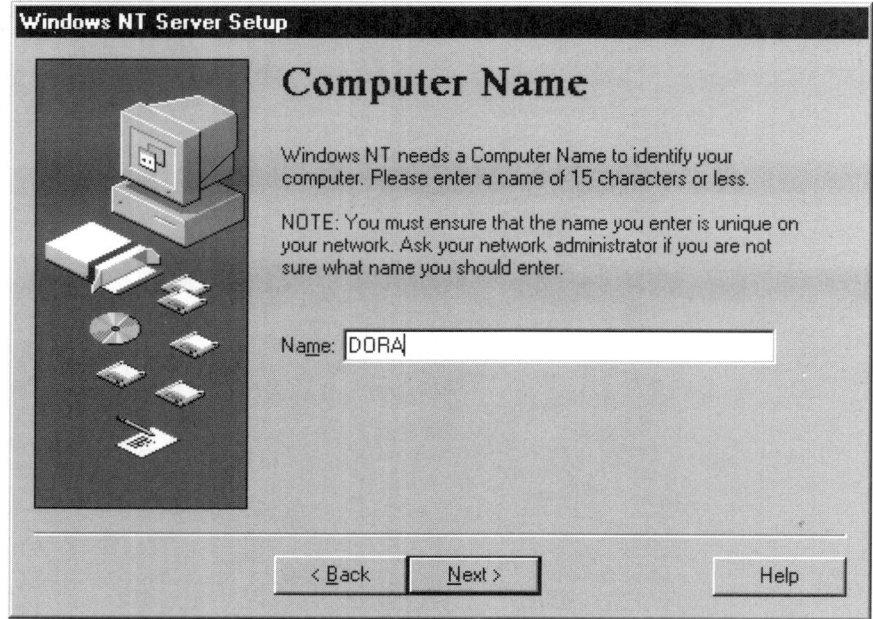

Figure 2-15: The Windows NT Server Setup window is where you give your computer a name.

Selecting the Type of Server

Things have looked easy up till now. You've had no hard choices, no difficult decisions. All of a sudden, Microsoft prompts you to enter a name to identify your computer. Systems administrators who are not experienced with Microsoft networks (Windows NT Server in particular) may find this prompt confusing, or, at the very least, thought provoking.

As Figure 2-16 shows, you must decide whether you are setting up a primary domain controller (PDC), a backup domain controller (BDC), or a stand-alone server. What's the difference?

A *stand-alone server* is the only server on the network, and the network model is called a workgroup. There can be other servers (such as a NetWare server), but this server is the only Windows NT 4 Server on the network. User information is entered at the server one time and is not shared between servers—this is the only server which has user information.

A *domain* is a network that (usually) has more than one server. With a domain, one server is designated as the PDC, which manages security for the entire domain. There are usually one or more BDC servers, too:

Each of these servers has a backup copy of the security information, which is automatically updated by the PDC. If anything happens to the PDC, a BDC is able to "take over" as a new PDC. If you only have one server, it can still be a domain controller (it is always a PDC).

With a domain, you can use a domain controller as a way to share login authorizations so that user identification information doesn't have to be updated manually on each server.

If you are unsure of which selection to take, configure your server as a domain and set the server as the PDC. Later, you may "demote" the server to a BDC if needed.

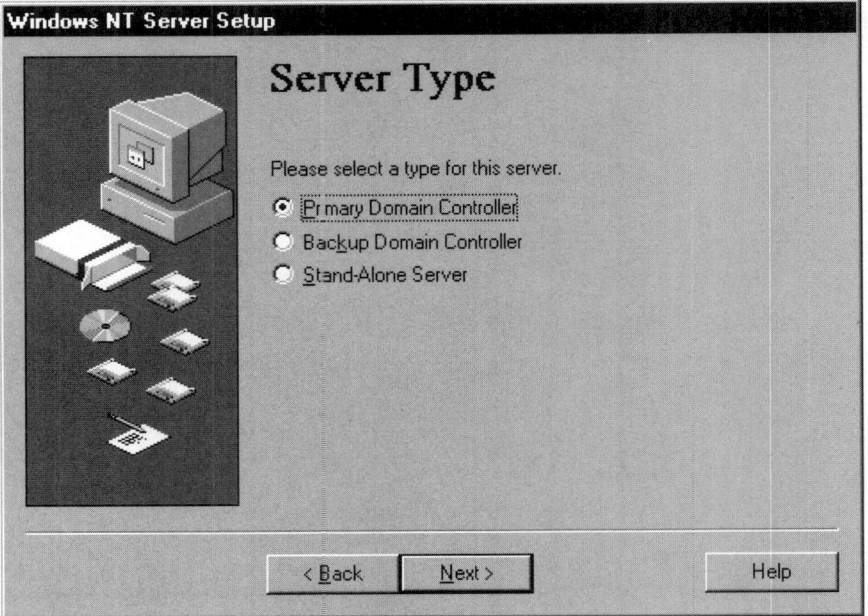

Figure 2-16: The Windows NT Server Setup Server Type window is where you select whether this is a domain or not.

Note: If you are unsure, set your system up as a Primary Domain Controller (PDC)—you cannot convert from a stand-alone server to a PDC at a later date, but instead would have to reinstall Windows NT 4 Server. Having a stand-alone server configured to run as a PDC doesn't add too much to the overhead of the system.

After selecting your server type, click on the Next button.

Setting Up the Administrator's Account

Next, the only userid that is created by the Setup Wizard is the administrator account. This account is the main account that the systems administrator uses to manage Windows NT 4 Server. A password must be specified for the administrator account, as shown in Figure 2-17.

Figure 2-17: The Windows NT Server Setup Administrator Account window is where you supply the administrator's password.

Select this password carefully. The administrator account is a powerful account and, if abused, could cause substantial problems. Also, forgetting the administrator account's password may result in having to reinstall Windows NT 4 Server! After entering the administrator's password, click on the Next button.

Specifying That You Want an ERD

You use a Windows NT Emergency Repair Disk (ERD) to fix the system when serious corruption or other problems prevent Windows NT from being booted. The Setup Wizard prompts you, as shown in Figure 2-18, to create this Emergency Repair Disk. Respond Yes! Even if you already have an Emergency Repair Disk, create a new one for each installation.

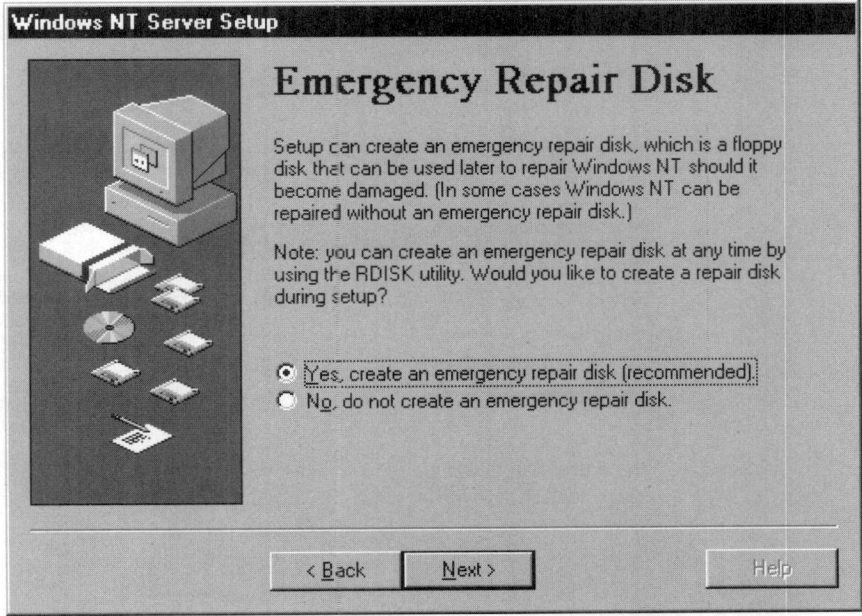

Figure 2-18: Use the Windows NT Server Setup Emergency Repair Disk window to create an Emergency Repair Disk.

When this disk is created, make sure that you mark it with a notation that describes which computer the disk is for. Without an Emergency Repair Disk, a number of simple problems could occur requiring reinstallation of Windows NT 4 Server to correct. After selecting whether you wish to create an ERD or not, click on the Next button.

Selecting Which Components to Install

The Setup Wizard next prompts you to select the Windows NT 4 Server components. Figure 2-19 shows the six main categories of components that I selected for this installation example. If you have sufficient space on your installation drive, you can select all components; this saves you from having to reinstall components later.

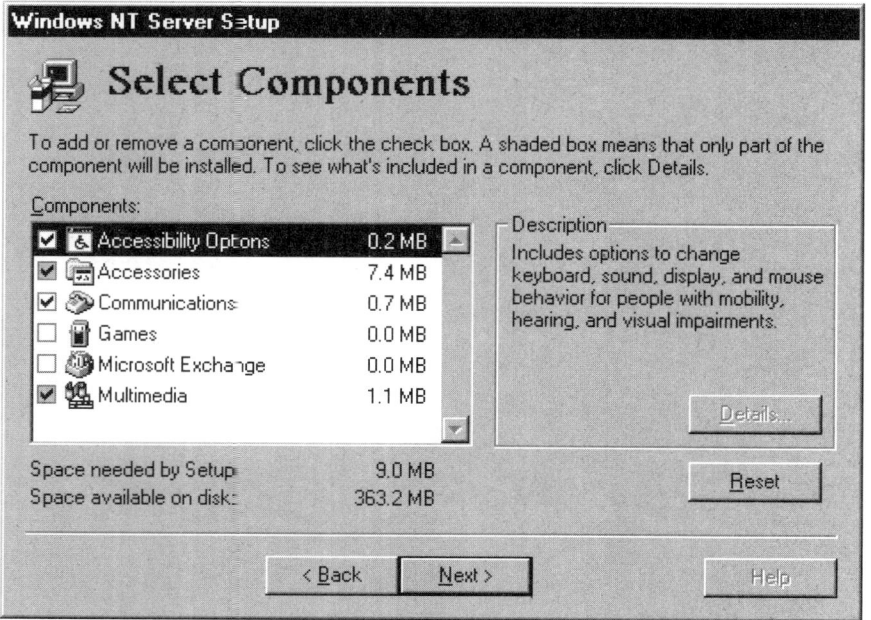

Figure 2-19: The Windows NT Server Setup Select Components window is where you select options to install.

- **Accessibility Options**—options that assist users who have an impairment or disability. Items in this category include keyboard, mouse, and sound support. An applet, called Accessibility Options, is added to the Control Panel, allowing customization of the Accessibility Options.

- **Accessories**—items that include a number of other useful utilities. Selecting all accessories at installation time may make the installation easier.

- **Communications**—Options in the Communications area include the HyperTerminal program for communications.

- **Games**—We all play games sometimes. The Games group includes a number of games such as Pinball, FreeCell, Solitaire, and Minesweeper. These games serve a very valid purpose in that you can use them to test the functionality of your installation. Install Games unless they are not allowed by your organization.

- **Exchange**—Microsoft Exchange includes the Exchange client (not server). Exchange is a very competent e-mail client that can be used with Microsoft Mail, Internet mail, Fax, and MSN mail.

- **Multimedia**—The Multimedia group includes the CD Player, Media Player, and a number of other useful utilities. If you have a CD-ROM drive and a sound card, I recommend that you select the Multimedia option.

After selecting options and setting details as necessary, click on the Next button.

Moving On to Networking

The next stage of the setup program is perhaps the most important part of your Windows NT 4 Server installation. Figure 2-20 shows step two, installing the network functionality. This stage of the installation is critical, because this is a server! Click on the Next button to begin installing network components.

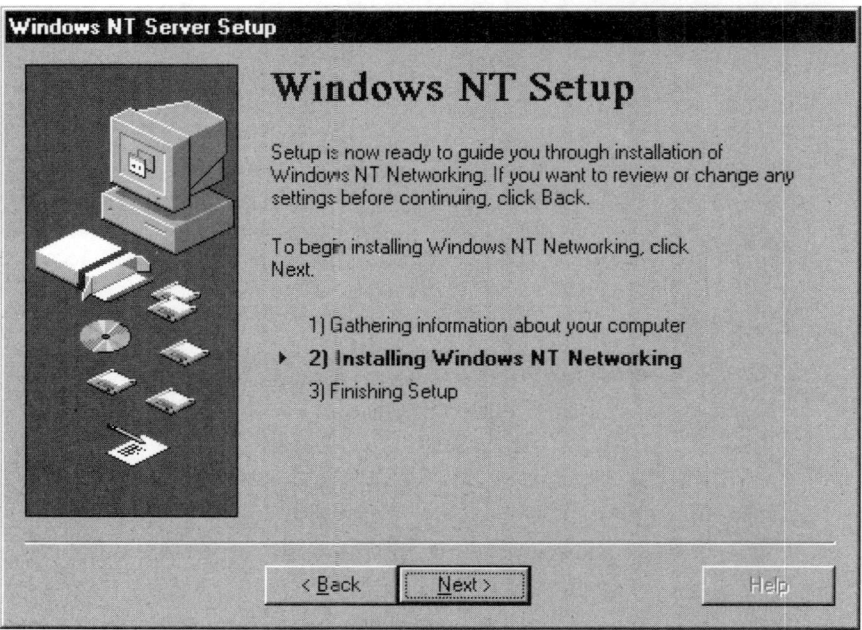

Figure 2-20: Use the Windows NT Server Setup Networking window to begin installing Windows NT Networking.

At this stage, your knowledge of both the system and the network is critical; notes and other information should be on hand at this stage.

Selecting Network Options

The first networking choice is how the server is connected to a network, as Figure 2-21 shows. You have two nonexclusive choices on this window.

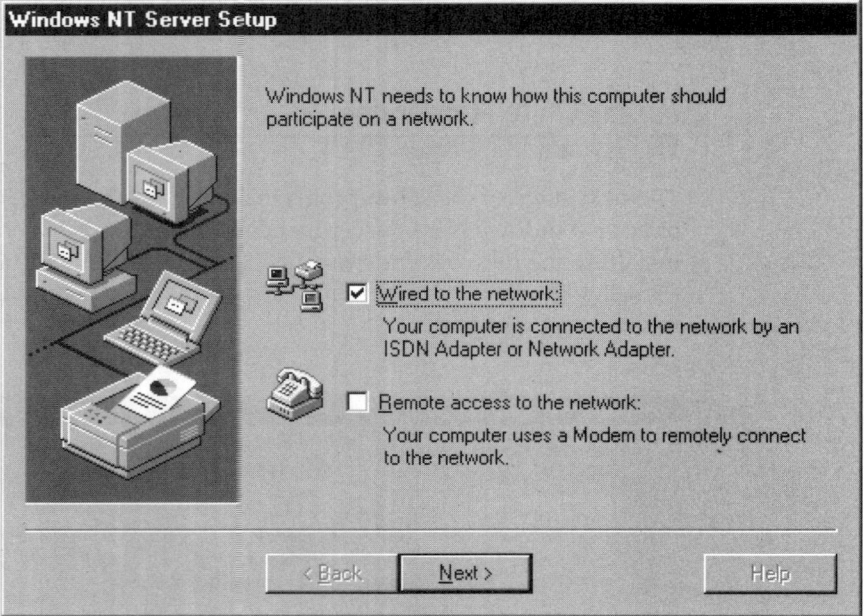

Figure 2-21: The Windows NT Server Setup Network Access window is where you select what network types to use.

- **Wired to the Network**—where the system is permanently connected to the network, using either a Network Interface Card (NIC) or via ISDN.

- **Remote Access to the Network (Modem)**—usually called Remote Access Server (RAS). This is where clients dial into the system using one (or more) modems connected to the system's serial ports.

Remember: If need be, you can select both choices. After selecting the network types, click on the Next button.

You are next prompted, by Setup Wizard, to install Microsoft's Internet Information Server (IIS) (see Figure 2-22). Doing so is optional. If you won't be using this server on either the Internet or an intranet, then there is no purpose in installing IIS. However, if at a later date you determine that you do need to install IIS, an icon on the desktop called "Install Internet Information Server" automatically installs IIS for you. After selecting whether to install IIS or not, click on the Next button.

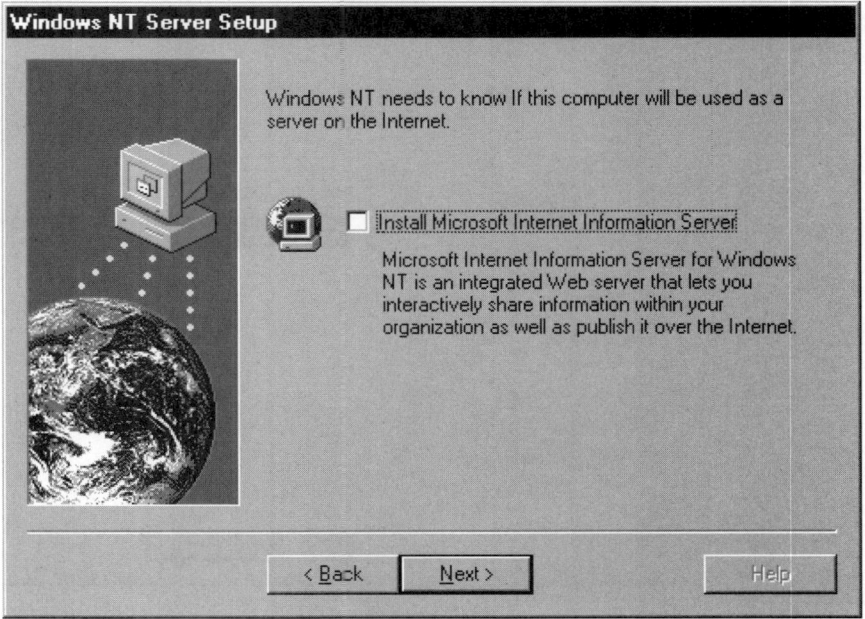

Figure 2-22: The Windows NT Server Setup Internet Connection window is where you specify whether you want to install the Microsoft Internet Information Server.

Note: The version of IIS that is shipped with Windows NT 4 Server installs under both Windows NT 4 Workstation and Windows 95. These versions (Windows NT 4 Workstation and Windows 95) have a more limited capability than the version that installs under Windows NT 4 Server.

The server's NIC is the next stage in the setup program. Generally, the Setup Wizard can detect the correct NIC when you select the Detect (or Find Next) button. The button's title changes from Detect to Find Next after the server has found the first NIC. Figure 2-23 shows the Network

Adapters after I clicked the Find Next button. You may have more than one NIC. If so, select all the installed NICs that you want to use. You don't need to select modems for RAS at this time. You can configure RAS later. If by chance your NIC is not detected, you can manually add it to the list of NICs available.

After detecting and selecting your NIC, click on the Next button.

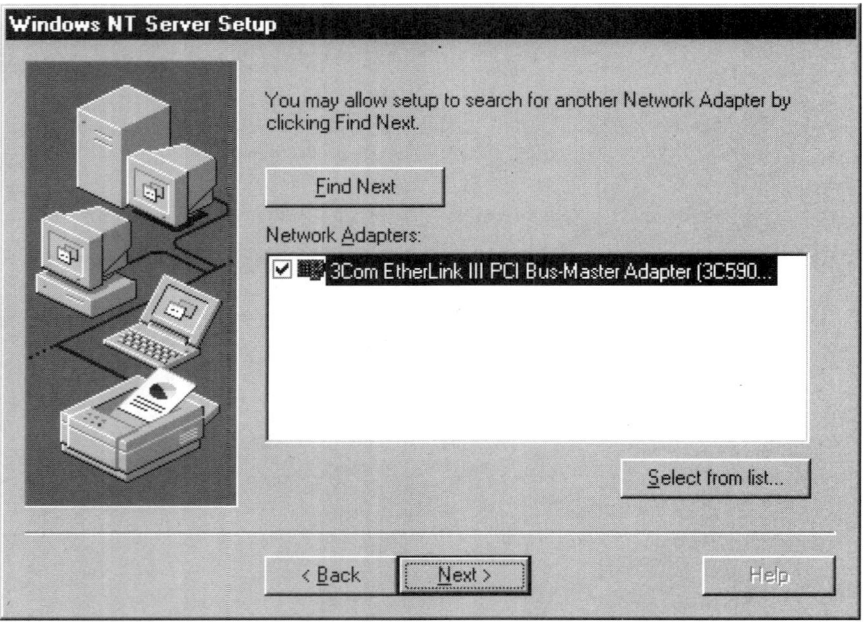

Figure 2-23: The Windows NT Server Setup Network Adapters selection window is where you select the correct network adapter.

Selecting Network Protocols & Services

You must also select the network protocol that you want to use. After installing Windows NT 4 Server, you can choose to add protocols. Realize, however, that the TCP/IP protocol is difficult to remove once installed. Figure 2-24 shows the Network Protocols selection window. After selecting the network protocols that you want to install, click on the Next button.

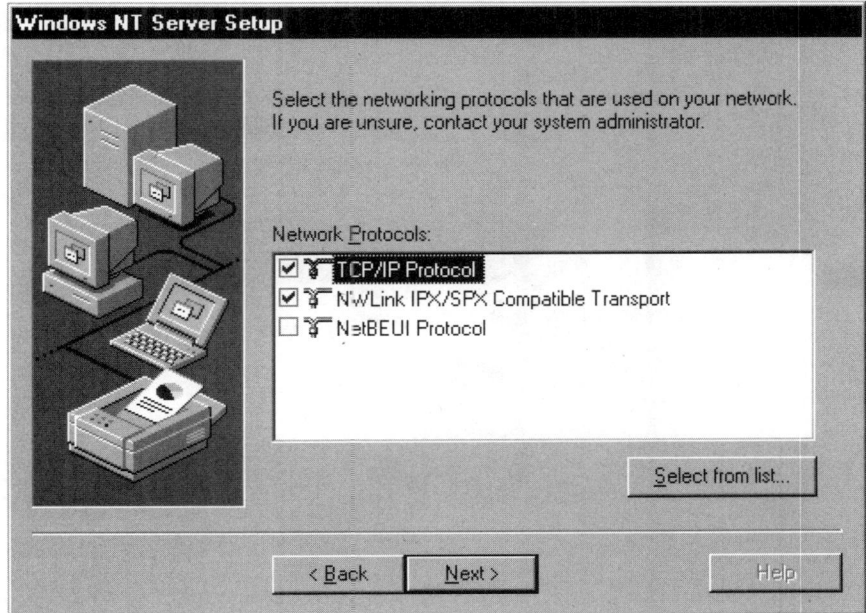

Figure 2-24: Use the Windows NT Server Setup Network Protocols selection window to select the network protocols.

The Selecting Services portion of the setup program may prove to be the most difficult portion of the network installation. A number of services are available, and if you are not familiar with the correct services to select from, you may have an unsuccessful Windows NT 4 Server installation.

Figure 2-25 shows the Network Services selection list. Clicking on the Select from list button allows you to select from all services listed in Table 2-4. After selecting the services to install, click on the Next button.

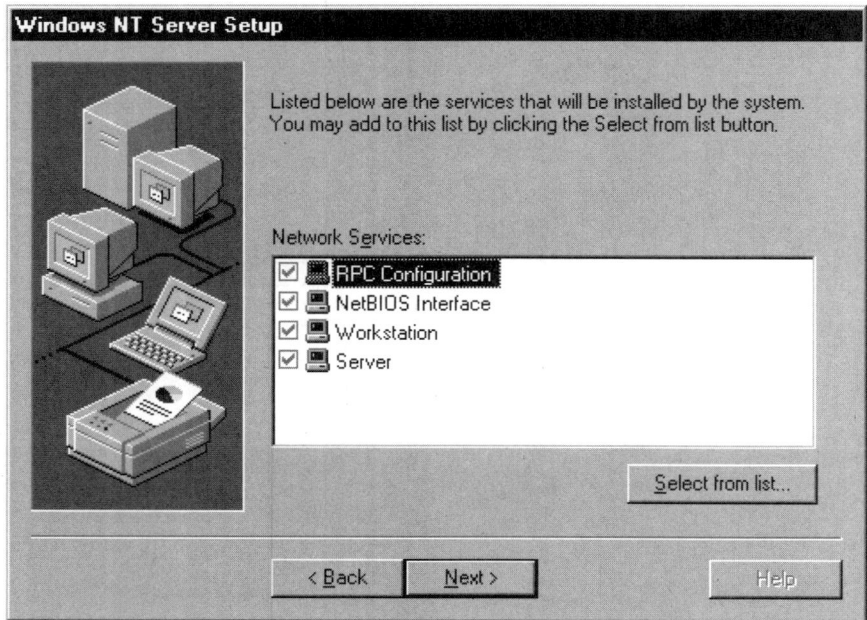

Figure 2-25: Use the Windows NT Server Setup Network Services window to select which services to install.

Table 2-4 lists the different services that the Setup Wizard makes available to you. These services are grouped into two categories: those available by default (you select them using the main Select Services page), and services that you choose by selecting optional services.

Generally, installing the services that Microsoft selects as defaults is a good idea. Usually, installing a service that you do not use will not cause problems.

Service	Default	Description
Remote Access Server	Yes	Allows you to dial into other servers and allows clients to dial into your server.
Remote Procedure Call (RPC) Configuration	Yes	Allows clients to execute procedures on the server.
NetBIOS Interface	Yes	Installs the NetBIOS network interface.
Workstation	Yes	Installs the workstation interface.
Server	Yes	Installs the server interface.
Dynamic Host Configuration Relay Agent	No	The agent. For more information about the Protocol (DHCP) DHCP Relay Agent, see the public specification RFC 1542, which you can retrieve, using FTP, at ds.internic.net in the RFC subfolder.
Gateway (and client) services for NetWare	No	Used to support Novell NetWare.
Microsoft Dynamic Host Configuration Protocol (DHCP) Server	No	For more information about the DHCP Relay Agent, see the public specification RFC 1542, which you can retrieve, using FTP, at ds.internic.net in the RFC folder.
Microsoft DNS Server	No	Allows an Internet/intranet TCP/IP network to resolve names at a local level.
NS IIS 2.0	No	The Microsoft Internet Information Server, this option allows you to install IIS.
Microsoft TCP/IP	No	Printers, connected directly to a TCP/IP protocol network, are supported by Windows NT 4 Server.

Service	Default	Description
Network Monitor Agent	No	Included with Microsoft Systems Management Server (SMS) is this utility. It is a network analyzer with the ability to capture real-time network data. Windows NT 4 Server includes Network Monitoring Agent Service that can be used with the Systems Management Server (SMS) Network Monitor utility.
Network Monitor Tools and Agent	No	Both the Network Monitor Agent and additional monitoring tools.
Remote Boot Service	No	Allows you to boot "diskless" workstations connected to the Windows NT 4 Server from the network.
Routing Information Protocol (RIP) for Internet Protocol	No	Routes network packets between two or more network adapters. This implementation is used for the Internet Protocol (IP).
Routing Information Protocol (RIP) for NwLink IPX/SPX Compatible Transport	No	Routes network packets between two or more network adapters. This implementation is used for the IPX/SPX transport.
Remote Procedure Call (RPC)support for Banyan		Allows clients to execute procedures on the server. This implementation is for the Banyan VINES network.
Service Advertising Protocol (SAP) Agent	No	NetWare clients use this to perform name resolution on NetWare networks. NetWare servers advertise their services through periodic SAP broadcasts.

Service	Default	Description
Services for Macintosh	No	Its features allow the Windows NT 4 Server to be connected to, and function with, an Apple Macintosh network.
Simple TCP/IP Services	No	Additional support for the TCP/IP protocol.
Simple Network Management Protocol (SNMP) Service	No	Windows NT 4 Server administrators use this to monitor and control remote hosts and gateways.
Windows Internet Name Service (WINS)	No	Resolves names for the TCP/IP protocol. Works much like a DNS server.

Table 2-4: Services you can select at installation time.

After you provide the necessary network information and click on the Next button, the Windows NT 4 Server setup program installs the components selected. See Figure 2-26.

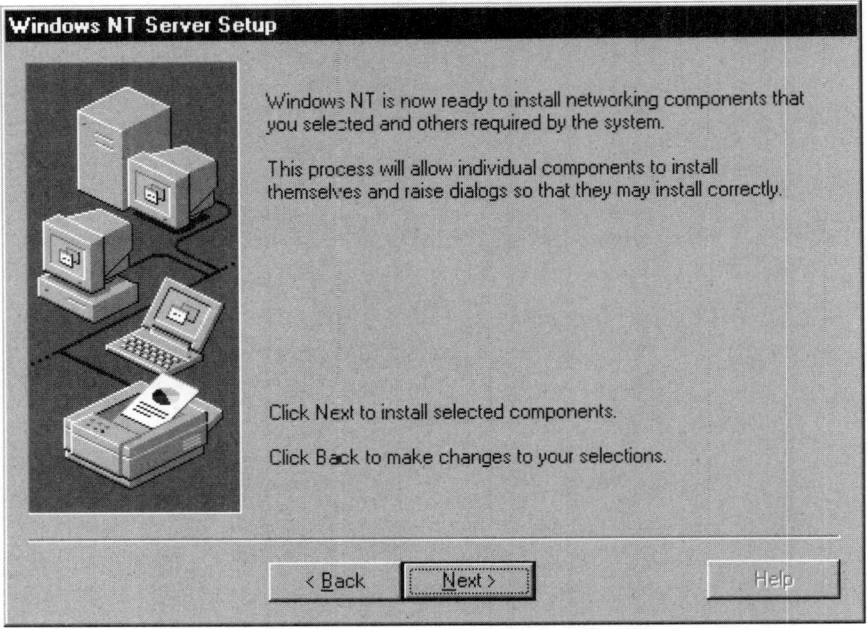

Figure 2-26: Click on Next to install selected components.

Configuring Server Pieces

The next step in the setup program is to configure the server portion of Windows NT 4 Server. The Setup Wizard prompts you to supply all the information that the setup program needs—respond to prompts as appropriate.

Earlier, if you chose to allow remote clients using a modem to access your computer (see Figure 2-21 shown previously), then the RAS modem (if you selected RAS) is now detected and configured. If you do not yet have your RAS modem installed, you can postpone this step till after the installation is complete. If your modem is not correctly detected, you may be able to select a compatible modem from the list. Knowing which other modems are similar to your modem is beneficial.

RAS is configured (if you have selected RAS) after the modem is detected and installed. Make sure that you configure whether this server can make calls (a client), receive calls (a server), or both.

TCP/IP configuration is the next step. You need to know the IP address of your server, the IP address of the Domain Name Server (DNS), and you may configure other parts of TCP/IP if necessary. If you selected TCP/IP, you will be prompted (see Figure 2-27) to use a DHCP server. If you have a DHCP server installed (on a different server), then you may wish to select Yes; otherwise, select the default button, No.

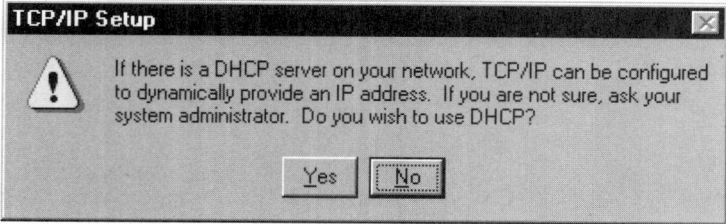

Figure 2-27: Find out: Do you wish to use a DHCP server to obtain the IP address?

The Microsoft TCP/IP Properties window is shown in Figure 2-28. You can display this window using the Control Panel's Network applet anytime after installation.

After configuring the TCP/IP properties, click on the OK button to continue.

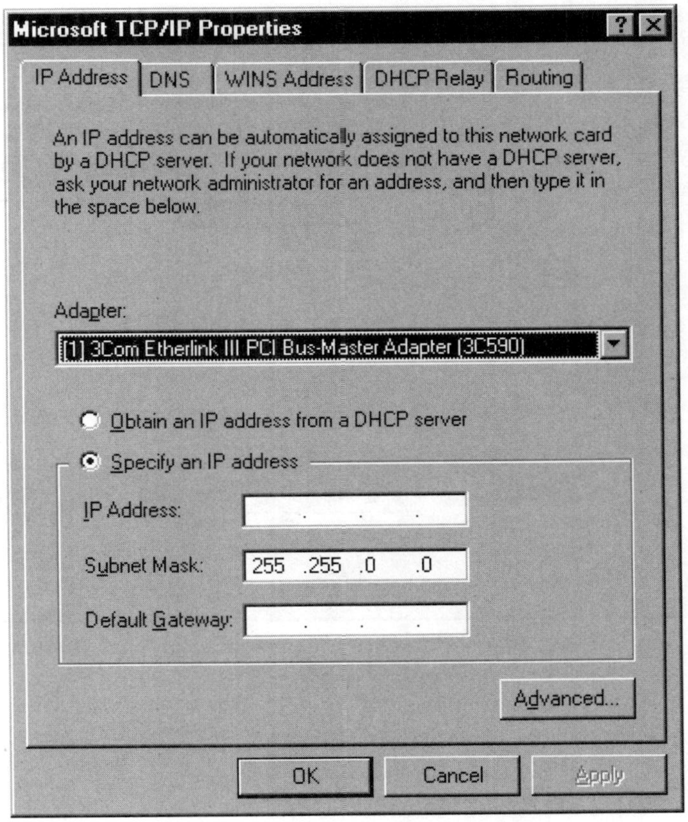

Figure 2-28: Microsoft TCP/IP Properties window.

The Setup Wizard reviews the current network configuration and allows you to make any modifications necessary. One caution: Though you can make almost any changes to the networking components to Windows NT 4 Server that you may need, be very careful not to delete the TCP/IP protocol, because you may be unable to reinstall it later without reinstalling Windows NT 4 Server.

The bindings (which "connect" the network components together) display, as shown in Figure 2-29. You can modify bindings as needed. After configuring the bindings, click on the Next button.

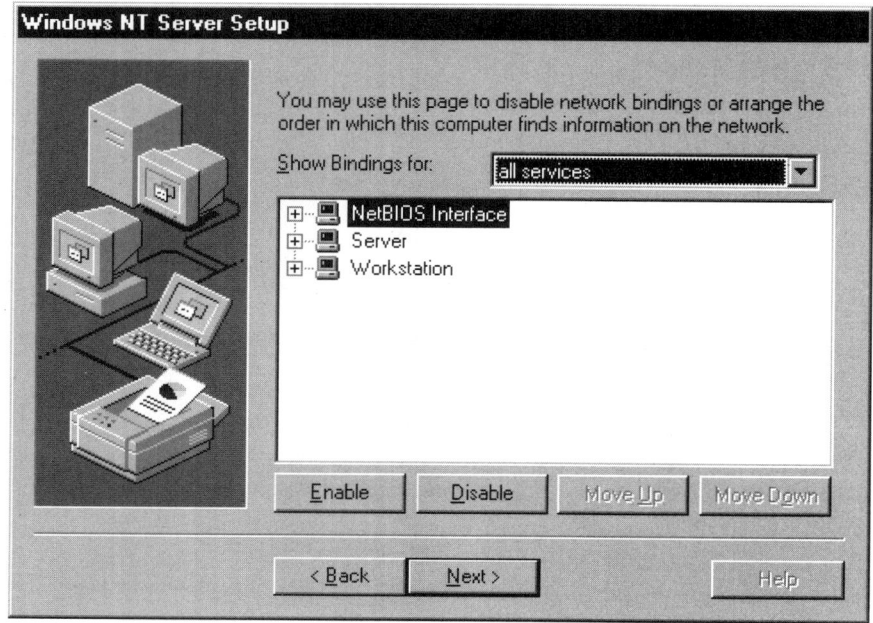

Figure 2-29: Use the Windows NT Server Setup Show Bindings window to review network bindings.

Starting the Network

After you accept the network configuration, Setup Wizard starts networking (see Figure 2-30) and finishes the installation of Windows NT 4 Server. Click on the Next button to start the network and continue with the installation.

You will need to provide the computer name and domain name when the network is started for the first time, as shown in Figure 2-31. If you selected a stand-alone server, then this prompt is for a Computer Name and a Workgroup instead of a Computer Name and a Domain. After entering your Computer Name and Domain, click on the Next button.

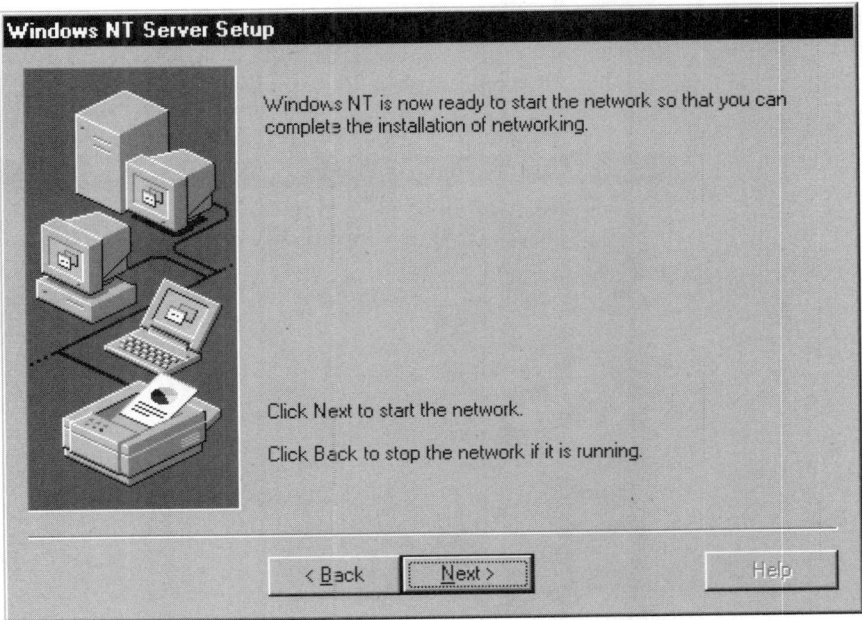

Figure 2-30: Use this window to start the network for the first time.

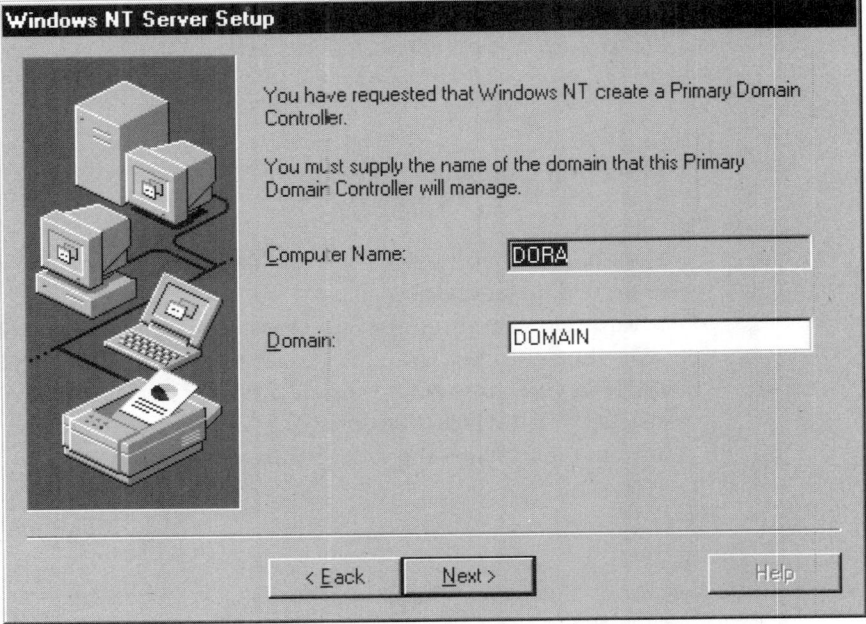

Figure 2-31: Use this window to supply the computer name and domain.

The Setup Wizard completes the configuration of the installation and notifies you using the status window, as shown in Figure 2-32. Click the Finish button to complete this stage of the installation.

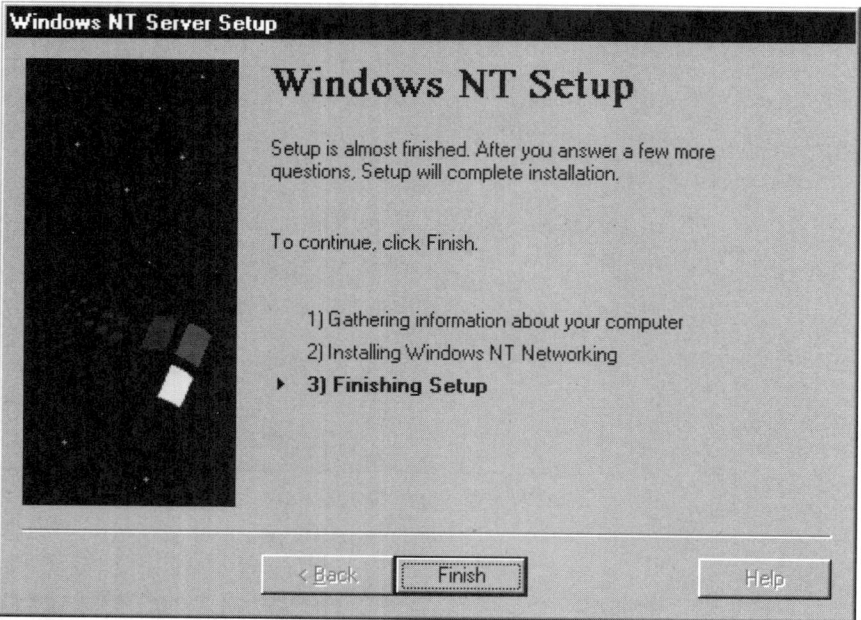

Figure 2-32: You are almost finished with the setup!

The Final Configuration

The final stages of installation are to configure some basic features such as time, date, and video display.

Time zone, and setting the correct time and date, is one of the final tasks the Setup Wizard handles; see Figure 2-33. Find your time zone, and if in your time zone you use daylight savings time (DST), you can instruct Windows NT 4 Server to allow for DST. Click on the Close button after you set the date and time information.

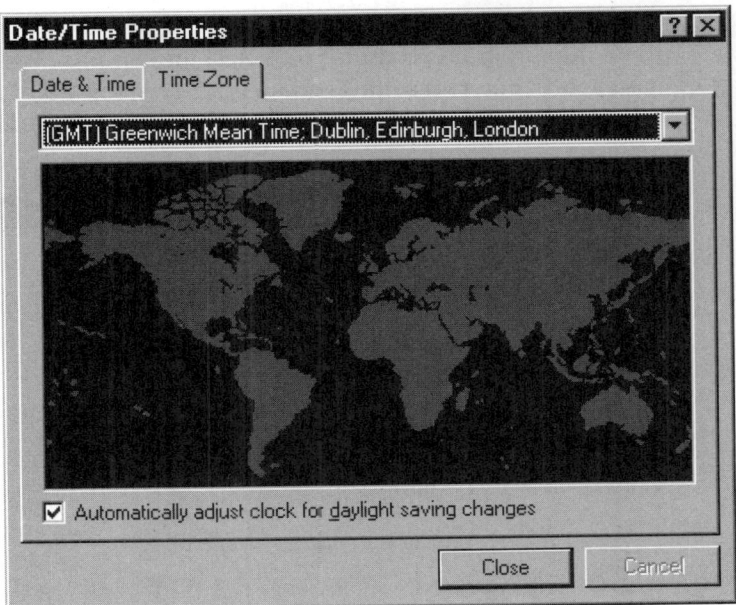

Figure 2-33: The Date/Time Properties dialog box.

If you have a video adapter that is more than a standard VGA adapter, Setup Wizard will detect it and prompt you to determine whether you wish to configure the adapter. For my Matrox Millennium, the Detected Display dialog box in Figure 2-34 appears. Click on the OK button to continue with the display configuration part of the installation.

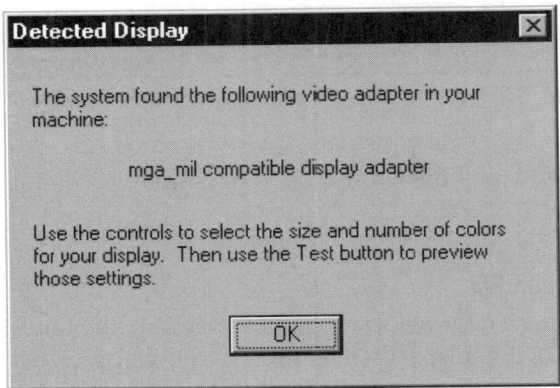

Figure 2-34: The Setup Wizard has detected a display.

The video configuration involves setting the resolution and color depth (the setup program prompts you to test the settings). Each video adapter has slightly different settings and parameters; some also allow setting refresh rates. Figure 2-35 shows the Display Properties dialog box.

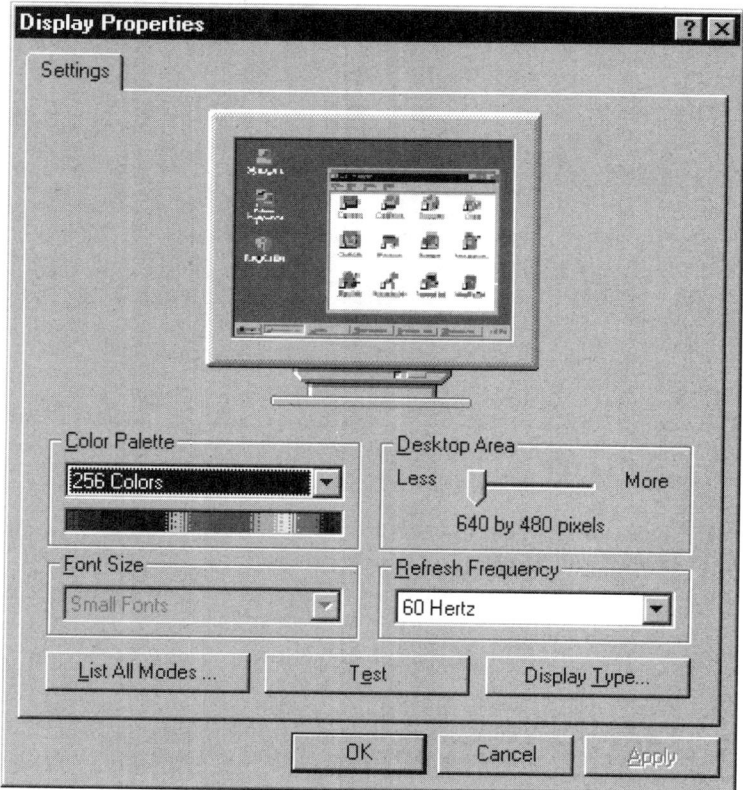

Figure 2-35: The Display Properties dialog box.

When you are finished setting your display options, click on the OK button.

Creating the ERD

The final step in the setup program is to create the Emergency Repair Disk (ERD), if you specified an ERD as shown previously in Figure 2-18. An ERD is vital to restoring a damaged installation of Windows NT 4 Server that no longer boots correctly. If by chance you chose not to create an ERD, when Windows NT 4 Server restarts, you can select the

RDISK.EXE utility (found in the Windows NT 4 Server folder) to create a new repair disk. Figure 2-36 shows the prompt to insert the disk that you want to use for the ERD. Insert a diskette in the A drive and click on the OK button to create the ERD disk.

Figure 2-36: Insert your ERD disk into the diskette drive.

Note: If you inadvertently leave one of your Windows NT 4 Server installation diskettes in the drive, the program is smart enough to tell you that the disk cannot be used for the ERD!

When the Emergency Repair Disk creation process is completed, the Setup Wizard reboots the computer for a final time. When the reboot is completed, you can log on as the systems administrator and configure your shares, users, and other devices specific to your installation.

One Final Reboot & a Test or Two!

The installation process end is marked with a dialog box (Figure 2-37) that prompts you to reboot the system. You must reboot to implement the features and components that you have installed. Click on the Restart Computer button to restart the computer.

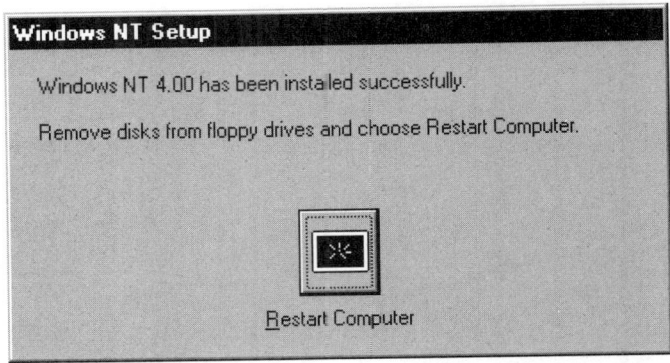

Figure 2-37: You are finished! A successful installation.

When installing Windows NT 4 Server, completely testing the installation is important. From a workstation, make sure that users can access shared devices such as drives and printers. Also test RAS (if installed) and other special features as needed.

Reinstall any applications that you want to run from the server if this was a clean installation. Examples of these applications are Microsoft BackOffice, Microsoft SQL Server, Microsoft Office, and other products that would normally run on this computer.

The preceding steps are typical for a simple, single-server system. Your installation may be quite different, but the general flow of any installation will be similar to the preceding description.

Configuring Network Services

After you install Windows NT 4 Server, you can manipulate Network protocols and services using the Control Panel's Network applet (see Figure 2-38). Start the Network applet by double-clicking on the Network icon in the Control Panel.

The first tab, Identification, is used to specify the domain or workgroup to which this server belongs. Also found on the Identification tab is the Change button, which displays the Identification Changes dialog box shown in Figure 2-39. With the Identification Changes dialog box, you can change the name and description of the server.

Note: Changing the name of a server may create immense confusion with users. The users must be aware of the server's new name so that they can change their configurations and links to shared resources. Don't change the server's name arbitrarily!

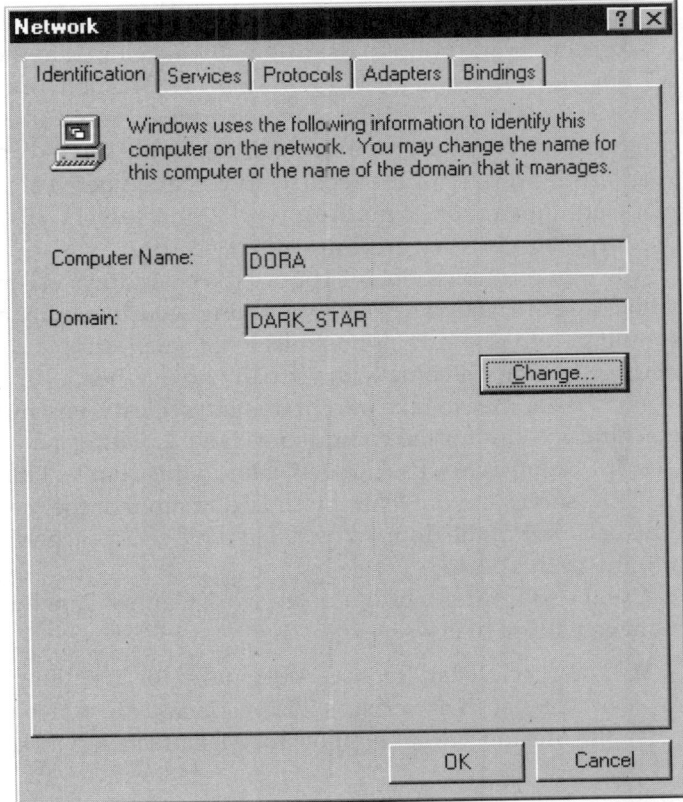

Figure 2-38: The Control Panel's Network applet, Identification tab.

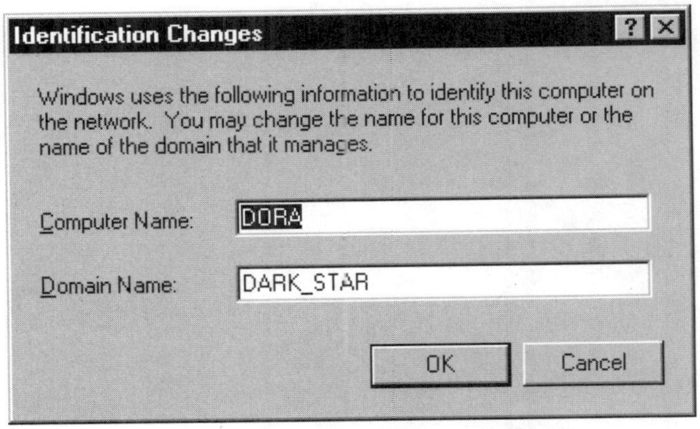

Figure 2-39: The Identification Changes dialog box.

Most Windows NT systems should be part of a domain instead of a workgroup. Workgroups were originally developed in the pre-Windows NT days for Windows for Workgroups 3.11. The network model for WfW 3.11 was a distributed model in which each system could share file and printer services with any other computer in the same workgroup. Workgroups did not share security information between servers, which made administration of multiple workgroup servers a real problem as the corporate network grew in size.

The workgroup model is supported by Windows NT but doesn't take advantage of Windows NT's networking security ability at all and should be avoided if at all possible. Even small, simple LANs may be managed using domains with virtually no overhead.

For a computer to take part in domain security, you must create a machine account for the computer as well. Creating a machine account (see "Managing Groups & Users" later in this chapter) means to inform the PDC server in your Windows NT domain that the machine should now be a part of the domain by using the User Manager for Domains administrative tool.

Use the following tabs of the Network Control Panel window to manage your network services:

- The Services tab (Figure 2-40) is used for installing higher-level services such as Services for the Macintosh, which contains all of the file and printer support for Macintosh networks.

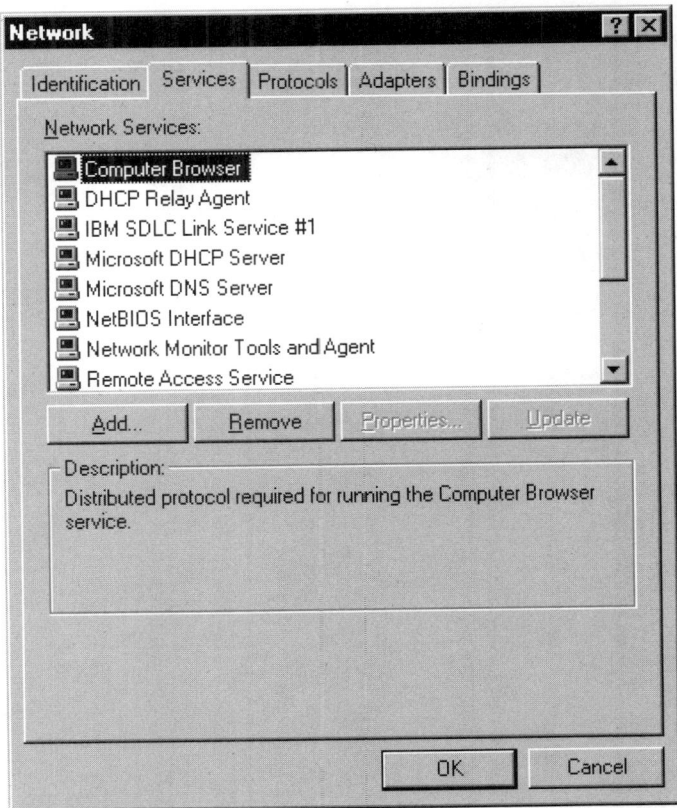

Figure 2-40: The Network applet's Services tab.

■ The Protocols tab (Figure 2-41) is used for adding, removing, and configuring protocols. Protocols are the "language" that computers use to talk to each other on a network. There are several commonly used protocols, however TCP/IP (used with the Internet), IPX/SPX (used with Novell NetWare), and NetBEUI are the most commonly used ones.

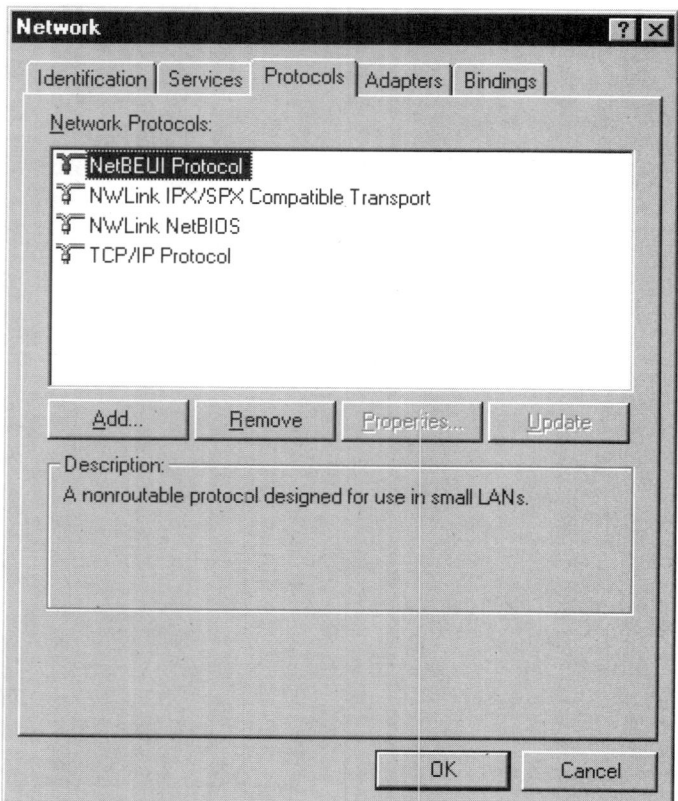

Figure 2-41: The Network applet's Protocols tab—DORA has almost everything installed.

- The Adapters tab (Figure 2-42) is used for adding, removing, and configuring network adapters. The network adapter (usually called an NIC—Network Interface Card) is the hardware that connects a computer to the physical network. Only one NIC is in the server shown in this figure, a 3Com 3C590 PCI-based Ethernet card.

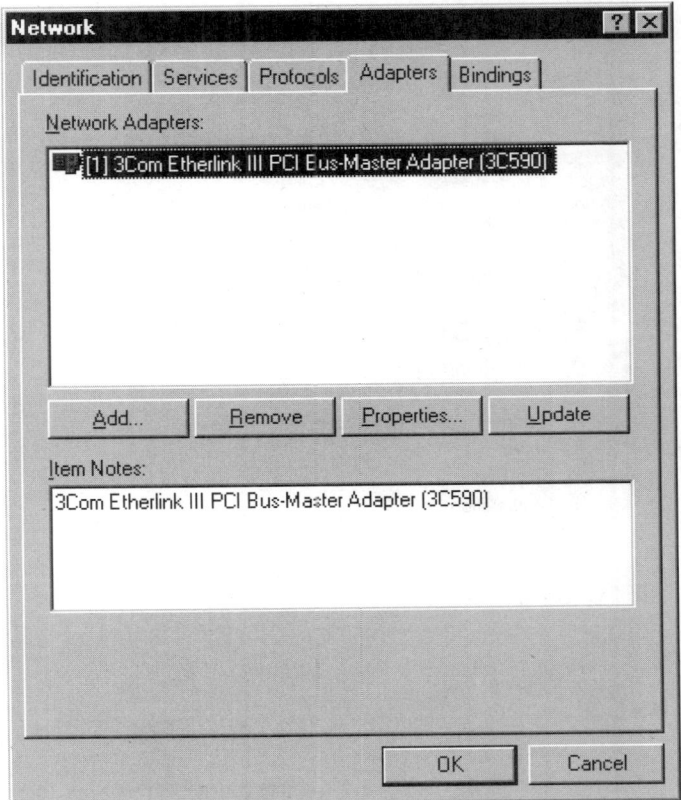

Figure 2-42: The Network applet's Adapters tab.

■ The Bindings tab (see Figure 2-43) simply keeps track of the mappings between services, protocols, and adapters. You can use this page to disable a particular relationship between two layers in the network protoccl suite. Typically, bindings refer to the relationship between NICs and protocols.

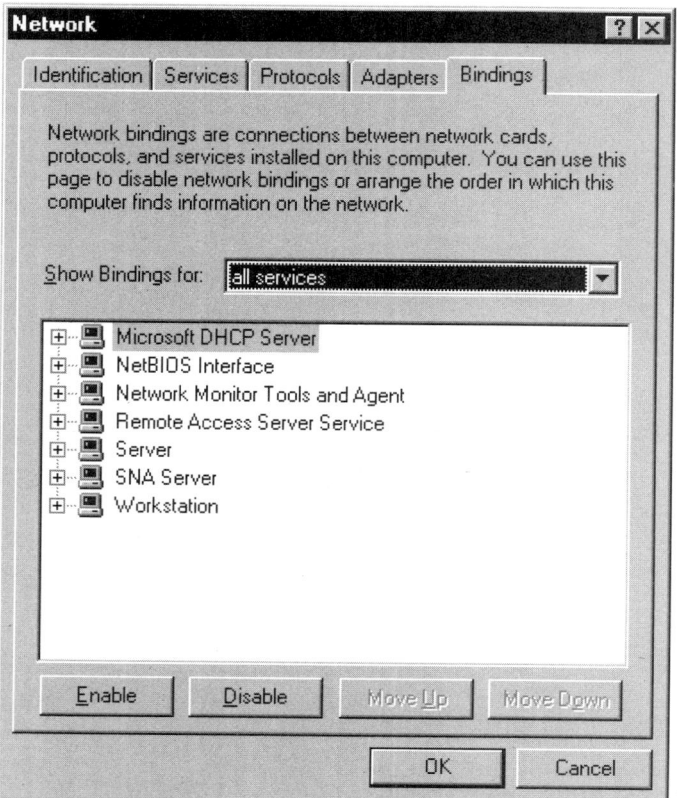

Figure 2-43: The Network applet's Bindings tab.

For example, assume that you have a Windows NT 4 Server that has two installed network cards. This network is divided into two sections, with the Windows NT 4 Server connecting the two parts of the network (this uses Windows NT 4 Server's router capabilities). For the sake of security, one network is running TCP/IP and is connected to the Internet, and the other network is not connected to the Internet and is not running TCP/IP protocol, either. In the bindings page, TCP/IP protocol is bound to the external (Internet side) and NIC would be enabled, while the TCP/IP protocol bound to the other NIC would be disabled.

Note: That is not the best way to handle this particular configuration. Using Microsoft's Proxy Server (code named Catapult) is a better solution, offering more security and flexibility.

Installing a New Protocol

Protocols (the "language" with which computers communicate with each other over a network) may be added if new computers, either servers or workstations (which don't support the currently installed protocols), are added to the network, or if the network is reconfigured.

For example, a network that becomes connected to the Internet will need the TCP/IP protocol, which is not always used with PC-based networks. Another example of adding a protocol is where it becomes necessary to support a Novell network (perhaps there are two networks at the organization, one Novell, one Windows NT 4 Server, and these two networks must be joined) with Windows NT 4 Servers.

Note: You can have more than one protocol on a network at one time. For example, the DarkStar network has TCP/IP, NetBEUI, and IPX/SPX all installed. Adding additional protocols should not significantly impact network performance.

To change protocols (either removing or adding), you must start the Windows NT 4 Server Control Panel (use Start Menu | Settings | Control Panel). In the Control Panel, double-click on the Network icon to open the Network applet.

1. Click on the Protocols tab. This will display a list of currently installed Network Protocols (see Figure 2-44). Below the list of installed protocols are four buttons: Add, Remove, Properties, and Update. Not all protocols have properties, so the Properties button may be disabled.

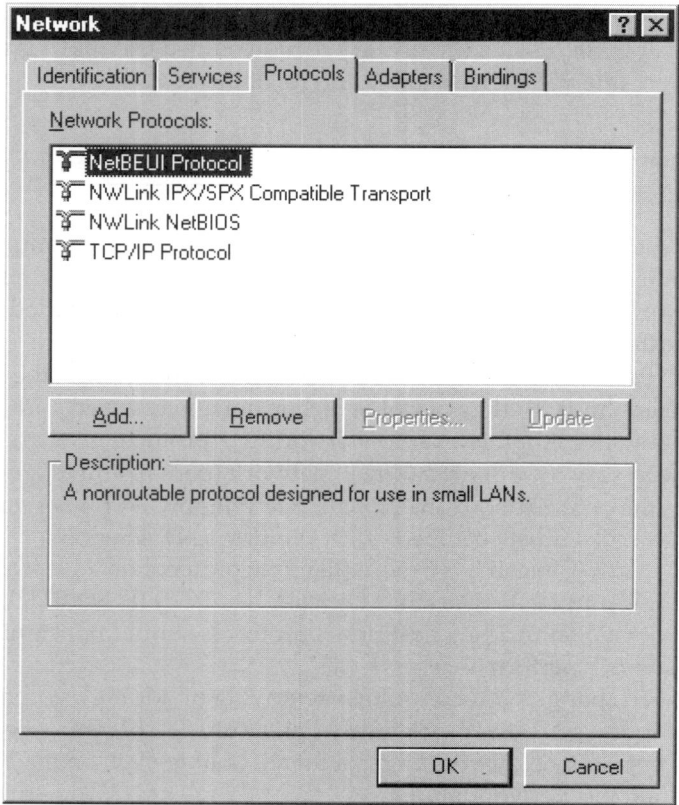

Figure 2-44: The Network applet's Protocols tab. Click on Add to add a protocol.

2. Click on the Add button to add a new protocol. The Select Network Protocol dialog (Figure 2-45) box will be displayed, listing all protocols that are available.

3. Select the Network Protocol to be added from the list, and then click OK. If you are adding a protocol that is not supplied with Windows NT 4 Server and you have an installation disk for the protocol, then click on the Have Disk button.

4. The Windows NT Setup program (which is used to install protocols) will prompt for the location of the Windows NT 4 Server CD. The default will be the CD drive from which Windows NT 4 Server was installed; however, you can change the location if necessary.

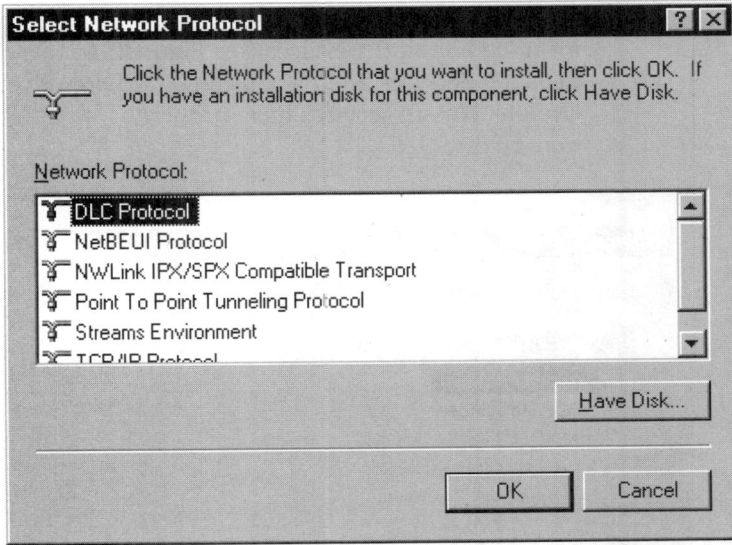

Figure 2-45: The Select Network Protocol dialog box. Select the protocol to be added, and then click on OK.

5. Most protocols will require configuration. If you're installing a protocol that requires configuration, Windows NT 4 Server will prompt for any needed information.

6. After the protocol has been installed, Windows NT 4 Server typically prompts to reboot to enable the protocol. If the server is currently in use and the protocol will not be needed until the next time the server will be rebooted, then you may defer the reboot to a later time.

Installing a New Network Service

The term *network service* covers a wide range of possible items. Though for most Windows NT 4 Server installations, only a few services may be needed, each installation is unique and will have a different set of services installed. The network services listed previously in Table 2-4 (p. 73-75) may be installed from the Windows NT 4 Server CD.

To change services (either removing or adding), you must start the Windows NT 4 Server Control Panel (use Start Menu | Settings | Control Panel). In the Control Panel, double-click on the Network icon to open the Network applet.

1. Click on the Services tab. This will display a list of currently installed Network Services (see Figure 2-46). Below the list of installed Services are four buttons: Add, Remove, Properties, and Update. Not all services have properties, so the Properties button may be disabled.

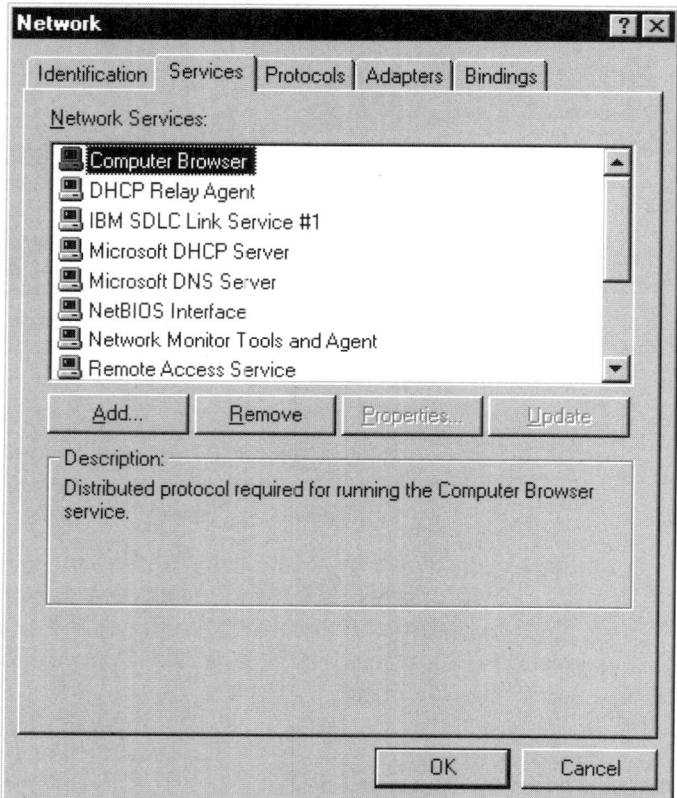

Figure 2-46: The Network applet's Services tab. Click on Add to add a service.

2. Click on the Add button to add a new service. The Select Network Service dialog (Figure 2-47) box will be displayed, listing all protocols that are available.

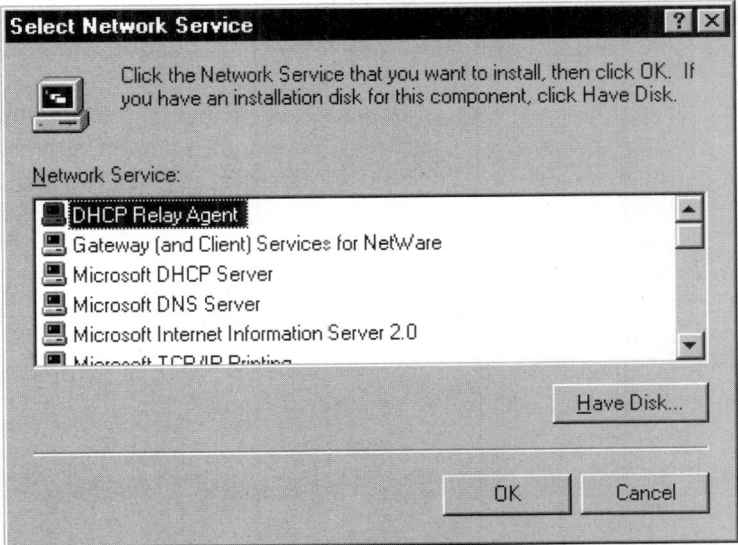

Figure 2-47: The Select Network Service dialog box. Select the service to be added, and then click on OK.

3. Select the Network Service to be added from the list, and then click on OK. If you are adding a service that is not supplied with Windows NT 4 Server and you have an installation disk for the service, then click on the Have Disk button.

4. The Windows NT Setup program (which is used to install services) will prompt for the location of the Windows NT 4 Server CD. The default will be the CD drive from which Windows NT 4 Server was installed; however, you may change the location if necessary.

5. Most services will require configuration. If you are installing a service that requires configuration, Windows NT 4 Server will prompt for any needed information.

6. After the service has been installed, Windows NT 4 Server may prompt to reboot to start the service. If the server is currently in use and the service will not be needed until the next time the server will be rebooted, then you can defer the reboot to a later time.

Managing Groups & Users

Windows NT 4 Server uses the User Manager for Domains to manage users and groups. The User Manager for Domains is started by selecting the Start Menu | Programs | Administrative Tools (Common) | User Manager for Domains. Once started, the User Manager for Domains will look like the one shown in Figure 2-48.

Note: For servers that are not using the domain model, the User Manager program is used to administer users. The execution of the User Manager program is very similar to the User Manager for Domains program, with the exception that workgroup networks don't support domain (global) groups.

```
┊ User Manager - DARK_STAR                                           _ □ ×
User  View  Policies  Options  Exchange  Help
```

Username	Full Name	Description
Administrator		Built-in account for administering the computer/domain
andrew	Andrew S	From TTG
BWaters	Bryan Waters	Bryan, one of this book's authors.
Guest		Built-in account for guest access to the computer/domain
IUSR_DORA	Internet Guest Account	Internet Server Anonymous Access
Jennifer	Jennifer Huntley	Ventana - Editor
LisaB	Lisa Bucki	Production Editor
LisaS	Lisa Swayne	
Long	Long is the 386 FAX comp	The FAX system
Peter	Peter D. Hipson	Peter's personal account
Pixel	Pixel is the 486 computer	486 test platform
smsadmin	SMS Administrator	Bogus
SQLExecutiveCmdExec	SQLExecutiveCmdExec	SQL Executive CmdExec Task Account

Groups	Description
Account Operators	Members can administer domain user and group accounts
Accounting	Accounting, AR, AP, Order processing.
Administrators	Members can fully administer the computer/domain
Backup Operators	Members can bypass file security to back up files
Domain Admins	Designated administrators of the domain
Domain Guests	All domain guests
Domain Users	All domain users
Guests	Users granted guest access to the computer/domain
Internet Users	Users who connect to the FTP/Gopher sites
Print Operators	Members can administer domain printers
Replicator	Supports file replication in a domain
Server Operators	Members can administer domain servers
Users	Ordinary users

Figure 2-48· The User Manager for Domains program administering the server DORA.

The User Manager for Domains main window is divided into two panes: The top pane lists individual users, whereas the lower pane lists local and global groups. Notice that there is, in the example shown, a group called Domain Users and a group called Users. The Domain Users group is a global group that is used with all servers which are part of the domain. The Users group is a local group, used with only the local server. Most systems administrators configure most users to be members of the Domain Users group, which adds flexibility; should a server be unavailable, Domain Users can continue to log on to other domain servers (if files and folders are properly replicated on other servers) without interruption to their work.

Two tasks must be performed with the User Manager for Domains: managing users and managing groups.

Managing Users

Users must be managed: People come and people go. As well, needs and requirements for users change as their jobs and the organization change. The User Manager for Domains program allows the systems administrator to manage the domain's users.

Three user-related tasks must be performed on a regular basis:

■ Adding users

■ Deleting users

■ Modifying and managing users

All organizations should have an established set of rules for accessing resources on the network. Parameters such as minimum password length, password aging, account disabling, and the like should be established and enforced. Whenever a user is managed using the User Manager for Domains program, the systems administrator should always check to make sure that none of the organization's rules for use have been violated.

Note: The Administrative Wizard allows some user management as well. Specifically, the Administrative Wizard allows adding new users and groups quickly and easily.

Adding Users

Adding a new user is a relatively straightforward task:

1. From User Manager for Domains, select the User | New User menu selection. This will display the New User dialog box (see Figure 2-49).

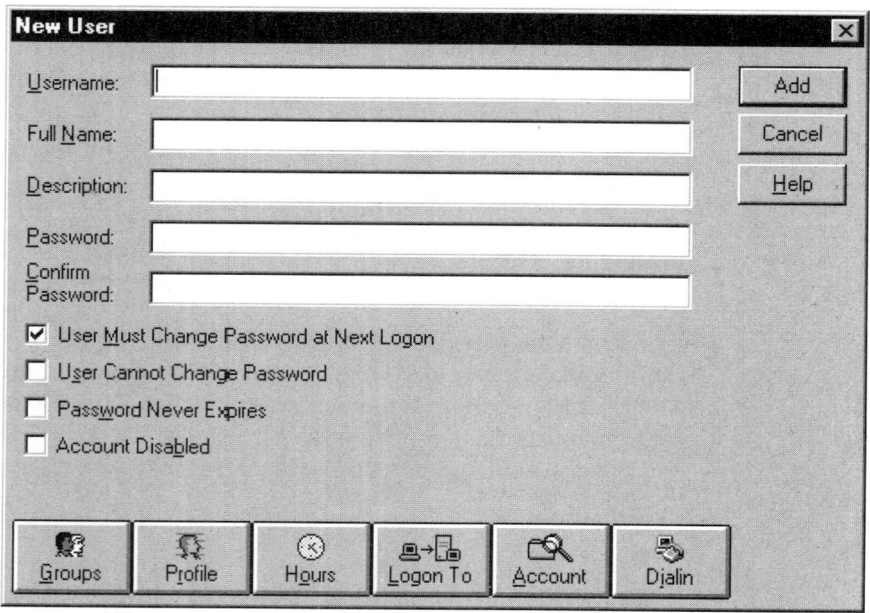

Figure 2-49: The New User dialog box.

2. In the New User dialog box, enter the Username (typically first initial and last name, or first name and last initial), the user's Full Name, and Description. There may be advantages to placing information in the Description field, which will enable finding the user (such as the user's telephone extension or office location), and perhaps the user's job title.

3. Provide an initial password. This initial password should be used for the initial logon by the user, and the user should be required to change the initial password on the first logon (see options, below). Typical choices for initial passwords are either eight random numbers and characters (alternate characters and

numbers, such as 9w0c5e3g), or two random words separated with a hyphen, such as blue-rocks. For the initial password, resist the urge to use either the user's username, a standard password, or no password; some users do not immediately log on to the network, and there is no point in compromising system security during the time between when the account is first created and when it is first used.

Warning

If a user cannot log on using the password given to the user, and the password is correct, consider that system security has been breached; another user probably has logged on, and was forced to change the password.

4. Set the account options. There are four main options for the account:

   ■ **User Must Change Password at Next Logon**—If this option is selected (which is the default), then the next time the user logs on, his or her password must be changed. This option is important in that it prevents the initial password from being discovered, and forces the user to select a password that is that user's choice.

   ■ **User Cannot Change Password**—Some organizations do not allow users to change passwords. Rather, the systems administrator will assign new passwords on a regular basis, and provide the user with the password used. Properly managed, this technique limits the problems of users setting their passwords to something that can be easily guessed.

   ■ **Password Never Expires**—Most organizations prefer that passwords expire after a certain period of time: typically monthly or bimonthly. This forces the user to change his or her password, which limits the problems when password spying is used. (Password spying is when someone looks "over the shoulder" when passwords are being entered; each time, the person gets one or two characters, and eventually will have the entire password.)

- **Account Disabled**—Pretty drastic, huh? Create the account and don't let the user use it. Well, actually, there is a reason for this. The user calls up the systems administrator while at his or her workstation, and the systems administrator then reenables the account. That way, the user immediately logs on, and resets his or her password. This greatly minimizes the problems of the initial password being misused.

5. Set the new user options. There are six buttons for setting user options:

   - **Groups**—The Groups button allows the systems administrator to change which groups the user will be a member of. Most organizations grant membership to the Domain Users (or Users) group, and any special, organizational groups (such as R&D or Accounting) as needed. Special users (such as operators) may be made members of administrative groups as needed, of course.

   - **Profile**—The Profile button allows setting up the user's profile. Profiles allow users who log on locally to have their own configurations and home folders. Profiles can be used in many creative ways to enhance the usability of the network.

   - **Hours**—Setting hours allows restricting access to the network to, say, business hours, or simply restricting the system during hours when no one should (logically) be accessing the network (say, from midnight until 7 a.m.). Each user can have specific hours of access set.

   - **Logon To**—Logon To allows the systems administrator to specify which workstation(s) the user is allowed to use when logging on to the network. For example, for users who are members of the accounting department, it may be wise to allow their accounts to be used on workstations in the accounting department.

   - **Account**—The account's expiration date (very useful for temporary employees), and whether the account is global (for regular users in the domain) or local (for users who are from an un-trusted domain).

   - **Dialin**—Some users should be allowed to dial into the network, whereas others should not be allowed the privilege. Each organization must determine which users should be legitimately allowed to dial into the network.

Deleting Users

To delete a user, select the user's name in the upper, Username list, and press the Del key. User Manager for Domains will caution you that when the user had been deleted, even if a new user with an identical name is created, the new user will not have the same privileges as the original user. In other words, once a user is deleted, that particular user is gone for good. You may create a new user with the same userid, but you will also have to reconfigure the new user completely.

Modifying Users

Modifying a user is very similar to the process of adding a new user. Select an existing user, in the upper, Username list, and press the Enter key. The User Properties dialog box (Figure 2-50) will be displayed where the user's entry may be edited.

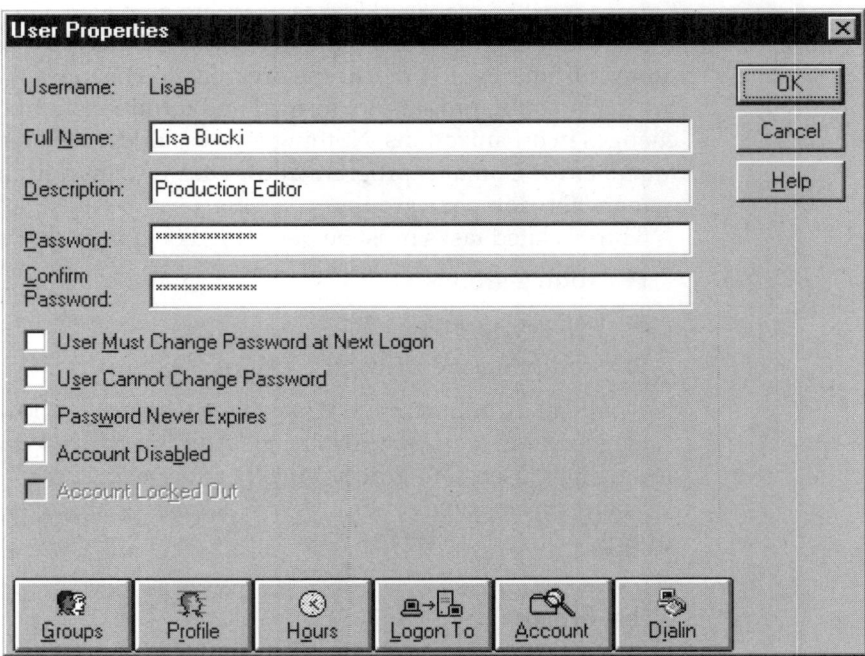

Figure 2-50: The User Properties dialog allows the systems administrator to modify a user's access.

Note: There is no way to retrieve or find out a user's password. If a user forgets his or her password, then a new password must be assigned.

The only difference between the User Properties dialog and the Add User dialog is that User Properties has a fourth option:

- **Account Locked Out**—This option, when checked, indicates that the user's account has been disabled by the system. This usually happens when the system detects possible security violations (such as excessive incorrect passwords, indicating that someone is trying to guess the password). This forces the potential security violation to the systems administrator's attention because the legitimate user is unable to use the account while it is locked out.

Managing Groups

Groups must be managed just as users are managed. Groups probably won't change as often as users do, but it will be necessary to manage groups, from time to time, as the organization changes. Departments merge and split, projects are formed and terminated, functionality changes in organizations. Nothing is as assured as change is. The User Manager for Domains program allows the systems administrator to manage the domain's groups.

Three related tasks must be performed on a regular basis:

- Adding groups
- Deleting groups
- Modifying and managing groups

Note: The Administrative Wizard (see Chapter 1) allows some group management as well. Specifically, the Administrative Wizard allows adding new users and groups quickly and easily.

There are two types of groups in a domain: global groups and local groups.

Global Groups

A global group is a collection of users who share some particular attributes (typically a job-related attribute, such as all working in R&D, for example). Global groups allow easy management of global user accounts, which are found on a domain.

Members of global groups cannot be granted permissions to use network resources. To allow users in a global group access network resources, you must assign the global group to a local group. That is, a global group may be a member of a local group. (However, local groups may not be members of global groups.)

Creating a New Global Group   Creating a new global group is a relatively straightforward task:

1. From the User Manager for Domains, select the User | New Global Group menu selection. This will display the New Global Group dialog box (see Figure 2-51).

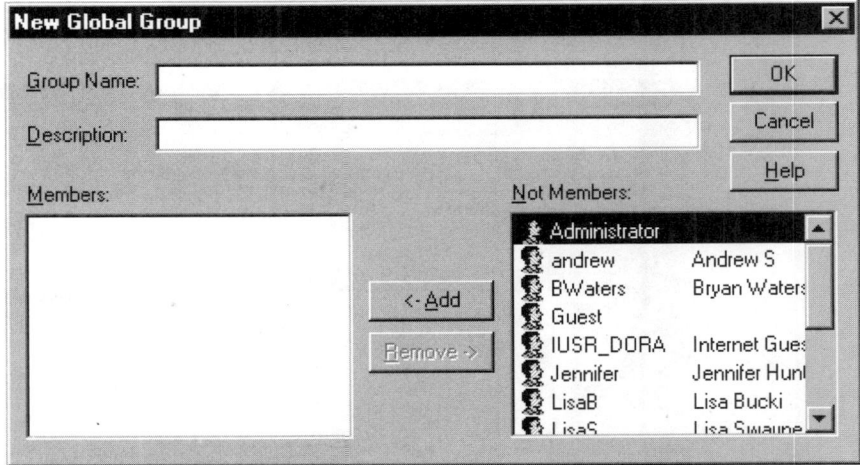

Figure 2-51: The New Global Group dialog box.

2. In the New Global Group dialog box, enter the Group Name (typically a department name or function), and a Description. There may be advantages to placing information in the Description field, which will enable locating the group (such as the group's manager or supervisor, or office location).

3. Add members using the Add button, whatever users are to be members of the Global group. Remember: Only users may be members of a global group.

4. When you have finished adding members to the new global group, click on the CK button to save the new global group.

Deleting a Global Group   To delete a global group, select the global group's name in the lower, Groups list, and press the Del key. User Manager for Domains will caution you that when the group has been deleted, even if a new global group with an identical name is created, the new global group will not have the same privileges as the original global group. In other words, once a global group is deleted, that particular global group is gone for good. You may create a new global group with the same name, but you will also have to reconfigure the new global group completely.

Modifying a Global Group   Modifying a global group is very similar to the process of adding a new global group. Select an existing global group, in the lower, Groups list, and press the Enter key. The Global Group Properties dialog box (Figure 2-52) will be displayed where the global group's entry may be edited.

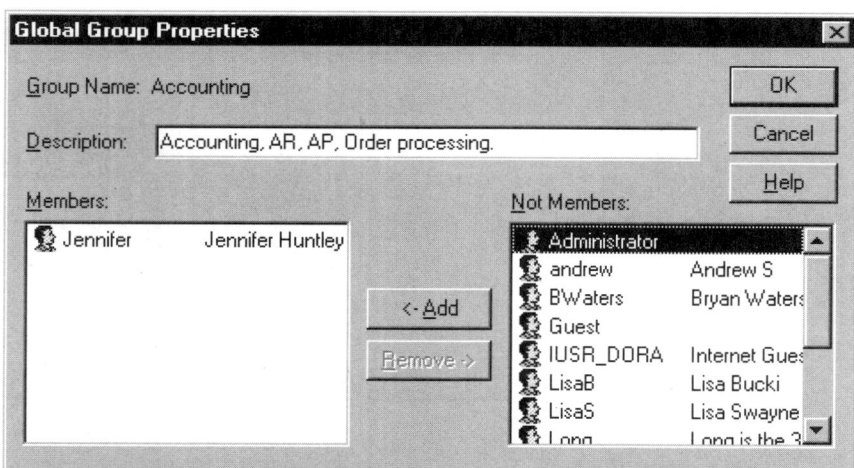

Figure 2-52: The Global Group Properties dialog allows the systems administrator to modify a global group's access.

The only difference between the Global Group Properties dialog box and the New Global Group dialog is that Global Group Properties will not allow changing the global group's name.

Note: There is no way to change a group's name once the group has been created. To rename a group, the group must be deleted and a new global group must be created in its place.

Local Groups

Unlike a global group, members of a local group may be allowed to access network resources. The resources that the local group may access are local to the domain in which the local group was created. Each and every member of a local group is extended the same access privileges that the local group has.

Smaller, single-domain organizations may find that local groups fulfill their entire needs for groups.

Creating a New Local Group   Creating a new local group is a relatively straightforward task:

1. From User Manager for Domains, select the User | New Local Group menu selection. This will display the New Local Group dialog box (see Figure 2-53).

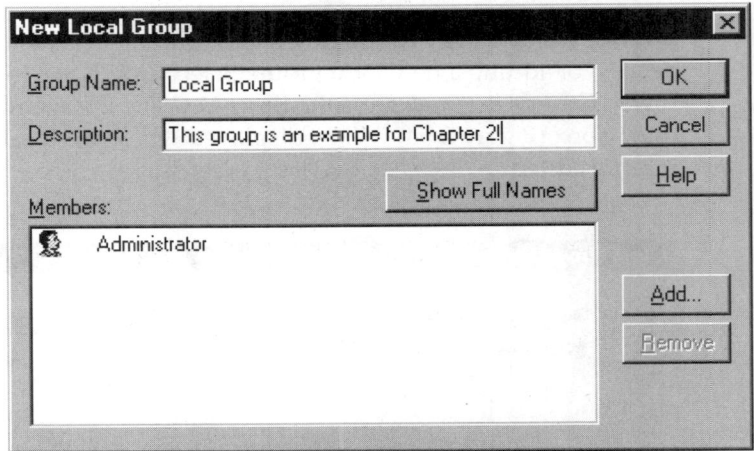

Figure 2-53: The New Local Group dialog box.

2. In the New Local Group dialog box, enter the Group Name (typically a department name or function), and a Description. There may be advantages to placing information in the Description field that will enable locating the group (such as the group's manager or supervisor, or office location).

3. Add members using the Add button (which will display the Add Users and Groups dialog), whatever users or global groups are to be members of the local group. Both users and global groups may be members of a local group.

4. After you have finished adding members to the new local group, click on the OK button to save the new local group.

Deleting a Local Group   To delete a local group, select the local group's name in the lower, Groups list, and press the Del key. User Manager for Domains will caution you that when the group has been deleted, even if a new local group with an identical name is created, the new local group will not have the same privileges as the original local group. In other words, after a local group is deleted, that particular local group is gone for good. You may create a new local group with the same name, but you will also have to reconfigure the new local group completely.

Modifying a Local Group   Modifying a local group is very similar to the process of adding a new local group. Select an existing local group, in the lower, Groups list, and press the Enter key. The Local Group Properties dialog box (Figure 2-54) will be displayed where the local group's entry may be edited.

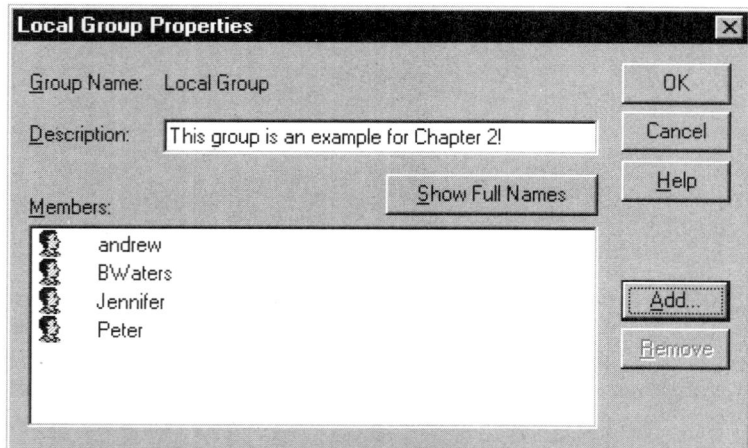

Figure 2-54: The Local Group Properties dialog allows the systems administrator to modify a local group's access.

Note: There is no way to change a group's name once the group has been created. To rename a group, the group must be deleted and a new local group must be created in its place.

The only difference between the Local Group Properties dialog box and the New Local Group dialog box is that Local Group Properties will not allow changing the local group's name.

Viewing Events With Event Viewer

The Windows NT Event Viewer system is another one of the tools that is extremely valuable but still under utilized. There are three classes of events that Event Viewer will allow you to monitor. These are the following:

- System events, which are generated by the Windows NT operating system and include information about driver failures or system components that fail to start.

- Security events, which log security events by monitoring the Windows NT network for possible breaches in security. By the way, only the Administrator can view the security log.

- Application events are used by applications to log specific events related to the operation of the application.

The Event viewer, started from the Start Menu | Programs | Administrative Tools (Common), is shown in Figure 2-55. In this figure, the system log is being displayed. To display either the security log, or the application log, select Log from the menu, and click on the log that is to be displayed.

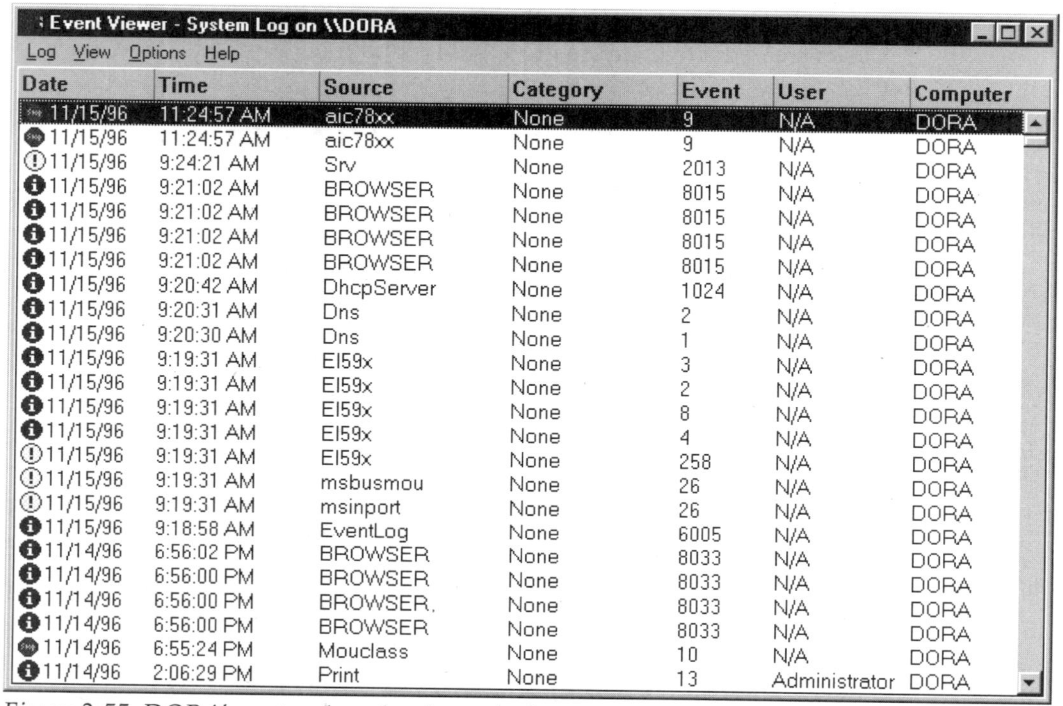

Date	Time	Source	Category	Event	User	Computer
11/15/96	11:24:57 AM	aic78xx	None	9	N/A	DORA
11/15/96	11:24:57 AM	aic78xx	None	9	N/A	DORA
11/15/96	9:24:21 AM	Srv	None	2013	N/A	DORA
11/15/96	9:21:02 AM	BROWSER	None	8015	N/A	DORA
11/15/96	9:21:02 AM	BROWSER	None	8015	N/A	DORA
11/15/96	9:21:02 AM	BROWSER	None	8015	N/A	DORA
11/15/96	9:21:02 AM	BROWSER	None	8015	N/A	DORA
11/15/96	9:20:42 AM	DhcpServer	None	1024	N/A	DORA
11/15/96	9:20:31 AM	Dns	None	2	N/A	DORA
11/15/96	9:20:30 AM	Dns	None	1	N/A	DORA
11/15/96	9:19:31 AM	EI59x	None	3	N/A	DORA
11/15/96	9:19:31 AM	EI59x	None	2	N/A	DORA
11/15/96	9:19:31 AM	EI59x	None	8	N/A	DORA
11/15/96	9:19:31 AM	EI59x	None	4	N/A	DORA
11/15/96	9:19:31 AM	EI59x	None	258	N/A	DORA
11/15/96	9:19:31 AM	msbusmou	None	26	N/A	DORA
11/15/96	9:19:31 AM	msinport	None	26	N/A	DORA
11/15/96	9:18:58 AM	EventLog	None	6005	N/A	DORA
11/14/96	6:56:02 PM	BROWSER	None	8033	N/A	DORA
11/14/96	6:56:00 PM	BROWSER	None	8033	N/A	DORA
11/14/96	6:56:00 PM	BROWSER	None	8033	N/A	DORA
11/14/96	6:56:00 PM	BROWSER	None	8033	N/A	DORA
11/14/96	6:55:24 PM	Mouclass	None	10	N/A	DORA
11/14/96	2:06:29 PM	Print	None	13	Administrator	DORA

Figure 2-55: DORA's system log, showing today's entries.

Note: The log can get quite large if not purged from time to time. Select Log | Clear All Events to clear the current logs.

After you become comfortable with using Event Viewer, you'll find that several features make it more useful, such as the ability to locate any specific log record using a search feature. It also has the ability to filter out records that look valid or didn't fail.

Managing Windows NT Services

Services are the life blood of Windows NT. A service is a component of Windows NT Server that runs either for all users, or for the currently logged-on user. Each service performs a specific task; for example, there is a service called Spooler that manages the Windows NT 4 Server printer queues.

Earlier in this chapter, you saw how to install certain types of services through the Control Panel's network dialog box. There is a catch, however. The services shown in this dialog box are not the only services present on the system. Because most of the server products under the BackOffice umbrella are service based, it will help to know how to find the Services dialog box as well as be able to stop and start any of these services.

Services may be managed by starting the Control Panel's Services applet, by clicking on the Services icon in the Control Panel. This will display the Services applet, as shown in Figure 2-56. An alternate way to display the Services applet is to launch the Server Manager by clicking on Start Menu | Programs | Administrative Tools (Common) | Server Manager. Then select the appropriate computer from the list of computers that appear in the Administrative window, and click on the menu item Computer | Services in the menu.

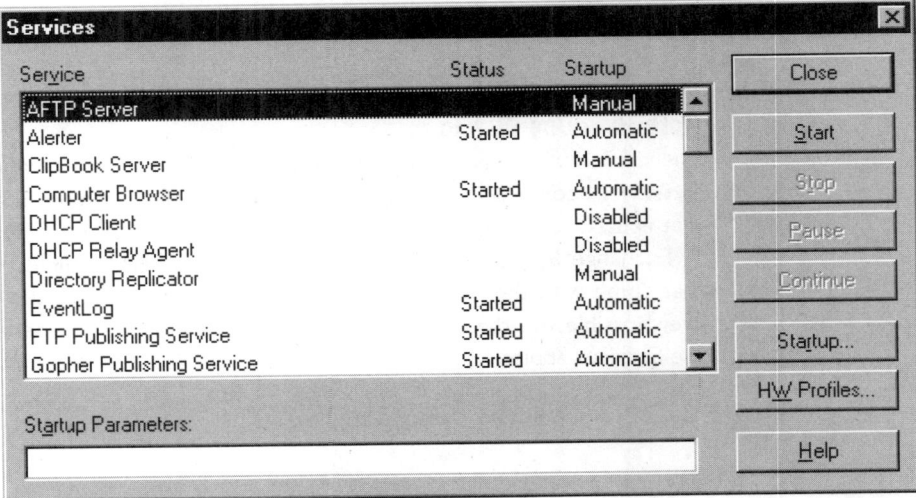

Figure 2-56: The Control Panel's Services applet.

Warning

Make sure that you know what a service does before you start or stop it. You can damage your system severely by accidentally incorrectly changing or reconfiguring the existing services on your system.

There are two main parameters that you can control for a service: its current state, and the start-up mode for the service.

The current state is simple. There are three states for a service:

- **Stopped**— The service is not loaded, or running.
- **Started**—The service is loaded and running.
- **Paused**—The service is loaded but not currently running.

The start-up mode has three substates as well. These are as follows:

- **Automatic**—will attempt to run before any other class of protocols or services.
- **Manual startup mode**—The service does not automatically start itself unless the user explicitly starts it.
- **Disabled**—Disabled is, well . . . it's disabled!

More Than One Way To . . .

There is more than one way to manage many services. Many components that run as services come with management applications; for example, IIS has a manager that is used to manage the various IIS services such as Web, FTP, and Gopher.

Exchange Server, SQL Server, and SMS are other examples of components that come with their own programs to start, stop, or pause the service. Whenever possible, use the components application to manage the service rather than the Services applet.

Starting a Service

To start a service, the Service Manager must be started, as described previously. After Services has started, select, in the Service list, the service that you would like to start. Click on the Start button to start the service. Confirm that the service has started by visually checking to see that the service's Status changes to Started.

Stopping a Service

To stop a service, the Service Manager must be started as described previously. After Services has started, select in the Service list the service that you would like to stop. Click on the Stop button to stop the service. Confirm that the service has stopped by visually checking to see that the service's Status changes to Stopped or becomes blank.

Setting the Startup Mode for a Service

To change a services start-up mode, the Service Manager must be started, as described previously. After Services has started, select in the Service list the service that you would like to change.

Click on the Startup button to display the Service on dialog box, as shown in Figure 2-57. Change the Startup Type and click on OK when done. Be cautious about changing the Log On As items; each service that uses a logon (such as SQLExecutive, shown in the example) will have specific logon requirements, and probably will have a special userid configured for the service. Changing the logon account to an account that doesn't have the proper privileges will cause the service to fail to properly start.

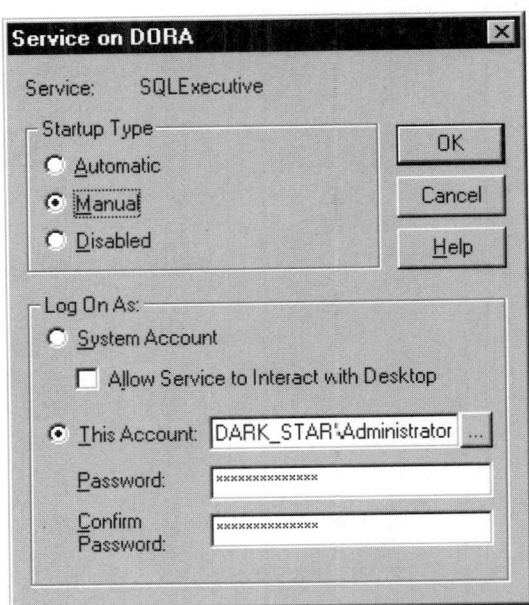

Figure 2-57: The Service on DORA dialog box, to change the SQLExecutive service.

Moving On

In this chapter, I showed a typical (yet simple) installation of Windows NT 4 Server. Although there were quite a few setup windows to step through, the Setup Wizard has greatly reduced the number of tasks performed by the systems administrator. Generally, most users will have few difficulties installing Windows NT 4 Server.

Now that you know how to get around some of the core features in Windows NT, the next chapter will show how to configure your disk storage system for maximum safety and efficiency. This also involves an in-depth discussion of the various file systems supported by Windows NT, along with their strengths and merits.

3

Windows NT 4 Server Fault Tolerance

D*ear Diary,*

Today was just one of those days. I should have realized it when I saw that new Italian Spyder sports car in the boss's parking space. But no, I missed the significance.

First that guy from maintenance who put up the new shelves . . . I never knew drill bits came in 14-inch lengths, but who would ever figure he'd drill right through the wall and then through our new SCSI drive system? Didn't he realize, when chunks of metal came out of the hole, that something was wrong? (Guess he didn't hear the screams coming from users, right?)

I could have forgiven him for the hole blunder, but then he gets out this long toggle bolt, shoves it 14 inches into the hole, and bolts the SCSI drive system to the wall.

My assistant Bob, who went to fix the drives, didn't realize that it had been bolted to the wall. (Can we blame him?) He removed the screws holding the cover on and tried to remove the cover. Well, I do have to give him credit for ingenuity; tying the rope to the back of the company delivery van to give a bit of extra pull was really something. Maintenance will be over tomorrow to fix the hole in the wall, though we are not sure where the SCSI drive system went—only that it did hit two cars in the parking lot before falling in the river.

Thank goodness for redundancy and fault tolerance . . .The second SCSI system was undamaged and we recovered. . . Well, sort of. Bob moved the second SCSI system to the edge of the table, where it was fine until about 3 PM. They say we only get earthquakes like that once every 20 years. What luck . . .Bob says it doesn't hurt too much, and we must count our blessings; he did save the second SCSI system when it fell on his foot.

We moved the SCSI system to the table over by the window (which should also be fixed tomorrow). That is the table Bob accidentally cleared off when he was trying to get the cover off of the first SCSI system. With luck, we had everything back up and running in no time.

Do you realize that R&D is right next to the back wall of the computer department? Bet what you didn't know is that they are working on new super-conducting magnet technologies . . . Well, the warning came when those refrigerator magnets we use to hold notes to the door of the backup tape cabinets went flying across the room. When I opened the cabinet door, the sight was a bit unnerving; every tape has been totally erased. In fact, I didn't realize that the magnet stuff that is coated on the tape could be pulled off the backing by a really, really strong magnet—well, now we know . . .

Damage from the earthquake keeps showing up; the sprinklers in the computer department (weren't they supposed to be disconnected?) went off a bit later. Fortunately, we got them turned off before anything other than all our documentation was ruined! Then the boss comes running in, wanting to know what's going on. What a sight—he slips on the wet floor, lands on the table by the window, and out goes our second SCSI system. Care to guess where the boss's new car was parked?

Well, diary, that is all for today. Tomorrow will be quieter, I'm sure, since all I have to do is go to the Unemployment Office.

Not everyone's day is *that* bad, but accidents happen, hardware fails, and people do make mistakes. Windows NT 4 Server has a number of features, called fault tolerance, that will help minimize the impact of failures and accidents. And with careful management, it is possible to even minimize the impact of human error.

One of the reasons that corporate MIS systems have always been run on mainframes and minicomputers is that these systems were designed and have been proven to be reliable running for years without total system failure. Even when various hardware would fail, the systems were designed to adapt and still keep running without hardly missing a beat. Fault tolerance was built in as a core design consideration.

Microcomputer operating systems have never really handled device or other system failures gracefully. The file systems were not well designed, forcing users to resort to arcane data recovery and hard-drive repair tools such as the Norton Utilities, whose usage became so widespread that it made its author, Peter Norton, both famous and a little rich.

As microcomputers have sought to capture more and more market share away from the minis and mainframes, features such as fault tolerance had to be added for them to be competitive. Windows NT was designed with fault tolerance in mind from day one.

This chapter will cover the NT fault-tolerance features and show you how to use the NT Disk Administrator to configure volume sets, stripe sets, and disk mirroring as well as introduce you to some of the details of RAID and fault-tolerant storage systems along the way.

What Is Fault Tolerance?

Fault tolerance is defined as the system's ability to recover from some catastrophic event (or fault) such as hardware or power failures. The recovery must be done in such a way that it ensures that no data is lost. As well, fault tolerance must ensure that work in progress is not compromised, interrupted, or corrupted.

The industry standard for fault tolerance is known as the RAID (Redundant Array of Independent Disks) Specification. The RAID Specification was designed to be a standard based around combining arrays of small disk drives that could recover from the failure of one or more drives and would be inexpensive to maintain and support, or even repair. There are six levels of compliance with the RAID standard that are described in "RAID Levels" later in this chapter.

Note: RAID was originally defined as Redundant Array of Inexpensive Drives. However, in today's world, virtually all drives are inexpensive! The term RAID was recently redefined as Redundant Array of Independent Disks, which more accurately describes it.

We use fault-tolerance systems to ensure data integrity whenever hardware failures occur. With Windows NT 4 Server, there is the WNFT (Windows NT Fault-Tolerance) system, which is able to fix bad sectors dynamically (sector sparing) and keeps redundant copies of the data using RAID technology. NT provides support for several levels of RAID (specifically, 0, 1, and 5) that allow for different levels of fault tolerance, including options that support full data recovery in case of failure of a hard drive.

Important Fault-Tolerance Terminology

Before continuing, it will be helpful to define some of the key terms used in this chapter and with fault tolerance in general:

RAID   Redundant Array of Independent Disks. Two, three, or more drives are combined into a single logical drive. There are a number of different RAID configurations, and RAID may or may not have fault tolerance.

SLED   Single Large Expensive Disk. Not often used in microcomputer servers. In today's world, where a 9GB drive costs under two thousand dollars, there is little incentive to purchase larger, expensive disks. Multiple 9GB drives can be logically connected using RAID to appear as a single larger drive.

MTBF   Mean Time Before Failure. Intended as an indication of reliability. MTBF is sometimes referred to as MTTF (Mean Time To Failure).

MTTR   Mean Time To Repair. Indicates how difficult a repair can be. For many RAID arrays, using hot-swappable (the drive may be removed while the system is powered up) components can reduce MTTR to a manageable period.

MTBDU   Mean Time Before Data Unavailability. Indicates how long data may be unavailable when a failure occurs.

Synchronized Disks   File data are written to multiple devices simultaneously, resulting in increased performance for writing file data since each drive can be writing data concurrently.

Nonsynchronized Disks   File data are written to a single device, resulting in a linear write access situation.

Parity Data   One or more extra bits of information stored with each byte of data. Parity may be used to detect errors, and reconstruct the data.

Infant Mortality   Used to describe failures early in the life of a device. The failure rate is much higher for the first few months of a drive's life than at any other time (other than the first few seconds after being dropped on the floor).

RAID Levels

RAID technology provides fault tolerance for Windows NT 4 Server (and other servers). RAID technology works by using an array of inexpensive disks to store data. The following levels of fault tolerance are available with RAID systems, though Windows NT 4 Server only supports (without additional hardware or software) RAID levels 0, 1, and 5:

- **RAID level 0**—disk striping only. Provides improved fixed-disk read performance by sequentially placing blocks of data on multiple disks. RAID level 0 disk striping by itself doesn't provide fault tolerance, only improved performance.

- **RAID level 1**—disk mirroring. Uses a set of drives to store identical copies of data on two fixed disk drives. Each write to one member of the mirror set is duplicated on the other member of the mirror set. If the drive in the mirror set fails, Windows NT 4 Server automatically uses the remaining operable disk.

The advantage of disk mirroring is that only two drives are required, while RAID 5 requires three or more disks. If the drive that fails is the boot disk, you must boot from your ERD (Emergency Repair Disk) and refresh the operating system on the second drive.

■ **RAID level 2**—disk striping. Writes blocks of data across two or more drives. A third (and perhaps fourth) drive stores error-correction code. In the event of a failure, an error-correcting code regenerates data that was contained on the failed drive. Level 2 is faster when reading than level 1. Level 2 is not used in current RAID systems because of its inefficient method of storing data.

■ **RAID level 3**—disk striping. Works much like level 2. With level 3, one disk drive is required to store parity information that allows you to recover the data from the other drives. The costs of implementing level 2 are lower, as the error-correcting code is smaller. Level 3 is used for applications such as client/server database systems (Microsoft SQL Server, for example), which use very large files.

■ **RAID level 4**—disk striping. Uses a technique similar to level 3, but the stripe blocks are larger for more efficiency.

■ **RAID level 5**—disk striping with parity. Level 5 uses level 4's larger blocks and stripes the parity data across all disks rather than storing parity information on a dedicated drive. The RAID system (Windows NT 4 Server) ensures that the parity and data are always stored on different drives. Though level 5 is slower writing data than level 1, the read performance is better.

■ **RAID level 6**—identical to level 5, with the addition of redundant hardware such as disk controllers and power supplies.

Windows NT Server lets you choose either RAID level 0 (striping), RAID level 1 (mirroring), or RAID level 5 (striping with parity). Both RAID levels 1 and 5 offer redundancy to keep Windows NT 4 Server operating even when a drive fails. RAID level 5 is currently the favored method of providing disk drive fault tolerance; it is more efficient, though level 5 does require three (or more) drives.

If there are multiple drive failures, then the system will fail: Windows NT 4 Server is unable to reconstruct the missing data when more than one drive in a RAID system fails. Low-cost (well under $200 per gigabyte and still falling) fixed-disk drives that offer excellent reliability, with advertised MTBF rates of 800,000 to 1,000,000 hours, are easily available. However, be very aggressive with backups when new drives are first installed.

Warning

Regardless of what level of RAID is implemented, RAID isn't effective if multiple drives are damaged. Natural disasters, especially lightning and flooding (or when the SCSI system falls out a window), can easily destroy all the drives in a RAID system at once.

Adaptec and several other companies offer total RAID products, which consist of hardware (controllers, drives, cables, and so on) and software. These products are valuable for large Windows NT 4 Server installations, though there is no reason why you cannot create your own RAID system with standard components and Windows NT 4 Server's built-in RAID support.

Windows NT File System Formats

For the purpose of backward compatibility, Windows NT supports two different file systems. It supports the FAT (File Allocation Table) file system for backward compatibility with DOS. In fact, this is the only file system supported on floppy disks Windows NT 4 Server also supports the NTFS (New Technology File System) file system, which is the native Windows NT file system.

The disk file system format (either FAT or NTFS) is a very important consideration. Choosing FAT maintains compatibility with both DOS and Windows 95; however, it is unlikely that a Windows NT 4 Server will be run using either of these operating systems. As well, FAT is less efficient, and lacks NTFS's fault-tolerance features. About the only time that FAT offers any distinct advantages over NTFS is for disk volumes that are smaller than about 300MB—in this situation the overhead of NTFS will consume a significant percentage of the drive space.

FAT is not suitable for any fault-tolerant system—FAT just does not have the necessary structure to enable fault tolerance. NTFS, however, was designed to be fault-tolerant and works well in a fault-tolerant environment.

Note: Although earlier versions of Windows NT supported HPFS (High Performance File System) used on OS/2, Windows NT 4 Server does not support HPFS. If you have HPFS volumes, they must be converted to NTFS before upgrading to Windows NT 4 Server.

While each file system has its own quirks and limitations, NTFS is the least constrained of them all and should be the file system used for all drives unless backward compatibility with another operating system is desired. NTFS is the only file system that supports file system object-level security.

Regardless of which file system is installed on the drives, all drive management is done using the Disk Administrator program, the topic of the next section.

Note: Although at the time of this writing Windows NT 4 Server does not support FAT-32, it is expected that Microsoft will add support to Windows NT for FAT-32 in the future.

Using the Disk Administrator

Windows NT 4 Server includes a program called Disk Administrator. Disk Administrator performs both FDISK and Formatting functions. All fault-tolerance settings are configured using the Disk Administrator program.

When you start Disk Administrator after installing a drive that has not been initialized, the Disk Administrator (Figure 3-1) offers to configure the drive automatically. The Disk Administrator program is started by choosing the Start Menu | Programs | Administrative Tools (Common) | Disk Administrator.

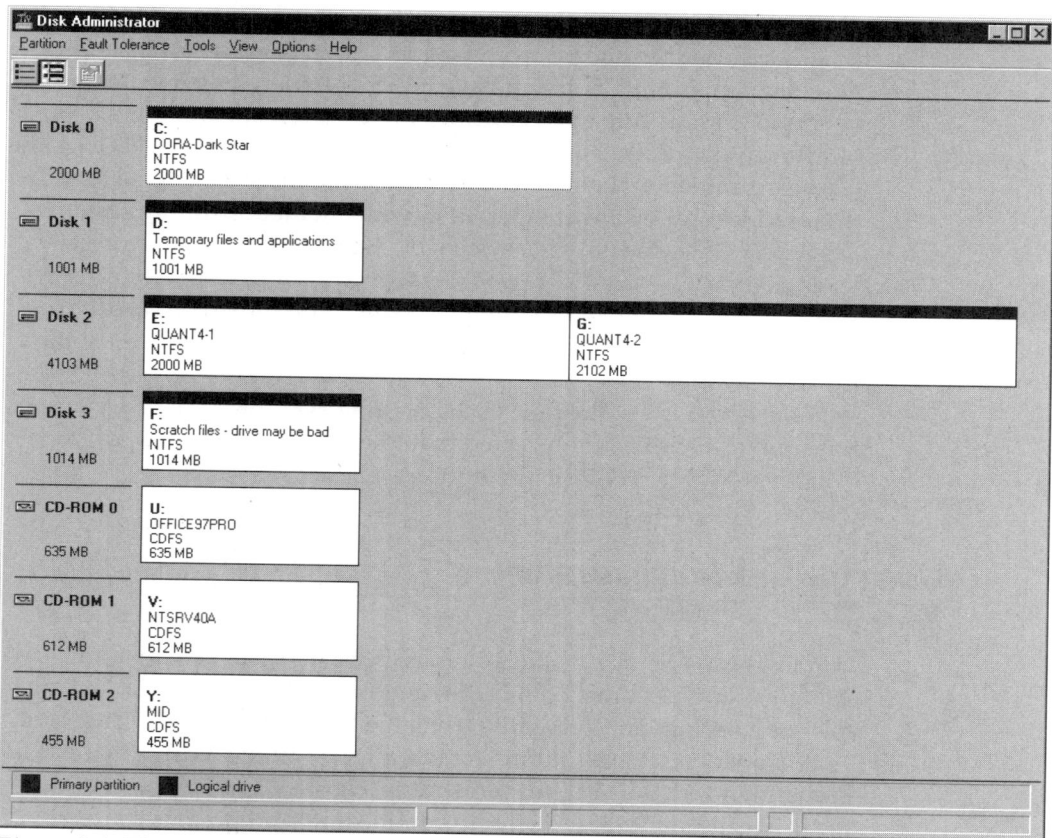

Figure 3-1: The Windows NT 4 Server Disk Administrator for the server DORA.

Disk Administrator can also manage fault tolerance, format and manage drives, and check and repair errors on drives.

Warning

Any time you work with Disk Administrator you must be careful. It is possible, with just a few clicks of the mouse, to delete, format, or otherwise destroy the contents of a drive. Always, always read all prompts, and be sure that your backup is current!

Working With Partitions

Working with partitions is sometimes a daunting task for a systems administrator. With MS-DOS, you can use a program called FDISK, which with a few keystrokes wipes out a drive's data with little hope of recovery. FDISK requires complicated keystroke sequences, munching of numbers, and is generally user-unfriendly, as well.

Disk Administrator makes working with partitions much more user-friendly. Installing a new drive can be as simple as connecting the drive, running Disk Administrator, and creating a partition.

Creating & Deleting Partitions

Partitions are created and deleted whenever a drive must be reconfigured. As well, whenever a new drive is added to the system, it will be necessary to create one or more partitions on the new drive. To create a new partition, follow these steps:

1. You must select a drive that has not been completely allocated.

2. Choose Partition | Create.

3. Create a new partition.

Warning

Deleting a partition will delete, permanently, any data that were contained on that partition. Be certain that there are adequate backups of the partition's data before deleting the partition!

If the entire drive has been allocated to partitions, then you must delete a partition to be able to create a new one. To delete a partition, choose Partition | Delete. Remember, deleting a partition deletes any data that has been written to that partition.

You can configure a drive into one or more partitions. When creating more than one partition, the second partition is called an extended partition. You must then divide the extended partition into multiple logical partitions that will appear as logical drives. Each logical drive will have a drive letter and will look like a separate drive to the user and operating system, even though the logical drive will not be on a separate physical drive. To create an extended partition, choose Partition | Create Extended.

Sometimes it is necessary to either combine or split partitions that have already been created. An example of this is when you have created multiple, small, FAT-based partitions and you wish to create a single large NTFS-based partition. To do so, follow these steps:

1. Back up the data. (Do not skip this step! Always back up your data before working with partitions.)

2. Delete the existing partitions by choosing Partition | Delete.

3. Create the new partition.

Using Volume Sets

There are times when you have a number of smaller drives (such as three 2GB drives) and you would really like to have a single 3GB drive. Sure, you could go out and purchase a new drive, but most of us would like to use the hardware we already have.

With Windows NT 4 Server, we can combine multiple hard drives into a single logical drive. This logical drive is called a volume set. To combine multiple hard drives, follow these steps:

1. Select free space on two or more drives.

2. In Disk Administrator, choose Partition | Create Volume Set.

3. The dialog box allows you to form a single logical drive from the drives selected in step 1, above. The size of the resulting volume set may be specified (within the limits set by Disk Administrator).

4. A volume set must be formatted with the NTFS file system (Tools | Format) to use volume sets. Format will prompt for the file system to use.

Note: When you are creating a volume set, the component drives do not need to be the same size, nor do you need to allocate all the space on the component drives to the volume set; you can have a 4GB drive and a 2GB drive. On the first drive, you can allocate 1GB of the 4GB drive to be the C partition and allocate the remaining 3GB on the drive, along with the 2GB on the second drive, to create a 5GB volume set. You do have to format the resulting partition with NTFS.

Once you have a volume set, you can extend the size of your logical drive by adding more drives. This is done by choosing Partition | Extend Volume Set in Disk Administrator. You can extend a volume set at any time, without the loss of data on the volume set.

Extending a volume set allows you to make an existing volume set larger by adding additional drives. However, once a drive has been included into a volume set, it cannot be removed without breaking the volume set and losing the volume set's data.

Note: Volume sets are not compatible with MS-DOS or Windows 95. If you are dual booting your system to either of these operating systems and anticipate needing to access the data on your volume set, do not create a volume set.

Creating Boot Partitions

One partition is used to boot or start a computer. This partition need not be the first partition (though it often is). Some systems have multiple, noncompatible operating systems (such as a Windows NT system and a UNIX system), each installed on their own partition.

You can make a choice between two different, incompatible operating systems by marking the partition containing the desired operating system as active—when the system is rebooted, the first active partition will be booted.

To mark a partition as the active partition, use Partition | Mark Active. This defines which partition contains the operating system and startup files (and which partition boots).

If you mark more than one partition as active, then the first active partition is the partition that boots.

Working With Configurations

Save and restore the current drive configuration (partitions, drive letters, striping, volume sets, etc.) with Partition | Configuration. You should save the configuration before you upgrade to a different operating system version and as a periodic measure to ease recovery in the event of an operating system failure.

To save your configuration information, follow these steps:

1. Choose Partition | Configuration | Save.

2. Insert a (blank) formatted floppy disk in drive A to save the current configuration. The configuration is automatically saved on the diskette in a file called system.

After saving configuration information, you can recover the configuration. You can do this in one of two ways:

- Choose Partition I Configuration I Restore. The configuration is restored from the file called system, contained on the floppy disk in drive A.

- Users who have multiple installations of Windows NT can search for another installation of Windows NT and load that installation's configuration. To do so, choose Partition I Configuration I Search. Drive letters and so on are restored but new partitions are not created or deleted.

When loading configurations, any changes made with Disk Administrator prior to searching (and loading a configuration for another installation of Windows NT) will be lost, with the possibility of data becoming inaccessible.

Committing Changes

Many of the changes to partitions and drives are not immediately written to the drive. To force Disk Administrator to write these changes, choose Partition I Commit Changes Now. This causes Disk Administrator to write all partition changes to the necessary locations.

If you do not commit changes, Disk Manager will prompt you to save (or discard) changes when you exit. There is no going back once the changes have been committed!

Working With Fault Tolerance

When your server reliability is a primary consideration, you may choose to either use a stripe set with parity (a RAID 5 implementation) or to create mirror sets. The Disk Administrator provides an easy way to work with mirror sets and stripe sets.

Using Mirror Sets

A mirror set is a configuration where all data is duplicated on two different physical drives. A mirror set is RAID level 1. If either of the physical drives fails, you can quickly and easily extract the copy of the data on the second drive in the mirror set. For systems that have online requirements (such as order processing and other real-time systems), a mirror set offers the highest degree of confidence in the system's data, with quick recovery times.

To create a mirror drive set, in Disk Administrator choose Fault Tolerance | Establish Mirror. You must have a free space on another physical drive that is the same size (or larger) than the partition you want to mirror. Both the primary partition and the mirror are referred to by the same drive letter. All data written to files on that drive letter are written to both physical drives.

If you have problems with the mirror set (or simply don't need to use mirroring for some reason), you can break apart the mirror volume set with Disk Administrator's Fault Tolerance | Break Mirror. This selection breaks the linkage between an existing mirrored drive set. The mirror (second drive) then is given its own drive letter. No files on either drive are lost; however, any writes to the original mirrored drive are no longer written to the mirror drive.

Stripe Sets

Similar to a volume set, stripe sets combine multiple hard drives into a single, large, logical volume. The differences between a stripe set and a volume set are:

- A stripe set requires that each component drive's space be identical in size. With a volume set, each component can be different in size.

- A stripe set offers enhanced performance as data are spread effectively between multiple drives. With a volume set, the data can be spread between multiple drives, but this is not guaranteed or even likely to happen.

- A stripe set is RAID level 0. RAID level 0 offers no enhanced data reliability. (RAID level 0 actually reduces data reliability, since if any part of a stripe set fails, the contents of the entire stripe set are lost.) A volume set is not part of the RAID specification.

- A stripe set can be created with parity, creating a RAID level 5 implementation, which offers enhanced reliability. More on this below.

- A failure of a stripe set drive when the stripe set is generated without parity usually results in the loss of all data in the stripe set. A failure of a stripe set drive when the stripe set is generated with parity often results in the loss of little or no data on the stripe set. A failure of a volume set drive typically results in the loss of at least some and perhaps all data on the stripe set.

For more information on stripe sets with parity, see the "Working With Fault Tolerance" section earlier in this chapter. Additional information on stripe sets with parity is found in the next section, where we cover fault-tolerant configurations.

To create stripe sets, choose Partition | Create Stripe Set. A stripe set is created in the same manner as a volume set. As mentioned in the list of differences between a stripe set and a volume set, there are additional restrictions to a stripe set: Each member of the stripe set must be the same size and on a different physical volume (Disk Administrator helps manage the size allocation for stripe sets).

Stripe Sets With Parity

As shown in the previous section, a stripe set (without parity) is created using two (or more) areas of free space, which are then built into a single larger volume. A basic stripe set has virtually no fault tolerance.

For a stripe set to have fault-tolerance protection, it is necessary to add parity-information stripes. In Windows NT 4 Server, disk striping with parity includes one parity stripe per row. A minimum of three physical drives are required when creating a stripe set with parity.

You can create a stripe set with parity, which implements RAID 5, using Fault Tolerance | Create Stripe Set With Parity.

Unlike mirrored sets, which are quickly recovered, when a failure occurs in a stripe set with parity, the drive's contents must be recovered using Fault Tolerance | Regenerate. When a volume created as a stripe set fails (typically catastrophically) the stripe set becomes an orphan.

To recover the stripe set, you must regenerate the data from the parity stripe. To regenerate the stripe set, you must select a new area of free space that is either equal to or larger than the other stripe set members and use Fault Tolerance | Regenerate.

Note: If you are using identical drives, then it is wise to have a spare drive (tested, formatted, and ready to use) in the event that you have a failure with your mirror or stripe set. Having a spare drive allows you to recover as quickly as possible, without having to purchase a new, replacement drive.

Using the Disk Administrator's Tools

The Disk Administrator's Tools menu items allow you to manipulate drives. Functions for formatting, error checking, and setting the drive label and letter are all available in the Tools menu. The Tools menu displays as the context menu when you right-click on a drive, making it easy to access these functions.

Formatting Drives

You must format both new drives that have never been formatted and drives that need to be cleaned. Cleaning is removing all files from the drive without using a delete command sequence.

Warning

When formatting drives that contain data, be sure that there are adaquate backups of the drive's contents. Once reformatted, the contents of the drive cannot be recovered except from a backup!

To format a drive, choose Tools | Change Format. You can format new drives and drives that were previously formatted. The Disk Administrator's format functionality is generally identical to the MS-DOS FORMAT command. The types of formatting supported include both FAT and NTFS for hard drives and FAT for floppy drives (a floppy drive cannot be formatted using the NTFS file system).

Checking for Errors

Periodically, all drives should be checked for errors, especially drives that use the FAT file system. Generally, an NTFS file system drive is not as likely to fail, but you cannot go wrong checking NTFS drives. To check a drive, use Tools | Check for Errors. A drive can be checked for errors (using CHKDSK's functionality) and you can optionally repair any errors detected.

For those drives that are currently being used (typically there are open files on the drive), a check for errors can be scheduled for a later time.

Labeling Drives

The volume label for any drive (excluding diskettes) can be set using Tools | Set Volume Label.

For a FAT volume, the label can be no more than 11 characters; an NTFS volume can have labels that are 31 or fewer characters long.

Assigning Drive Letters

You can modify the drive letter assigned to any hard drive or CD-ROM drive using Tools | Assign Drive Letter. For example, on our network all CD-ROM drives use drive letters that range from S to Z. All clients establish links to the CD-ROM drives using the same letters, so that S is

the same CD-ROM drive on all machines, both the server and the client
users. However, be careful when changing a drive letter assignment as
many MS-DOS and Windows 95 applications assume that a drive is at a
specific location.

Tip

*Assign your CD-ROM drives to higher letters (such as S, T, . . .) so
that added hard drives may be contiguous using lower letters (such as
C, D, . . .).*

Viewing Properties

To display the properties of the current selection, use Tools | Properties.
The Properties menu item displays the Volume Properties dialog box, as
shown in Figure 3-2.

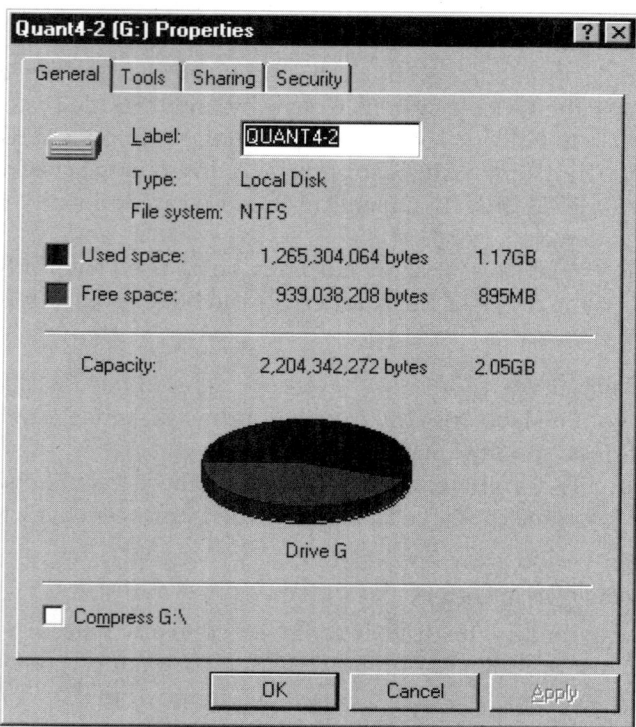

Figure 3-2: The Disk Administrator's Volume Properties dialog box.

Moving On

This chapter has discussed some of the concepts of fault tolerance and how to implement its techniques on your Windows NT-based computers.

Windows NT supports RAID level 0 with the stripe sets, RAID level 1 with mirror sets, and RAID level 5 with stripe sets with parity. This support provides several options to ensure data integrity and system tolerance from hard drive failure, which tends to be more common than you might imagine.

Next we will discuss the issues and details of configuring a Windows NT 4 Server operating on a network.

4

Configuring & Administering Windows NT Networks

The main benefit of Windows NT Server is that is provides much more than just the file and printer services that have become the de facto standard features of a PC-based network operating system. Windows NT is also an ideal applications server. It runs robust client-server applications (such as SQL Server) and information services (such as FTP and so on) with the Internet Information Server (IIS). Windows NT supports an e-mail server that easily scales up to handle the largest organization and it even handles network management support systems such as Systems Management Server.

The one thing that all of these benefits have in common is that they rely on a network connection. It is necessary to have a network connection for any of the above-mentioned applications to be able to function at all.

This chapter will concentrate on the basics of Windows NT network configuration and administration and will include a discussion of the network protocols Windows NT supports. This chapter introduces the Windows NT networking model and provides a tour of the Windows NT network utilities.

Workgroups vs. Domains

Before Windows NT Server was introduced, a version of the Windows operating system was enhanced to provide a distributed network service and was sold under the name of Windows for Workgroups 3.11. The basic concept was that all workstations that were configured to the same workgroup could share their files and printers with each other. It was a crude networking model, but for a period of time became quite popular, probably due to the growth in popularity of the Windows operating system.

For the sake of backward compatibility, Windows NT supports workgroups, and a Windows NT workstation can even join a workgroup if necessary.

A Windows NT domain is a centralized networking model relying on a central primary domain controller to maintain security, user accounts, and directory services with the assistance of backup domain controllers. The main benefit of this model is that it is manageable from a security perspective as well as just a practical perspective.

With a domain, one server serves as the primary security authenticator. This server is called the PDC (primary domain controller). There may be zero or more BDCs (backup domain controllers). The PDC will handle all security authentication and management. If at any time the PDC becomes unavailable, then one of the BDCs (if any) will be "promoted" to become the new PDC. This provides a degree of fault tolerance to the network.

Setting Up Windows NT Domains

During the Windows NT 4 Server installation, the server's role in the network must be specified. Choices are either PDC, BDC, or stand-alone (workgroup) server. To have a domain server, either PDC or BDC must be selected at installation time. It is not possible to change an existing installation of Windows NT 4 Server from stand-alone server to being a domain controller.

PDCs may be "demoted" to BDC at any time there is a BDC available to become a new PDC. This would be done were it necessary to take the PDC down for maintenance. As well, a BDC may be promoted to PDC, an action which will demote the current PDC to BDC status. When a network is started, the server that was established as the PDC will continue in the same role. If the PDC is unavailable, then a BDC will need to be promoted to be the new PDC. When the original PDC later becomes available, it will become a BDC.

In an ideal Windows NT network, one Windows NT server is specified as the PDC and (typically) the other Windows NT servers on the network will be BDCs. There is no limit on the number of BDCs that may be part of a network. The BDC's job is to handle authentication and validation requests as well as directory services when the PDC is, for whatever reason, unable to respond.

It is important to think about the structure of your network ahead of time so that you don't end up having to make major changes after you have already configured your entire network, user accounts and all.

A single Windows NT domain can handle up to 10,000 users. For most companies, that means that a single domain would work just fine with a couple of domain controllers. In most cases, with fewer users than this you will not have to create more than one domain. However, there may be cases where you will want to create multiple domains regardless of size. For example, suppose a department in a company needs to have tighter restrictions for accessing the Internet and also needs much stricter control over the user accounts and security policy than does the rest of the company. For that reason, a subnet and a separate domain can be created and given their own PDC.

If a choice is made to create multiple domains, then ask the question as to whether the two domains need to share information. If they do, then you will probably need to create a *trust* relationship to allow sharing of user account and security information. Using trust relationships, network size is virtually unlimited!

Changing the Domain

Computers and people move in the organization, which can affect domains. It is not uncommon for a person and their workstation to move to a different domain, and the network must be made aware of this change.

Tip

It is less common, but not unknown, to move servers from one domain to another. This does happen, however: Changing a server's domain membership is the same as changing a workstation's domain membership.

To change the domain that a Windows NT 4 Server or a Windows NT 4 Workstation belongs to, follow these steps:

1. Start the Control Panel (Start Menu | Settings | Control Panel). Once the Control Panel has started, double-click the Network icon to start the Network applet.

2. Select the Identification tab of the Network dialog.

3. Click the Change button, which displays the Identification Changes dialog, as shown in Figure 4-1.

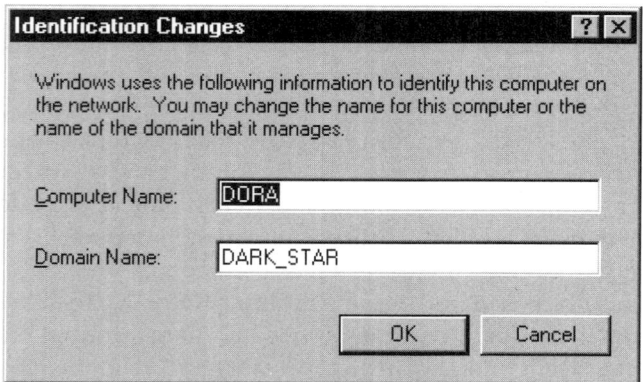

Figure 4-1: The Identification Changes dialog box is used to change the computer name and domain name.

4. Simply enter a new computer name or domain name in the corresponding text boxes as needed.

5. Click OK when done.

Tip

Windows 95 workstations are changed in a similar manner, with the changes being entered into the Identification tab, rather than using an Identification Changes dialog box. In addition, with Windows 95, the domain name is always entered into the Workgroup position, and Windows 95 supports a description field as well.

Computer Accounts in a Domain

Every Windows NT computer that wants to be part of a domain must be explicitly added to the domain, either through the automatic computer account creation process that was just presented or through explicitly adding the Windows NT machine to the domain using the server manager. This ensures that the domain controllers for the domain know about the machine and will update directory services and user account information for that Windows NT computer.

Trusting Relationships With Other Domains

The concept of a trust relationship is to allow a domain to provide shared access to information to another domain. This is done by having a domain specifically state that it *trusts* another domain; in this case, the trusted domain shares its user account information with the trusting domain for authentication purposes. At this point, users in the trusted domain are able to access resources in the trusting domain.

However, a trust relationship between two domains is a one-way street, as illustrated in Figure 4-2. Just because the Corporate domain trusts the East Coast domain doesn't imply reciprocation. The East Coast domain has to explicitly state that it also trusts the Corporate domain before there is a two-way exchange of information.

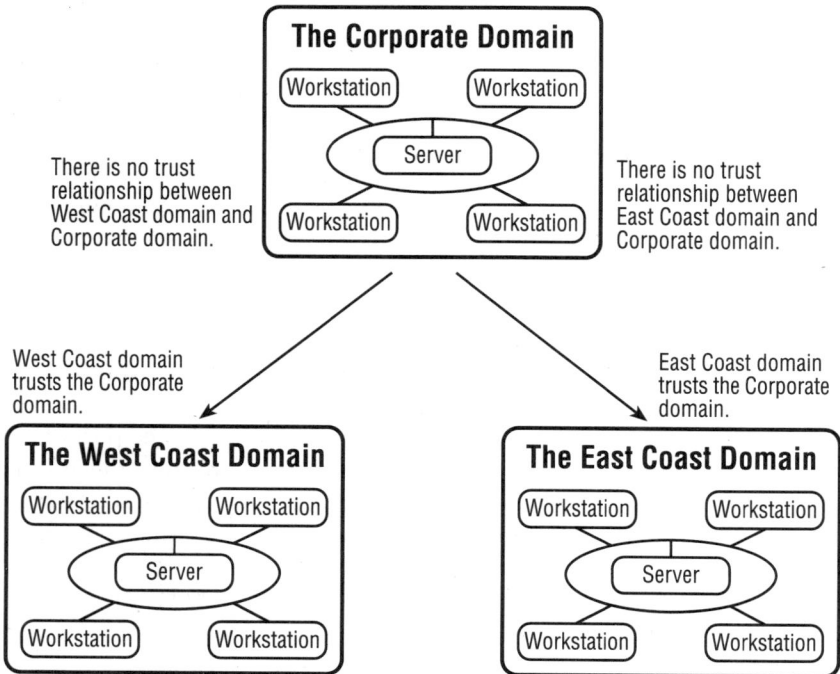

Figure 4-2: A trust relationship, with a main corporate domain and two other domains.

Figure 4-1 shows that the East Coast domain and the West Coast domain both trust the Corporate domain. This trust is not returned, however, since the Corporate domain does not have a trust relationship with either of the other domains. This is an example of a master domain, as described in the section, "Master Domains."

The Windows NT concept of domain combined with trust relationships can be used to create a number of different network models that can help keep a large network manageable. Several possible models are:

- Single domain
- Master domain
- Multiple master domains
- Multiple domains with trust relationships

Single Domain

In this model, there is a single domain that manages all domain resources, including file servers and user accounts. This is by far the simplest model.

In a single domain, there is only one PDC; zero, one, or more BDC(s); and a single network. Management is performed locally, for only the single domain. Configuring and setting up a single domain is easy: Install Windows NT 4 Server as a PDC and specify the domain name to be used.

Master Domains

The master domain model is used when there are multiple domains, perhaps for different departments in a company, that need to be managed from a central location (see Figure 4-1).

The first step is to install and configure each of the separate domains for the departments. Once this is accomplished, you then create a master domain that is trusted by each of the subdomains. This allows the network administrator to manage all user accounts in a single location (the master domain) and have that information propagated to each of the subdomains by means of the trust relationship.

With master domains, there is one PDC and zero, one, or more BDC(s) for each subdomain. There is a single network. Management is performed locally for all the domains in the master domain.

Because this model is still managing all user accounts in one domain, it is also subject to the domain limit of 10,000 users.

Multiple Master Domains

The multiple master domains model uses a similar approach to the single master domain model, with extra master domains added where all of the master domains trust each other and all of the subdomains trust all of the master domains.

With multiple master domains, there is one PDC and zero, one, or more BDC(s) for each subdomain. There are multiple networks. Management is performed locally or remotely as needed.

Because this model does not attempt to manage all user accounts using one domain, it is not subject to the domain limit of 10,000 users.

Multiple Domains With Trust Relationships

The final model, which is perhaps simpler than the multiple master domains model, is multiple domains where each of the domains trusts the others. Figure 4-3 shows a multiple master domains relationship.

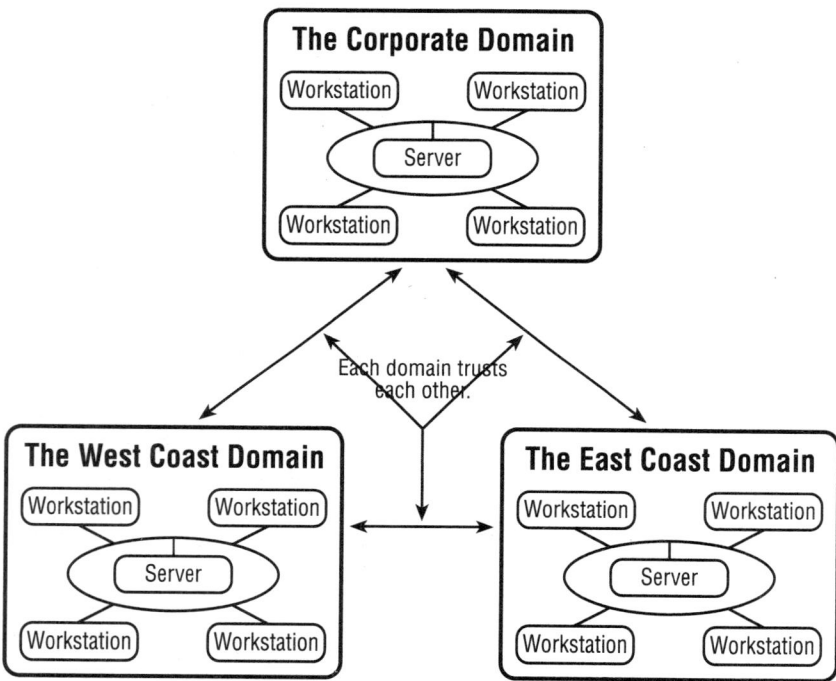

Figure 4-3: Multiple domains that trust each other.

Establishing a Trust Relationship

The process for establishing trust relationships must be performed on both the trusting and the trusted domains. The application that is used to establish trust relationships is the User Manager for Domains, which is started by choosing Start Menu | Programs | Administrative Tools (Common) | User Manager for Domains.

Creating a trust relationship is a two-stage process—each domain must configure the trust relationship.

The Trust Relationships dialog box (choose Policies | Trust Relationships from the User Manager for Domains main menu), shown in Figure 4-4, shows that no trust relationships have been established.

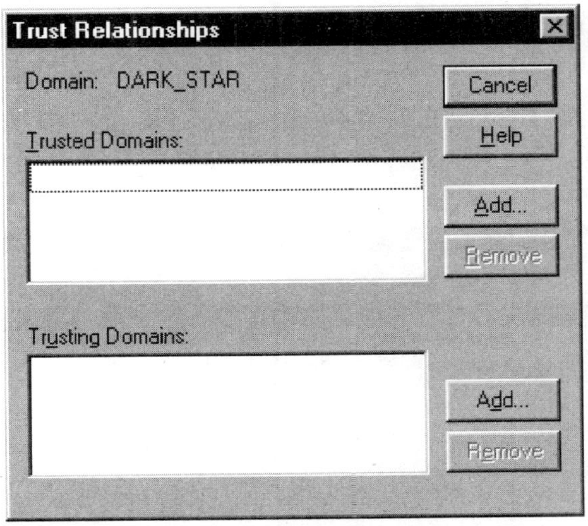

Figure 4-4: The Trust Relationships dialog box.

A trusted domain's users and groups are allowed user rights, resource permissions, and local group memberships on the trusting domain. See Chapter 2 for more information about local and global groups.

A trusting domain allows users from a trusted domain to have user rights, resource permissions, and local group memberships on the trusting domain.

To create a trust relationship, you must:

1. On the domain that will be trusted, click the Add button next to the Trusting Domains list and add a trusting domain.

2. On the domain that was added to the Trusting Domains list in Step One, you must start the User Manager, go to the Trust Relationships dialog, and add the trusted domain to the Trusted Domains list by clicking the Add button next to the Trusted Domains list.

Never, ever, remove one side of a trust relationship without removing the other side. Both sides (trusted and trusting) must agree on the relationship.

Using the Server Manager

The Server Manager (Figure 4-5) is a core tool for maintaining and monitoring all of the computers in a domain.

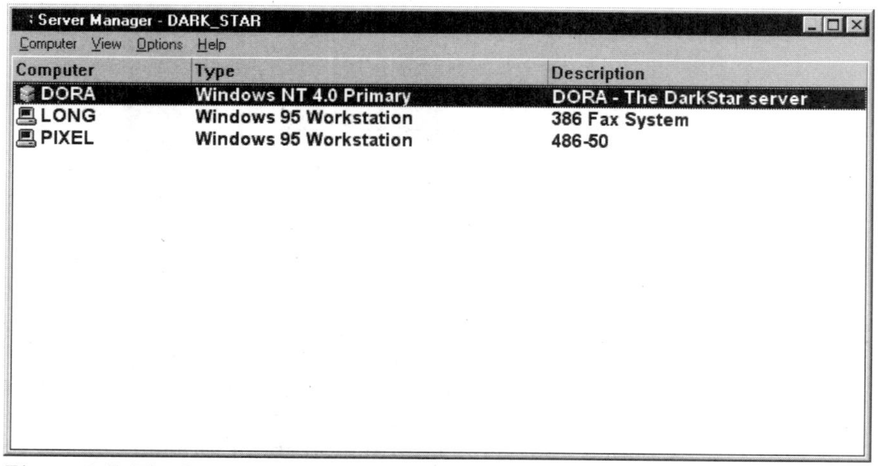

Figure 4-5: The Server Manager program.

The Server Manager is responsible for:

- Adding and removing computer accounts to/from the domain.
- Computer properties, statistics, and current usage and connections.
- Viewing, starting, and stopping services.

The Server Manger is started by choosing Start
Menu | Programs | Administrative Tools (Common) | Server Manager.

Adding a Computer to the Domain

With Windows NT 4 Server, a computer may not access resources on a domain unless it has been added to the domain. When a computer is added to a domain, it is given an account in the domain directory database.

To add a computer to a Windows NT domain, you perform the following steps:

1. Start the Server Manager (Start Menu | Programs | Administrative Tools (Common) | Server Manager).

2. Choose Computer | Add to Domain from the menu. In the Add Computer To Domain dialog box (see Figure 4-6), click the correct computer type, and enter the name for the computer to add.

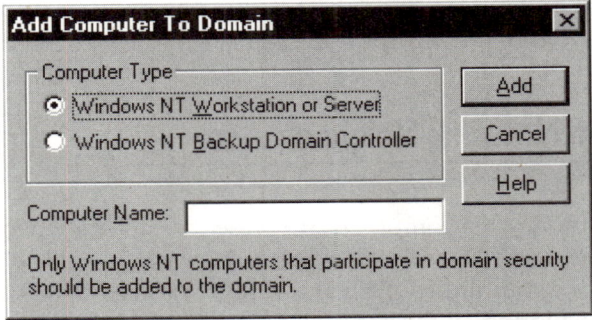

Figure 4-6: The Add Computer To Domain; click the correct computer type, and fill in the computer name.

Generally, only Windows NT computers (either workstations or servers) should be added to a domain.

Removing a Computer From a Domain

With Windows NT 4 Server, a computer that has been included into a domain may explicitly be removed from the domain using the Domain Manager. When a computer is removed from a domain, its account is removed from the domain directory database.

To remove a computer from a Windows NT domain, use the following steps:

1. Start the Server Manager (Start Menu | Programs | Administrative Tools (Common) | Server Manager).

2. Select the computer to be removed from the domain in the list, and either press Del or choose Computer | Remove From Domain from the menu.

3. The Server Manager will prompt for confirmation.

When moving a computer from one domain to another, always remove it from the previous domain first.

Browsing the Network Neighborhood

Determining what computers are present on the network is a simple task using the new Windows NT 4 Server Network Neighborhood (see Figure 4-7). This application, which was first introduced with Windows 95, makes exploring on the network a simple and easy task.

There are Network Neighborhood icons in the Windows NT Explorer and on the Windows NT 4 Server desktop. The simplest way to start the Network Neighborhood is to double-click the Network Neighborhood icon on the desktop. If Explorer is open, however, you can select Network Neighborhood to display it from within Explorer (see Figure 4-8 for a view of Network Neighborhood in Explorer).

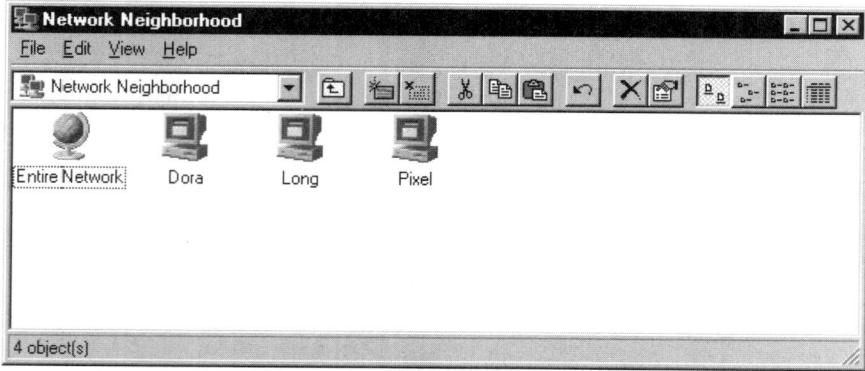

Figure 4-7: The Network Neighborhood showing the DarkStar network.

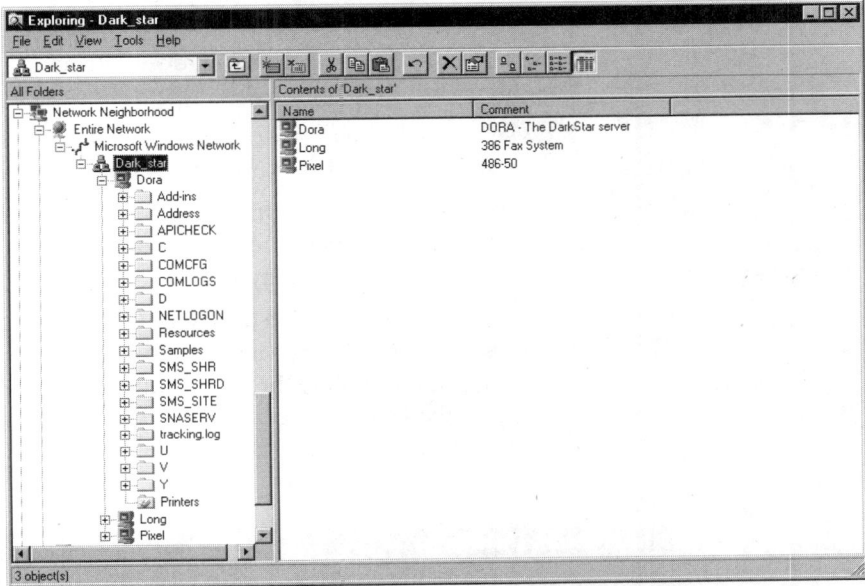

Figure 4-8: The Network Neighborhood when viewed from Explorer.

Mapping a Network Drive

The process of accessing a shared disk object (usually a folder, or perhaps an entire shared drive) using a local drive letter is referred to as *mapping a network drive.*

Tip

An object being mapped need not be on another server: A local folder that is shared may be mapped to a drive letter as well. This is a functionality very similar to the seldom-used MS-DOS SUBST command.

It is useful, once a shared object must be accessed more than one time, to map it to a local drive for convenient access. That way, the shared object may be accessed using the more familiar drive letter, rather than the more complex UNC (Uniform Naming Convention) name. See the section "Mapping a Network Drive to a UNC Name" for more on UNC names.

To map a shared object to a local drive:

1. Start Network Neighborhood by double-clicking the Network Neighborhood icon on the desktop.

2. Browse through the network and servers until you find the server and the share that you want to map to a local drive.

3. Choose Tools | Map Network Drive from the menu (or right-click the object to be mapped and select Map Network Drive from the context menu that is displayed).

4. In the Map Network Drive dialog box (see Figure 4-9) that displays, change the drive letter in the Drive drop-down list box to another drive letter if the default drive is not acceptable. To connect to the shared object using a different username, enter the username in the Connect As box.

Figure 4-9: The Map Network Drive dialog box, connecting to DORA's share called Address.

5. Click the Reconnect at Logon option so that Windows NT will automatically remap this drive for you the next time you log on.

6. Click OK when done.

Deleting a Mapped Network Drive

Many users map drives with wild abandon. Then their 26 drive letters get used up, and there is that panicked, "Now what do I do?"

Any network objects that are mapped to drive letters may be deleted by starting the Windows NT Explorer (Start Menu | Programs | Windows NT Explorer) and following these steps:

1. Select the mapped drive to be deleted.

2. Right-click on the drive, and select Disconnect from the pop-up menu.

An alternate way of disconnecting network drives is to:

1. Choose Tools | Disconnect Network Drive from the menu.

2. In the Disconnect Network Drive dialog box (see Figure 4-10), select the drive to be disconnected and click OK.

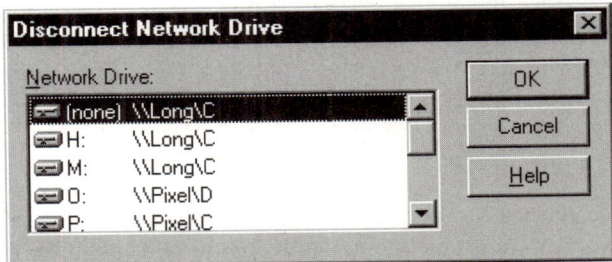

Figure 4-10: Disconnecting a drive using the Disconnect Network Drive dialog box.

Mapping a Network Drive to a UNC Name

UNC names, which consist of the server, share, and object names, are an alternative way to access a network shared drive. Again, the process of accessing a shared disk resource using a local drive letter is referred to as mapping a network drive.

To connect to a network drive using a UNC name, simply refer to the drive using the UNC conventions:

    \\server\share

where *server* is the server's name and *share* is the share name. For example, the server Long, on the DarkStar network, has a share called C. To access this shared drive, to do a directory from an MS-DOS window, for instance, the UNC name could be used:

```
dir \\long\c
 Volume in drive \\long\c is USB
 Volume Serial Number is 2C6A-15E3

 Directory of \\long\c

 10/22/96  05:34p   63      AUTOEXEC.BAT
 10/22/96  02:19p   19      AUTOEXEC.DOS
 08/24/96  11:11a   93,812  COMMAND.COM
 10/22/96  02:08p   21      CONFIG.DOS
 10/22/96  06:32p   21      CONFIG.SYS
 10/22/96  04:00p   21      CONFIG.WIN
 07/11/95  09:50a   25,473  MSCDEX.EXE
 10/22/96  05:49p   <DIR>   MWW
 10/22/96  02:59p   2,293   NETLOG.TXT
 10/22/96  03:01p   <DIR>   PROGRA~1      Program Files
 01/07/94  03:57p   38,256  SLCD.SYS
 10/22/96  02:54p   <DIR>   WINDOWS
 12 File(s)   159,979 bytes 680,820,736 bytes free
```

UNC names can be useful for applications that understand them; however, many times using a UNC name will result in more typing on the user's part!

Configuring Remote Networking

A feature of Windows NT that becomes extremely useful now that telecommuting has become more popular is the RAS (Remote Access Server) built in to Windows NT. RAS allows a user to dial in from a remote location over standard telephone lines, log on to the network, and have the same services and capabilities (albeit a little slower as a result of the modem speeds) as if he or she were connected directly to the network.

DUN (Dial-Up Networking) is used to connect a Windows NT 4 Server system to a remote computer system.

If you are not using RAS or DUN, then there is no need to consider installing, configuring, or tuning these services.

RAS runs as a service on a Windows NT Server and is administered through the use of the Remote Access Admin program (see Figure 4-11). Start the Remote Access Admin program by choosing Start Menu | Programs | Administrative Tools (Common) | Remote Access Admin.

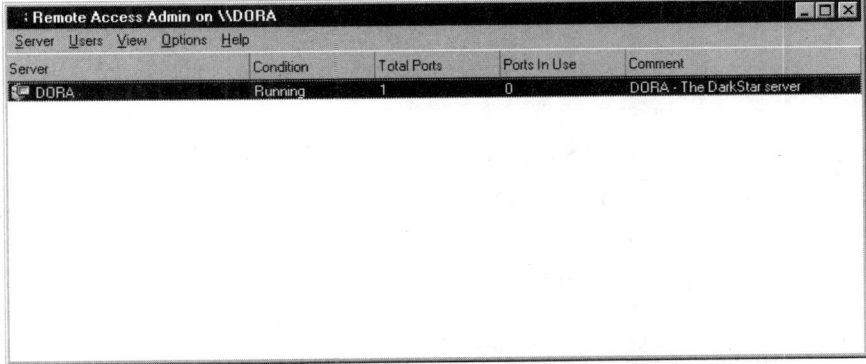

Figure 4-11: The Remote Access Admin program, with one server (DORA) running.

What Is RAS & Where Did DUN Come From?

With Windows NT 4 Server, RAS (Remote Access Server) is for incoming connections (the server side), while DUN (Dial-Up Networking) is for outgoing connections (the client side). The two collectively are usually called RAS/DUN. DUN is configured with the Dial-Up Networking Administrator, while RAS is configured from the Control Panel's Network applet's Services tab.

Configuring Dial-Up Networking (DUN)

In this section, I'll cover Windows NT 4 Server's use of the TCP/IP protocol for DUN. You can have a RAS connection that uses either the IPX/SPX-compatible or NetBEUI protocols, but TCP/IP is more common.

You can configure both RAS and DUN to use TCP/IP, NetBEUI, or IPX/SPX-compatible protocols. Neither NetBEUI nor IPX/SPX are difficult to configure. However, TCP/IP seems to be more complex and daunting to users who are less experienced.

Installing DUN for the IPX/SPX or NetBEUI Protocols

To install the DUN service for IPX/SPX or NetBEUI, use the Control Panel's Network applet. To select services to install, follow the steps below:

1. Start the Control Panel's Network applet.

2. Select the Services tab.

3. Click the Add button. The Select Network Service dialog box appears.

4. Select the services component you wish to install from the Network Service list.

Installing DUN for the TCP/IP Protocol

Unlike TCP/IP for an NIC, TCP/IP for DUN is not configured under the Control Panel's Network applet. Rather, to configure TCP/IP for DUN, follow the steps below:

1. Access the Dial-Up Networking program (Start Menu | Programs | Accessoriess | Dial-Up Networking). See Figure 4-12.

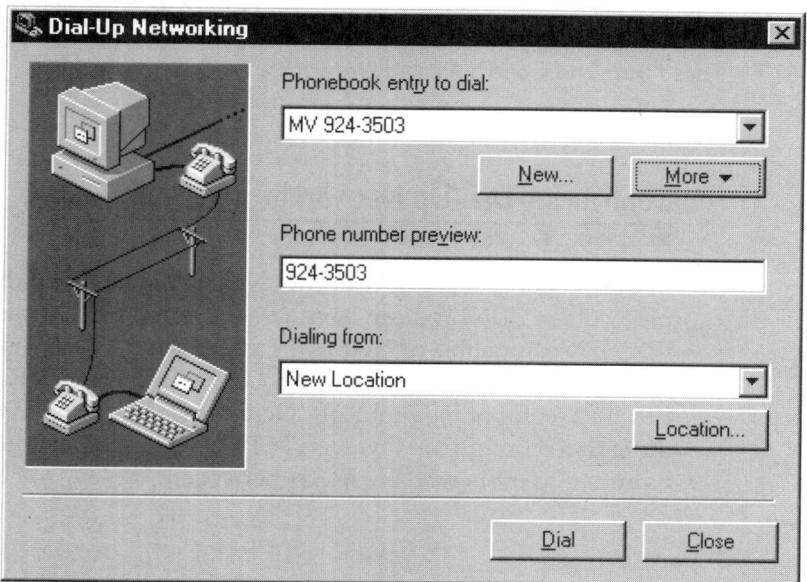

Figure 4-12: The Dial-Up Networking program.

2. With the Dial-Up Networking program, you can add, configure, or remove dial-up connections and set phone numbers and dialing locations. Readers who have experience with dial-up networking for Windows 95 will find many of the concepts in the DUN program for Windows NT 4 Server familiar. In addition, future releases of Windows 95 will strive towards making the DUN program uniform in both platforms.

   As Figure 4-12 shows, the Dial-Up Networking program allows you to select an existing configuration or to create a new configuration. In all cases, you need to know the telephone number to call (for outgoing DUN connections), the protocol of the receiving end (such as PPP), and other configuration information such as the TCP/IP parameters.

3. In the Dial-Up Networking program, you can also configure the modem properties. You can have as many modems connected to your system as you have serial ports. Most users have only one (or perhaps two) modems; however, some systems have multiple modems, perhaps of differing types. You can attach any modem to a phonebook entry as desired, and you can have more than one phonebook entry for each modem.

Creating a DUN Configuration

A DUN configuration describes a logical connection to a remote host. The configuration includes information about the modem to be used, telephone numbers, and host configuration.

   In this section, you will learn to create a new DUN configuration (called a phonebook entry) using the name Internet-1. This phonebook entry is the one that I actually use when I connect to the Internet using my ISP's dial-up PPP service.

Specifying an Entry Name   To create a new phonebook entry, select the New button. The New Phonebook Entry Wizard displays, as shown in Figure 4-13.

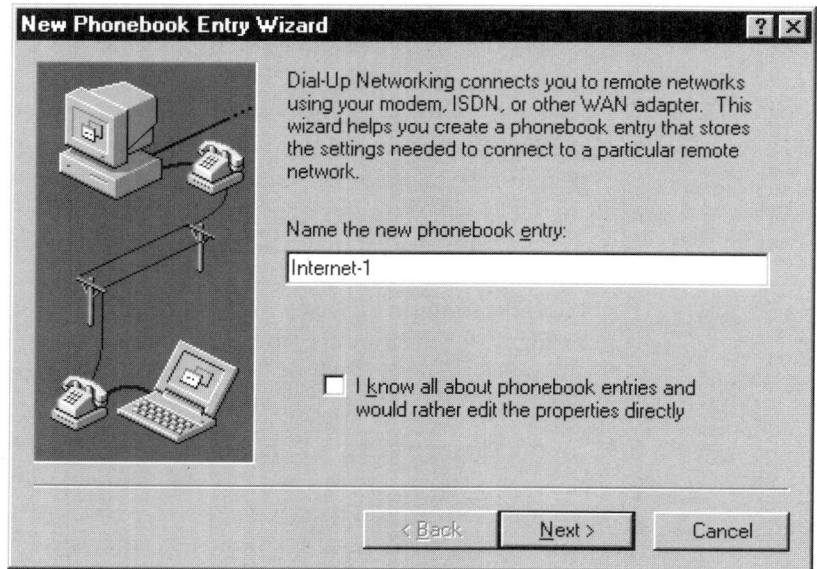

Figure 4-13: The New Phonebook Entry Wizard's first dialog box.

To specify a phonebook entry name, follow the steps below:

1. In the first dialog box of the New Phonebook Entry Wizard, you must enter the name for this entry (Internet-1).

2. Do not click the I Know All About Phonebook Entries . . . check box. If you do, you will have to manually specify the properties for the phonebook (DUN) entry.

3. Click Next to set the Server options.

Specifying Server Options   On the next dialog box of the New Phonebook Entry Wizard (titled Server and shown in Figure 4-14), you can specify options for calling an Internet Service Provider.

1. Use the check boxes provided to specify the following Server options:

   ■ Check the I Am Calling the Internet check box if you are calling an Internet Service Provider (in many cases this will be true).

■ Check the middle check box if you want to send logon information such as the password as plain text (many Internet Service Providers don't support encrypted logons).

■ Check the bottom check box if the server you are connecting to cannot provide TCP/IP configuration (such as the assigned node address).

2. When you are finished, click Next.

Tip

If in doubt as to whether to check these items or not, you can experiment: Don't check the Send My Plain Text Password . . . option, and check the The Non-Windows NT Server I Am Calling . . . option. If you are unable to successfully connect to your server, then try different combinations of these two options.

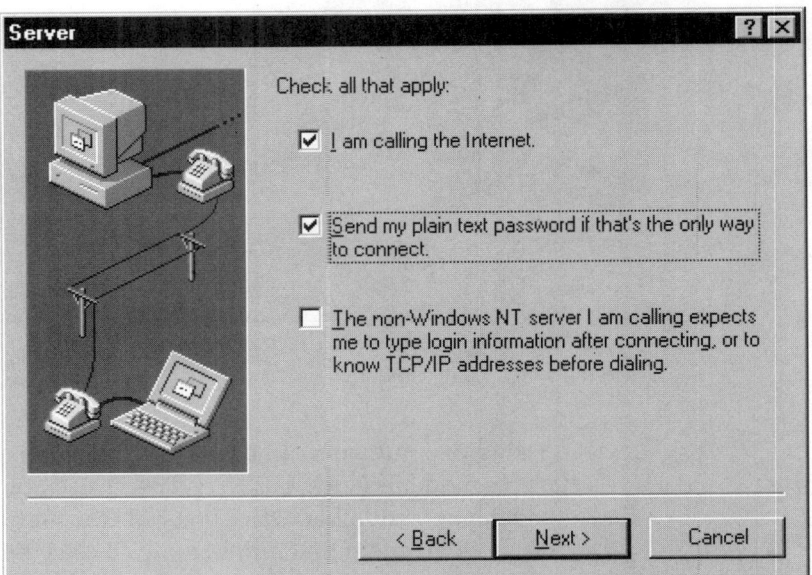

Figure 4-14: The New Phonebook Entry Wizard's second dialog box, titled Server.

Specifying Phone Numbers   To specify phone numbers to use to connect to the server, follow the steps below:

1. On the next dialog box of the New Phonebook Entry Wizard (Figure 4-15), enter the telephone numbers to connect to the server. You can enter one or more numbers.

2. To enter alternate numbers, click the Alternates button. DUN dials the first number, and if it cannot connect (if the line is busy, for example), then it attempts to connect to the second number.

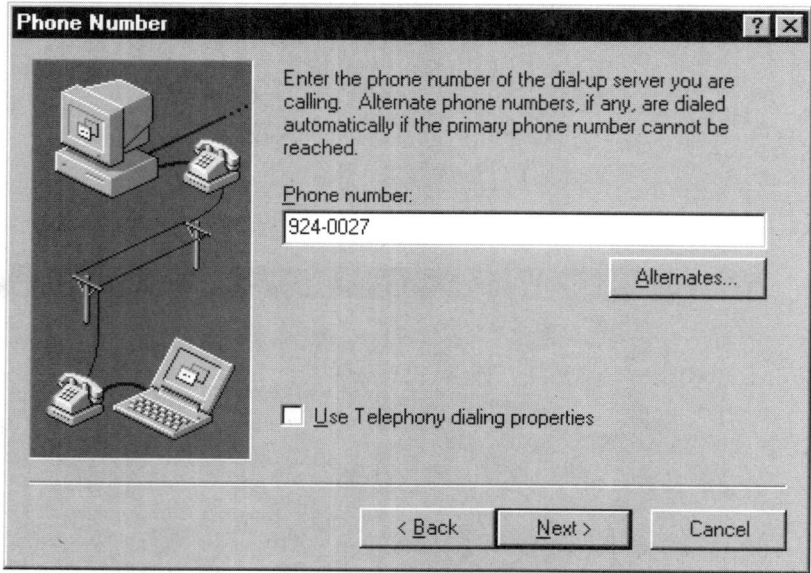

Figure 4-15: The New Phonebook Entry Wizard's third dialog box, titled Phone Number.

Using two numbers can be useful when your server has two types of modems (such as 28.8 and 14.4), each type having its own telephone number. DUN first calls the number that matches your modem, and if that number fails, it calls the second number. Connecting to the second number might mean that you have to accept the possibility of degraded performance if the second number connects to less capable modems.

3. Additionally, you can select the Use Telephony Dialing Properties check box. The established dialing properties are used if you choose this option. This feature is useful for long distance numbers or for numbers that have special dialing requirements.

Tip

You can also configure telephony dialing properties using the Control Panel's Modems applet. To configure telephony dialing properties, follow the steps below:

1. *Open the Control Panel's Modems applet. The main window for the Modems Properties dialog box appears.*

2. *Click the Dialing Properties button to display the Dialing Properties dialog box.*

Finishing & Configuring DUN Entries   The next screen of the New Phonebook Entry Wizard (see Figure 4-16) simply shows you that the setup of the new phonebook entry, Internet-1, is complete. Click the Finish button to save Internet-1.

If you need to go back and make a change, click the Back button to go back and change any parameter. If you'd like to delete the new phonebook entry, click Cancel.

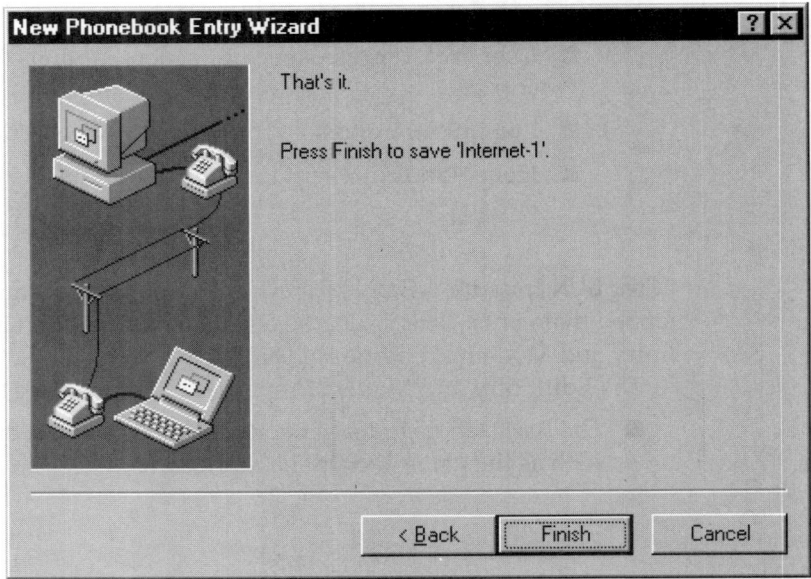

Figure 4-16: The New Phonebook Entry Wizard's fourth, and final, dialog box.

After creating a phonebook entry, you can edit the entry's properties. Generally, all entries require some manual configuration. To select an entry to edit, follow the steps below:

1. Access the Dial-Up Networking program. (Start Menu | Programs | Applications | Dial-Up Networking). See Figure 4-12.

2. Select an entry's name in the Phonebook Entry to Dial drop-down list box.

3. The More button on the main Dial-Up Networking program dialog box, as shown in Figure 4-12, displays a pop-up menu with the following choices:

   - **Edit Entry and Modem Properties**—allows you to change DUN entry properties. See the section, "Editing DUN Properties" for more information.

   - **Clone Entry and Modem Properties**—copies a DUN entry and allows you to immediately modify the entry.

   - **Delete Entry**—deletes an entry.

   - **Create Shortcut to Entry**—creates a shortcut for the DUN entry on your desktop or in the Start program.

   - **Monitor Status**—monitors the DUN connection.

   - **Operator Assisted or Manual Dialing**—allows you to manually dial the number, such as when you are on a laptop computer in a hotel or when making an international call.

   - **User Preferences**—specifies general options for the DUN entry.

   - **Logon Preferences**—specifies systems administrator options.

   - **Help**—finds more information about the DUN program options.

Editing DUN Properties   DUN properties are set using a standard Windows tabbed dialog box. This dialog box is displayed by choosing More | Edit Entry and Modem Properties in Dial-Up Networking.

The Edit Entry and Modem Properties dialog has five tabs:

   - The Basic tab includes general information about the DUN entry, such as the name and phone number.

- The Server tab includes specific server settings, such as the type of connection and the network protocol used.

- The Script tab allows you to create a logon script that makes manual logon much easier.

- The Security tab includes authentication properties.

- The X.25 tab includes options for the X.25 protocol, which is only supported by a few ISPs, including CompuServe and SprintNet.

Configuring Remote Access Server (RAS)

The previous section describes the procedures for configuring DUN (Dial-Up Networking). This section describes configuration of RAS (Remote Access Server). There is substantial overlap between RAS and DUN: It is common to refer to both together as RAS/DUN, though the configuration of each is slightly different.

Tip

If RAS has not been installed, install it from the Control Panel's Network applet. Select the Services tab and click the Add button. From the list of services to be added, select RAS and click OK.

As we mentioned above, RAS is the server side, just as DUN is the client side, of networking by modem. Both RAS and DUN interact, are able to use the same modems, and share similar properties and configurations. There are differences, however, and in this section we cover some of these differences.

To configure RAS, follow the steps below:

1. Open the Control Panel's Network applet.

2. Select the Services tab.

3. Choose Remote Access Service from the Network Services list, as shown in Figure 4-17.

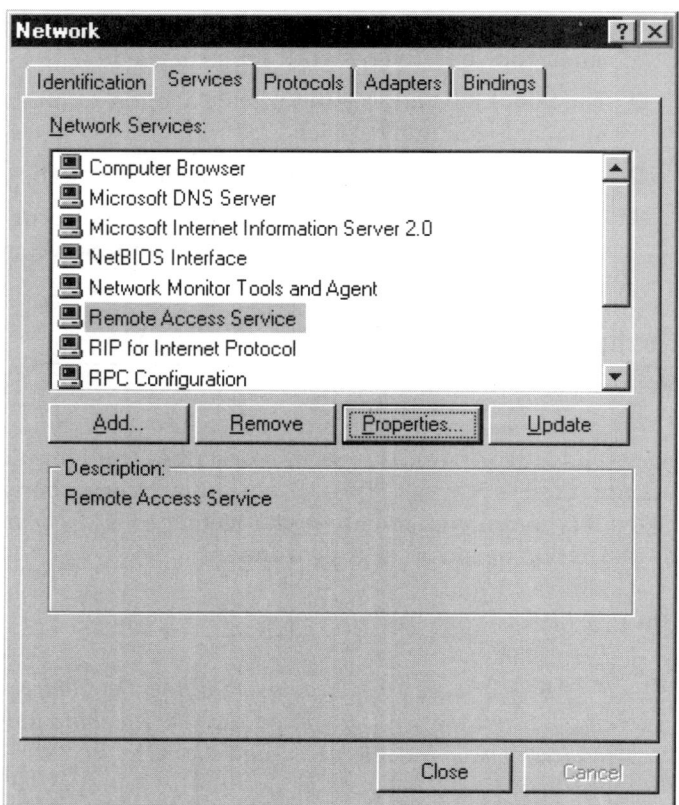

Figure 4-17: The Network Services list box with Remote Access Service highlighted.

4. Click the Properties button. The Remote Access Setup dialog displays, as shown in Figure 4-18. This dialog box lists each port that is configured for RAS, the device connected to each port (typically, the modem), and the type of device (such as modem, though other devices such as ISDN are also supported).

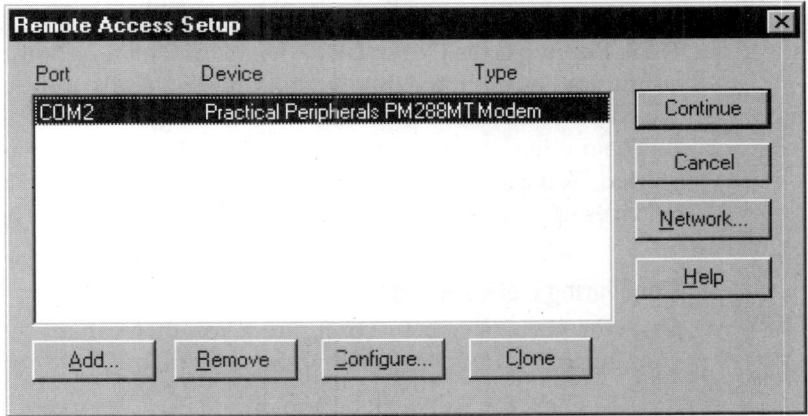

Figure 4-18: A single modem is listed on this Remote Access Setup dialog box.

From the Remote Access Setup dialog, you can add, remove, clone, and configure ports.

Configuring a RAS Port

To configure a Remote Access Setup port, follow the steps below:

1. Select the port using the Remote Access Setup dialog box.

2. Click the Configure button. The Configure Port Usage dialog displays, as shown in Figure 4-19.

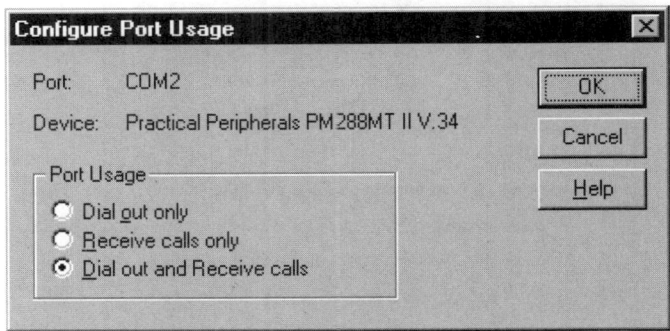

Figure 4-19: The Configure Port Usage dialog.

The Configure Port Usage dialog allows you to dedicate the port to RAS (Receive Calls Only), DUN (Dial Out Only), or both. When a port is configured as both, the modem both receives calls and places calls, as was done in our example.

The modem doesn't answer calls if the RAS service has not been started. You can set RAS to start automatically (use the Control Panel's Services applet) or manually (using the RAS Monitor program).

Configuring Network Protocols for the Port

Once the ports have been configured, you then can set the network configuration. To do this, follow the steps below:

1. Click the Network button on the Remote Access Setup dialog box. The Network Configuration dialog box displays, as shown in Figure 4-20.

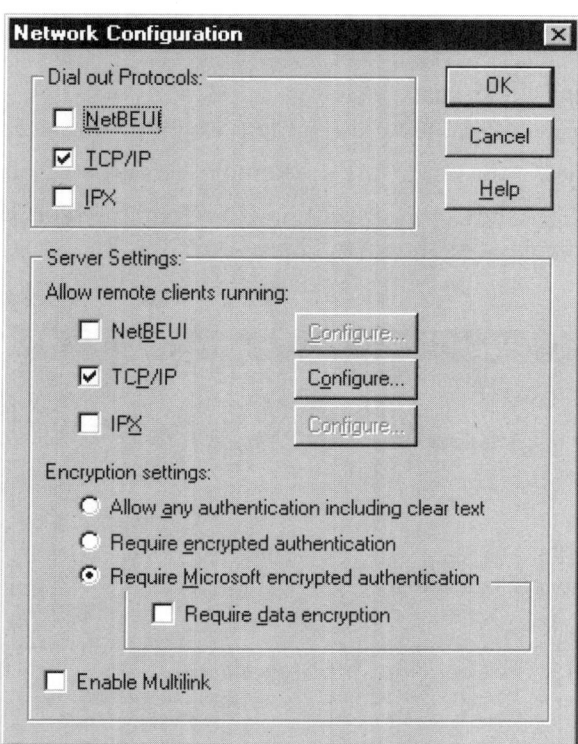

Figure 4-20: The Network Configuration dialog box.

2. Set the DUN and RAS network protocols on the Network Configuration dialog box. Typically, you specify TCP/IP, but NetBEUI and IPX protocols are also supported. Select those protocols you are relatively certain the server supports because DUN attempts to negotiate each protocol, which may seriously impact the performance at logon time.

Configuring NetBEUI   To configure the NetBEUI protocol, follow the steps below:

1. Click the Configure button next to the NetBEUI check box in Server Settings on the Network Configuration dialog box (see Figure 4-20). The RAS Server NetBEUI Configuration dialog box appears, as shown in Figure 4-21.

2. Use the RAS Server NetBEUI Configuration dialog box to restrict a NetBEUI client to accessing resources on this server only or to allow the client to access resources across your entire network.

Warning

Be careful: Allowing remote sites full access to your network can be dangerous! Remember, Windows NT 4 Server is a router and does not restrict access to other servers (including Windows NT 4 Workstation and Windows 95 clients who are sharing resources on the network).

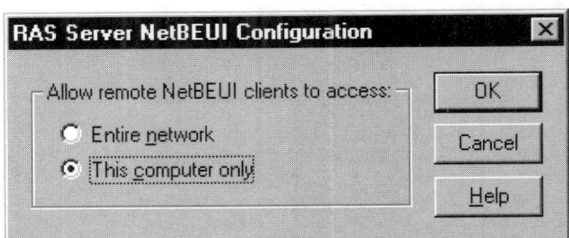

Figure 4-21: The RAS Server NetBEUI Configuration dialog.

Configuring TCP/IP   To configure the TCP/IP protocol, follow the steps below:

1. Click the Configure button next to the TCP/IP check box in Server Settings on the Network Configuration dialog box (see Figure 4-20). The RAS Server TCP/IP Configuration dialog box appears, as shown in Figure 4-22.

2. Use the RAS Server TCP/IP Configuration dialog box to restrict a TCP/IP client to accessing resources on this server only or to allow the client to access resources across your entire network.

For the TCP/IP protocol, you can specify that the client receives an IP address from a DHCP server or from a static pool. In addition, you can specify that a client user can request a specific IP address. (The latter option is useful for users who expect the same IP address assignment each time they connect.)

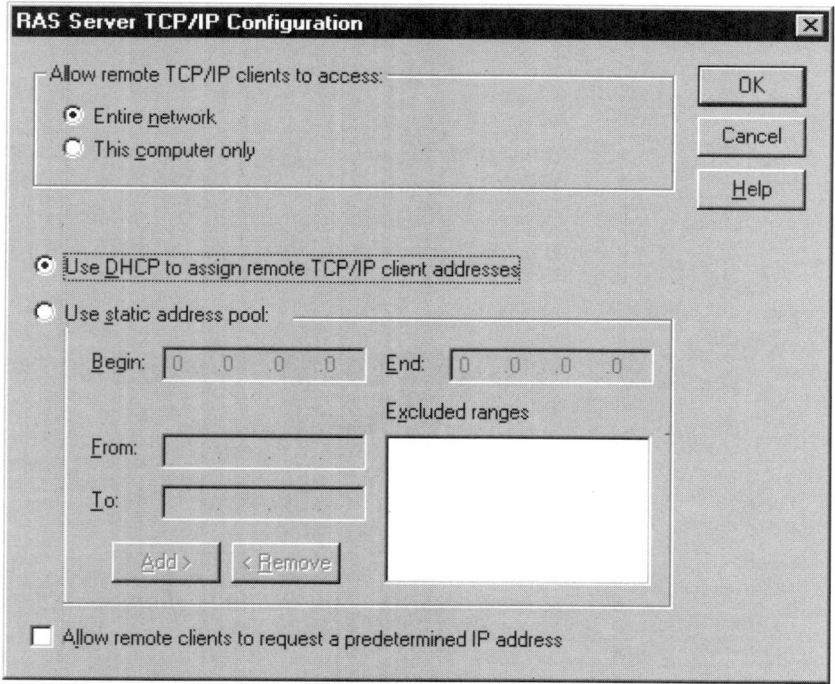

Figure 4-22: The RAS Server TCP/IP Configuration dialog.

Configuring IPX   To configure the IPX protocol, follow the steps below:

1. Click the Configure button next to the IPX check box in Server Settings on the Network Configuration dialog box (see Figure 4-20). The RAS Server IPX Configuration dialog box appears, as shown in Figure 4-23.

2. Use the RAS Server IPX Configuration dialog box to restrict an IPX client to accessing resources on this server only or to allow the client to access resources across your entire network.

3. For the IPX protocol, you can specify that the client receives a network number automatically or that network numbers are allocated from within the range you specify. Additional options allow assigning the same network number to all clients or allowing a client to request a specific IPX node number.

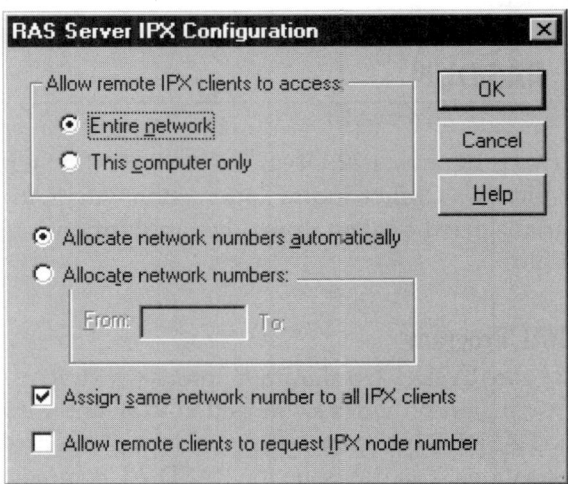

Figure 4-23: The RAS Server IPX Configuration dialog.

Setting Other Network Configuration Options   Other items in the Network Configuration dialog include Encryption Settings, which enables the encryption used for authentication, and Enable Multilink, which allows a client to connect to the server using multiple ports.

To use the Encryption settings, follow the steps below:

1. You can choose between Allow Any Authentication Including Clear Text, Require Encrypted Authentication, and Require Microsoft Encrypted Authentication.

2. If you choose to require Microsoft encrypted authentication, you can also choose to require data encryption.

The final check box in the Network Configuration dialog box is Enable Multilink. Enable Multilink allows a client to connect to the server using multiple ports. Typically, this is done using ISDN's multiple channel features. However, this facility is not restricted to ISDN; regular modem lines can also be multilinked. For example, a user can connect using two 28.8 kbps modems and get a throughput of about 56K. The actual throughput may vary from the theoretical value for a number of reasons, such as quality, server loading, and other factors that are not necessarily easy to predict.

Managing RAS/DUN

There are two programs, RASDIAL and RASADMIN, which allow console (typically a CMD window) interaction with RAS/DUN. Each of these programs may be called from other applications or from a batch command file.

The RASDIAL Program

You can use the RASDIAL program to interact with RAS/DUN. It starts the RAS system and provides a connection to an entry that is specified.

With the RASDIAL program, you can dial a phonebook entry and make substitutions. You can issue the RASDIAL command from a command line, a batch command file, or as a call process from another application.

RASDIAL requires that you provide a Dial-Up Networking phonebook entry name. You usually have to provide a login username and password if either is different from your current Windows NT logon username and password. The userid and the password would follow the phonebook entry name in the command:

```
RASDIAL PHONEBOOK USERID PASSWORD
```

When you use RASDIAL without any parameters, RASDIAL displays the status of any currently open RAS/DUN connections, as shown below:

```
Windows NT Version 4.0 C:\WinNT
Rasdial
Connected to
MV 924-3503
Command completed successfully.

Windows NT Version 4.0 C:\WinNT
```

Table 4-1 shows the various parameters you can specify on the RASDIAL program.

Option	Description
/domain	You can specify the /domain:domain option to allow the specification of a domain name. This parameter is optional and is only used with servers that support domain names (such as Windows NT Server).
/phone	Specifying the /phone:phonenumber option allows you to override the telephone number in the phonebook entry. This parameter is optional.
/callback	The /callback:callbacknumber option allows the specification of a callback telephone number. The number specified overrides the number found in the phonebook entry. This parameter is optional.
/phonebook	You can override the current phonebook using the /phonebook:phonebookpath option. This parameter is optional.
/disconnect	You can disconnect from connections using the /disconnect option. You can specify the phonebook (connection) entry name to disconnect from a specific connection. The only other parameter that you can specify with the /disconnect option is entryname.
/?	To receive online help for RASDIAL's command syntax, use the /? Help option.

Table 4-1: RASDIAL program parameters.

The RASADMIN Program

You can use the RASADMIN program to manage RAS/DUN connections. The RASADMIN command starts the Remote Access Admin program (see Figure 4-11).

Tip

You can also start the Remote Access Admin program from a command prompt with the command RASADMIN or from Start Menu | Programs | Administrative Tools (Common) | Remote Access Admin.

Figure 4-11 shows a single port active for dial-up users. Were a user to connect to my server (DORA) using this port, they would see my network as if they were locally connected, except that they must set the Network Browsers for both Windows NT 4 Workstation and Windows 95 to browse a *slow* network.

RASADMIN allows the administrator to start, pause, or stop the Remote Access Services. Remember: RAS is incoming connections, while DUN is for outgoing connections. You can also use Remote Access Admin to configure ports and to view potential and current users.

The shortcut for Remote Access Admin is found in Start Menu | Programs | Administrative Tools (Common).

Configuring the RAS Server

Once you have the RAS Server service installed, you must configure the RAS accounts for people to be able to dial in remotely. Start the Remote Access Admin program, and follow these steps to grant user rights to dial in:

1. Choose Users | Permissions in the Remote Access Admin menu. This will display the Remote Access Permissions dialog box, as shown in Figure 4-24.

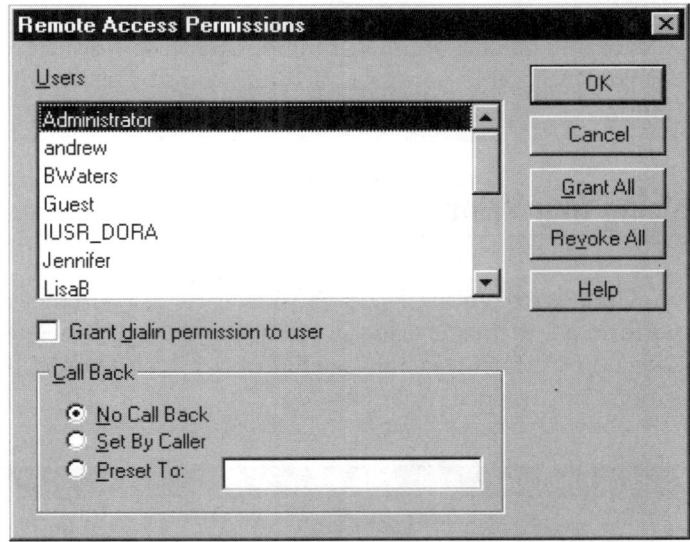

Figure 4-24: The Remote Access Permissions dialog box.

2. For each user that is to be granted dial-in privileges, select the User in the list and then check the Grant dialin permission to User check box.

3. For users who have been granted dial-in permission, configure the call back option. Call back can be configured as:

■ No Call Back means that the user will be able to connect directly to the server without the server attempting to call back the user.

■ Set By Caller tells RAS to call the user back at the telephone number specified by the user. Useful when the user is calling from a location where the call is long distance.

■ Preset To tells RAS to call the user back at a predefined number. This provides a high level of security by ensuring that the user is at the location he or she is supposed to be.

4. When done granting permissions, click the OK button.

When setting permissions, you can grant all users permission to use RAS dial-in by clicking the Grant All button. In addition, it is possible to revoke RAS dial-in permissions for all users by clicking the Revoke All button.

Optimizing Your Windows NT Installation

Now that we have changed almost every setting on the computer, let's perform a few final checks. Open up the Control Panel's System applet. Select the Performance tab (see Figure 4-25), and you will see the Application Performance slider bar.

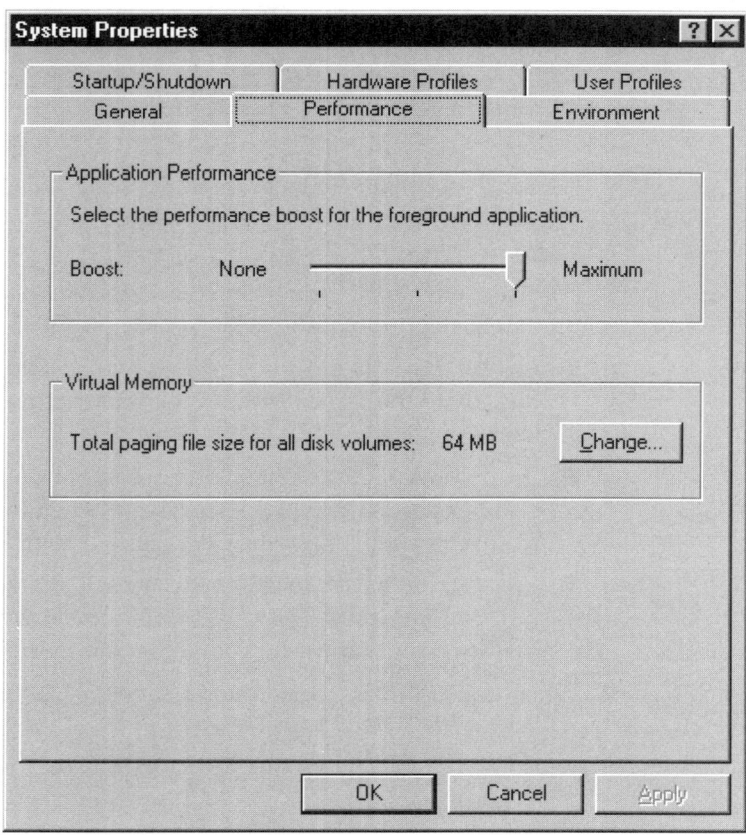

Figure 4-25: Setting the balance between foreground applications and server tasks.

For a server, this bar should be all the way to the left, not optimizing for applications at all, but instead boosting network traffic and services.

For a workstation, this bar should be all the way to the right, optimizing foreground applications and minimizing network traffic and services.

For systems that are performing both workstation and server tasks, this bar should be centered, which will balance performance between both applications and the server aspects of the system.

Virtual memory must also be configured to optimize the system's performance. This is done by clicking the Change button in the System Properties dialog's Performance tab. The Virtual Memory dialog box (see Figure 4-26) lets you set which drives to use for virtual memory's paging file(s).

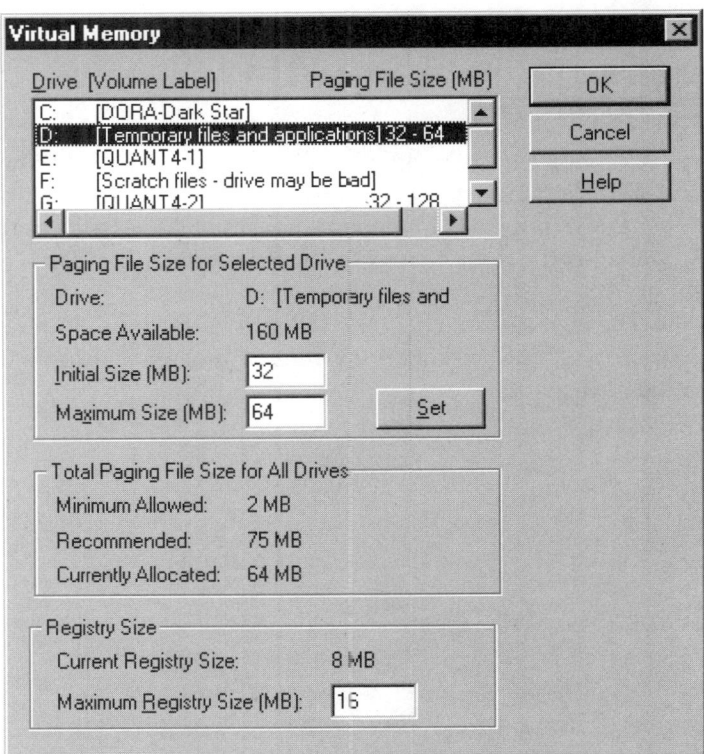

Figure 4-26: The Virtual Memory dialog box showing several paging files configured.

There are several rules of thumb for setting virtual memory:

- Try to use a drive other than the one on which Windows NT 4 Server is installed.

- Try to use a drive that does not have I/O intensive applications or databases installed.

- Try to use a drive that has a high-performance figure. Avoid IDE drives (which on a server should not exist) or SCSI drives, which are slow.

- Try to use drives that are not too full.

- Try to split the virtual memory's paging file between two or more drives to improve I/O performance.

Moving On

This chapter introduced you to the concepts behind Windows NT's networking model. It also covered some of the core utilities and services behind Windows NT's networking capabilities, such as the Server Manager, the Remote Access Service, and the Dial-Up Networking Service.

The next several chapters will introduce you to Windows NT's interoperability with various other networks, starting with NetWare in the next chapter.

5

Integrating Windows NT With NetWare & Banyan Vines

This chapter covers some of the components supplied with Windows NT 4 Server that allow you to work with Novell NetWare and Banyan Vines. Novell's NetWare is still the most popular PC-based server and network system. Banyan Vines has some limited support in the PC server and network market; however, the popularity of Vines is rather limited compared to other networking alternatives such as Windows NT 4 Server and Novell.

Note: Windows NT 4 Server's native networking and the networking that comes with OS/2 are similar. Chapter 4, "Network Configuration and Administration," covered both.

For Novell and Banyan networks, the services that you can configure include:

- **Novell's NetWare**—These services include the gateway (and client) services that make it easier for Windows NT clients to access NetWare shares on the network, the RIP (Routing Information Protocol) services that exchange information between routers, and the SAP agent that resolves names on NetWare networks.

- **Banyan VINES Networks**—These services enable and support the RPC (Remote Procedure Call) protocol on Banyan VINES networks.

If you are not using NetWare or Banyan LANs, you don't need to consider installing, configurir g, or tuning these services. Installing unneeded network componer ts can create problems because each protocol consumes system re-ources, including network bandwidth.

Configuration is often a par- of installation; here, it is a critical step in getting Windows NT 4 Server up and running effectively. Windows NT 4 Server usually performs much better if you, the systems administrator, configure the system optimally First, you install; then, you configure the installatior; and finally, you tune the configuration for optimal performance.

Configuration and tuning are interrelated, to a certain extent. For example, changes in the configuration commonly affect system performance. If and when you make changes in the configuration, especially when you add new services (and servers, such as IIS), you should consider the impact on system performance.

Configuring NetWare Services

Novell's NetWare is currently the most popular microcomputer network today. Though Windows NT 4 Server is making significant inroads into the networking market, NetWare will be around for some time to come.

Note: Novell's popularity will be affected by Windows NT 4 Server, as noted in Chapter 1's introduc-ion.

Running both a NetWare server and a Windows NT 4 Server on a single network is often necessary. Some applications look for NetWare networks; also, when you convert from NetWare to Windows NT 4 Server, you should run both networks together until you can determine that the Windows NT 4 Server is working correctly.

Configuring Gateway Services

The Gateway Service for NetWare allows Windows NT 4 Server to perform as a gateway for a Novell NetWare network. This allows the Windows client users to access the NetWare resources even if the clients are not running a NetWare redirector.

You can install the Gateway Services for NetWare at the time that you install Windows NT 4 Server, or you can do so later, using the Control Panel's Network applet.

To install the Gateway Service for NetWare after you install Windows NT 4 Server, follow these steps:

1. Start the Control Panel's Network applet.

2. Select the Services tab.

3. Click the Add button. The Select Network Service dialog box appears.

4. Select the Gateway Service for NetWare from the Network Service list. Windows NT 4 Server copies any needed files from the Windows NT 4 Server distribution CD, then prompts you to reboot.

5. Reboot your computer.

6. Log back on to Windows NT 4 Server. The Gateway Service for NetWare automatically displays the Select Preferred Server for NetWare dialog box, as shown in Figure 5-1. The options in this dialog box are similar to those in the Gateway Service for NetWare dialog box shown in Figure 5-2.

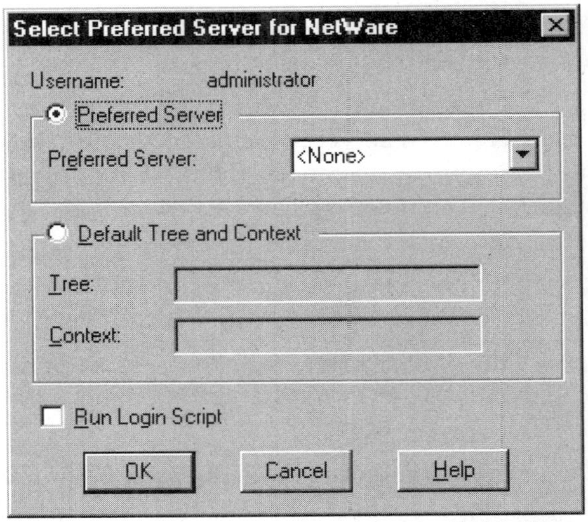

Figure 5-1: The Select Preferred Server for NetWare.

The NetWare gateway is intended to allow sites that must utilize both Windows NT and NetWare networks to perform efficiently.

To start the NetWare gateway from a command prompt, follow these steps:

1. Issue the command:

   ```
   net start "gateway service for netware"
   ```

2. Press Enter.

The NetWare gateway will start. Issuing the net start command will start the NetWare gateway for only the current session.

To start the NetWare gateway using the Windows NT 4 Server Control Panel, follow these steps:

1. Start the Control Panel's Services applet. The Services dialog box appears.

2. Click the Startup button.

3. Click the Automatic radio button in the Service dialog's Startup Type group box. When a service's startup is set to Automatic, the service starts each time that Windows NT 4 Server is booted.

4. Set up user accounts and groups to configure the gateway service for NetWare.

5. Following the addition of user accounts, configure the gateway service for NetWare by using the Control Panel's Gateway Service for NetWare dialog box, as shown in Figure 5-2.

6. Set the Preferred Server (the current NetWare server, if there is one, is shown for reference). The preferred server is the server to which the Gateway Service for NetWare connects.

7. Optionally, set the Default Tree and Context, which allows you to set both the tree and the name context. The Default Tree and Context options are new to Windows NT 4.

8. Specify the desired print options. The Print Options, Add Form Feed, Notify When Printed, and Print Banner, all apply to printer output.

9. If you wish, you can choose to require a client user to use a NetWare login script by clicking the Run Login Script check box.

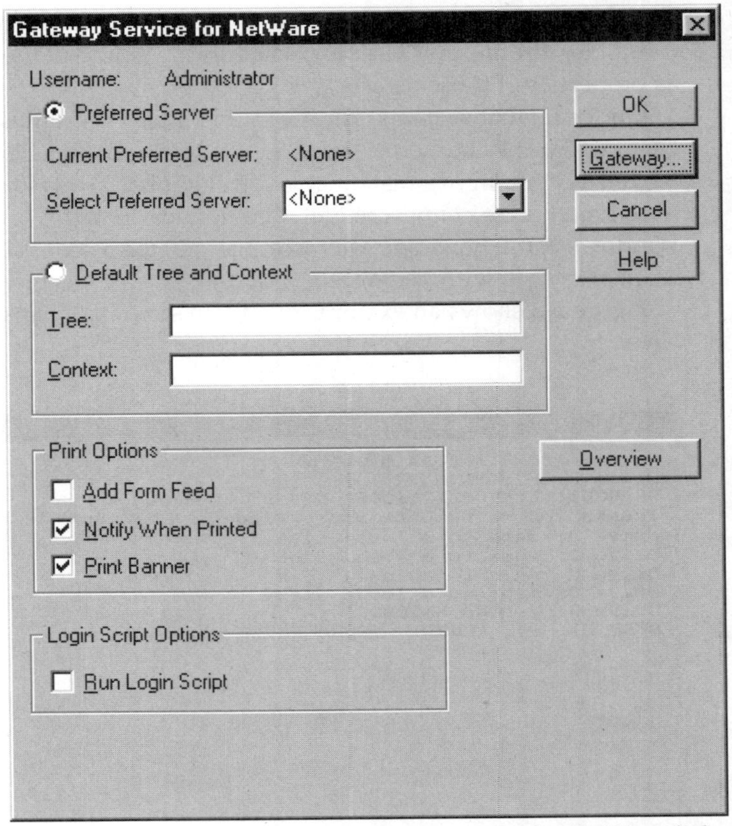

Figure 5-2: The Control Panel Gateway Service for NetWare dialog box.

Novell Login Scripting

Novell NetWare networks use scripting (which look, and work, in a fashion similar to a batch file) to configure each client user. For NetWare networks that preceded NetWare 4 (that is, NetWare 3.x) or for NetWare 4, which is using the bindery, NetWare uses a login script called NET$LOG.DAT. That script normally is stored in the PUBLIC directory on the NetWare server.

Each NetWare client user will have his or her own private scripts, typically stored in MAIL subdirectories (as the LOGIN file). Login scripts are edited using the SYSCON utility.

Note: For Novell NDS (NetWare Directory Services) servers, the Container, Profile, and User login scripts are stored in the NDS database as properties of those objects.

One issue that systems administrators must confront is whether the client will use Windows 95 or Windows NT NetWare client software, or Novell's client. In the past, the Novell client has always been the preferred method to connect to NetWare networks; with Windows 95 and Windows NT 4, however, Microsoft has created a set of client drivers that work very well with NetWare.

Figure 5-3 shows an example of a login script that runs on a Windows client.

```
Login Script Processor for Netware                          _ □ ×
Welcome to <<< DORA_N >>>
Drive V: = DORA_N\SYS:
SEARCH1: Z:\PUBLIC [DORA_N\SYS: \PUBLIC]
Thanks for using Dark_Star: Windows NT Server is HERE!
Drive A: maps to a local disk.
Drive B: maps to a local disk.
Drive C: maps to a local disk.
Drive D: maps to a local disk.
Drive Z: = DORA_N\SYS: \
SEARCH1: = Z:\PUBLIC [DORA_N\SYS: \PUBLIC]
```

Figure 5-3: An example of a NetWare login script.

Novell networks have some problems as to loading TSRs and other resident software components. Some components may be loaded using the autoexec.bat file, whereas others must be loaded using other techniques.

When you run NDIS 3.1 drivers:

autoexec.bat	Applications used with MS-DOS or Windows that do not require IPX/SPX support.
winstart.bat	Windows-based applications that do not require IPX/SPX support (place winstart.bat in the Windows root directory).
Loaded at a command prompt	MS-DOS based applications that require IPX/SPX support.

When you run ODI drivers:

autoexec.bat	Applications used with MS-DOS or Windows that require IPX/SPX support, where the application is loaded after the loading of IPXODI in the autoexec.bat file.

Configuring RIP Services

RIP (Routing Information Protocol) for NWLink IPX/SPX Compatible Transport, which I call "RIP for NWLink," allows NetWare routers to share routing information.

Installing RIP for NWLink

To install RIP for NWLink, you must have the NWLink IPX/SPX Compatible Transport (IPX/SPX) protocol installed. When the IPX/SPX protocol is installed, NWLink NetBIOS is installed automatically.

To install RIP for NWLink, follow these steps:

1. Select the Control Panel's Network applet.

2. Select the Services tab.

3. Click the Add button. The Select Network Service dialog box appears.

4. Select RIP for NWLink IPX/SPX Compatible Transport from the Network Service list. The Windows NT 4 Server distribution CD will be prompted if it is necessary to retrieve files for the installation.

The installation process for RIP for NWLink is simple. A single prompt appears: "Netbios Broadcast Propagation (broadcast of type 20 packets) is currently enabled. Do you want to disable it?" (see Figure 5-4). When you use NetBIOS over IPX, or if you are not certain whether you need this feature, you should enable the NetBIOS Broadcast Propagation.

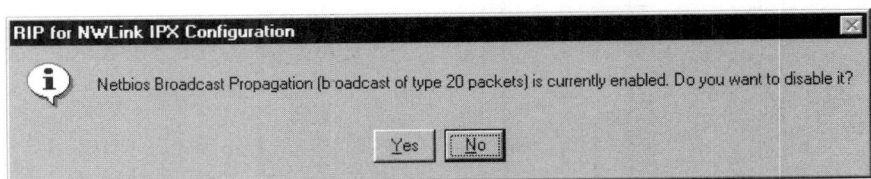

Figure 5-4: The RIP for NWLink IPX Configuration message box.

Later, if you decide that you don't want NetBIOS Broadcast Propagation, follow these steps:

1. Select the Control Panel's Network applet.

2. Select the Services tab. Click on the Add button to display the Add Services dialog box.

3. Select the RIP for NWLink IPX.

4. Select Properties.

5. Respond to the message box that prompts you to enable (or disable) NetBIOS Broadcast Propagation.

Using the IPXROUTE Utility

To manage RIP for NWLink, you use the command line IPXROUTE utility. This utility allows you to configure and otherwise manage RIP for NWLink. An example of IPXROUTE is shown in Figure 5-5.

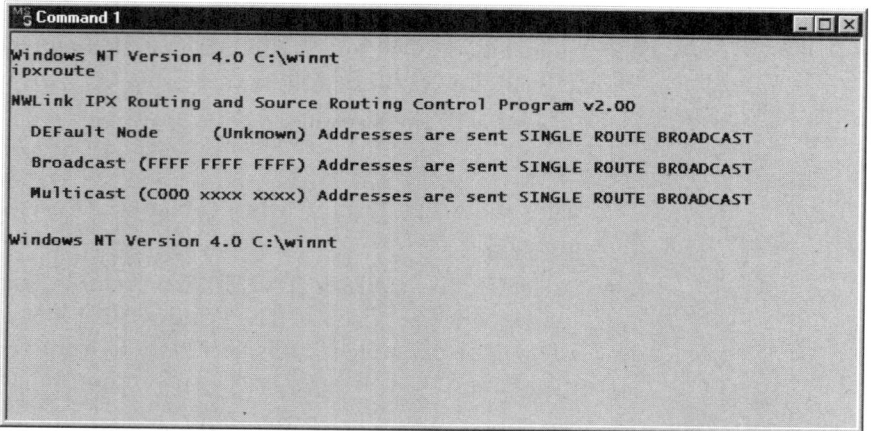

Figure 5-5: The IPXROUTE utility showing defaults.

The IPXROUTE program allows you to configure RIP for NWLink. You display and modify information contained in the routing tables using the IPXROUTE program.

Entering the command IPXROUTE servers, displays a line of information about each server. For example, the output that I received was:

```
IPX Address                 Server Type      Server Name
-----------------------------------------------------------
00000000.00a0246b331f          1600          DORA
```

Limit the types of servers listed with the /type= qualifier (for example, IPXROUTE servers /type=1600 limits the servers to type 1600).

Issuing the IPXROUTE table command lists the current routing table. The list is empty if the routing table has no entries.

Configuring your IPX routing with the IPXROUTE config command, with board=n (where n is a zero-based index to the NIC—that is, Network Interface Card—to configure), provides optional support for the following options:

■ **clear**—clears the existing routing table.

■ **def**—sends packets destined to all unknown addresses (using an ALL ROUTE broadcast).

■ **gbr**—sends packets destined for the address FFFF-FFFF-FFFF (using an ALL ROUTE broadcast).

■ **mbr**—sends packets for the multicast address C000-xxxx-xxxx (using an ALL ROUTE broadcast).

■ **remove=xxxxxxxxxxx**—removes the mac specified by the address xxxxxxxxxxx from the routing table.

When you enter parameters, you should separate them by spaces.

Configuring SAP Agent

NetWare clients use SAP (Service Advertising Protocol) when resolving names on a NetWare-compatible network is necessary. A NetWare-compatible server broadcasts SAP messages. IPX routers and servers then store both the broadcasting server's name and address for later use.

To install the SAP Agent, follow these steps:

1. Start the Control Panel's Network applet.

2. Select the Services tab.

3. Click the Add button. The Select Network Service dialog box appears.

4. Select SAP Agent.

5. Click OK.

To remove SAP Agent, follow these steps:

1. Select the Control Panel's Network applet.

2. Select the Services tab.

3. Select SAP Agent. Then, click the Remove button to remove the service.

The SAP Agent is not configurable. Your only options are to install or remove the service. Removing SAP Agent can cause problems if you don't simultaneously remove any services that use SAP Agent.

Configuring SNMP Service

Microsoft Simple Network Management Protocol (SNMP) is a network-management protocol. SNMP manages both TCP/IP networks and networks using NetWare's IPX protocol.

Tip

SNMP is a large and complex component of Windows NT 4 Server. You can obtain more information on SNMP from both the Microsoft Windows NT 4 Resource Kit and TechNet.

You use SNMP to communicate between the SNMP management program and an SNMP agent program (which runs on the host system). SNMP is a standard defined by a number of RFCs (Request for Comments).

The first step in configuring SNMP is to install the service. You can install SNMP at the same time that you install Windows NT 4 Server, or at a later time, using the Control Panel's Network applet. Both methods are identical and produce the same results.

Note: To install SNMP for the IPX protocol, you must also install the TCP/IP protocol.

You must install SNMP on all Windows NT 4 Servers that will use SNMP, and on any Windows NT 4 workstations that will act as SNMP agents.

To install SNMP, follow these steps:

1. Start the Control Panel's Network applet.

2. Select the Services tab.

3. Select SNMP Service. The SNMP configuration dialog box appears. The Agent tab is shown in Figure 5-6.

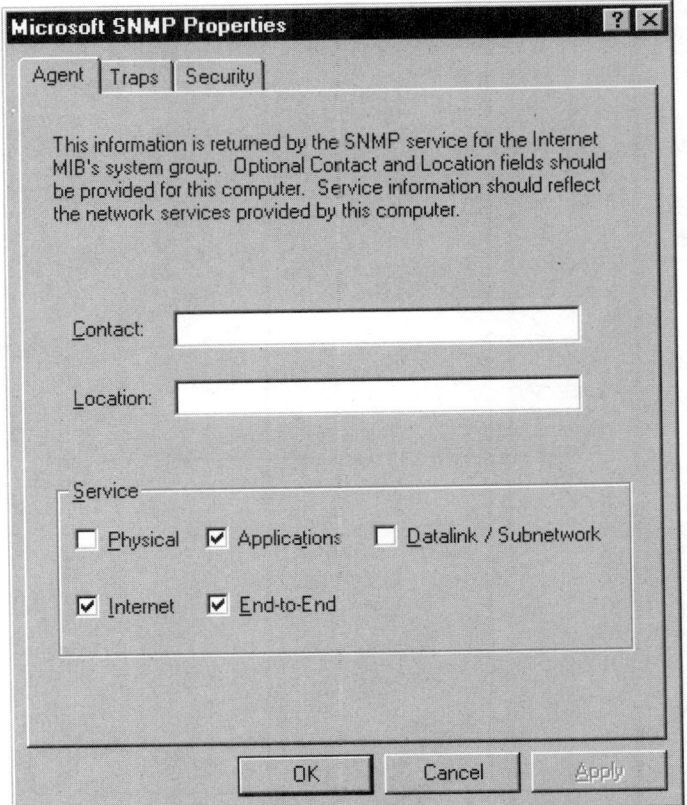

Figure 5-6: The Microsoft SNMP Properties dialog, Agent tab.

4. Use the Agent tab to establish the contact and location for the monitor agent. Both the Contact and Location are optional; you must, however, select the applicable Service items as needed.

5. Use the Traps tab, as shown in Figure 5-7, to configure the trap destinations. A trap destination can be a name, an IP address, or an IPX address. A community name is a group of hosts to which a server, running the SNMP service, belongs. This name is then placed in SNMP packets when traps are sent. The default community name is Public, which is defined in the RFC as the community common to all hosts.

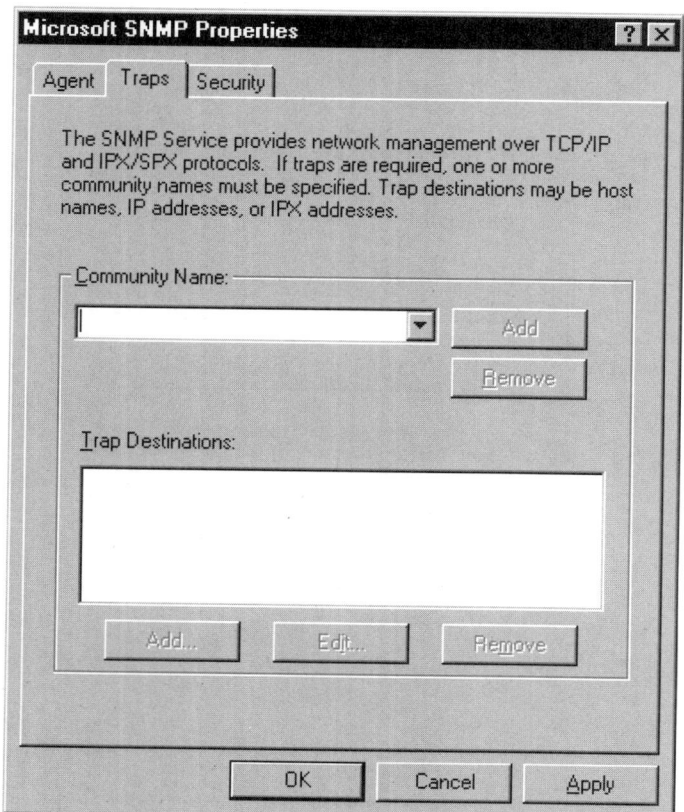

Figure 5-7: The Microsoft SNMP Properties dialog, Traps tab.

6. Use the Security tab, shown in Figure 5-8, to configure SNMP security. In the Security tab, you can select community names (which you may have created in the Traps tab or in the Security tab). You also select to have authentication traps sent (when an authentication request is rejected). The Security tab also allows you to select to receive SNMP packets from either of the following: all hosts or only a specified group of hosts.

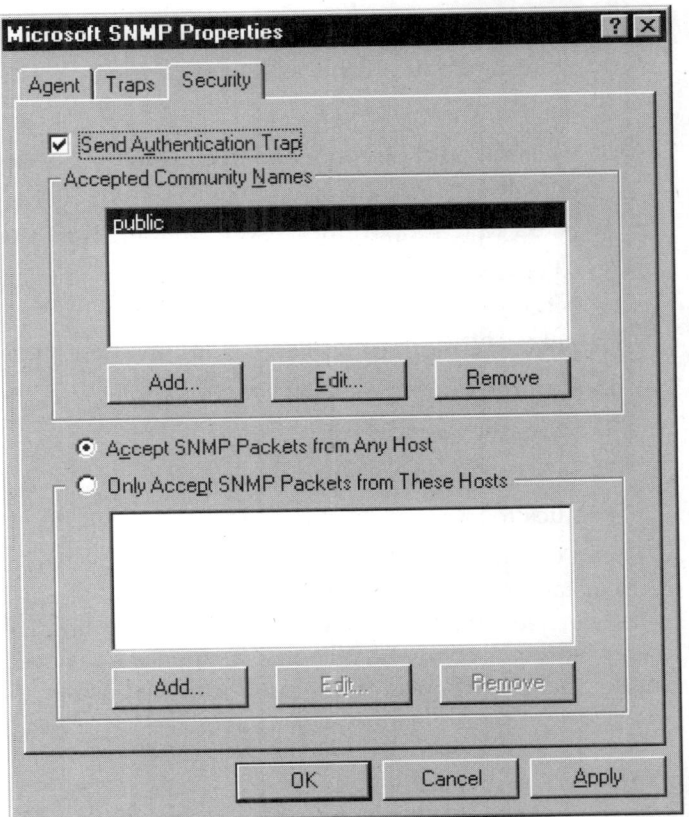

Figure 5-8: The Microsoft SNMP Properties dialog, Security tab.

You can reconfigure SNMP as needed at any time, using the Control Panel's Network applet.

Configuring Services for Banyan

The Banyan Visual Networking System (VINES) supports multitasking for multiple users. Although VINES was designed using the UNIX operating system, a VINES LAN can also support DOS, OS/2, and Macintosh workstations. VINES's capability to move across operating system platforms makes network building with VINES an easy task. You can add RPC (Remote Procedure Call) support for Banyan using the Windows NT 4 Server Control Panel.

To install the RPC support for Banyan, follow these steps:

1. Start the Control Panel's Network applet.

2. Select the Services tab.

3. Click the Add button. The Select Network Service dialog box appears.

4. Select RPC support for Banyan from the Network Service list.

5. Click OK. The necessary files will be copied from the Windows NT 4 Server distribution CD as needed.

To remove RPC support for Banyan, follow these steps:

1. Start the Control Panel's Network applet.

2. Select the Services tab.

3. Select RPC support for Banyan.

4. Click the Remove button.

The RPC support for Banyan is not configurable. Your only options are to install or remove the service.

Banyan networks have some problems as to loading TSRs and other resident software components. Some components may be loaded using the autoexec.bat file, whereas others must be loaded using other techniques.

Moving On

I just showed you how to make accessing some of the most popular network services easier for Windows NT clients. The services that I chose to describe are Novell NetWare and Banyan VINES. In this chapter, I explained how to access Novell NetWare shares on the network, and how to enable RPC protocol on Banyan VINES networks.

In the next chapter, you will learn how to integrate Macintoshes and NT Servers on the same network.

6

Building a Hybrid Macintosh & PC Network

The Macintosh is one of the machines that falls into a realm similar to religion. You don't say anything bad about it because you never know when a Macintosh fanatic might be around the corner. Please don't get me wrong: I don't mean to be sarcastic (I started working on the first Lisa computer before Microsoft could even say that it did Windows). I used to be one of those Macintosh fanatics myself.

Anyway, in every company I have ever worked for, the Macintosh has been ever present and always in the same niche areas. Art and graphics design. Digital music composition and sound design. Video processing. And, of course, the few diehard PowerBook users.

In each of these companies, having some sort of connectivity between the two types of computers has always been important. In fact, in some cases, that connectivity has been critical to the success of the company.

There is really only one option for integrating your Windows NT network with Macs. That option is to configure a Windows NT Server or two as hybrid Macintosh and Windows NT servers, and use these hybrid servers as shared file and printer servers from both the Macintosh and the PC side of the network.

Windows NT includes a feature called Services for Macintosh. This feature is built in to the operating system to allow Windows NT to behave as if it were an AppleShare server running on an AppleTalk network.

This chapter shows you how to install and configure the Services for Macintosh feature of Windows NT, and points out a few quirks along the way.

Installing Services for Macintosh

The Services for Macintosh component is installed using the Control Panel's Network applet. To install Services for Macintosh, follow these steps:

1. Start the Control Panel's Network applet by opening the Control Panel and double-clicking the Network icon.

2. Select the Services tab.

3. Click on the Add button. The Select Network Service dialog box appears.

4. Select Services for Macintosh from the Network Service list. Any files necessary will be copied from the Windows NT 4 Server distribution CD.

If you are not using Macintosh workstations, you don't need to consider installing, configuring, or tuning this service. Installing unneeded network components can create problems, because each protocol consumes system resources, including network bandwidth.

Configuring Services for Macintosh

After you install Services for Macintosh, the Microsoft AppleTalk Protocol Properties dialog box will be displayed. This dialog box is also displayed any time that you select Services for Macintosh in the Control Panel's Networking applet's Services tab and click on Properties.

The Microsoft AppleTalk Protocol Properties dialog box has two tabs: General and Routing.

Use the General tab (Figure 6-1) to specify the Default Adapter (all Apple Macintosh users should be connected to the same adapter, if possible), and default zone. For an initial installation, a Default Zone should be specified. The zone will be presented to Apple Macintosh users when selecting items in Chooser.

What's a Zone?

A zone in Macintosh networking terminology is much the same as a Windows for Workgroups workgroup or a limited Windows NT domain. I say limited because a Macintosh zone does not necessarily imply integrated user account management or other Windows NT-like services.

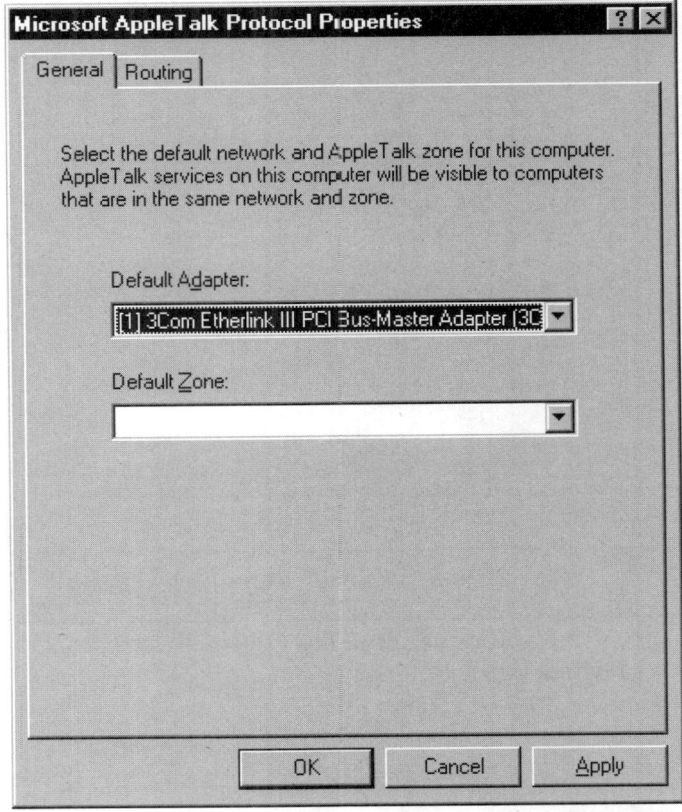

Figure 6-1: The Microsoft AppleTalk Protocol Properties dialog box's General tab.

Use the Routing tab (Figure 6-2) to specify whether routing is enabled. If routing is not enabled then no other option in the Routing tab may be set. If routing is enabled, then for each adapter, you can make a choice to use this router to seed the network, specify a Network Range, and configure zones.

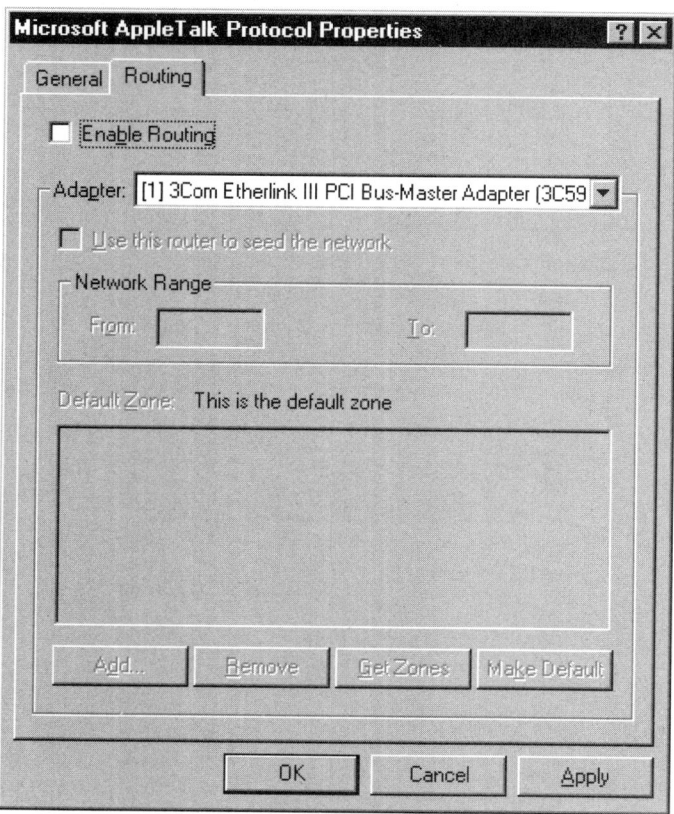

Figure 6-2: The Microsoft AppleTalk Protocol Properties dialog box's Routing tab.

Configuring File Servers & Print Services

When Services for Macintosh is installed, two new services are added to the Windows NT 4 Server:

- **File Server for Macintosh.** This service allows the system to manage Apple Macintosh clients' access to Windows NT 4 Server shared Macintosh volumes.

- **Print Server for Macintosh.** The service allows the system to manage Apple Macintosh clients' access to Windows NT 4 Server shared printer queues.

You can configure each of these services to start automatically, start manually, or be disabled by using the Control Panel's Services applet. The default is for the Services for Macintosh to start automatically at system start-up time.

Note: Apple Macintosh users may access only Macintosh-compatible volumes. Services for Macintosh configures a Macintosh-compatible volume for you, as part of the installation process.

Configuring Connections to Macintosh Clients

When you install Services for Macintosh, a new Control Panel applet, called MacFile, is created. The MacFile applet allows you to configure the connection to Apple Macintosh clients. Starting the MacFile applet displays the main window shown in Figure 6-3.

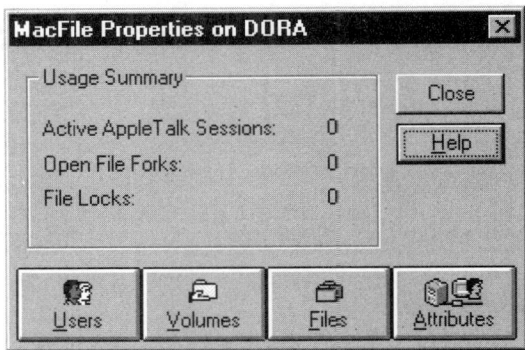

Figure 6-3: The MacFile Properties dialog box.

The MacFile window has three items in the Usage Summary area. All three show numeric counts:

- **Active AppleTalk Sessions.** The Active AppleTalk Sessions counter allows you to determine how many actual connections to Apple Macintosh clients have been established.

- **Open File Forks.** The Open File Forks counter indicates how many files, resource, and data forks combined are currently open.

- **File Locks.** The File Locks counter indicates how many file forks (one of two sub-files of a Macintosh file) are currently locked by Apple Macintosh clients.

Using the MacFile window, you can configure users, volumes, files, and attributes of a Macintosh LAN from Windows NT 4 Server.

Users

Click on the Users button to display the Macintosh Users dialog box (Figure 6-4). Use this dialog box to determine which users are currently connected to the system and how many volumes are open.

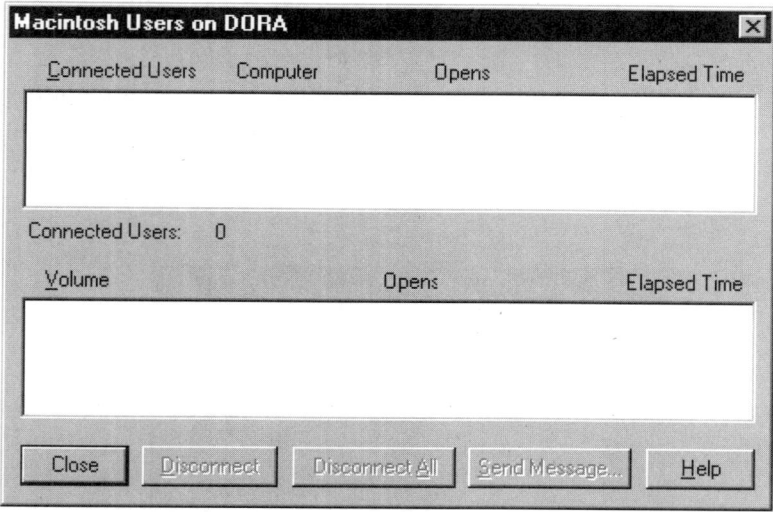

Figure 6-4: The Macintosh Users dialog box shows that no Apple Macintosh clients are currently connected.

In the Macintosh Users on dialog box, you can view, disconnect, and send messages to a single user or multiple users.

Viewing Users   The Default mode of the Macintosh Users on dialog box is set to allow you to view those Apple Macintosh users who are currently connected to the server shown in the Macintosh Users on dialog box.

The dialog box also lists shared volumes and the number of objects currently opened on each volume.

Disconnect   Individual Apple Macintosh users may be forcibly disconnected from the server if necessary. To disconnect a specific Apple Macintosh user, select the user in the Connected Users list, and then click on the Disconnect button.

Disconnect All   All Apple Macintosh users may be forcibly disconnected from the server if necessary. To disconnect all Apple Macintosh users, click the button labeled Disconnect All.

Warning

Disconnecting a user could cause the user to lose data. Be sure to warn the user so that any open files may be closed as necessary. Disconnecting all users probably will cause users to lose data. Be sure to warn the users so that any open files may be closed as necessary.

Send Message   Apple Macintosh users may be sent a message by the systems administrator (for example, to warn that the server is being removed from service). To send a message to a specific Apple Macintosh user, select the user in the Connected Users list, and click on the Send Message button.

Volumes

Click on the Volumes button to display the Macintosh-Accessible Volumes dialog box. This dialog box (see Figure 6-5) shows the Macintosh volumes that Macintosh clients can access. A Macintosh volume is typically created at the same time that Services for Macintosh is installed.

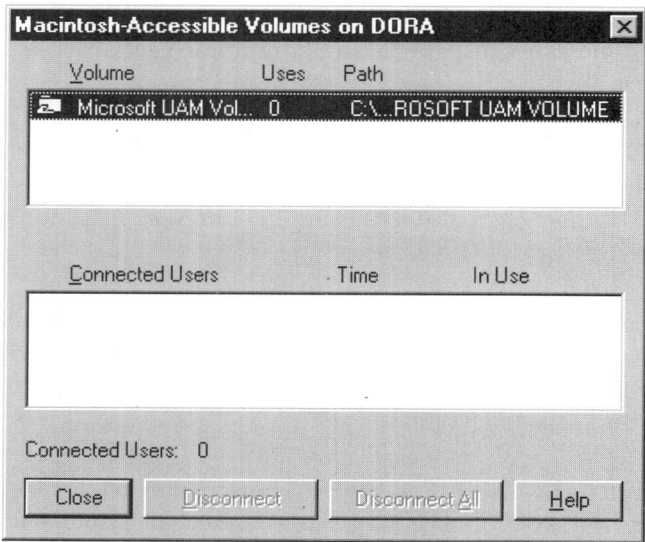

Figure 6-5: The Macintosh-Accessible Volumes dialog box, showing the default Apple Macintosh-compatible volume.

Each volume that is compatible with the Apple Macintosh file system (Apple Macintosh users may access only Macintosh-compatible volumes) is listed in the Volume (upper) list of the Macintosh-Accessible Volumes on dialog box. The Connected Users (lower) list of the Macintosh-Accessible Volumes on dialog box contains a list of all connected users.

In the Macintosh-Accessible Volumes on dialog box, you can view and disconnect connected users.

Viewing Users   The Default mode of the Macintosh-Accessible Volumes on dialog box is set to allow you to view those Apple Macintosh-compatible volumes that are shared, and any users who are currently connected to these volumes.

Disconnect   Individual Apple Macintosh users may be forcibly disconnected from a volume on the server if necessary. To disconnect a specific Apple Macintosh user from a volume, select the user in the Connected Users list, and then click on the Disconnect button.

Disconnect All   All Apple Macintosh users who are connected to Macintosh-Accessible Volumes may be forcibly disconnected if necessary. To disconnect all Apple Macintosh users, click the button labeled Disconnect All.

Warning

Disconnecting all users probably will cause users to lose data. Be sure to warn the users so that any open files may be closed as necessary.

Configuring Files

Click on the Files button to display the Files Opened by Macintosh Users dialog box (see Figure 6-6). This dialog box shows the Macintosh files currently opened by Macintosh clients. A Macintosh file is located on a Macintosh-accessible volume, as described previously.

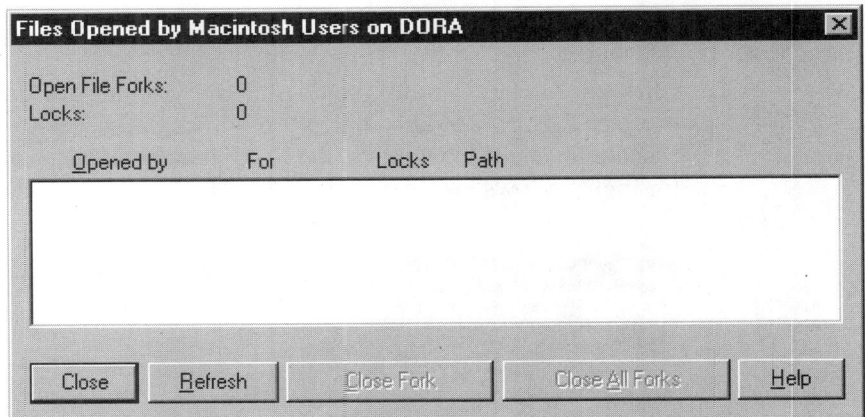

Figure 6-6: The Files Opened by Macintosh Users on dialog box show that no files are currently opened by Apple Macintosh users.

In the Files Opened by Macintosh Users on dialog box, you can view, refresh, and close currently opened forks.

Viewing Users   The Default mode of the Files Opened by Macintosh Users on dialog box is set to allow you to view the forks that are open, as well as to view locks and the Apple Macintosh user who has the fork opened. (That user's name appears within a list of other users.)

Refresh   The display of opened forks may be updated by clicking on the Refresh button. Refreshing the display is a good idea if the Files Opened by Macintosh Users on dialog box has been opened for any extended period of time.

Close Fork   Individually opened files may be forcibly closed on the server if necessary. To close an individual file, select the file in the Opened by list, and click on the Close Fork button.

Warning

Closing an open file could cause the user to lose data. Be sure to warn the user so that the user is aware of the situation.

Close All Forks   All opened files may be forcibly closed on the server if necessary. To close all open files, click on the Close All Forks button.

Attributes

Click the Attributes button to display the MacFile Attributes of dialog box (see Figure 6-7). This dialog box shows the server configuration for Macintosh clients. Generally, the MacFile attributes are similar to those for the Windows NT 4 Server.

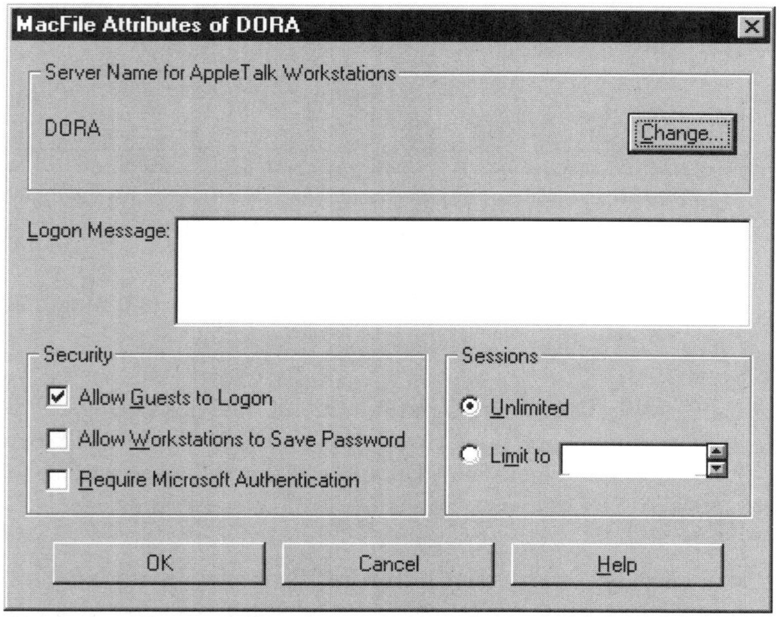

Figure 6-7: The MacFile Attributes of dialog box. Nothing is configured yet; I'll fill this dialog box in later.

In the MacFile Attributes of dialog box, you can set three important parameters: Logon Message, Security, and Sessions.

Logon Message   Whenever an Apple Macintosh user connects to the Windows NT 4 Server, a logon message will be presented to the user. Setting this message to a meaningful string makes good use of this feature. For example, in my Windows NT 4 Server, I set the Logon Message to "Welcome to the DarkStar network, report all problems to the System Administrator at Extension x20."

A logon message can have up to four lines of text.

Security   You can choose from among three nonexclusive security options:

- **Allow Guests to Logon**—allows any user who does not have a Windows NT 4 Server account to log on to the server.

- **Allow Workstations to Save Password**—allows the workstation to save the password so that the next time the user needs the object, the password will not have to be reentered. This option, if selected, may have a detrimental effect on Windows NT 4 Server security.

- **Require Microsoft Authentication**—forces the Apple Macintosh user to log on using the MS UAM security module. This option enhances security because it encrypts the password information.

Sessions   Sessions may be limited to a certain, specified number of users, or they may be unlimited. For smaller networks in which the number of Apple Macintosh users is known, specifying Unlimited is the easiest choice. Larger networks may wish, for performance or licensing reasons, to limit sessions to a specific number of users.

Creating Apple Macintosh-Compatible Volumes

To create an Apple Macintosh-Compatible volume, you must start the Windows NT 4 Server File Manager program. To start File Manager, use Start Menu | Programs | Administrative Tools (Common) | File Manager.

In File Manager (see Figure 6-8), you can perform the same tasks as you can with Explorer (create folders, for example). Also, when you install Services for Macintosh, a new menu item will be added to File Manager, called MacFile.

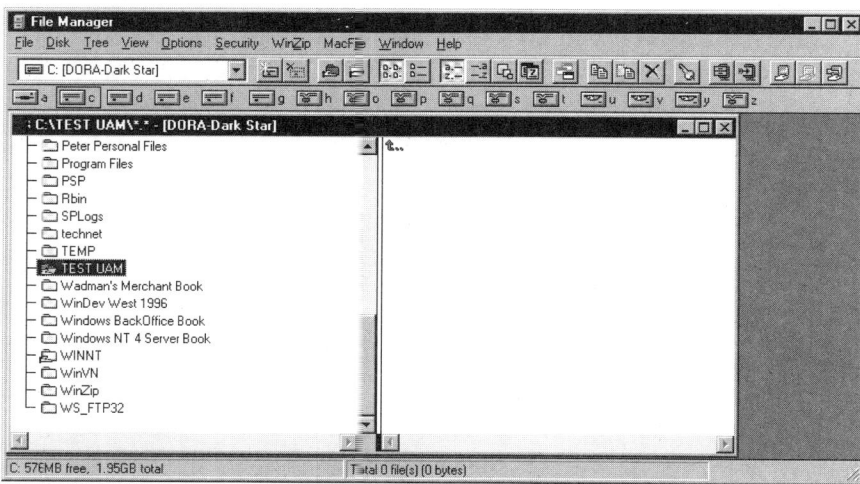

Figure 6-8: The Windows NT 4 Server File Manager program, with the MacFile menu selection.

Note: MacFile is added to File Manager's menu but not to Explorer's. No, I can't explain it!

The MacFile menu selection has selections to create an Apple Macintosh-Compatible volume (from an existing folder), modify or view an existing Apple Macintosh-Compatible volume, or delete an existing Apple Macintosh-Compatible volume.

The MacFile menu selection also allows modification of permissions, and file type associations.

Creating a Macintosh-Accessible Volume

To create an Apple Macintosh-Accessible volume, first create a new folder on the drive and click on the MacFile | Create Volume menu selection. The Create Macintosh-Accessible Volume dialog box (Figure 6-9) will
be displayed.

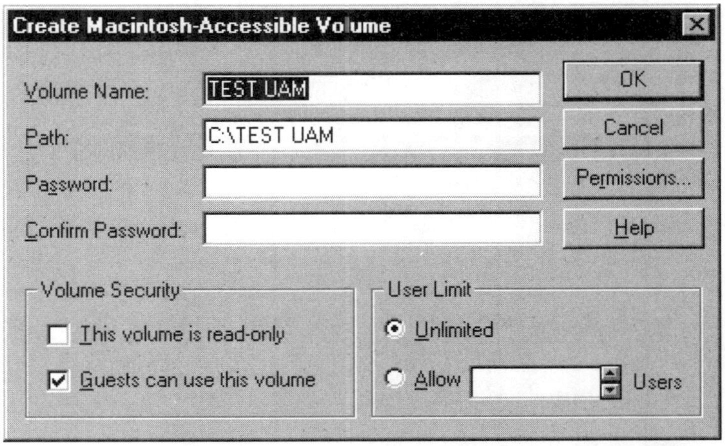

Figure 6-9: Use the Create Macintosh-Accessible Volume dialog box to create a new Apple Macintosh-Compatible volume from a folder.

In the Create Macintosh-Accessible Volume dialog box, you must specify the Volume Name and Path. You will be given defaults (based on the folder currently selected in the File Manager's currently active window), though these defaults may be changed as needed.

You may also specify optional password, security specifications (such as read-only and whether guests may access the volume), and user limits; initially, however, the defaults may prove to be adequate.

View/Modify Macintosh-Accessible Volumes

To view the properties of an Apple Macintosh-Accessible volume, select the MacFile | View/Modify Volumes menu selection. The View/Modify Macintosh-Accessible Volumes dialog box (Figure 6-10) will be displayed.

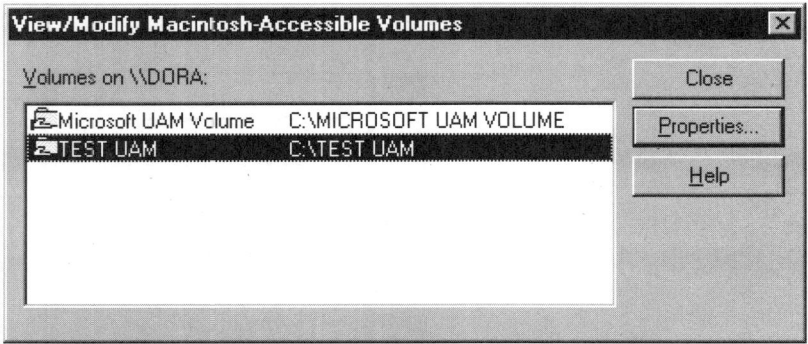

Figure 6-10: Use the View/Modify Macintosh-Accessible Volumes dialog to select an Apple Macintosh-compatible volume.

In the View/Modify Macintosh-Accessible Volumes dialog box, select the volume whose properties are to be displayed and click on the Properties button to display the Properties of Macintosh-Accessible Volume dialog box (Figure 6-11). In the Properties of Macintosh-Accessible Volume dialog box, the Volume Name and Path may not be modified.

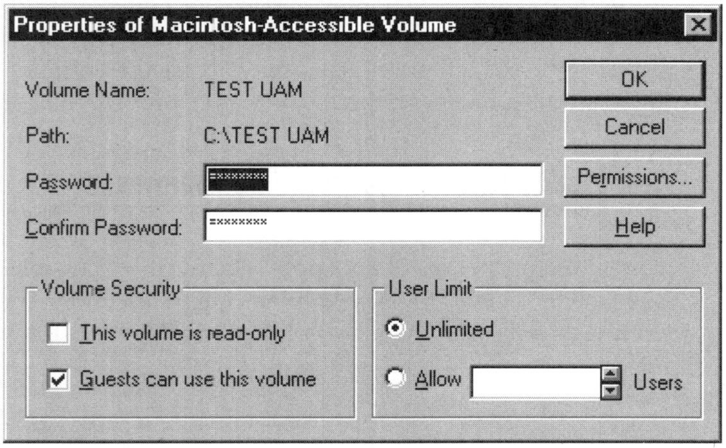

Figure 6-11: Modify a Macintosh-Accessible Volume's password, security, and user limits.

The password, security specifications (such as read-only and whether guests may access the volume), and user limits may be modified in the Properties of Macintosh-Accessible Volume dialog as desired.

Remove Macintosh-Accessible Volumes

To remove an existing Apple Macintosh-Accessible volume, select the
MacFile | Remove Volumes menu selection. The Remove Macintosh-
Accessible Volumes dialog box (Figure 6-12) will be displayed.

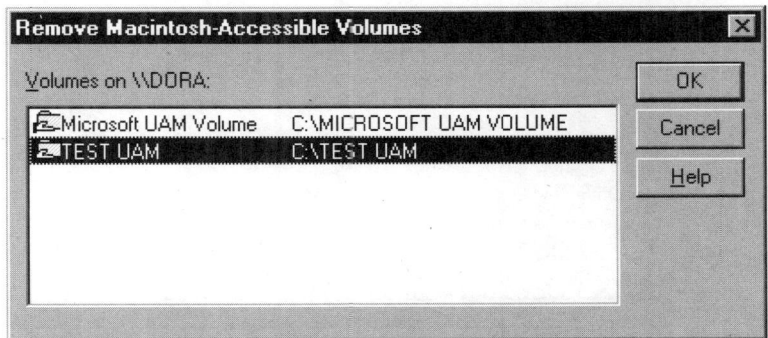

*Figure 6-12: Use the Remove Macintosh-Accessible Volumes dialog box
to remove an Apple Macintosh-Compatible volume.*

When you click on the OK button in the Remove Macintosh-Accessible
Volumes dialog box, you will see a confirming prompt before the volume
is deleted.

Permissions

To view the permissions of an Apple Macintosh-Accessible volume,
select the MacFile | Permissions menu selection. The Macintosh View of
Directory Permissions dialog box (Figure 6-13) will be displayed.

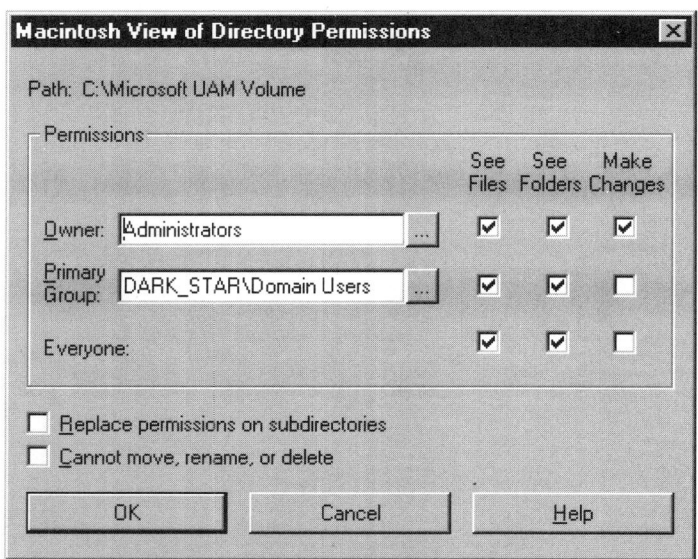

Figure 6-13: Use the Macintosh View of Directory Permissions dialog box to view the Macintosh-Accessible volume's permissions, in a format similar to that found on an Apple Macintosh.

You can set various permissions and restrictions on what users may do using the Macintosh View of Directory Permissions dialog box. Restrictions include:

- **Owner.** You can set an Owner, and the Owner of the Macintosh-Accessible volume may have the following permissions: See Files, See Folders, and Make Changes.

- **Primary Group.** You can set the Primary Group, and members of the Primary Group of the Macintosh-Accessible volume may have the following permissions: See Files, See Folders, and Make Changes.

- **Everyone.** The Everyone group may have the following permissions: See Files, See Folders, and Make Changes.

For all volumes, you can set the option to replace permissions for subdirectories, as well as global restrictions on moving, renaming, and deleting.

Apple Macintosh File Associations

To view the associations of files on an Apple Macintosh-Accessible volume, select the MacFile | Associate menu selection. The Associate dialog box (Figure 6-14) will be displayed.

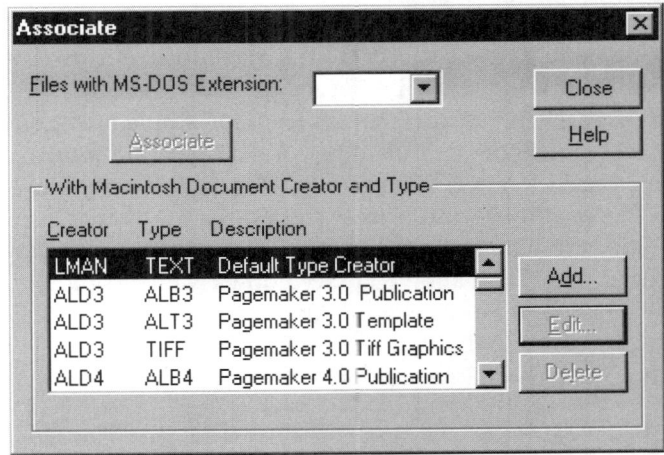

Figure 6-14: Use the Associate dialog box to view the Macintosh-Accessible volume's files associations. Experience with Apple Macintoshes will be helpful here

You can set various associations; when you work with Apple Macintosh file associations, however, following Apple Macintosh conventions is best whenever possible.

Sharing Network Printers With the Macintosh

Creating a Macintosh printer server on a Windows NT 4 Server running Services for Macintosh is rather easy:

1. You install the printer on the server as normal. No special options or configurations need be selected.

2. Launch Server Manager (Start Menu | Programs | Administrative Tools (Common) | Server Manager) and select the Windows NT Server that is to share the printer for Apple Macintosh clients. Select Computer | Services in the Server Manager's menu, make sure that Print Server for the Macintosh is started, and click on the Close button.

That's it! Print Server for the Macintosh automatically recognizes printers that are shared on the Windows NT Server and makes them available on the Apple Macintosh network zone as well.

Connecting to a Windows NT 4 Server Domain

To log on to the new server from a Macintosh, ensure that your Macintosh and Windows NT 4 Server are both connected to the network properly. Then, launch Chooser from the Apple menu on the Macintosh. Select AppleShare and then the correct server from the list of servers that appears; click on OK. You can then log on to the Windows NT 4 Server and access the file and printer shares that are available on the server.

I need to note one quirk. AppleShare names and passwords are shorter than those allowed by Windows NT. If Apple Macintosh users have usernames or passwords that are too long, they may find it impossible to log on to the Windows NT Server as a result. If this happens, shorten the username and/or password as necessary.

Moving On

In this chapter, you saw how to configure a Windows NT Server to operate as an AppleShare server and provide file and printer services to all the Macintoshes on your network.

In the next chapter, I discuss the built-in support for integrating with UNIX systems along with a discussion of a few third-party options to help Windows NT integrate even tighter with UNIX.

7

Supporting UNIX Networks With Windows NT 4 Server

Like the Apple Macintosh, UNIX has gained little support in the business environment. UNIX's strongest users are those involved in education, and Internet/intranet users and research and development has provided some support for the UNIX platform.

Windows NT 4 Server works well in a mixed UNIX and Windows networking model. This configuration allows easy transition between UNIX and Windows networking. All the commands shown in this chapter are workstation based—they work with Windows NT workstations connected to UNIX servers. Generally, there are components for Windows NT 4 Server (either built-in, or available from third-party suppliers) to emulate UNIX functionalities, such as Finger and Telnet.

There are many, many flavors of UNIX, some running on specialized platforms, others based on the PC (Intel and others). Some versions of UNIX are freeware; some are rather expensive investments, with high overhead costs. Generally, larger UNIX systems are found on the Internet (which until recently was almost entirely UNIX based, with a smattering of VAX VMS and mainframe computers filling out the playing field).

Interestingly enough, NT stops just short of fully supporting UNIX. I was surprised to find out that even though the support for TCP/IP and related protocols, including some of the cooler protocols such as FTP, Gopher, and HTTP, was built in to NT, they left out one of the more useful protocols—Sun's NFS protocol, which essentially allows file sharing among UNIX systems.

The purpose of this chapter is to expose you to some of the UNIX-specific utilities that may come in handy and also to make you aware of the steps that must be taken to get a UNIX system to communicate with a server connected to the network.

All utilities discussed in this chapter are usable with Internet-connected computers. As well, there are a number of excellent aftermarket products that will provide enhanced capabilities for Windows NT 4 Server users, such as the ever popular WS-FTP32 program, which is a Windows-based 32-bit replacement for the command-line-driven FTP program included with Windows NT 4 Server.

UNIX Utilities for Windows NT

If you have a need to use UNIX-based utilities, you should be aware that they are all based on the DOS command line. There are not any Windows NT 4 Server UNIX utilities available with a graphical interface. The UNIX utilities listed in see Table 7-1 have been helpful to the author at one time or another.

The UNIX utilities are grouped into two broad categories: diagnostic and connectivity. The diagnostic UNIX utilities are used to assist the user in configuring and diagnosing problems with the network. The connectivity utilities are used for communications and performing nondiagnostic tasks over the network.

Utility Name	Category	Description
ARP	Diagnostic	Displays and modifies the IP-to-Physical address translation tables used by address resolution protocol (ARP).
FINGER	Connectivity	Displays information about a user on a specified system running the Finger service. Output varies based on the remote system.
FTP	Connectivity	File Transfer Protocol. Transfers files between computers that support the FTP file transfer protocol.
HOSTNAME	Diagnostic	Displays the name of the current host (server).

Utility Name	Category	Description
IPCONFIG	Diagnostic	Displays a summary of the IP configuration for the computer for each NIC (Network Interface Card).
LPQ	Diagnostic	Checks status of line printer queues. This utility is not installed on Windows NT 4 Server by default.
LPR	Connectivity	Prints file to line printer. This utility is not installed on Windows NT 4 Server by default.
NBSTAT	Diagnostic	A tool used to troubleshoot NetBIOS name resolution problems. Use NBSTAT to remove or correct preloaded NetBIOS name entries. This utility is not installed on Windows NT 4 Server.
NETSTAT	Diagnostic	Displays a summary of active connections to the computer.
PING	Diagnostic	Sends messages requesting a response to the specified computer on the network and times the response.
RCP	Connectivity	Copies files to and from any other computer that is running RCP services.
REXEC	Connectivity	Runs commands on remote hosts running the REXEC service. REXEC authenticates the username on the remote host before executing the specified command.
ROUTE	Diagnostic	Manages the network TCP/IP routing tables.
RSH	Connectivity	Runs commands on remote hosts running the RSH service.
TELNET	Connectivity	Establishes a terminal session on the remote computer.
TFTP	Connectivity	Trivial File Transfer Protocol. Works like FTP, but is simpler and easier to use. Programs such as WS_FTP32 make TFTP unnecessary.
TRACERT	Diagnostic	Traces and displays the routing to a remote computer on the network.

Table 7-1: UNIX utilities built in to Windows NT.

Just a suggestion: Some of the utilities listed in Table 7-1 (such as REXEC and LPR) may cause undesirable actions (such as printing files) on the host server. Be careful that the results of the command are what you expected!

Each of the UNIX utilities is described in detail in the sections that follow.

Note: UNIX, unlike Windows NT 4 Server, is rather case sensitive. Options in uppercase must be entered in uppercase, not lowercase. The same goes for usernames, passwords, and usually filenames, too.

ARP

The ARP (Address Resolution Protocol) utility is a diagnostic program that is used to display and modify the IP-to-Physical address translation tables used by address resolution protocol (ARP). If ARP is not being used, the ARP utility will return the message, "No ARP Entries Found."

An example of running ARP on my Windows NT 4 Server is:

```
C:\ >arp -a

Interface: 99.125.78.23 on Interface 2
  Internet Address    Physical Address    Type
  99.125.78.250       00-80-ad-04-b1-47   dynamic

C:\ >
```

This example shows that there is a single NIC, which has an IP address bound to it, and that the NIC's physical address is 00-80-ad-04-b1-47. Each NIC will have a unique physical address, which is assigned by the NIC's manufacturer.

FINGER

The FINGER utility is a connectivity program used to obtain information about users on a remote system.

The FINGER utility supports the option –l (the lowercase letter L, not the number 1), which will display the information in a long list format.

Figure 7-1 shows several examples of the FINGER utility. The first example, finger @mv.com, displayed a list of all active users on the computer at the address mv.com. The second example, finger mem@mv.com, displays information about the user mem (Mr. Mark Mallett, who is MV's owner). Oh, yes, MV is my ISP, and I now know that Mark is currently connected.

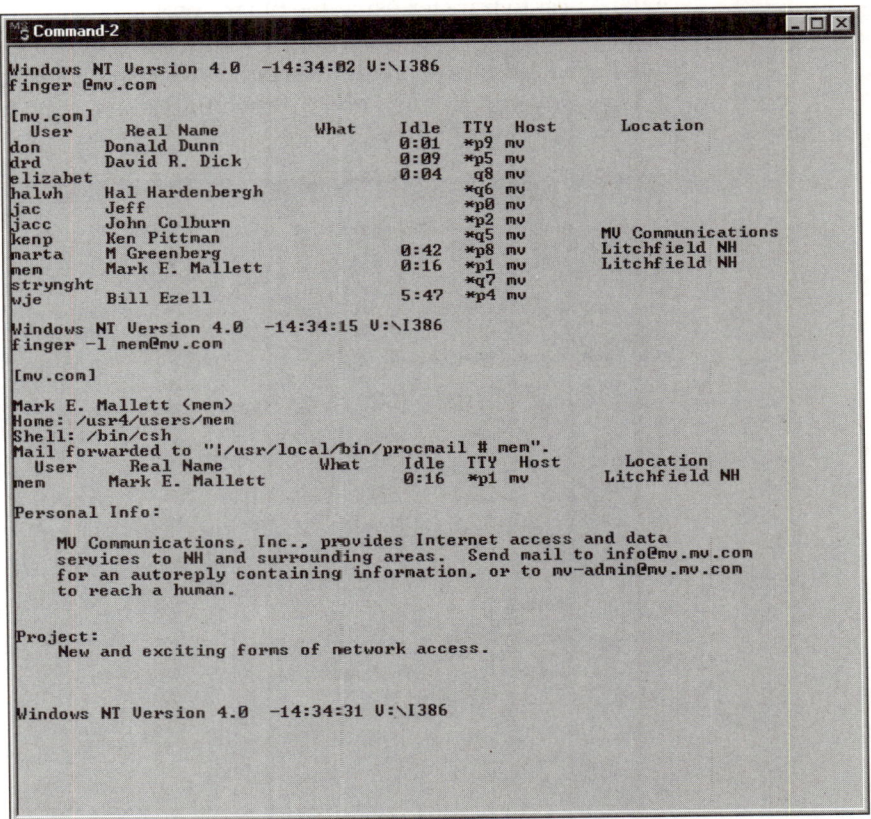

Figure 7-1: Using FINGER to find out about a server and its users.

FTP

The FTP utility is a connectivity program used to transfer files between computers that support File Transfer Protocol (FTP). For Windows NT 4 Server servers, Microsoft's IIS (Internet Information Server) provides the best method to implement an FTP server.

The FTP utility is a command-line-driven program that is far from user friendly. Figure 7-2 shows the FTP utility connecting to the DarkStar server (darkstar.mv.com) and transferring a file, joke121.txt, to the local drive.

FTP transfers may be either ASCII or binary; however, in most cases it will be best to transfer using the binary protocol to avoid any possible corruption of the files. Also realize that files are transferred in their native format and there are utilities on UNIX systems for file compression that are not compatible with PC-based utilities.

```
Command-2                                                                    _

Windows NT Version 4.0  -15:12:28 C:\WINNT
ftp darkstar
Connected to darkstar.mv.com.
220 darkstar Microsoft FTP Service (Version 2.0).
User (darkstar.mv.com:(none)): anonymous
331 Anonymous access allowed, send identity (e-mail name) as password.
Password:
230-Welcome
230 Anonymous user logged in.
ftp> ls
200 PORT command successful.
150 Opening ASCII mode data connection for file list.
Joke120.txt
Joke121.txt
Joke122.txt
Joke123.txt
Joke125.txt
JOKE126.TXT
Joke127.txt
Joke128.txt
Joke129.txt
226 Transfer complete.
117 bytes received in 0.00 seconds (117000.00 Kbytes/sec)
ftp> get joke121.txt
200 PORT command successful.
150 Opening ASCII mode data connection for joke121.txt(1727 bytes).
226 Transfer complete.
1727 bytes received in 0.07 seconds (24.67 Kbytes/sec)
ftp> bye
221 Bye

Windows NT Version 4.0  -15:13:15 C:\WINNT
```

Figure 7-2: Using FTP to get a joke!

HOSTNAME

The HOSTNAME utility is a diagnostic program that is used to display information about the hostname. The hostname is the name for the server. For example, typing HOSTNAME in a DOS window displays the following information:

```
Windows NT Version 4.0  -14:34:31 V:\I386
hostname
darkstar

Windows NT Version 4.0  -14:38:48 V:\I386
```

The hostname may be set using the Control Panel's Network applet.

IPCONFIG

The IPCONFIG utility is a diagnostic program that is used to display information about the current IP configuration for the local computer. Each NIC will be listed, along with any WAN (wide area network) wrappers that are configured.

Figure 7-3 shows an example of running the IPCONFIG utility.

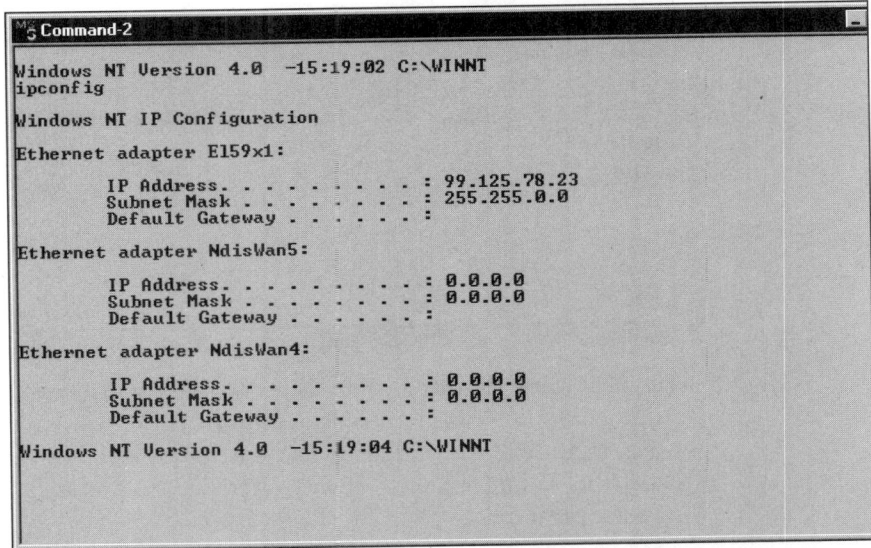

Figure 7-3: The IPCONFIG utility shows my IP address and WAN configuration.

LPQ

The LPQ (Line Printer Queue) utility is a diagnostic program that is used to display information about a TCP/IP printer queue. This utility may not be installed on Windows NT 4 Server by default, but it can be installed manually if necessary.

Figure 7-4 shows the LPQ utility listing two files that have been printed to a TCP/IP printer queue.

```
Command-2                                                    _ □ ✕
Windows NT Version 4.0  -15:49:16 C:\
lpq -S dora -P GenTCP -1
                        Windows NT LPD Server
                          Printer GenTCP (Paused)

Owner         Status      Jobname          Job-Id    Size    Pages  Priority
Administrat  Waiting    Microsoft Word - CH    1     90316     3       1
Administrat  Waiting    Microsoft Word - CH    2     176640   10       1


Windows NT Version 4.0  -15:49:35 C:\
```

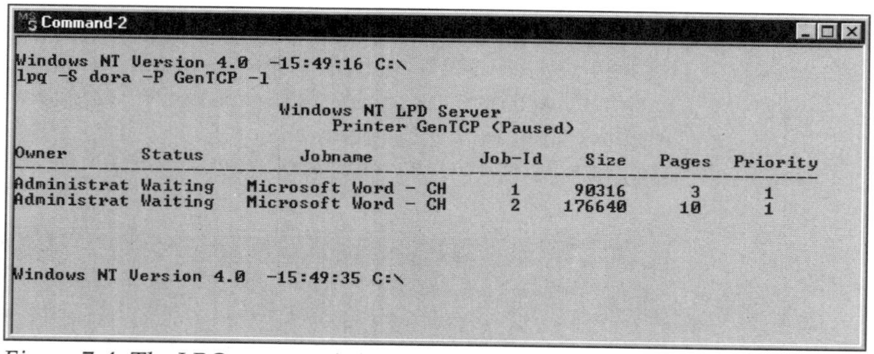

Figure 7-4: The LPQ command showing two files in DORA's TCP/IP printer queue.

LPR

The LPR (Line PRinter) utility is a connectivity program that is used to print a file to a TCP/IP printer queue. The LPR utility has several options, including setting the job name (using the –J option), the print job's class (the –C option), and setting other options that may be unique to a specific print queue.

NBSTAT

The NBSTAT utility is a diagnostic program that is used to troubleshoot NetBIOS name resolution issues. If you are not using NetBIOS over TCP/IP, then NBSTAT is not needed.

NBSTAT is not currently shipped with Windows NT 4 Server.

NETSTAT

The NETSTAT utility is a diagnostic program that is used to display the status of all current TCP/IP connections to the Windows NT 4 Server. An example of the results of running NETSTAT are:

```
Windows NT Version 4.0  -15:49:35 C:\
netstat

Active Connections

   Proto  Local Address    Foreign Address  State
   TCP    dora:nbsession   PIXEL:1025       ESTABLISHED
   TCP    darkstar:1026    localhost:1027   ESTABLISHED
   TCP    darkstar:1027    localhost:1026   ESTABLISHED

Windows NT Version 4.C  -17:29:03 C:\
```

PING

The PING utility is a diagnostic program that is used to display information about how long it takes to send and receive messages from a remote computer.

The PING utility works by sending a message to the remote computer simply requesting that the remote computer respond. The amount of time the message takes to reach the remote host is then displayed for the user. Three examples of the PING utility are shown in Figure 7-5. In the first example, ping microsoft.com (which is on the other side of the country from me) shows that the message takes just under 300 milliseconds to reach me. Ping mv.com (which is my ISP) shows that a message from my ISP to me takes about 130 ms, or just under half as long as it takes to send messages across the entire United States. Of course you can also ping yourself (as I did) and the ping time will be virtually unmeasurable (that is < 10 ms).

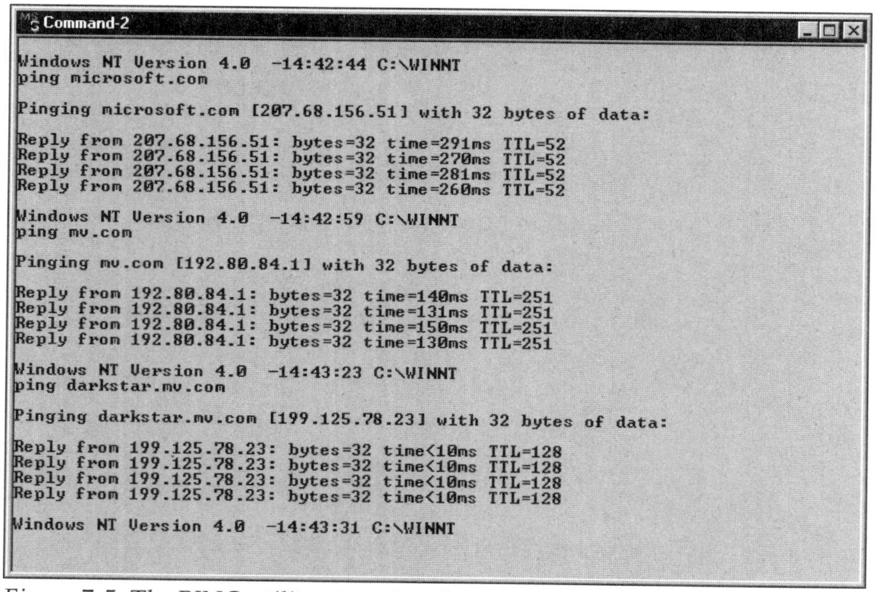

```
Command-2                                                          _ □ ×

Windows NT Version 4.0  -14:42:44 C:\WINNT
ping microsoft.com

Pinging microsoft.com [207.68.156.51] with 32 bytes of data:

Reply from 207.68.156.51: bytes=32 time=291ms TTL=52
Reply from 207.68.156.51: bytes=32 time=270ms TTL=52
Reply from 207.68.156.51: bytes=32 time=281ms TTL=52
Reply from 207.68.156.51: bytes=32 time=260ms TTL=52

Windows NT Version 4.0  -14:42:59 C:\WINNT
ping mv.com

Pinging mv.com [192.80.84.1] with 32 bytes of data:

Reply from 192.80.84.1: bytes=32 time=140ms TTL=251
Reply from 192.80.84.1: bytes=32 time=131ms TTL=251
Reply from 192.80.84.1: bytes=32 time=150ms TTL=251
Reply from 192.80.84.1: bytes=32 time=130ms TTL=251

Windows NT Version 4.0  -14:43:23 C:\WINNT
ping darkstar.mv.com

Pinging darkstar.mv.com [199.125.78.23] with 32 bytes of data:

Reply from 199.125.78.23: bytes=32 time<10ms TTL=128
Reply from 199.125.78.23: bytes=32 time<10ms TTL=128
Reply from 199.125.78.23: bytes=32 time<10ms TTL=128
Reply from 199.125.78.23: bytes=32 time<10ms TTL=128

Windows NT Version 4.0  -14:43:31 C:\WINNT
```

Figure 7-5: The PING utility at work—three examples.

RCP

The RCP utility is a connectivity program that is used to copy files between the Windows NT computer and a computer that is running the UNIX rshd (Remote SHell Daemon). (A service is called a daemon under UNIX.) Support for RCP is not available from all UNIX servers.

Note: The rshd service is not available on Windows NT 4 Server. The RCP command will only copy files between a Windows NT computer and a UNIX server—and not between two Windows NT computers.

REXEC

The REXEC utility is a connectivity program that is used to execute commands on a remote UNIX system. A username and password must be supplied to enable a connection to the remote system.

ROUTE

The ROUTE utility is a diagnostic program that is used to examine and modify the system routing tables. For example, Figure 7-6 shows the routing table for the server DORA. (DORA is running Windows NT 4 Server; that does not, however, affect the ROUTE utility's output.)

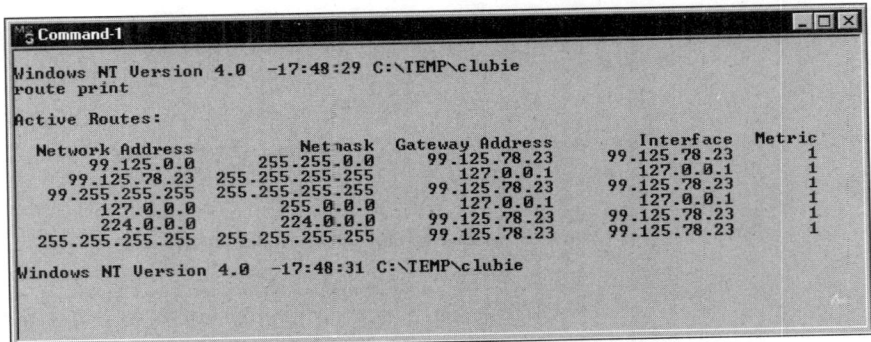

Figure 7-6: Displaying a routing table with the ROUTE utility.

RSH

The RSH utility is a connectivity program that is used to execute commands on a remote host. RSH works in a manner similar to the REXEC command.

Telnet

The Telnet utility is a connectivity program that is used to connect to a remote computer. Many UNIX computers use locally attached terminals for users (UNIX is a multiuser operating system). A logical terminal (typically an application called Telnet) may be logically connected to a UNIX computer using a network connection instead of a local serial port.

TELNET is the remote terminal protocol usually used by UNIX computers and also the name for a Telnet-compatible terminal program. Figure 7-7 shows Telnet connected to a computer as part of an online session.

```
 Telnet - metro.jussieu.fr                                        _ □ ×
Connect  Edit  Terminal  Help
Do you want to continue [Yes] : y


Departure station [no default answer] : alewife
Arrival station [no default answer] : park

Several station names match what you typed (park)
They are:
(1) Forge Park/495      (3) Melrose/Cedar Park (5) Science Park
(2) Hyde Park           (4) Park Street

Choose (with its number) your station : 4

Estimated time = 15 minutes

Line 'Red', Direction 'Braintree' or 'Ashmont'
        Alewife
        Davis
        Porter
        Harvard Square
        Central
        Kendall/MIT
        Charles/Massachusetts General Hospital
        Park Street
Do you want to continue [Yes] : █
```

Figure 7-7: A Telnet session to a computer in France telling me how to get there on the Boston subway.

About that session shown in Figure 7-7 . . . I connected to a computer located in France and then was able to retrieve information about the Boston subway! How's that for international cooperation?

TFTP

TFTP (Trivial File Transfer Protocol) is a connectivity program that is used to transfer files between a Windows NT system and a UNIX server. TFTP does not allow connections to a Windows NT 4 Server, as connects using TFTP do not support user authentication.

TFTP works like FTP, but is simpler and easier to use. Programs such as WS_FTP32 make TFTP unnecessary. Windows 95 and the TCP/IP 32 products do not include the TFTP utility.

TRACERT

The TRACERT utility is a diagnostic program that is used to display information about how long it takes to send and receive messages from a remote computer and the specific routing that messages take between a client and the host.

The TRACERT utility works by sending a series of messages with incrementing TTL (Time to Live) parameter values. The messages simply request that the remote computer respond. The amount of time that the message takes is then displayed for the user. Two examples of the TRACERT utility are shown in Figure 7-8. In the first example, tracert microsoft.com (which is on the other side of the country from me) showed that the connection passes through a number of different routers before it reaches Microsoft. Using tracert whitehouse.gov (which is where the president of the United States lives) shows that a message from me to the president takes about 10 steps, or just a few steps less than what it takes to connect to a computer across the entire United States. Bet you didn't realize I had such close communications with him, did you?

```
Command-2                                                                    _ □ ×

Windows NT Version 4.0  -14:54:01 C:\WINNT
tracert microsoft.com

Tracing route to microsoft.com [207.68.137.62]
over a maximum of 30 hops:

  1      *          *          *       Request timed out.
  2      *          *          *       Request timed out.
  3      *          *          *       Request timed out.
  4    140 ms     140 ms     140 ms   gw-sprint.mv.net [199.125.85.138]
  5    240 ms     211 ms     250 ms   sl-fw-3-S2/2-T1.sprintlink.net [144.228.169.65]

  6    371 ms     240 ms     270 ms   sl-fw-5-F1/0.sprintlink.net [144.228.30.5]
  7    270 ms     261 ms     220 ms   sl-kc-2-H2/0-T3.sprintlink.net [144.228.10.77]
  8    290 ms     231 ms     230 ms   sl-chi-15-H2/0-T3.sprintlink.net [144.228.10.69]

  9    340 ms     321 ms     260 ms   sl-sea-2-H2/0-T3.sprintlink.net [144.228.10.61]

 10    260 ms     271 ms     290 ms   sl-sea-5-F0/0.sprintlink.net [144.228.90.5]
 11    330 ms     331 ms     330 ms   sl-mic-2-H-T3.sprintlink.net [144.228.95.10]
 12    310 ms     431 ms     270 ms   207.68.145.45
 13    320 ms     321 ms     280 ms   207.68.137.62

Trace complete.

Windows NT Version 4.0  -14:55:57 C:\WINNT
tracert whitehouse.gov

Tracing route to whitehouse.gov [198.137.241.30]
over a maximum of 30 hops:

  1      *          *          *       Request timed out.
  2      *          *          *       Request timed out.
  3      *          *          *       Request timed out.
  4    191 ms     140 ms     150 ms   gw-sprint.mv.net [199.125.85.138]
  5    200 ms     191 ms     180 ms   sl-fw-3-S2/2-T1.sprintlink.net [144.228.169.65]

  6    370 ms     431 ms     230 ms   sl-fw-5-F1/0.sprintlink.net [144.228.30.5]
  7    280 ms     271 ms     250 ms   sl-dc-8-H3/0-T3.sprintlink.net [144.228.10.17]
  8    230 ms     271 ms     230 ms   sl-dc-17-F0/0.sprintlink.net [144.228.20.17]
  9    270 ms     261 ms     230 ms   sl-eop-1-S0-T1.sprintlink.net [144.228.72.66]
 10    290 ms     251 ms     240 ms   whitehouse.gov [198.137.241.30]

Trace complete.

Windows NT Version 4.0  -14:57:27 C:\WINNT
```

Figure 7-8: Using TRACERT to find Microsoft and the president!

What Is a TTL & Who Cares How Long It Has to Live?

What is a TTL (Time to Live) parameter?

A TTL value is a number that is part of every TCP packet (the "message") on the network. Each time a packet is forwarded, the TTL value is decremented. When the TTL value reaches zero, the packet is returned to the sender with information on the returning router.

Why do we use a TTL parameter?

The first use for the TTL parameter is the TRACERT command. Well, we are sure that TTL was not developed to simply facilitate the TRACERT command. Rather, TTL is used to limit the distance that a packet travels on the network. This helps reduce the number of undesired packets floating around on the network. In reality, most systems set the TTL value very high (sometimes as high as 255), which means that the packet rarely "times out."

Not all routers will properly return a packet when the TTL reaches zero, so the results of a TRACERT command cannot be considered to be 100 percent accurate all the time.

Sharing Files With a UNIX System

Windows NT Server provides file services to PCs through the Server Message Block (SMB) protocol, which is not compatible with UNIX workstations. For UNIX systems, file transfer is done using the NFS (Network File System) protocol or the FTP service.

Windows NT 4 Server does not directly support NFS. However, there are a number of non-Microsoft products to add NFS support to Windows NT 4 Server, including:

- BW-Connect from Beame & Whiteside, Inc.
- Chameleon/32NFS from NetManage, Inc.
- DiskShare from Intergraph Corporation
- NFSWare from Process Software

Each of the above products provides for all NFS clients (PC, UNIX, and any other NFS clients). These solutions will allow sharing to UNIX clients files on NTFS, FAT, and CDFS systems. Unlike Windows NT 3.51, Windows NT 4 Server does not support HPFS file systems.

Most NFS system add-ons will support sharing of network drives that are located on other servers (such as Novell NetWare or other platforms). This is done by creating a link to the drive to be shared using NFS and telling the NFS add-on about the drive. Some NFS system add-ons also enable the exporting of network drives.

In previous chapters, we have stepped through what is involved in mixing Macs, NetWare file servers, and NT servers all on the same network, but when a UNIX system is added to the mix, all of a sudden you are reduced to transferring files in-house by FTP, which is a little crude for any significant amount of use.

When it was necessary to integrate a Silicon Graphics Irix Workstation with an existing Windows NT 4 Server network, it didn't take too long to determine that there was no really solid solution.

A copy of Chameleon/NFS32 was installed, and after a little fuss with the installation the Irix workstation, (with UNIX installed), and the NT Server communicated and shared files just fine.

NT Servers Everywhere (or the CIFS)

I said in the beginning of this chapter that it is surprising Microsoft didn't go the extra mile to support UNIX more fully. Well, I may have spoken too soon! Microsoft has proposed a standard that it intends to introduce across the Internet called the Common Internet File System (CIFS). If this new standard becomes accepted and becomes a part of future versions of Windows NT Server, perhaps the lack of support for native NFS will not present that big a problem.

The Microsoft TCP/IP Print Service

One feature of Windows NT 4 Server is its ability to be a print server for a UNIX workstation. To configure a UNIX-compatible printer, it is necessary to install the Microsoft TCP/IP Print Service and then configure a printer as appropriate.

Installing TCP/IP Print Service

The TCP/IP Print Service component is installed using the Control Panel's Network applet. To install TCP/IP Print Service, follow these steps:

1. Start the Control Panel's Network applet by opening the Control Panel and double-clicking the Network icon.

2. Select the Services tab.

3. Click the Add button. The Select Network Service dialog box appears.

4. Select Microsoft TCP/IP Printing from the Network Service list.

If you are not using TCP/IP protocol, either for a connection to the Internet or to connect to an intranet, there is little need to consider installing, configuring, or tuning this service. Installing unneeded network components can create problems, as each protocol consumes system resources, including network bandwidth.

Once Microsoft TCP/IP Print Service is installed, use the Control Panel's Services applet (see Figure 7-9) to ensure that the TCP/IP Print Service has been started for your system.

The TCP/IP Print Service is not automatically started for you by default when the server boots, although you can (and should, if TCP/IP Print Services are to be used on a regular basis) change that setting using the Control Panel's Services applet.

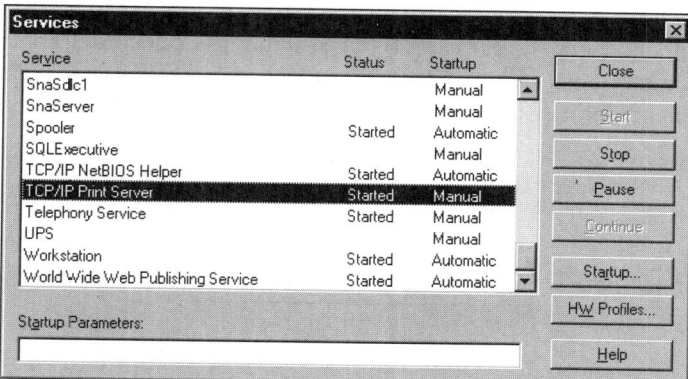

Figure 7-9: Starting the TCP/IP Print Service, which is not started by default.

Configuring a Local Printer to Be Accessible From UNIX

To allow a UNIX workstation to use a printer on the local network, you need to install a special printer port. To install a UNIX-compatible printer port:

Note: A UNIX printer port is configured using an existing printer. If there are no installed printers that are suitable for use with UNIX, then a printer must be installed. Just a hint: Keep this printer's name simple; it will have to be typed in later during the installation of the UNIX-compatible printer port generation phase.

1. Open the Printer folder from Start Menu | Settings. Double-click the Add Printer icon to launch the Add Printer Wizard.

2. In the first pane of the Add Printer Wizard, click the My Computer option and then click the Next button.

3. Click the Add Port button on the second pane of the Add Printer Wizard (See Figure 7-10). This will display the Printer Ports dialog box, as shown in Figure 7-11.

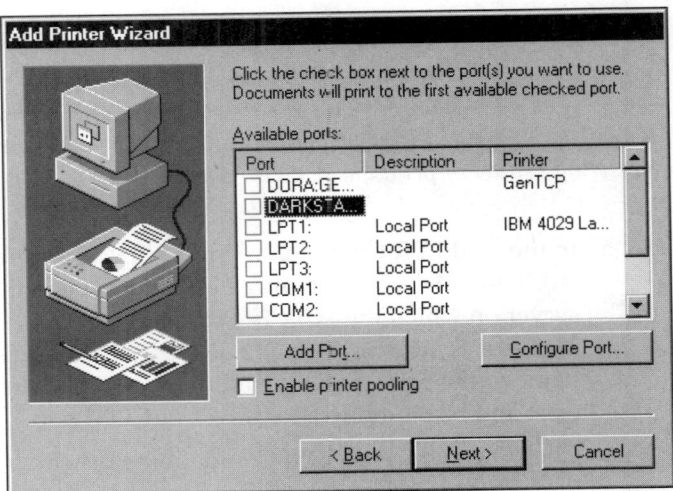

Figure 7-10: Adding a UNIX-compatible port in the Add Printer Wizard's second pane.

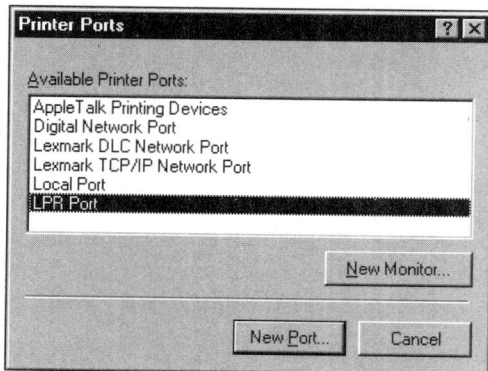

Figure 7-11: Use the Printer Ports dialog box to add an LPR Port.

4. In the Printer Ports dialog, select LPR Port and click New Port. The Add LPR compatible printer dialog box (Figure 7-12) will be displayed.

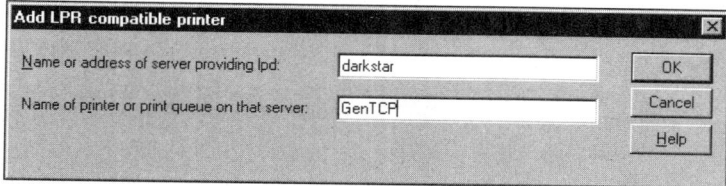

Figure 7-12: The Add LPR Compatible Printer dialog box—enter the server and an existing printer or print queue name.

5. In the Add LPR Compatible Printer dialog box's Name or Address of Server Providing Lpd field, type in the name of the server on which the TCP/IP Print Service is installed. In the Name of Printer or Print Queue on That Server field, type in the name of the printer being added. (Note: this printer must already exist and be bound to a local LPT or COM port.)

6. Click OK in the Add LPR Compatible Printer dialog box to create the LPR port. If Windows NT 4 Server displays an error message, check to make sure that the TCP/IP Printer Service is running and retry adding the port.

7. Click Close in the Printer Ports dialog box.

8. The newly created port should be selected (with a check mark) in the Available Ports list. If not selected, select it. Click the Next button.

9. Select the vendor and model of the printer you are installing (this should match both the printer itself and the printer specified in Step 5) and click Next. A message that the printer driver is already installed may be displayed. If so, it is safe to keep the existing driver.

10. Provide a name for the new print queue. Keep this name simple, yet descriptive. If at a later time there is a need to change the printer queue's name, you can do so in the Printers folder (Start Menu | Settings | Printers). Do not use this printer as the default printer for Windows applications: Click the No button in this step.

11. Click Next and configure sharing as desired for your configuration. When you are done configuring sharing, click Next.

12. There is generally no need to print a test page. However, if you are unsure of the installation, printing a test page will confirm that the drivers have been properly installed. Click Finish to complete the installation of the UNIX-compatible printer queue.

The printer port may be tested using a UNIX workstation.

Simple TCP/IP Services

Windows NT 4 Server supports a set of Simple TCP/IP Services. These Simple TCP/IP Services are usable with any client workstation having support for them. Consult the client workstation's documentation for more information about Simple TCP/IP Services support. Simple TCP/IP Services may be installed either when installing Windows NT 4 Server or at a later time, as shown below.

Note: Don't confuse Simple TCP/IP Services with the TCP/IP protocol. Simple TCP/IP Services is a group of specialized services that the server offers to TCP/IP clients. You don't need to install Simple TCP/IP Services to use TCP/IP.

Installing Simple TCP/IP Services

The Simple TCP/IP Services component is installed using the Control Panel's Network applet. To install Simple TCP/IP Services, follow these steps:

1. Start the Control Panel's Network applet by opening the Control Panel and double-clicking the Network icon.

2. Select the Services tab.

3. Click the Add button. The Select Network Service dialog box appears.

4. Select Simple TCP/IP Services from the Network Service list.

If you are not using TCP/IP protocol, either for a connection to the Internet or to connect to an intranet, there is little need to consider installing, configuring, or tuning this service. Installing unneeded network components can create problems, as each protocol consumes system resources, including network bandwidth.

Services Included

The Simple TCP/IP Services provide support for CHARGEN, DAYTIME, DISCARD, ECHO, and QUOTE, and while most (except for QUOTE) of the Simple TCP/IP Services cannot be configured, in this section there is a quick description of each service.

Simple TCP/IP Services is server based. You will notice no changes in how your Windows NT 4 Server functions. Simple TCP/IP Services supports client users, who have support for CHARGEN, DAYTIME, DISCARD, ECHO, or QUOTE. The services included in Simple TCP/IP Services are:

- **ECHO**—returns received data verbatim. The ECHO service is defined in RFC 862.

- **DISCARD**—discards or throws away any data received. The DISCARD service is defined in RFC 863.

- **CHARGEN**—sends predetermined data to the client regardless of the client's input. The client can send any data to the CHARGEN service; Microsoft recommends, however, that you use a recognizable pattern. The CHARGEN service is defined in RFC 864.

- **QUOTE**—sends a "quote of the day" to the client upon request. QUOTE ignores all text in the client's request. Quotes are defined in the file %SystemRoot%\system32\drivers\etc\quotes, where %SystemRoot% is the folder where Windows NT 4 Server is installed. You can add a quote having one or more lines with a maximum length of 512 characters (about six 80-character lines). The QUOTE service is defined in RFC 865. This constitutes the sole configuration option for the Simple TCP/IP Services: changing the quotes!

Note: The quotes provided by Microsoft are getting a bit stale. Consider revising the quote list before placing your quote server online.

Moving On

In this chapter, we discussed some of the support that is built in to Windows NT for UNIX workstations. We also briefly covered a third-party product that allows UNIX workstations to mount directories that exist on an NT workstation.

The next chapter really dives into the issues of connecting to the Internet and what that means with NT.

8

Connecting to the Internet With Windows NT Server

Since the Internet became the electronic highway of choice for e-mail, file transfer, and electronic information sharing, the importance of connecting to it has grown significantly. Until recently, e-mail transfer was the primary reason to connect to the Internet, and most networks used various types of gateways as a bridge between a LAN-based e-mail system and the Internet. Networks other than government and university networks did not necessarily use TCP/IP as their network protocol.

Since 1993, there has been an explosion in the number of individuals and corporate networks that are connected to the Internet. A company is considered to be behind the times if they don't have a corporate Web site. Business cards almost always include name, title, address, phone and fax numbers, and an e-mail address. Until very recently, the only practical way to connect to the Internet was to use a UNIX server. However, with the advent of Windows NT 4 Server, it has become possible to connect to the Internet without relying on UNIX-based systems and a small horde of UNIX system gurus (who have always been very difficult to manage!).

All connections to the Internet are done though an ISP (Internet Service Provider). The ISP will become the connection point, and the relationship with the ISP will be much like a marriage—a long-term love/hate relationship in most cases!

Windows NT Server provides the most sophisticated non-UNIX-based solution to connect to the Internet that is available today. As an added bonus, it also beats, hands-down, any UNIX-based solution for ease of configuration and ease of use.

This chapter, though oriented toward readers who are setting up an ISP, is fully applicable to any organization that is using Windows NT 4 Server to connect to the Internet. It will cover details for connecting an NT-based network to the Internet, including the understanding and configuration of such critical services as DNS (Domain Name Server) and DHCP (Dynamic Host Configuration Protocol).

Setting Up as an Internet Service Provider

Windows NT 4 Server makes a logical choice as the platform to use when setting up as an ISP (Internet Service Provider). Both operating system and hardware provide good support, and Windows NT 4 Server is becoming more popular with ISPs. Even if the connection to the Internet is used for users within the organization, all the functionalities of an ISP can and should be implemented.

The solutions outlined in this chapter will work just fine for many Internet connections. If there is a need for larger bandwidths or you are interested in setting up an Internet Access Provider of your own, check out the report titled "Starting an Internet Access Provider," written by Alexander T. Weinert (http://www.databahn.net/library/inet/howto). This report is not nearly as complete as the name suggests, but it does give a very good idea of what is necessary to set up an ISP. There are even a couple of warnings and disclaimers about trying to do so and still have a life, family, and the chance to sleep.

ISPs usually have client users who dial in. The client users may be the general public, or they may be employees of the ISP—as in the case where the ISP is a company seeking to simply expand utilization of expensive Internet communications facilities. Client users are an ISP's customers. Many times, if your company is well run, client users will be loyal, providing a long-term source of income.

IPSs require a permanent connection to the Internet. Most connections are done through SprintLink, MCI, AT&T, Pacific Bell, HLC, other ISPs, or communications companies who offer connectivity services.

A Threat or a Promise?

The ISP business is a growing and changing business! The most common problem that new ISPs have is financial in nature: Rates are low, competition is fierce, and falling behind in customer billing is a sure way to run out of cash—the lifeblood of any business.

As with any business, make sure you have sufficient working capital to carry the business through whatever growth problems you may experience.

Install, and use, a competent accounting system. Billing systems based on flat rates or actual usage are most commonly used. Some ISPs ask for (and usually get) advance payments, especially for their lower-rate or flat-rate fares. Consider EFT (Electronic Funds Transfers) or direct credit card billing as methods to ensure prompt payments from client users. Both your bank and the credit card companies can provide information on these types of billing.

Also, consider obtaining legal advice; contracts with client users should be written to limit the ISP's liability regardless of fault.

Consider insurance ... all kinds of insurance, including liability insurance just in case a customer files a lawsuit against the ISP. Property insurance is also a wise investment.

Many ISPs start as small organizations, many times run from people's homes. Windows NT 4 Server makes an ideal platform for new ISPs. Commonly available low-cost hardware and software and Windows NT 4 Server's ease of configuration are advantages that other systems, UNIX for example, may not offer. Small beginnings shouldn't limit your potential for growth. Many smaller communities may never be reached by the large ISPs (such as MSN, Sprint, or AT&T's WorldNet). A community of 5 to 10 thousand homes can be a viable market for a small ISP. Companies with only a few dozen employees can function well providing Internet access for their employees either for business or personal use.

One justification for setting up your company as an ISP is to help to pay for a high-cost, high-speed, connection to the Internet. For example, if your company needs a T1 line (see "Connecting to a Point of Presence," later in the chapter) and it is only used during business hours, then offering ISP services may substantially increase the usage during evening hours and help pay for the T1 line.

In this type of situation, you can offer greatly reduced rates for those times when your company is not utilizing the full bandwidth of the connection as an incentive to client users—unlimited evening time, for example. Or running your system as a private ISP accessible only by your own employees during off hours (free or at cost, perhaps) may provide an attractive fringe benefit to the employees.

The Windows NT 4 Server must be reliably connected to the Internet. Such a connection must be fast enough to satisfy client user needs. Connecting to the Internet is a two-part process: You must have an Internet site to connect to (called a PoP, or Point of Presence, which is different than POP, which stands for Post Office Protocol), and the physical connection (telephone line, optical cable, or satellite) must be established.

Physical Connections

Most organizations (PoPs) used to connect to the Internet will assist you in negotiating with whatever entity (usually the telephone company) will be providing the physical connection.

Connections to the Internet are measured by speed:

- Dial-up connections allow speeds of up to 33.6 kbps. Although dial-up connections are not useful for connecting a multiuser network to the Internet, they are useful for client users to connect to your site.

- ISDN (Integrated Services Digital Network) allows speeds of 56,000 to 128,000 (56 to 128 kbps). Usable for very small Windows NT 4 Server network sites (isolated, small communities and organizations) and for client user dial in. ISDN may well disappear as newer technology becomes more popular.

- Frame Relay provides rates that are compatible with ISDN, with multiple circuits combined to provide even higher rates.

- T1 speeds are adequate for most small and mid-sized ISPs. T1 supports rates up to 1,500 kbps (roughly 12 to 25 times faster than ISDN), though "fractional" T1 circuits, which operate at slower speeds, may be configured.

- Ethernet, for comparison, offers speeds of 10,000 kbps (10 mbps), which places most networks between T1 and T3 performancewise.

- T3 speeds are adequate for even large networks. Smaller sites will not find the performance of T3 worth the costs. When configuring T3, consider the advantage of having multiple T1 lines to diverse sites—redundancy of connections can be very valuable. T3 speeds are 45,000 kbps.

- FDDI (Fiber Distributed Data Interface) is used only for the very largest networks and organizations. Speeds of 100,000 kbps make these circuits fast, but expensive. Multiple T3 lines can be advantageous where reliability is a factor.

Many smaller organizations start with a leased 56 kbps line, which will support a minimal number of users. An upgrade to T1 is made as soon as the client user load permits.

Incoming lines, connected to modems, connect client users with the Internet. When possible, make sure the lines are available and are in good condition. Be sure you have a firm commitment from the local telephone company before selecting your site; it may be possible that sufficient lines will not be available to your proposed site.

Note: Don't "short plan." Many organizations that offer ISP services quickly grow to hundreds of incoming lines within a few weeks or months. If the telephone company cannot provide the necessary service, your organization will be in trouble! Get commitments from communications, hardware, and software providers in writing!

Connecting to a Point of Presence

You connect your network to a Point of Presence (PoP). Larger organizations will usually try to connect to two different and geographically separate PoPs. That way, if something happens to one connection (such as a communications cable being cut), the other connection will continue to handle the workload.

PoPs range from other ISPs and large communications companies to telephone companies and interstate telephone carriers.

Connecting to Another ISP

The easiest way to get started with your Internet connection is to forge an agreement with an ISP in a neighboring area. Carefully search out ISPs:

- Look for a company that is not too remotely located (remember, costs for high-speed communications lines are based on distance).

- The ISP will become a silent, invisible "partner" in your operations. All your services will eventually be fed through them. If they are unable to provide good service, it will reflect badly on your operation.

- Consider expansion. Make sure that you and your PoP will not be competing for the same markets later. This type of situation may well make a working relationship difficult.

Smaller (and often larger) ISPs are usually eager to find a way to increase their business.

Some hints, which have led to successful ISP startups, include:

- Forge a relationship with a local college and offer to provide services to the college in exchange for assistance in setting up your site and facilities. Then the college becomes your first (and largest) account.

- Form a partnership with an existing ISP in a neighboring town or area. Technology, infrastructure, support, and possibly even hardware can be the benefits of such a relationship.

SprintLink

Sprint offers SprintLink, which provides a number of flexible connections to the Internet. Sprint is probably one of the largest players in the Internet game, and one of the best organized.

For many ISPs, Sprint can offer excellent connectivity: SprintLink has main hubs located in Anaheim, Seattle, Cheyenne, Kansas City, Fort Worth, Atlanta, Washington, DC, Pennsylvania, and Chicago.

In addition to SprintLink's main hubs, there are over 300 other SprintLink PoPs. Each of them can be used by organizations to connect to the Internet.

MCI

MCI Communications states that they are willing to provide support to ISPs up to and including providing equipment that has been configured and tested.

MCI also provides other support, such as assisting in providing Web page creation and router and DNS setup. Like SprintLink, MCI offers a large number of PoPs used by organizations to connect to the Internet.

Other PoPs

Companies offering Internet connectivity include:

- **AT&T WorldNet**—A competitor to both SprintLink and MCI, AT&T is becoming a noted player in the Internet connectivity market.

- **HLC**—HLC.internet is a company that specializes in network connectivity only. HLC.internet is not a long distance carrier and therefore may be more focused on connecting to the Internet.

- **Pacific Bell**—PacBell, serving California, is a "local" telephone company (local phone companies provide local telephone service) that has become a player in the PoP market. Unlike many other local telephone companies, PacBell has boldly moved into advanced communications with an aggressive ISDN program.

There are companies other than those listed above offering connectivity to the Internet. One way to find out which companies are establishing PoPs in your local area is to interview other ISPs in your region.

Multi-homed Systems

Most ISPs try to connect to the Internet through two sites. Referred to as multihoming, this allows some redundancy in the event of communications problems. However connecting to two sites can increase the costs—especially if the communications costs are high.

An extreme in multi-homing exists when the ISP maintains communications that are 100 percent separate; communications to the two (or more) sites that the ISP is connected to leave the ISP's facilities from different locations (such as the front and rear of the building), so that there is no common point or location that could cause a disruption in communications. There is nothing worse than having an errant truck knock down the pole carrying both sets of communications lines! Splitting the dial-in client user access lines this way is also important; if your incoming dial-in lines fail, the effect is the same as if the link to the Internet is lost.

If your site is large enough, consider direct backup satellite communications. Generally thought of as too slow for main communications links, satellite communications can be an effective backup to land-based lines.

Factors that influence whether, and how, you wish to multi-home your system include the distance from the PoP (if the distance is very short, the risks of a catastrophic communications failure are somewhat reduced, as are the potential costs of an outage).

At the present time, many occasional (home users) client users are accustomed to periodic failures and slowness on the Internet. Business users, however, will expect a reliable connection. Well, actually we all are used to a certain amount of slowness and failure in connecting to the Internet: The Internet has grown noticeably slower in the past two years, and continues to slow as heavy growth outstrips the ability of the Internet backbone to carry this increased traffic.

Protocols & Servers

ISPs using Windows NT 4 Server should offer the following protocols:

- **WWW (World Wide Web)**—provides a hypertext, multimedia database to Internet users. Many client users will expect a WWW server to be active at the ISP's server site. Provisions for client users' home pages should be made.

- **FTP (File Transfer Protocol)**—allows Internet users to transfer files between the server and an Internet client.

- **Gopher**—allows users to view information from text documents easily. A somewhat better user interface than FTP, though not as good as WWW.

- **IRC (Internet Relay Chat)**—the "CB radio" of the Internet. Allows interactive textual chat, file, and sound transfers between two or more users.

Other items you'll want to provide your users are:

- **RA (Real Audio)**—allows client users to receive audio in real-time from an RA server.

- **VDOLive (Streaming Video)**—allows client users to receive video from a VDOLive server.

The Microsoft BackOffice products include a number of servers and services that are meant for use by organizations who are connecting to the Internet and offering ISP services, either internally or to external users. These products were described in more detail in the section "What Is Microsoft BackOffice?" in Chapter 1.

News Servers

A news server is a product that allows a user to connect to the ISP's server and retrieve postings from newsgroups. A newsgroup is a collection of messages posted by users, arranged into categories. Client connection software includes: Microsoft's News Reader, Forté's Agent (available in both commercial and freeware versions), and WinVN, a public domain news reader.

Windows NT 4 Server does not include a news server. Aftermarket products, such as NetManage's product or a news server from Net-Shopper, will generally be a satisfactory solution. The freeware version of the NetManage IntraNet Forum Server is a multithreaded, standards-based, NNTP-compliant, fully integrated NT service. (NNTP is Network News Transfer Protocol, used to implement newsgroups.) This server provides an organization with fast access to create and/or participate in newsgroups for public or private use. Using a standards-based NNTP news reader (such as NETNews, provided with NetManage Chameleon), your company can communicate in privately created newsgroup discussions or in any of the 15,000+ established newsgroup discussions in the Internet community.

Telnet Servers

Telnet provides a console interface with the server computer. With Windows NT 4 Server, the console interface is a CMD command prompt.

There is one company, Ataman, with a Telnet server for Windows NT 4 Server. Telnet is very useful for remote administration over the Internet.

When users log on to the system using the Telnet service, they are presented with an interface similar to a CMD prompt. Users are given privileges based on the Windows NT 4 Server userid's specified privileges.

The Ataman TCP Remote Logon Services (ATRLS) provide rlogind, telnetd, and rexecd services for Windows NT. Each remote user executes in their own security context. The ATRLS runs as a Windows NT service—no one needs to be logged on to the console. Rlogind and telnetd services support full-screen console-mode apps.

Mail List Servers

When a message is received for a mail list, a mail list server forwards it to all other members of the list. This way, each member of a specific list will receive copies of every message. Mail list servers typically handle many lists concurrently and automatically handle other tasks, such as administration.

Net-Shopper is another entry into the mail list servers market. Their product is closely related to e-mail products (EMWAC's e-mail server will also provide mail list services).

Net-Shopper's interNeTlist is a list server contained within the SMTP and POST services supplied by NTMail. The trail or full key enables it. The SMTP server will accept messages and redirect them to the list server for processing. Once the list server has processed them, it creates mail messages that are automatically treated as lower-priority mail.

SMTP/POP3 Services

Although Microsoft Exchange Server offers many of the mail services an organization needs, it doesn't support POP-3 protocol.

Since an ISP will have clients who are not using Microsoft Exchange for e-mail, it is necessary to have a POP-3-compatible e-mail server. Fortunately there are several choices for e-mail products for ISPs running under Windows NT 4 Server, such as NetManage's JetMail, and EMWAC Internet Mail Services.

NetManage's JetMail Server is an Internet standards-based electronic mail server for ISPs. Simple to set up and configure, JetMail is a quick and inexpensive e-mail server. JetMail is available for both Windows 95 and Windows NT platforms.

EMWAC offers e-mail servers for Windows NT 4 Server:

- **Freeware EMWAC Internet Mail Services**—Internet mail (SMTP/POP-3) is necessary for all ISPs. It is only possible to use Exchange if the client users are all using it, something that public ISPs cannot be assured of.

- **EMAIL**—The EMWAC Internet Mail Services for Windows NT (known as IMS) are a suite of server programs that allow you to use Windows NT as a mail server for Internet mail. The EMWAC IMS requires an NTFS partition and Windows NT 3.51 or higher. With IMS, your Windows NT machine can receive messages from the Internet, put them in individual users' incoming mailboxes, accept outgoing mail from users, and relay that mail to its destination anywhere on the Internet. It supports mail aliases and can also run (optionally moderated) mailing lists.

Ipswitch offers a number of products, including an e-mail server that is very interesting.

IMail Server for Windows NT is a high-performance SMTP/POP-3 e-mail server that will help you manage your Internet and corporate intranet electronic mail—efficiently and economically. Easy to administer through a simple, intuitive graphical user interface, it offers businesses an attractive alternative to more complex, higher-priced UNIX-based systems. Easy-to-use features improve productivity, and unlike other Internet mail products, IMail Server for Windows NT is nonproprietary.

As the foundation of an integrated family of Internet server software products, IMail Server for Windows NT is available for a range of scalable, price/performance platforms that include Intel, DEC/Alpha, and PowerPC. It can be used with Ipswitch's IMail Client for Windows or any other POP-3 mail client, giving you complete flexibility in setting up a total mail solution that incorporates disparate mail clients.

Finger Services

Fingers? Keep your fingers off of my computer. No, not that kind of finger service! A finger server returns information about all users on the server (or a specific user) to the client.

EMWAC's Freeware Finger Server is a finger server that will provide basic finger capabilities. Though all Internet sites do not support finger, it can be a useful service. Since the Freeware Finger Server is easy to obtain, install, and configure, running a finger server is not difficult.

Other Interesting Products

There are a number of sources for products that should be very interesting to Windows NT 4 Server-based ISPs.

WAIS Servers   EMWAC offers a freeware WAIS server. A WAIS (Wide Area Information Servers) allows users to query indexes of distributed databases and retrieve data. Windows NT's Resource Kit included a WAIS server, and when Microsoft releases the Resource Kit for Windows NT 4 Server, a WAIS server should be included.

EMWAC also offers the WAIS Toolkit based on freeWAIS 0.3 to assist in configuring and setting up freeWAIS 0.3 (the freeware WAIS server).

Time & Scheduling   Extreme Software offers a product that can be used effectively by Windows NT 4 Server-based ISPs. This product, ntcrond, is a powerful replacement for the Windows NT AT command. Extreme Software's Internet site is www.dfw.net/~gparsons.

The ntcrond command is a Windows NT service that emulates the UNIX crond command-scheduling utility. UNIX's crond was developed by AT&T and Hewlett Packard for UNIX. With ntcrond, Windows NT users may schedule the execution of commands at specified dates and times.

Accounting & Billing   Not a Windows NT 4 Server issue, but critical to your success as an ISP is that you are able to bill your client users promptly and accurately.

Windows NT 4 Server, in the event log, maintains logon information that can be extracted to provide information about usage by client users. Extracting this information might be difficult were it not for a product called Crystal Reports (version 4.5 or later), which will allow you to create reports based on the event log.

Creative usage of Crystal Reports can result in a system that actually prints out detailed invoices for your client users. Or Crystal Reports can simply summarize the data and write a report to the disk, which might then be used by an accounting program to generate invoices.

Client or User Connectivity

Hardware is one of the more critical issues when working with PC-compatible microcomputers. The PC has always been limited when it comes to communications (IBM's original thoughts were that no one would ever need more than two serial ports), and if we are to use a Windows NT 4 Server PC-based system as an ISP, we must be able to connect modems, lots of modems, to the server.

I/O Boards

Question: How do I connect a hundred modems to Windows NT 4 Server? Answer: Digiboards . . . Lots of 'em! Well, many of us would ask, "What's a Digiboard?"

Most microcomputers come equipped with two to four serial ports. For a single-user system, four serial ports are usually sufficient. However, if you are running a PC-compatible system (with ISA, PCI, MC, or EISA bus configurations) you can add up to 255 serial ports to your server by using a product such as the Digiboard.

Digi's multiserial port products are typically configured as either 4, 8, or 16 serial ports. Speeds may be set from 50 bps to 56 kbps, and many models contain internal buffering and communications management. The use of onboard processing allows these products to only minimally load the server. All I/O to the serial ports is done using drivers provided by Digi, providing a seamless interface with Windows NT 4 Server.

More information on Digi's products can be obtained from their Web site at http://www.dgii.com.

Modems & Connection Lines

Considering just how few choices there are for I/O boards, there are many choices for modems. Among the selections are rack mount modems and standard commercial modems such as the Practical Peripherals PM288MT modem (because it's small, this modem can be stacked for good density); modems from virtually every modem manufacturer are basically acceptable. Also check the section, above, called "Physical Connections."

Despite what we may think, selecting higher-priced, commercial quality modems may not be cost effective. Modem technology continues to change quickly, and modems must be replaced frequently, not because they fail, but because they don't offer features demanded by users. Reliability is seldom a problem; even inexpensive modems, once working, seem to be as reliable as their more expensive cousins.

Note: Modem technology has taken another step when at least one manufacturer announced a new technology that will, under certain conditions, allow performance faster than the current maximum of about 38K. By next year, who knows what speeds will be available to dial-up modem users!

With modems you must have a plan to test and ensure that they are working correctly. Generally, a telephone hunt group (which allows client users to dial a single number and be connected to any of a number of different phone lines) will start at a predefined line and search in order until a line that is currently unused is found. This means that the first modems and lines will see more usage than the last ones.

Gateways & Proxy Servers

A gateway is a hardware and/or software product connecting two networks. For example, gateways connect parts of the Internet together.

As a network connected to the Internet, you use a product such as Microsoft Proxy Server to connect your client users with the Internet.

Using Microsoft Proxy Server, your network is isolated from users, yet users are able to, transparently, interact with the Internet.

For more information on Proxy Servers, refer to Section IV, "Microsoft Proxy Server."

Overview of TCP/IP

The TCP/IP protocol suite was developed by the Department of Defense to connect the various incompatible networks that were being used by government agencies. TCP/IP is named after TCP and IP, which are two of the major protocols in the suite. In fact, TCP is a more involved and sophisticated protocol running on top of the IP protocol. TCP stands for Transmission Control Protocol and IP stands for Internet Protocol.

TCP/IP comprises a collection of protocols that were designed to send *packets* of data over the Internet (actually, it was ARPANET at the time TCP/IP was designed). The packets are blocks of data composed of the actual data itself as well as a header that contains addressing information for delivery of the data. The packets are referred to as *datagrams*. The datagram format is defined by the IP protocol.

The IP protocol provides the most basic level of data delivery available. More advanced protocols are built on top of the IP protocol for both general data transfer and special purpose services. The most significant of the special purpose protocols are ICMP, ARP, RIP, and DNS. The two general purpose protocols are TCP and UPD.

IP protocol assigns an address (a 32-bit value, which is subdivided into four 8-bit octets). Each item on the network is assigned a unique IP address.

Domain names are used to provide a more user friendly interface between users and IP addresses. It would be difficult to remember that 199.127.78.23 is the address for my Windows NT Server; however, it is much more easy to remember my domain name: darkstar.mv.com.

ICMP (Internet Control Message Protocol)

ICMP is actually not built on top of but is part of IP. ICMP is responsible for flow control, error reporting, and checking the status of remote hosts. Flow control, in this case, is similar to flow control mechanisms built into asynchronous serial communications. To accomplish this function, IP sends an ICMP Source Quench Message back to the sender when data is arriving too fast to process.

The error reporting functions of IP center around informing the sender that a destination is unreachable or that a particular route is not optimal.

The most visible function of ICMP is the Echo service on which the PING utility is based. This function works by automatically echoing any transmitted data back to the sender.

ARP (Address Resolution Protocol)

The address resolution protocol (ARP) is responsible for the translation of the physical network. The function of this protocol is discussed in greater detail in the section "Understanding IP Addresses" later in the chapter.

RIP (Routing Information Protocol)

The most basic type of routing is done by setting up static routing tables that define the gateway or router to which to send data packets. The Routing Information Protocol updates these tables dynamically based on information sent by systems configured to send route updates. RIP automatically updates routing tables to follow the optimal routes.

DNS (Domain Name Server)

DNS is responsible for translating host and domain names to IP addresses. Due to the sheer size of the Internet, DNS is designed to be a distributed database system where each portion of the database is managed by discrete name servers. Typically, each workstation on a network that is running TCP/IP is configured to use a specific name server to resolve network addresses. If the server that is queried to resolve a name to an address does not have the information available, it will query another server that is authoritative for the name in question.

UDP (User Datagram Protocol)

UDP (User Datagram Protocol), along with TCP, is one of the general transmission protocols providing a very specific delivery service. Its basic design goal is to deliver data packets as quickly and with as little overhead as possible. The significance of this fact is that UDP does not provide for any guarantee of packet delivery. The packet is sent and it may or may not arrive at its destination.

TCP (Transmission Control Protocol)

TCP is a bidirectional connection-oriented protocol that guarantees reliable data delivery. To accomplish its guarantee of data delivery, TCP will resend the data repeatedly until the destination sends an acknowledgment message. Because of the extreme amount of data verification and receipt acknowledgment that is exchanged when data is transmitted, this protocol trades off efficiency for reliability.

Managing IP Addresses

IP addresses are used to identify each machine on a TCP/IP network. Typically, TCP/IP networks are subdivided into smaller subnetworks to make their management easier. Subnet masks are used to allow a router to determine whether a specific IP address will be found in a certain subnetwork.

Understanding IP Addresses

Every machine that uses TCP/IP and is connected to the Internet must use an address. This address has no relation to the physical network address built into the network card. IP addresses are 4-byte values that are traditionally displayed as four decimal numbers separated by periods.

Part of each address represents the network on which a host computer is located and the remainder represents the address of the computer on that network. The addressing scheme for IP was carefully designed to be hardware independent. If you look at the snapshot screen (Figure 8-1) from the WinIPCfg application that is provided with Windows 95, you will see an entry for an adapter address (44-45-53-54-00-00) and an entry for the IP address (199.125.78.23).

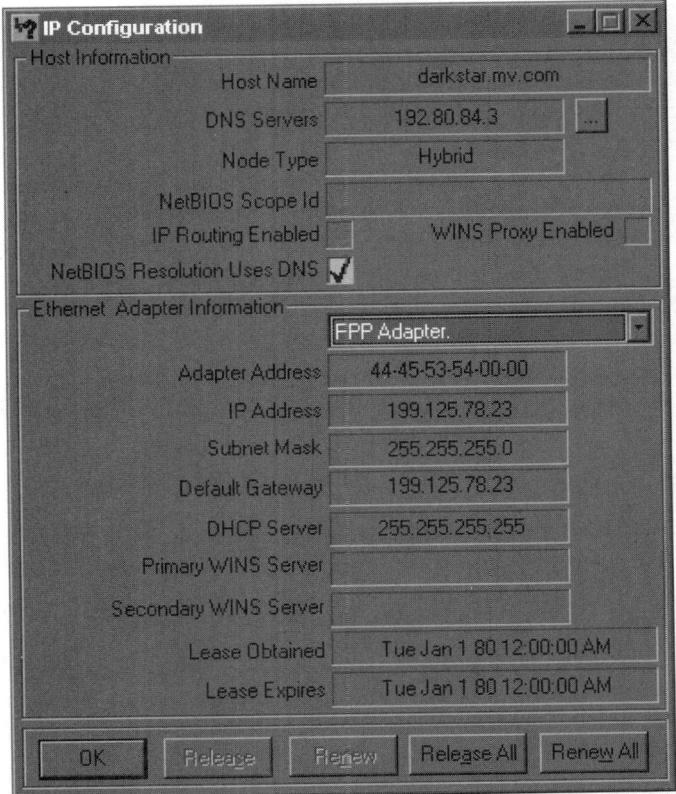

Figure 8-1: WinIPCfg's IP Configuration dialog showing the Adapter Address.

Note: The adapter address (44-45-53-54-00-00) is for the dial-up networking adapter, not the NIC installed in the computer. Usually, the adapter address is the same for all dial-up networking adapters.

The adapter address corresponds to the physical network transports address and is different than the IP address. Physical addresses are completely dependent on the type of network you have configured. If you have an Ethernet-based network, then for one computer to talk to another computer on that network, it must know the physical address of the second computer.

Of course, there is also the ability to broadcast a message from one computer to all computers on the local network, but this tends to clog up the network and any protocol that relies heavily on broadcasting will have problems scaling to support a larger number of workstations on the network.

How do two computers talk to each other on a TCP/IP-based network? Well, the originating computer must somehow obtain the IP address of the computer with which it needs to communicate. This is normally done by using a DNS server to translate a host name into an IP address, but more on that later. Once it has the IP address, it still needs to do some extra work to be able to communicate directly with the receiving computer. We already know that it is necessary to obtain the physical network address of a computer to send a direct message.

TCP/IP handles through the ARP protocol by broadcasting a request to the entire local area network to determine the computer that is associated with that IP address. The appropriate computer responds with a message acknowledging ownership of the IP address and sends the physical network address along as well. This IP-to-network address pair is entered into a table on the original computer so that the next time it needs to talk to that computer, it does not have to broadcast a general request for IP address ownership.

All of the workstations on an IP network will quickly build a table corresponding to the core servers on the local area network, and packet flow from that point on happens in an extremely efficient point-to-point manner.

Before we get into the discussion of IP addresses, I want to address one more topic. What about computers that are not on the local area network? Obviously, broadcasting a message to these computers will simply not work. At least I hope it should be obvious. A worldwide broadcast would be a little tough, right? So when you want to send a message to another computer that is not in your local network, what happens?

Note: IP addresses consist of a 32-bit value, expressed as four 8-bit bytes. All IP addresses are written in a unique format called doted decimal notation: w.x.y.z, where w is the first byte, and z is the last byte in the IP address.

Let's start by assuming we have an IP address for that remote computer. In the previous example, we simply broadcasted a message asking for the guilty computer to respond. Actually, I left out a step. Before the broadcast, the IP address was examined to determine whether it was on the local network at all. This was done by using the subnet mask to compare the source and destination computer's IP address. I will explain the details to you in the next section, but I assure you this is easily done. It is 255.255.255.0 or three 255s followed by a zero. The IP address for the computer, 199.125.78.23, is similar in structure but is not as repetitive.

The purpose of the subnet mask is to define which part of the IP address is used to identify the network to which the computer is connected. Each field or position in the subnet mask that has a 255 corresponds to a field that identifies the network IP address. The part of the subnet mask that contains a 0 corresponds to the computer's address on that network. So if we take the two addresses and only compare the parts of the address that correspond to 255s in the subnet mask, we know that the computers will be on the same network if those numbers match. Right?

One more example: The address for my computer is 199.125.78.23, and the address for a computer I want to communicate with is 207.196.34.8. Because of the subnet mask, I can compare the two network addresses to see if the second computer is local as follows:

IP Addresses	199.125. 78. 23	207.196. 34. 8
Subnet Mask	255.255.255. 0	255.255.255. 0
Network Address	199.125. 78. 23	207.196. 34

Since the network addresses of the two computers still don't match, TCP/IP knows that these two computers can't communicate directly. The default gateway is the place that all IP packets that can't be sent directly are sent to insure delivery. In other words, the default gateway routes IP packets to and from computers on the local network to computers elsewhere on the Internet.

Since Internet addresses are globally unique and there are only a limited number of addresses available to allocate, the address domain for the Internet was divided into Classes A, B, and C. Each class contains a certain number of computers that it will support, with a Class A network address supporting the largest number of host computers and a Class C supporting only 255. Table 8-1 lists the address classes and also shows the subnet masks that are used with each.

Value of the First Byte of the IP Address	Subnet Mask	Number of Host Addresses	Description
1 to 128	255.0.0.0	16,581,375	Class A addresses
128 to 191	255.255.0.0	65,025	Class B addresses
192 to 223	255.255.255.0	255	Class C addresses
127.0.0.1	N/A	1	Local loopback address
127.0.0.0	N/A	1	Address of local network

Table 8-1: IP network address classes and special cases.

All of new addresses issued are Class C addresses. In fact, even if you need more than 255 host addresses, you will have to apply for multiple Class C addresses.

Just as an aside, even though the number of available addresses seems large, the addresses are still nearly depleted and have caused a quiet crisis on the Internet. Keep your eye out in the next few years for some changes to be made to the addressing scheme.

Understanding the Subnet Mask

A subnet mask is used by the IP protocol to determine whether an IP address exists on the local network or not. Any TCP/IP packets destined for IP addresses that are not on the local network must be forwarded to the gateway to be routed to their destination.

To determine whether an IP address is on the local network, the subnet mask is bitwise ANDed with the IP address of the local computer (the computer which originated the packet). The subnet mask is also ANDed with the destination IP address. The results of these two operations are compared, and if they are equal, then the IP address is found on the local network.

If the address is local, then a direct connection is made to that address. If the address is not local, the packet will be routed to the default gateway, which will in turn route the packet to the destination address.

This is not as complicated as it may sound. For Class C addresses, the most common subnet mask is 255.255.255.0, as shown in Table 8-1. With a subnet mask of 255.255.255.0, the first 3 bytes of the address are used for the comparison. The last byte of the IP address is the local portion (called the host part).

The question at this point is, if you just use 255.255.255.0 and get on with it, why all the fuss? Well, because even if you don't ever use it, there is a little more to the subnet mask than meets the eye.

The subnet mask is really used to specify which part of an address specifies the network (the part of the network that is external) and which part specifies the host (the local part of the network) address. When you get a Class C address, you are being handed the entire first 3 bytes of the address: the network part of the IP address. These 3 bytes are all that the rest of the Internet knows about your network. With a standard subnet mask of 255.255.255.0, the local part of the network has the potential to have up to 254 valid addresses.

Maybe there is a need to subdivide the network into more than one part. For example, perhaps the site consists of two buildings, each of which is connected to a different Ethernet network, joined with the Windows NT 4 Server. Let's call these two buildings the East Building, and the West Building. Each of the two halves of the network (you could divide the network into two, six, or even more smaller parts; more on that a bit later) would be separate, except for the connection through the Windows NT 4 Server.

Each part of the newly divided network would then have to have its own subnet mask. Now, there is nothing stopping you from creating a subnet from a Class C address (which, if not split has 254 addresses). You do so by specifying a different subnet mask than the by now boring 255.255.255.0.

Things can get a little involved at this point, but stay with me; this is a bit important. Ignore the 3 bytes of the Internet part of the Class C address for now. Instead, the final byte is being split into a new network component and a new host component, and we are only going to consider this final byte.

A bit of background helps here: Some IP addresses are not valid because they're being used for special purposes. For example, an address (either host or network) consisting of all 0s specifies the local host or the network and not a specific computer on the network. As well, an address may not be all 1s, as this address specifies a broadcast message. So, for a standard Class C address, there are really only 254 usable addresses: w.x.y.0 and w.x.y.255 are not usable.

Now, let's assume that there is one Class C address that must be subdivided into two subnetworks: one for the East Building, and one for the West Building.

To do this, we use bits in the last byte of the subnet mask to further subdivide our network. The most optimum mask for our needs would seem to be to use 1 bit, 255.255.255.128 (which would, in theory, split our address space into two equal pieces) if it weren't for one problem: This would create an invalid network subnet! Why? Because, remember above where it was pointed out that an address that was all 0s or all 1s was invalid . . . OK, do you see it? One bit would only allow either a 1 or a 0, neither of which would be valid!

Okay, let's review: An IP address is divided into two parts: the network part, and the host part. The network part of the IP address is always a set of contiguous bits on the left side of the address, while the host part of an IP address is the remaining bits on the right side of the IP address. A Class C address has 3 bytes (24 bits) for the network part, and 1 byte (8 bits) for the host part.

The subnet mask determines where the division between the host part of the IP address and the network part of the IP address is. To split a Class C address into two subnetworks, it is necessary to use a subnet mask of 255.255.255.192 (which has 2 bits to specify the network component of the address)! Looking at that subnet mask in binary format makes this more clear:

```
255        .255      .255      .192
1111 1111.1111 1111.1111 1111.1100 0000
```

In the example above, we can see that we need to add 2 bits on the right end of the network part of the IP address, taking away 2 bits from the left end of the host part of the IP address. We need 2 bits, because 1 bit would not allow us to have a non-all-0s, non-all-1s address. The decimal value for the binary number 1100 0000 is 192. To make this a bit simpler, Table 8-2 lists valid values for a subnet. These values can be used in any field of the subnet mask, though they are typically only used in the last byte position as currently only Class C addresses are being assigned.

Because a host address may not be all *0*s or all *1*s, each of the possible network options is missing a small block of addresses at the beginning and end of the range of addresses. If you examine Table 8-2, you will see that depending on the subnet mask you use, you get various trade-offs between the number of subnets you can create and the number of valid addresses per subnet.

The custom subnet address that provides the most bang for your buck in terms of address retention is 255.255.255.240 at 196. The problem is that this subnet configuration requires you to create 14 subnets with 14 addresses per subnet. This is not going to help us with our example situation at all where we wanted to create 2 subnets, each of which needed to have as many host addresses as possible. Even though we lost more than half of our addresses, the subnet mask that makes the most sense in this situation is 255.255.255.192. This gives us 2 subnets with 62 addresses each. Figure 8-2 shows the subnet addresses for each segment of the network and also shows the addresses for each workstation.

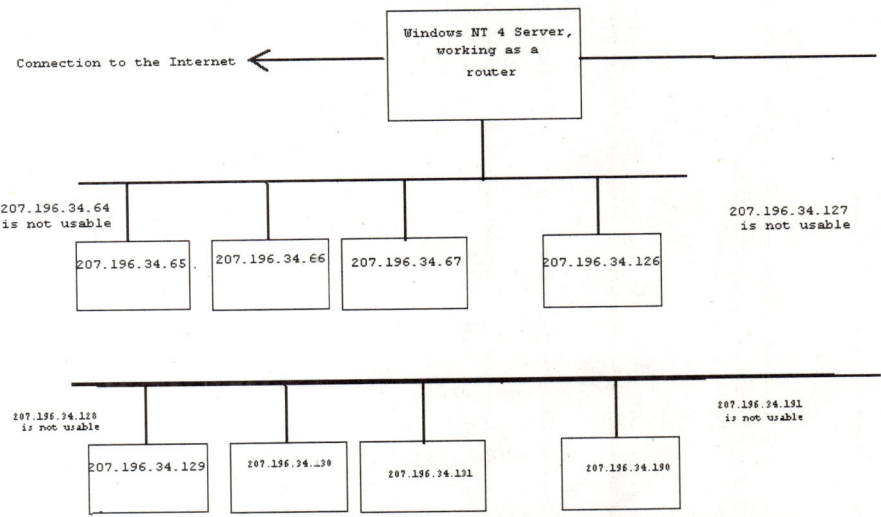

Figure 8-2: A Class C address divided equally between two subnetworks.

Subnet Mask	Subnet Description	Subnet Addresses	Total Addresses Available
255.255.255.0	1 subnet 254 addresses	x.y.z.0	254
255.255.255.128	illegal subnet	*	*
255.255.255.192	2 subnets 62 addresses each	x.y.z.64 x.y.z.128	124
255.255.255.224	6 subnets 30 addresses each	x.y.z.32 x.y.z.64 x.y.z.96 x.y.z.128 x.y.z.160 x.y.z.192	180
255.255.255.240	14 subnets 14 addresses each	x.y.z.16 x.y.z.32 x.y.z.48 x.y.z.64 x.y.z.80 x.y.z.96 x.y.z.112 x.y.z.128 x.y.z.144 x.y.z.160 x.y.z.176 x.y.z.192 x.y.z.208 x.y.z.224	196
255.255.255.248	30 subnets 6 addresses each	x.y.z.8 x.y.z.16 x.y.z.24 x.y.z.32, etc.	180
255.255.255.252	62 subnets 2 addresses each	x.y.z.4 x.y.z.8 x.y.z.12 x.y.z.16, etc.	124

Table 8-2: Possible subnet masks for Class C addresses.

So how is Table 8-2 used to create subnets with a Class C address? First, determine how many subnets are wanted and how many computers are to be on each subnet. Use the Subnet Description column and the Total Addresses Available column to determine the best use of your network IP address. Once you have determined the table entry that works for your situation, use the Subnet Mask column to determine the subnet mask to use for your subnets. Next, look at the Subnet Addresses column to determine the address range for each of your subnets.

Continuing with the example above, choose a subnet mask of 255.255.255.192. This gives 2 subnetworks with 62 addresses (hosts) each. According to the Subnet Address column of the table, the network addresses for this subnet mask are 64 and 128. (Addresses 0 and 255 are both invalid; they contain either all 0s or all 1s.) This leaves 2 usable subnets, each having 64 minus 2 (the 0 and all 1s addresses cannot be used), giving 62 addresses in total.

The first subnet address range is 207.196.34.65 (and not 207.196.34.64) to 207.196.34.126 (and not 207.196.34.127), and the next address range is 207.196.34.129 to 207.196.34.190. Take another look at Figure 8-2.

Tip

Remember: Host addresses that are all 0s are the address for the network itself and cannot be used as a host address.

Host addresses that are all 1s are addresses for broadcast messages to all hosts on the network and cannot be used for an individual host.

As another quick example, look at the final row in Table 8-2. The subnet mask 255.255.255.252 allows 62 subnets of 2 addresses each. Looking at each host address in the first subnet, we see we have addresses ending in binary 00, 01, 10, and 11. These addresses represent the 4 possible combinations of the 2 host bits in the IP address. However, since a host address may not be all 0s (00) or all 1s (11), only 2 values constitute valid IP addresses: 01 and 10.

Obtaining IP Addresses

There is good news and bad news. First the bad news: You absolutely must understand the addressing scheme used by TCP/IP. It is absolutely critical that you understand the subtleties of IP addresses if you are attempting to connect a LAN to the Internet and expect to have things work right. Now for the good news: It is not nearly as complicated as it seems and after the initial leap of understanding is an easy and robust protocol to manage.

Remember that IP addresses have to be fixed and global. This means that there must be a global addressing scheme where all addresses are unique and also implies that there is someone who maintains and allocates Internet addresses. To insure that these addresses are indeed globally unique, all addresses are allocated by a group called the InterNIC.

To receive an InterNIC address, you should contact your service provider. Most will apply for the address for you, but you may have occasion to apply for a new domain address or modify your existing address in some way. To find out how to apply for a domain address, you can contact the InterNIC at the following URL:

```
http://www.internic.net/
```

As a network connected to the Internet, you will have a group of IP addresses (usually a Class C, or a partial Class C address), which you will then assign to your client users.

IP addresses are assigned statically or dynamically. All client software used to connect with ISPs (such as Windows 95 and Windows NT's DUN) can handle dynamic IP address allocations.

Using a system such as Microsoft Proxy Server (Catapult) allows you to isolate your client user's IP address from the Internet. This allows your ISP site to exist with a minimum number of assigned IP addresses—which makes management of the system much easier.

IP Spoofing

IP Spoofing . . . My first comment, when I first encountered the term *IP Spoofing* was "What the heck is this?" Actually IP Spoofing is one of the more interesting things to be produced!

Note: IP Spoofing is also used to break into computer systems on the Internet. With it, the attackers can remain relatively anonymous; the IP address they are using will not be properly reported to anyone attempting to monitor their activity.

Earlier in this book, I commented on the shortage of IP addresses. As a result of the shortage, it can be difficult to obtain IP addresses to support an ISP's operations. Using IP Spoofing, you can circumvent this problem. With only one IP address, you can offer Internet connectivity to an almost unlimited number of client users!

With IP Spoofing, your server will have one IP address on the Internet. All your users, however, will have local, private IP addresses, which will not appear directly on the Internet; instead, all communications between your users and the Internet will be routed through Microsoft Proxy Server. Microsoft Proxy Server will receive requests from users and forward them to the recipient on the Internet. Prior to forwarding the requests, however, Microsoft Proxy Server will change the IP address from the client's local, private IP address to the server's IP address. When information is received from the Internet, Microsoft Proxy Server will determine which user this information is intended for and forward the information to the correct user.

IP Spoofing allows the server to have a single IP address on the Internet, while each and every user on the network (whether dial-up or directly connected) will seem to have their own IP address. A basic win/win situation: The Internet wins, because only one IP address is allocated to your site; the user wins, as they are actually isolated behind your router and impervious to any security risks from the Internet; and you win, because you don't have to obtain separate IP addresses for each active client.

Using Proxy Server

The Microsoft Proxy Server (Catapult) gives you the easiest way to provide fast and secure Internet access to both dial-in and directly connected users. Its ability to manage IP addresses and security make the Microsoft Proxy Server very interesting. Microsoft Proxy Server is covered in Section IV, "Microsoft Proxy Server."

A proxy server provides a security barrier (firewall) between your internal network and the Internet. This prevents other Internet sites from accessing information on your internal network.

With a proxy server working like a firewall, no other user on the Internet is able to access any computers (client users) on your side of the proxy server, while at the same time you can pass legitimate information freely between the Internet and client users.

Windows NT 4 Server users may use WINS to implement a proxy server or simply use the Microsoft Proxy Server, described above.

Microsoft Proxy Server provides these benefits:

■ Access control managed by user, service, port, and Internet domain, for both inbound and outbound connections.

■ Compatibility with most Internet protocols and Windows Sockets-based applications. On your Windows NT 4 Server, you can use both IPX/SPX and TCP/IP.

■ Designed to be used with Windows NT 4 Server. It is easily installed, with excellent linkages with Windows NT 4 Server's security, networking, and user interface.

■ Fast, makes only small demands on the system, and users will not notice that they are isolated from the Internet.

■ Security, preventing any access from external sources to your own private network. It also isolates the client user from the Internet.

■ Support for data encryption using Secure Sockets Layer (SSL) tunneling.

As a released product, Microsoft Proxy Server is included with various versions of Microsoft BackOffice and as a separate product.

Using DHCP

DHCP (Dynamic Host Configuration Protocol) is used to manage assignment of addresses and other configuration information to workstations on a network that is using IP protocol. When a network is running a DHCP server, any workstation configured to use DHCP will request the server to allocate an IP address and to supply the other basic configuration information required by TCP/IP. This can include the default gateway, DNS servers, WINS configuration, and so on.

To use DHCP, you must first install the DHCP service and run the DHCP Manager (see Figure 8-3) to configure the service.

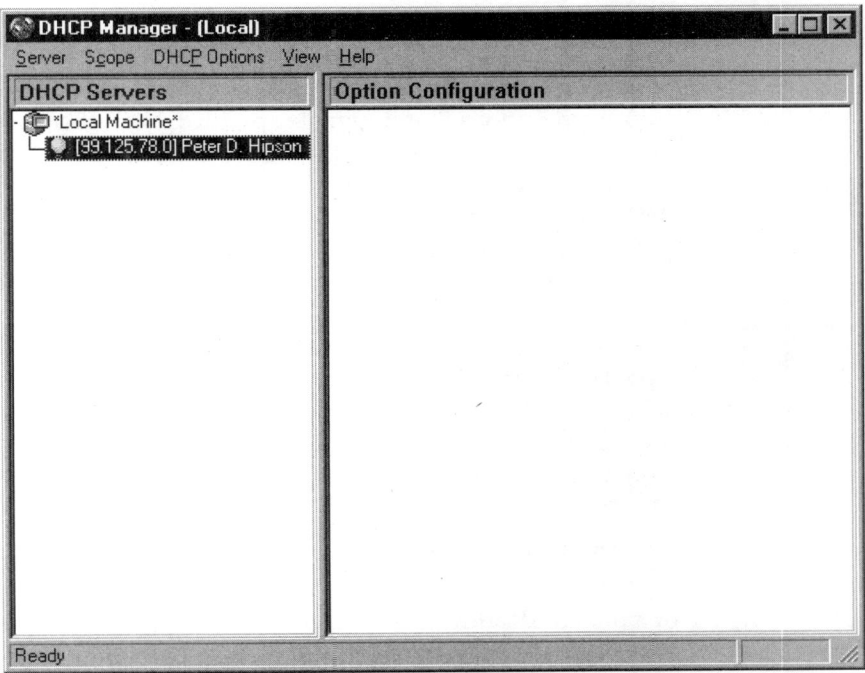

Figure 8-3: The DHCP Manager managing a local DHCP server.

The DHCP service is installed using the Control Panel's Network applet. To install the DHCP service, follow these steps:

1. Start the Control Panel's Network applet by opening the Control Panel and double-clicking the Network icon.

2. Select the Services tab.

3. Click the Add button. The Select Network Service dialog box appears.

4. Select Microsoft DHCP Server from the Network Service list and click the OK button.

If you are not using TCP/IP protocol, there is little need to consider installing, configuring, or tuning this service. DHCP allows allocation of IP addresses from a pool of addresses. This functionality is usually reserved for when users connect and disconnect frequently from the network, such as when establishing an ISP. Installing unneeded network components can create problems, as each protocol consumes system resources, including network bandwidth.

DHCP Scopes

After installing DHCP you will need to create and activate DHCP scopes. A DHCP scope is simply a range of IP addresses that also have some associated options that designate specific DHCP client-configuration information. For example, let's use the Class C address of 207.198.123.0 and configure a DHCP server that will be used for the workstations on this network. The first step is to set up and configure all of the servers with static IP addresses. It is necessary that the IP addresses for the servers remain constant. Let's reserve the first 15 addresses of our Class C for servers only.

Using the remaining addresses, we create a DHCP server that creates a pool of addresses, called a scope, that ranges from 207.198.123.16 to 207.198.123.254. If necessary, ranges of addresses may be excluded from the scope's range. (This allows reserving specific IP addresses for fixed assignment.)

Creating a DHCP Scope

DHCP scopes must be created for DHCP to work. DHCP scopes consist of a pool of IP addresses that DHCP is then able to assign to client users.

1. Launch DHCP Manager using Start Menu | Programs | Administrative Tools (Common) | DHCP Manager.

2. Select the desired DHCP server. In Figure 8-3, there is only one server, marked as *Local Machine*.

3. Select Scope | Create in the DHCP Manager's menu. The Create Scope dialog box (Figure 8-4) will be displayed.

4. Fill in the Start Address and End Address fields for the IP address pool. Also fill in the Subnet Mask field. (A Class C subnet mask would be 255.255.255.0; see the description of subnet masks in "Understanding the Subnet Mask" earlier in the chapter.)

5. If there are any addresses to exclude from that range (addresses that will be assigned permanently to a computer on the network), enter the excluded addresses in the Exclusion Range fields and click the Add button.

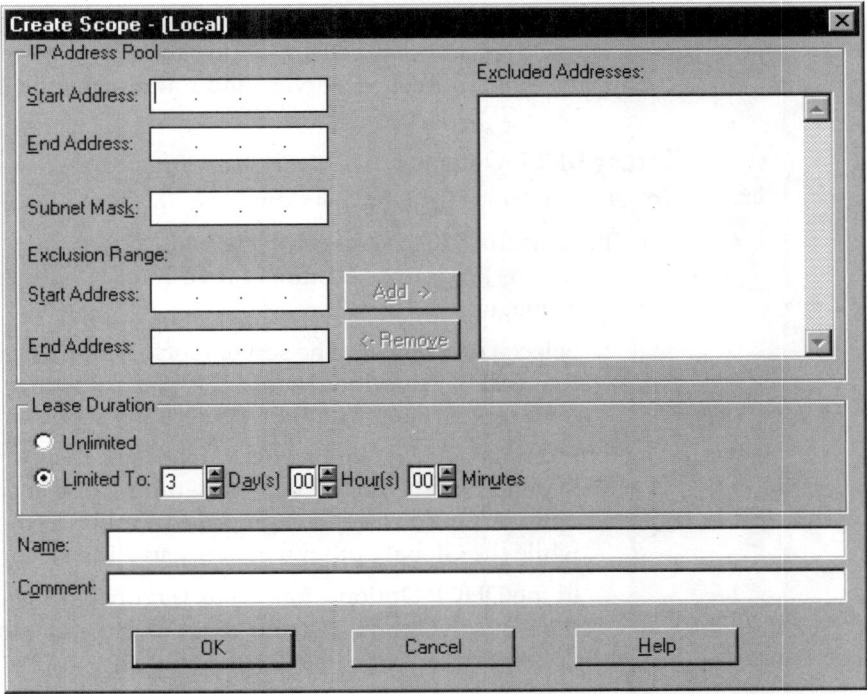

Figure 8-4: The Create Scope (Local) dialog box—fill in address, subnet, and any exclusion ranges.

6. Select the desired lease duration. With DHCP, you can have an address that expires after a specific period of time, requiring the workstation to renew its lease after that point. This has certain security benefits as a feature. The unlimited lease option will not require a renewal.

7. In the Name and Comment text boxes near the bottom of the dialog box, enter a name for the scope along with a comment. The scope's name will be displayed in the DHCP Manager's main window once the scope has been created.

8. Click OK when you are done creating the scope.

Once the scope is created, the DHCP Manager will prompt to activate the scope. Use the Activate and Deactivate options under the Scope menu to enable and disable scopes as appropriate.

Now that a scope has been created, you need to specify the options to associate with it. Although DHCP allows for a huge selection of options, the typical options are DNS servers and routers (default gateway).

Setting DHCP Options

To set any options for DHCP follow these steps:

1. Launch DHCP Manager using Start Menu | Programs | Administrative Tools (Common) | DHCP Manager.

2. Select a scope under the server (such as the *Local Machine*) that will have options set for it. If you are setting global options for a server (Global Options), select any scope in the server.

3. From the DHCP Options menu, choose either Scope or Global, depending on whether you are setting scope-specific or global options. Options set for a scope are applied to the scope only, while the Global option will apply to all scopes in the server.

4. In the DHCP Options dialog box (Figure 8-5), select options from the Unused Options list and click Add to make the selected option active.

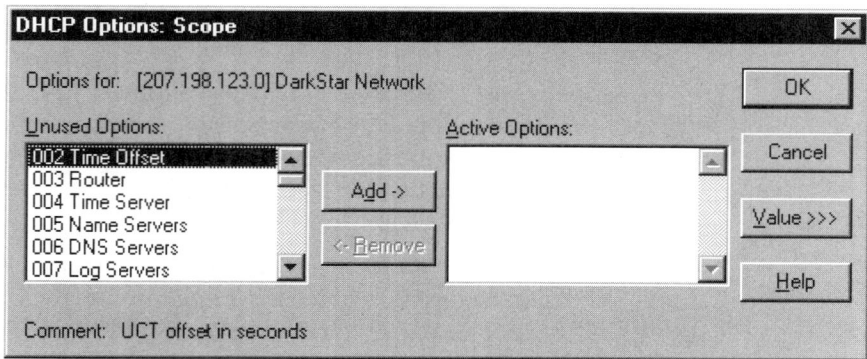

Figure 8-5: The DHCP Options: Scope dialog box.

5. After activating the desired options, click the Value button and enter the appropriate values for each selected option.

6. When you are done setting options, click the OK button to save any changes.

Once you have DHCP up and running, you should have a much easier time of managing the TCP/IP configuration for workstations on the local network.

Managing Domain Names

Domain names establish our identity on the Internet. InterNIC maintains a Web site at http://www.internic.net/. There is generally a one-to-one relationship between a domain name and an IP address. In some cases, however, more than one domain name will resolve to a single IP address. For a few of the busiest sites on the Internet, a single domain name will resolve to a number of different IP addresses—this is done to share the load between multiple servers.

When working with networks that are connected to the Internet, the host names and local IP addresses must be coordinated with the Internet address governing body, InterNIC. For local networks, the hosts file may be used to resolve names without having to use a DNS. For most networks, however, a DNS (Domain Name Server) must be used to resolve domain names to IP addresses.

Understanding Domain Names

On the Internet, computers usually have a name that is more people friendly than an IP address. The DNS is the TCP/IP service that allows a workstation to refer to other computers on the network using their names, such as www.microsoft.com. Each segment of the name is separated by periods, with the first segment of the name specifying the name of the computer and the rest of the name referring to the domain to which the computer is connected. The last segment of the name is the top-level domain to which all other domains belong. The key top-level domains are listed in Table 8-3.

Name	Description
.com	Commercial organizations
.net	Networks
.edu	Educational organizations, post secondary
.gov	Federal government organizations (levels of government lower than the federal level must use their geographical name)
.org	Noncommercial organizations
.mil	Military organizations
.countrycode	A code for a country, such as .US for the United States

Table 8-3: Top-level domain names.

Even though it is not typically used, each of the top-level domains belongs to the root domain that is represented by a period at the end of the name. For example, ftp.microsoft.com. is a fully qualified domain name that is read as follows: www is a host computer belonging to the *microsoft* domain, which belongs to the top-level domain *com*, which in turn is a member of the root domain represented by the final period. You will find that this final period is most commonly used when configuring a DNS server.

Now that we have covered the domain naming system, let's discuss the two options for configuring a workstation to translate domain names.

Registering Domain Names

Now you have done all of the work required to get a DNS server up and running—all that is needed for the computers that will use this DNS server as their primary DNS server. However, if your domain needs to be accessed by computers on the Internet, you will need to register your domain with your parent domains.

The easiest way to do so is to use the information provided by the DNS Registration information page on the World Wide Web at http://www.dns.net/dnsrd/registration.html. After you have registered with the root servers, any computer on the Internet will be able to access your computer by name instead of just by IP address. Follow the instructions carefully, since this will cost you $100 if you are registering your domain name for the first time.

To register your DNS server in the reverse address domain, download the application from InterNIC, fill the application in, and mail it to hostmaster@internic.net. There is no charge for registering a reverse address domain.

Registering a domain name is not difficult:

1. Set up your DNS servers to recognize the name. InterNIC will check to make sure this has been done, so configure the DNS first! Remember, a DNS is hierarchical in nature; you will need to coordinate with your PoP to ensure that their DNS has the correct information, also.

2. At the Web site http://rs.internic.net/cgi-bin/itts/domain, fill in the registration form. InterNIC charges $100 for the initial registration (which includes a two-year registration), and $50 per year after the second year. InterNIC will send invoices, which may be paid by check or credit card.

What's a valid domain name? InterNIC will provide the rules (length, valid characters, and so on), and you may also search the database for your intended name to ensure that no other organization has registered the same name. If there is a registration of the same name, but with a different suffix (*yourname*.net already exists, where you want to register *yourname*.com), you should try to find a different name to register. Consider adding a hyphen (*your-name*.com) or spelling the name differently.

If your intended name is so important to you that no other name can be used, consider contacting the current holder of the name; you may be able to purchase rights to the name. Generally, Internet domain names are given out on the basis of first come, first served. You may be able to force an existing user to cease using a name (if the name were your trademark or your company name), and such an action might be expensive and difficult.

Note: It is considered very, very bad form to threaten an individual or organization who has registered a name you wish to register. Consider that they may have a very legitimate claim to the name and the fact that they were there first.

ISPs will register their domain names and maybe domain names of permanently connected commercial client users. Many ISPs will assist other users in registering a domain name, usually for no charge. Virtually all occasional client users will use names that are under your domain name and as such are not registered with InterNIC.

Each of your ISP client users will have a name in your domain. For example, if your domain name is ourtown.com and you had a user named Westheimer, the user might be given the name westheimer.ourtown.com. Of course, an ISP should always work with the client user to make sure the name is acceptable and that there are no duplicates. Many ISPs have automated their database of client user records to allow quick searches for duplicate names.

Using the HOSTS File

Before the DNS service was created, each workstation was required to have a file that resided locally containing a translation table with each host name and its associated IP address. There was no required structure or consistency in the naming process and also no way to guarantee that the local HOSTS file was up-to-date. Windows NT supports the HOSTS file, although it is really only useful for very small networks since it is extremely difficult to maintain; some sort of procedure is required to keep the HOSTS file up-to-date for all workstations on a network.

The Windows NT HOSTS file exists in the <SystemRoot>\system32\drivers\etc folder. Listing 8-1 shows the sample HOSTS file supplied with Windows NT 4 Server, which contains one entry. This entry is for the name localhost mapped to the address 127.0.0.1:

Listing 8-1: Default HOSTS file supplied with Windows NT 4 Server.

```
# Copyright (c) 1993-1995 Microsoft Corp.
#
# This is a sample HOSTS file used by Microsoft TCP/IP for Windows NT.
#
# This file contains the mappings of IP addresses to host names. Each
# entry should be kept on an individual line. The IP address should
# be placed in the first column followed by the corresponding host name.
# The IP address and the host name should be separated by at least one
# space.
#
# Additionally, comments (such as these) may be inserted on individual
# lines or following the machine name denoted by a '#' symbol.
#
# For example:
#
#      102.54.94.97     rhino.acme.com          # source server
#       38.25.63.10     x.acme.com              # x client host

127.0.0.1          localhost
```

That really is all there is to it. You simply add an entry for every machine you need to access and copy this file to each workstation on the network. It is not difficult to see why the HOSTS file can quickly become difficult to manage.

Using the DNS Server

The preceding section showed how to create a HOSTS file for a Windows NT Network. The HOSTS file must include all mappings to every computer that needs to be accessed from the workstation. For this to work properly, every workstation must have an up-to-date copy of this file.

Now, just for the fun of it, let's assume we have a network with only 10 workstations and a couple of servers and that none of these machines need to talk to any other computer outside of the local network. In this case, a HOSTS file may be a viable option. But what happens when the number of workstations grows? Or when the number of external hosts that need to be accessed grows? This would become an unmanageable situation, to say the least.

This is why the DNS was created. The original Internet was completely driven by a master HOSTS file that was maintained by a group now known as the InterNIC. This HOSTS file became unmanageable so quickly that it forced the creation of a system that allowed each group or network on the Internet to be responsible for its own maintenance.

There are several basic functions that a DNS server provides for TCP/IP-based workstations:

■ Converting names to IP addresses (address resolution).

■ Converting IP addresses to names (reverse address resolution).

■ Forwarding resolution queries to root domain servers for names outside of the servers own authority.

To convert names to IP addresses, the DNS server must have a list of name/IP address pairs for all computers that exist in the domain. This is the domain database. For each IP address that needs to be translated in reverse, the DNS server needs a similar mapping to translate the address to a name. This is the reverse address domain database. The other significant piece of the DNS server's data is a list of root servers to forward requests that are outside of the DNS server's jurisdiction. This, for reasons the authors can't explain, is referred to as the cache.

Another terminology point you should know before we start working with DNS is the definition of a zone. A zone in DNS terminology roughly corresponds to a domain, with the exception that it may not always be the entire domain. For example, you could have a DNS server for a company's domain, but also have a separate DNS server for a subdomain within the master domain. A zone is the portion of any domain for which a particular DNS server is responsible. When a zone for a DNS server does not include the entire domain, it is because the DNS server has delegated portions of the domain to another DNS server.

Usually, because it is such an integral service, there is more than one DNS server available for any particular network. DNS Manager supports the ability to have multiple DNS servers that are authoritative for the same zone by allowing the creation of primary and secondary servers. When a secondary server is created, it automatically replicates the data from the primary DNS server in much the same fashion as a backup Windows NT domain controller replicates user account information from the primary Windows NT domain controller.

Historically, DNS has been based on a collection of text files that correspond to each of the zones supported by the DNS server. If you have a need to understand how these data files work, you should start by examining the sample data files in the %SystemRoot%\system32\dns\samples directory. After you follow the configuration steps listed in "Installing a DNS Server," the Windows NT DNS Manager will create similar files automatically, which will be placed in the %SystemRoot%\system32\dns directory. Examining and comparing these files to the files in the samples directory will help you to better understand the structure of the DNS databases, even though with the DNS Manager there is no need to work directly with these data files.

Installing a DNS Server

To install and configure a DNS server for your Windows NT domain, you will take the following basic steps:

1. Start the Control Panel's Network applet by opening the Control Panel and double-clicking the Network icon.

2. Select the Services tab.

3. Click the Add button. The Select Network Service dialog box appears.

4. Select Microsoft DNS Server from the Network Service list and click the OK button.

If you are not using TCP/IP protocol for an internal network, there is little need to consider installing, configuring, or tuning this service. Installing unneeded network components can create problems, as each protocol consumes system resources including network bandwidth.

After installing the DNS service, you will use the Domain Name Service Manager to define and configure a new server. Start the Domain Name Service Manager by choosing Start Menu I Programs I Administrative Tools (Common) I DNS Manager. Follow these quick steps to get started:

1. Select DNS I New Server from the Domain Name Service Manager menu and define a new server, as shown in Figure 8-6.

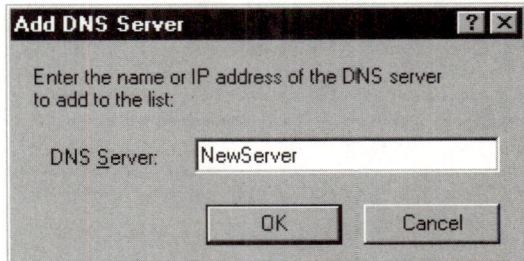

Figure 8-6: The Add DNS Server dialog box. Enter the server's name and click OK.

2. Now select the server that you just created (in the Domain Name Service Manager) and create a zone for each domain for which the DNS server will be responsible. (See "Creating a New Zone" later in the chapter for more information on creating zones.)

3. Choose DNS I New Record and in the New Resource Record dialog box (Figure 8-7), create an A (address) record to translate names to IP addresses. Enter both a host name and the host's IP address. Make sure that Create Associated PTR Record is checked!

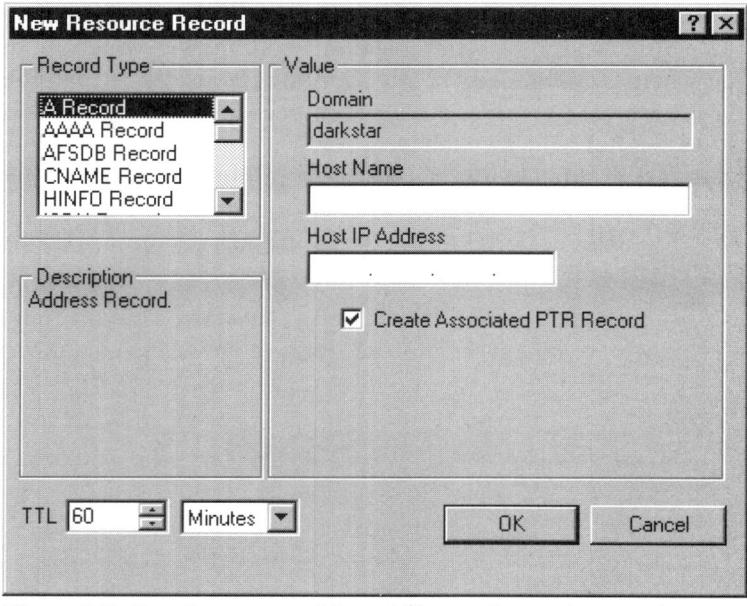

Figure 8-7: Creating a new address (A) record resource record.

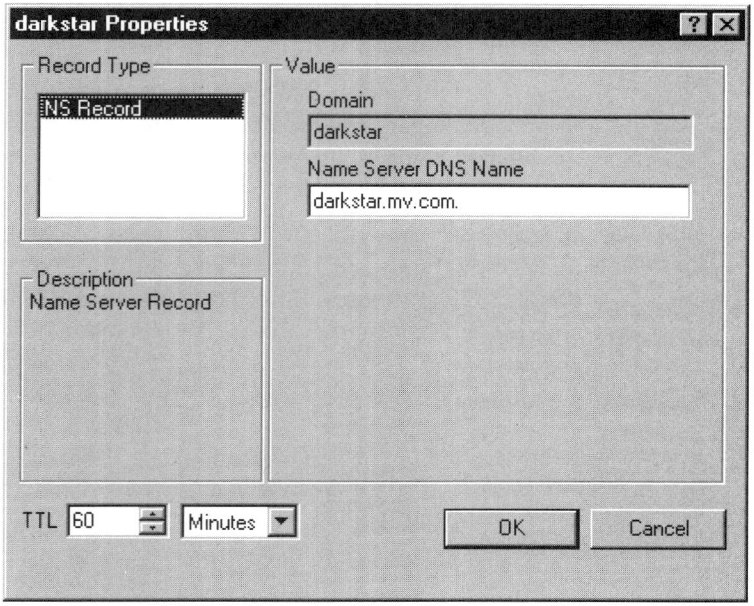

Figure 8-8: An NS record's properties.

4. Enter the appropriate Name Server records (NS) to specify all of the DNS servers that are responsible for this domain. This includes the secondary and the primary DNS server. See Figure 8-8 for an example of an NS record.

5. Enter address records (Step 3) for computers with more than one name.

Zones

If you look at Figure 8-9, in the left pane of the DNS Manager window, you will see the tree Cache | arpa | in-addr. In the right pane, there are a number a records listed. Several of these zones are reserved zones and are created automatically by DNS Manager. They are for special case reverse address resolution and should not be modified. These special zones are as follows:

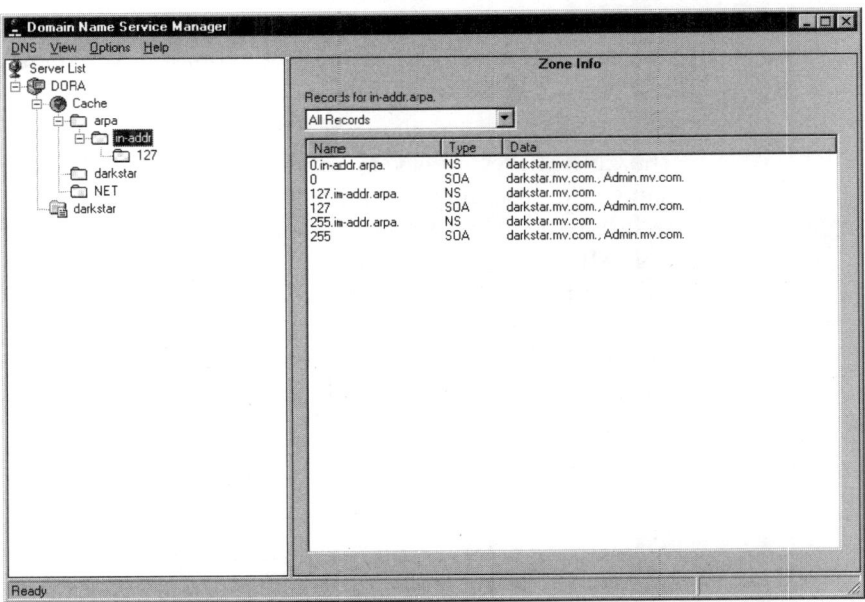

Figure 8-9: The arpa in-addr tree in the Domain Name Service Manager.

- 0.in-addr.arpa—domain address
- 127.in-addr.arpa—reserved address for loopback network
- 255.in-addr.arpa—broadcast address

Record Types

Each zone database has a collection of records that correspond to the various types of entries that were just mentioned. This section lists each of the basic record types and how they are used.

A (Address) Record

The address record specifies a name to IP address mapping. The information needed for this record is the name of the computer and its associated IP address. You will want specify a name for each workstation on your network with a static IP address.

For computers that are using DHCP, the best solution for dynamic resolution is to use WINS to resolve the computer name. This can be done with a special record type supported by Microsoft DNS Manager that defers all resolution requests for computers that are direct members of a domain to the local WINS server.

CNAME (Canonical Name or Alias) Record

The CNAME record is very simply a way of giving a computer multiple names. You use canonical names or aliases by creating an address (A) record for a host computer using the actual name for a computer. Then a CNAME record is created that translates an alias name into the actual name of the computer so that an address record can be located.

For example, you might want to do this if you have a server running on your network that you also want to act as an FTP server or a Web server but have already given the computer another name.
Example:

```
Fileserver    IN    A       205.187.234.201
ftp           IN    CNAME   fileserver
```

Note: The notation used for this example corresponds to the notation used by UNIX servers and only serves to show the required information for the specific record types. The IN stands for Internet record class and is pretty much the only record class left in use and so has become somewhat redundant.

MX (Mail Exchange Record)

You have probably always sent mail to names such as
someone@company.com instead of *someone@mailserv.company.com*. To
simplify the Internet mail addressing scheme, DNS provides the MX
record to allow the specification of a mail server for each domain. Using
the same example just given, this is done as follows:

```
company.com. IN    MX    mailserv
mailserv     IN    A     207.199.42.34
```

A mail system that wants to send mail to *company.com* will first query
its DNS server for the MX record and then use the returned data to
resolve the address of the mail server.

Notice the period at the end of the domain name for the MX record.
As mentioned, this indicates that the domain name is fully qualified and
requires no other information appended. The name *mailserv* for the mail
server name does not have an appended period. When the DNS server
resolves this name, it automatically appends *company.com* to the end of
the name since it is part of the current zone.

NS (Name Server Record)

The NS record is used to specify name servers for a domain. While this
record may seem a little redundant (the address must already be known
if a client is already talking to the server), it still serves a purpose. First, it
documents both the primary and secondary DNS servers for any specific
domain, and second, it is also used to specify delegation of subdomains
to other DNS servers.

As we will see in a moment, this is one of the records that DNS
Manager automatically creates for you when a new zone is created.

At this point, it should be noted that the delegation of domains is not
a simple process using DNS and can cause the propagation of invalid
information through major domain servers if done improperly. I strongly
recommend researching the DNS and BIND service more extensively
when using DNS servers in such a manner.

PTR (Pointer Record)

The PTR record is the opposite of the A record and provides an IP
address to name mapping.

SOA (Start of Authority Record)

The SOA record (see Figure 8-10) exists in every zone database specifying the information about the domain for which the zone is authoritative.

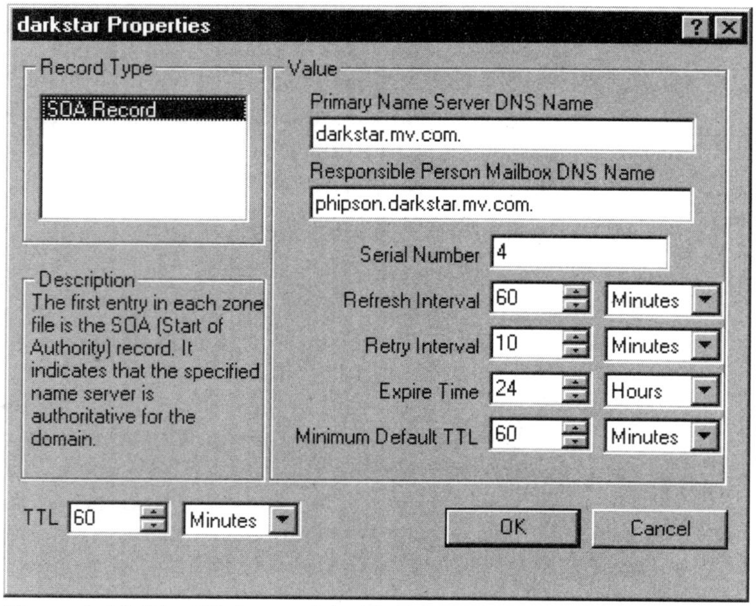

Figure 8-10: The SOA record for DarkStar.

The DNS Manager will automatically create this record when you create a new zone. Until you fully understand each of the SOA parameters, you should not try to change the default values. The defaults will work for most simple DNS server installations.

Configuring the DNS Server

If you are running TCP/IP with a network of any significant size, then DNS support is probably needed. Some ISPs will handle your DNS needs for you. For small networks that do not require any support other than a publicly available mail server address, this may be adequate.

However, as soon as the network's needs become more sophisticated, such as making an FTP server available to the rest of the world (with its own name) or even creating internal subnets, it becomes much more advantageous to operate a local DNS server. While DNS is not a simple service, it is definitely one worth understanding even if you choose not to run your own DNS server.

Microsoft's new DNS Manager (Figure 8-11), provided with Windows NT 4.0, makes setting up a DNS server a much more manageable task. The next few sections will give you the background you need to configure a DNS server for a single domain and also show you how to use DNS Manager.

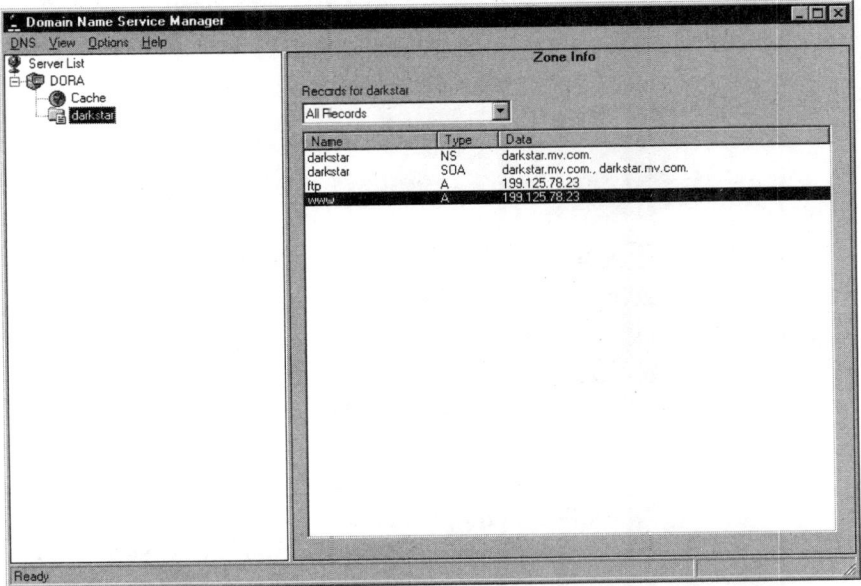

Figure 8-11: The Microsoft DNS Manager—a graphical way to manage a DNS.

Creating a New Zone

To create a new zone, it is necessary to know if the zone is to be a primary or secondary zone. Typically, a primary zone is created. To create a primary zone:

1. Start DNS Manager (Start Menu | Programs | Administrative Tools (Common) | DNS Manager).

2. In the server list (the left pane), select the appropriate server in which to create the new zone.

3. Choose DNS | New Zone from the menu. In the Creating New Zone Wizard's first window (Figure 8-12), click Primary, then click Next.

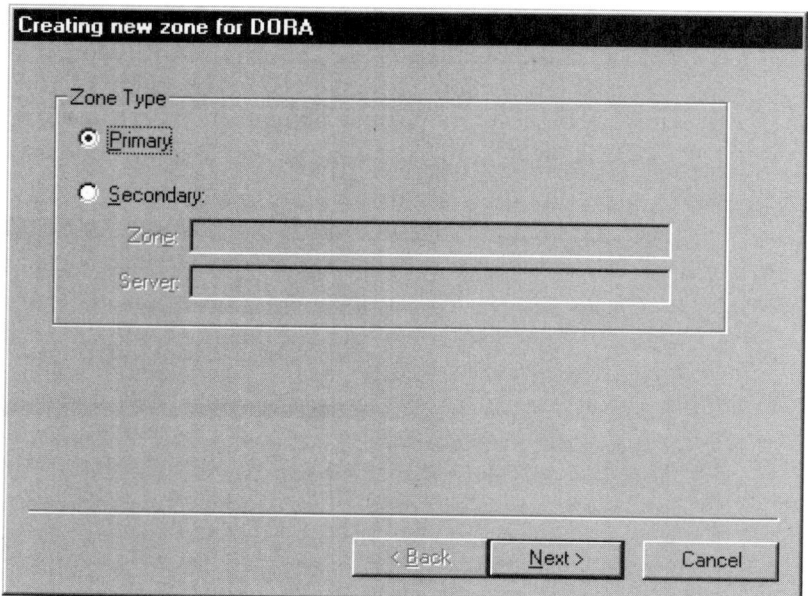

Figure 8-12: Creating New Zone Wizard's first window.

4. In the Creating New Zone Wizard's second window (Figure 8-13), enter the zone name that is the same as the domain name you registered with the InterNIC. Or if you are not connected to the Internet, make one up. After entering the zone name, enter a name for the database file in which to store the zone records (in the Zone File field). The name of the file is not important as long as it does not conflict with the name of any other zone file. (Usually the Domain Name Service Manager's default name will be satisfactory.)

   If you look in %SystemRoot%\system32\dns directory after creating the zone, you can examine this file with any normal text editor to see an example of a raw DNS zone database file.

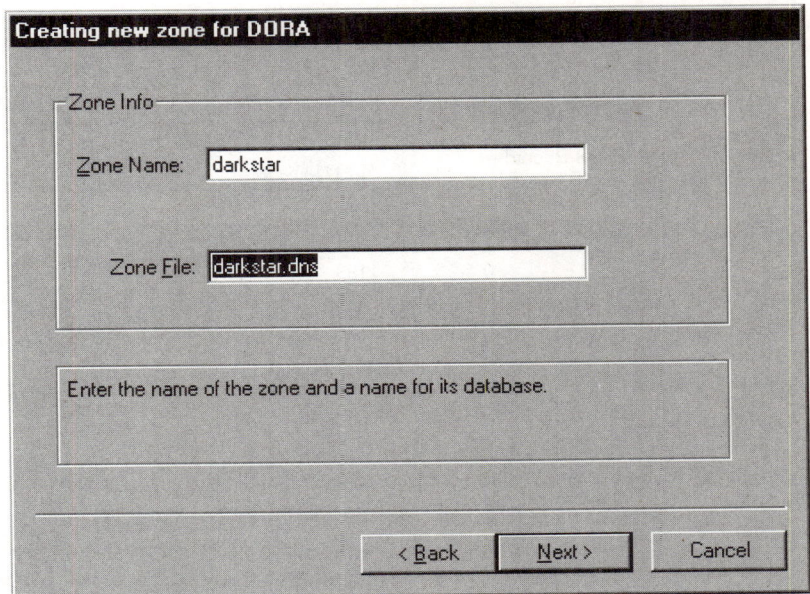

Figure 8-13: Filling in the Zone Name and Zone File fields—use the name registered with InterNIC for the zone name when working with the Internet.

5. Press the Next button, and then click the Finish button.

The new zone should appear under the server that was selected when you started the Add Zone wizard. If you select the zone entry, you will see two default records that were automatically created: the SOA record and an initial NS record corresponding to the server in which the zone was created.

Creating Address Records for the Zone

To create new address records, select the zone to be updated, then follow these steps:

1. Choose DNS | New Record from the Domain Name Service Manager's menu. The New Resource Record (Figure 8-14) dialog will be displayed.

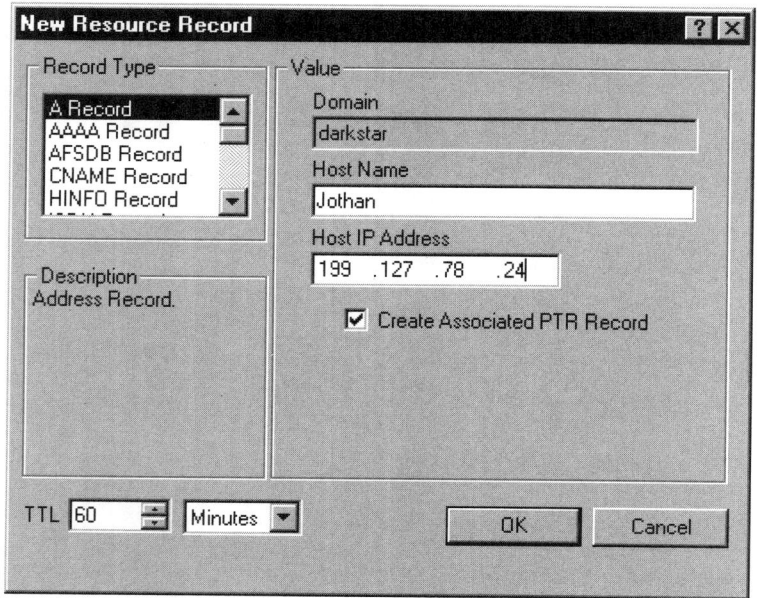

Figure 8-14: Adding an address record for a computer on the local network.

2. Click A Record in the Record Type list, and enter the computer name and the associated IP address in the Host Name and Host IP Address fields. Make sure that the Create Associated PTR Record is also selected to automatically create a PTR record.

3. Click OK to add the record to the DNS database.

Creating CNAME Records for the Zone

To create new CNAME records, select the zone to be updated, then follow these steps:

1. Choose DNS | New Record from the Domain Name Service Manager menu.

2. Click CNAME Record in the Record Type list and enter the alias name and the host name, as shown in Figure 8-15.

3. Click OK.

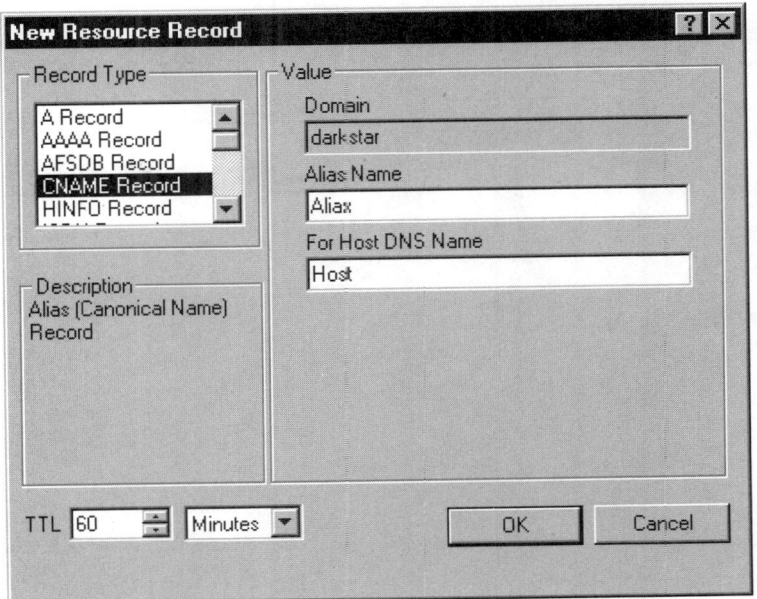

Figure 8-15: Adding a new CNAME record in the New Resource Record dialog box.

Note: When you are adding a CNAME record, ensure that the computer listed in the For Host DNS Name field, in the CNAME record, has a corresponding A (address) record.

Creating a Reverse Address Zone

A reverse address zone (used to look up names for a given IP address) is created using the following steps:

1. Create a new reverse address zone, using the following naming convention: Use the IP address of the network, in reverse, followed by in-addr.arpa. as the zone name. For example, if the network is a Class C address of 207.198.123.0 the zone name would be 123.198.207.in-addr.arpa. Again, the name of the data file doesn't matter as much other than to ensure that the filenames do not overlap. (Windows NT 4 Server supports long filenames, which allows the default filename to be used.)

2. Create PTR records (see Figure 8-16) for each of the computers that have A records in your main zone. Select the reverse address zone, and choose DNS | Add Record. Select PTR Record in the Record Type list, and then enter the IP address and host DNS name.

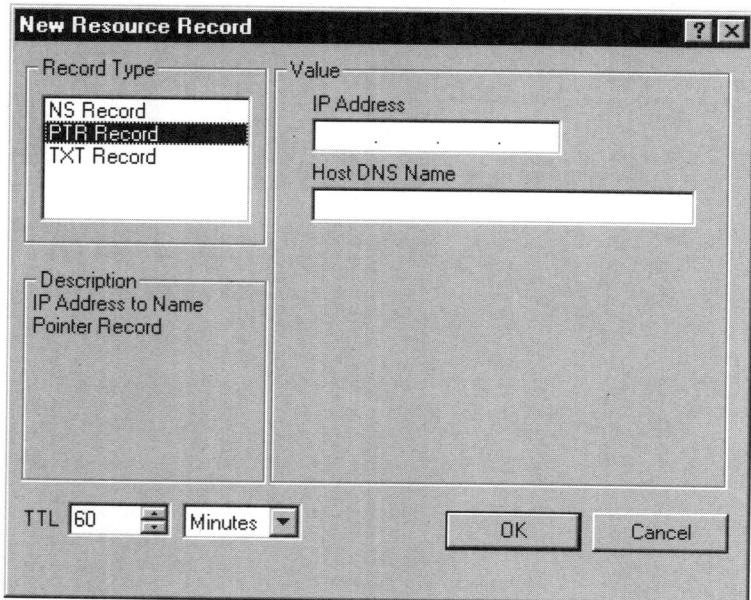

Figure 8-16: Adding a PTR record in the New Resource Record dialog box for a reverse name lookup.

3. Click OK when done.

4. Repeat Steps 2 and 3 for each address record in the DNS zone.

Cache Database

The cache database is automatically provided by the Domain Name Service Manager. This database contains a pointer to all of the important root servers for the clients of the DNS server to be able to access the computers on the Internet.

Creating a Mail Server Exchange

Mail server records are used to resolve requests for e-mail addresses. For example, not every domain will have a mail server; instead, e-mail for many domains could be sent to a single centralized e-mail server, using MX records.

1. Select the desired zone in which to create the address record.

2. Choose DNS | New Record from the Domain Name Service Manager's menu.

3. In the New Resource Record dialog box (Figure 8-17) ensure that the MX Record entry is selected in the Record Type scroll box, fill in the Mail Exchange Server DNS Name field and enter a preference number. The preference numbers are relative to each other so that if you have multiple MX records, a host trying to send mail to your network will give the lower numbers a higher preference.

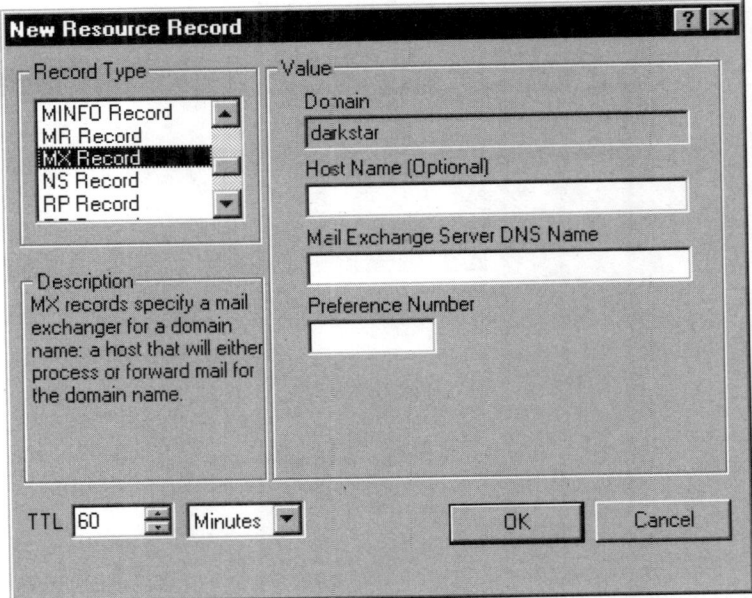

Figure 8-17: Creating a mail zone (MX Record) in the DNS server.

4. Click the OK button.

Note: Oh yes, be sure that the computer listed in the MX record has a corresponding A (address) record.

Creating a Secondary Zone

The preceding sections covered creating and managing a primary zone. However, it is also necessary to create a backup or secondary domain server.

1. Start the DNS Manager (use Start Menu | Programs | Administrative Tools (Common) | DNS Manager).

2. In the server list, select the appropriate server in which to create the new zone.

3. Choose DNS | New Zone from the Domain Name Service Manager's menu and click Secondary in the Zone Type section of the Creating New Zone Wizard (see Figure 8-18).

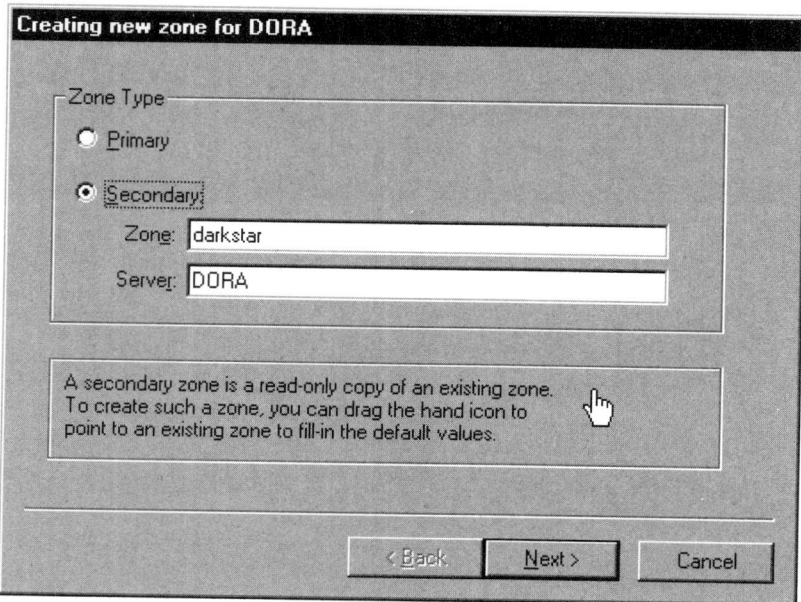

Figure 8-18: Drag the hand icon to an existing zone to copy the zone's attributes.

At this point, if you have DNS Manager configured to view both the primary and the secondary DNS servers, you will be able to simply drag the hand icon to the zone that you want to select.

4. Click the Next Button. The Zone Info section (Figure 8-19) should be filled in if the hand icon was used to initialize the new zone. This zone information must be updated since it is the same as the initializing zone; adding a postfix of _secondary is one alternative name.

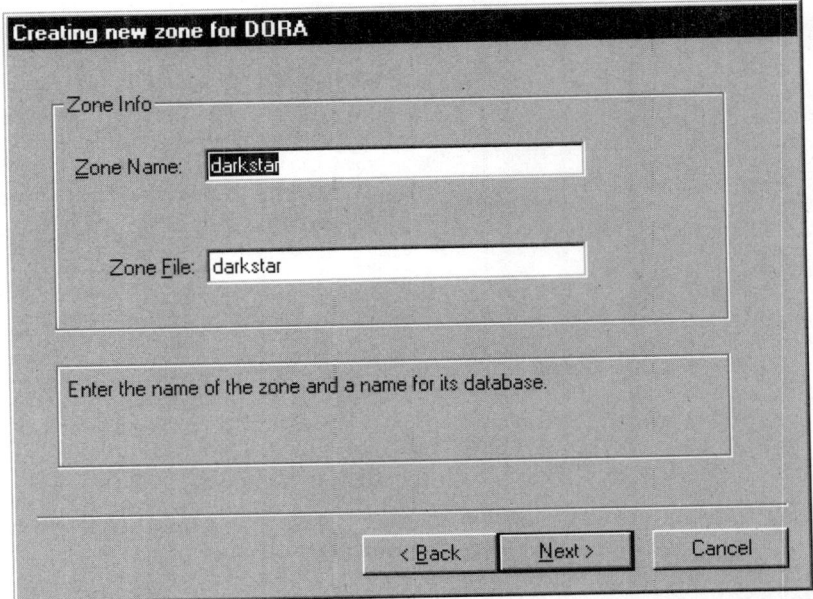

Figure 8-19: The Zone Name and Zone File fields must be changed to be unique when using the hand tool to copy an existing zone.

5. If the hand icon was used to select the DNS server and zone, there should already be an entry in the Creating new zone for dialog box (Figure 8-20) that appears. Otherwise, in the IP Master(s) field, enter the IP address of the server on which the primary zone resides.

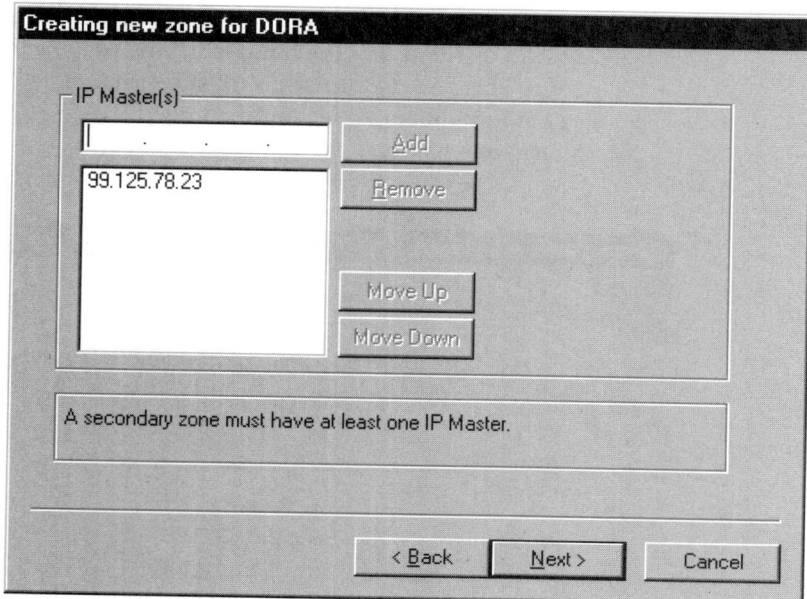

Figure 8-20: The IP Master(s) wizard box where an IP master must be selected.

6. Click Next, then click Finish.

A secondary DNS server zone that will replicate and cache the information in the primary zone has been created.

Using WINS

The Windows Internet Name Service (WINS) is a dynamic computer name resolution service that allows the network to resolve machine names to IP addresses even for systems using DHCP, which assigns addresses on the fly. WINS Manager (Figure 8-21) is a very hands-off utility. The only thing that you really have to do to support WINS is to open the static mappings database and inform WINS of all of the machines on your network with hard-code IP addresses.

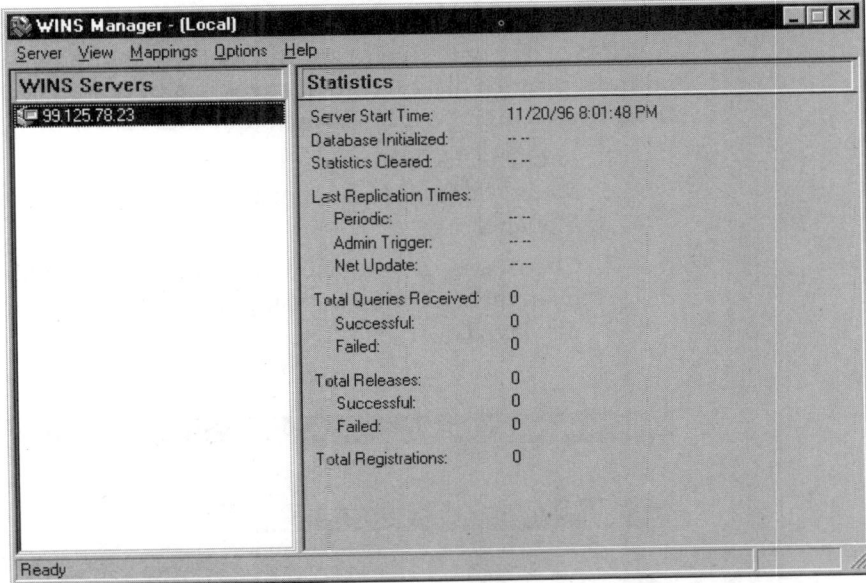

Figure 8-21: The WINS Manager at work.

Installing the WINS Service

The WINS Service must be installed before it can be used. To install WINS on a Windows NT Server, follow these steps:

1. Start the Control Panel's Network applet by opening the Control Panel and double-clicking the Network icon.

2. Select the Services tab.

3. Click the Add button. The Select Network Service dialog box appears.

4. Select Windows Internet Naming Service from the Network Service list and click the OK button.

Adding Static IP Addresses to a WINS Server

A WINS server will need to know about any statically assigned IP addresses (much like exclusion ranges in a DHCP server). To add static IP addresses to the WINS server, follow these steps:

1. Launch DHCP Manager using Start
   Menu | Programs | Administrative Tools (Common) | WINS
   Manager.

2. Choose Mappings | Static Mappings in the WINS Manager's main menu. The Static Mappings dialog box (Figure 8-22) will be displayed.

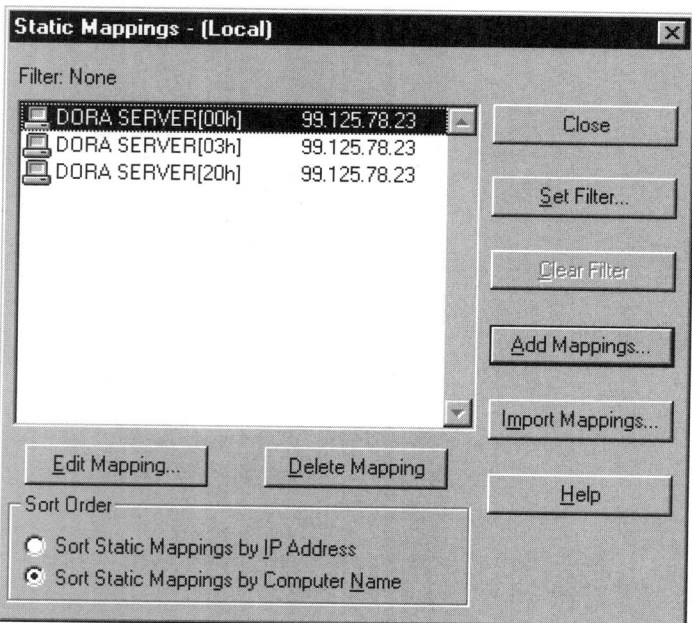

Figure 8-22: Displaying WINS Manager's static mappings in the Static Mappings dialog box.

3. Click the Add Mappings button. The Add Static Mappings dialog box (Figure 8-23) will be displayed. Enter a name (descriptive) and the address that will be mapped statically for this name. Also set the type for this static mapping: Unique, Group, Domain Name, Internet group, or Multihomed.

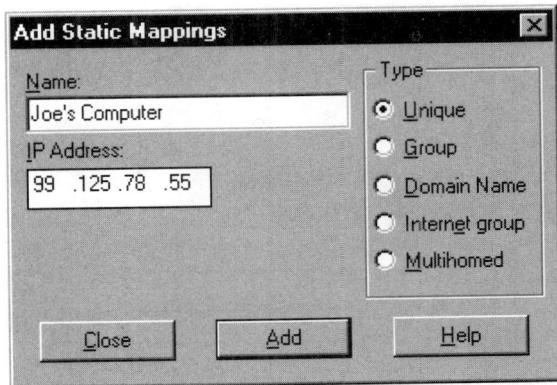

Figure 8-23: The Add Static Mappings dialog where a name is mapped permanently to an IP address.

4. Enter in the name and IP address of each computer on the network with a static IP address and click Add each time.

5. After all static IP addresses have been entered, click Close in the Add Static Mappings dialog box. For each statically mapped IP address, three records will be added to the Static Mappings list, a type 00h, 03h, and 20h.

6. After the static IP addresses have been entered, click Close in the Static Mappings dialog box.

Configuring a Workstation to Use WINS

Each workstation that will be using WINS to obtain an IP address must be configured to use WINS. This process is done on the workstation, not on the Windows NT 4 Server. The following steps apply to computers running Windows NT 4, either server or workstation versions:

1. Choose Start Menu | Settings | Control Panel. In the Control Panel, double-click the Network icon.

2. Select the Protocol tab and click TCP/IP Protocol in the Network Protocols list. Then click the Properties button to display the Microsoft TCP/IP Properties dialog box as shown in Figure 8-24.

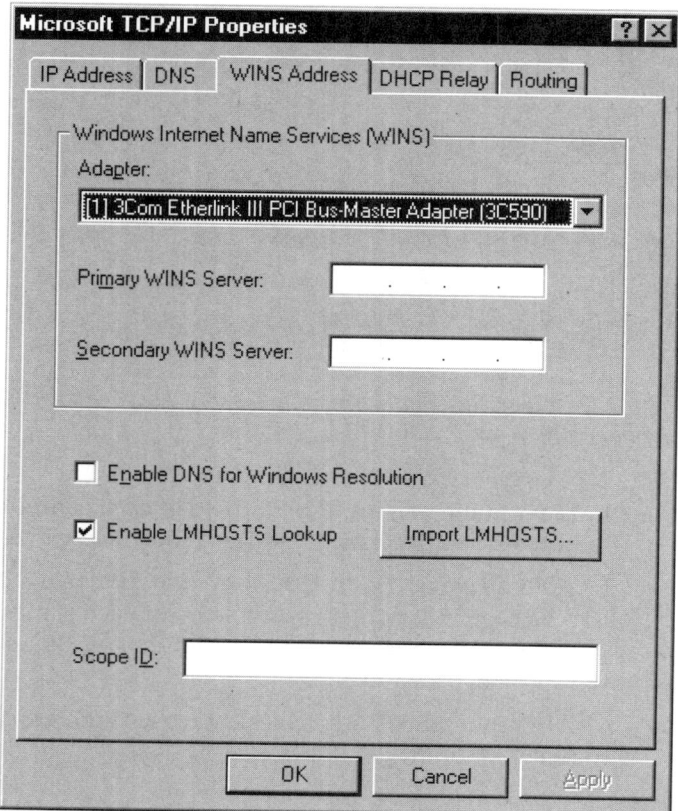

Figure 8-24: The Microsoft TCP/IP Properties dialog box WINS Address tab.

3. In the Primary WINS Server box, enter the IP address of the WINS server to be used, and if there is a secondary WINS server, enter its address in the Secondary WINS Server box.

4. Click OK when you are done configuring the WINS server.

WINS is used for mapping NetBIOS names to TCP/IP addresses and is discussed in detail in Chapter 4. It is possible, however, to use WINS as a backup service to DNS for resolving computer names that do not have explicit A (address) records in the appropriate zone. This is done by simply adding a WINS record to the appropriate zone. When a computer name is resolved for that zone, the DNS server will first check to see if an A record exists. If not, then it will use the WINS server address listed in the WINS record to try and resolve the address.

Creating a WINS Record in a Zone

1. In the Domain Name Service Manager program, select the zone in which to create the WINS address record.

2. Choose DNS | Properties from the Domain Name Service Manager's menu.

3. Select the WINS Lookup tab in the Zone Properties dialog box (Figure 8-25).

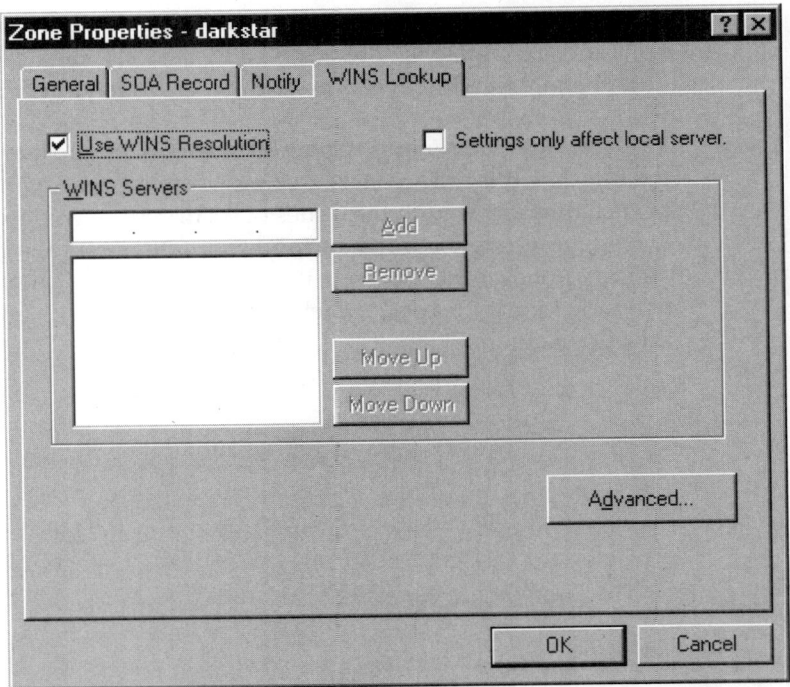

Figure 8-25: The WINS Lookup tab in the Zone Properties dialog box.

4. Check the Use WINS Resolution check box.

5. Enter the addresses of one or more WINS servers in the WINS Server edit box and click Add for each WINS server.

6. Click OK when done adding WINS servers.

Moving On

This chapter dealt with connecting a Windows NT 4 Server network with the Internet. The chapter covered issues such as how to make the connection, how to manage the network, and how Internet addresses work.

Some special services, including DNS, DHCP, and WINS, all used to help manage Internet addresses and names, were covered in this chapter too.

While in the process of connecting to the Internet, there was so much to do that the whole concept of security never really came up. Now that your entire company's network is connected, not only can users get out onto the Internet, but everyone else can get in to your company's network as well.

Regardless of previous network security, with the live connection to the Internet, it is time to start dealing with the security problem. The next chapter deals with the issues of security for Windows NT Networks and suggests a few guidelines for developing your own in-house security policy. Network security differs from physical security in that network security may be breached by an attack that is physically outside the organization.

9

Windows NT 4 Server Security

$\mathbf{I}$n this chapter, I cover both system and physical security, users, groups, permissions, ownership, and other issues related to security.

Security is paramount to networks, and doubly so when connected to the Internet. Whenever a network server is used, you need to maintain confidentiality for both users' and corporate data.

Threats to security come from inside the organization (disgruntled or simply unethical employees) and outside (hackers, visitors, experimenters, and others who may or may not have a relationship with the organization).

Note: If you have not already read Chapter 3, then you should take a quick look at it. Fault tolerance is closely related to security, the topic of this chapter.

System Security

When I speak of system security, I am typically talking about non-physical security. System security means securing from hackers and other people who should not have access.

Many companies take the mistaken attitude that system break-ins happen to "the other guy." Heck, *someone* has to be that other guy! And because *I've* protected *my* system, it may well be you who gets hit.

What happens, and why? System attacks can come from outside sources (usually through either your RAS dial-in connection or perhaps a permanent Internet connection), whereas internal attacks can result from a number of factors, most of which are easily prevented:

- Employees whose employment is being terminated, either by their choice or the company's. Many companies tend to think that an employee who has resigned is not a threat. Wrong. More than one company has lost its customer list to a competitor when a departing sales manager carries the customer list, on a diskette, to his or her new job. Whenever an employee leaves, immediately remove that employee's computer access privileges!

  I won't even discuss what happens when an employee has been dismissed and that employee's computer access privileges have not been terminated: files erased, entire drives formatted, subtle changes made in databases and accounting systems, and all sorts of vandalism and mischief are frequent.

- Dissatisfied and unethical employees are a constant threat. Often, these people are not recognized—audit policies (discussed later) can be an effective tool in spotting misdeeds and trespasses by employees.

- Outside vendors, temporary staff, and other nonemployees who have access to the system should be closely monitored. Be cautious about items being removed from the computer room such as tapes and diskettes, especially when critical or sensitive data is being managed.

- When a drive fails, you might be able to recover the data on the drive using some very simple techniques. You may choose not to bother recovering the data (possibly an expensive task, and unnecessary if you have adequate backups of the data). However, if the drive is returned to a dealer, given away, or tossed in the trash, the drive's data may be recovered, thereby compromising your security.

- When a drive is removed from service, radical steps, including physical destruction of the drive, may be called for. A few well-placed whacks with the office hammer will render the typical hard drive irrevocably unreadable! If the drive must be returned to the manufacturer for warranty service, ship it directly to the manufacturer yourself if possible: don't delegate this task to the dealer, because you have no control over what happens to the drive after it leaves your premises.

Note: Here at DarkStar, we turn our old hard drives into wind chimes. It turns out that the hard drive disks, when removed from the drives, are wonderfully vibrant!

Network Security

Is your network secure? Probably not. Cables and wires often go to unused offices (which may not even be located in your company). Imagine this: someone moves into an office, plugs into the network jack on the wall, and ends up connected to the network for the company next door! If you are that company next door, this can be a problem.

With 10BaseT and other UTP (Unshielded Twisted Pair) networks, which use cabling that resembles telephone wires, the network wiring is frequently routed to a "cable closet" that is connected with similar cable closets on other floors in the building. You can easily connect to the wrong cable inadvertently and find your network routed to virtually any location in the building. Frequent cable audits, determining that each hub jack is routed to a workstation you can account for, are necessary. Unannounced spot checks can be useful in detecting problems. Never underestimate employees; the urge to make changes without proper security considerations is almost irresistible!

Networks made of fiber optic media are inherently much more secure—it is very difficult to "tap" into a fiber optic connection.

Wireless networks are becoming more common. Once considered toys, a wireless network today can save literally 50 percent of the cost of wiring a complex network. Most wireless networks are reasonably secure; however, you must evaluate security on a case-by-case basis.

Wireless networks come in two varieties: infrared and radio based. Both cover a limited area, but the radio-based units are better able to penetrate walls, floors, and ceilings. Infrared units don't go through walls (though some windows may allow some signal to escape); however, infrared units are typically usable only where there are cubicles with open areas through which the infrared signal can pass—infrared is really "line of sight."

Believe It or Not?

Due to an unquenchable thirst for diet cola, I had the cola company install a direct cola pipeline into my office. Imagine my surprise when I returned from a month-long trip and found that my cola bill was still quite high. A check of the pipeline showed that the guy in the next office had tapped my pipeline and was enjoying a free cola (or two).

Be aware of patterns of usage that are unusual, such as high usage during nonoffice hours, sudden surges in usage on accounts that normally don't get much usage, or an unjustifiable increase in remote accesses. All of these changes indicate probable security problems.

Internet & Intranets

An important goal today is to be on the information superhighway—the Internet. This book has devoted lots of coverage to Internet topics, and I am sure that your computer, if it's not already connected to the Internet, will be connected one day.

The Internet is so big that estimating its size is difficult. On the Internet are students, hackers, children, even (arrgh) politicians! The bottom line is that there are people out there who are just waiting for your computer to be placed on the Internet so that they can try to break into it. With Windows NT, you are at a slight advantage—many of the evildoers are oriented toward UNIX-based computers (once almost 100 percent UNIX-based, the Internet continues to have a very large community of UNIX machines).

The most common protection against an attack from the Internet is a device called a *firewall*. This device is placed between your network and the Internet. Programmed with the IP addresses of those networks and computers that are not considered to be a security risk, the firewall totally blocks attempts to access your network from the Internet by others.

A number of companies produce firewalls, including Cisco, 3Com, Cypress, and Network 1. You should contact each of these companies to determine their offerings.

Securing RAS

RAS (Remote Access Server) can be made very secure if you are able to work with the restrictions that security requires. When you configure RAS, you may choose to allow only those clients that follow the Windows NT security model.

First, you manage RAS configuration from the Control Panel's Network applet, by setting the Remote Access Server network service's properties. Figure 9-1 shows the Remote Access Setup dialog that displays when you click on Properties in the Network applet.

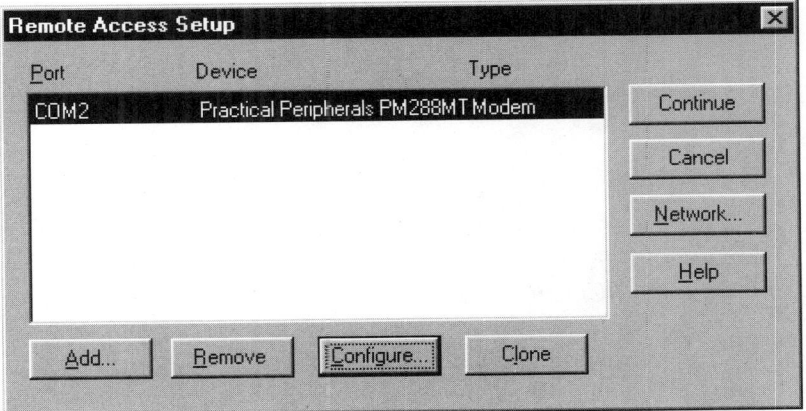

Figure 9-1: The Remote Access Setup dialog box.

As Figure 9-2 shows, each modem (there is a single modem, connected to COM2 in my example) in the RAS pool may be configured to the following:

- **Dial out only**—The modem is used for DUN (Dial-up Networking) only, and no incoming calls are received on this modem. The phone can ring for hours, Windows NT 4 Server won't answer.

- **Receive calls only**—The modem is used for RAS only, all incoming calls are answered, but users are unable to use this modem for dialing out. This is usually an administrative choice intended to keep local users from using the modem when it may be needed for incoming calls.

- **Dial out and Receive calls**—allows both incoming and outgoing calls on this modem.

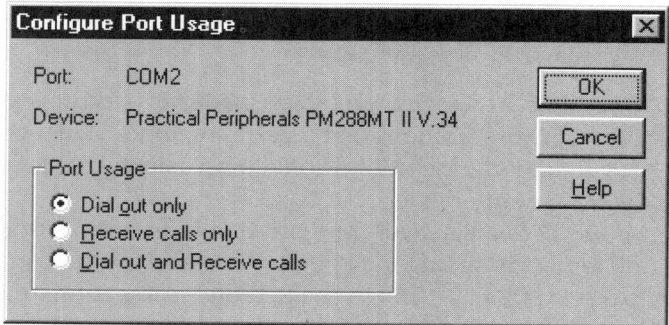

Figure 9-2: The Configure Port Usage dialog.

If you are not hosting clients (no one will be calling in to your computer), then set the modem to Dial out only. That way, a hacker will not be able to enter your system using a dial-in modem.

Tip

Some telephone systems have facilities to monitor telephone line usage from several sites. Here at DarkStar, my telephone displays usage for all data lines, so I can see, at a glance, which data lines are in use. If I see a data line in use during a time when it perhaps should not be, I can quickly check to determine whether the usage is legitimate.

Clicking on the Network button displays the Network Configuration dialog box (Figure 9-3). Set only those protocols that are required. You'll gain no advantage by offering an unsupported protocol—and this can lead to abuse if a hacker is able to use a protocol that you don't need. Many networks offer only TCP/IP protocol, because TCP/IP is used for most dial-up Internet connections.

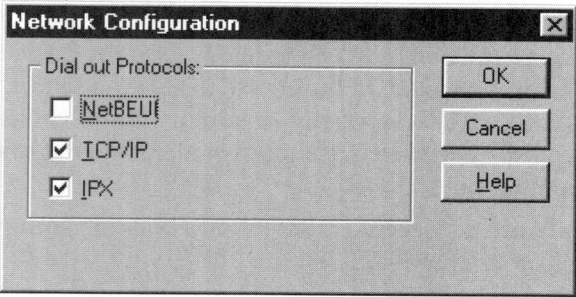

Figure 9-3: The Network Configuration dialog box when dial-in is not authorized.

When you check either Receive calls only or Dial out and Receive calls in the Configure Port Usage dialog box (Figure 9-2), then the Network Configuration dialog box shown in Figure 9-4 displays.

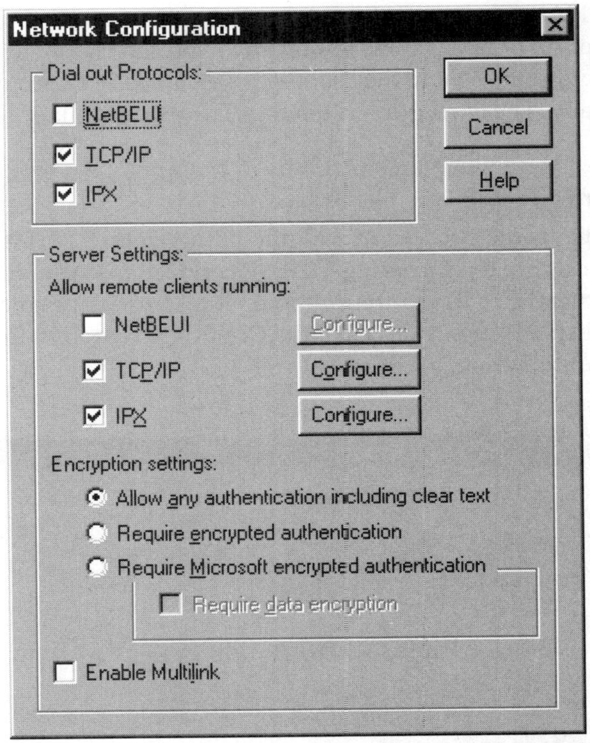

Figure 9-4: The Network Configuration dialog box when dial-in is authorized.

Most dial-up network connections to the Internet need only TCP/IP protocol. Some private connections use NetBEUI or IPX protocols also, so check all protocols that your installation needs to support. Configure each protocol by clicking on the appropriate Configure button.

Encryption settings allow you to greatly enhance the security of your dial-in links. You may choose the following:

■ **Allow any authentication (user ID and password) including clear text**—the weakest level of security and should be avoided if possible. Use this level of encryption only if you have clients who are not using Windows NT as their operating system.

■ **Require encrypted authentication**—allows you to restrict authentication to one of the encrypted protocols (except that PAP—
Password Authentication Protocol—is not supported).

■ **Require Microsoft encrypted authentication**—allows use of MS-
CHAP (Challenge-Handshake Authentication Protocol) protocol
only. If you select this option, then you can choose to also encrypt the
data being sent to the client—this enhances data security substantially! The encryption is the RSA Data Security, Inc.'s RC4 algorithm.

Configuring TCP/IP

When clients are allowed to dial into your Windows NT 4 Server, you
must configure the incoming TCP/IP connections. You do this using the
RAS Server TCP/IP Configuration dialog, shown in Figure 9-5. This
dialog displays when you click the Configure button in the Network
Configuration dialog (Figure 9-4).

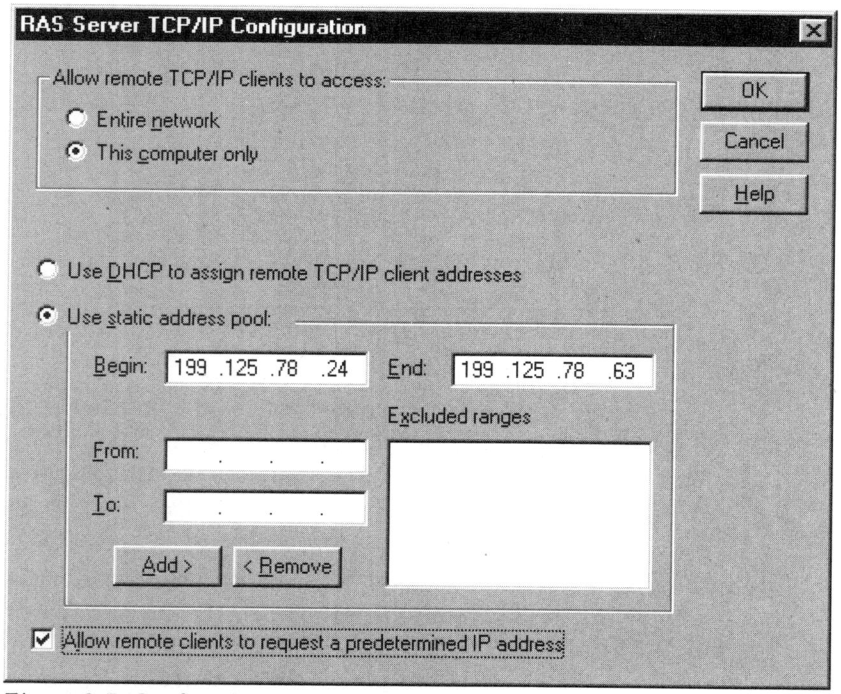

Figure 9-5: Configuring TCP/IP for RAS connections.

Problems . . . RAS Won't Start, You Say?

If you get a message telling you that RAS will not start, and that RAS returned an error code, check the error log.

You can review the Windows NT 4 Server error log by selecting Start Menu | Programs | Administrative Tools (Common) | Event Viewer.

In the event log, you will see an entry with the same date and time as the attempt to start RAS. Open this event, and if the event ID is 7024, and the error returned is 1066, then the problem is simple to fix—RAS cannot start if you have not defined at least one modem with receive calls active!

For security, limit dial-in clients to resources found only on the Windows NT 4 Server. Do this by clicking the This computer only radio button. This protects other servers (and other workstations with shared resources over the network) from possible attack from dial-in clients.

Note: Disabling access to other resources on the network means that you're turning off Windows NT 4 Server's routing capabilities!

Also, you must specify how TCP/IP addresses are assigned to dial-in clients:

- TCP/IP addresses may be assigned using a DHCP server. If you have more than one Windows NT 4 Server with dial-in connections, then using a DHCP server is the most efficient method to assign TCP/IP addresses.

- TCP/IP addresses may be assigned from a fixed pool (generally a satisfactory solution using DHCP/WINS servers, or you can have a single server managing IP addresses). You must provide a beginning address, an ending address, and any addresses to be excluded from assignment.

You may choose to allow a dial-in client to specify his or her TCP/IP address. The address that the client specifies must be routed to the server.

Security considerations include making only this server's resources visible to the client, and perhaps using a fixed TCP/IP address.

Configuring IPX & NetBEUI

If you allow IPX or NetBEUI protocol clients, then you use their configuration dialogs. As with TCP/IP, you can limit dial-in clients to resources found only on the Windows NT 4 Server. Do this by clicking on the This computer only radio button.

Like TCP/IP, IPX protocol assigns an address (called the *network number*) to the client. You may choose to either allocate network numbers automatically, or restrict the network numbers to a specific range.

Remote Access Admin

You start the Windows NT 4 Server Remote Access Admin program by selecting Start Menu | Programs | Administrative Tools (Common) | Remote Access Admin.

The Remote Access Admin program contains several security-related functions. Selecting Users | Permissions displays the Remote Access Permissions dialog box (see Figure 9-6). This dialog box allows you to specify which of your Windows NT 4 Server users have permission to log on remotely using RAS. You may also set the user's call-back status:

- **No Call Back**—tells Remote Access Admin that this client user may connect directly. It is often needed for client users who call from multiple locations (sales representatives, for example).

- **Set by Caller**—tells Remote Access Admin that the client user will specify the callback number. This allows some after-the-fact auditing of phone numbers used to access the system. This option is useful in reducing costs, because the caller (Windows NT 4 Server) will be paying for the call, not the client user.

- **Preset To**—forces the user to be at a specific number. RAS calls back to the preset number, and the client user's computer has to answer. This option is useful when you must strictly control access to the network.

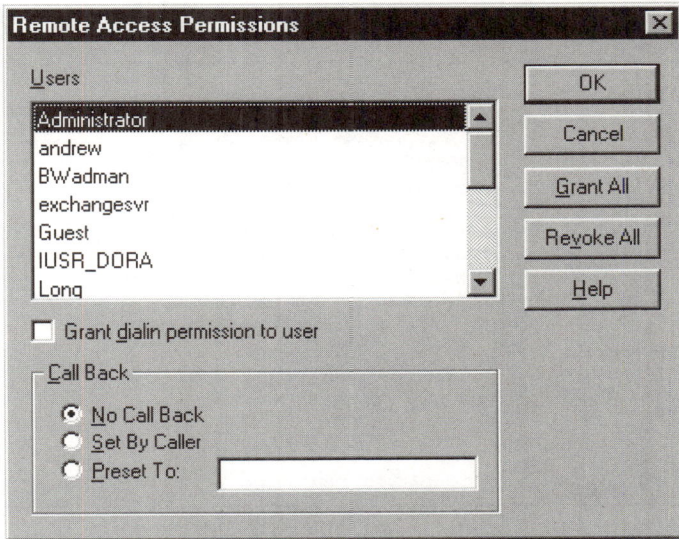

Figure 9-6: The Remote Access Permissions dialog box.

RAS offers a great deal of flexibility, but it also exposes your server, and possibly your network, to compromise from outside. Don't configure or use RAS unless you understand the risks involved.

To enable logging for dial-in RAS client users, you must enable logging in the system registry. The key for logging is found in HKEY_LOCAL_MACHINE\SYSTEM\CurrentControlSet\ ServicesRasMan\PPP as the variable "Logging." Set the Logging variable to 1 to enable logging of PPP connections. Figure 9-7 shows the registry editor with the Logging variable selected.

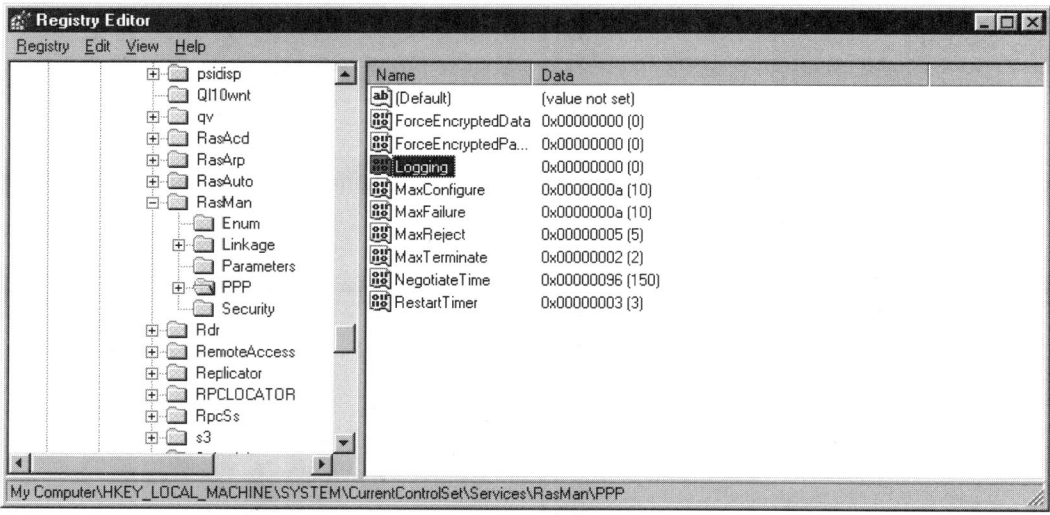

Figure 9-7: The Registry Editor, ready to change the RAS logging mode.

After setting the logging mode, you need to restart RAS for the change to take effect.

Groups

After you have secured your system, you'll need to turn your attention to user security. Organizing users into logical groups helps manage users and security. A group doesn't have any special privileges initially; however, you may assign privileges to a group if desired.

To create a group, select User | New Global Group or User | New Local Group in User Manager for Domains. The main difference between a local group and global group is that a local group can be used only in the database in which it was defined. A global group can be a member of a local group. No restriction exists on how many global or local groups you can create, but keep it to a manageable number. You can add members to a group at any time.

Create groups for each part of your organization—for example, you may have groups for accounting, sales, administration, data processing, research and development, and so on. You may also create groups based on functionality, though Windows NT 4 Server has a number of preconfigured groups, such as the following:

- **Account Operators**—users who can establish and modify user accounts.
- **Administrators**—can administer the server and the domain.
- **Backup Operators**—possess the necessary privilege of accessing files for backup purposes.
- **Domain Admins**—a global group that consists of administrators who administer the domain.
- **Domain Guests**—a global group that consists of guests to the domain.
- **Domain Users**—a global group that consists of users in the domain.
- **Guests**—users with limited access to the computer and domain.
- **Print Operators**—can administer print queues.
- **Replicator**—supports file replication in a domain.
- **Server Operators**—manage the domain servers.
- **Users**—users with more privileges than guests, but fewer privileges than administrators.

Groups may be assigned rights, as described later in the chapter in "Rights & Privileges."

Users

Simply put, users are why we are here. A user is anyone who either logs on directly to the server or makes a network connection to the server.

Users are given privileges and rights and must be managed. Users who will be logging on locally may have a somewhat different configuration. For locally logged-on users, you may choose to create a profile. A profile defines how Windows NT 4 Server will appear to users, and users may choose to customize parts of the system (such as the desktop) to meet their own needs and desires.

Note: When using FTP, with accounts, any user who is to be allowed a nonanonymous logon to the IIS FTP Server must be granted the Right to Logon Locally privilege.

To create a user account on Windows NT 4 Server, you should already have created any groups to which you will be assigning the user. Assigning users to a group when creating user accounts is slightly easier than assigning users to a group when you create groups last.

Defining Users

To define a user account on Windows NT 4 Server, select the User Manager's User | New User menu selection. The New User dialog box (Figure 9-8) displays.

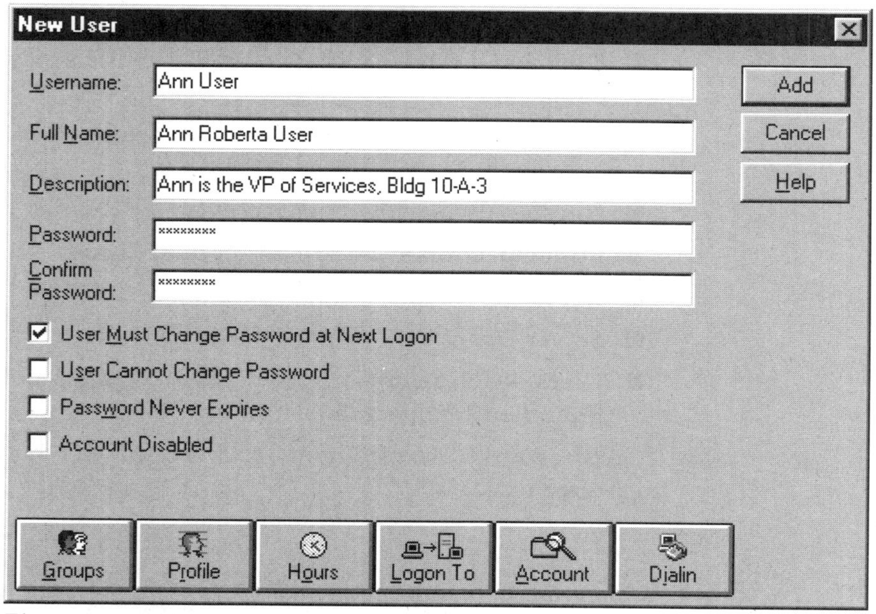

Figure 9-8: Adding a new user.

Fill in the Username, Full Name, Description, Password, and Confirm Password edit boxes. Even though a user account may be created without a password, I do not recommend that any accounts (even guest accounts that have only read-only privilege) be created without passwords. Also set, as appropriate, the User Must Change Password at Next Logon, User Cannot Change Password, Password Never Expires, and Account Disabled check boxes.

At the bottom of the New User dialog box is a set of six buttons: Groups, Profile, Hours, Logon To, Account, and Dialin. These function as follows:

■ The Groups button displays the Group Memberships dialog box. The default group is Domain Users. Add any other groups that you wish this user to be a member of. Remember, groups are not exclusive—a user account may be a member of multiple groups. If you select more than one group, you can one select one group as the primary group; if there are conflicting rights in groups assigned to the user, then the right specified in the primary group takes precedence. More on groups in "Working With Users & Groups" later in this chapter.

- Click on the Profile button to add profile information. The user must have been granted the right to log on locally in order to use profiles. (Profiles are discussed later, under "Defining Profiles.")

- The Hours button displays the Logon Hours dialog box. A user may be restricted to accessing the server only during certain hours; a server who is working on a shift basis may be restricted from using the user during shifts other than the one to which he or she is currently assigned. All users may be restricted from accessing the server at certain hours for maintenance purposes. Some nonessential users may be restricted from accessing the server during peak load times.

- Click on the Logon To button to restrict the user's access to the server from specific workstations. For example, you can restrict a person who is working in the R&D department to use workstations only in the R&D area (and not in Accounting, for example).

- Click on the Account button to set account options. The Account Information dialog box allows you to set several options. A life span of an account can be set to either never expire or to expire on a specific date. You may also set the account type—either a domain (global) account, which will be used throughout the domain, or a local account.

- Click on the Dialin button to set the dial-in privileges for this user. You may prohibit users from dialing into the server (using RAS). If you permit a user to dial in to the server, then you may specify a call-back protocol for this user—either No Call Back (the user dials in and is connected directly to the server), Set by Caller (the user configures the call-back number when he or she calls in), or Preset To (the call back is fixed to a single number).

After you have set all necessary information for the user, click on the Add button to add the new user to the user database.

Defining Profiles

For users who have the right to log on locally, you may establish a profile. Profiles contain information such as Application Data, Desktop, Favorites, Personal, SendTo, and the Start Menu. To enable profiles for a given user, use the User Manager, select the user, and display the user's properties.

Not all users need to have a profile defined. If only a limited number of users have the right to log on locally (to actually log on at the server, in addition to logging on through a workstation), establishing a profile for each may be best.

When a user's properties are displayed (see Figure 9-9), you can click on the Profile button to display the User Environment Profile dialog box, shown in Figure 9-10.

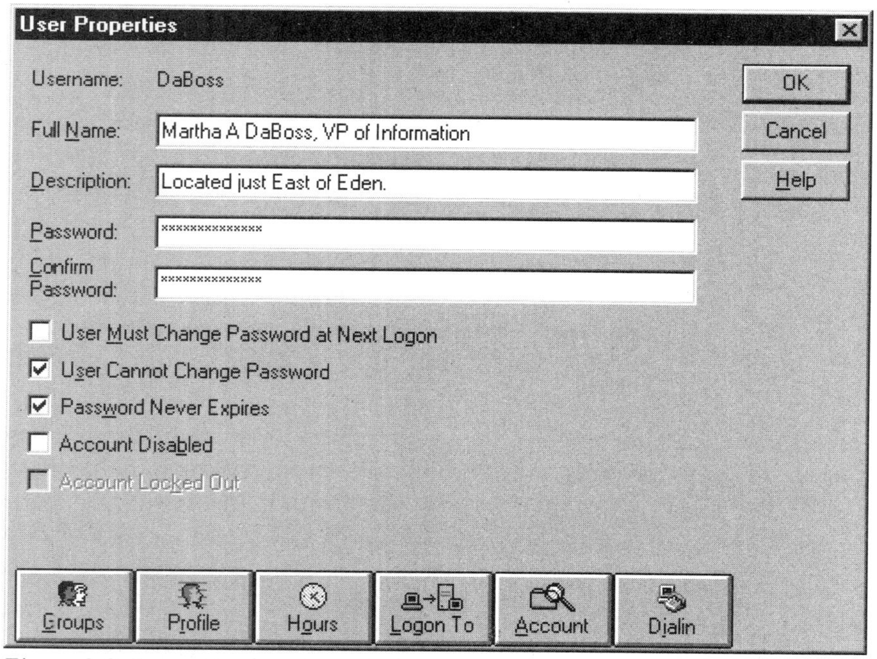

Figure 9-9: Properties for a typical user.

Note: In Figure 9-9, the Account Locked Out button is enabled only when the account has been locked out. See "Account Lockout," later in this chapter for information about locking out users.

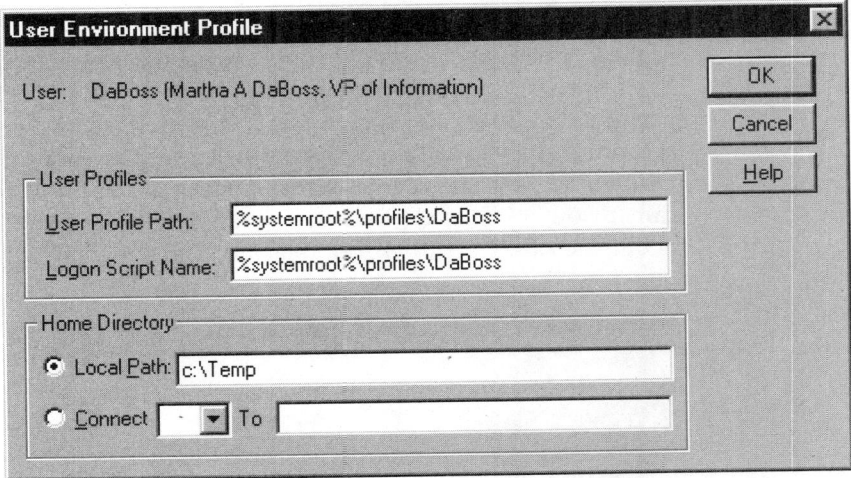

Figure 9-10: User Environment Profile—for DaBoss.

In the User Environment Profile dialog are three items:

■ **User Profile Path**—a fully qualified path name where the user's profile will be stored. The default location is in the %systemroot%\system32 folder, which is not a good location for a profile. A better choice is the %systemRoot%\profiles folder, which has been established for user profiles.

■ **Logon Script Name**—a BAT, CMD, or other executable filename that executes whenever the user logs on. Maintenance, setup, and other commands can be placed in the Logon Script file. If the user logs on from a DOS-based workstation, then the logon script must be a BAT file. The typical logon script path for users who log on remotely is \%systemroot%\system32\system32\repl\import\ scripts, although you may establish a different path (such as the \users folder) for logon scripts.

■ **Home Directory**—the initial folder whenever a File Open or File Save As dialog is displayed. As well, any CMD sessions also default to the Home Directory. You may specify either a local folder (specified in the Local Path edit box) or a virtual drive connected to a shared network folder. You may specify the environment variable %USERNAME% to insert the current user's name for the Home Directory: \users\%USERNAME%.

Using the System Applet

In the Control Panel's System applet, select the tab marked User Profiles. The System Properties dialog box (shown in Figure 9-11) shows four user profiles defined on the server DORA. One profile (Administrator) is the account that I use. DaBoss is the profile created for this chapter. The other two profiles, exchangesvr and smsmanager, are accounts created automatically by other installed products, Exchange Server and SMS Manager. I use neither account very often, but they are available if needed.

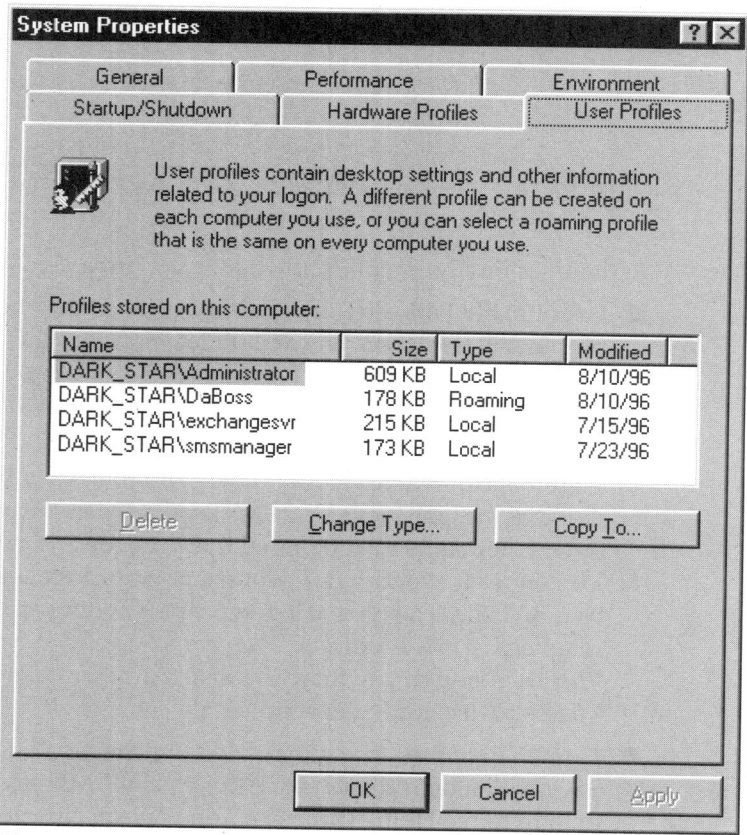

Figure 9-11: Four User Profiles in the Control Panel's System applet.

You can change the type of profile as needed. For example, DaBoss's profile is currently roaming (a roaming profile is always retrieved from the server, if available), whereas Administrator's profile is local (a local profile is always loaded from the local machine). When using a roaming profile, you can specify the profile be cached to improve performance. If a roaming profile is not available, then a local profile is used. If two users log on with the same roaming profile, the last user to log off will be the one whose settings are saved.

Figure 9-12 shows the Change Type dialog box for user DaBoss. Specified for this user is a roaming profile, which will be cached if the connection is defined as slow.

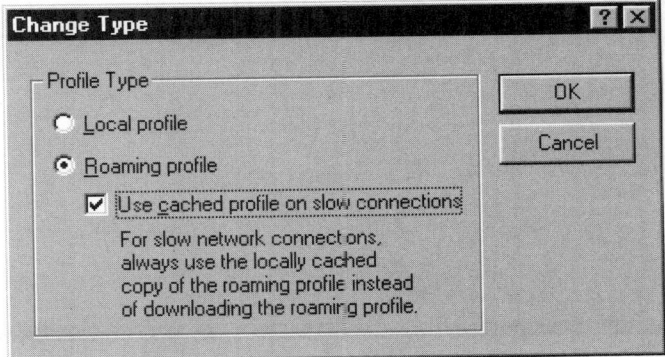

Figure 9-12: Changing a profile's type.

Working With Users & Groups

Maintaining control over users can be a difficult task. Large organizations can have thousands of users, creating a nightmare for the system administrator. In this book, I assume that you have configured a domain, and that you are working on the primary domain server (PDS).

Fortunately, Windows NT 4 Server provides several features and tools to make user management less difficult. First, it is important to understand that *anyone* who interacts with Windows NT 4 Server is a user. You are a user, and everyone else is a user.

Groups are logical collections of users. A group may be managed as a whole, and members of a group may in turn be granted (or denied) privileges as needed.

You manage users through the User Manager for Domains program, found in Start Menu | Programs | Administrative Tools (Common) | User Manager for Domains. When the User Manager for Domains program starts (Figure 9-13), a display of both users and groups will be provided. All users belong to one or more groups. For example, a user may be a member of both the Administrators group and the Domain Users group simultaneously.

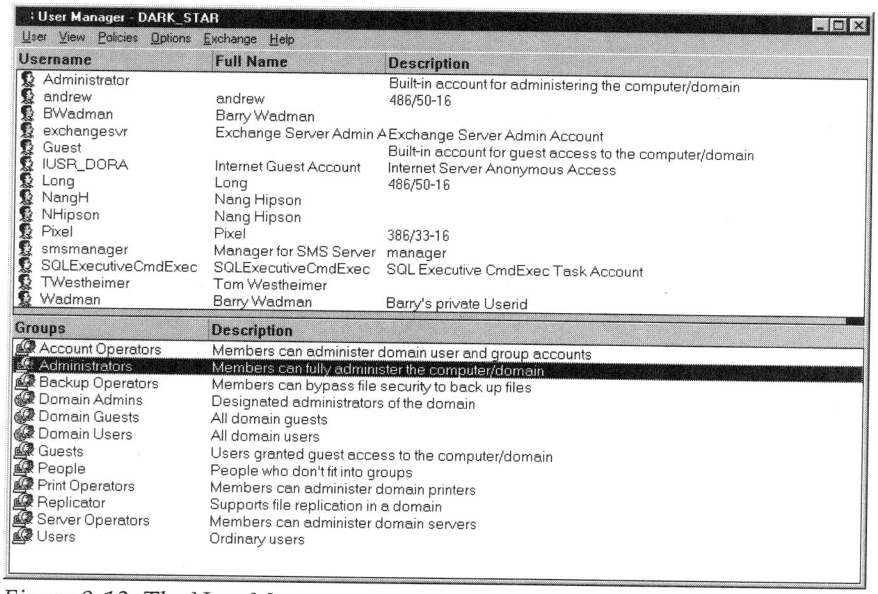

Figure 9-13: The User Manager.

Rights & Privileges

Both groups and users are assigned privileges called *rights*. Groups created by default have a set of default rights. New groups, which you create, do not have any special rights.

To grant your groups any special rights, select Policies | User Rights from the menu. Most groups do not need to have any special rights assigned. Most user base groups need only the Access this computer from network right.

Rights are categorized into two broad classifications: regular rights and advanced rights. Advanced rights include rights given to very special user accounts that must perform special tasks. Usually, you will not have to assign advanced user rights; when an application or system requiring advanced user rights is installed, it will create a user account and assign whatever rights are needed. From time to time, however, you may need to know where advanced user rights are set. User Manager's Policies | User Rights menu selection displays the User Rights Policy dialog, as shown in Figure 9-14.

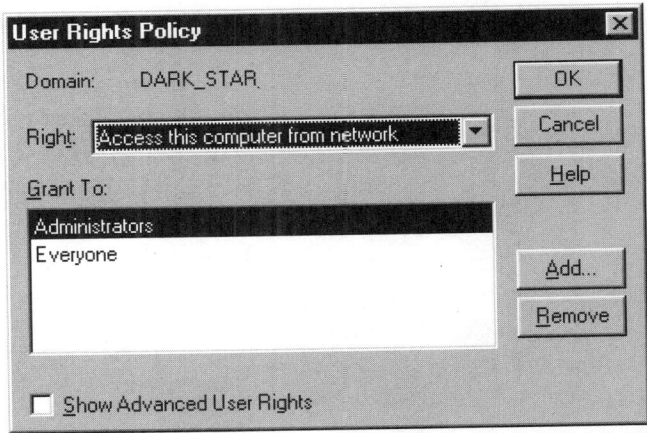

Figure 9-14: The User Rights Policy dialog lets you add and remove rights.

To grant a right to a group or a user, in the User Rights Policy dialog click on the Add button, and in the Add Users and Groups dialog box, select the user account or group that you plan to grant the right to. To remove a right from a group or a user, select the user or group in the Grant To: list and then click on the Remove button.

The various rights supported by Windows NT 4 Server are shown in Table 9-1. Rights should not be granted indiscriminately, because many of the rights may be used to compromise system security if misused.

Right	Basic?	Notes
Access this computer from network	X	Everybody has this right. It is the default right for all users.
Act as part of the operating system		Used by services, and not by users.
Add workstations to domain	X	Usually domain account managers, if you have one.
Back up files and directories	X	Backup operators—you may define zero, one, or more backup operators.
Bypass traverse checking		Everybody has this right. It is the default right for all users.
Change the system time	X	Usually assigned to administrators and server operators; you may want to create other privileged users who are able to change system time. Be aware of the impact of an improper change of time—many transactions will be timestamped with the incorrect time.
Create a pagefile		Usually, only administrators create pagefiles.
Create a token object		Creation of token objects is a special right that is normally assigned when the user account that needs this right is created.
Create permanent shared objects		Creation of permanent shared objects is a special right that is normally assigned when the user account that needs this right is created.
Debug programs		Normally, only administrators are allowed to debug programs, but at times, maintenance or development staff may need this right.

Right	Basic?	Notes
Force shutdown from a remote system	X	Administrators and server operators are assigned this right. You would not normally want other user accounts to be able to shut down the server remotely.
Generate security audits		Not normally assigned; could be useful to administrators or server operators.
Increase quotas		This right is usually granted to administrators. Server operators may need this right; determine this on a case-by-case basis.
Increase scheduling priority		Administrators have this right, though server operators may benefit from being granted this right.
Load and unload device drivers	X	This right is assigned to administrators.
Lock pages in memory		This right is not assigned to any group or user by default.
Log on as a batch job		Assigned to individual user accounts as needed when these accounts are created. Not normally assigned manually; however, you may find a use for this right.
Log on as a service		The administrator group is given this right, and individual accounts created to work with services are also granted this right on a user-by-user basis.
Log on locally	X	Most administrative and operator user accounts may log on locally. As well, the IIS guest account has this right. This right can be assigned to many users who would have a need to log on at the server, but this right should not be granted indiscriminately.

Right	Basic?	Notes
Manage auditing and security log	X	Usually granted to administrators, the audit log is useful for monitoring security problems.
Modify firmware environment values		This right is usually granted only to administrators.
Profile single process		This right is usually granted only to administrators.
Profile system performance		This right is usually granted only to administrators.
Replace a process level token		This right is usually granted only to administrators.
Restore files and directories	X	Granted to administrators, backup operators, server operators, and individual user accounts that need this right.
Shut down the system	X	This right is usually granted only to administrators.
Take ownership of files or other objects	X	This right is usually granted only to administrators, though it may be granted to other trusted operators and users who need this privilege.

Table 9-1: User rights, both basic and advanced.

Printing a List of Users

Having a list of users is useful should you need to recreate the user database. By printing this list, you can look up users and do other user-management tasks even when access to the server is not available. The User Manager program is not able to print (or save to disk) the list of users. However, the command-based NET command does support listing of user accounts and detailed information about user accounts. Though the process to produce a list of users is a bit convoluted (you must create a command file using an editor), you can, using the steps outlined below, generate a list of all user accounts.

Note: The same basic process can also be used to document groups. To generate a detailed list of user accounts, follow these steps:

1. When logged on as an administrator, open a command prompt window.

2. Issue the command NET USERS >TEMP.BAT. An example of the output from this command is shown in Figure 9-15.

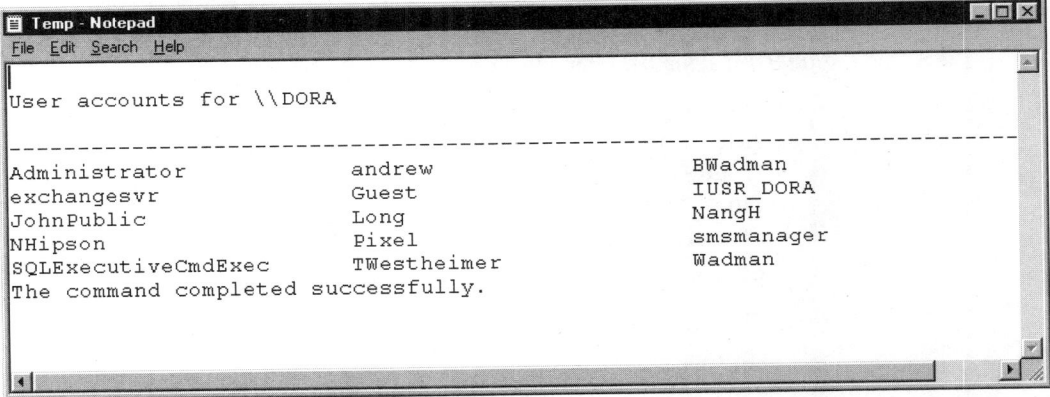

Figure 9-15: The output from NET USERS>TEMP.BAT.

3. Edit the output from the command (the file temp.bat) using any text-based editor. Split the three columns of user account names into a single column, and delete all information from the file except for the user account names. Figure 9-16 shows the temp.bat file after these changes.

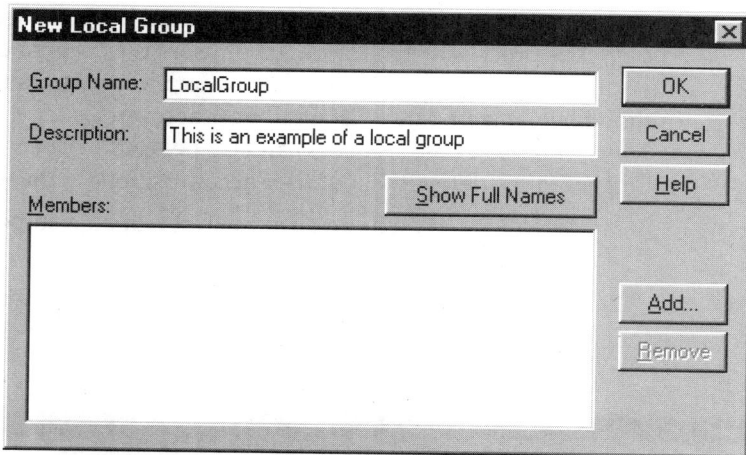

Figure 9-16: Temp.bat after editing.

4. Add, in front of each user account name, the command NET USERS. After each user account name, add >> USERLIST.DAT. Finally, add a header line at the beginning of the file: ECHO "List of users as of (date)" > USERLIST.DAT.

5. Save temp.bat, and from your command prompt, execute it!

6. The file userlist.dat will contain a detailed list of all user accounts.

Warning

Information contained in the user list could be used to compromise system security. Keep this list secure! When you no longer need it, dispose of this list in a secure manner. Do not leave the userlist.dat file on the server without protecting it from access by unauthorized users!

Backing Up the User List

OK, if you can print a list of users, can you back up the user database? The answer, short and sweet, is not really. However, Windows NT 4 Server does automatically back up the user account list when you have both a primary domain controller (PDC) and a backup domain controller (BDC) configured.

The whole purpose of a domain with a PDC and BDCs is to allow the account information to be maintained in one location, and be available from more than one location. If the PDC cannot function (for any reason, such as being shut down), then a BDC is promoted to become the PDC. The BDC has its own copy of user account information (this information is replicated between the PDC and any BDCs).

If for some reason you must create a new, clean PDC installation, you don't have to reenter the user information:

1. Create the new PDC server initially configured as a BDC.

2. Bring the new server up on the network.

3. The current PDC replicates the current user account information to the new server.

4. Manually promote the new server to be the PDC (this process automatically demotes the current PDC to be a BDC).

Voilà, your new server now has the complete list of user accounts (and all other security information such as groups and rights).

Account Policy

In Windows NT 4 Server, all accounts have a set of basic policies. These policies can be used to enhance system security. Figure 9-17 shows the Account Policy dialog that displays when you select Policies | Account in User Manager.

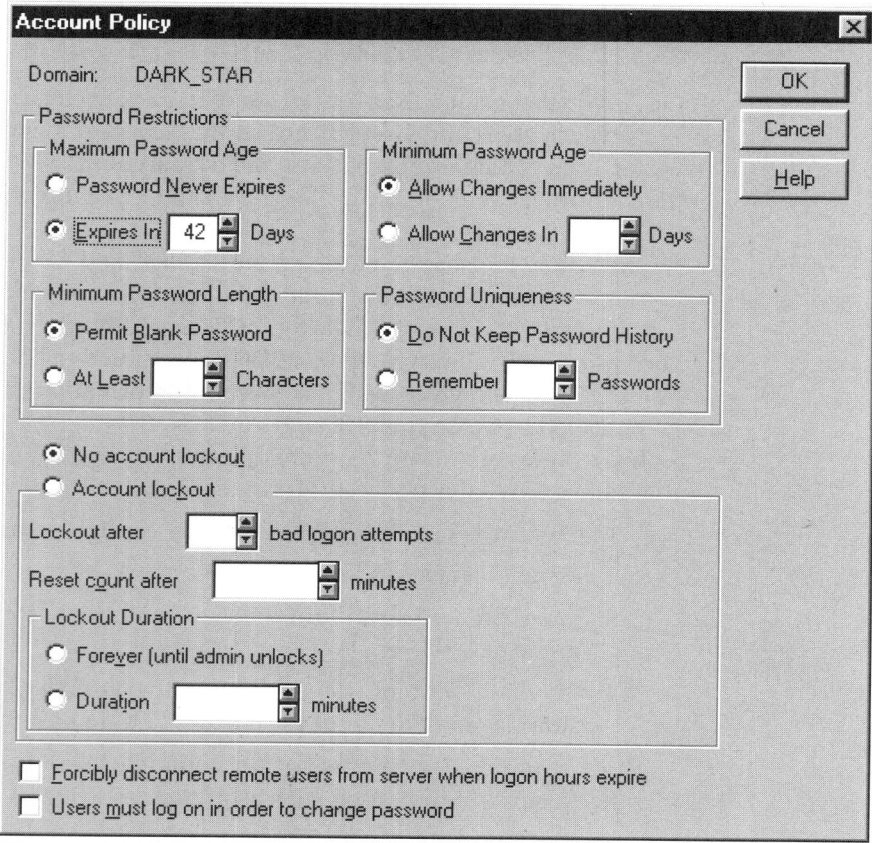

Figure 9-17: Default account policies.

Password Restrictions

For user accounts, you may set a number of password restrictions:

- **Maximum Password Age**—allows you to force passwords to expire after a fixed period of time. Choosing Password Never Expires forces Windows NT 4 Server to never have a password expire. Most organizations find it advantageous to have passwords expire on a monthly basis.

- **Minimum Password Age**—allows you to set the minimum time the user must wait before changing his or her password. Most organizations don't restrict password changes.

- **Minimum Password Length**—permits you to specify a minimum password size. You may specify either that the user may have a blank password (never a good idea, in my opinion), or that the password must have At Least <number> Characters. The minimum <number> of characters should be at least six, and preferably eight or more.

- **Password Uniqueness**—helps prevent users from having fixed lists of passwords that they rotate on a regular basis. If you implement this feature, set the number of passwords remembered to at least eight! The typical number, four, is not sufficient.

Account Lockout

Locking out an account when security violations may have occurred is an effective tool in stopping such practices as password guessing.

If you set Account Lockout, you can specify that the account is locked out after a specified number of bad log on attempts (bad password attempts). The typical number of consecutive bad log on attempts permitted is four, though in organizations in which security is critical, this number may be set to two or even one.

The count of bad log on attempts is typically reset after a predefined period of time, usually 30 minutes. Some organizations set this time to as much as 24 hours.

Lockout duration can be either a fixed period of time (the default of 30 minutes is typical for many organizations), or "Forever." If you select Forever, then when an account has been locked out, the administrator must unlock the account using the Account Locked Out check box in the User Properties dialog box (see Figure 9-9).

For highest security, select Forever (Until Admin Unlocks). If you do so, then when a user's account is locked out, the administrator will always be aware of the situation.

Tip

Just because a user's account has been locked doesn't mean that the user is doing anything wrong. This can happen for a number of reasons, including (in no particular order):

- *The user has a poor memory for passwords.*
- *The user has a problem typing passwords.*
- *Someone is attempting to access the user's account improperly.*
- *The user was given the wrong password.*
- *There are network communication difficulties.*

A user may be restricted to a limited number of hours of connection to the server. When the connection hours have expired, the user is not allowed to log on again until either the next authorized time period or the authorized hours have been changed. You can tell Windows NT 4 Server to force a user to be disconnected when the logon hours expire.

Users should always be required to log on to change passwords. This helps prevent someone from changing a password for a user account without authority.

Audit Policy

The Windows NT 4 Server audit facilities allow you to monitor a number of events. Events may be audited when successful or when a failure occurs. Display the Audit Policy dialog box (Figure 9-18) by selecting Policies | Audit from the User Manager's menu.

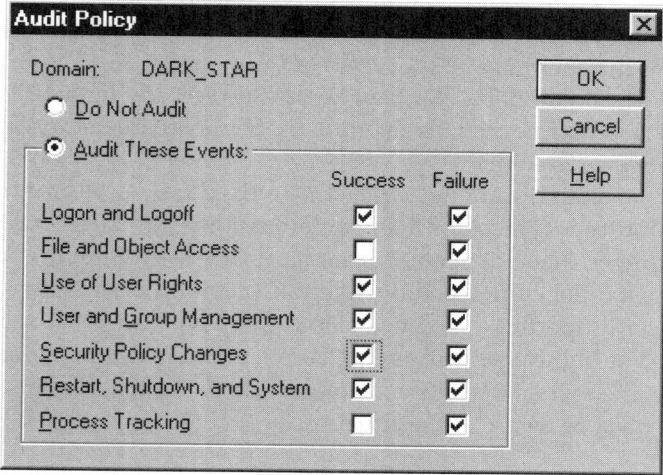

Figure 9-18: Establishing Audit policies.

Generally, if you are monitoring success, you should also monitor failure:

- **Logon and Logoff** —audits user logon and logoff. When auditing success, you will be able to determine who is using the system. Auditing failure allows you to detect possible attempts to log on improperly.

- **File and Object Access**—audits whenever files or objects are accessed from the server. The information from the success audit can be extensive. Failure information can help detect attempts to browse files and objects that are not permitted for the user.

- **Use of User Rights**—any user rights other than logon or logoff.

- **User and Group Management**—audits changes to users and groups.

- **Security Policy Changes**—audits changes to user rights, audit, or trust relationship policies.

- **Restart, Shutdown, and System**—audits starts, shutdowns, or any event that could compromise system security.

- **Process Tracking**—audits actions related to program activation and termination and other related actions.

Auditing information is sent to the security log. Use the Event Viewer (Start Menu | Programs | Administrative Tools (Common) | Event Viewer) to view audit information.

Trust Relationships

A trust relationship is the method by which two separate domains establish that they "trust" each other. Creating a trust relationship is a two-stage process—each domain must configure the trust relationship.

The Trust Relationships dialog box (select Policies | Trust Relationships from the User Manager menu), shown in Figure 9-19, shows that no trust relationships have been established.

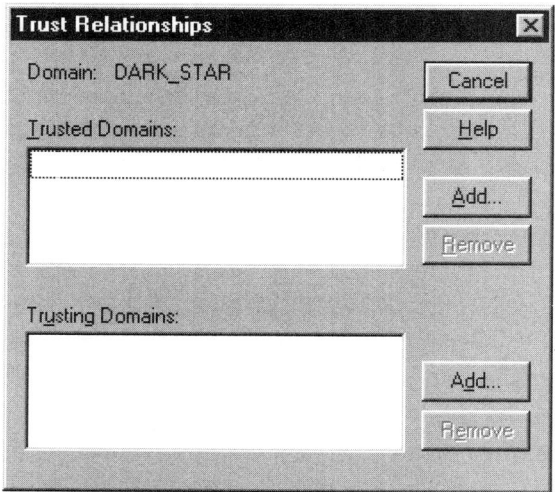

Figure 9-19: The Trust Relationships dialog box.

A trusted domain's users and groups are allowed user rights, resource permissions, and local group memberships on the trusting domain.

A trusting domain allows users from a trusted domain user to have user rights, resource permissions, and local group memberships on the trusting domain.

To create a trust relationship, you must do the following:

1. On the domain that will be trusted, select the Add button next to the Trusting Domains: list and add a trusting domain.

2. On the domain that was added to the Trusting Domain: list in step one, you must start the User Manager, go to the Trust Relationships dialog box, and add the trusted domain to the Trusted Domains: list by selecting the Add button next to the Trusted Domains: list.

Warning

Never, ever remove one side of a trust relationship without removing the other side. Both sides (trusted and trusting) must agree on the relationship.

Physical Security

Most servers are shared resources. Generally, most of us need to meet a set of conflicting goals—the server must be located convenient to administration, users, and other resources (including printers, power, and network connections).

Server Locations

Planning your server location and security may be difficult. Existing installations may dictate the server's location, smaller companies that are growing larger may feel that security is unimportant (and will feel that way until there is a security problem), and, let's face it, planning is difficult.

Even if operating systems claim to be secure, as Windows NT 4 Server does, the bottom line is that if your server is not physically secure, then no amount of operating system security will make the system secure. Some physical security points of mine include:

- Place the servers, drives, backup devices, and backup media in a computer room that has restricted access.

- Use combination or electronic locks on the computer room. Like passwords, change the combinations frequently. Dual-lock the computer room for maximum security so that it takes two people to open the door.

- Ensure that the computer room cannot be accessed through a raised computer room floor from outside the room.

- Check the ceilings! Dropped or suspended ceilings usually offer no barrier to people moving from room to room through the ceiling using only a simple stepladder.

- Windows in the computer room should be protected with alarms that cannot be disabled except by the security staff, whether the windows are internal or external.

- Secure your network cables. Be very cautious of network cables that run between discontinuous floors, or run through common raceways.

- A lot of damage can be done to a server by a remote user who is using an account with administrator privileges. Make sure to keep passwords and user ID lists confidential.

- Have you installed Microsoft SQL Server? Be sure that the Microsoft SQL Server "sa" account has a password!

Power Security—the UPS

The first rumble of thunder, and you start getting nervous. Out goes the message, "There is a storm coming, save your data frequently." Well, for users, that is half a solution.

Most network servers run with some form of Uninterruptible Power Supply (UPS). This device typically consists of a rechargeable battery and a converter that converts the battery's power to power that the server can use.

Windows NT 4 Server has UPS communications features that are very useful. You can perform a number of tasks when power fails:

- Notify users that a power failure occurred at the server.

- If power is not restored in a reasonable period, begin a system shutdown.

Configuring a UPS requires the UPS to be able to send some form of message to the server that power has failed. This is done by connecting the UPS to the server using a serial cable. For example, many better UPS systems notify the server when power fails, when a low battery power condition exists, and when the UPS is shutting down (either because batteries have been exhausted or the UPS is overheating).

The Windows NT 4 Server Control Panel's UPS applet, shown in Figure 9-20, shows a typical configuration. Every UPS is unique, so you will need to consult with the documentation supplied with your UPS to determine which features are supported and how to configure these features.

The UPS Configuration group box allows you to select which signals the UPS sends to the server. UPS communications are very simple, and not all UPS systems support the different signals. You can select whichever signals your UPS provides, and configure for those signals. Make sure that the UPS Interface Voltage polarity is set correctly!

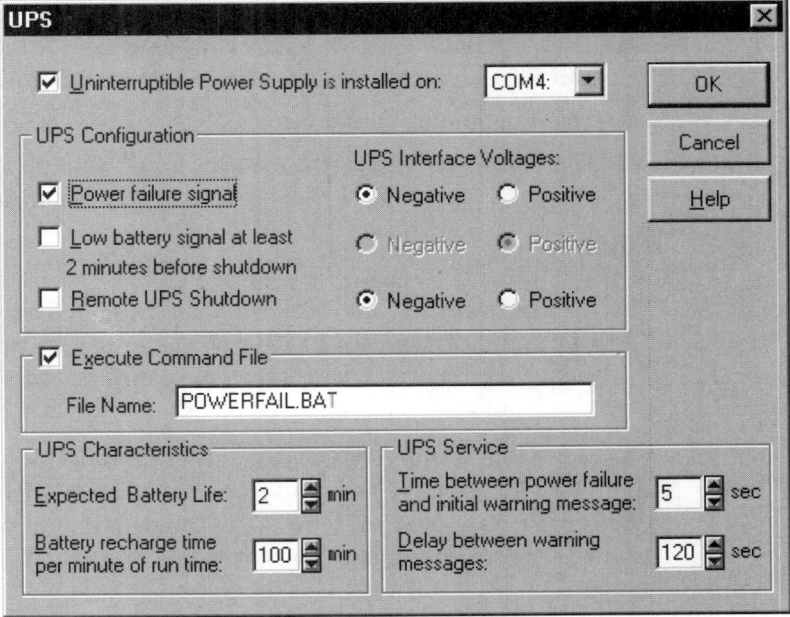

Figure 9-20: The Control Panel's UPS applet.

UPS Communications

UPS systems communicate using the serial port's control lines. Each line is assigned a use by Windows NT 4 Server:

CTS (Clear-to-send) signals that the power has failed. CTS will either go negative or positive when power fails. Enable the Power failure signal check box to use this feature.

DCD (Data-carrier-detect) signals that the battery level is dropping to a critical level. Enable the Low battery signal at least 2 minutes before shutdown to use this feature.

DTR (Data-terminal-ready) signals that the UPS is in the process of being shut down. Enable the Remote UPS Shutdown to use this feature.

If you're using any adapters or extension cables, make sure that they correctly carry these signals! Test the installation: Pull the plug and see what happens (but do this when no users are on the server).

You can have the server automatically execute a command file (EXE, COM, BAT, or CMD) located in the WinNT\System32 folder. This command file executes just before the system is shut down when:

- The time limits specified expired.
- The UPS signaled that the system should shut down.

Warning

Microsoft states that the command file specified in Execute Command File must execute within 30 seconds or the server may not properly shut down. Making this command file as simple as possible is a wise idea!

A second part of the UPS system configuration is found in the Control Panel's Service applet, where you configure the UPS service Startup Type to Automatic, as shown in Figure 9-21. The default, for most systems, is that the UPS service is manually started.

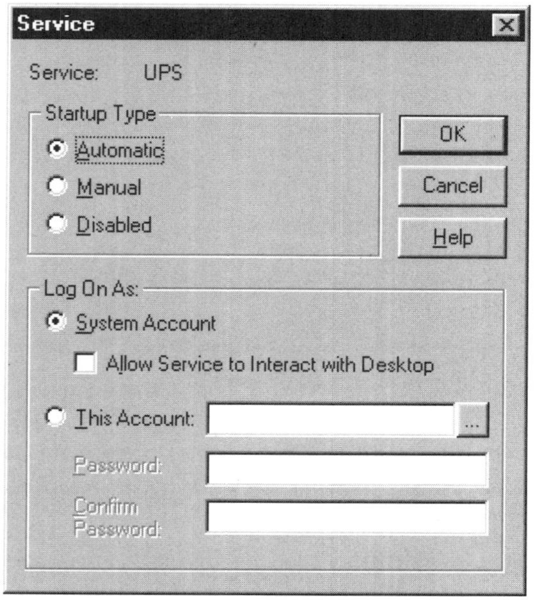

Figure 9-21: Changing UPS startup to Automatic.

Environmental Security

Ever wonder how hot it gets inside your server? Wonder how much dust those little fans deposit on the inside of the system? Wonder what would happen if your computer fell into a lake?

Temperature is a critical problem with computers. Back in the good old days, we used huge air conditioners to cool the computers. Today, a small room air conditioner is all that is needed, but in many environments, some form of air conditioning is still needed. Generally, you should not have to worry about overheating if the ambient air temperature is about 70°F (or 22°C). When the air temperature exceeds this value by more than 15 percent, then overheating becomes a real threat.

Some hardware has overheating protection, but many servers do not have sufficient protection and should be monitored whenever possible. Even simple electronic thermometers (such as what Radio Shack sells) will monitor the temperature of a server adequately. In the two servers here at DarkStar, I continually monitor both the temperature near the CPU and the temperature of the power supply. Several fans have failed, and these monitors have helped prevent disaster! Give serious consideration to multiple fans. The external SCSI drive unit on the DORA server has five fans—a single fan failure will not cause immediate problems there.

Dust and dirt in the air is a major problem. Corrosive atmospheres can wreak havoc for computers; be certain that servers are not exposed to any substances (gases, salt air, and so on) that could cause corrosion. All computers, especially servers, should be taken apart at regular intervals and cleaned of dust. Dust traps air and can lead to overheating. A small air compressor, or canned air, is adequate to clean most computers. A carefully used vacuum cleaner can be used, but caution must be exercised so as not to damage components while cleaning.

Moving On

In this chapter, I delved into security, users, groups, and auditing. For most organizations, security is a major part of the system administrator's job. Most Windows NT 4 Server security is managed using the Domain User Manager. Physical security is also an issue covered in this chapter. Without physical security, the most carefully managed Windows NT 4 Server will never be secure.

This concludes the Windows NT 4 Server section of the book. The next section overviews Microsoft SQL Server 6.5.

Microsoft SQL Server 6.5

10

Understanding SQL Databases

To fully understand what Microsoft SQL Server is, you must first understand the concept of databases. There are two general database systems: shared (or distributed) and client/server. The differences between client/server databases and shared databases lie in where the "work" is being done.

In a client/server database system, the database is located on a server. The server also hosts a software system that interfaces the clients with the database. All the clients do (typically) is take the information that the server provides and format/display the data for the user. Typically, the client does little or no processing of data.

Microsoft SQL Server 6.5 and Oracle Server are just two examples of client/server database servers. Generally, despite the fact that the server does much of the work in a client/server system, client/server systems are generally more robust, and offer better performance when faced with greater loads. In a client/server environment, it is most unusual for a server to be developed in-house, whereas the client-side software is typically developed in-house.

In a shared or distributed database, the data is usually found on one (or more, if distributed) servers, but all the processing is done at the client site. The client retrieves, sorts, and processes records, and the server (or servers) merely functions as a file server, sharing the database with the client users. Microsoft Access is an example of a shared database system. Designed as a desktop database system, Access is actually able to serve well in a lightly loaded environment. However, when the number of concurrent users increases, the performance of a multiuser Access database system falters.

This chapter describes Microsoft SQL Server 6.5 and some of the utilities that are included with it.

The one thing computers do better than anything else is process information. No matter what the task, it almost always comes down to acquiring, storing, and reporting or otherwise manipulating information. This single fact was responsible for creating companies such as Oracle, Informix, and Sybase and has enticed Microsoft to enter the database market in a big way.

This chapter starts by providing a background to the different types of database systems and standards at work in the database industry and then introduces you to Microsoft SQL Server as one of the premier client/server database applications in the industry.

The Anatomy of a Database

A database, in the very simplest of terms, is nothing more than a collection of data (called a table), organized as a number of rows, consisting of one or more columns of information. We can take that view a bit further, but taking a visual view of a conceptual database table (Figure 10-1) shows this relationship very well.

au_id	au_lname	au_fname	phone	address	city	state	zip	contract
172-32-1176	White	Johnson	408 496-7223	10932 Bigge Rd.	Menlo Park	CA	94025	1
213-46-8915	Green	Marjorie	415 986-7020	309 63rd St. #411	Oakland	CA	94618	1
238-95-7766	Carson	Cheryl	415 548-7723	589 Darwin Ln.	Berkeley	CA	94705	1
267-41-2394	O'Leary	Michael	408 286-2428	22 Cleveland Av. #14	San Jose	CA	95128	1
274-80-9391	Straight	Dean	415 834-2919	5420 College Av.	Oakland	CA	94609	1
341-22-1782	Smith	Meander	913 843-0462	10 Mississippi Dr.	Lawrence	KS	66044	0
409-56-7008	Bennet	Abraham	415 658-9932	6223 Bateman St.	Berkeley	CA	94705	1
427-17-2319	Dull	Ann	415 836-7128	3410 Blonde St.	Palo Alto	CA	94301	1
472-27-2349	Gringlesby	Burt	707 938-6445	PO Box 792	Covelo	CA	95428	1
486-29-1786	Locksley	Charlene	415 585-4620	18 Broadway Av.	San Francisco	CA	94130	1
527-72-3246	Greene	Morningstar	615 297-2723	22 Graybar House Rd.	Nashville	TN	37215	0
648-92-1872	Blotchet-Halls	Reginald	503 745-6402	55 Hillsdale Bl.	Corvallis	OR	97330	1
672-71-3249	Yokomoto	Akiko	415 935-4228	3 Silver Ct.	Walnut Creek	CA	94595	1
712-45-1867	del Castillo	Innes	615 996-8275	2286 Cram Pl. #86	Ann Arbor	MI	48105	1
722-51-5454	DeFrance	Michel	219 547-9982	3 Balding Pl.	Gary	IN	46403	1
724-08-9931	Stringer	Dirk	415 843-2991	5420 Telegraph Av.	Oakland	CA	94609	0
724-80-9391	MacFeather	Stearns	415 354-7128	44 Upland Hts.	Oakland	CA	94612	1
756-30-7391	Karsen	Livia	415 534-9219	5720 McAuley St.	Oakland	CA	94609	1
807-91-6654	Panteley	Sylvia	301 946-8853	1956 Arlington Pl.	Rockville	MD	20853	1
846-92-7186	Hunter	Sheryl	415 836-7128	3410 Blonde St.	Palo Alto	CA	94301	1
893-72-1158	McBadden	Heather	707 448-4982	301 Putnam	Vacaville	CA	95688	0
899-46-2035	Ringer	Anne	801 826-0752	67 Seventh Av.	Salt Lake City	UT	84152	1
998-72-3567	Ringer	Albert	801 826-0752	67 Seventh Av.	Salt Lake City	UT	84152	1

Figure 10-1: A typical table in a database; the top row contains the column names.

In Figure 10-1, we see a header row at the top of the table, which contains the column names (such as au_id, au_lname, etc.). There are nine columns of information, and 23 rows of data. (The table in this example is the *authors* table from the *pubs* database, which is included with Microsoft SQL Server 6.5.)

Information is retrieved from a table, typically based on restricting criteria (for example, retrieve all authors who live in California). Once retrieved, the data is then presented to the user (interactively on the screen, or perhaps as a printed report). Sounds simple, right?

Things get more complex as the amount of data increases. It is not uncommon for database tables to have 50,000 to 1,000,000 rows of data. The problems of searching and selecting rows from such a large amount of data are paramount. Many simpler database systems that perform well when working with a few thousand rows of data completely fail when given larger amounts of data to manage! But not SQL Server, since it is optimized to work well with large amounts of data.

Of Rows & Columns

Each table in the database (remember, there may be many tables, or only one) consists of rows and columns. A row consists of one datum for each column in the table. Rows are self-evident—just take a quick look at Figure 10-1 if you are unsure of what a row is.

A column, however, represents a particular type of information, perhaps formatted in a particular way. For example, as Figure 10-1 shows, there is a column called *state*, which contains the two-character postal abbreviation for the author's state.

A column may have an index to enable searching and sorting (we will talk more about indexes in the next part of this chapter), and each row has attributes that describe the data contained in the column. Table 10-1 lists both the Microsoft SQL Server 6.5 datatypes and a brief description of each datatype.

Datatype	Description
bit	Bit values, either a logical zero or one value.
tinyint	A value between 0 and 255.
image	Image information, of variable size.
varbinary	A binary field, of a maximum size defined at the time the table is created.
binary	A binary field, of a size defined at the time the table is created.
timestamp	Time and date field.
text	A text field, 16 bytes in size.
char	A text field of predefined size.
numeric	A numeric field, size defined at the time the table is created.
decimal	A numeric field, size defined at the time the table is created.
money	Fields that will contain money value (two decimal places). Field is 8 bytes long.
smallmoney	Fields that will contain money value (two decimal places). Field is 4 bytes long.
int	An integer value, 4 bytes long.
smallint	An integer value, 2 bytes long.
float	A floating-point value, either 4 or 8 bytes long (8 bytes are used for precisions of 8 or greater).
real	A floating-point value, 4 bytes long.
datetime	A date and time field.
smalldatetime	A date and time field with less precision than datetime.
varchar	A text field of a maximum predefined size.

Table 10-1: The Microsoft SQL Server 6.5 datatypes for a column in a table.

As Table 10-1 shows, Microsoft SQL Server offers a rich array of datatypes for columns. Actually, datatypes are defined in the SQL standards, so that a database from another database system will probably be easy to implement using Microsoft SQL Server 6.5.

Of Indexes & Sorting

Indexes are objects that the database system creates. Many database systems store indexes as special tables (which are not visible, to you or anyone else). An index is a sorted list of all the values in the specified column, with a pointer to the record that the value is from. Because the index is sorted, it is easy to find a specific record based upon a value found in the index column.

When data is placed in a table, there can be several problems. For example, let's say there are 5,000 rows of data in our authors table (again, refer to Figure 10-1). If we want to list all authors who live in Oakland, California, we might formulate our request as:

```
SELECT authors.au_id, authors.au_lname,
authors.au_fname, authors.phone, authors.address,
authors.city, authors.state, authors.zip,
authors.contract
FROM "pubs.dbo".authors authors
WHERE (authors.city='Oakland' and authors.state='CA')
```

The above example (an actual SQL statement) will list all authors who have their city listed as Oakland, as Figure 10-2 shows.

The results of this query then could be formatted into a report and printed, or perhaps presented to the user as an interactive display.

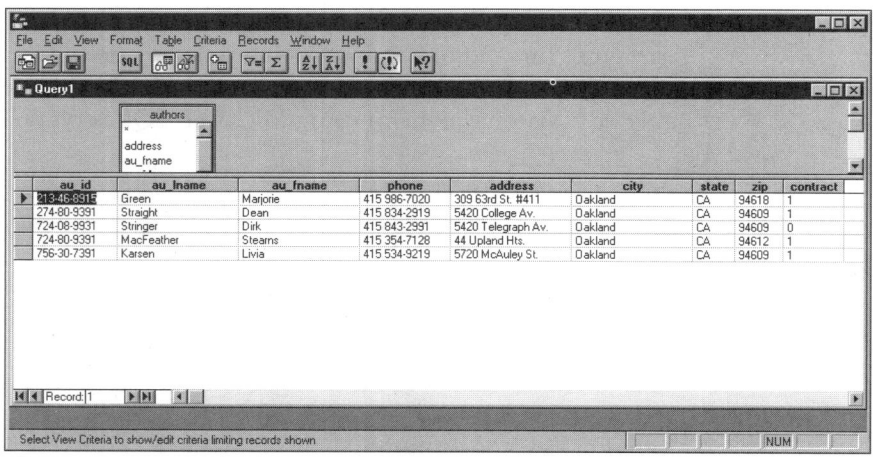

Figure 10-2: Only these authors live in Oakland.

Okay, so what's the big deal? Why are indexes necessary? Were the authors table to really have thousands of authors in it (rather than the paltry 23 the example database has), then the time spent searching each record could become significant very quickly: Imagine having to go through thousands of records, one by one, searching for Oakland?

The solution is to create an index, because with an index, searching is made much easier. Let's define an index:

in·dex (în'dêks') *noun*

1. *Abbr.* **ind.** Something that serves to guide, point out, or otherwise facilitate reference, especially: **a.** An alphabetized list of names, places, and subjects treated in a printed work, giving the page or pages on which each item is mentioned. **b.** A thumb index. **c.** A table, file, or catalog.[1]

So an index is an alphabetized list . . . really, it is! Now, just how does this make things easier when searching for Oakland? First, Microsoft SQL Server would do a binary search to find Oakland. A binary search takes only a few comparisons to determine whether a particular value will be found in the list. (The exact number of comparisons needed, were there 65,000 records in the table, would be about 16.)

---

[1] *The American Heritage® Dictionary of the English Language, Third Edition* copyright © 1992 by Houghton Mifflin Company.

How Is a Binary Search Done?

Start here: First, the search routine determines the middle of the list to be searched. For example, if a list has 23 entries, then the middle entry would be the 12th entry. The middle entry is then compared with the desired value. If it matches (more luck than anything else), then the search ends.

If the middle entry does not match, then the search routine determines whether the middle entry is greater or less than the desired value. If it is less than the desired value, then the search routine must check the second half of the list. If it is greater than the desired value, then the search routine must check the first half of the list.

If the remaining list consists of two or fewer entries, then the search is over, and the desired value was not found!

Otherwise, go to *Start here* and try, try again.

For example, if the list contains the names Ann, Kathleen, Nancy, Paul, and Peter, and the desired name is Paul, then the first midpoint would be Nancy. Since Paul is greater than Nancy, we would limit our search to the upper half of the list. Again, the midpoint of the upper half of the list is Paul, which is a match. In this example, the match was found using only two comparisons!

Once a single record matching the search criteria (Oakland) was found, the index list would be "walked" forward and backward until no more matches to Oakland were found. Since the index is sorted, all instances of Oakland will be grouped together, making the search very fast!

"Cool," you say, "let's make indexes for all of our columns. That way regardless of which column is searched on, the results will be fast!" Well, there is a down side to indexes (a gotcha). When a column is indexed and a new row is added, the index must be "fixed." The new row's value must be inserted into the index. This process of rebuilding the index is not as difficult as it may appear. The location where the new row would be placed is found, and the current value in this location is saved in a special place along with the new row's value. Then in the location in the index where these two values would have been found, a flag is placed telling the database system that the special place must be searched for a match. This does make inserting records faster, but slows searching, as the binary search algorithm must take into account the process of adding records. Figure 10-3 shows an example of an index that has had a row added.

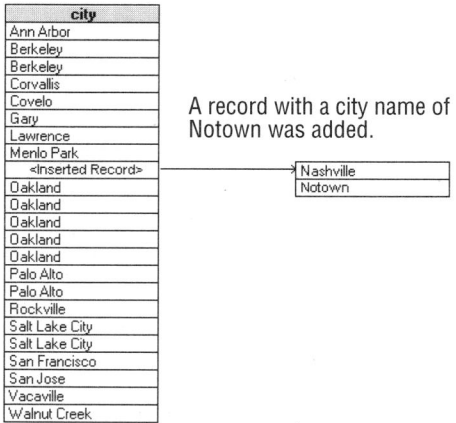

Figure 10-3: Adding a row to an indexed column makes things more difficult.

Once records have been added to an indexed table, it is generally desirable to rebuild the indexes. Different database systems use different techniques.

Devices, Transaction Logs & Such

Typically, when a database is created, it is best to also create a new database device (a database device is the actual file where the database's data will be stored). Actually, for nontrivial databases, it would be best to create two devices: one for the database itself and a second device for the transaction log.

The transaction log consists of all updates (changed or added rows, for example) to the database since the last backup. Transaction logs are optional—for databases that are not critical and for databases that are on secure, fault-tolerant devices, the need for a transaction log is minimal.

If at all possible, create these two devices on different physical devices (or on a fault-tolerant device). Though there are no hard and fast rules for how large to make the transaction log device, a quick rule of thumb would be to use a size that is between 10 percent and 50 percent of the size of the database. Transaction log sizes vary greatly depending on the update activity of the database (databases that are very actively used will need a larger transaction log) and the frequency of backups. A more frequently backed-up database will not need as large a transaction log.

Overview of Relational Databases

Before we go any further, let's understand the database market. The first distinction that must be made is between personal information processing and enterprise or corporate information processing. The difference between the two has nothing to do with the nature of the information being processed but rather with the way it is used. For example, a spreadsheet or desktop database application such as Microsoft Access is a personal information processor. The information being processed can be monthly sales figures or cooking recipes. When you need to have information that is up-to-date and immediately available to a large number of people, you must have a system capable of processing information at the enterprise level. An example of this might be a corporate accounting system.

There are a number of "standardized" database types that are commonly found on computers.

Types of Databases

There are three general classes of database systems: desktop, host based, and client/server. Let's take at look at each in a little more detail. In addition, databases themselves are typically organized as flat, object oriented, or relational.

Desktop Database Systems

Desktop database systems are database applications that run completely on the user's computer. The only way a desktop database system can support multiple users is by relying on network operating systems' file-sharing capabilities.

The biggest problem with desktop database systems is performance, especially when the database file itself is stored on a server and must load all data to be processed into the user machine's RAM. As an example of how inefficient this can be, imagine two users searching for all records that fit given criteria, and for some reason they happen to be using the same criteria.

USER 1 begins first by loading every record in the database (transferred across the network) to the user's machine where it is compared against the search criteria and then discarded. USER 2 begins the same search, immediately following the same exact procedure. In both cases, all of the data is transferred across the network at great expense only to be discarded, with the exception of the records that match the criteria.

If that seems incredibly inefficient to you, well, that is because it is! Imagine if a request could be made to only return the records that matched the criteria and where all of the processing was performed on the machine on which the database existed. Moreover, imagine if the second request was made and the search did not have to be repeated, since it had just been successfully completed.

Host-based Database Systems

Host-based database systems are the oldest DBMSes (database management systems), with all of the software and data residing on a mainframe or minicomputer and all user communication happening from a dumb terminal.

The biggest problem with this model is the expense of maintaining and administering the database. The hardware, which is centralized, is usually expensive. The software component usually requires a small army of the initiated and elite to manage the system and the database.

Client/Server Database Systems

If you haven't noticed by now, the desktop database model requires all of the processing to reside on the client, and the host database model requires all processing to happen on the host or server. Both of these models have extreme drawbacks and built-in constraints as far as scalability. The desktop model doesn't scale well due to the mere fact that the larger the database and the more users you have, the more inefficient the database becomes until performance becomes abysmal. The host model doesn't scale well due to the sheer expense of increasing capacity for the system.

The basic premise behind the client/server model is to distribute the processing between the client and the server in a balance that makes sense. Microsoft's SQL Server is an example of this class of database.

Object-oriented Database Systems

The object-oriented database model follows the tenets of object-oriented design, which are that each element or component of an architecture be designed to include not only the data associated with the object, but also the intelligence to manipulate itself in the appropriate way. For example, an employee object in an object-oriented database would know how to give itself a raise and a promotion as well as knowing how to terminate itself. Of course, security is addressed as well, by only allowing users of the database with the correct authorization to ask an employee object to terminate itself.

ODBC (Open Database Connectivity)

As you may have already realized, one of the biggest problems with enterprise-wide computing is the fact that when a large organization tries to integrate systems that were designed completely out of context with each other, they encounter a nightmare of compatibility problems.

For example, in a hypothetical organization there is an accounting system running on an IBM mainframe, a warehouse inventory tracking system running on an Oracle database server, and the sales department has just implemented a new and improved sales and fulfillment system complete with electronic update capability from field sales reps.

You have been given the task of creating a management information system that can create consolidated reports using the appropriate information from each system. What do you do? No, the correct answer is not "Quit!" However, not too long ago this would have been a very difficult task, relying on special gateways to be available from the database company vendors or from third parties.

However, Microsoft developed a technology called ODBC (Open Database Connectivity) just for this purpose. ODBC is roughly equivalent to database drivers in the sense that you think of video driver or sound driver. The idea is that if an application uses ODBC and you have the proper drivers available, then you can access it. With the situation posed, you can actually create an ODBC-based management information system that uses the correct ODBC drivers to pull data from each database for consolidation into a report.

Relational Databases

Dr. E. F. Codd published a series of papers in 1969 describing a database design model known as the Relational Database Model. The Relational Database Model has since become the accepted model for almost all database design.

There are several other competing models, some with an academic basis and others with a practical basis. The Relational Database Model was designed as an answer to the alternative that is still widely practiced today; it doesn't really have a proper name but can be described as "Lazy, Inefficient Database Design." Since there is not a published body of work, it is best described by pointing out the problems with the technique.

Let's look at an example. Imagine you have been asked to create a database to track library books for a small publisher. The publisher still uses a manual system with cards, but needs to be able to automatically update the inventory. To do this, it is necessary to track the author's name; the address, including city, state, and zip code; the book's ISBN and name; and other information about the author and book itself.

In Table 10-2 is a simple field layout for a table in a theoretical database that can track this information.

Field Name	Data Type(Length)	Description
au_fname	CHAR(32)	First and last name of the author
address	CHAR(64)	Street address
city	CHAR(24)	City
state	CHAR(2)	Two-character state postal code
Zip	CHAR(9)	Zip + 4. Character to preserve leading zeros.
ISBN	CHAR(64)	Book's ISBN
BookTitle	CHAR(64)	Book's title
royaltyper	INT	Author's royalty rate
title_id	CHAR(3)	Book's ID code
au_id	CHAR(12)	Usually the author's SSAN
au_ord	INT	Number of books ordered to date

Table 10-2: Columns in an example database.

To understand the problem with this table layout, let's look at a few records of data (see Table 10-3).

au_fname	address	city	state	ZIP	ISBN	BookTitle	royaltyper	title_id	au_id	au_ord
Peter D. Hipson	13 South Shore Drive	Oakland	CA	99302	123.12.1	Database Developer's Guide with VC++	12	DDG	123-43-1234	3
Peter D. Hipson	13 South Shore Drive	Oakland	CA	99302	543.21.2	What Every VC++ Programmer Should Know	13	WEV	123-43-1234	5
Peter D. Hipson	13 South Shore Drive	Oakland	CA	99302	222.68.34	The Windows NT 4 Server Book	12	WNS	123-43-1234	5
Bryan Waters	321 Down Rd.	Oakland	CA	99302	123.12.123	The Expert Guide to Computers	2	EGC	243-43-2344	5
Barry Wadman	23 West Concord Road	Weston	MA	01234	598.38.234	The Merchant Server Book.	5	MSB	321-98-0023	1

Table 10-3: A table with redundant information.

Notice that with the layout in Table 10-3, we are forced to repeat the author's name and address for each record. This is extremely awkward and may well waste substantial disk space in a large database. To save typing time when entering data, it might be possible to only enter all of the data in the first record and then just enter the name and the book data in each record that follows. This would be dangerous; if the first record is deleted for any reason, the address information would be lost.

It is exactly this sort of poor database design that relational database design was created to address. In a relational model, a minimum of information is duplicated. With the previous design, we have duplicated information all over the place. Examine Figure 10-4 to see what this database table looks like in a more relational form.

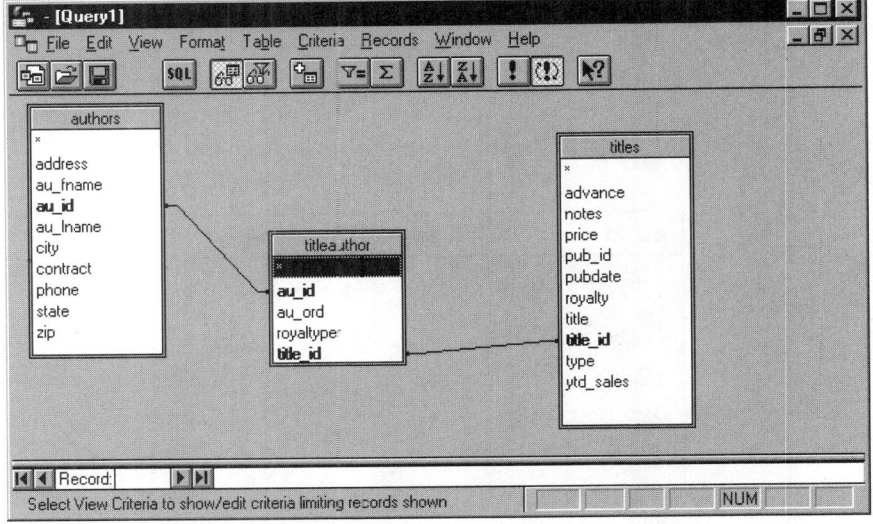

Figure 10-4: A relational database.

The new authors table has had a field added called au_id that is used to provide a reference or key field to link the two tables together. It also helps uniquely identify an individual author, especially if there are two or more authors with similar or even the same name. It happens!

Now the authors table looks like Table 10-4. This table has one record for each author and contains no information about any books that the author may have written.

au_id	au_fname	address	city	state	ZIP
123-43-1234	Peter D. Hipson	13 South Shore Drive	Jaffrey	NH	03452
243-43-2344	Bryan Waters	321 Down Rd.	Oakland	CA	99302
321-98-0023	Barry Wadman	23 West Concord Road	Weston	MA	01234

Table 10-4: The authors table (not all columns are shown).

The titleauthor table (see Table 10-5) contains three fields that were previously in the original table design. The titleauthor table contains the au_id as well. Fields such as the au_id field are referred to as key fields. Two tables that are associated by a key field link are referred to as a relation. A relation can be one-to-many as is this one, meaning that for every record in the authors table, there can be many records in the written titleauthor table. Or it can be one-to-one (each record in the authors table would have a single corresponding record in the titleauthor table), even many-to-one (where zero, one, or more records would have a single corresponding record in the titleauthor table).

The titleauthor table contains only information on books, with the au_id field used to identify the book's author.

au_id	au_ord	royaltyper	title_id
123-43-1234	2	12	VCG
123-43-1234	5	13	WEV
123-43-1234	2	12	WNS
243-43-2344	3	2	EGC
321-98-0023	1	5	MSB

Table 10-5: The titleauthor table (not all columns are shown).

Blasphemy or Common Sense?

Now for something that might be considered blasphemy by database theorists: You can overdo anything to death, and some database designs are so normalized that the design becomes unusable. For example, while it may be correct form to normalize a database to the nth degree, it may not always be a practical decision to do so. Just keep that in mind. If it doesn't seem right for your application or database project, even if the rules of relational database design dictate otherwise, then don't do it.

The primary goals of the relational model are as follows:

- **Data integrity.** Maintenance of the data is important, with assurances that the data's accuracy is maintained.

- **Efficiency.** The performance of the database system is also critical. For many systems, if the database is not sufficiently efficient, the performance degradation will lead to other problems, such as an inability to meet goals.

- **Security.** When databases are insecure, there is a potential for incurred financial losses.

Note: Most of the above example comes from the Microsoft SQL Server 6.5's sample database called pubs. It is an example of a publisher's database system that manages information about authors, books, stores, and the like. Study this example (use the MS Query program that is included with Microsoft SQL Server 6.5 to view the database).

Using SQL to Query Databases

Fundamentally, SQL (Structured Query Language) is a programming language. It is through the use of SQL that all work ultimately ends up being performed. Even when using a front-end program such as Microsoft Access to connect with an SQL database, Access generates SQL commands to send to the database server.

To give you an idea of how rich SQL actually is, you should know that everything you will learn in this section of the book, indeed everything you can do with SQL Server, can be done using SQL commands. Unfortunately, SQL is not for the faint of heart. It won't be too difficult if you have a programming background of some sort. Beyond that, you may be better off just learning the useful command or two and relying on the graphical interface for the remainder, unless your work is pushing to learn SQL.

Fortunately, since Microsoft SQL Server 6.5 has an extremely rich graphical interface, a lot of the tasks that at one time could only be performed using SQL can now be done with the SQL Enterprise Manager (see Figure 10-5). There may be little or no need to use SQL at all unless you begin designing databases.

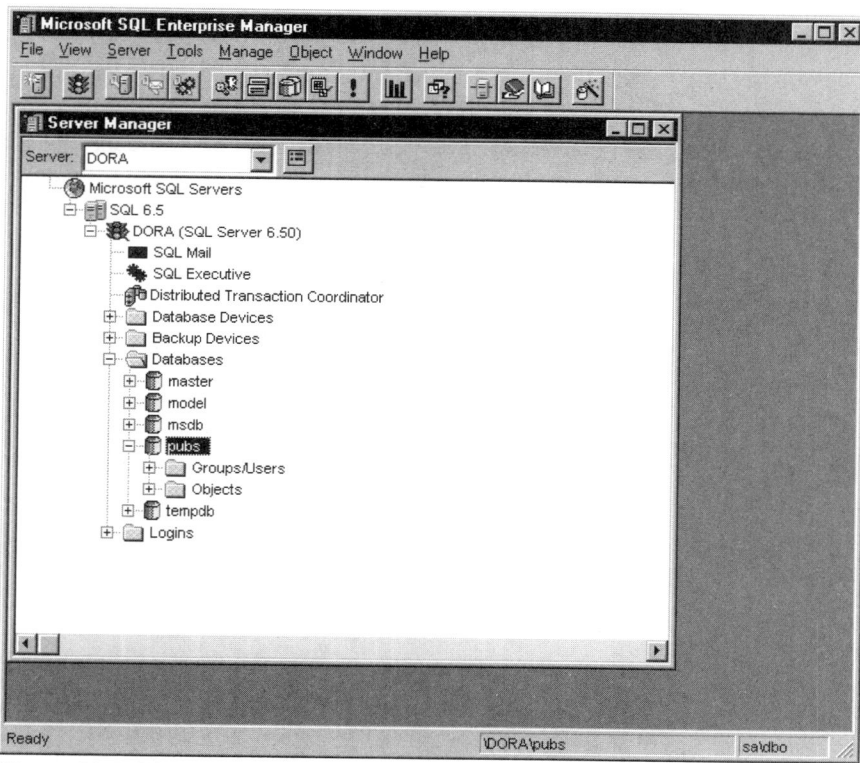

Figure 10-5: The Microsoft SQL Enterprise Manager.

For example, the following SQL statement is used to create a table used to log information from the IIS Servers (this SQL statement is from the file logtemp.sql, found in the %SystemRoot%\system32\inetsrv folder):

```
create table inetlog          (
ClientHost varchar(255),
username varchar(255),
LogTime datetime,
service varchar( 255),
machine varchar( 255),
serverip varchar( 50),
processingtime int,
bytesrecvd int,
bytessent int,
servicestatus int,
win32status int,
operation varchar( 255),
target varchar(255),
parameters varchar(255)          );
```

Moving On

In this chapter, I covered the Microsoft SQL Server 6.5 system. Microsoft SQL Server 6.5 is part of the Microsoft BackOffice product and forms the cornerstone of Microsoft's client/server thrust.

Chapter 11 walks you through the process of installing and configuring SQL Server and SQL devices. Then Chapter 12 shows you how to maintain your server's configuration, as well as add users and grant access permissions to databases.

Chapter 13 shows you how to create and maintain databases.

Chapter 14 shows you how to back up and restore SQL databases and devices and includes setting up features such as replication and mirroring for fault tolerance.

Installing & Configuring Microsoft SQL Server

Microsoft SQL Server 6.5 is installed using the main Microsoft BackOffice installation program or from the setup program, which is located on the Microsoft SQL Server 6.5 CD that comes with Microsoft BackOffice.

In this chapter we cover three main topics: Microsoft SQL Server 6.5's selling points, installation of Microsoft SQL Server 6.5, and the key components that are included with Microsoft SQL Server 6.5.

In the latter part of the chapter is a section describing the interface that allows a Web page designer to use Microsoft SQL Server 6.5 to create dynamic Web pages based on tables and queries.

In all, installation of Microsoft SQL Server 6.5 is not difficult: The setup program will configure the installation as needed, prompting for information.

Microsoft SQL Server 6.5 Selling Points

Microsoft SQL Server has a staggering number of features, especially when you get into the SQL language itself and actually start creating database queries and designing Server applications. From a systems administrator's viewpoint, the following features are the most critical:

- Scalable high-performance architecture
- Advanced data replication

- Support for large databases
- Integration with Performance Monitor
- Support for ODBC (Open Database Connectivity)
- Automated database maintenance
- Centralized database management
- Graphical administration tools

Scalability & Performance

Microsoft SQL Server 6.5 scales by taking advantage of symmetric multi-processing as well as by using clustering. This allows significant performance enhancements to be implemented with simple hardware upgrades.

Microsoft SQL Server 6.5 uses multithreading. Using mulitthreading allows the server to take advantage of multi-CPU architecture while incurring low overhead as a result.

With Microsoft SQL Server, every time another user connects to the database, another thread is started to handle that user. Multithreaded techniques are another method of improving multiuser performance.

Threads are simply another separate execution path that can either run simultaneously, using time slicing, on a single CPU or run on separate CPUs on a multi-CPU system. Other database applications actually start another process (that basically serves the same purpose but has a huge amount of overhead associated with it and impacts the number of simultaneous connections a single server can handle).

Replication

Database replication is a feature built in to Microsoft SQL Server that is equivalent to NT's ability to replicate (or mirror) storage devices. There are actually two levels of replication in Microsoft SQL Server: database replication and device mirroring.

Database replication maintains an exact copy of the database on another device or even another server through a Publish and Subscribe model. The database is published from the server on which it resides and is then subscribed to by either the same server or another server for the purpose of duplicating all changes to the published database.

Device mirroring works at a lower level and simply involves creating two devices for databases. The first is the actual storage device and the second is the mirror device. All changes to the original device are mirrored by the mirror device. This model does not take into account the fact that a database can exist across multiple devices.

A device in this context is a Microsoft SQL Server device, which is not the same as a hardware device.

Integration With Performance Monitor

Microsoft SQL Server also supplies full integration with Performance Monitor (see Figure 11-1) for tuning and optimization. The following classes of counters are supplied:

- Cache access
- User connections
- Active transactions
- I/O statistics
- Database lock statistics
- Log space statistics per database
- Replication statistics

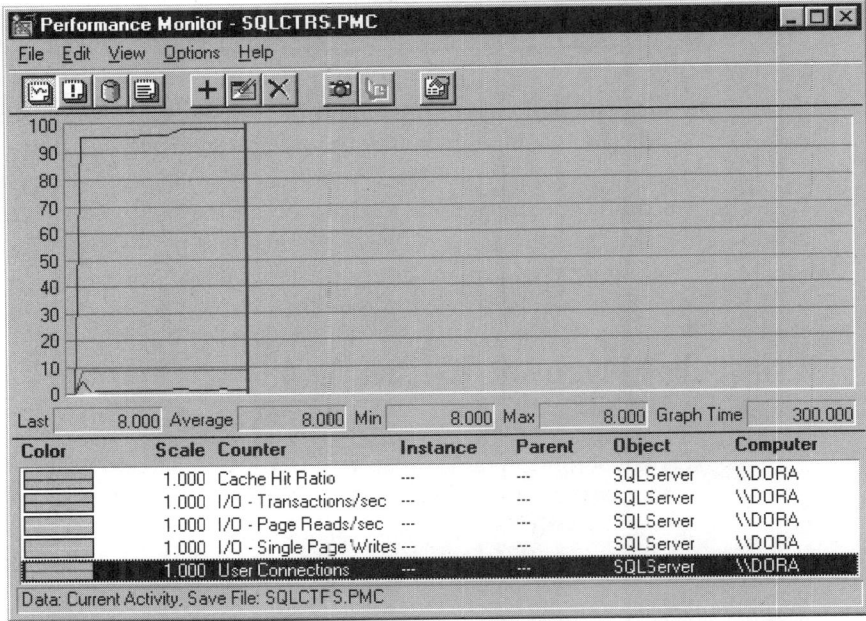

Figure 11-1: Monitoring Microsoft SQL Server 6.5's performance.

Support for ODBC

Microsoft SQL Server is fully supported by 32-bit ODBC drivers, allowing you complete access to Microsoft SQL Server databases from any application that supports ODBC. This includes the following:

- Access
- Word
- Excel
- FoxPro
- Crystal Reports
- Custom applications written in many languages

Microsoft SQL Server 6.5 is a multiuser relational database management system (DBMS). There are 16-bit and 32-bit ODBC drivers for Microsoft SQL Server 6.5. The 16-bit ODBC drivers are used with 16-bit applications (typically those applications written for Windows 3.x that have not yet been ported to the 32-bit world of Windows 95 and Windows NT).

Microsoft SQL Server 6.5 uses SQL to access data in an SQL Server database. Typically, a client communicates with Microsoft SQL Server 6.5 using a network, including LANs, WANs, and even the Internet.

Automated Database Maintenance

Microsoft SQL Server has a built-in task scheduler so that you can define and schedule tasks to be performed automatically (on a regular basis and at the most appropriate time). This includes database backups (dumps) as well as time-consuming tasks such as rebuilding indexes for large databases.

Automated database maintenance will be discussed throughout the following chapters for every task that is supported by the SQL Scheduler.

Installing Microsoft SQL Server 6.5

The installation of Microsoft SQL Server 6.5 is straightforward. First, the majority of users install from a CD, though a few use network connections (usually from a networked CD-ROM drive, but possibly from a temporary directory). Regardless of the source you use, the process is basically the same: Place the CD-ROM in your CD-ROM drive and run the setup program (SETUP.EXE) from the CD. Make sure you run the correct version; there is a folder for each CPU architecture (I386 for Intel, MIPS, ALPHA, and PPC).

Note: Like other Windows NT Server products, Microsoft SQL Server 6.5 is available in versions to support all of the current Windows NT 4 Server platforms, including Digital Alpha, MIPS, and Intel.

Preparing for Setup

To prepare for setup, an account to be used by Microsoft SQL Server 6.5 must be created. This account is used both by the setup program and by Microsoft SQL Server 6.5 to perform various administrative tasks. The account must have the following attributes:

- Member of the Administrators group (has administrator privilege) on the server that will be running Microsoft SQL Server 6.5.

- Logon as a Service right.

- A password that never expires. (Though this account could be created with no password, a nontrivial password should be assigned; accounts with the administrator privilege have substantial power on the Windows NT 4 Server.)

- The ability to log on at all hours (if the account is a domain account).

Figure 11-2 shows the New User dialog box creating the account in the User Manager for Domains (Start Menu | Programs | Administrative Tools (Common) | User Manager for Domains). The name chosen (SQLService) is arbitrary; any name that is significant may be used. When installing multiple SQL Servers, the same account may be used for all installations.

Warning

Only the very brave, or foolish, attempt to run Microsoft Exchange Server, Microsoft SNA Server, and Microsoft SQL Server at the same time on the same Pentium uni-processor server. To do so, you need to have a very fast Pentium (at least a 200MHz) and a minimum of 128MB of RAM.

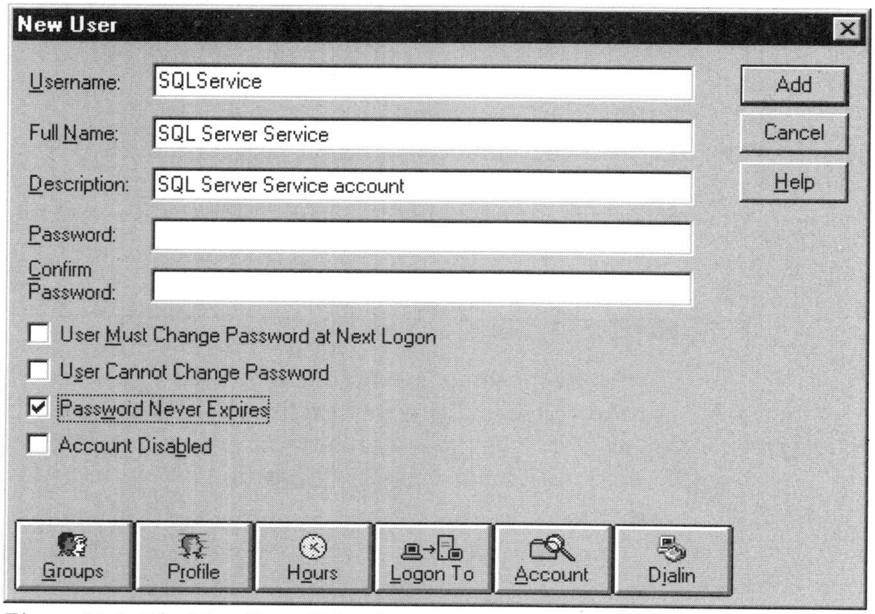

Figure 11-2: The New User dialog box creating an account.

When you are creating an SQL account, make sure that User Must Change Password at Next Logon is not checked. Follow these steps:

1. Click the Groups button in the New User dialog box, and ensure that the new account has been made a member of the Administrators group, as shown in Figure 11-3.

2. Set the new SQL account's logon information (in the New User dialog box) and group membership.

3. Save the account by clicking the Add button.

4. Dismiss the New User dialog by clicking the Cancel button.

5. In the User Manager for Domains, choose Policies | User Rights from the menu. The User Rights Policy dialog box (see Figure 11-4) will be displayed.

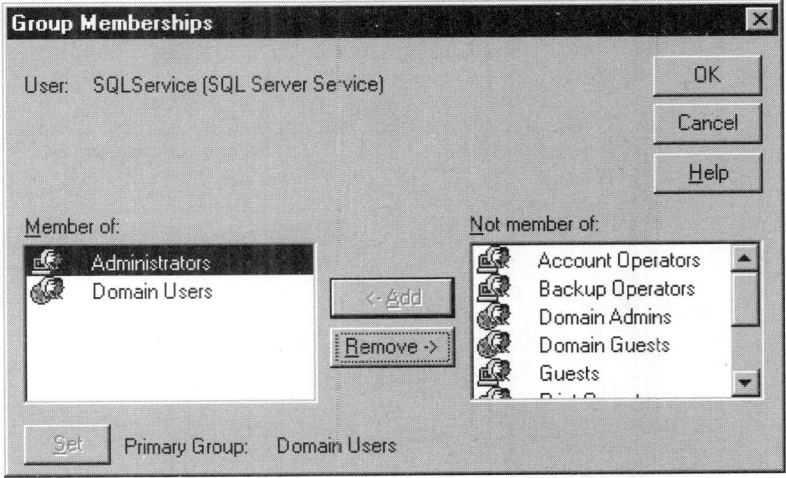

Figure 11-3: Make the account a member of the Administrators group.

6. Check the Show Advanced User Rights check box (at the bottom of the User Rights Policy dialog box), and then select Log On as a Service in the Right drop-down list box.

7. Click the Add button to display the Add Users and Groups dialog box, which lets you assign users (and groups) this right (see Figure 11-5).

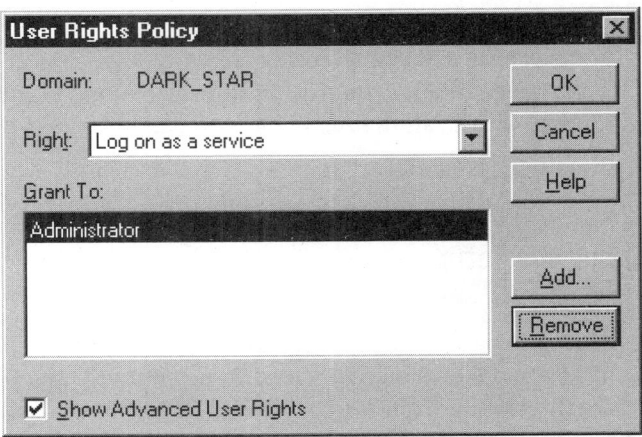

Figure 11-4: Use the User Rights Policy dialog box to give a user the right to log on as a service.

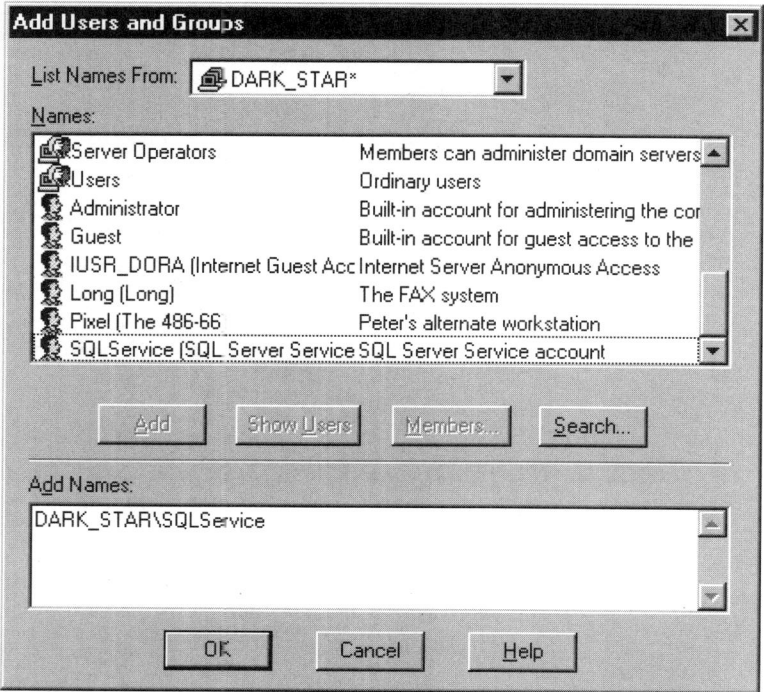

Figure 11-5: Give users and groups the right to log on as a service.

8. In the Add Users and Groups dialog box, click the Show Users button to include users in the Names list.

9. Select the account that was created for Microsoft SQL Server 6.5 to use, and click the Add button. The name of the account should then appear in the Add Names list as shown in Figure 11-5.

10. Finally, click OK.

Starting the Setup

The setup program is straightforward. Figure 11-6 shows the initial setup screen, which the user sees when running setup for the first time. Users who are upgrading from Microsoft SQL Server 6.0 will notice that there are few differences in the setup program between the two versions of Microsoft SQL Server.

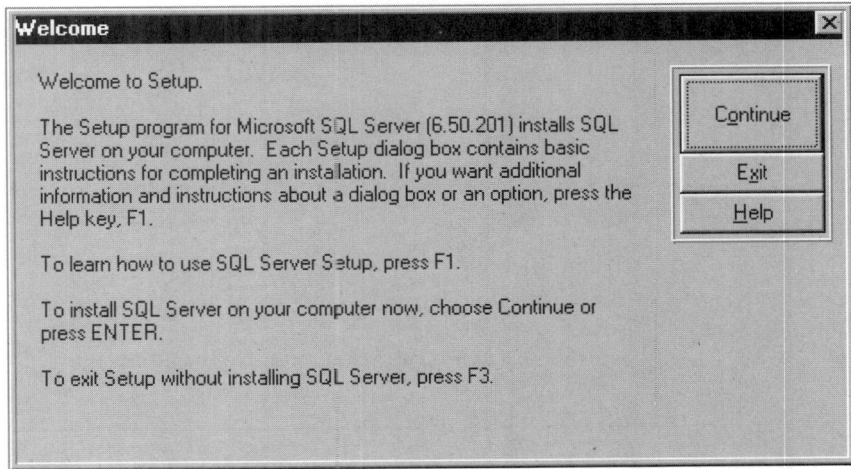

Figure 11-6: Welcome to the Microsoft SQL Server setup.

Note: Prompts for installation vary slightly depending on which options are selected. In this chapter, I cover new installations only, outlining the steps that the Microsoft SQL Server setup program takes to install Microsoft SQL Server.

Once setup starts, you are prompted for your name, company, and product ID (found on the back of the CD holder).

Setup Options

Once name, company, and product ID information have been entered and confirmed, the Microsoft SQL Server 6.5 - Options dialog box appears, as shown in Figure 11-7.

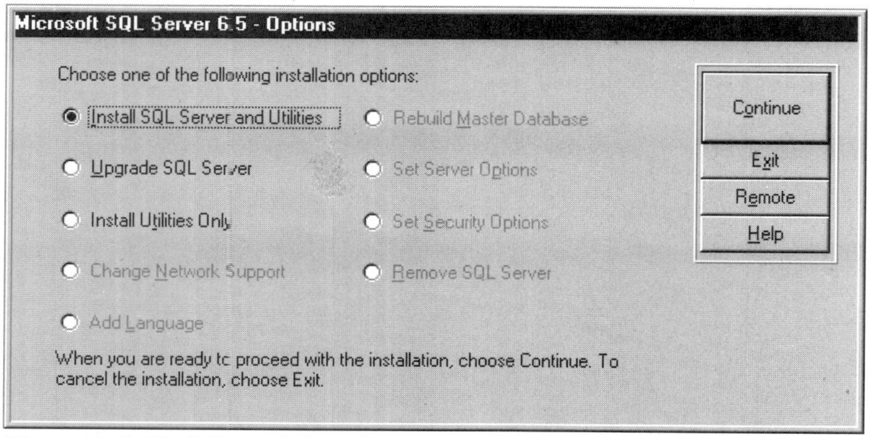

Figure 11-7: The Microsoft SQL Server 6.5 - Options dialog box.

In the Options dialog box, you can perform only one task at a time, but the setup program redisplays the Options dialog box after performing each of the following tasks:

- **Install SQL Server and Utilities**—available only if you do not already have a copy of Microsoft SQL Server installed. With this option, you create a new installation of Microsoft SQL Server.

- **Upgrade SQL Server**—available only if there is an existing installation of Microsoft SQL Server (any version that can be upgraded). The currently installed version of Microsoft SQL Server upgrades to Microsoft SQL Server 6.5.

- **Install Utilities Only**—allows you to install the support utilities. If you have an existing installation of Microsoft SQL Server (which installed utilities), then this option is disabled. In most situations, the utilities are installed at the same time as the SQL server.

- **Change Network Support**—lets you change the net library options. Select Help for more information about this or any other option.

- **Add Language**—adds support for a different language.

- **Rebuild Master Database**—rebuilds the master database, if damaged. You can also change character sets and sort orders with this option.

- **Set Server Options**—allows you to set different server options.
- **Set Security Options**—lets you change the security options of login mode, mappings, and auditing.
- **Remove SQL Server**—allows you to "get rid" of SQL Server. This option deletes most of the Microsoft SQL Server files and cleans the Registry as needed.

Most installations consist of either a clean installation of Microsoft SQL Server or an upgrade of an existing Microsoft SQL Server.

Setting the Licensing Mode

Microsoft server products require that a licensing mode be selected at installation time. The two choices, Per Server and Per Seat, should be familiar. If in doubt when installing Microsoft SQL Server, select the Per Server licensing mode—your license agreement allows a one-time change from Per Server to Per Seat.

When you choose the licensing mode (Figure 11-8), you must also indicate how many client licenses you have purchased. Since Microsoft SQL Server is sold in a number of different packages (most of which vary only in the number of bundled client licenses included), you should review the product you have purchased and coordinate with your management to ensure that the correct number of client licenses have been obtained.

Warning

Licensing Microsoft SQL Server clients is a complex affair. In some cases, you do not need to have a client license. Consult the current Microsoft EULA (End User License Agreement) and your management to determine what your license requirements are—there is no reason to purchase more client licenses than you are required to obtain.

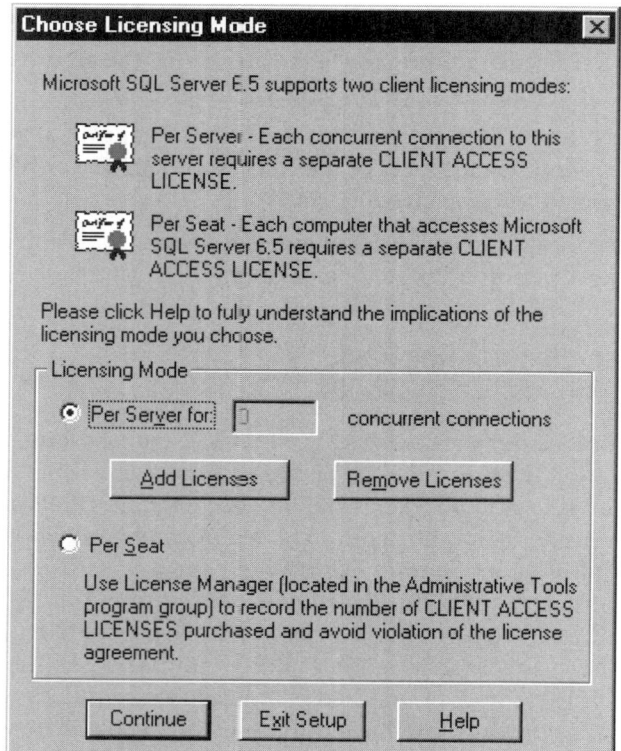

Figure 11-8: Make sure the correct licensing mode is selected.

The SQL Installation Folder

After selecting the licensing mode (and configuring the number of client licenses, if necessary), the next step is to assign a location (drive and folder) to install Microsoft SQL Server 6.5 in. The default location (on drive C: in a folder named \mssql) may not be optimal. It is best that Microsoft SQL Server 6.5 be installed on a drive that is not used for either Windows NT 4 Server or the Windows NT 4 Server paging file, as performance may otherwise be seriously degraded. Figure 11-9 shows the default installation drive and path.

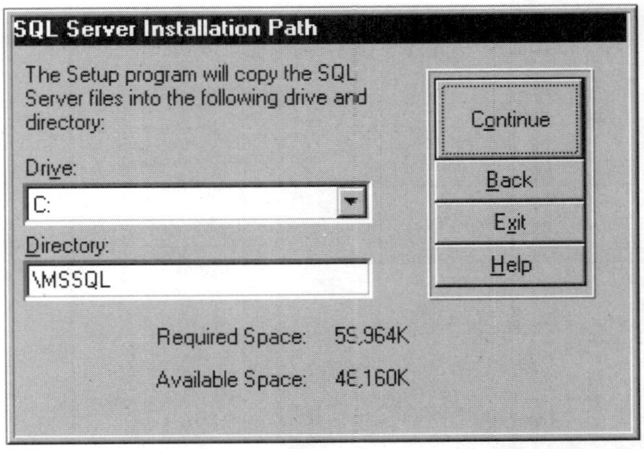

Figure 11-9: The default location in which to install Microsoft SQL Server 6.5.

In the SQL Server Installation Path dialog box, change the drive to the drive that is best for Microsoft SQL Server 6.5. It is recommended that the default directory (but not the default drive) be used, unless there is already an existing directory with the same name already in existence on the target drive. Be careful not to overwrite an existing installation of Microsoft SQL Server!

The SQL Master Database

Microsoft SQL Server stores all of your data and other information in a master database file. The setup program creates this file, and you are prompted for the initial size. Later, should your needs grow, you may expand the file's size. However, try to anticipate your initial requirements, and set the file's size to this requirement.

As Figure 11-10 shows, the setup program recommends a minimum size of 25MB for an initial master database. However, I recommend that you set the size between 35MB and 50MB for the initial database; more if you are planning to import a large dataset from another source.

Note: SMS Server and other Microsoft BackOffice products that use Microsoft SQL Server 6.5 will resize the database as needed. It is not necessary to consider which BackOffice products are being installed at this stage.

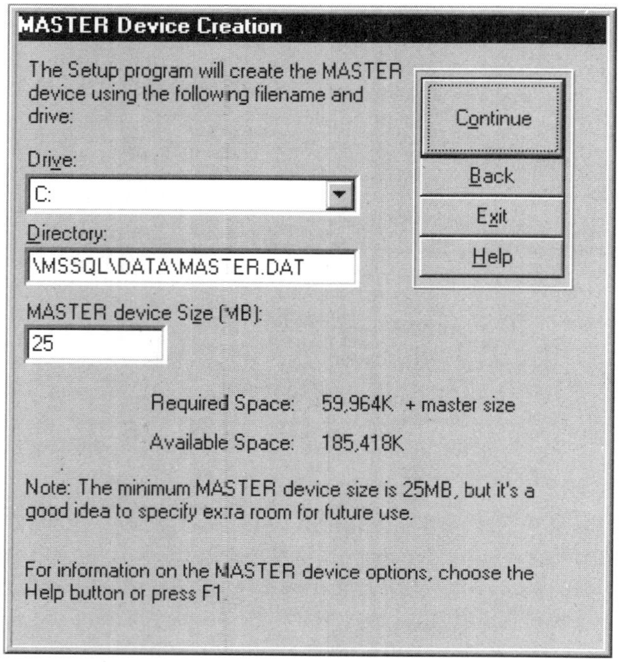

MASTER Device Creation

The Setup program will create the MASTER device using the following filename and drive:

Drive:
```
C:
```

Directory:
```
\MSSQL\DATA\MASTER.DAT
```

MASTER device Size (MB):
```
25
```

Continue
Back
Exit
Help

Required Space: 59,964K + master size

Available Space: 185,418K

Note: The minimum MASTER device size is 25MB, but it's a good idea to specify extra room for future use.

For information on the MASTER device options, choose the Help button or press F1.

Figure 11-10: Setting the initial database size.

After installing Microsoft SQL Server 6.5, the database may be resized. Often, as the needs for Microsoft SQL Server 6.5 grow, the size of the database grows, too. It is unwise to make the master database too large initially, however, as this would serve no useful purpose.

Note: The setup program may be used to rebuild the master database, also. Rebuilding the master database will result in loss of all data stored in the database. The files master.da@ and master.al@ are used to rebuild the master database. When Microsoft SQL Server 6.5 has been installed with the default character set and sort order, master.da@ is used to replace master.dat (the SQL master database file). When Microsoft SQL Server 6.5 has been installed with a nonstandard character set or sort order, master.al@ is used to replace master.dat. master.al@ contains scripts which then configure the database to match the desired character set and sort order. Therefore, when nonstandard character sets or sort orders are specified, the time needed to build (or rebuild) the master database will be longer.

Microsoft SQL Documentation—Books OnLine

Most of the documentation for Microsoft SQL Server is contained in a Books OnLine database. You can choose to install the entire set of documentation on your hard drive or execute the Books OnLine from the CD. If you plan on having the Microsoft SQL Server CD available when running Microsoft SQL Server, then running from the CD is acceptable; however, if your CD-ROM drive resources are limited, then I recommend that you install the Books OnLine on the hard drive. You can choose not to install the Books OnLine, but keep in mind that there are very few Microsoft SQL Server users who are experienced enough that they don't need assistance.

Other Installation Options

Installation options, which you choose after determining the location for the Books OnLine, allow you to set the character set (for American users, select English) and sort orders. (Generally, if you are not using English, review the sort order to make sure it matches the language you are using; otherwise select the default.)

You may also choose to install additional network support at this stage. Two final options (Auto Start SQL Server at Boot Time and Auto Start SQL Executive at Boot Time) allow you to choose to have Microsoft SQL Server started automatically each time the system is booted. This happens not when you log on, but when Windows NT 4 Server is started. There is a choice to have the Microsoft SQL Server Executive program run automatically at boot time as well.

The Administrator's Userid

The final required information is the userid for the installation user, in the SQL Executive Log On Account dialog box (see Figure 11-11). Setup must log on as this user to complete the setup. The default is the userid used to install Microsoft SQL Server 6.5. This userid must have Administrative privileges and Log On as a Service rights, and the password must be supplied. Once the userid and password have been verified, the setup program installs Microsoft SQL Server, generally with no further prompts.

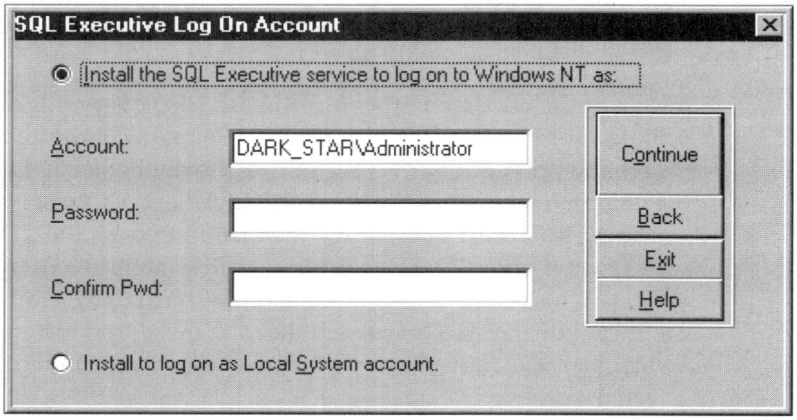

Figure 11-11: Either specify a userid, or select the Local System account.

Rather than use the installer's userid, use the userid created before installation as described earlier in "Preparing for Setup."

Tip

> *If setup displays a message "ISQL.EXE could not be executed. Please check the relevant OUT file. Setup could not connect to the SQL Server," then the userid used for setup did not have the correct privileges. Retry the installation after correcting the userid privileges, or install using the Install to Log on as Local System Account option in the SQL Executive Log On Account dialog box during installation. After correcting the problem, rerun the Microsoft SQL Server 6.5 setup program.*

When setup is finished, you should have a fully functional installation of Microsoft SQL Server. You will have, in the All Users group, a program group called Microsoft SQL Server 6.5.

Warning

> *If at a point near the end of the installation you receive a critical error message that a file with the extension CPL could not be copied to the system32 folder, then you probably have the Control Panel program running. Close Control Panel, and click the Retry button. If you click Cancel, setup will not correctly complete.*

The Microsoft SQL Server 6.5 system consists of the actual SQL Server and a set of utilities and programs that assist the user and administrator in using Microsoft SQL Server 6.5.

Again, this chapter provides an overview of Microsoft SQL Server 6.5 installation. Other chapters in this section of the book provide an overview of the major components that make up Microsoft SQL Server 6.5. However, a good book dedicated completely to Microsoft SQL Server 6.5 might be a wise investment for anyone who is serious about working with Microsoft SQL Server 6.5.

Note: If you are installing Microsoft SQL Server 6.5 to support another service, such as Microsoft Systems Management Server or Microsoft Exchange Server, then a complete understanding of Microsoft SQL Server 6.5 may not be necessary. Other Microsoft BackOffice products, which use Microsoft SQL Server 6.5 to manage data, generally do not require substantial manual interaction with Microsoft SQL Server.

After installation, all the component parts of Microsoft SQL Server may be found in Start Menu | Programs | Microsoft SQL Server 6.5.

Key Components of SQL Server 6.5

There are a number of supporting applications and components that are supplied with Microsoft SQL Server 6.5. The remainder of this chapter describes each of them.

ISQL/w

The ISQL/w utility queries an SQL Server. To start the ISQL/w utility, choose ISQL_w in the Start Menu | Programs | Administrative Tools (Common) | Microsoft SQL Server 6.5 group. You can do an analysis and view statistical information about the query. ISQL/w is able to perform more than one query at a given time. ISQL/w is shown in Figure 11-12 with an example query being executed.

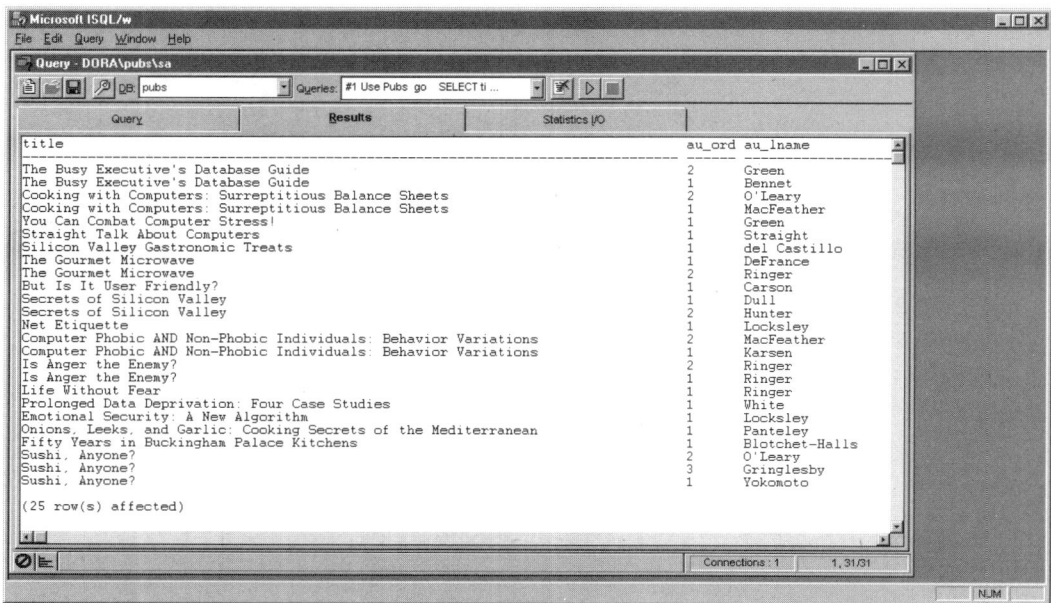

Figure 11-12: ISQL/w with a query's result set.

Note: Unlike MS Query, ISQL/w works only with Microsoft SQL Server databases. If you need to perform queries on any other ODBC data source, you will need to use MS Query, rather than ISQL/w.

You can use the File menu to connect to and disconnect from servers, create new queries, open and close existing queries, and configure the look and feel of ISQL/w. You can use the Query menu to execute and cancel a query (which you would want to do if the query is not responding correctly or is returning excessive amounts of data). ISQL/w has a toolbar and status bar available in each query window. Many of the menus are represented in the toolbar, which is unfortunately not customizable.

Microsoft ODBC SQL Server Driver Help File

The Microsoft ODBC SQL Server Driver help file is used when you need assistance on topics related to ODBC. To start the help file, choose Microsoft ODBC SQL Server Driver in the Start Menu | Programs | Microsoft SQL Server 6.5 group. ODBC is the engine that clients use to connect to a data source such as Microsoft SQL Server 6.5.

While ODBC is used only by clients, it is important that a Microsoft SQL Server 6.5 administrator understand how ODBC works.

MS Query

Microsoft Query (often referred to as MS Query) is a general-purpose query tool. To start Microsoft Query, choose MS Query in the Start Menu | Programs | Microsoft SQL Server 6.5 group. Not only is it usable with Microsoft SQL Server 6.5, MS Query is also able to query any data source in which there exists an ODBC driver.

MS Query is a reasonably flexible tool. It is available in both 16- and 32-bit versions (though you would be less likely to utilize the 16-bit version of MS Query).

Note: MS Query is typically installed in the %SystemRoot%\msapps\ msquery folder (where %SystemRoot% is the drive and folder where Windows NT 4 Server has been installed) and not in your Microsoft SQL Server 6.5 base directory.

Like ISQL/w, MS Query is basically a menu-driven application. Figure 11-13 shows MS Query after a basic query has been executed. This simple query (which lists all the data in the authors table), in native SQL format, is:

```
SELECT authors.au_id, authors.au_fname,
   authors.au_lname, authors.address,
   authors.city, authors.state, authors.zip,
   authors.phone, authors.contract
   FROM "pubs.dbo".authors authors
```

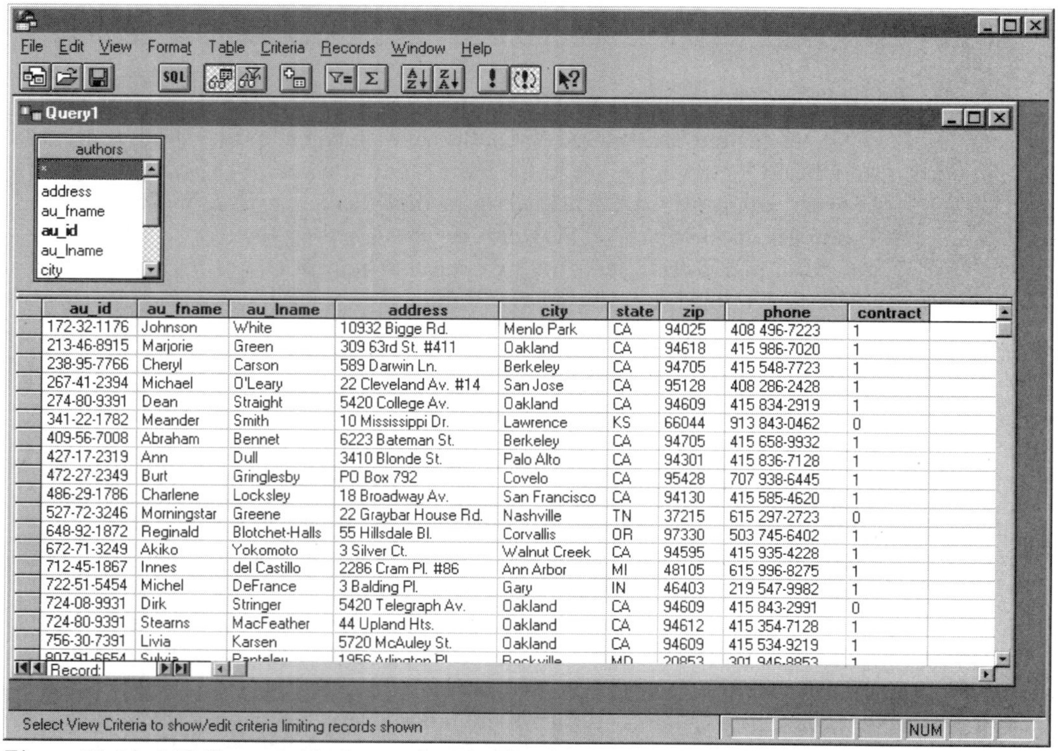

Figure 11-13: MS Query with the results of a simple query.

Generally, MS Query displays the query graphically. To view the actual SQL statement, click the SQL button in the toolbar. This displays the SQL dialog, as shown in Figure 11-14. It is possible to modify this SQL statement, and when the OK button is clicked, the modified SQL statement executes.

Figure 11-14: The MS Query SQL dialog.

MS Query has a toolbar and status bar to make interacting with it very easy.

You can use the File menu to create and save a new query, open or close an existing query, execute a query, and view a table definition. You can use the View menu to add new tables to your query and view SQL statements that fetch data. You can use the Table menu to add or remove tables or create, remove, or reorder joins between tables. The Records menu allows you to add, remove, or edit columns; sort data; go to a specific location in the data; enable editing of records in the database; perform a query immediately; and perform a query immediately after it has changed.

MS Query is a rather powerful tool, which makes it very useful for developing client applications. MS Query is also part of many of the other Microsoft applications environments, such as Microsoft Office, Access, Visual C++, and Visual Basic, where front-end applications are typically developed.

The Readme File

The readme.txt file is an important part of any software package. Contained within this file are a number of important topics:

- Installing or upgrading SQL Server 6.5.
- Xp_sqlregister extended stored procedure.
- Running sqlole65.sql.
- Using Microsoft distributed transaction coordinator.

SQL Client Configuration Utility

Started from the Start Menu | Programs | Microsoft SQL Server 6.5 group, the SQL Client Configuration Utility displays, as its main window, a tabbed dialog box. The three tabs in this dialog box are:

- **DBLibrary**—configures the DB library.
- **Net Library**—configures the network library.
- **Advanced**—configures the advanced client options.

In the SQL Client Configuration Utility there is also a button labeled Locate. This button searches the system for the libraries used by SQL Client Configuration Utility and Microsoft SQL Server 6.5. Clicking Locate displays the dialog box shown in Figure 11-15.

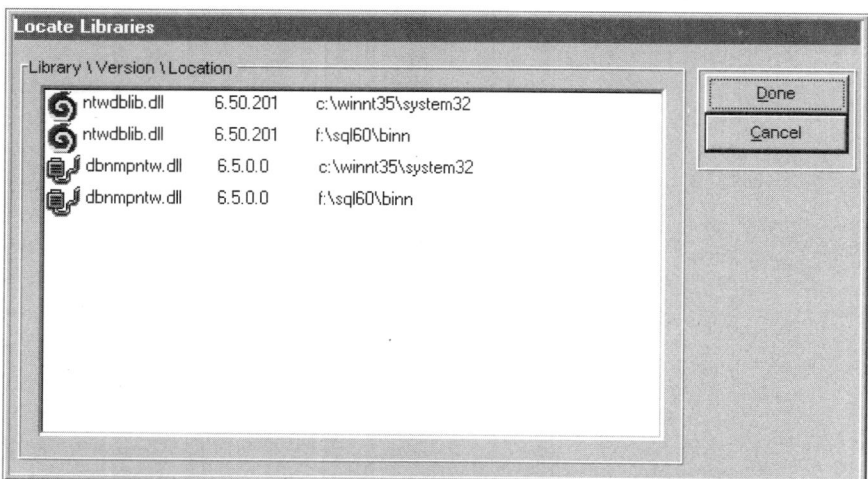

Figure 11-15: The SQL Client Configuration Utility's Locate Libraries dialog.

The Locate Libraries dialog has no controls other than Done and Cancel. With the Locate Libraries dialog, you can specify a library (click on the library name or icon in the list) other than the default library that SQL Client Configuration Utility names. Once you have selected a library, click the Done button.

The DBLibrary Tab

The DBLibrary tab (see Figure 11-16) configures the DB (database) library options. There are two options in this tab:

- Automatic ANSI to OEM, which enables the automatic conversion of objects from ANSI character sets to OEM character sets. It is useful when the OEM line-drawing characters have been used in an object.

- Use International Settings, which enables international settings for the DB library.

In addition to the above two options, you are also presented with statistical information about the DB library.

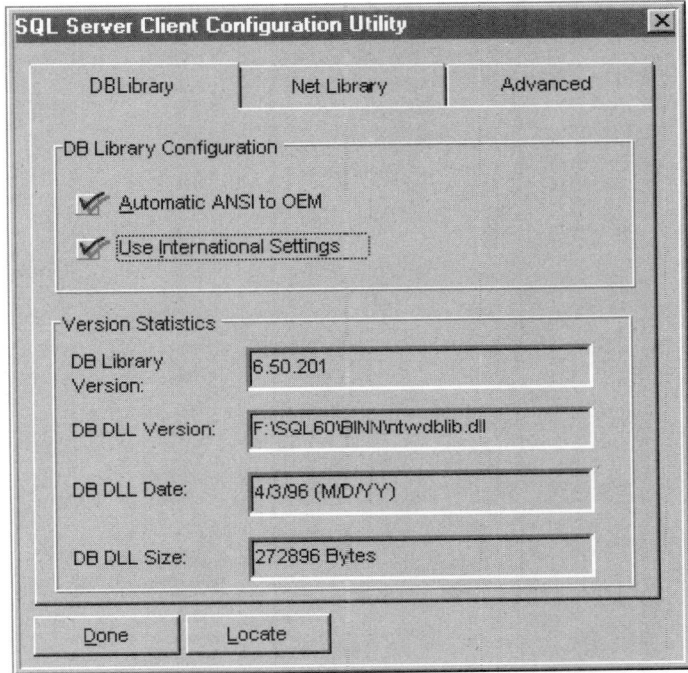

Figure 11-16: The SQL Server Client Configuration Utility's DBLibrary tab.

The Net Library Tab

The Net Library tab (see Figure 11-17) allows you to configure the network protocol for Microsoft SQL Server 6.5. The Net Library tab has only one option that may be set: Default Network. In the Default Network, you can choose one of the following network protocols:

- Named Pipes
- Multi-protocol
- NWLink IPX/SPX
- TCP/IP Sockets
- Banyan VINES

The default is Named Pipes, which will serve for most installations. There is no Defaults button in the SQL Client Configuration Utility, so be sure to note what the current default is.

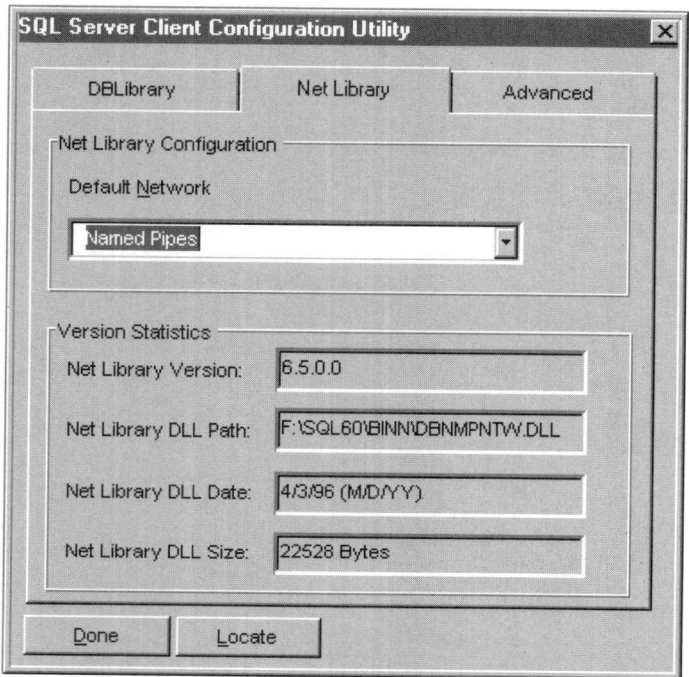

Figure 11-17: The SQL Server Client Configuration Utility's Net Library tab.

The Advanced Tab

The SQL Client Configuration Utility Advanced tab (see Figure 11-18) configures advanced options. You are able to set the configuration for multiple servers in this tab by specifying both a server name and a DLL name (which is actually the protocol as described in "The Net Library Tab").

Using the Advanced tab, you are able to specify different net protocols for different servers, if this is necessary. You may also specify a connect string for each entry.

The process for using the Advanced tab is to fill in both the Server and DLL Name boxes in the Client Configuration group box. You may optionally fill in a connection string, too. After filling in the server and DLL names, click Add/Modify to add the entry to the list of current entries.

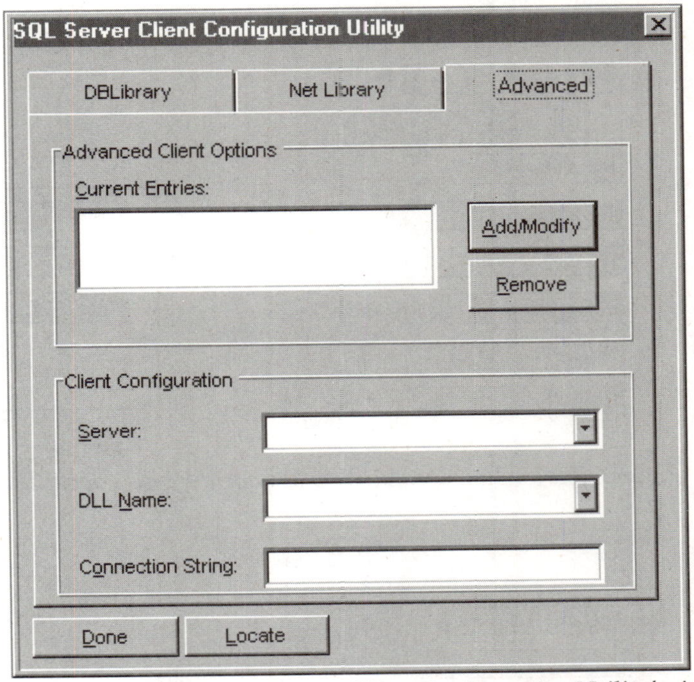

Figure 11-18: The SQL Server Client Configuration Utility's Advanced tab.

SQL Distributed Management Objects Help

The SQL Distributed Management Objects Help file contains descriptive text for each of the object classes in Microsoft SQL Server 6.5. To start the help file, choose SQL Distributed Management Objects in the Start Menu | Programs | Microsoft SQL Server 6.5 group. Descriptions of the objects are given for both Visual Basic and Visual C++ (MFC) contexts whenever appropriate.

Figure 11-19 illustrates the application-related objects. When in SQL Distributed Management Objects, you are able to click on any object and a hypertext jump will take you to the description of the object.

Figures 11-19, 11-20, and 11-21 show relationships between various objects in the SQL hierarchy. Figure 11-20 illustrates server-related objects, and Figure 11-21 illustrates database-related objects.

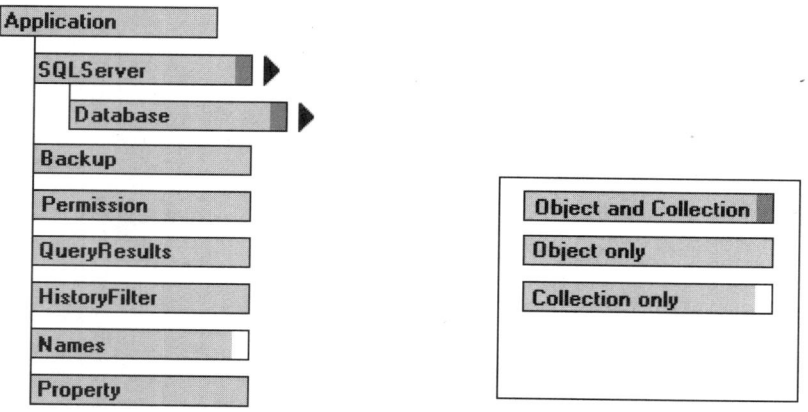

Figure 11-19: SQL Distributed Management Objects application objects.

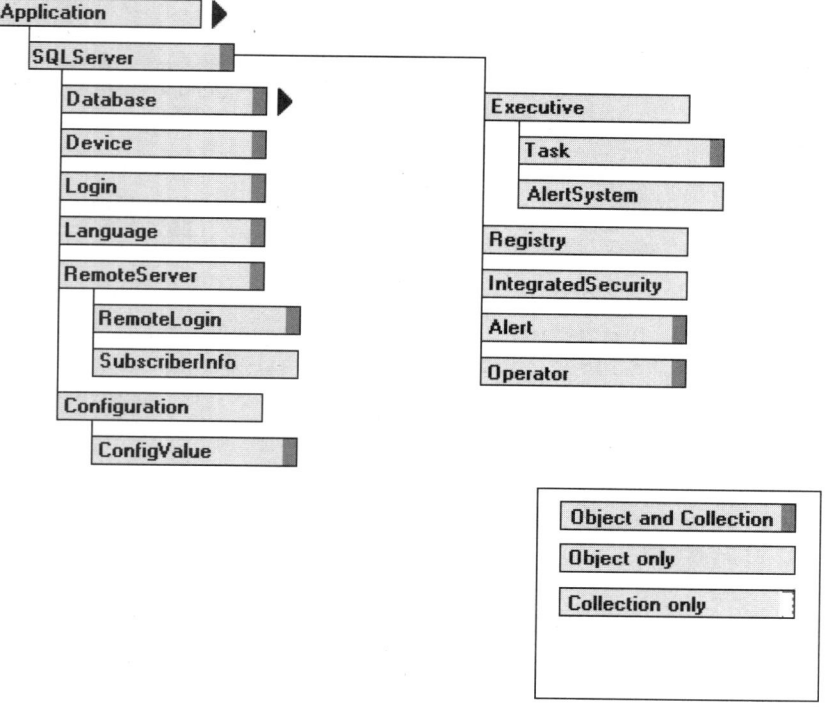

Figure 11-20: SQL Distributed Management Objects server objects.

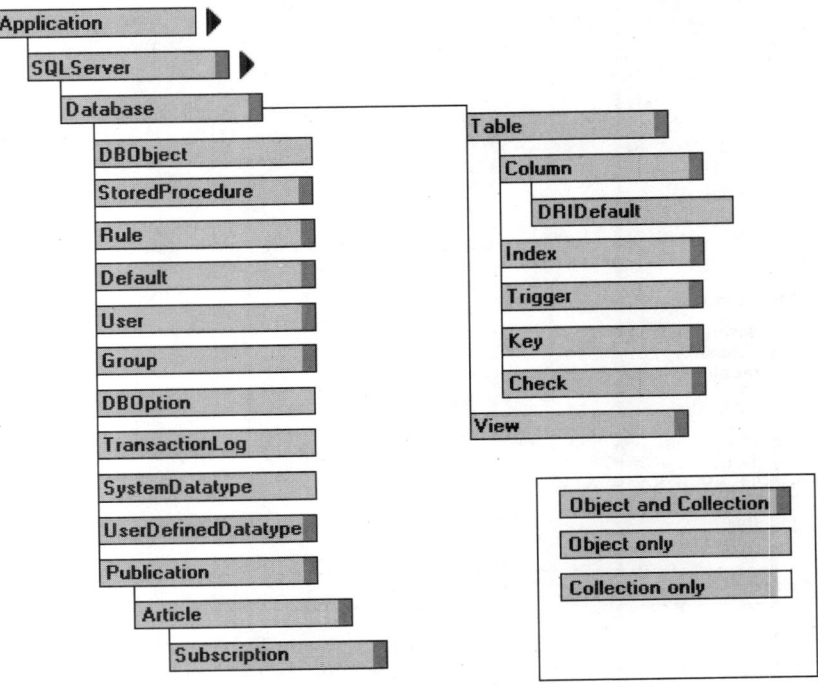

Figure 11-21: SQL Distributed Management Objects database objects.

The SQL Distributed Management Objects Help file is useful for designing and programming Microsoft SQL Server 6.5. There are examples for most items for both Visual Basic programmers and for those of us who are addicted to Visual C++.

As an example, an important database design tool would be the ability to insert a new column of information into an existing table. The InsertColumn method allows you to do this, as shown in Figure 11-22. To use InsertColumn, complete the following steps:

1. Select Database in the Contents page (see Figure 11-22).

2. Click on the Table box.

3. After the Table Object page is shown, click on the Methods hyperlink. This displays a list of all the table methods.

4. Click on the InsertColumn item in the list. Voila! You now have a new column.

In Figure 11-22, you see the description for the InsertColumn method, examples of both Visual Basic and Visual C++ usage, and descriptions of the elements of the InsertColumn method.

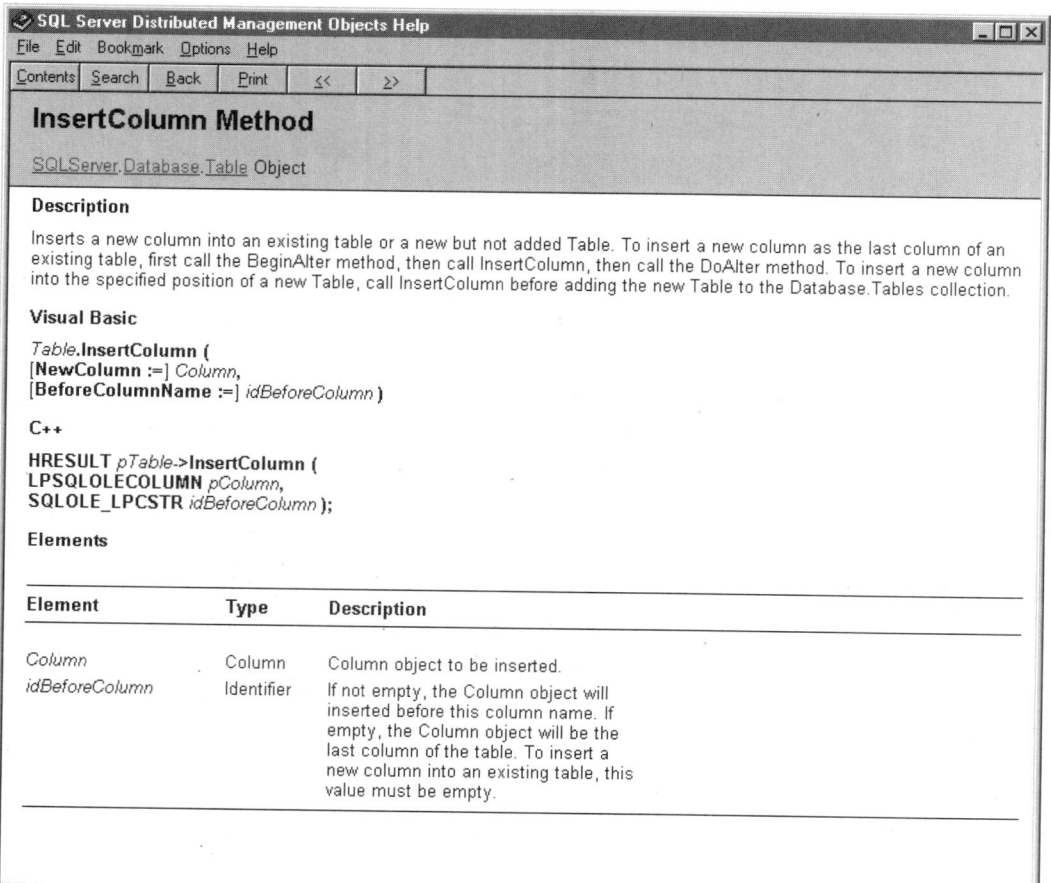

Figure 11-22: SQL Distributed Management Objects documenting the InsertColumn method.

If you are not programming Microsoft SQL Server 6.5 using Visual Basic or Visual C++, you will probably not find much use for the SQL Distributed Management Objects Help file.

SQL Enterprise Manager

The SQL Enterprise Manager is the core management tool for Microsoft SQL Server 6.5. The SQL Enterprise Manager is the tool that modifies, backs up, and generally interacts with Microsoft SQL Server 6.5. You launch SQL Enterprise Manager from the Start Menu, using the Programs | Microsoft SQL Server 6.5 group.

SQL Enterprise Manager is a complex program with many options and features. Due to SQL Enterprise Manager's complexity, this chapter only presents an overview of what it is capable of doing.

When launched, SQL Enterprise Manager presents a display similar to the one shown in Figure 11-23 (the displayed data will reflect your server's configuration). This figure shows SQL Enterprise Manager managing the Microsoft SQL Server 6.5 on DORA.

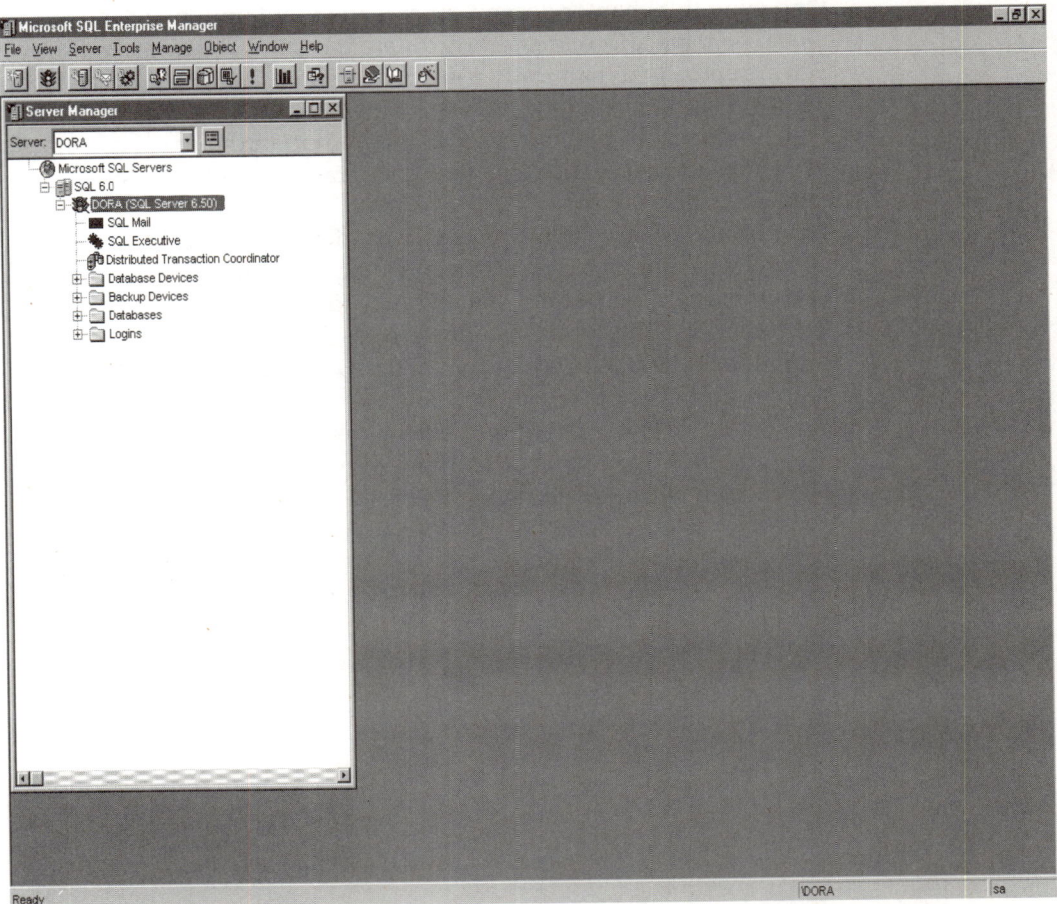

Figure 11-23: SQL Enterprise Manager managing Microsoft SQL Server 6.5 on DORA.

Notice in Figure 11-23 that only the SQL Server has been started. The SQL Mail, SQL Executive, and the Distributed Transaction Coordinator (DTC) have not been started. If you wanted to start these services, you would start them in SQL Enterprise Manager or in the SQL Service Manager. To start an SQL service (the SQL Server), right-click on the service and choose Start from the context menu that is displayed.

Also shown in Figure 11-23 are four other services, which I will cover shortly.

When connected to an SQL server, the SQL Enterprise Manager program has a complex menu structure.

One thing this chapter doesn't cover is the proliferation of context menus. There are approximately 35 different context menus—some of which are actually dynamically constructed based on need at the time of display.

SQL Enterprise Manager uses a relatively standard menu structure. However, because it is such a complex program, it is easy to "lose" functionality.

Definition: LFD (Lost Functionality Disorder), a condition that strikes accomplished computer users, is usually diagnosed when they are discovered mumbling at their desks, "I know how to do it, I just don't know where to find it." The current treatment is rest—and soothing words.

From the Server menu, you can manage SQL Servers, SQL Mail, SQL Executive, and distributed transaction coordination. From the Manage menu, you can work with logins, devices, disks, replications, users, groups, and indexes, among other things. From the Objects menu, you can work with permissions, dependencies, and the like.

Database Devices

If you click the plus sign next to the Database Devices item in the tree shown at the left side of Figure 11-23, it expands into a set of subitems: Master, MSDBData, and MSDBLog. The Master device is the master database, the MSDBData device is the scheduling database, and the MDSB log device is the transaction log.

Each of the Database Devices items, when double-clicked (or when you choose Edit from the context menu), displays a dialog box similar to the one shown in Figure 11-24.

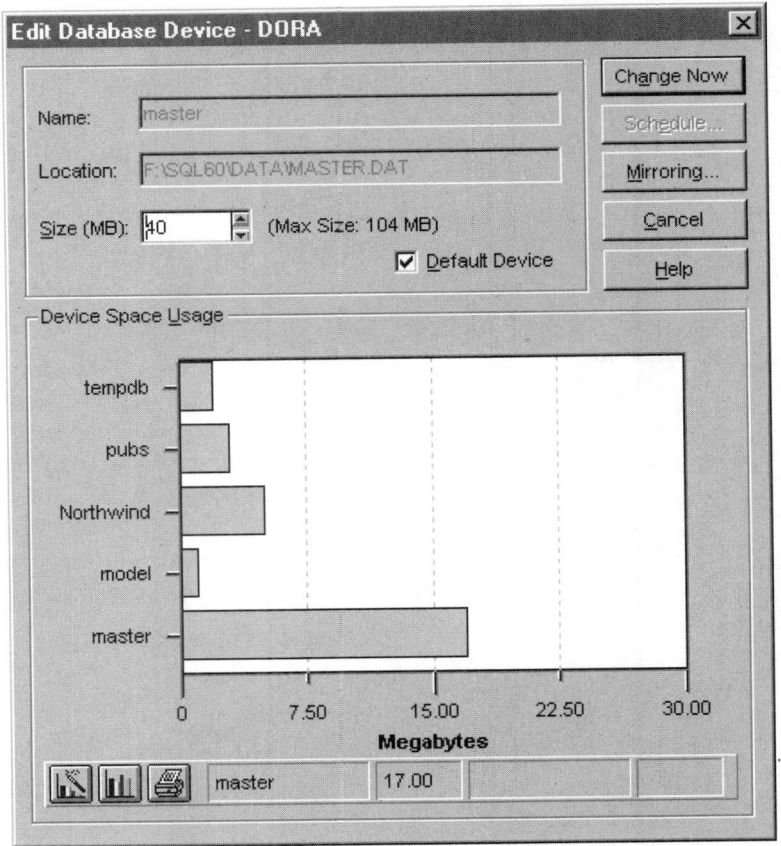

Figure 11-24: The Edit Database Device dialog box.

Note: You cannot change the location of the Database Services items from the Edit Database Device dialog box. Use the New Device selection (select Microsoft SQL Enterprise Manager's Manage | Database Devices) to create a new Database Services item on a different drive.

You can use the context menus to add new devices, edit and delete existing devices, and mirror existing devices.

Backup Devices

Backup devices are used to back up your SQL database. Your choices include both tape and disk storage. When using disk storage to back up, it is possible to choose any local hard drive. You cannot select networked devices, nor can diskette drives be selected in this context. When selecting tape devices, you can choose to skip headers.

Using the context menu you can create new backup devices, delete existing backup devices, restore devices, and refresh the list of backup devices.

Note: It does not make a great deal of sense to back up a file to the same drive. If the drive were to fail, then both copies of the file would be lost. No security there!

Databases

In the SQL Enterprise Manager's Server Manager window (shown in Figure 11-23), click the plus sign next to the Databases folder.

Data in Microsoft SQL Server 6.5 is stored in a hierarchical manner. The highest level is a database object. Stored in the database in Microsoft SQL Server 6.5 are Groups/Users and Objects. Under Objects comes Tables. Within Tables are columns and rows of data. Figure 11-25 shows the hierarchy for the pubs database, a sample database of publisher data.

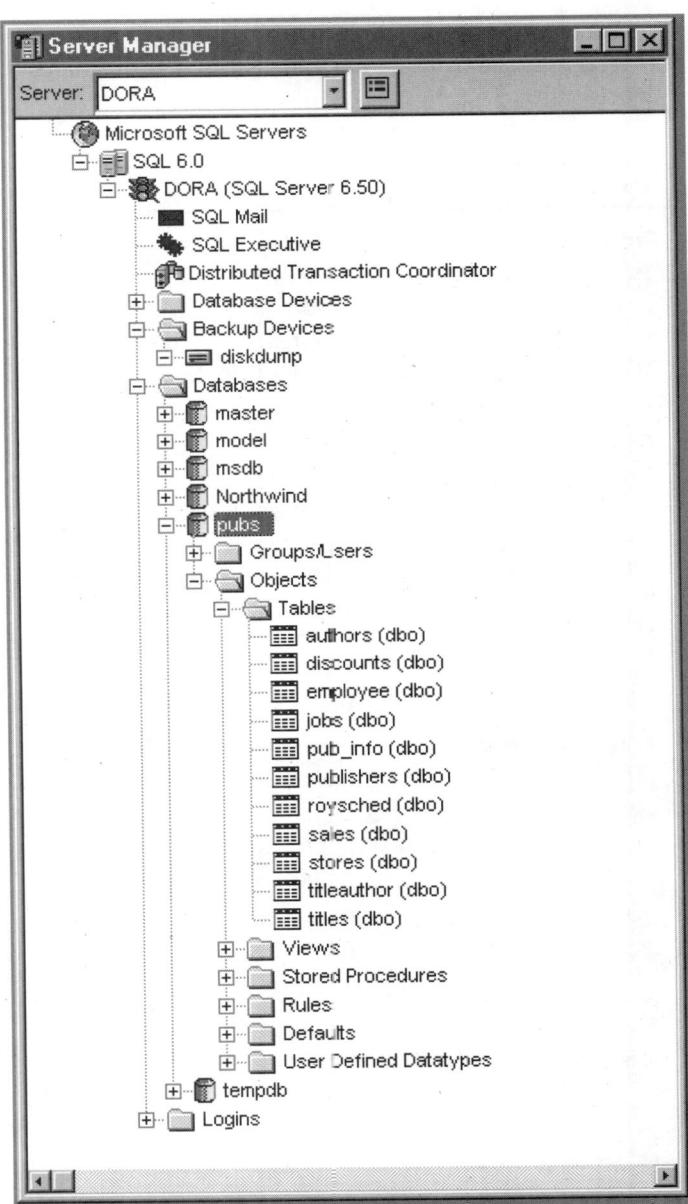

Figure 11-25: The pubs database in Microsoft SQL Server 6.5.

Also note that in addition to tables there are a number of other items stored under the Objects tree item. Table 11-1 describes the items in the Objects tree.

Item	Description
Tables	A table contains rows of data. Each row consists of one or more columns, each column having a particular set of attributes, such as name and datatype. A row of data is usually referred to as a record in the database.
Views	A view is a virtual table that represents an alternative way of looking at the data in one (or more) tables. A typical use is to allow a user to see some but not all of the data contained in a table. For example, you may allow users to see employee names and titles, but not salary information. To do so, create a view that contains only the information you wish the user to see.
Stored Procedures	A stored procedure is a set of commands saved with the database in the Microsoft SQL Server 6.5. Stored procedures offer improved performance as they execute at the server, not the client.
Rules	Rules, which are bound to columns or user-defined datatypes, specify acceptable values that can be inserted into a column or user-defined datatype.
Defaults	Defaults allow you to specify a default value when the user fails to provide data for a column or a user-defined datatype.
User-Defined Datatypes	A user-defined datatype is created by the user and defined in terms of existing system datatypes.

Table 11-1: Items in the Objects tree.

Figure 11-26 shows the user-defined datatypes from the pubs database. In pubs there are three user-defined datatypes, empid, id, and tid.

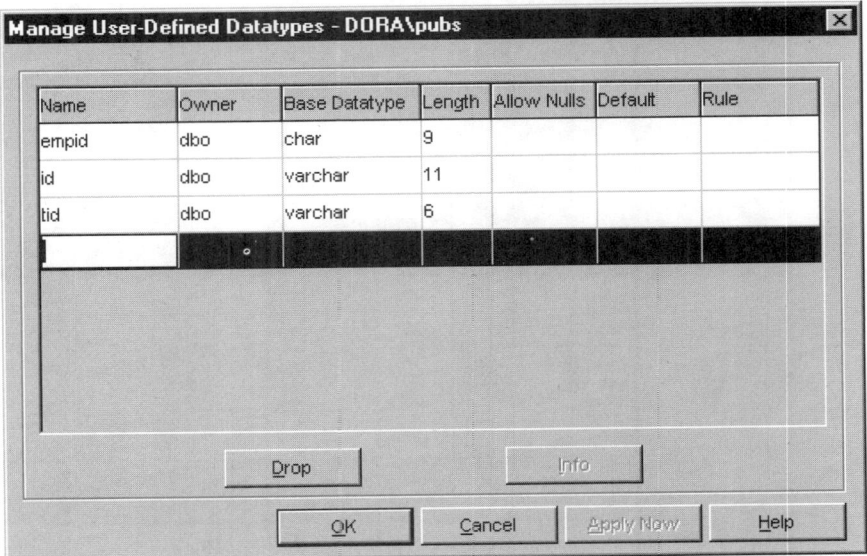

Name	Owner	Base Datatype	Length	Allow Nulls	Default	Rule
empid	dbo	char	9			
id	dbo	varchar	11			
tid	dbo	varchar	6			

Figure 11-26: The three user-defined datatypes in pubs.

Generally, user-defined datatypes are simply a way to qualify an existing datatype. For example, in Figure 11-26, the tid datatype is simply a varchar type with its length defined as six characters. Each database could have zero, one, or more user-defined datatypes.

Logins

The last item in the Service Manager window tree is Logins. Logins contains the status of all authorized users. Each user may be queried using the context menu's Edit selection (or simply double-click a user's name to display the Manage Logins dialog box). Figure 11-27 shows the sa login. Note that this dialog shows what privileges each login ID has.

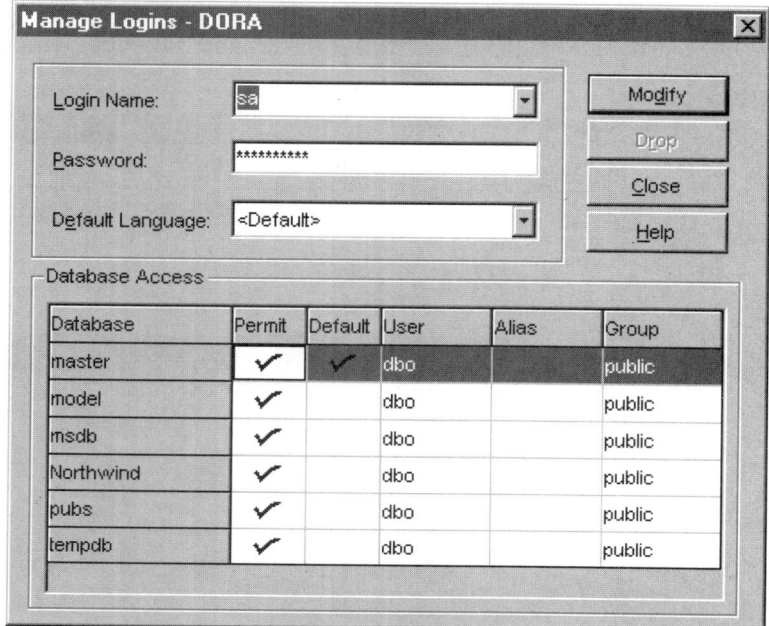

Figure 11-27: The Manage Logins dialog box.

SQL Performance Monitor

The SQL Performance Monitor is a powerful system-monitoring tool that monitors Microsoft SQL Server 6.5 performance as well as Windows NT 4 Server's performance.

To start the SQL Performance Monitor, choose the SQL Performance Monitor from the Start Menu I Programs I Microsoft SQL Server 6.5 group. SQL Performance Monitor is actually a call to Windows NT 4 Server's Performance Monitor using a modified parameter file to include monitoring of Microsoft SQL Server 6.5 parameters. You can display performance data in a number of formats.

The SQL Performance Monitor is a powerful application with many options. As it is simply a monitoring tool (and therefore rather benign), it is an easy application to "play" with. Starting SQL Performance Monitor launches it in the graph mode, as shown in Figure 11-28.

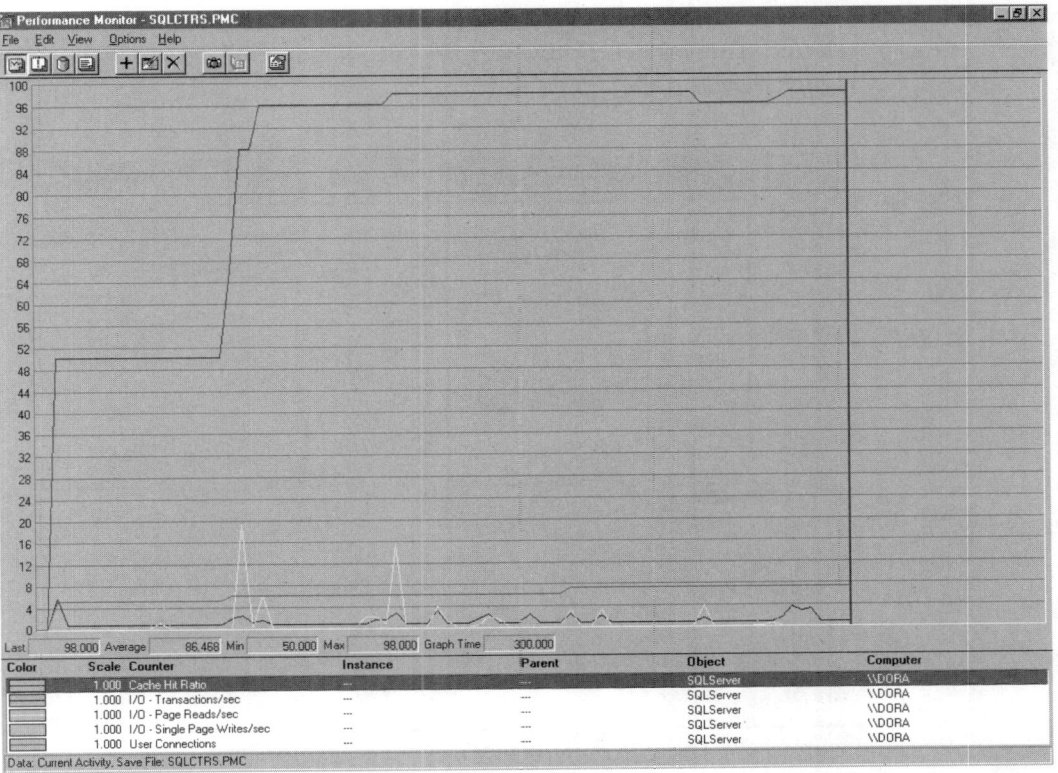

Figure 11-28: The SQL Performance Monitor main window.

Tip

> *Because SQL Performance Monitor is Windows NT 4 Server's Performance Monitor, it may make sense to include this application in your startup group so it can be easily accessed, especially at times when you are optimizing server performance.*

With the SQL Performance Monitor, you can monitor parameters in the categories such as processor, cache, Internet services, network services, and many SQL Server services, among others.

To add a parameter to the SQL Performance Monitor, choose Edit | Add to Chart (shortcut key is Ctrl+I). This displays the Add to Chart dialog box, as shown in Figure 11-29.

Each of these categories has between 10 and 30 subitems that can be selected. There is descriptive text for each item as well, as shown in Figure 11-29.

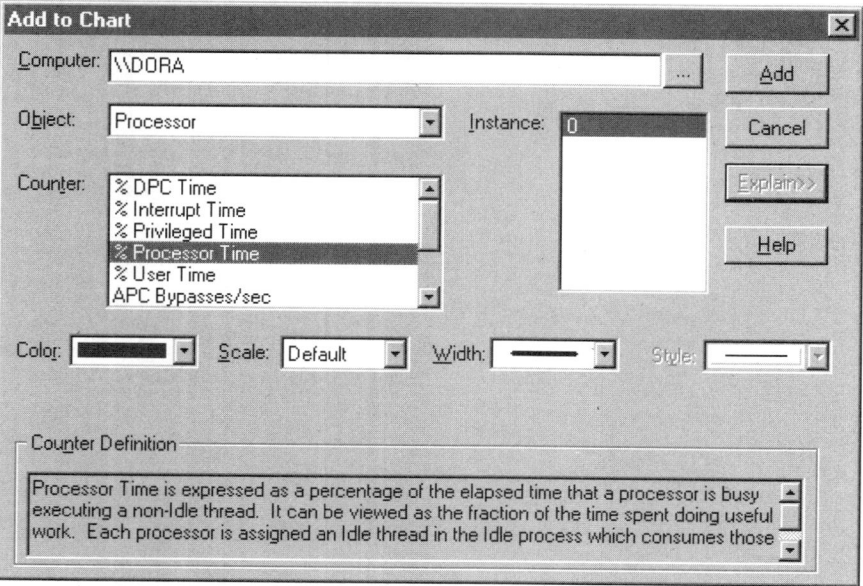

Figure 11-29: The SQL Performance Monitor's Add to Chart dialog.

Tip

For more information about the Windows NT 4 Server Performance Monitor, see Chapters 8 and 9.

SQL Security Manager

The SQL Security Manager manages Microsoft SQL Server's security features. Start SQL Security Manager from the Microsoft SQL Server program group (Start Menu | Programs | Microsoft SQL Server 6.5). Microsoft SQL Server 6.5 Security Manager allows you to manage Microsoft SQL Server users and defaults. Shown in Figure 11-30 is SQL Security Manager's main window, with users displayed.

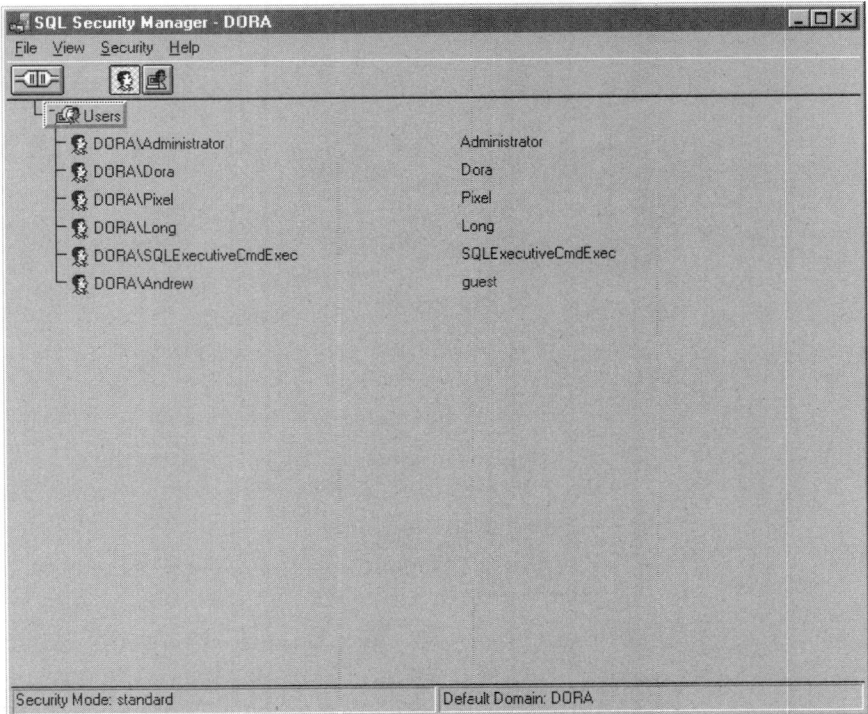

Figure 11-30: The SQL Security Manager main window.

SQL Security Manager shows both users and administrators for the Microsoft SQL Server. Administrators are defined as users who have sa privilege (sa stands for systems administrator), while users have no special privileges.

To add Windows NT 4 Server users to the list of allowed Microsoft SQL Server users, choose the Security | Grant New menu selection. In the Grant User Privilege dialog that displays, select Users in the Grant Privilege list; then click the Grant button. The SQL Security Manager then enumerates the Windows NT 4 Server user list and adds new users to the list of SQL userids.

In the menu for SQL Security Manager, you can choose File | Configure and SQL Security Manager displays the Configure dialog box, as shown in Figure 11-31.

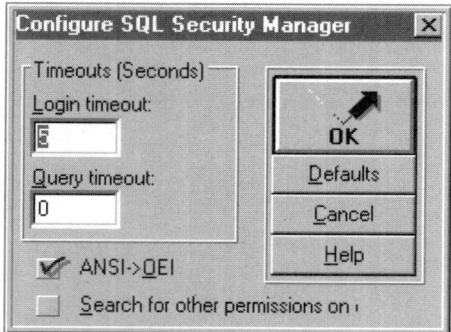

Figure 11-31: The Configure SQL Security Manager's dialog box.

This dialog box has the following options:

- **The Login Timeout text box**—specifies the time, in seconds, that Microsoft SQL Server 6.5 waits prior to terminating an incomplete login attempt.

- **The Query Timeout text box**—specifies the time, in seconds, that Microsoft SQL Server 6.5 waits to retrieve a query result.

- **The ANSI->OEI check box**—enables or disables the automatic ANSI-to-OEI character set conversion. The conversion assists in correcting any problems that may arise when displaying extended characters as graphics. On Windows NT-based computers, these characters normally display as letters with diacritical marks. You need to disconnect and then reconnect to Microsoft SQL Server 6.5 for this selection to take effect.

Note: This option affects not only Microsoft SQL Server 6.5, but also all Windows- and Windows NT-based applications using the DB-Library API.

- **The Search for Other Permissions on check box** —indicates to Microsoft SQL Server 6.5 that when a login ID is dropped, all permission paths are searched. If any other permission paths exist, they are dropped as well.

Note: Selecting the Search for Other Permissions on Drop option may result in a performance degradation of Microsoft SQL Server 6.5.

- You can use the Defaults button to restore the SQL Security Manager to the default values for these options.

For user-level accounts you can display account details: Simply double-click on a user's name in the Users tree (in the SQL Security Manager window). The Account Detail dialog box is shown in Figure 11-32. This dialog displays a number of pieces of information about the user, as the figure shows.

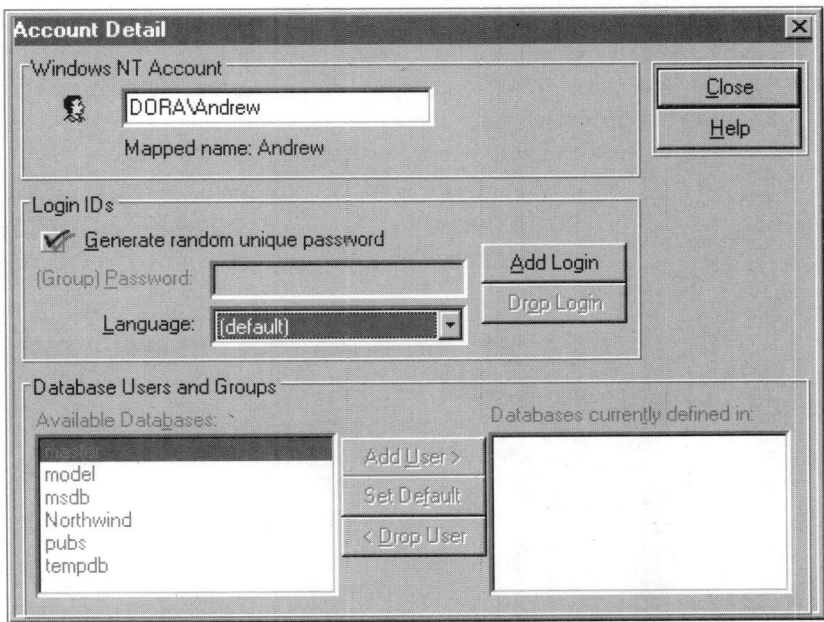

Figure 11-32: The SQL Security Manager's Account Detail dialog box.

SQL Server Books Online

SQL Server Books Online offers a full set of documentation for Microsoft SQL Server 6.5. To start the documentation, choose SQL Server Books Online in the Start Menu | Programs | Microsoft SQL Server 6.5 group. When using SQL Server Books Online, you are presented with the standard Books Online program used with many of Microsoft's products.

Each of the books offers a vast number of topics and valuable information. Whenever you need to find an answer about Microsoft SQL Server 6.5 and are not certain where to look, check SQL Server Books Online. Odds are, this is where you will find your answers!

SQL Server Web Assistant

The SQL Server Web Assistant is a very useful tool if you are interfacing your Web site with Microsoft SQL Server 6.5. With SQL Server Web Assistant, you are able to publish tables as Web pages automatically.

The entire SQL Server Web Assistant program is a wizard. That is, you will be prompted for various information and when the SQL Server Web Assistant program completes, it generates the necessary Web page and the program ends.

Running SQL Server Web Assistant is easy:

1. Select the SQL Server Web Assistant icon in the Start Menu | Programs | Microsoft SQL Server 6.5 group. The application launches with the window shown in Figure 11-33.

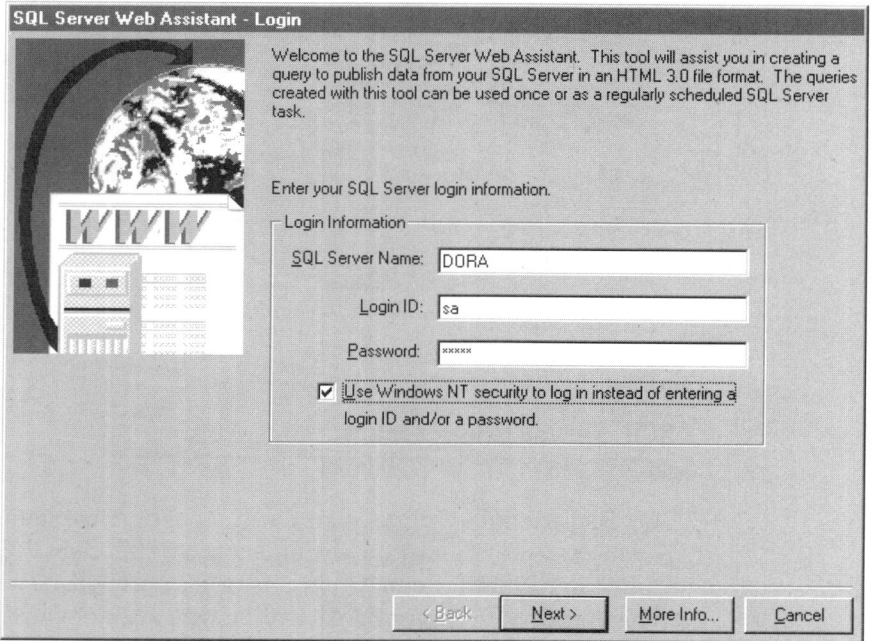

Figure 11-33: The SQL Server Web Assistant Login window.

2. In the initial window, enter Microsoft SQL Server 6.5 login information, including a server name, login name, and password. You may choose to use Windows NT's security rather than using Microsoft SQL Server 6.5 security.

   Using Windows NT's security means that you will be logged on to the SQL server using your current logon userid and password. After entering the necessary login information, click the Next button.

3. The second window, after SQL Server Web Assistant logs in to Microsoft SQL Server 6.5, displays a tree view of the different databases available. Figure 11-34 shows this window, with pubs database tree opened. Figure 11-34 does not show that I have also selected the titles table and the title, ytd_sales, and pubdate columns in the titles table to be included in my query. I've not selected any other criteria, but you probably would want a WHERE clause, and perhaps a SORTED BY clause, too.

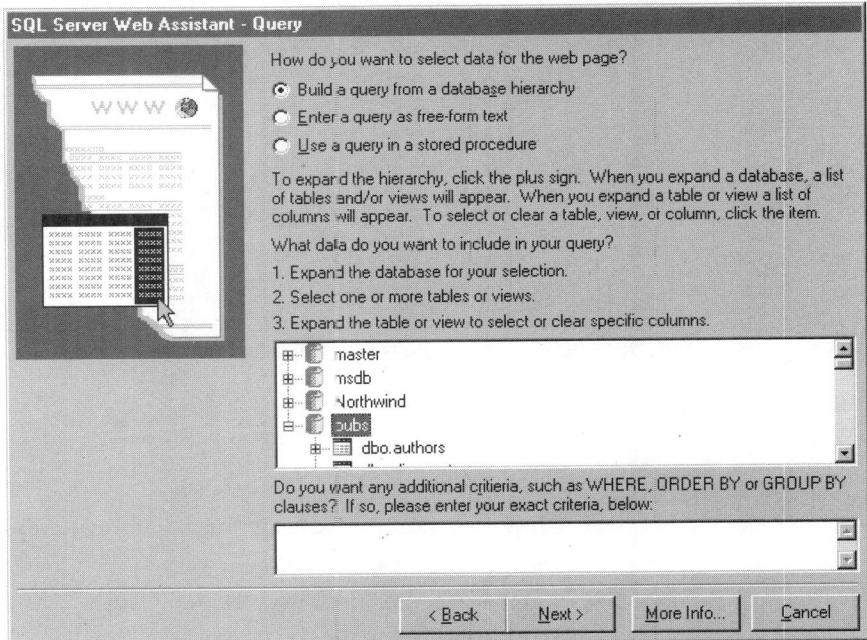

Figure 11-34: The SQL Server Web Assistant Query window.

4. Once you have selected the tables (and columns, if you do not want all of the columns in the selected tables) and entered any optional criteria, click the Next button. The third wizard window, shown in Figure 11-35, allows you to set scheduling options.

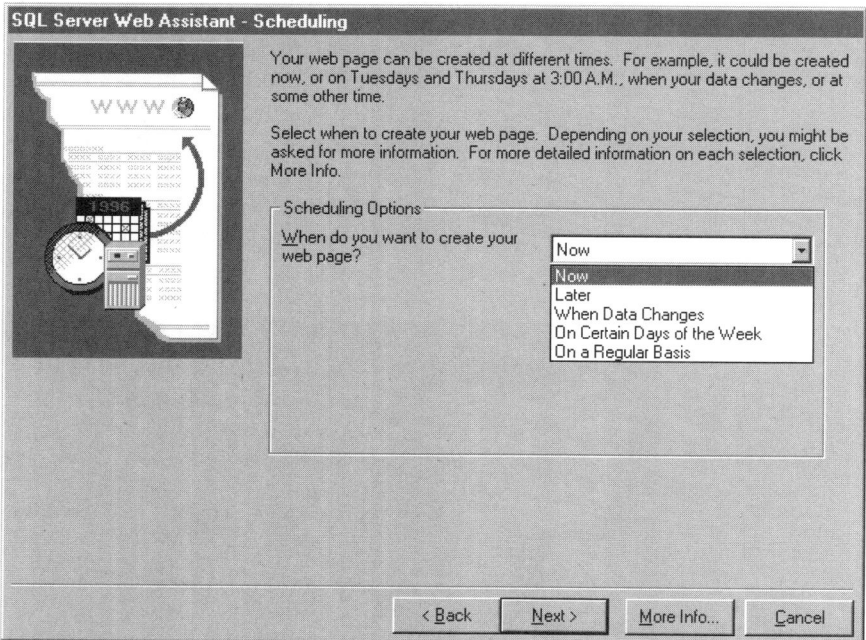

Figure 11-35: The SQL Server Web Assistant Scheduling window.

5. You have five choices in the SQL Server Web Assistant Scheduling window:

■ **Now**—executes the query immediately and the Web page is generated from this query.

■ **Later**—executes the query at a later time. You specify the date (and time) when the query executes.

■ **When Data Changes**—executes the query when data in the column(s) you specify changes.

■ **On Certain Days of the Week**—executes the query on the day (or days) and time specified.

■ **On a Regular Basis**—executes the query at the specified interval. For example, every two hours, every day, at a given time.

6. Select a schedule option that reflects the volatility of your data— if your data changes frequently, schedule the page to be updated more frequently. If the data is relatively static, then a less frequent updating is required. Once you have selected the schedule

(and provided any schedule-specific information required, such as day, time, or interval), click the Next button.

7. The fourth window, shown in Figure 11-36, defines the final format for your Web page. You specify a name for this page, a source template or title and table information, and whether you wish to have any URL (Uniform Resource Locator) information included in your Web page.

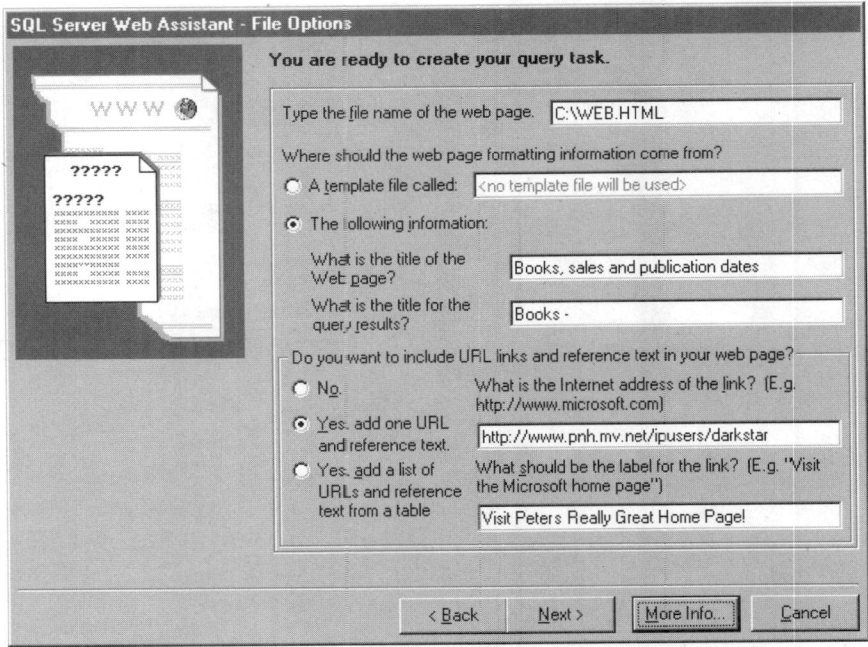

Figure 11-36: The SQL Server Web Assistant File Options window.

8. In the File Options window is a radio button labeled A Template File Called, which is followed by a text box. You can specify a template file into which the results table will be inserted. The template file is for a standard HTML document, with a marker <%insert_data_here%>. Where the <%insert_data_here%> marker is found, the table created by the query is inserted. This lets you customize a complex HTML document by adding (dynamically) data from a Microsoft SQL Server 6.5 database table.

When you specify a template file, then all other options in the File Options dialog box (except for the Web page name) are disabled.

9. The fifth and final window in SQL Server Web Assistant is the Formatting window, shown in Figure 11-37. This window allows you to specify the appearance of your Web page, including the title format and level (Header 1 through Header 6) and the font and attributes of the data table. You can also specify whether you want a time and date stamp, column or view column names, and whether you wish to limit the number of rows returned by the query.

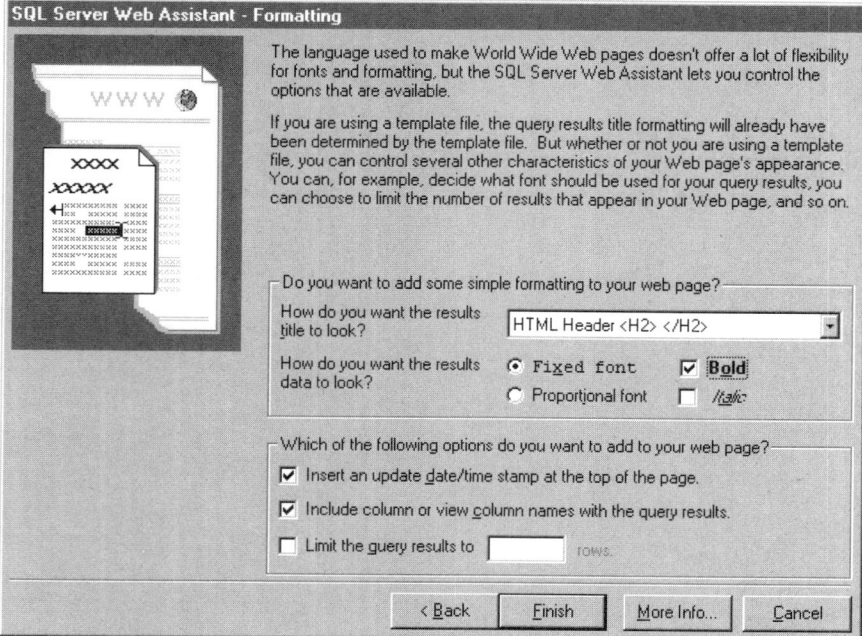

Figure 11-37: The SQL Server Web Assistant Formatting window.

The final results (as seen using Microsoft Internet Explorer) are shown in Figure 11-38. The Web page shows information about books and includes the link to my home page.

This page would be much more complex if a template were designed and used. The technique for using a template is simple and effective, allowing you to use your background, text, footers, headers, and so on. For professional results, a template is recommended.

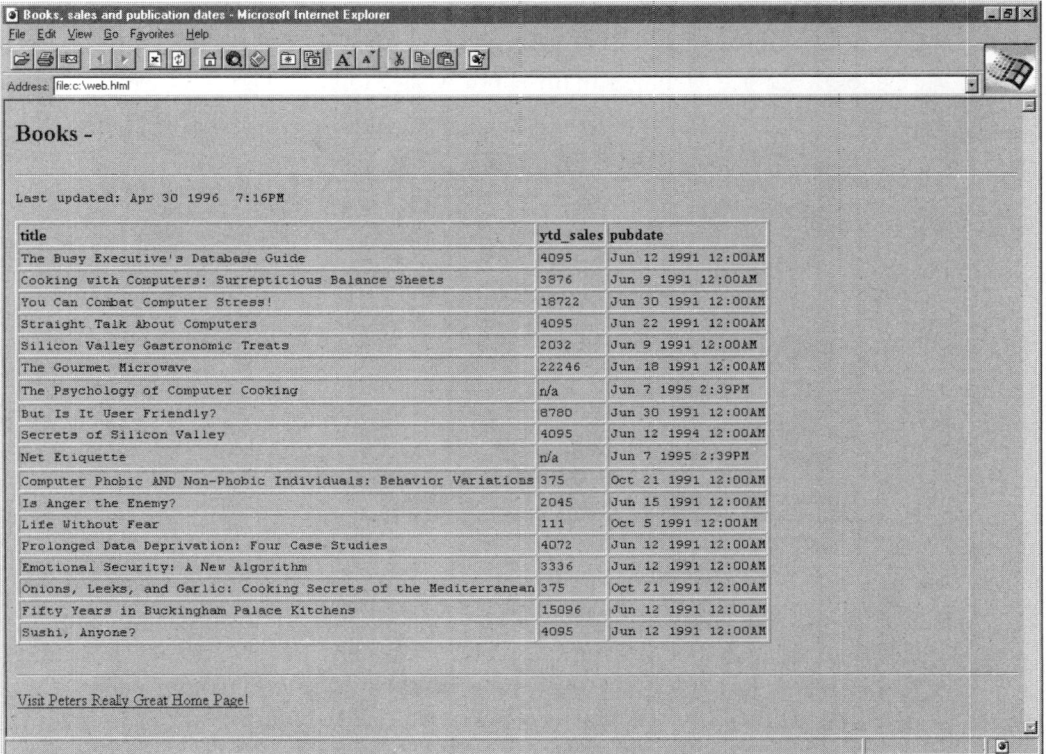

Figure 11-38: The SQL Server Web Assistant-created web.html document.

SQL Service Manager

The SQL Service Manager is the initial interface with Microsoft SQL Server 6.5. The SQL Service Manager is the way the administrator starts, stops, or pauses Microsoft SQL Server 6.5. You launch SQL Service Manager from the Start Menu, using the Programs I Microsoft SQL Server 6.5 group.

Using SQL Service Manager is easy. The user interface consists of a "traffic signal"-type control (a frequently used control with Microsoft SQL Server 6.5) with three buttons: red, yellow, and green. The functionality of each button is documented right in the control:

- **Red**—stop Microsoft SQL Server 6.5.
- **Yellow**—pause Microsoft SQL Server 6.5.
- **Green**—start Microsoft SQL Server 6.5.

The current state of Microsoft SQL Server 6.5 is indicated by whichever button is brighter and is also shown in the status bar at the bottom of the SQL Service Manager main window, as shown in Figure 11-39.

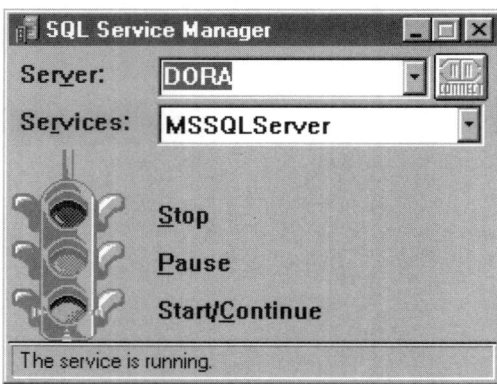

Figure 11-39: SQL Service Manager's main window.

The Microsoft SQL Service Manager allows you to connect to and manage SQL Servers remotely. Shown in Figure 11-39 are two drop-down lists: Server and Services. A button allows you to connect to a server (the button is disabled in Figure 11-39) when you select a remote server that is not currently connected in the Server combo box control.

Use the Server drop-down list to work with either a local Microsoft SQL Server or a remote Microsoft SQL Server. When you select a server, you must then connect to that server, supplying the necessary password and other logon information as necessary.

The Services drop-down list allows you to stop, pause, or start/continue the following services:

- **MSDTC**—The Microsoft Distributed Transaction Coordinator (MSDTC) coordinates transactions across a network of Windows NT and Windows 95 clients and servers. Using MSDTC, Microsoft SQL Server 6.5 is able to do several things. It is possible to update data that reside on two or more Microsoft SQL Server 6.5 systems. It is also possible to participate in transactions controlled by X/Open DTP XA-compliant transaction-processing monitors. MSDTC provides a graphical user interface for distributed transactions.

- **MSSQLServer**—The Microsoft SQL Server is the core component of Microsoft SQL Server 6.5.

- **SQLExecutive**—The SQLExecutive is the service for the SQL executive. The SQLExecutive resides on the Windows NT 4 Server on which Microsoft SQL Server 6.5 runs. The SQLExecutive provides the Microsoft SQL Server 6.5 scheduling engine and offers robust and varied task scheduling and alerting abilities. SQLExecutive is able to work in large client-server environments. SQLExecutive is also sometimes referred to as SQL Executive, both in this book and in the Microsoft SQL Server 6.5 documentation and programs.

Once you've selected the server and services, to manage them you double-click on the Start/Continue, Pause, and Stop buttons.

SQL Setup

The SQL Setup utility is the same program you used to install Microsoft SQL Server 6.5. The setup program can be rerun at any time to refresh, modify, or totally reinstall Microsoft SQL Server 6.5 if desired.

Warning

Use caution when you have an actively used database. Make sure you have adequate backups of all the information in the database: schema, miscellaneous items, data—all must be backed up, and frequently.

Most options may be specified whenever SQL Setup is rerun. This gives the user the opportunity to change basic Microsoft SQL Server 6.5 options, if desired.

Though it is not a good idea to reinstall a product arbitrarily, if you find that your installation is not reliable, has unexplained crashes, or hangs for no apparent reason, a reinstall may be in order. If you find that more than one application fails, however, check hardware or other system components for the problem area.

SQL Trace

The SQL Trace utility monitors Microsoft SQL Server 6.5. To start the SQL Trace utility, choose SQL Trace from the Start Menu | Programs | Microsoft SQL Server 6.5 group. You may choose which events you wish to monitor (the defaults are to monitor virtually everything) and how you wish the monitoring to be performed.

Figure 11-40 shows the SQL Trace utility tracing the execution of a simple SQL query. This query successfully returned a number of rows of information to the user.

Figure 11-40: SQL Trace at work.

The SQL Trace program has a number of options, described in the following paragraphs.

To connect to an SQL server, use the File I Connect menu selection. Once you make a connection, you can begin tracing operations. Also, when finished tracing a specific SQL Server, choose File I Disconnect to disconnect from the currently connected SQL Server.

You can use the File menu to create new filters, modify or delete existing filters, or start, pause, or stop tracing with existing filters. You can use the View menu to monitor the filter that is currently being used in the tracing. You can use the Tools menu to audit or monitor the SQL Server, putting the results in a file, and configure what is traced. Many of these menu items are represented on a toolbar, which is unfortunately not customizable.

Moving On

This chapter covered the installation of Microsoft SQL Server 6.5. Installing Microsoft SQL Server 6.5 is easy and requires selecting only a minimal number of options to complete.

Also covered in this chapter were some of Microsoft SQL Server 6.5's selling points and descriptions of its key components.

Using Microsoft SQL Server allows organizations to completely manage data access. Microsoft SQL Server and client applications can be made to do almost any information management task required.

The next chapter covers maintenance and administration of Microsoft SQL Server 6.5. The degree of maintenance necessary is based on what Microsoft SQL Server 6.5 is being used for: When Microsoft SQL Server 6.5 is used solely to support other Microsoft BackOffice products, substantially less effort need be expended working with Microsoft SQL Server 6.5.

12

Maintaining & Administering Microsoft SQL Server

Microsoft SQL Server 6.5 is managed using the Microsoft SQL Enterprise Manager program (Start Menu | Programs | Microsoft SQL Server 6.5).

There are some typical administrative tasks that are performed on Microsoft SQL Server 6.5, including managing security and user logins. Both of them are done using the Microsoft SQL Server 6.5 Enterprise Manager program (as shown later in this chapter). Many other items, such as scheduled tasks, may be done using the Manager program as well.

Microsoft SQL Server 6.5 is not difficult to manage. As mentioned in the previous chapters, if the only reason Microsoft SQL Server 6.5 is being installed is to support other Microsoft BackOffice products, the systems administrator's need to fully understand the inner workings of Microsoft SQL Server 6.5 is minimized. The BackOffice products that use Microsoft SQL Server 6.5 are fully integrated with Microsoft SQL Server 6.5—and to use them, it is unnecessary to have an in-depth understanding of Microsoft SQL Server 6.5.

Microsoft SQL Server 6.5 may be started using one of the following three techniques:

- Start automatically when the server is booted. This technique can be configured when Microsoft SQL Server 6.5 is installed or from the Enterprise Manager program.

- Use Service Manager, which allows starting Microsoft SQL Server 6.5 or one of its component parts.

- Use Enterprise Manager, which allows starting of either Microsoft SQL Server 6.5 or a component part.

Starting SQL Server 6.5 Using the Service Manager

When Microsoft SQL Server 6.5 is installed, you have the option to configure it to start at boot time. See "Other Installation Options" in Chapter 11 for more information on configuring automatic startup at boot time.

If automatic startup was selected during installation, Microsoft SQL Server 6.5 will start each time the server is booted. For many organizations, SQL Server must be running at all times: Both users and applications (such as Microsoft SMS Server and Microsoft Exchange Server) will expect it to be running prior to their starting.

If SQL Server is not started at boot time, it must be started manually prior to being used. To start it, choose the SQL Service Manager from Start Menu | Programs | Administrative Tools (Common) | SQL Server 6.5 | SQL Service Manager. The SQL Service Manager program (see Figure 12-1) has a simple user interface that lets you start, pause, and stop SQL services on the selected server.

The SQL Service Manager lets you start any of the following SQL Server's services:

- **MSDTC**—the Microsoft Distributed Transaction Coordinator manages transactions across a network of Windows NT- and Windows 95-based systems.

- **MSSQLServer**—the main component of Microsoft SQL Server 6.5; the actual SQL Server.

- **SQLExecutive**—provides scheduling capabilities, including replication, backups, DBCC (DataBase Consistency Checker) operations, and administrative maintenance tasks.

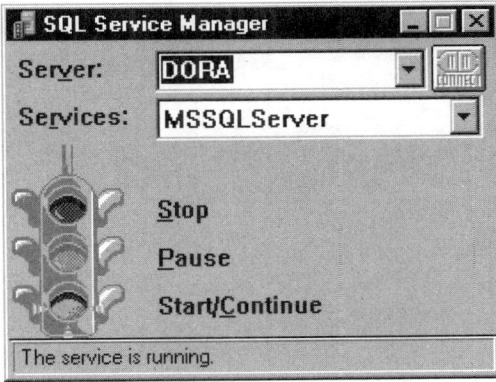

Figure 12-1: The SQL Service Manager—the green light (at the bottom, just like a traffic signal) shows that the SQL Server on DORA is running.

To use Microsoft SQL Server 6.5, only the MSSQLServer service must be started. Both the MSDTC and SQLExecutive services are (at least initially) optional: Microsoft SQL Server 6.5 will operate correctly without either of these services being started. Some users of Microsoft SQL Server 6.5 (such as those who use the Web page wizard, described in Chapter 11) will need to use these features.

The Microsoft SQL Enterprise Manager

The Microsoft SQL Enterprise Manager (Figure 12-2) is the main program used to manage and administer Microsoft SQL Server 6.5. Start Microsoft SQL Enterprise Manager by selecting Start Menu | Programs | Administrative Tools (Common) | SQL Server 6.5 | SQL Enterprise Manager.

The Microsoft SQL Enterprise Manager is used to perform virtually all management functions. Many SQL Server administrators will leave the Enterprise running much of the time.

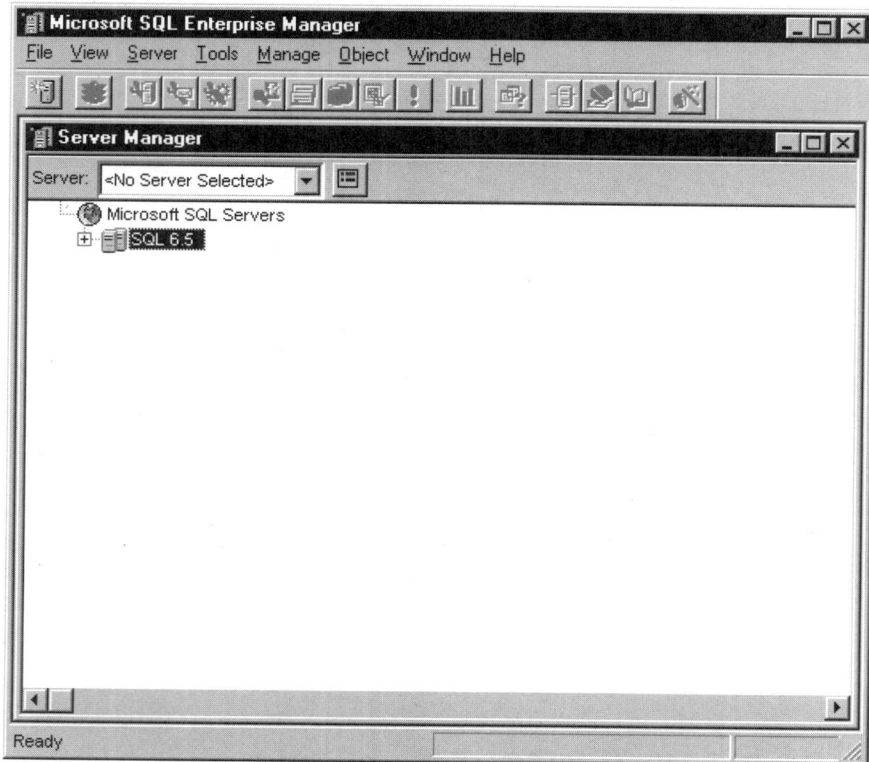

Figure 12-2: Microsoft SQL Enterprise Manager—select a server to manage in the Server drop-down list.

SQL Enterprise Manager will display a tree view of Microsoft SQL Servers and a subtree item named SQL 6.5 for those servers running Microsoft SQL Server 6.5.

Selecting a server in the Server control (which contains the text <No Server Selected> when there is no server selected) will display the selected server's status (Figure 12-3).

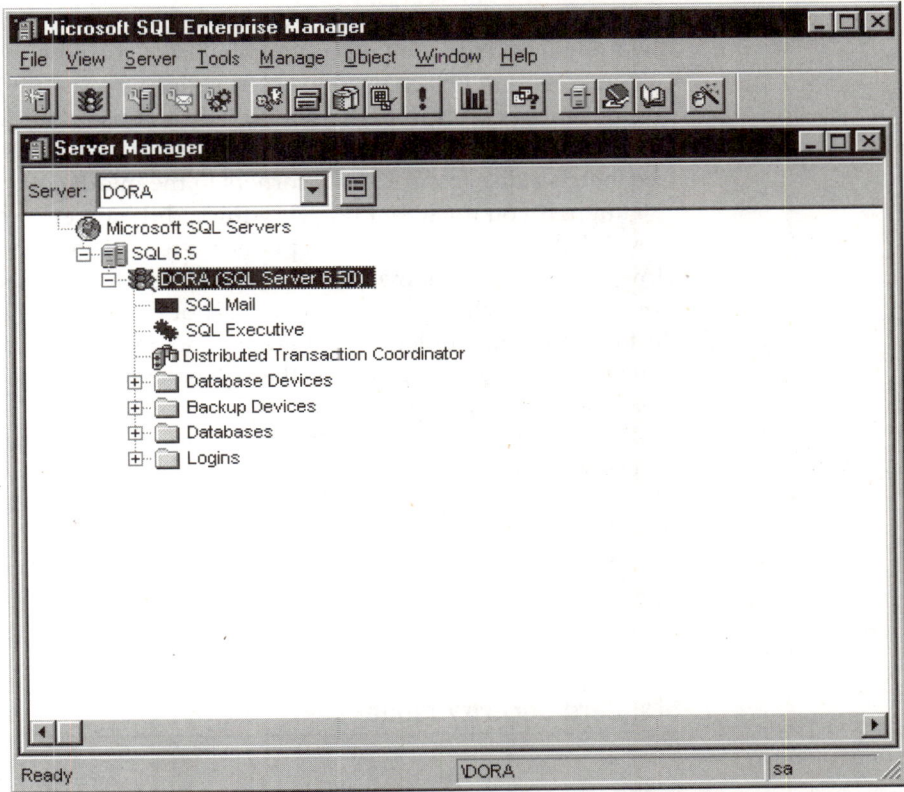

Figure 12-3: Microsoft SQL Enterprise Manager ready to manage DORA's SQL Server.

A server may be managed by selecting the server and expanding the server's tree display (by clicking the plus sign in the box to the left of the server's name). This chapter reviews basic management tasks, such as configuring users and logins, managing databases, and other features as described below.

Managing Logins & Security

Microsoft SQL Server 6.5 is a client/server database system. The data are maintained and then given to client users as they request it. Generally, security must be maintained: There is a compelling desire to not allow the wrong people to access data in an organization's database. For example, it would be unwise to allow anyone outside the personnel or accounting departments to access employee data such as salary information. As well, it would be best to maintain confidentiality of customer lists, so that the customer list can't be compromised. Imagine what might happen if the orders table were improperly modified by an unscrupulous employee; there could be the possibility that your organization might be delivering free merchandise to dark street corners in the middle of the night!

Laugh, if you must, but this very thing did happen to one company; they delivered an expensive telephone system to a manhole in a street. How? Easy—many deliveries of parts and cable were made to manholes (for telephone cabling teams), so it was not that unusual a delivery destination. The problem was there was no one from the company there to receive the merchandise. Yes, there was someone there, but they didn't work for the company!

Before we can delve too deeply into the issues of managing logins, it is necessary to look at the Microsoft SQL Server 6.5 security modes. Microsoft SQL Server 6.5 supports two ways to validate users: either from Microsoft SQL Server 6.5's internal login list or by using Windows NT 4 Server's security validation facilities. These modes are set using the Microsoft SQL Server 6.5 Enterprise Manager program. Microsoft SQL Server 6.5 allows both security models to be used at the same time.

Standard Security Mode

In the standard security mode, all login validation is done internally by Microsoft SQL Server 6.5 using built-in lists of users. The systems administrator creates the user lists, and any user who must access data from Microsoft SQL Server 6.5 must have a login name created for that access.

With the standard security mode, it is necessary to maintain a separate list of users for Microsoft SQL Server 6.5. Should the organization be large, with many users, this duplication of security lists (one for Microsoft SQL Server 6.5 and one for Windows NT 4 Server) may prove to be a considerable burden.

Windows NT Integrated Mode

In the Windows NT integrated security mode, all login validation is done internally by Windows NT 4 Server using the built-in Windows NT 4 Server security system. All user validation is done from the regular list of Windows NT 4 Server users; typically, the user is validated using the login name they used to log on.

With the Windows NT integrated security mode, it is not necessary to maintain a separate list of users for Microsoft SQL Server 6.5, making administration work a little bit easier. However, a down side is that special care would have to be made to ensure that each Windows NT 4 Server user is able to access only that data they are authorized to access (by defining permissions on a database-by-database basis).

Mixed Mode

With the mixed mode, there are two types of login validation:

- Mixed security mode, where all login validation is done with the Microsoft SQL Server 6.5, using built-in lists of users.
- Windows NT 4 Server user list, where login validation is done by Windows NT 4 Server.

A user may be validated using either technique. Using the mixed security mode lets you create access to Microsoft SQL Server 6.5 without allowing access to the Windows NT 4 Server, while at the same time allowing all Windows NT 4 Server users access to the Microsoft SQL Server 6.5. Mixed security mode is often used in many organizations.

Configuring Security Options

To configure security (and username validation), display the Server Configuration/Options dialog box. First select the server to be managed, in the Server Manager window (see Figure 12-3). The Server Configuration/Options dialog box is displayed by choosing Server I SQL Server I Configure in the Microsoft SQL Enterprise Manager main menu. Finally, click on Security Options to display the Security Options tab (Figure 12-4).

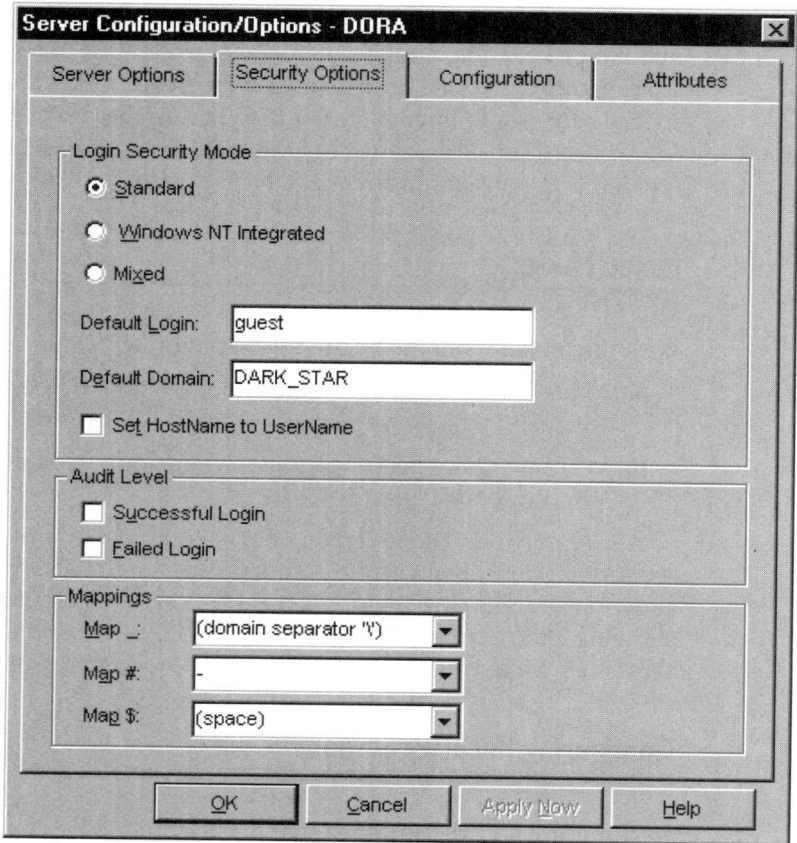

Figure 12-4: The Security Options tab—this server uses only the standard (SQL Server) security mode.

The Security Options tab has three main sections: Login Security Mode, Audit Level, and Mappings.

Login Security Mode

Setting the login security mode (as described in the previous section) lets the systems administrator configure how security is managed. The most common problem I see when Microsoft SQL Server 6.5 is installed is that the login security mode is not set the way it is expected to be set. The default is to use only Microsoft SQL Server 6.5's security—and there are only a very few usernames created by default when Microsoft SQL Server 6.5 is installed.

The first choice in the Security Options tab is to configure the login security mode; if you select either the Windows NT Integrated option or the Mixed option, the Windows NT 4 Server security system will either manage or assist in the management of login security.

There is a place to add a default login and default domain, also. The login name is used to allow users who are not members of the syslogins to access Microsoft SQL Server 6.5.

Tip

The login name specified (either by default or entered) must be added to the Microsoft SQL Server 6.5 login list! No end-user login name (other than the systems administrator's account, sa) is created when Microsoft SQL Server 6.5 is installed. If you use the provided name for the Default Login name (guest), add a login name also.

The final selection in the Login Security Mode section of the Security Options tab is the Set HostName to UserName check box, which allows the user's username to be placed in the hostname field in the client login record.

Audit Level

Two choices in the Audit Level section of the Security Options tab allow logging of both successful and failed logins. For many Microsoft SQL Server 6.5 installations, it may be best to log both failures and successful logins. If at a later time it is determined that this level of auditing is not necessary, then the auditing level may be changed as needed.

Mappings

Mappings are used to change invalid characters found in usernames to characters that Microsoft SQL Server 6.5 is able to handle. For example, the space character may be mapped to the $ character. Most installations will simply use the defaults for these characters.

Managing User Login Names

When using Microsoft SQL Server 6.5 security (either as the sole login validator or in conjunction with Windows NT 4 Server user security), users must be added, deleted, and managed in Microsoft SQL Server 6.5's user database.

There are several methods to manage login names:

- The Server Manager window, when a server is selected, will display the currently configured logins (see Figure 12-5) and allow the systems administrator to manage logins.

- Simply double-clicking a login name will display the Manage Logins (Figure 12-6) dialog box, with the user selected.

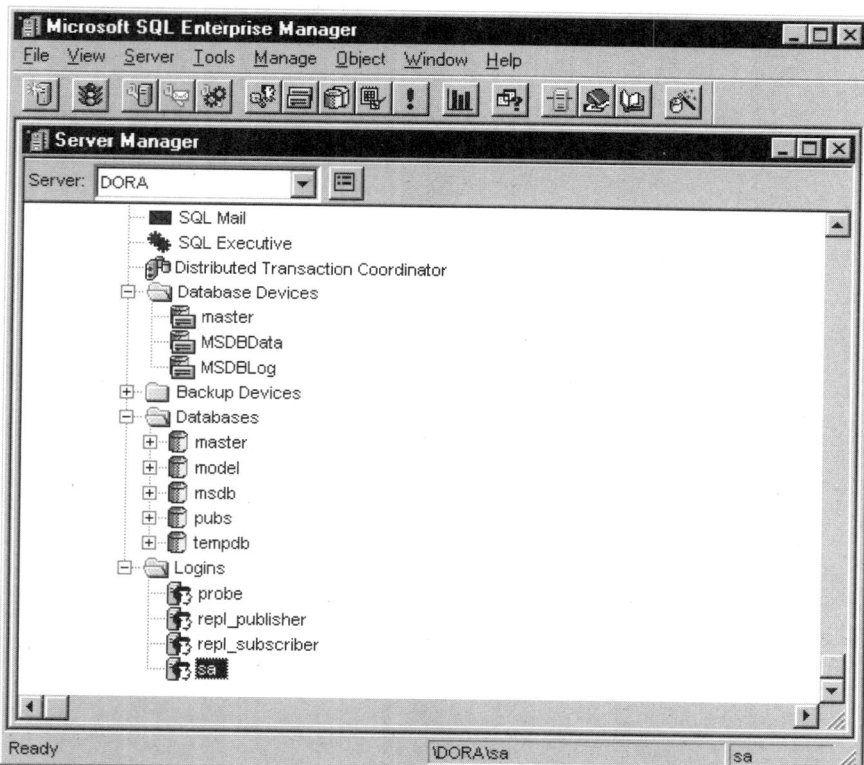

Figure 12-5: Manage users from the Server Manager window by expanding the Logins tree.

In addition, selecting Manage I Logins from the Microsoft SQL Enterprise Manager main menu will display the Manage Logins dialog box (Figure 12-6). In the Manage Logins dialog box, select a userid to manage or the <New Login> entry to create a new userid (select both from the Login Name drop-down list).

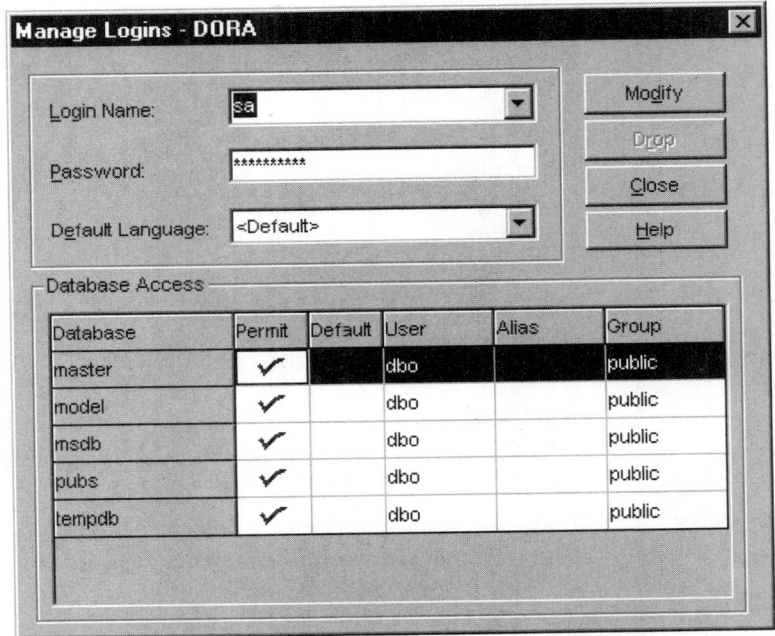

Figure 12-6: Display the Manage Logins dialog box to manage users, too.

Regardless of where, or how, the Manage Logins dialog box is displayed, the management process is identical. To manage an existing login name, select that name in the Login Name control at the top of the Manage Logins dialog box. Once the login name has been selected, the current settings for that login name will be displayed. Figure 12-6 shows the login name sa (the systems administrator's login), with the password (which is not displayed, but which may be changed), the default language, and the database access permissions.

Adding Users

To create a new login name (we will use the name *Westheimer* for our example), simply follow these steps:

1. Display the Manage Logins dialog box, and select <New Login> in the Login Name drop-down list. As soon as <New Login> is selected, the Manage Logins dialog box will clear, allowing you to enter the information for the new user.

2. Enter the user's name (Westheimer in our example), and a password (COMPUCARE). Make sure the password is non-trivial!

3. Select a language if the default language is not appropriate. Selecting languages is usually only necessary when dealing with a multilingual country (such as Canada) or for organizations that are international in scope.

4. In the Database Access section of the Manage Logins dialog box, select whether the user will be granted access by clicking in the Permit column for the database. One database will be defined as the default for the login name.

5. For each database, it is possible to specify a different username. Type in this name correctly!

6. If necessary, select an alias to be used when accessing the selected database. The alias must already exist in the login name list for the SQL Server. When specifying an alias, neither a username nor a group may be specified.

7. If using groups (groups make user management easier; for example there may be a group for accounting and a group for sales), specify which group the user belongs to.

8. Click the Add button to add the new user.

Once a login name (see Figure 12-7) for a user has been added, any of the configuration information specified when the user was created may be modified as needed. Typically, new databases will be added to the Microsoft SQL Server 6.5, and it will be necessary to either grant or deny access to these new databases as needed.

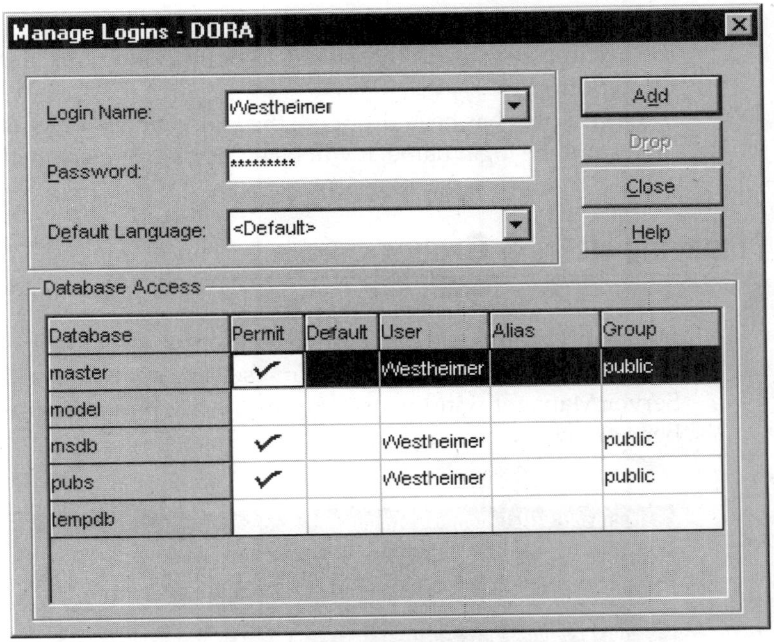

Figure 12-7: Adding the login name Westheimer.

Modifying Users

To modify the attributes for an existing login name, select the existing login name in the Server Manager's Logins list and double-click it. (An alternative method to add, modify, or drop a login name is to right-click and select an action from the displayed context menu.)

The user's password, default language, and database access rights may be changed as desired. It is not possible to change the login name, however; to do so it will be necessary to create a new login name.

Any time a password is entered, Microsoft SQL Server 6.5 will require that the password be confirmed. Remember that passwords are case specific!

Dropping Users

Whenever a user is no longer to be allowed to access the Microsoft SQL Server 6.5, it is necessary to remove the user's login name. This process is called *dropping*. To drop a login name, select the name in the Logins list and using the right button on the mouse, display the context menu. In the context menu, select Drop to remove this user. (Or select the user in the Login Name list in the Manage Logins dialog box and click the Drop button.)

Once a user has been dropped, the login name and its attributes are lost. To restore the login name, it will be necessary to re-create the login name.

Managing Users & Groups

Users and groups are database level groupings of login names. To manage either users or groups, first select a specific database in the Server Manager window (see Figure 12-8, where the pubs database has been selected).

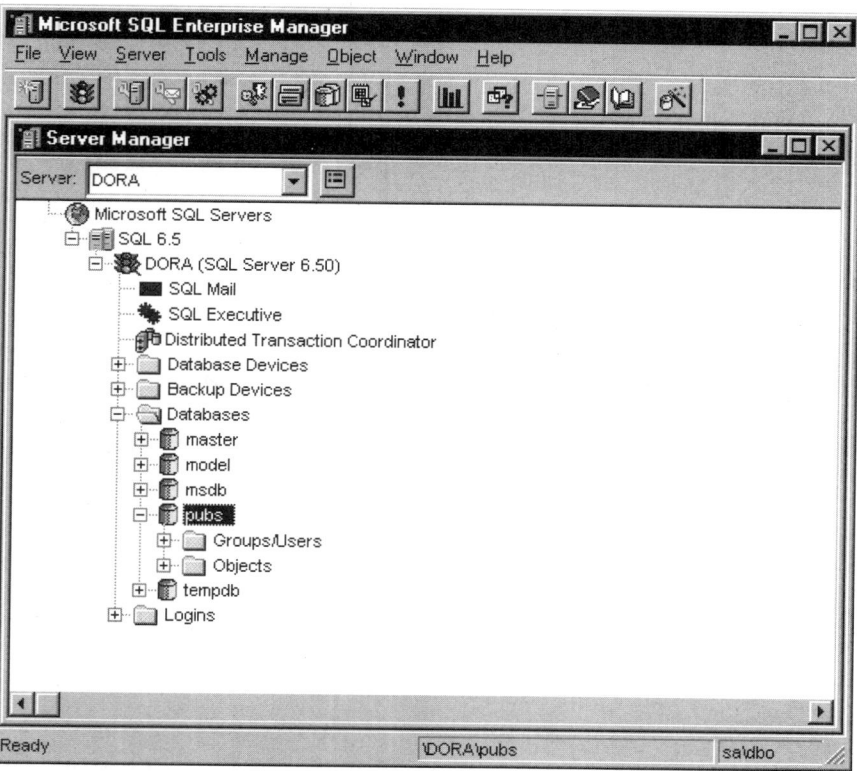

Figure 12-8: The pubs table selected so that users and groups may be managed.

Once a database has been selected, choose Manage I Users or Manage I Groups from the Microsoft SQL Enterprise Manager main menu.

Managing Users

Choosing Manage I Users in the Microsoft SQL Enterprise Manager main menu will display the Manage Users dialog box (see Figure 12-9). In the User Name control, select an existing user or select <New User> to create a new user.

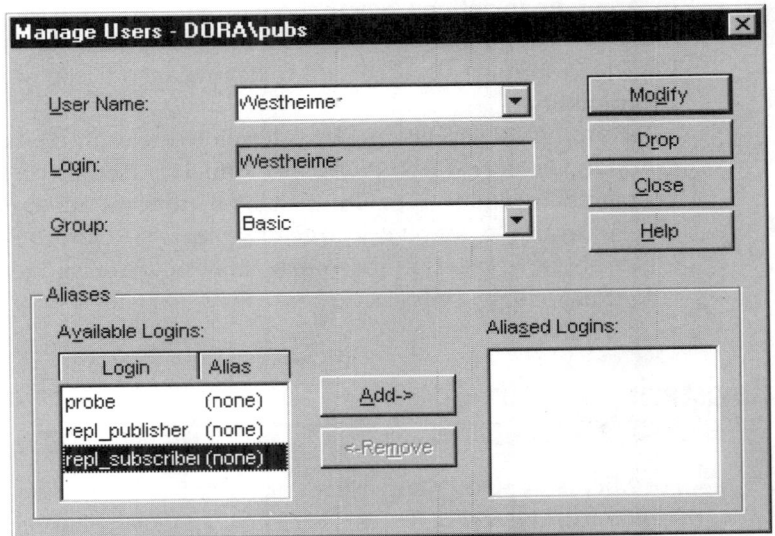

Figure 12-9: Managing user Westheimer (who is in the Basic group).

For each user, one or more optional aliases may be assigned (using any existing login name in the Available Logins list).

Managing Groups

Groups are useful for managing users based on some external (to Microsoft SQL Server 6.5) criteria. Such a criteria might be job function (accounting, personnel management, sales, corporate management, and so on), task, or department or division.

Choosing Manage | Groups in the Microsoft SQL Enterprise Manager main menu will display the Manage Groups dialog box. In the Group control, select an existing user or select <New Group> to create a new group.

For each group, one or more users may be assigned (using any existing login name in the Users list). Though it is possible to create a group that does not have any users, such a group would not serve any useful purpose until one or more users are assigned.

Server Groups

In larger organizations, where there is more than one Microsoft SQL Server 6.5 running, the servers may be grouped into logical groupings. Logical groupings allow servers to be managed based on, for example, functionality.

Groupings of servers might well follow the examples given above for groupings of users (accounting, personnel management, sales, corporate management, and so on). Groups may be formed under other groups, too. For example, for a very large organization, a group called Accounting might have several subgroups: Accounts Payable, Accounts Receivable, and General Ledger.

Registering Servers

For Microsoft SQL Enterprise Manager to be able to manage a server, the server must be *registered*. This is done by choosing Server | Register Server from Microsoft SQL Enterprise Manager's main menu. The Register Server dialog box (Figure 12-10) is used to register a Microsoft SQL Server 6.5 server.

To register a server, the server's name must be specified (usually the server's name will be in the Server drop-down list box; if not, however, click the Servers button to display a list of available servers).

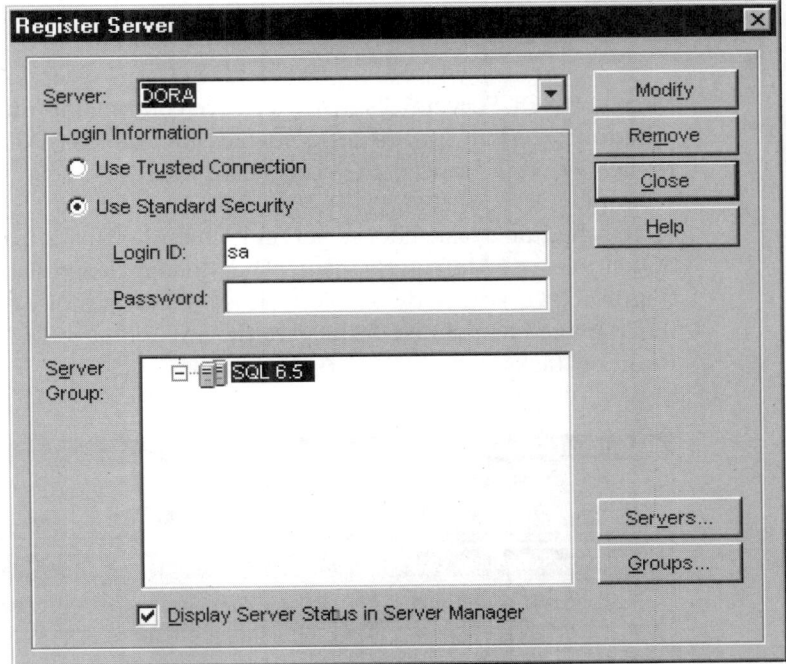

Figure 12-10: DORA is about to be registered. We use standard security for this server.

Once the server has been selected, the server's login information may be specified. Typically, Microsoft SQL Server 6.5 is managed using the sa account. The password for the sa account was specified when Microsoft SQL Server 6.5 was installed (the password may be changed using the techniques described in "Managing User Login Names"). Select the correct security model (typically the Standard Security model is selected as a default).

Once a server has been registered, various management functions may be performed on that server. To manage any Microsoft SQL Server 6.5 server, the server must be running—Microsoft SQL Enterprise Manager provides for starting and stopping a Microsoft SQL Server 6.5 server if necessary.

Scheduled Tasks

Microsoft SQL Server 6.5's SQLExecutive component functions as a task scheduler. Certain specific tasks such as commands (EXE, COM, or BAT), replication, or a Transact SQL command file may be executed by the scheduler.

To schedule a task, choose Server | Scheduled Tasks from Microsoft SQL Enterprise Manager's menu. The Manage Scheduled Tasks window (Figure 12-11) will be displayed (this is a window, not a dialog box). In the Managed Scheduled Tasks window are two tabs: Task List and Running Tasks.

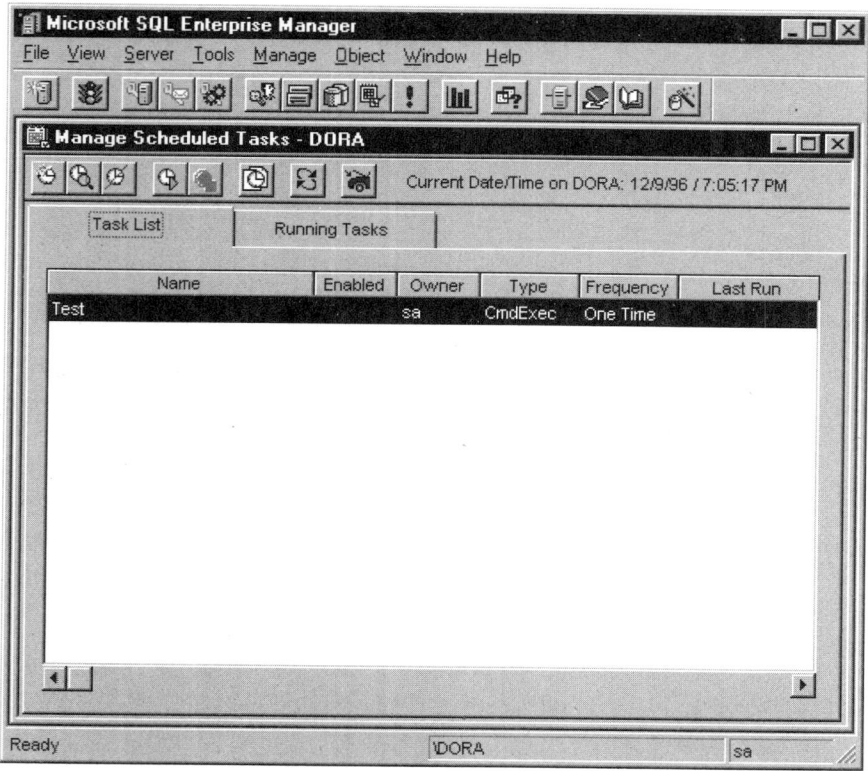

Figure 12-11: The Manage Scheduled Tasks window with a single task listed.

The Manage Scheduled Tasks window has its own toolbar: the eight buttons on the toolbar are, from left to right:

- **New**—allows creation of a new task. The task's name, type, database, and command must be selected. For tasks that are command based (and which therefore do not affect a database), the database may not be meaningful, however. New tasks may be scheduled to run on demand (the Run Task button must be clicked to run the task), one time (at a date and time specified), or recurring (daily, weekly, or monthly).

- **Edit**—used to modify an existing task. Any of the parameters specified when the task was created may be modified at any time.

- **Delete**—used to delete a task when its usefulness has come to an end.

- **Run Task**—executes any task on demand. For tasks that are scheduled as run on demand, the Run Task button is the method to start the task executing.

- **Stop Task**—used with a currently running task (click on the Running Tasks tab to display running tasks); execution may be halted by clicking on the Stop Task button.

- **View History**—displays a log listing of each task's execution. When a task executes, much information is kept on the task.

- **Refresh**—updates the display (primarily used with the Running Tasks tab).

- **Task Engine Options**—displays the Task Engine Options dialog box. Options are all log oriented (number of lines in the task log, number of lines per task, and a button to clear the current task history log).

Task List Tab

The Task List tab (see Figure 12-11) shows all currently available tasks, regardless of their status. Tasks scheduled to run one time only are listed after they have been executed, for example, as are recurring tasks.

Running Tasks Tab

The Running Tasks tab (see Figure 12-11) shows currently running tasks. Generally, most tasks will take little time to execute (TSQL [Transact SQL] tasks may take longer to execute than a command type task), so a task may well have completed its job before it's displayed in the Running Tasks tab.

Refresh the contents of the Running Tasks tab by clicking on the Refresh button (the seventh button on the Manage Scheduled Tasks toolbar).

Alerts/Operators

Alerts are sent to specific operators (typically the operators would include the systems administrator) when events or errors occur that require attention.

The Microsoft SQL Enterprise Manager program's Server | Alerts/Operators menu selection is used to display the Manage Alerts and Operators window.

For alerts (select the Alerts tab, shown in Figure 12-12), each error or alert defined may be sent to one or more individuals. Each recipient may be notified using direct e-mail or an e-mail-based pager.

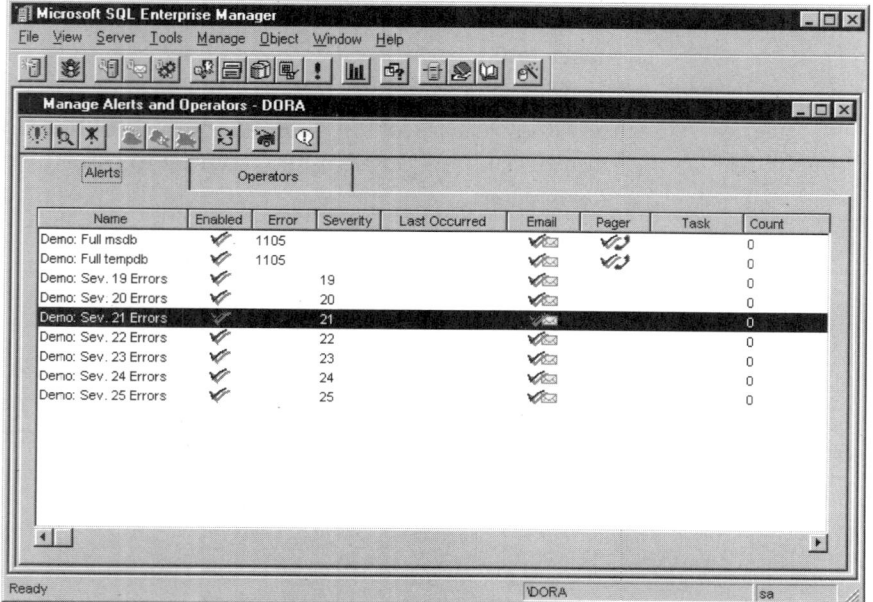

Figure 12-12: Example alerts created by default for Microsoft SQL Server 6.5.

Each operator is created by first selecting the Operators tab in the Manage Alerts and Operators window and then clicking the New Operator button (fourth button from the left) on the Manage Alerts and Operator's toolbar.

When an operator is created (or modified) the New Operator (or Edit Operator) dialog box is displayed (the Edit Operator dialog box is shown in Figure 12-13).

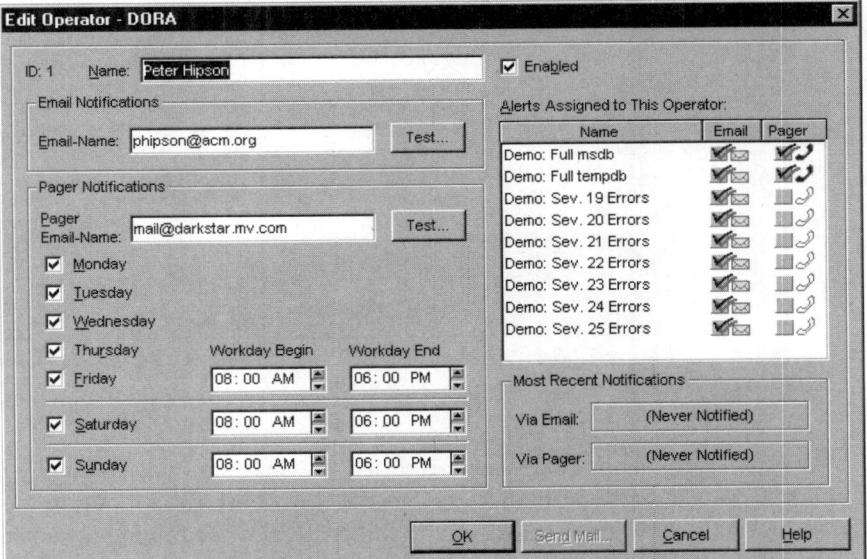

Figure 12-13: Editing an alert operator—sending messages to tell what's happened to the SQL Server.

For pager notifications, the operator's working hours may be specified. Remember that for critical problems, and senior staff, working hours can be 24 hours per day. (But don't page anyone without properly coordinating with them what hours they will be available.)

Messages

The Microsoft SQL Server contains over 2,700 error messages, which may be logged. It is also possible to add additional (user-defined) messages if desired. Figure 12-14 shows the Microsoft SQL Server Messages dialog box.

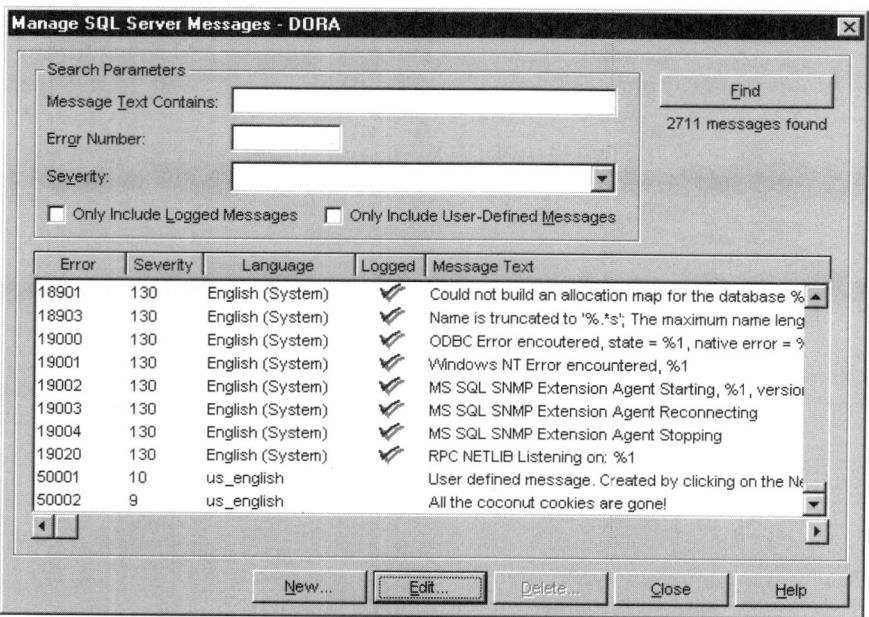

Figure 12-14: Microsoft SQL Server Messages, including two user-defined messages.

Though any user-defined messages may be created, be careful not to create so many messages that they become difficult to manage.

There is a search capability to allow searching for a specific word or string in a message, a message error number, or a message's severity. As well, searches can be made on only logged messages or only user-defined messages. For each message, you can set whether a message is logged (or not); when a message is not logged, it will be suppressed in the Windows NT event log.

Working With Remote Servers

Microsoft SQL Enterprise Manager is able to manage remote SQL servers. Choosing Server | Remote Servers from the Microsoft SQL Enterprise Manager menu will display the Manage Remote Servers dialog box (shown in Figure 12-15).

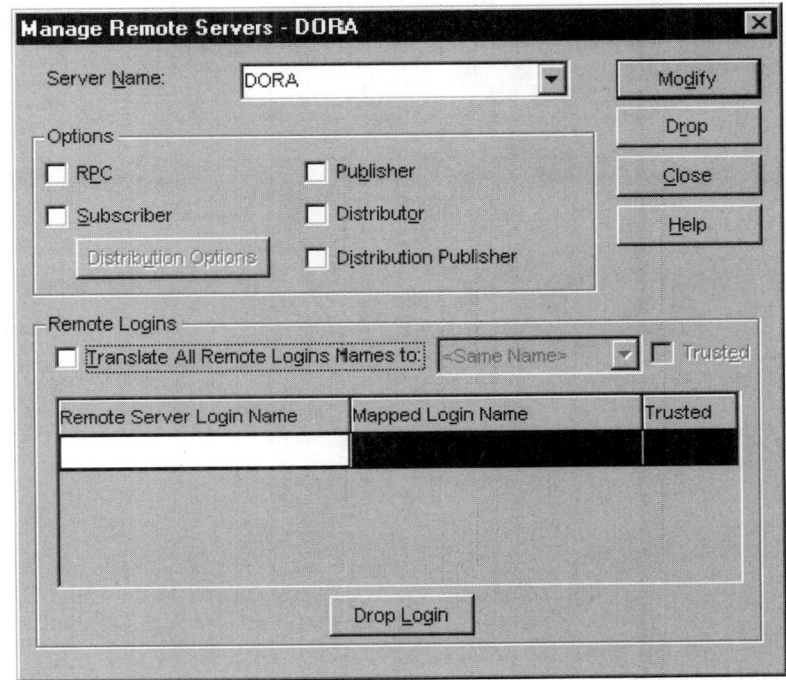

Figure 12-15: The Manage Remote Servers dialog box with DORA selected.

If your organization does not have any remote SQL servers, this option is not needed.

Viewing Current Activity

To determine the current activity (what the Microsoft SQL Server is doing) choose Server | Current Activity from the Microsoft SQL Enterprise Manager menu. The Current Activity window has three tabs: User Activity, Detail Activity (see Figure 12-16), and Object Locks.

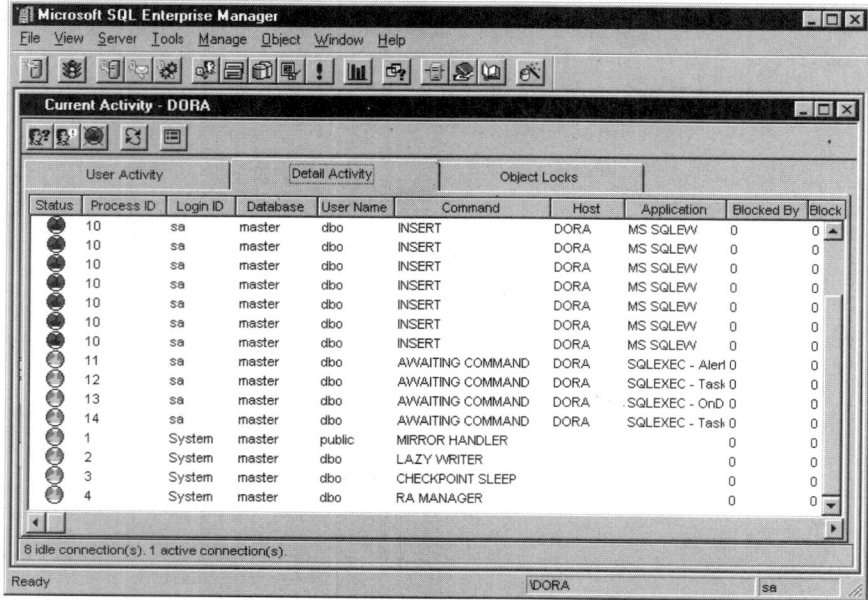

Figure 12-16: Detail activity for the Microsoft SQL Server named DORA.

The Current Activity window has a toolbar with five buttons:

- **Details**—displays detailed information about the selected object in the list.

- **Send Message**—sends a message to the user with the specified login ID.

- **Kill Process**—kills the specified process. Use with caution: The effects may be far reaching if there are users who are depending on the process.

- **Refresh**—updates the currently displayed tab.

- **Display Legend**—displays a legend that explains the status symbols.

Viewing the Error Log

The error log (which contains more information than just errors) is viewed by choosing Server | Error Log from the Microsoft SQL Enterprise Manager menu. The log lists actions such as the starting of the server and any other significant actions.

Figure 12-17 shows the Server Error Log's first few entries. The first entries show the server starting (information includes version numbers, useful when debugging problems that may be version specific), errors, and recover actions.

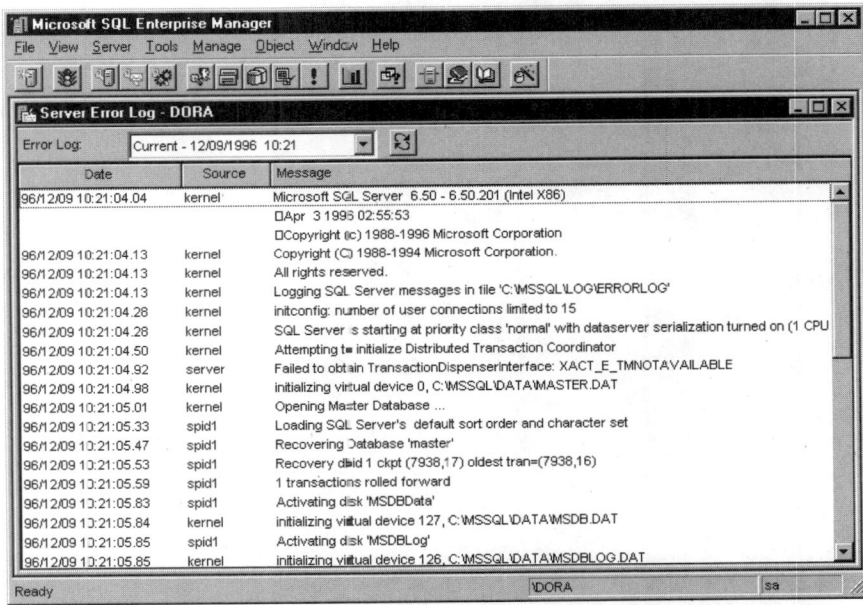

Figure 12-17: The Server Error Log showing a normal startup for Microsoft SQL Server 6.5.

Moving On

This chapter covered managing and configuring Microsoft SQL Server 6.5, focusing on the Microsoft SQL Server 6.5 security modes, creating login names, auditing, groups, and tasks.

The next chapter covers creating and using Microsoft SQL Server 6.5 databases. The database is the heart and soul of Microsoft SQL Server 6.5.

## 13

Creating & Using SQL Server Databases

Microsoft SQL Server 6.5 gives client users access to information. Often that information is contained in databases. Microsoft SQL Server 6.5 is able to make a large number of databases available to users (the actual number of databases that Microsoft SQL Server 6.5 is able to make available depends on a number of factors, most of which are based on hardware).

In this chapter, we'll focus on databases and the role of Microsoft SQL Server 6.5 in creating and using them. First we'll look at what a database is and the process of creating one. Then we'll get into basic maintenance of databases once they've been created.

The Parts of a Microsoft SQL Server 6.5 Database

In Microsoft SQL Server 6.5, each database is divided into a number of components. The actual data (in the tables) is but one part of a database. Groups, users, and objects are also parts of a database.

An SQL database is made up of tables, views, stored procedures, rules, defaults, and user-defined datatypes. Each of these items will be described in this chapter.

Groups & Users

Groups and users (see Chapter 12 for more on groups and users) are
used to manage access to a specific database.

Groups are typically logical groupings of individuals (usually by
some common attribute such as department, job function, or the like). A
specific user may belong to one, and only one, group at any given time.
An example of groups is shown in Figure 13-1, where there are two
groups: Public (created by default by Microsoft SQL Server 6.5) and
PowerUsers, a group our systems administrator created to allow certain
users who provide in-house support access to the database.

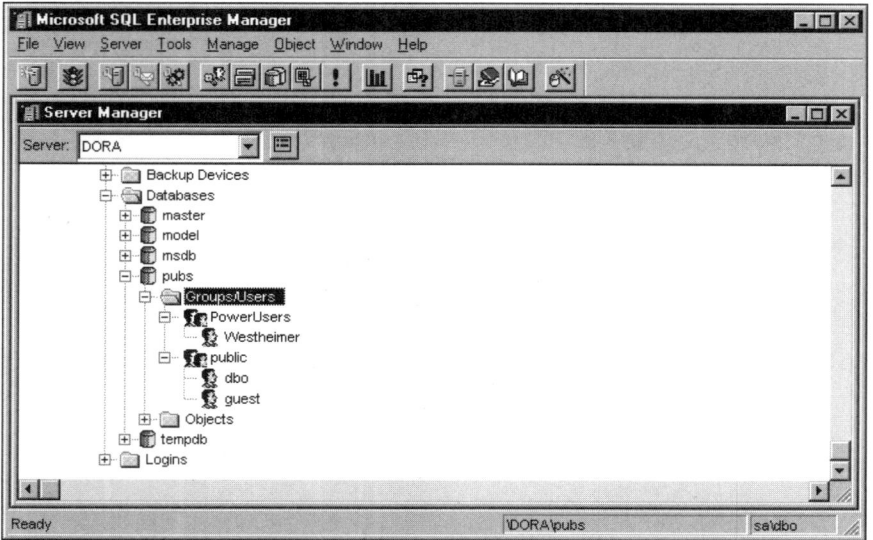

*Figure 13-1: User Westheimer is in the PowerUsers group—he provides in-
house support to other users.*

Right-click on the Groups/Users folder (Figure 13-1) to display the
pop-up menu. The choices on the menu are New User, New Group, and
Refresh. Clicking New Group lets you create a new group, and clicking
New User lets you create a new user. To remove an existing group (or
user), select the group (or user) and right-click. Choose Drop (or Delete if
working with users).

Group management is done by double-clicking the group (see Figure 13-2). Once you are done adding and removing users from the group, click OK to close the dialog box.

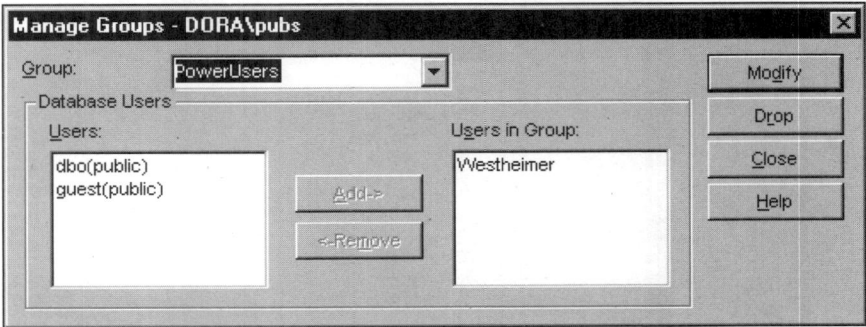

Figure 13-2: The Manage Groups dialog box—a user is added to the PowerUsers group.

Objects

Objects are a collection of the parts that make up the database: views, stored procedures, rules, defaults, and user-defined datatypes. The following sections go into more detail about each of these objects.

Tables

Tables consist of the actual data that forms the database. Typically, a database consists of many tables (the pubs database, as shown in Figure 13-3, contains 11 distinct tables).

A database comprises data objects. The data objects are arranged in a table format, made up of rows of data objects. Each table also contains one or more columns (where each column contains data objects having identical attributes). If you remember that columns define data objects, and that rows contain the data objects, then the concept of databases and tables will not be too difficult to understand.

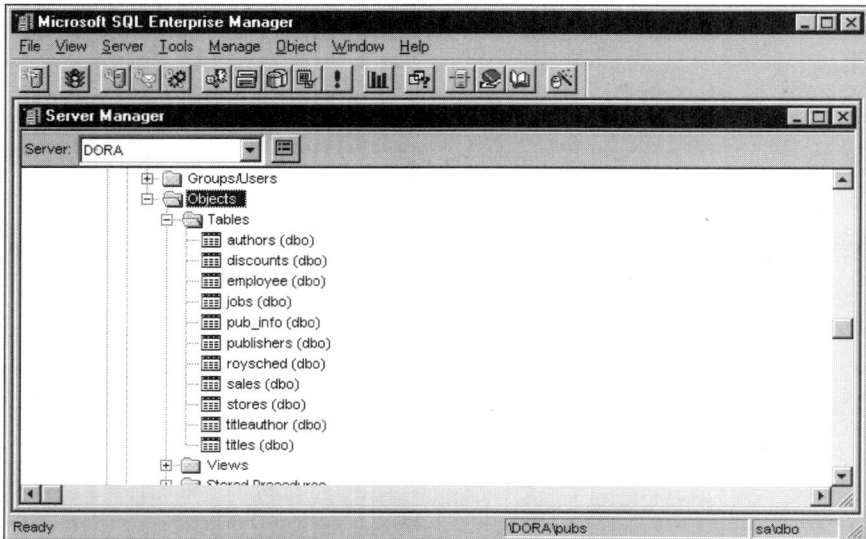

Figure 13-3: The pubs database has 11 tables, virtually everything that a publisher might need to manage his or her business.

Views

A view is more than what we see when we look out a window. For a database, a view represents a particular display of data from the database. The pubs database has a single view (called titleview) that displays the titles of the publisher's books.

Figure 13-4 shows MS Query displaying the titleview view. This view returned 25 records.

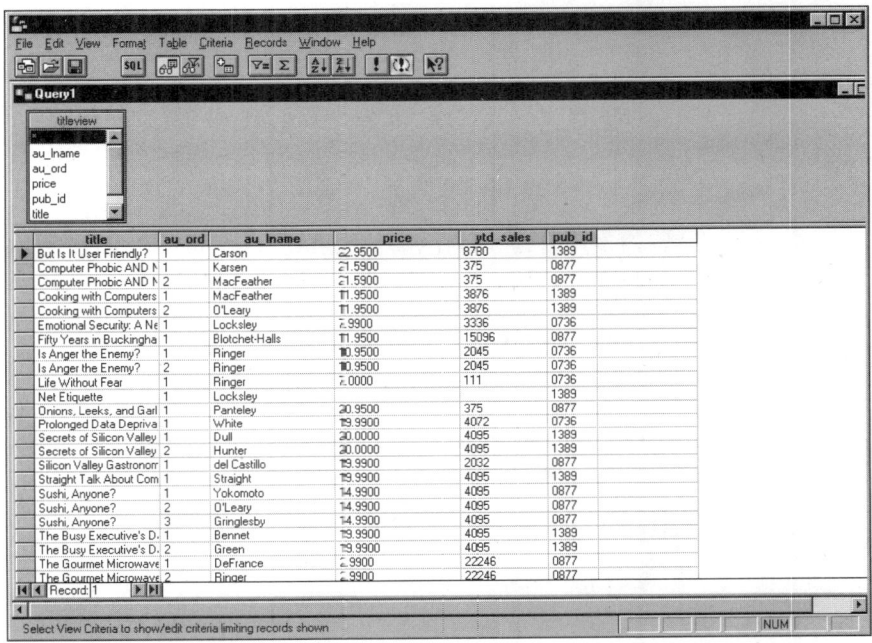

Figure 13-4: The titleview view has 25 records.

First and foremost, a view (from the systems administrator's view-point) is a series of SQL statements. The titleview view (shown below) has three statements. I've added comments to the listing explaining what each statement does:

```
/* First check to see if the view       */
/* exists, and delete it if it is there  */

if exists (select * from sysobjects where
id = object_id('dbo.titleview') and
sysstat & 0xf = 2) drop view dbo.titleview

GO /* the command GO executes the previous command */

/* Next create the view, named titleview */

CREATE VIEW titleview
AS
select title, au_ord, au_lname, price,
```

```
ytd_sales, pub_id
from authors, titles, titleauthor
where authors.au_id = titleauthor.au_id
AND titles.title_id = titleauthor.title_id

GO /* the command GO executes the previous command */

/* Finally, allow virtually all users (with guest */
/* privileges or better) to manipulate the view  */

GRANT  SELECT ,  INSERT ,  DELETE ,  UPDATE  ON dbo.titleview
TO guest

GO /* the command GO executes the previous command */
```

Tip

Why can't I see my view? A view is not listed in the Server Manager's listings of tables or any other objects. Rest assured: Users will be able to access the view. Saving a view executes the SQL statements that create the view.

Views may be edited (or simply deleted) at any time. Once a view is dropped, it becomes inaccessible to any users who may have had the view open. If you plan to drop a view that is used, it may be best to send a broadcast message to all users telling them so.

Stored Procedures

A stored procedure consists of a group of SQL statements. The SQL statements consist of complete procedures (that is, there are both SQL statements and program flow control statements).

Microsoft SQL Server 6.5 will save the stored procedures so that client users can later execute them. Upon the first execution, the stored procedure is compiled and executed, resulting in increased performance.

An example of a stored procedure is:

```
/* First check to see if the procedure exists  */
/* and drop it if it is already there (so that */
/* we can re-define the stored procedure       */
```

```
if exists (select * from sysobjects where
id = object_id('dbo.byroyalty') and
sysstat & 0xf = 4) drop procedure dbo.byroyalty

GO /* the command GO executes the previous command */

/* Next define the procedure 'byroyalty' to      */
/* return the column au_id,  for all authors  */
/* who's royalty rate is equal to the given     */
/* royalty rate                                 */
CREATE PROCEDURE byroyalty @percentage int
AS
select titleauthor.au_id, au_fname, au_lname
from titleauthor
LEFT JOIN  authors on titleauthor.au_id = authors.au_id
where titleauthor.royaltyper = @percentage

GO /* the command GO executes the previous command */

/* Allow all users to execute the byroyalty procedure */

GRANT  EXECUTE  ON dbo.byroyalty  TO public
GO /* the command GO executes the previous command */

/* Allow guests to execute the byroyalty procedure */

GRANT  EXECUTE  ON dbo.byroyalty  TO guest
GO /* the command GO executes the previous command */
```

When a user executes this stored procedure, the returned rows from the query are as shown in Figure 13-5. This example is not the same one supplied by Microsoft with Microsoft SQL Server 6.5. I've added several additional columns (including the authors' first and last names), using a join, so that Figure 13-5 would better represent the concept of stored procedures.

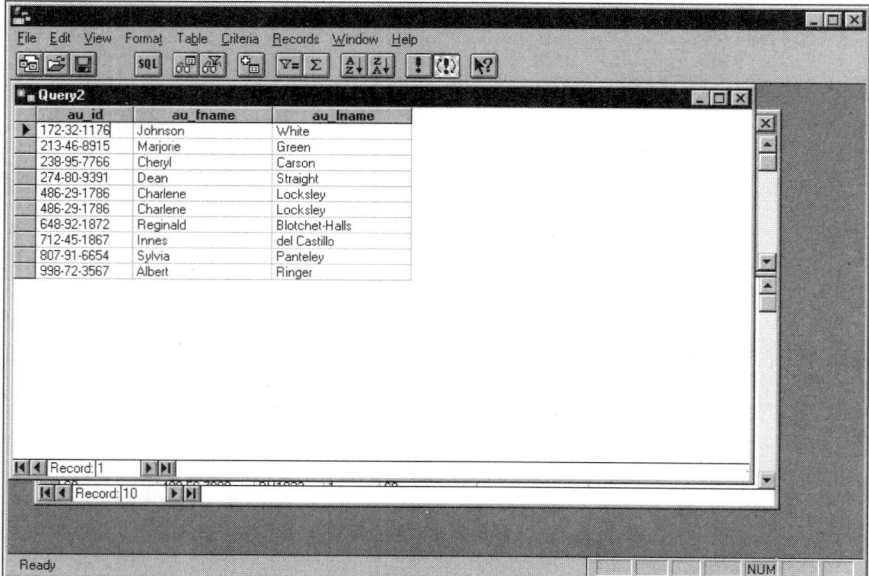

Figure 13-5: The byroyalty stored procedure returns these records.

The main advantage of stored procedures is an improvement in system performance. Executing stored procedures (which are saved in a "compiled" format) are faster than sending SQL commands from the client to the server.

Rules

A rule is an object that is bound to either a column or a user-defined datatype. The rule is used to validate data entered into a column when a client user either updates or inserts rows into the table.

There are two types of rule checks possible with rules:

■ Value within a range (which may be single ended, where the other end of the range is infinity). For example, @value > 10, which is single ended, limits the numeric parameter entered by the client to greater than 10. And, you can limit the number entered to a value between 10 and 30, @value > 10 AND @value < 30 (this example is not single ended). Figure 13-6 shows an example of this type of rule.

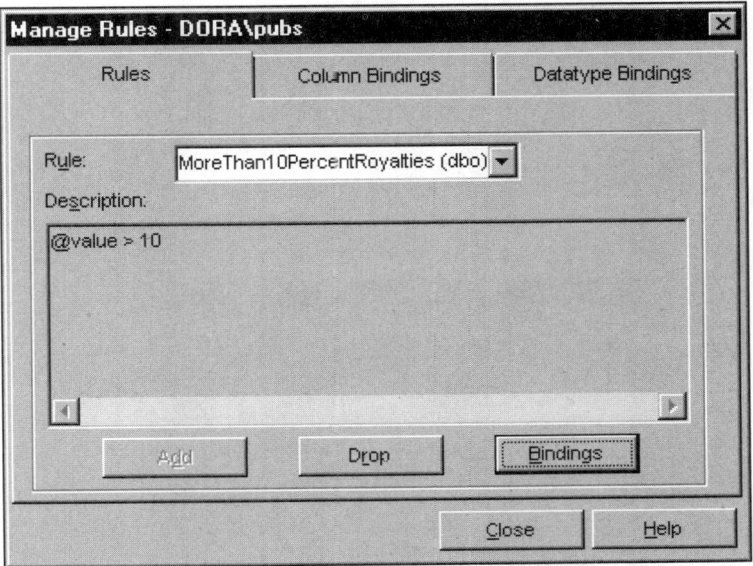

Figure 13-6: A rule limits the value to greater than 10.

■ Value from a list (which may be numeric or character). For example, if you limit the states entered for an author to only those states in the New England region, @value in("MA", "NH", "VT", "CT", "RI", "ME").

After a rule is created, it must be bound to one or more data columns. Figure 13-6 shows the Manage Rules dialog box, Manage Rules window, which is displayed after a rule has been added. Clicking on the Column Bindings tab will let you bind columns to the rule. Any column in any table may be bound to a rule (more than one column may be bound if appropriate). In the example in Figure 13-7, the column royaltyper is bound to the rule Between10and30, a rule that limits royalties to be greater than 10 percent and less than 30 percent.

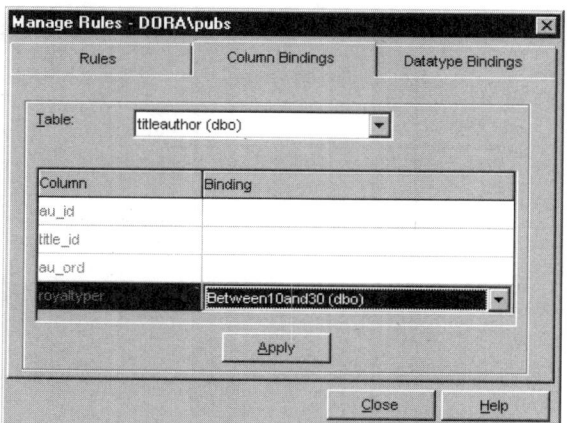

Figure 13-7: Binding a rule to the royaltyper column.

When a rule is violated, the client application will receive an error notification. Each application will display a different error message. Figure 13-8 shows the error that occurred when an attempt was made to add a record that had a royalty of 8 percent.

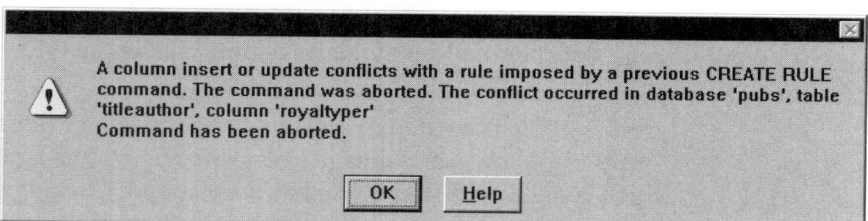

Figure 13-8: Errors happen when rules are not followed.

Defaults

Defaults are used when a value is not specified for a column in which a data value is required. Specifying a default allows Microsoft SQL Server 6.5 to fill in a value for the user.

Figure 13-9 shows the Manage Defaults dialog, which is very similar to the Rules dialog box.

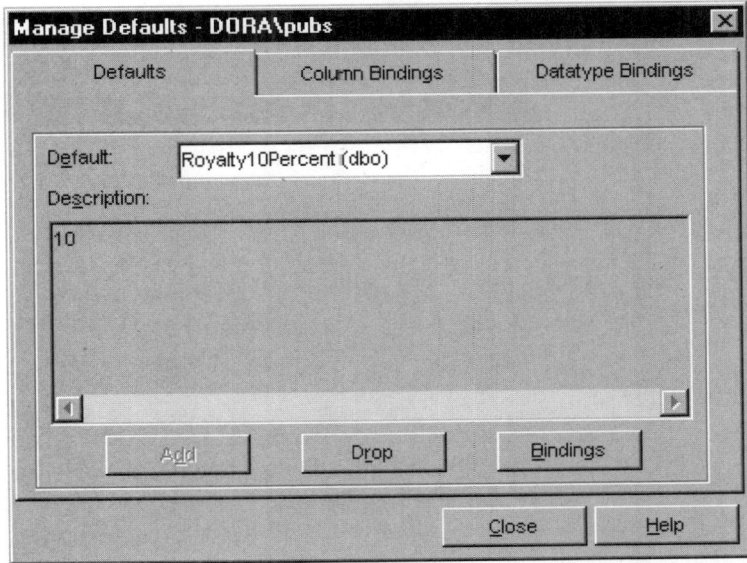

Figure 13-9: Set a default for a column that must have a default value when the user does not specify a value.

User-defined Datatypes

User-defined datatypes are one of the more powerful features of Microsoft SQL Server 6.5. A datatype may be defined so that it has certain specific attributes (including rules and default values).

For example, the pubs database has three user-defined data types:

- empid is a character string datatype that is 9 characters long.

- id is a variable length string with a maximum length of 11 characters.

- tid is a variable length string with a maximum length of 6 characters.

Figure 13-10 shows the Manage User-Defined Datatypes dialog box listing these three datatypes. Though in the example none of the user-defined datatypes have default values (or rules), setting a default value or rule would be as easy as selecting it in the list.

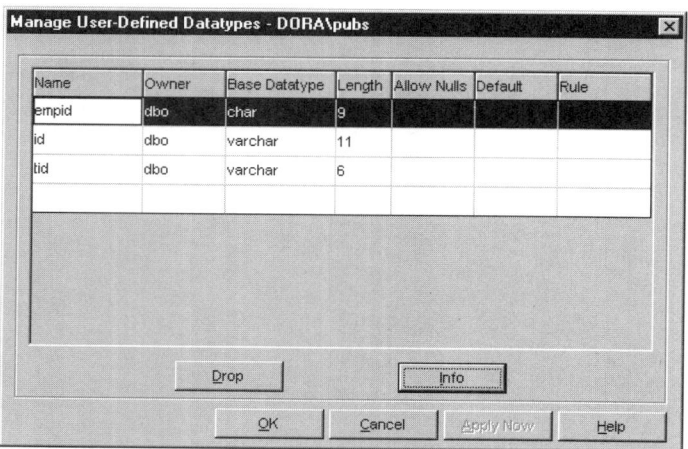

Figure 13-10: Three user-defined datatypes in the pubs database.

Creating Databases

Creating databases is a fundamental part of database management. Databases are usually created by programmers when a database system is designed. Users seldom create databases, though it may be possible that a user would create a database from time to time.

This section reviews creating a database using Microsoft SQL Enterprise Manager. The process is rather straightforward:

1. Select Databases in the tree view in the Microsoft SQL Server Enterprise Manager's Server Manager window (see Figure 13-11). Right-click to display the context menu.

2. Choose New Database in the context menu to display the New Database dialog box (see Figure 13-12).

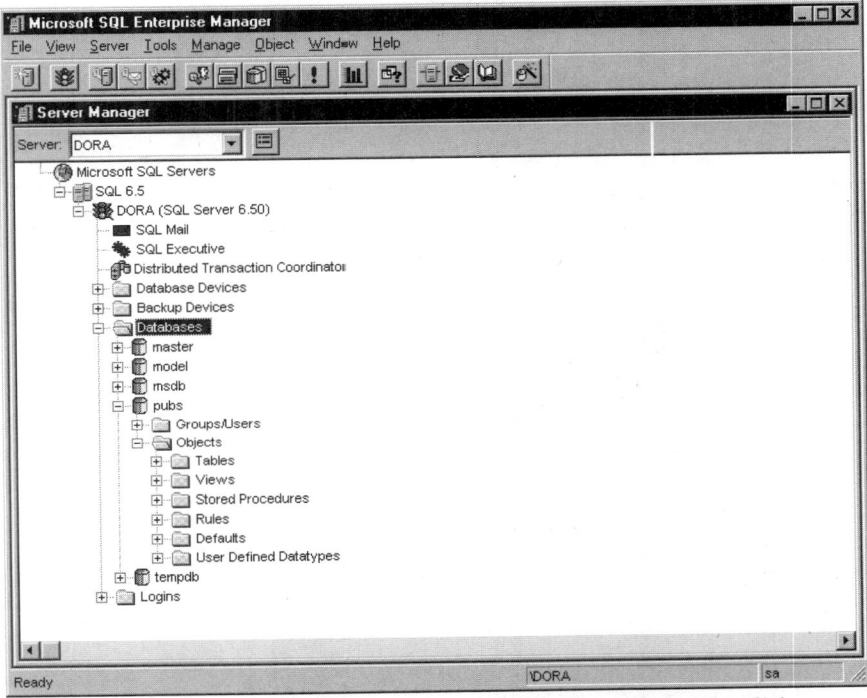

Figure 13-11: Server Manager window—select Databases and right-click.

3. In the New Database dialog box, enter the name of the database to be created (Figure 13-12 has the name Example entered already).

4. For a user database, select Master in the Data Device drop-down list. A log device may also be configured, if desired. The log device is used to maintain the transaction log.

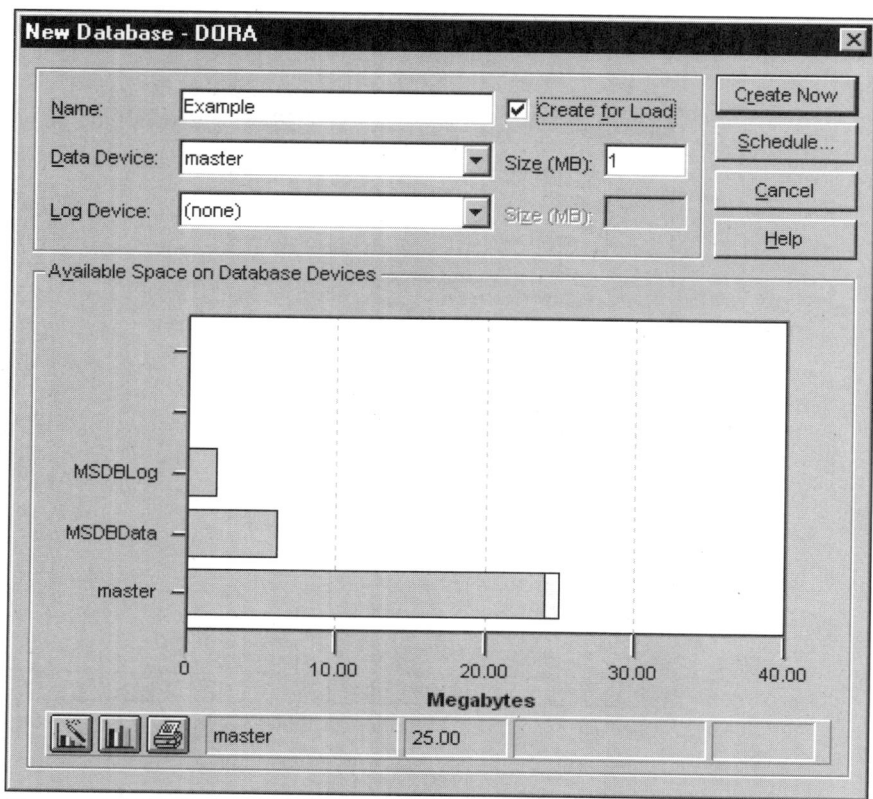

Figure 13-12: Create a new database using the New Database dialog box.

5. Once the new database has been configured, click the Create Now button to create the database. It may take some time for Microsoft SQL Server 6.5 to actually create the database; while it is being created, the new database may not be used.

Like creating databases, both new devices (which "hold" or store a database) and transaction logs (used to save, or track, changes to a database) may also be created as needed.

New devices can be created either by choosing the Microsoft SQL Enterprise Manager's Manage | Database Devices menu selection (which displays the Manage Database Device window) or from the Server Manager window's list of database devices (use the right [context] mouse button to display a context menu).

Tip

In the Manage Database Devices window, there is a Bar Graph Options button (the middle button on the bottom of the window), which lets you set options. The Graph Mode settings include Selectable and Stretched. The default setting, Stretched, does not allow selecting a database device for edit or deletion. To select a device, first change the Bar Graph Options' Graph Mode to Selectable. Why was this done this way? Got me!

Creating Tables

Tables are where the database's actual data are stored. Each table will consist of one or more columns, where a column defines a specific data object's attributes, and zero or more rows of data objects. Of course, a table with zero rows of data usually won't be of much use.

Tables may be created in either of two ways:

- First, use an SQL statement.
- Second, use the graphical table creation facilities that are part of Microsoft SQL Enterprise Manager.

Generally, users will use SQL statements to create tables, while administrators (and sometimes programmers) will use Microsoft SQL Enterprise Manager.

Creating Tables With SQL Statements

Creating a table using an SQL statement is a method that will typically require little or no user interaction. Once an SQL programmer writes the SQL statement(s), the user will execute the statements without much thought as to what is happening. Typically, SQL scripts are written with a text editor or directly; those that are written directly are written using either the Microsoft SQL Server Enterprise Manager or perhaps MS Query. Regardless of how an SQL script is written, they all function the same. With Microsoft SQL Server 6.5, scripts are never "compiled" as a separate step; rather, when they are executed, the script may be processed by Microsoft SQL Server 6.5 to convert the script into a format that is more usable and faster.

For example, the following SQL script will create a new table:

```
if exists (select * from sysobjects where id =
        object_id('inetlog') and sysstat & 0xf = 3)
        drop table inetlog
GO

create table inetlog
(
  ClientHost varchar(255),
  username varchar(255),
  LogTime datetime,
  service varchar( 255),
  machine varchar( 255),
  serverip varchar( 50),
  processingtime int,
  bytesrecvd int,
  bytessent int,
  servicestatus int,
  win32status int,
  operation varchar( 255),
  target varchar(255),
  parameters varchar(255)
)

GO
```

The script shown above is used to create a log file for the Microsoft Internet Server's log files. Unlike the example that Microsoft provides, the above SQL script checks to ensure that there is not already an existing table with the same name.

Creating Tables With Microsoft SQL Enterprise Manager

In addition to creating a table using a script, it is also possible to create a table using the Microsoft SQL Server Enterprise manager. Usually management decides how a table is created; for organizations that have a large number of programmers, using scripts may be more efficient because it may be unwise to have each programmer using Microsoft SQL Server Enterprise Manager! The risk of a programmer causing unintended "damage" may be too great.

To create a new table with the Microsoft SQL Enterprise Manager:

1. Click on the database in the Server Manager window to select it.

2. Expand the tree for the database to expose the Objects folder. Right-click the Objects folder to display the context menu.

3. Choose New Table from the context menu to display the Manage Tables dialog box, as shown in Figure 13-13.

4. In the Manage Tables dialog box, enter each column in the database (column name, datatype, size, whether nulls are allowed, and the default value, if any). When all the columns have been defined, click the Save button (located to the right of the Table name list box) in the Manage Tables toolbar.

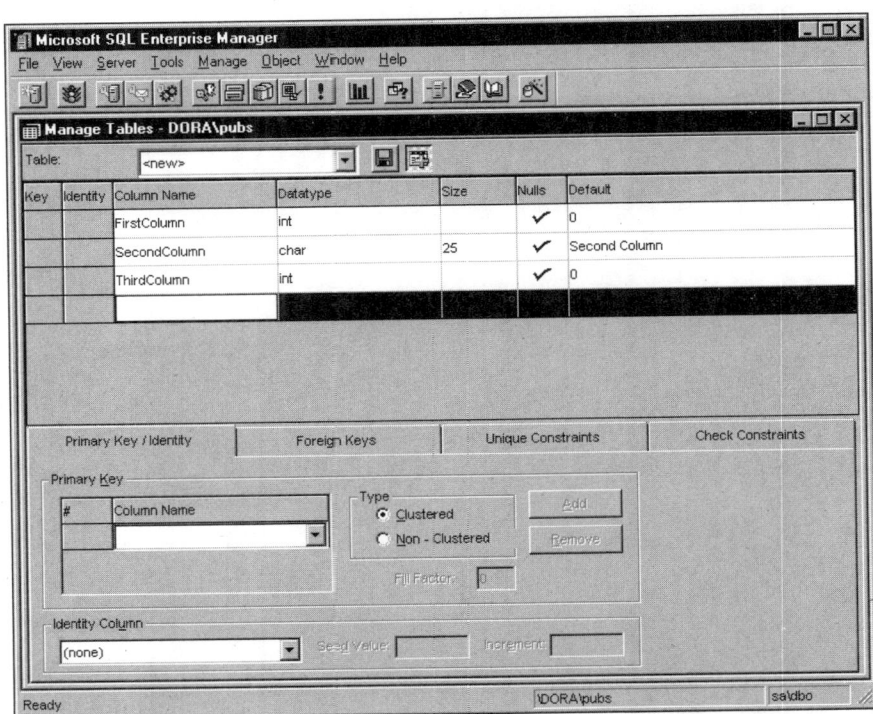

Figure 13-13: First define the columns in the table, then click the Save button to name the table.

Note: If entering a text (character) default value, enter the value using quotes!

Once the table has been created, there is still the option to create new columns or modify any existing columns.

If any columns should be indexed, select the Advanced Features button (which is next to the Save button). In the Advanced Features section of the Manage Tables dialog box, identify the Primary Key/Identity. Foreign Keys, Unique Constants, and Check Constraints also are set in the Advanced Features section.

There are a few tasks that must be performed with indexes. For example, indexes must be rebuilt when a table is modified substantially (when a large number of records are added, deleted, or modified).

Microsoft SQL Server 6.5's Manage Indexes dialog box (Figure 13-14) has a Rebuild button that is used to force SQL Server to rebuild the index. To display the Rebuild Indexes dialog box, start the Microsoft SQL Enterprise Manager program (Start Menu | Programs | SQL Server 6.5 | Microsoft SQL Enterprise Manager). Then, in the Server Manager window, choose a database. Finally, choose Manage | Indexes from the menu.

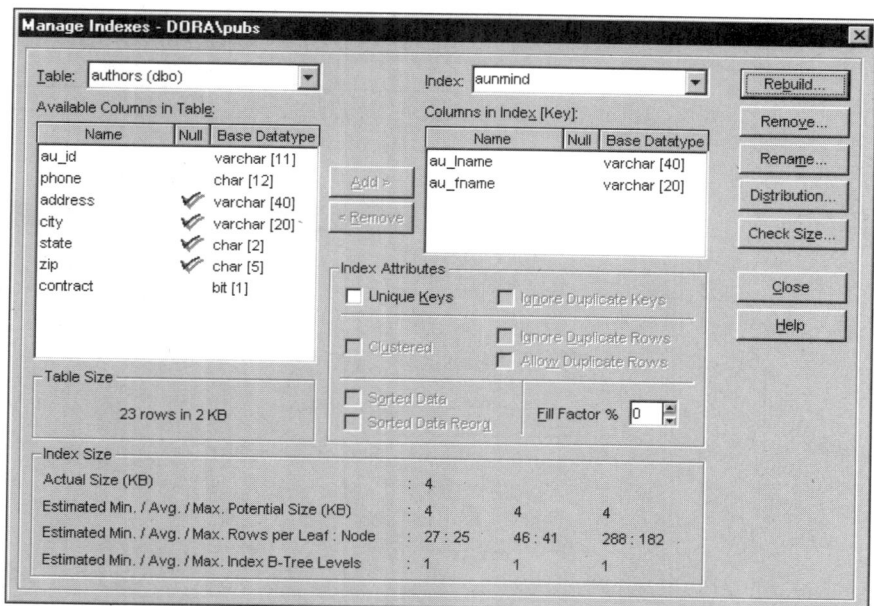

Figure 13-14: The Manage Indexes dialog box displays indexes for each table in the currently selected database.

Microsoft SQL Server 6.5 allows creating indexes that are based on more than one column. For example, the index (called aunmind) that is shown in Figure 13-14 has two columns: au_lname and au_fname. This technique is useful when both columns contain many similar values. Names are a classic example: There is a small number of commonly used first names and a somewhat larger number of commonly used last names, but when used together they usually form a unique combination.

Other features that the Rebuild Indexes dialog box allows include:

- **Adding a new index.** A new index may be added to a table by selecting the column to be indexed in the Available Columns in Table list and clicking the Add button.

- **Removing an index.** An index may be removed by selecting the index in the Columns in Index list and clicking the Remove button.

- **Distribution of values in an index.** The distribution of values in an index may be checked by clicking the Distribution button. The Index Distribution Statistics dialog box (see Figure 13-15) lists the steps in the first column of the index.

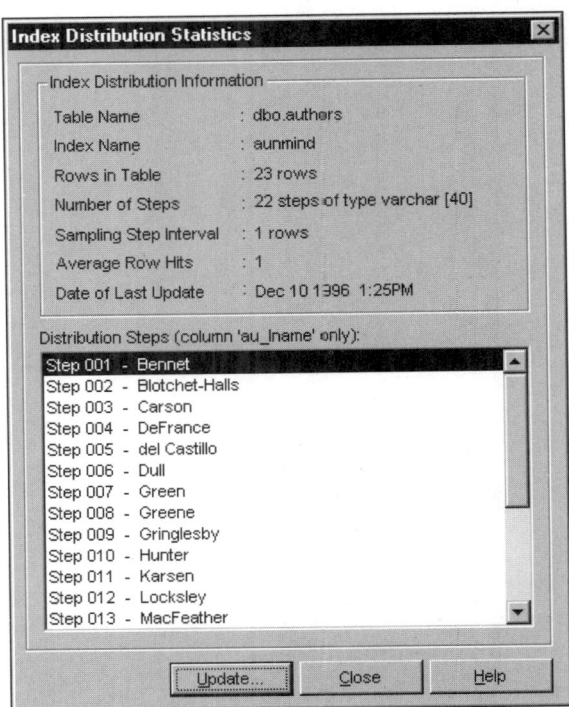

Figure 13-15: The Index Distribution Statistics dialog box shows how the names are distributed in the au_lname column in the index.

- **Check Size is used to recompute the size of the index.** Figure 13-14 shows, at the bottom, the index size statistics for the index in our example.

- **Rename allows the index to be renamed.** Things change, and sometimes we tire of the same names all the time. An index may have any name desired.

Moving On

This chapter covered the parts of a database and creating and managing databases and tables with Microsoft SQL Server 6.5. We started out by establishing what a database and a table consist of. Then we covered how databases, devices, tables, and so on are created. Finally, the chapter showed how to create databases and tables.

The next chapter covers maintenance and replication of Microsoft SQL Server 6.5 databases. The old rule applies: Back it up or lose it!

14

Backing Up SQL Server Databases

Microsoft SQL Server 6.5 offers a number of different techniques to allow backing up or otherwise saving the database files that it uses. These techniques include standard backup practices, replication, and other techniques.

This chapter will introduce backup techniques (which are basic and easy to do). Using replication (which is more complex, but then, replication offers capabilities that normal backup techniques don't—including faster recovery from problems and errors) is easy, in that the replication facilities are built into Microsoft SQL Server 6.5. Replication is a bit beyond the scope of this book, however.

Default Devices & Databases

Microsoft SQL Server 6.5 uses a series of database files, typically located in the folder mssql\data (the default locations are specified when Microsoft SQL Server 6.5 is installed), to store both the database tables and other related information. These database files must be backed up, so that they can be restored in the event there is an error condition.

Each of these database files is called a database device. As installed, Microsoft SQL Server 6.5 installs three database devices: master, MSDBData, and MSDBLog.

The master devices are created during installation of Microsoft SQL Server 6.5. The master database contains systemwide configuration information. The master, model, pubs, and tempdb databases are saved in the master device because they are usually small and are not used by users much. The msdb database is saved in the MSDBData and MSDBLog devices. Whenever changes are made to the master, model, pubs, or tempdb databases, the master device should be backed up.

Initially, there is a tendency to create new databases in the master device. Though there is nothing inherently wrong with this technique, more experienced Microsoft SQL Server 6.5 programmers and administrators will create a new device for each major database that will be running on Microsoft SQL Server 6.5. This allows restoration of a single database without having any impact on any other databases that are being used.

Tip

Kimberly L. Tripp (a training and consulting specialist) of SYSolutions, Inc., recommends that if the tempdb database must be altered, then it is best to alter it on another separate physical device to improve performance. An excellent discussion of the process of creating a fault-tolerant Microsoft SQL Server 6.5 configuration titled "Designing a Fault-Tolerant MS SQL Server" and written by Kimberly can be found on the Microsoft TechNet CD (available as a subscription from Microsoft).

The msdb database, also created when Microsoft SQL Server 6.5 is installed, is created in its own database device. Microsoft SQL Server 6.5 uses the msdb database to save historical information about scheduled events, tasks, operators, and alerts. As the number of events and such can grow rather large, using two database devices allows easier expansion of this database because the expansion of the msdb database components won't affect other objects.

Note: Any database may have transaction logging configured. Though optional, using a transaction log enhances the recoverability in the event that there is a problem with the database file and it must be restored from a backup. Always keep the transaction log on a separate physical device if possible—this will enhance recoverability.

Making a Backup of a Database

A backup is a copy of an object. The backup may be used later to recover the object if the original copy should become damaged for some reason. Backups may be saved to a number of different media, such as disk drives, optical devices, hard disks, or other devices, and although the actual backup is not usable directly by Microsoft SQL Server 6.5, a restored copy of the backup will be usable.

Tip

Don't Laugh: Floppy disks continue to be a valuable backup medium, as today's newer "floppy" technologies allow storage of large amounts of data on removable media. Newer technologies allow storing of from 20 to 1000MB of data on a single device. Even a 1.44MB floppy can be used to store useful amounts of information, including the schema of virtually any database!

To backup a database in Microsoft SQL Enterprise Manager's Server Manager window:

1. Select the database to be backed up. In Figure 14-1, the pubs database has been selected for backup.

2. Next, right-click pubs and select Backup/Restore from the context menu.

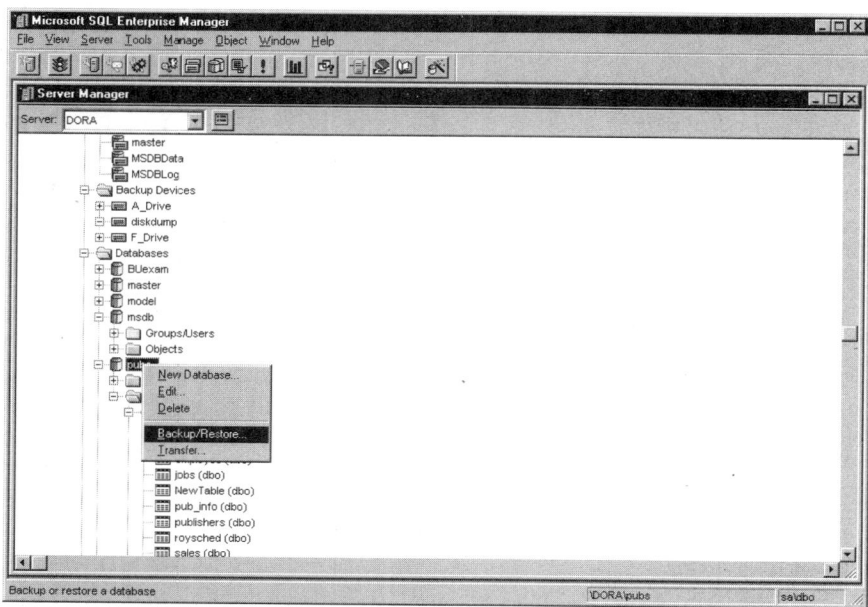

Figure 14-1: Select Backup/Restore from the context menu to display the Database Backup/Restore dialog box.

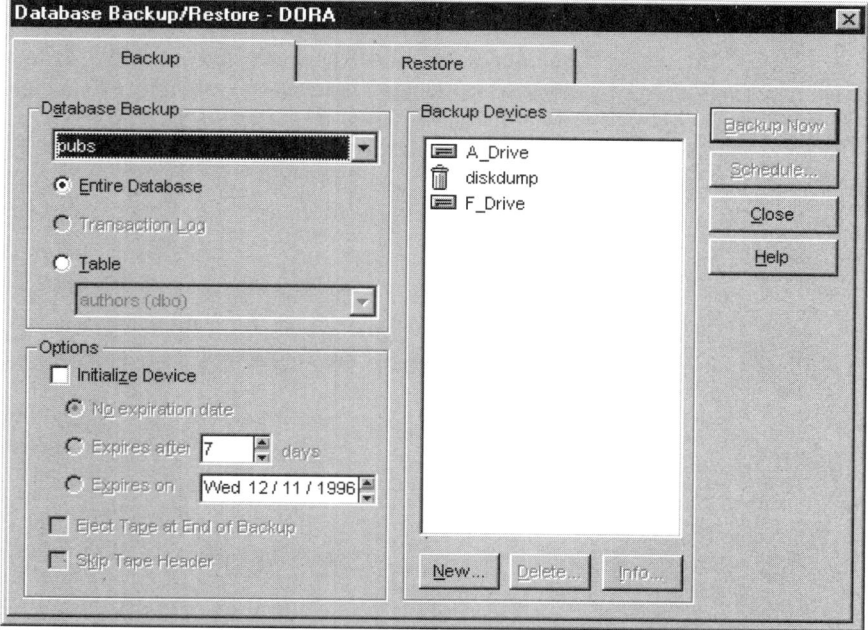

Figure 14-2: Configure the backup using the Database Backup/Restore dialog box.

3. Once the Database Eackup/Restore dialog box (Figure 14-2) is displayed, select the Backup tab.

4. In the Backup tab, there are a number of options that must be configured. The first choice is whether to back up the entire database, transaction log, or tables. These options are in the Database Backup section:

■ **Entire Database**—all data, tables, rules, defaults. . . everything. . . will be backed up.

■ **Transaction Log**—back up the transaction log (if active—this option will be disabled if transaction logging is not enabled on the selected database).

■ **Table**—backs up a specific table (some databases have many static tables that, because they do not change, need not be frequently backed up). When selecting Table, it is also necessary to specify which table will be the target of the backup operation.

5. In the Backup Devices section of the Backup tab, specify where the backup is to be written. The only device, available by default, is a device called diskdump. It is possible to create new backup devices by clicking the New button, which will display the New Backup Device dialog box (Figure 14-3). Name the new backup device, select the device's attributes, and click Create.

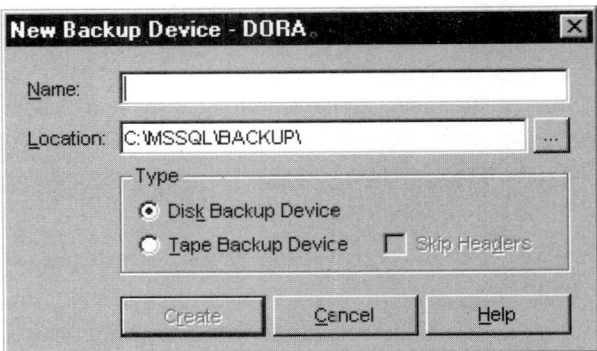

Figure 14-3: The New Backup Device dialog—specify either a disk or tape device.

6. In the Options section of the Backup tab, set whatever options are needed for this backup: selecting Initialize Device will configure the backup device (this process is different from initializing a drive; the current contents of the device are not deleted, though the dump device itself is rewritten if initialized).

Note: A new backup device must be initialized before it can be used. Failure to initialize the backup device will result in an error: "The volume label of backup device '<device name>' could not be obtained." If this error is received, select the Initialize Device button.

7. Click the Backup Now button in the Backup tab to perform the backup immediately, or click the Schedule button to schedule the backup to be performed at a later time.

Restoring a Backup of a Database

Restoring a database, a transaction log, or even a table is possible using the Microsoft SQL Enterprise Manager. Reloading the most recent backup and the transaction log restores a database. This allows recovering virtually all of the database's data.

Restoration may be done either on a table-by-table, or database-by-database basis.

Restoring Databases, Transaction Logs, or Tables

When restoring, it may be advantageous to restore either the entire database, the transaction logs, or individual tables. It is possible to restore the information that has been backed up in several passes to obtain the latest (or fullest) set of data.

To restore a database, transaction log, or table in Microsoft SQL Enterprise Manager's Server Manager window:

1. Select the database to be restored to. In Figure 14-1, the pubs database has been selected for backup.

2. Next, right-click, and select Backup/Restore from the context menu.

3. Once the Database Backup/Restore dialog box is displayed, select the Restore tab (Figure 14-4). In the Restore tab, there are a number of options that must be configured.

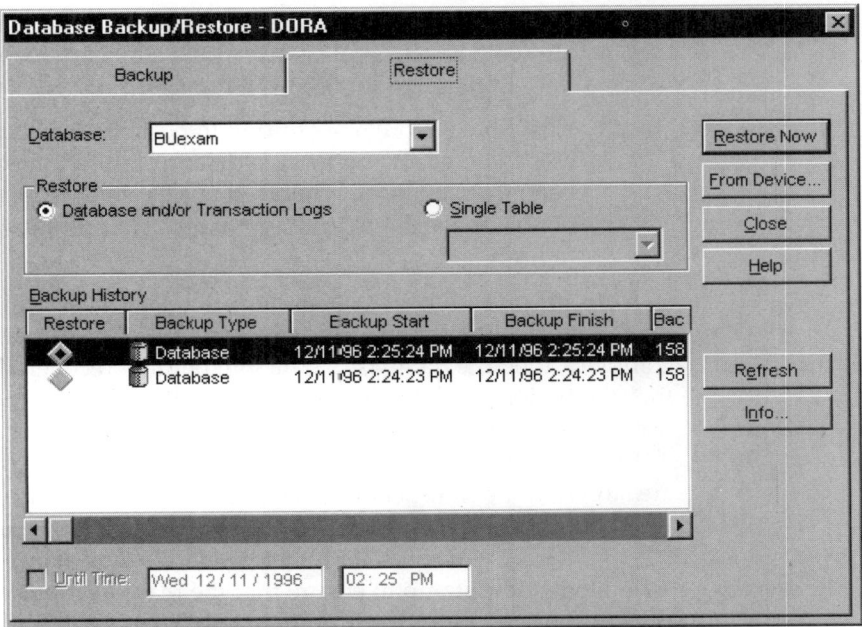

Figure 14-4: Configure the restore using the Restore tab in the Database Backup/ Restore dialog box.

4. Choose which database to restore from the Database drop-down list. The default will be the database that was selected when the Database Backup/Restore dialog box was displayed.

5. Choose whether to restore the database and/or transaction logs or specific tables. These options are in the Restore section of the Restore tab:

■ **Database and/or Transaction Logs**—recovers all data, tables, rules, defaults . . . everything . . . when restoring a database.

■ **Single Table**—restores a specific table. When selecting Single Table, it is also necessary to specify which table will be restored in the restore operation.

6. From the Backup History list, select which backup to restore. It may be possible that the most recent backup is not an acceptable candidate for restoration (maybe the database was corrupted before the most recent backup was done), and an earlier backup must be restored.

The transaction logs can be a "lifesaver" in this situation, allowing an earlier backup of the database to be restored and then updated to (hopefully) its current status.

7. Click the Restore Now button to perform the restore immediately. There is no method to defer a restoration (nor is there a need to; backups are deferred until a time when the database is not being used—a database that is being restored will never be in use!).

Note: When a database is restored, all data that was in the database will be replaced with data from the backup. If the transaction log is complete, then the database's data will be fully recovered. However, if the transaction log does not reflect all modifications to the data made by users, it is possible that data may have been lost.

When a transaction log is restored, all changes to the database, which are stored in the transaction log, will be reapplied to the database. A transaction log is restored chronologically, oldest to newest. Microsoft SQL Server 6.5 will check both the database's time stamp and the transaction log's time stamp to ensure that the reapplication of the transactions is consistent and correct. There may be more than one transaction log; a very large database will be only infrequently backed up. Rather, a daily backup will be made of the transaction log, and then the actual database may only be backed up on a weekly basis.

Why back up the transaction logs on a daily basis? This is done to limit the exposure to risk of data loss in the event that the device(s), which are being used to store the database and the transaction log, fail.

Note: For more information about maintaining data integrity, fault tolerance, RAID, and mirroring (of disk drives), refer to Chapter 3.

Restoring Databases After a Failure

When a database (or a database device) is "damaged" due to a hardware failure (the drive died!), it is important to run what is called the *DBCC* SQL statement (DBBC stands for Database Consistency Checker). The DBCC will check to ensure that the database contents are correct and as accurate as possible (no, DBCC won't perform miracles—damaged or lost data will remain lost).

Alternate uses for DBCC include checking memory usage, decreasing the size of a database, and checking performance statistics.

No matter how often database dumps (backups) are performed, Microsoft recommends that DBCC CHECKDB, DBCC CHECKALLOC, and DBCC CHECKCATALOG be run on databases before backing up or after restoring.

Whenever restoring a database from a backup, the database must not be in use. When a database must be restored because of a hardware failure, follow these steps:

1. Use a DBCC to ensure that the system is stable, and as "correct" as possible.

2. Use a drop command to drop the damaged database or database table(s) that are to be restored. Dropping a table will remove the table (with all the data it contains) and all indexes and permissions. Once dropped, the table cannot be recovered without restoring it from a backup. When dropping a table, you must own the table or database to drop it. Tables that client users have open may not be dropped. To drop an entire database, select the database in the Server Manager window, and right-click. From the context menu, select Delete. Drop is a fancy name for deleting!

3. From the Microsoft SQL Enterprise Manager, re-create the database.

4. Restore the database or table from the backup (as described above in "Restoring Databases, Transaction Logs, or Tables").

Details About the DBCC

DBCC is not well documented. Not well at all. The only information available about DBCC is contained in the Transact SQL help, and even that information is not complete. As Kimberly Tripp (a trainer and consultant with SYSolutions) puts it: Other DBCC flags "are, it seems, transmitted in secret ceremonies at midnight in microcomputer graveyards." In addition, DBCC is not part of any standard, and there is little guarantee that a specific DBCC trace flag will work with future versions of Microsoft SQL Server 6.5!

Table 14-1 lists all DBCC options that the author is aware of. Options in uppercase are documented by Microsoft as supported by Microsoft SQL Server 6.5. Options in lowercase are DBCC options that may or may not be supported by Microsoft SQL Server 6.5, but are documented as being part of "standard SQL" by some sources.

```
allocdump( dbid, page )
bhash( { print_bufs I no_print }, bucket_limit )
buffer( [ dbid ][, objid ][, nbufs ], printopt = { 0 I 1 I 2 }, buftype )
bytes( startaddress, length )
CHECKALLOC [(database_name [, NOINDEX])] I
checkalloc[ ( dbname [, fix I nofix ] ) ]
CHECKCATALOG [(database_name)] I
CHECKDB [(database_name [, NOINDEX])] I
checkdb[( dbname [, skip_ncindex ] ) ]
CHECKTABLE (table_name [, NOINDEX I index_id]) I
checktable( tablename I tabid [, skip_ncindex ] )
dbinfo( [ dbname ] )
DBREPAIR (database_name, DROPDB) I
dbrepair( dbid, option = { dropdb I fixindex I fixsysindex }, table, indexid )
dbtable( dbid )
delete_row( dbid, pageid, delete_by_row = { 1 I 0 }, rownum )
des( [ dbid ][, objid ] )
dllname (FREE) I
extentcheck( dbid, objid, indexid, sort = {1I0} )
extentdump( dbid, page )
extentzap( dbid, objid, indexid, sort )
findnotfullextents( dbid, objid, indexid, sort = { 1 I 0 } )
fix_al( [ dbname ] )
help( dbcc_command )
ind( dbid, objid, printopt = { 0 I 1 I 2 } )
indexalloc(tablenameItabid, indid, [full I optimized I fast],[fix I nofix])
```

```
INPUTBUFFER (spid) |

locateindexpgs( dbid, objid, page, indexid, level )

lock

log( [dbid][,objid][,page][,row][,nrecords][,type={-1.36}],printopt={0|1} )

memusage

MEMUSAGE |

netmemshow( option = {1 | 2 | 3} )

netmemusage

NEWALLOC [(database_name [, NOINDEX])] |

newalloc( dbname, option = { 1 | 2 | 3 } )

OPENTRAN ({database_name} | {database_id}) [WITH TABLERESULTS] |

OUTPUTBUFFER (spid) |

page( dbid, pagenum [, printopt={0|1|2} ][, cache={0|1} ][, logical={1|0} ] )

PERFMON |

pglinkage( dbid, start, number, printopt={0|1|2}, target, order={1|0} )

PINTABLE (database_id, table_id) |

pktmemshow( option = {spid} )

procbuf( dbid, objid, nbufs, printopt = { 0 | 1 } )

prtipage( dbid, objid, indexid, indexpage )

pss( suid, spid, printopt = { 1 | 0 } )

rebuildextents( dbid, objid, indexid )

resource

show_bucket( dbid, pageid, lookup_type )

SHOW_STATISTICS (table_name, index_name) |

SHOWCONTIG (table_id, [index_id]) |

SHRINKDB (database_name [, new_size [, 'MASTEROVERRIDE']]) |

SQLPERF ({IOSTATS | LRUSTATS | NETSTATS | RASTATS [, CLEAR]}
              |{THREADS} | {LOGSPACE}) |

tab( dbid, objid, printopt = { 0 | 1 | 2 } )

tablealloc(tablename|tabid, [full | optimized | fast],[fix | nofix])
```

TEXTALL [({database_name I database_id}[, FULL I FAST])] I

TEXTALLOC [({table_name I table_id}[, FULL I FAST])] I

TRACEOFF (trace#) I

traceoff(tracenum [, tracenum ...])

TRACEON (trace#) I

traceon(tracenum [, tracenum ...])

TRACESTATUS (trace# [, trace#...]) I

undo(dbid, pageno, rowno)

UNPINTABLE (database_id, table_id) I

UPDATEUSAGE ({0 I database_name} [, table_name [, index_id]]) I

USEROPTIONS

[WITH NO_INFOMSGS]

Table 14-1: DBCC options both from Microsoft and from other sources.

Moving On

This chapter covered the basics of backing up and restoring databases, transaction logs, and tables. Using proper backup techniques (combined with the fault-tolerance techniques described earlier in this book) will help to ensure that data contained in a Microsoft SQL Server 6.5 database will not be lost.

This chapter concludes our coverage of Microsoft SQL Server 6.5. The next section covers Microsoft SMS (Systems Management Server). Chapters in the next section include an overview of Microsoft SMS, inventory management, software distribution and installation, and remote control and in-house customer service.

Microsoft Systems
Management Server (SMS)

15

Overview of Microsoft SMS

$\mathbf{M}$icrosoft Systems Management Server (SMS) version 1.2 is an important part of Microsoft BackOffice in environments where there are systems that must be managed from a central location.

SMS is able to monitor both hardware and software, distribute software (and upgrades), and audit the usage of software.

Note: Microsoft Systems Management Server is a fairly large system. Microsoft SQL Server must be installed (and running) to install or use SMS. See Section II for information about installing and using Microsoft SQL Server.

SMS supports a number of different clients, including:

- Windows NT Server and Windows NT Workstation.

- Microsoft LAN Manager 2.1 (and later) with OS/2, DOS, and/or Windows 3.x clients.

- Microsoft Network Client for MS-DOS 3.0.

- NetWare 3.1x with MS-DOS and/or Windows 3.x clients.

- NetWare 4.x with MS-DOS clients.

- Apple Macintosh System 7.x clients.

- IBM LAN Server 3.0/3.1 running OS/2 clients.

Note: Microsoft Systems Management Server and its documentation were produced prior to the release of Windows 95. Although Windows 95 clients are not specifically listed, Windows 95 is supported. One of the few times that Windows 95 is mentioned is in the discussion about managing the distribution of the update to Windows 95 using SMS.

What's New in SMS Version 1.2?

SMS 1.2 offers a number of new functionalities over SMS 1.1. These improvements include:

- Windows NT Remote Control, which:

  - Allows the systems administrator to take over the screen and keyboard of any Windows 95, or Windows NT 3.51 (or later) system.

  - Allows the systems administrator to pass through Alt+Tab, request the Task List, or even pass through Ctrl+Alt+Del by using the special viewer buttons. This means that he or she can log on as a new user remotely.

  - Fully conforms to the Windows NT Security model.

  - Supports Winsock.

- SNMP trap forwarding and receiving, which:

  - Allows all Windows NT events to be forwarded as SNMP traps to other management consoles, including Hewlett-Packard's OpenView or IBM's NetView for AIX.

  - Lets the systems administrator filter forwarded SNMP traps to allow forwarding of only specific traps.

  - Receives traps from other SMS servers, Hewlett-Packard's OpenView, or devices such as routers or hubs.

  - Allows incoming traps to be filtered by source or trap type or even by the number of times a trap is received or the time delay between traps.

- Using SMS for inventory as a service for Windows NT clients, which:

  - Allows the systems administrator to run Inventory as a service on Windows NT clients, which in turn allows Inventory to function regardless of the client's logon status.

- Allows all Windows NT clients that do not have actively logged on users to be inventoried.
- Is more efficient because Inventory runs in the background rather than as part of the login process. This also improves the logon performance.

■ A faster, multithreaded Dataloader, which:

- Is used to move MIF (Management Information Format) files, improving system performance.
- Loads MIF files from local computers to the central SQL Server database.
- Because it is faster, will be especially useful for larger SMS installations where it must manage substantial amounts of data.

Other miscellaneous new and nifty features supported in version 1.2 of SMS include:

■ Over 5,000 applications in the AUDIT inventory database. The systems administrator may add new packages as needed.

■ An improved ISV (Independent Software Vendor) application launching facility.

■ Support for local settings and localized servers.

Installing SMS

Microsoft Systems Management Server is a very large product and requires substantial system resources. Microsoft suggests that an Intel 486 might run SMS, though performance will be degraded.

Even a midrange Pentium (100 MHz) processor and 32MB of RAM can become bogged down running SMS, especially if Microsoft SQL Server must also run on the same CPU. However, if you run Microsoft SQL Server on a different computer than SMS, you may find that a lower-powered system is adequate.

Warning

Only the very brave, or foolish, attempt to run Microsoft Exchange Server, Microsoft SNA Server, and Microsoft SQL Server at the same time on the same Pentium uniprocessor server. To do so, you need to have a very fast Pentium (at least a 200 MHz) and a minimum of 128MB of RAM.

Preparing to Install SMS

To install SMS, you must first install Microsoft SQL Server. Additionally, you must do the following prior to installing SMS:

1. Create an account (using the Windows NT 4 Server's User Manager for Domains program) for the SMS Administrator program to use. Typically the systems administrator does not use the account directly. Often this account will be named smsadmin and will need to have both Administrative and Log On as a Service privileges.

2. Create an account on your Microsoft SQL Server for the SMS Administrator program to use. This account must have Create Database, Dump Database, and Dump Transaction permissions for the master database. The default administration login for Microsoft SQL Server, the sa (systems administrator) account, also has these privileges.

3. Ensure that you have sufficient disk space for the SMS product. Microsoft suggests that the installation may require between 500MB and 1000MB of disk space. You should also make sure that the Microsoft SQL Server database is large enough to hold the anticipated information that will be stored in it. (SMS setup allocates about 53MB for the SMS SQL database.)

Note: The version of Microsoft Systems Management Server shown in this example is from Microsoft BackOffice. The stand-alone version of SMS can have slight disk and memory differences.

Starting the Installation

Once you have prepared your system (installed Microsoft SQL Server and set up the necessary userids), you may begin the installation of SMS. To install, you should either start the Microsoft BackOffice setup program (if you are using the Microsoft BackOffice version) or the SMS setup program (if you are using the stand-alone version).

After following the typical prompts for userid, organization, and product serial number, you will see the first significant dialog the SMS setup program presents, the Primary Site Configuration Information dialog box, shown in Figure 15-1. The following are the steps you will take to complete this part of the installation:

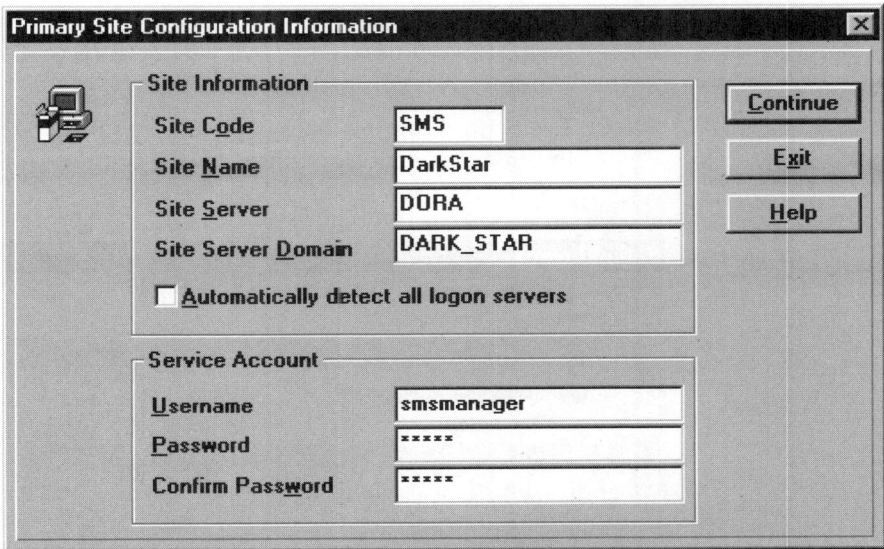

Figure 15-1: The Primary Site Configuration Information dialog.

1. Create a three-character site code in the Site Code text box. The site code uniquely identifies this SMS site, and therefore you must take steps to ensure that the site code itself is unique.

2. Fill in the Site Name text box. The site name is the "people readable" name that labels the site and therefore should be meaningful (for example, Sales, for the sales office).

3. Both the Site Server and Site Server Domain text boxes will be filled in with default values, which for the majority of the sites will be acceptable. Change these names if desired.

4. If you want to configure SMS to check for additional logon servers, check the Automatically Detect All Logon Servers check box.

5. In the Service Account area, enter the Windows NT 4 Server userid created to manage SMS. Make sure you enter the correct password for this account.

6. Click the Continue button.

Note: The Confirm Password edit box ensures that you typed the same password two times. It does not ensure the password is the correct one for Windows NT 4 Server.

7. The Setup Progress dialog appears (see Figure 15-2). As the name implies, this dialog box displays the progress of the setup.

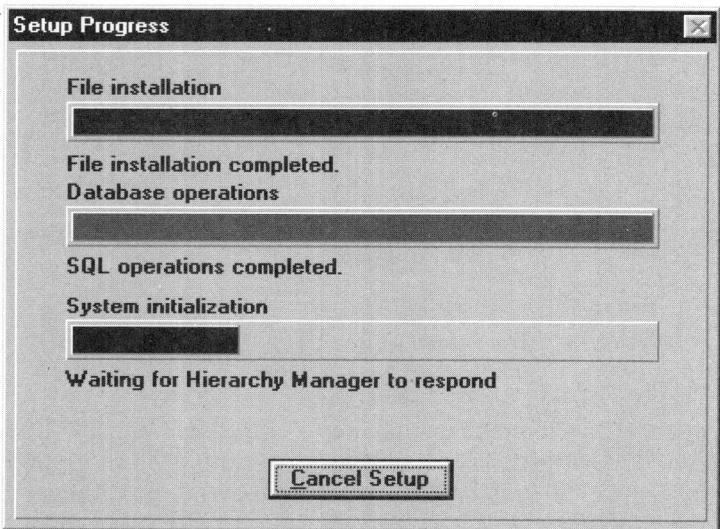

Figure 15-2: The Setup Progress dialog.

Note: If you get a message that the Hierarchy Manager doesn't respond, check the userid you provided in the Primary Site Configuration Information dialog and make sure that it has the necessary privileges. Remember, a userid may not be saved to the system until the User Manager for Domains program exits.

8. If you do not have the Network Monitor Driver installed, the SMS setup program prompts you to do so near the end of the setup process (see Figure 15-3). You can activate the Control Panel at this stage in the setup and add the Network Monitor Driver.

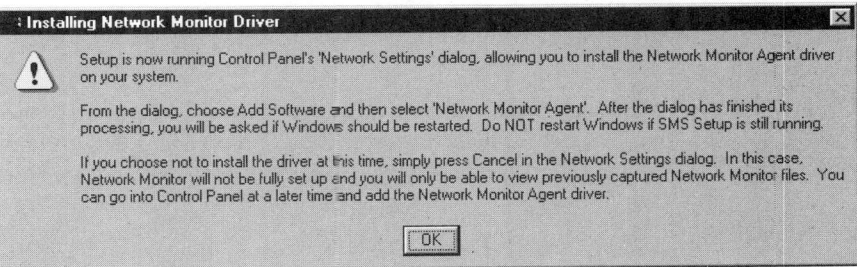

Figure 15-3: Prompt to add the Network Monitor Driver.

The prompt to add the Network Monitor Driver is not quite correct for Windows NT 4 Server (it was written for Windows NT 3.5x Server). Figure 15-4 shows the Control Panel's Network applet, with the Services tab displayed. Click the Add button in the Services tab and then follow the instructions in the Select Network Service dialog to install the Network Monitor Agent.

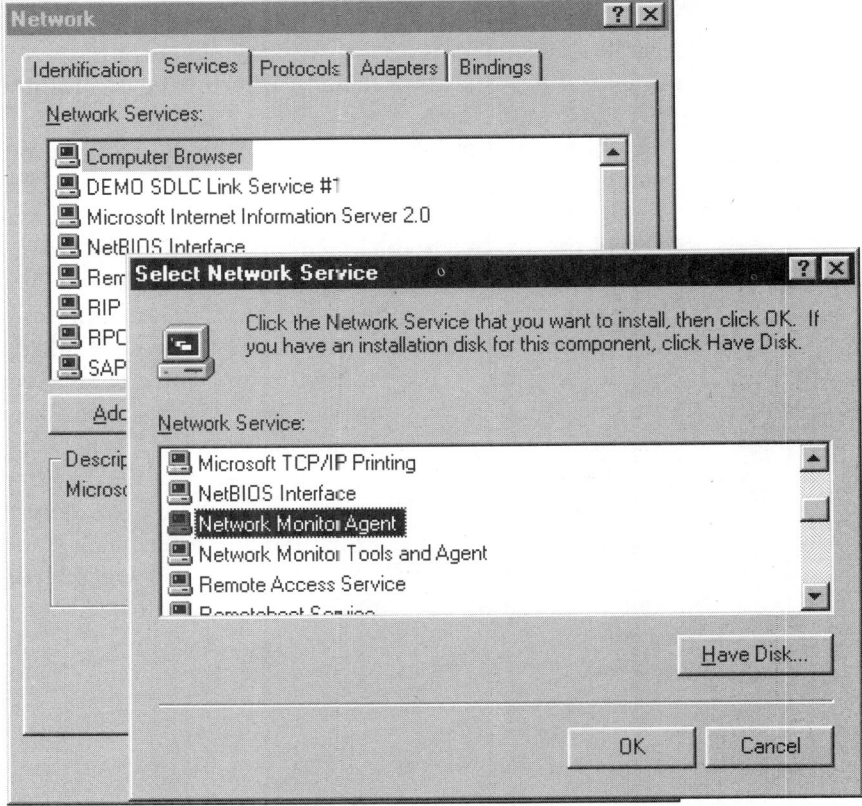

Figure 15-4: The Control Panel's Network applet.

Warning

As the message shown in Figure 15-3 states, when the Control Panel's Network applet is closed, it will prompt to restart the system. Do not restart Windows NT 4 Server at this time—wait until the SMS setup program has finished!

9. After you have installed all the component parts of SMS, the setup program displays its Completion dialog box. Once you dismiss the Completion dialog box, restart Windows NT 4 Server so that the installation of the Network Monitor Driver will be complete.

Installing SMS Clients

Installing clients for SMS requires an initial visit to each workstation. The systems administrator or the user (if he or she is comfortable with such a task) can install clients.

In the main SMS folder (called SMS by default) is a folder called \sms\site.srv\maincfg.box\client.src, which contains the files needed to install the SMS clients for most operating environments; it also contains the files needed to run the Macintosh Installer command. A Macintosh client requires special handling, using the Services for Macintosh (see Chapter 6 for details on the Services for Macintosh).

Throughout this section, we assume that you installed SMS in the default \sms folder. The SMS setup program creates several shares for you, sms_shr, sms_shrd, and sms_site. These shares allow clients (and other Microsoft Systems Management Servers) to access your SMS.

In this section, I'll give you an overview of the installation of an MS-DOS client, which is really being installed on a Windows 95 system. The installation is simple, requiring that you run a batch command from a DOS command window. Table 15-1 contains the batch commands for different operating environments.

Command	Environment
RUNSMS.BAT	DOS, Windows-95, Windows 3.x, and Windows NT
RUNSMS.CMD	OS/2 (no versions are specified)

Table 15-1: Commands to install Microsoft Systems Management Server clients.

Note: When you install SMS on an NTFS partition, check to make sure that client users have permission to access the SMS folder(s).

If the user doesn't have the necessary permissions, they will not be able to access the SMS system correctly.

To install the Microsoft Systems Management Server client for Windows 95, follow these steps:

1. On the client machine, establish a link to the sms_shr folder (which is created by the SMS setup program) using the Windows 95 Network Neighborhood and assign the folder a drive letter (for this example, we will use L:).

2. Open an Explorer window for the sms_shr folder and run the command to install the SMS client setup program: runsms.bat.

3. The runsms client setup program then installs the necessary files and prompts the user for any required user actions. With most environments, you have to restart the client system to complete the installation.

If at any time you change your mind about the SMS client software, you can use the Deinstal command to remove the client software from the system.

After the installation of SMS client software is complete, an inventory of the client system will be performed.

Note: The inventory of the client system may not be as accurate as, for example, the Windows 95 Control Panel's inventory. Minor differences may be noted; for example, one Windows 95 client with a Microsoft mouse installed was listed as having no mouse.

The Personal Computer Properties dialog displays properties about the client system including, but not limited to, the following: processor information, network information, disk and memory information, and other hardware-related information (see Figure 15-5). There are also several diagnostic properties available, such as the Network Monitor (see Figure 15-6).

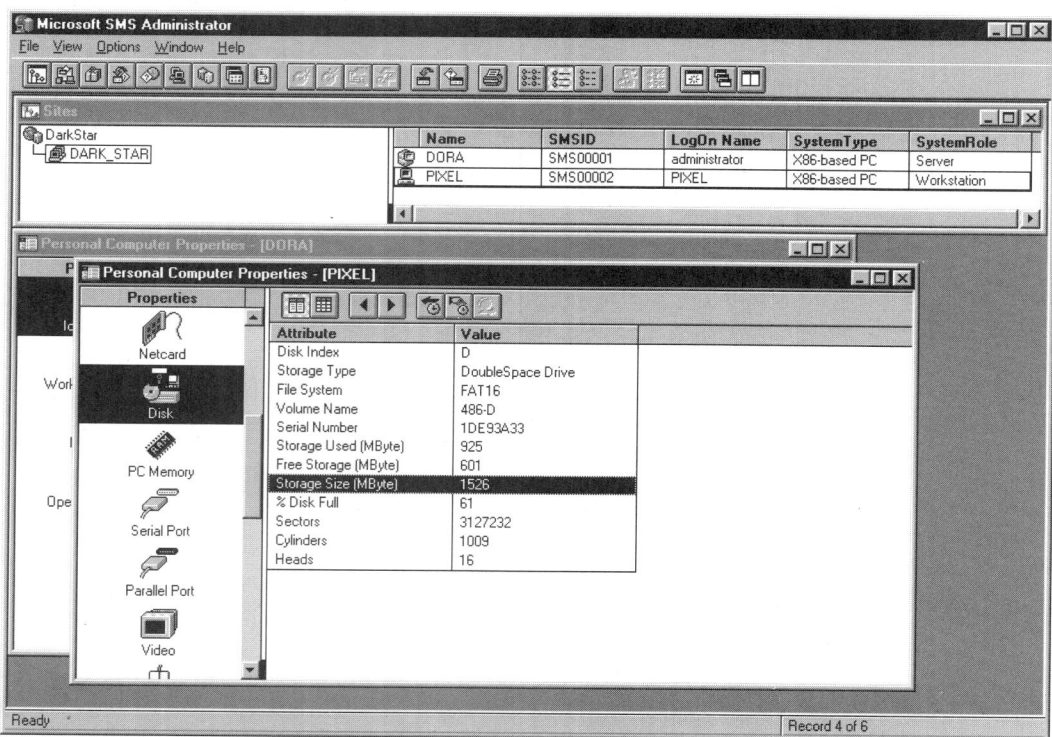

Figure 15-5: The Personal Computer Properties dialog.

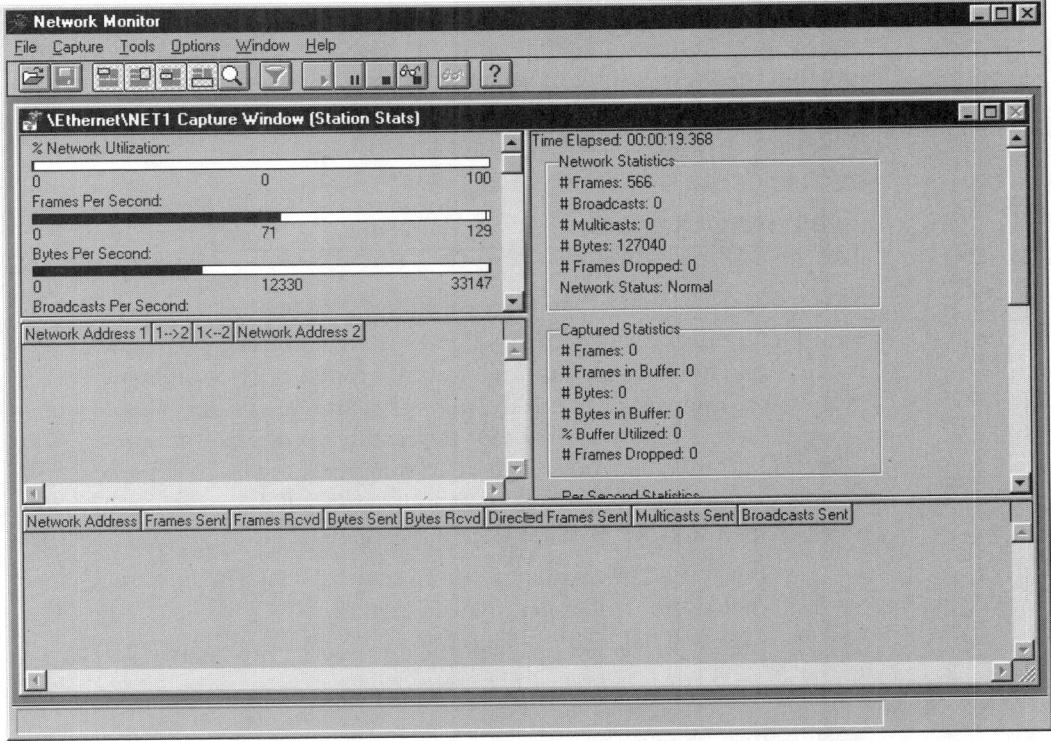

Figure 15-6: The Network Monitor monitoring a client workstation's network activity.

Using the SMS Administrator

The SMS Administrator program is the main interface with SMS. This section provides an overview of the SMS Administrator and how it is used.

This chapter covers the basics of using the SMS Administrator. The following three chapters describe, in detail, how to perform the following specific tasks with SMS:

- Chapter 16 describes how to use the SMS Inventory Management facilities.

- Chapter 17 describes how to distribute and install software using SMS.

- Chapter 18 describes the usage of the SMS remote control and diagnostic facilities.

We really will only be able to cover a very limited subset of SMS and the SMS Administrator program in this book. SMS is such a large product that readers needing more information should seek out publications dedicated to Microsoft Systems Management Server and also check Microsoft's TechNet CD for the latest information.

Submitting Queries

SMS allows you to easily interact with the SMS SQL database and provides a number of predefined queries for your use.

You can choose from a number of predefined queries or create an ad-hoc query. You can also limit the queries search to specific sites. Some queries have different formats for the results. In this example, we searched for all computers with disks that are more than 80 percent full (an easy search at the Dark_Star domain, since all drives seem to be full most of the time). To perform such a query:

1. From the File menu, choose Execute Query. The Execute Query dialog box will appear (see Figure 15-7).

2. In the Query text box, select Computers With Nearly Full Disks.

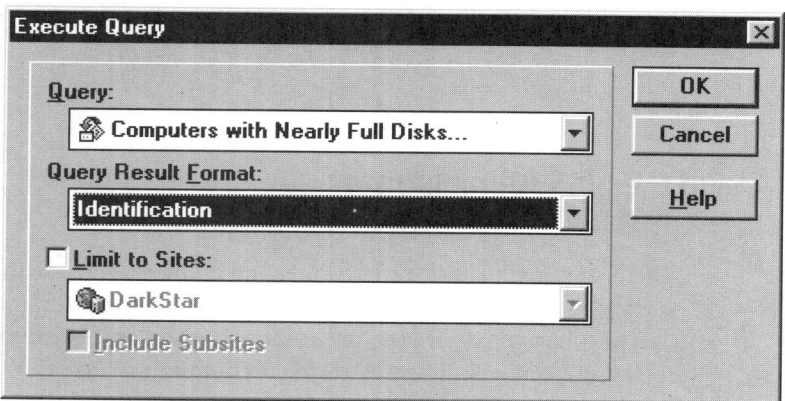

Figure 15-7: The Execute Query dialog box.

3. In the Query Result Format text box, select Identification. Click the OK button.

4. A dialog box will appear that prompts for what percentage of each disk needs be to be full. In this example, we specified 80 percent. The results of the query are shown in Figure 15-8.

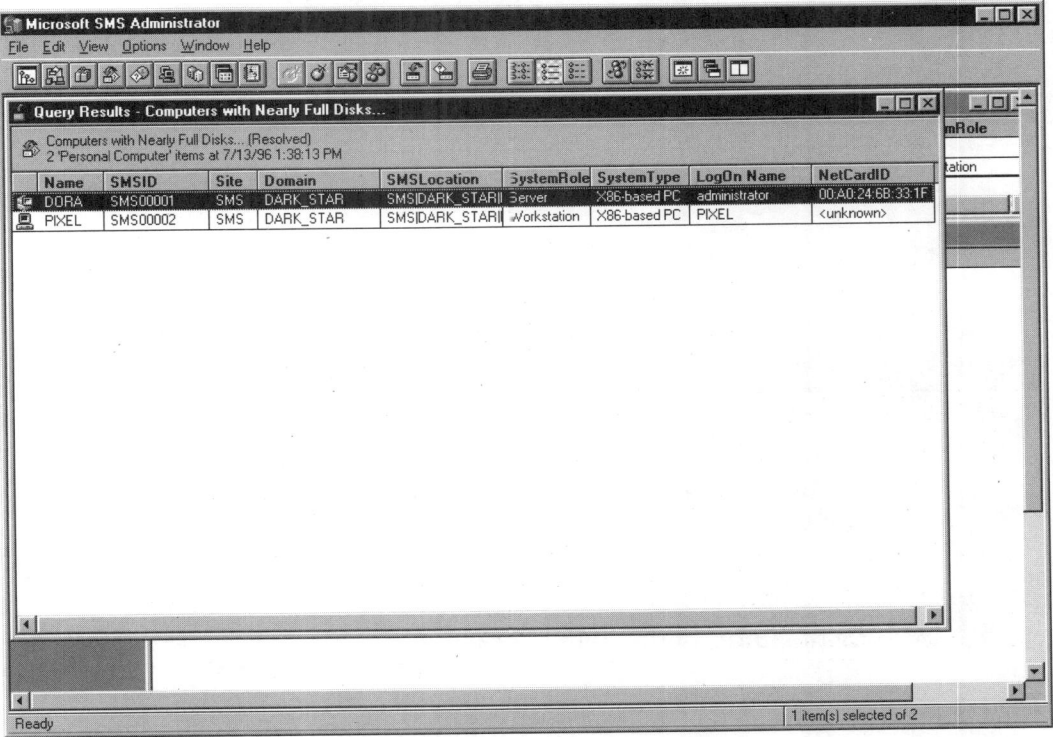

Figure 15-8: Results of a Computers With Nearly Full Disks query.

Displaying Queries

SMS has the Queries window to display (select File | Open from the SMS Administrator's menu) the available queries on the SMS database. Figure 15-9 shows the default queries that come with SMS. Once a query has been selected, it may be submitted for execution.

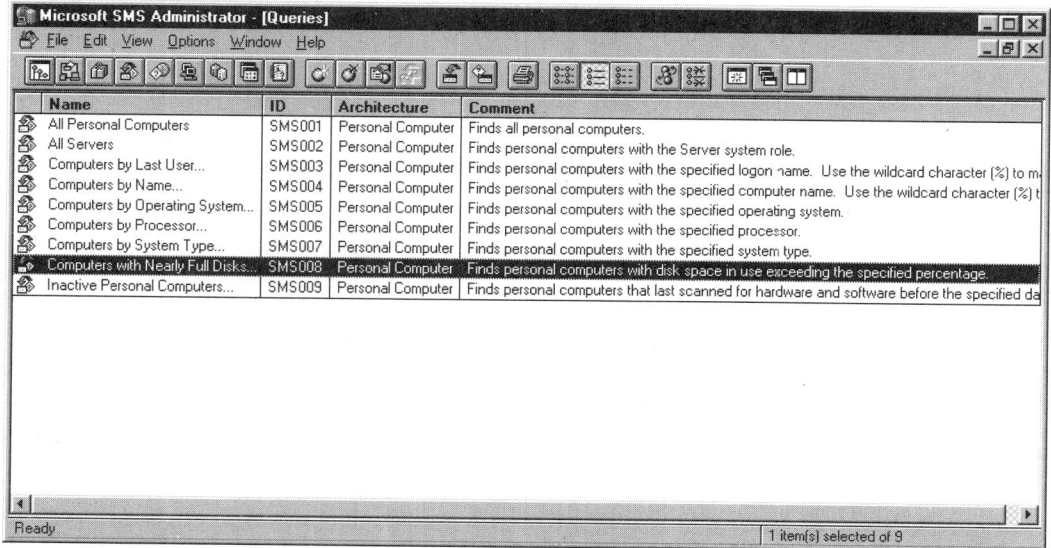

Figure 15-9: The Queries window.

You can create additional queries. The default queries may be customized as well. For example, you can limit the scope of a query or limit the output information.

Listing Sites in the SMS Hierarchy

SMS's Sites window (select File | Open from the SMS Administrator's menu) displays a listing of the sites in the SMS's hierarchy. Figure 15-10 shows an example of the Sites window.

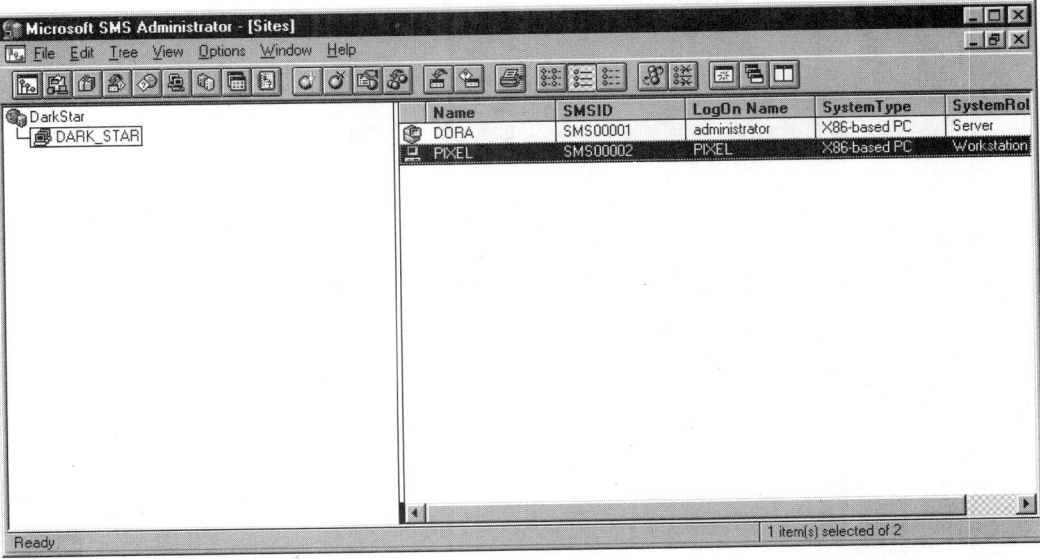

Figure 15-10: The Sites window.

Generally, all systems in the site will be listed in the Sites window, and you will use the Sites window when adding to machine groups and site groups (both machine groups and site groups are described below). Most SMS Administrator users will leave the Sites window open all the time, as it is frequently used.

Displaying & Creating Packages

SMS's Packages window (select File | Open from the SMS Administrator's menu) displays the currently defined packages. A package is an action that you want to take place on the client systems. When creating a package, you define the command to be executed, where the command will be found (the command's path), and the platform on which the command is intended to run. Figure 15-11 shows a list of packages defined in our example installation.

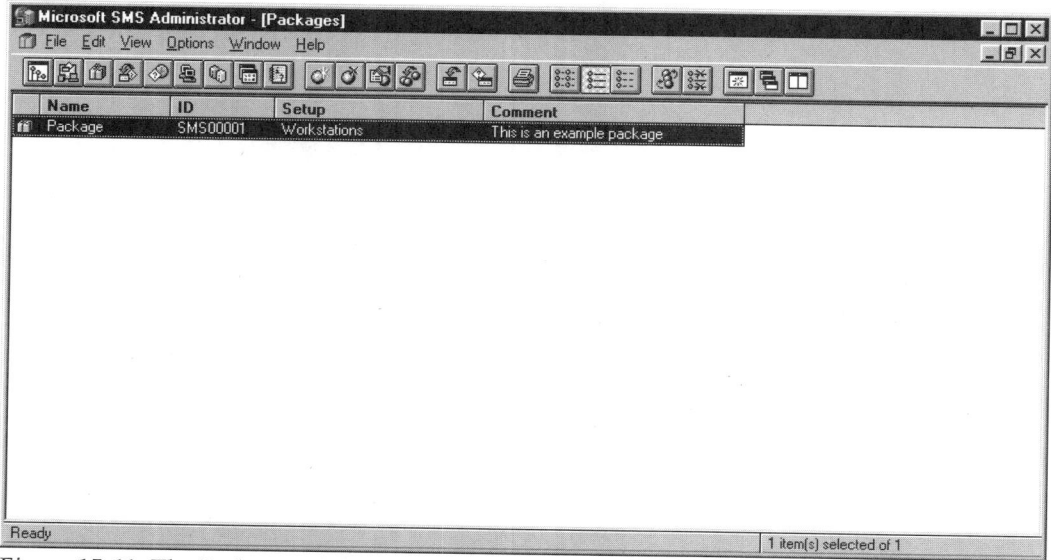

Figure 15-11: The Packages window.

When creating a package, you will be presented with several configuration dialog boxes. Figure 15-12 shows the Command Line Properties dialog box, which defines the actual command that executes. You also specify the platform for the command—in our example we can only execute the Pinball game under Windows 95 and Windows NT.

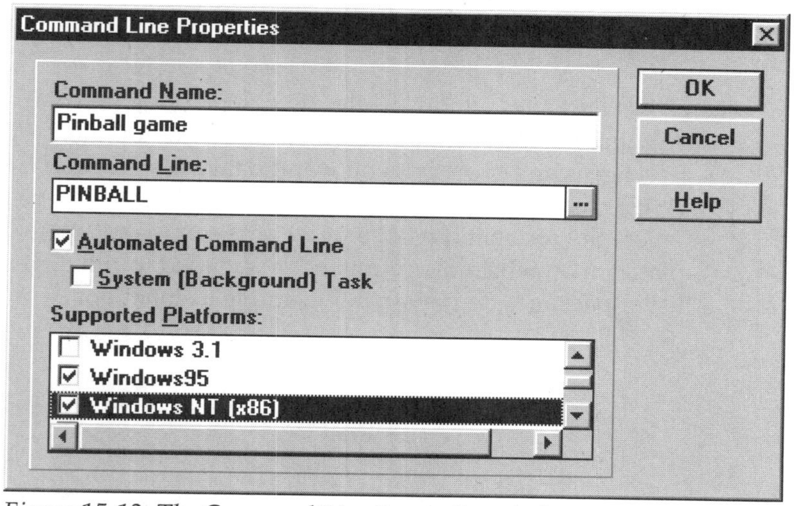

Figure 15-12: The Command Line Properties window.

Typical uses for packages include installing or upgrading software, testing, and running other administrative tasks. To enable a package to be executed on clients, you have to create a job, which is the topic of the next section.

Displaying & Creating Jobs

SMS has the Jobs window (select File | Open from the SMS Administrator's menu) to display the status of any existing jobs. To create a job, open the Jobs window and select File | New from the menu.

Prior to creating jobs, you must create a package (which is the task that the job will perform). Figure 15-13 shows the Jobs window.

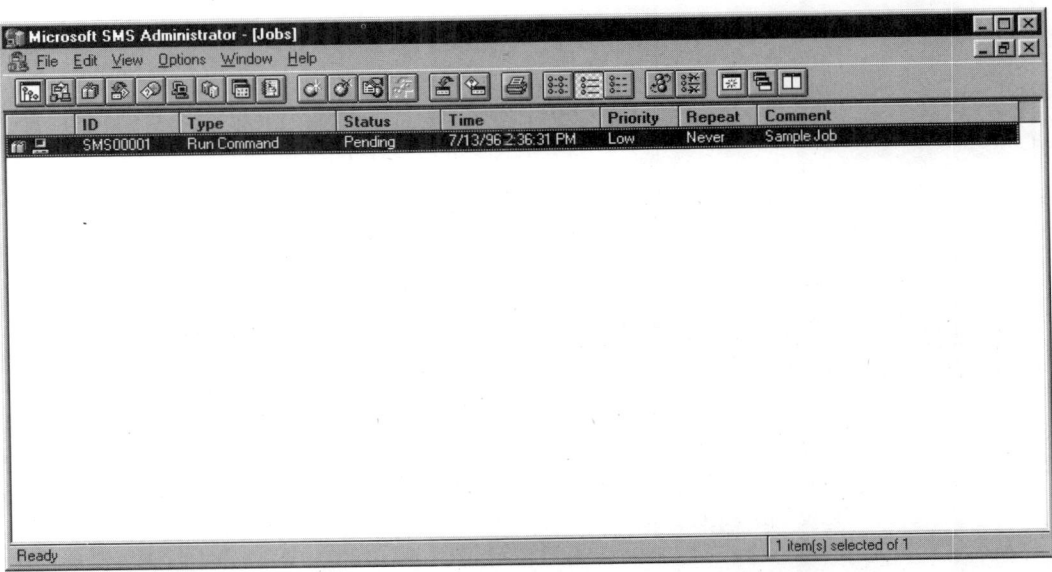

Figure 15-13: The Jobs window.

You can assign priorities to jobs as well as manipulate the schedule for the jobs. For example, you can make the execution of a job optional for a period of time and then mandatory after a certain date. At some later date, you may want the job to expire—users who have not executed the job by the expiration date probably don't need that specific job.

Displaying & Creating Alerts

SMS's Alerts window (select File | Open from the SMS Administrator's menu) displays information about alerts that have been created. To create an alert, open the Alerts window and from the menu select File | New. The Alerts window is shown in Figure 15-14.

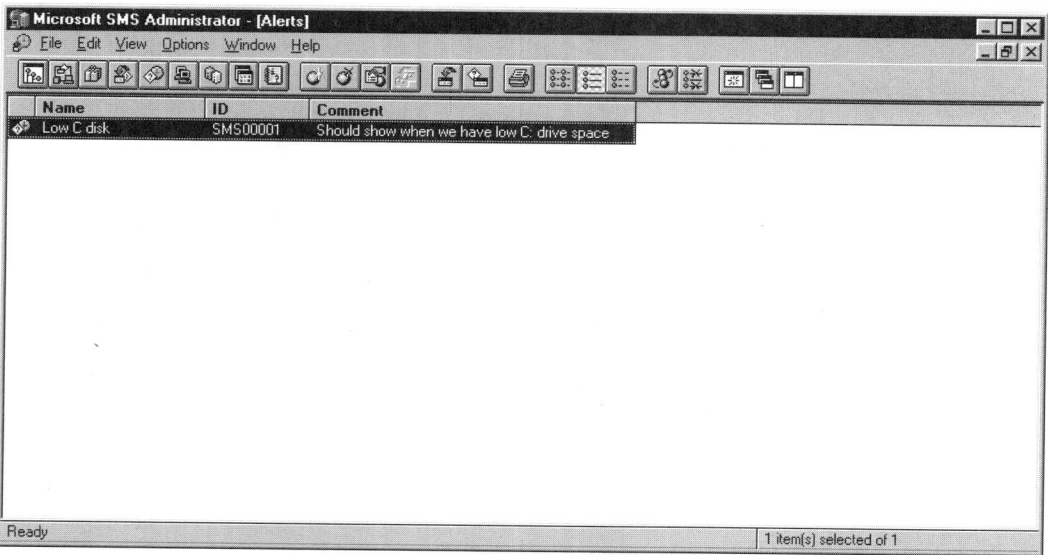

Figure 15-14: The Alerts window.

An alert can be as simple as checking the hard drives on the client systems to ensure that there is sufficient free space. For example, the alert shown in Figure 15-14 produced the message box shown in Figure 15-15.

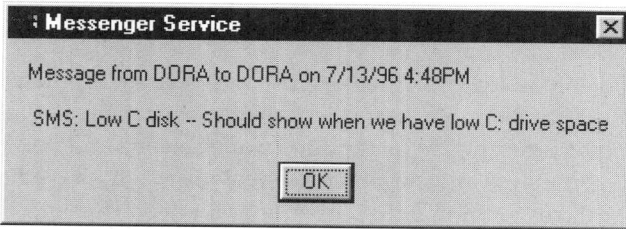

Figure 15-15: An alert message.

Notice how both the alert name and the comment are incorporated into the message, which is a good reason to make sure both the name and comment make sense and are accurate.

Displaying & Creating Machine Groups

SMS's Machine Groups window (select File | Open from the SMS Administrator's menu) displays information about machine groups. Machine groups create a logical grouping of a number of machines. For example, there might be a machine group for the R&D department, a machine group for the accounting department, and a machine group for the administrative department. Figure 15-16 shows the Machine Groups window, with a single group (called Group 1) comprising two machines.

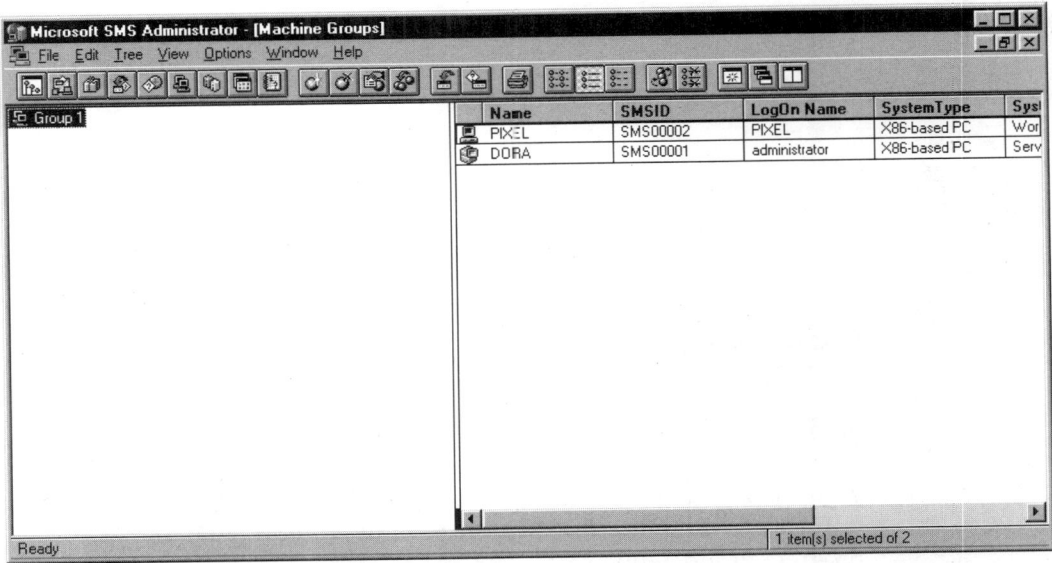

Figure 15-16: The Machine Groups window.

Displaying Site Groups

SMS's Site Groups window (select File | Open from the SMS Administrator's menu) displays information about sites. Generally (but not always), sites are geographically separated parts of your organization.

Figure 15-17 shows the Site Groups window, with a single site defined (well, actually the DarkStar site is it, the only location on the author's system!).

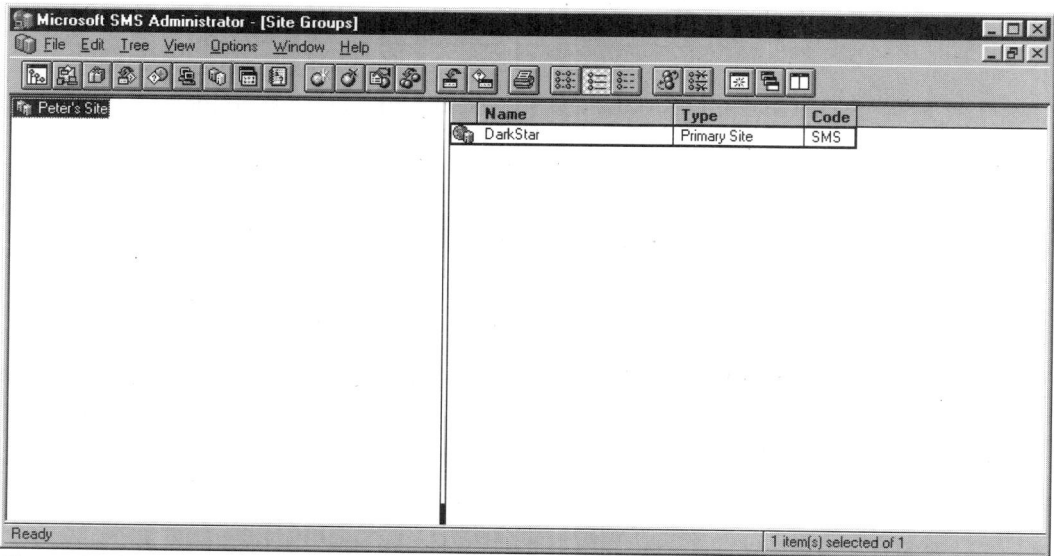

Figure 15-17: The Site Groups window.

Displaying Program Groups

SMS's Program Groups (select File I Open from the SMS Administrator's menu) window displays information about program groups. Program groups manage programs.

Figure 15-18 shows the Program Groups window, with a single program group defined.

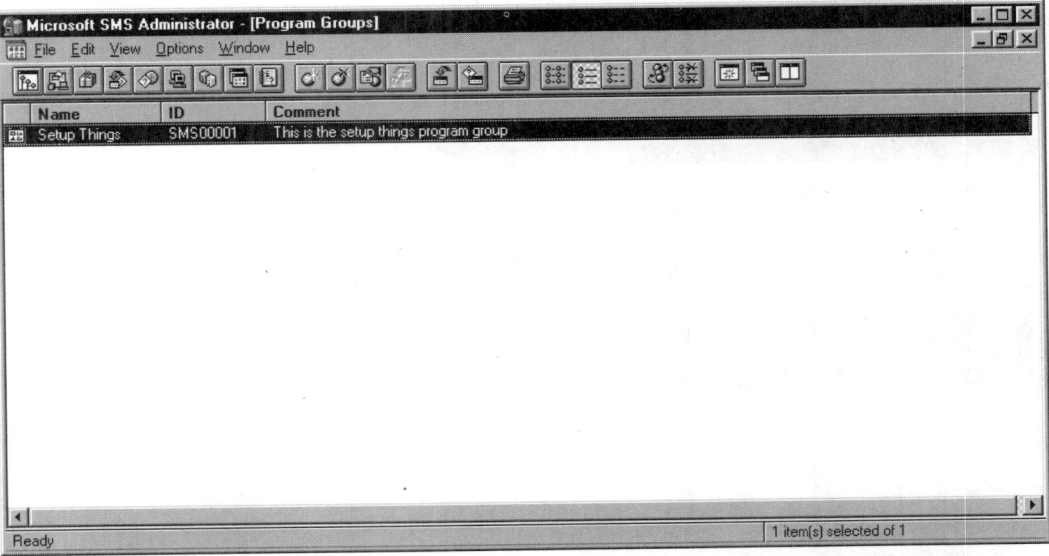

Figure 15-18: The Program Groups window.

Displaying Events

SMS's Events window (select File I Open from the SMS Administrator's menu) displays information about events that have occurred in the SMS. Event information is extracted from the Windows NT 4 Server Event Log (filtered, so that only event information relevant to SMS is displayed. This is done by selecting events of the SMSEvent type.)

Figure 15-19 shows the Events Window, with a number of events listed. You can then query each event to determine whether it is significant or may be safely ignored.

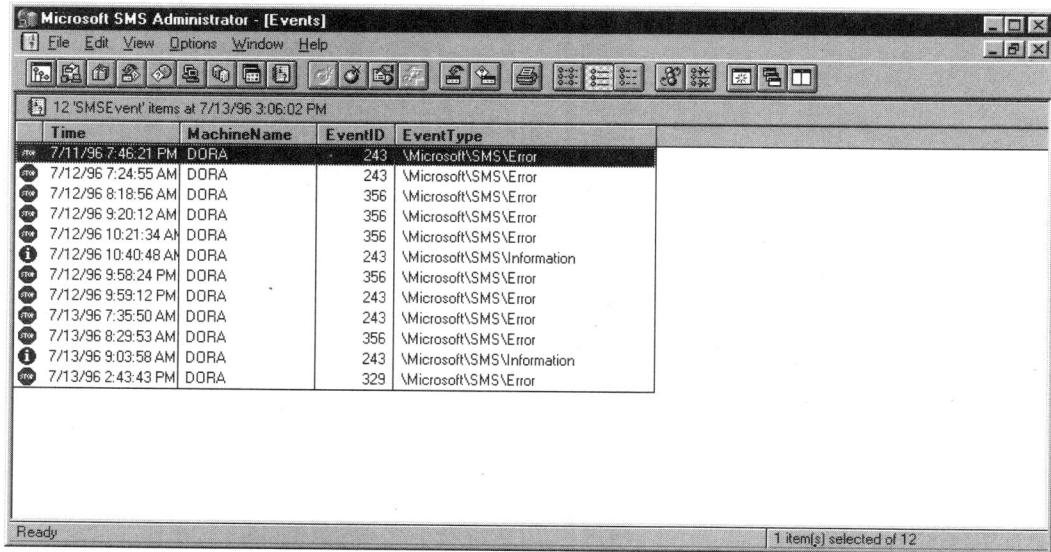

Figure 15-19: The Events window.

Displaying SQL Server Messages

SMS's SQL Server Messages window (select File | Open in the SMS Administrator's menu) displays any message received from the Microsoft SQL Server. Generally, such messages are important, so you should monitor the SQL Error window frequently when using SMS.

Figure 15-20 shows the SQL Server Messages window, with one entry: 7/13/96 3:07:09 PM - 0 new entries. The bottom line with this entry—there is nothing wrong with the SQL Server!

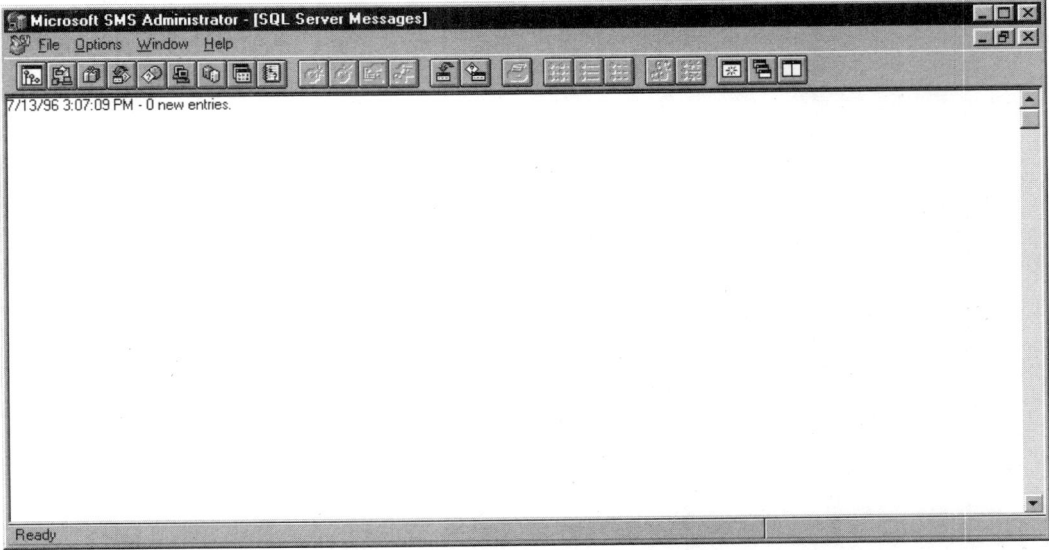

Figure 15-20: The SQL Server Messages window.

Moving On

This chapter introduced Microsoft Systems Management Server; we showed you how to install SMS, and we showed you some of its basic features. SMS works with Microsoft SQL Server, which also must be installed, either locally or on a server accessible to the SMS machine.

In the next three chapters, we will cover the SMS's features: Inventory Management, Software Distribution and Installation, and Remote Control and Diagnostics.

## 16

Microsoft SMS Inventory Management

In this chapter, we describe Microsoft SMS (Systems Management Server) version 1.2 inventory features. We deal primarily with Windows 95 client workstations. The differences between a Windows 95 workstation and a Windows NT workstation are slight, and the processes and procedures to install client software on either platform are identical. When managing Novell NetWare clients, a somewhat more complex installation process must be followed.

The whole concept of SMS is the ability to maintain an inventory of the clients on a network. This inventory consists of both client hardware and software components. There are four primary client and server inventory tasks performed by SMS:

- Automatic identification, and inventory, of servers and clients. This inventory assists the systems administrator to determine what servers and clients are found on the network.

- Installation of Client Management Agent, used by SMS to manage the client. The Client Management Agent is installed without the systems administrator having to visit each workstation.

- Detailed hardware and software inventories, allowing the systems administrator to determine what hardware and software is installed. Includes the ability to maintain a historical database of inventories.

- Software audits, allowing the systems administrator to determine what software is installed and the software's licensing status.

> **Tip**
>
> *After installing the client software, it can take up to 15 minutes for the SMS system to recognize a new client. Other tasks may take time to complete, also.*

Installing the Client Management Agent

One of the first tasks for the systems administrator is to install client software on each client that will be used with SMS. Client software installation is typically an easy task, consisting of execution of a batch file.

> **Tip**
>
> *Don't forget: Each client must have an SMS client license!*

Installing Windows Clients

The steps to install SMS client-side software for Windows (and OS/2) users who are using Windows networking are very simple:

1. At each client computer, map the SMS server's share named sms_shr to a drive letter using Network Neighborhood (or a DOS command prompt net use command). The drive letter for this share is not critical, however.

2. Under Windows, open a DOS Command session.

3. In the root folder of sms_shr, run the DOS batch command file runsms.bat. (If installing under OS/2, use runsms.cmd.)

4. The batch command file runsms.bat will install the necessary client software. Once client software is installed, the workstation must be restarted to configure the software.

5. Configure the client software. When the client workstation is restarted, the user will be prompted to provide MIF (Management Information Format) information about the user, and the workstation, as shown in Figure 16-1.

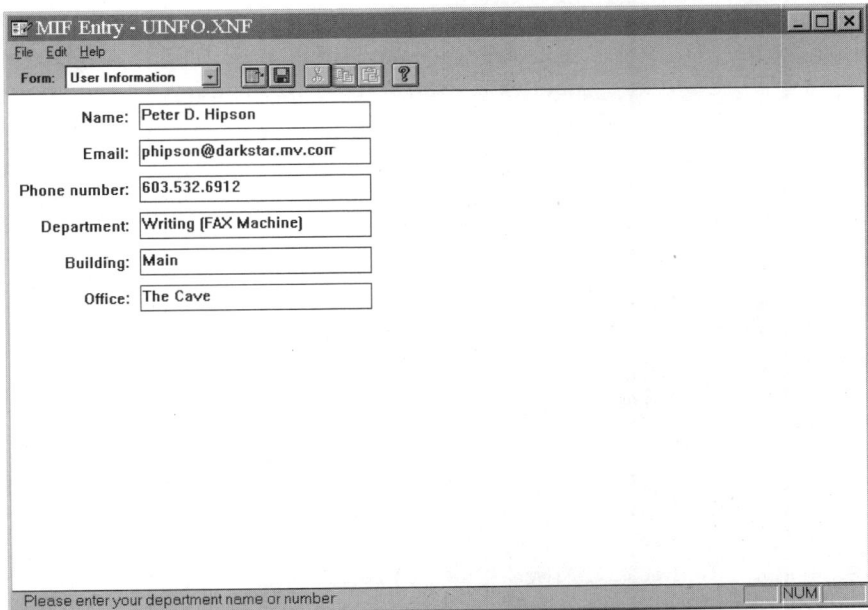

Figure 16-1: Entering MIF information, the client workstation's user.

6. After the client user has saved and exited the MIF Entry program (which may be rerun at any later time; see "Working With SMS Client Software" later in this chapter), the client workstation will send inventory information to the SMS server.

Installing NetWare Clients

For Novell NetWare, the client installation process is a bit different than for a Microsoft Windows-based network:

1. At the Novell NetWare client computer, map the SMS server's share named sms_shr. The drive letter for this share is not critical, however.

2. Under Windows, open a DOS Command session.

3. In the root folder of sms_shr, run the DOS batch command file runsms.bat. (If installing under OS/2, use runsms.cmd.)

4. The batch command file runsms.bat will install the necessary client software. Once client software is installed, the workstation must be restarted to configure the software.

5. Configure the client software. When the client workstation is restarted, the user will be prompted to provide MIF information about the user, and the workstation, as shown in Figure 16-1.

6. After the client user has saved and exited the MIF Entry program (which may be rerun at any later time; see "Working With SMS Client Software" later in this chapter), the client workstation will send inventory information to the SMS server.

What Time Is It?

Microsoft recommends that the time on each SMS client workstation be synchronized with the SMS server. Regardless of the reason, synchronizing the clocks on each computer on a network is a very, very good idea.

To synchronize clocks, designate a server (such as the SMS server) as the master clock. Then write a batch command file (perhaps called settime.bat) that contains the command:

Net time \\sms_server /set /y

Where \\sms_server is the name of the server which serves as the master clock.

Add this batch file to each workstation's startup group, with properties set to execute minimized, and close the window when the command exits. This command will then execute each time the workstation is started, ensuring that the clocks on all workstations are set to a single time.

Of course, you must maintain the time on your server. If there is Internet access, an accurate time can be obtained at http://www.flinet.com/~emeyers/nbstim.html. This utility will obtain the time by dialing into the NBS time standard, reset the clock, and then tell you just how far your clock was off from the actual time.

Of course, time is relative; accuracy must take into consideration transmission delays.

Working With SMS Client Software

When client-side software is installed (see "Installing the Client Management Agent" above, for installation instructions), a program group is created called SMS Client. This program group is shown in Figure 16-2. There are six items placed in the SMS Client program group:

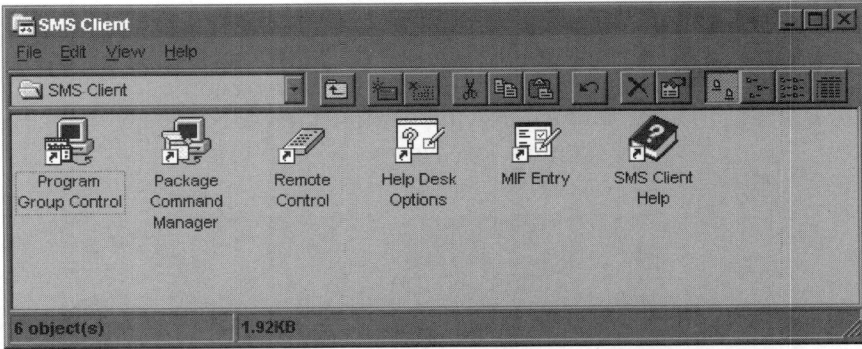

Figure 16-2: The SMS Client program group, a typical client installation.

- Program Group Control is an application that initializes and manages the environment for the SMS client. Program Group Control is run automatically by the SMS client.

- Package Command Manager is used when a package (usually a software application) is received by the workstation from the SMS server. The Package Command Manager will list pending, archived, and previously executed packages. Any package that has not already been executed may be executed by selecting Command | Execute from the Package Command Manager's main menu. This process is described in Chapter 17.

- Remote Control is a utility that is used to allow the SMS administrator to "take control" of the client workstation. Using the Remote Control application allows the systems administrator to diagnose and fix problems on the workstation without having to travel to the workstation. This process is described in Chapter 18.

- Help Desk Options allows the client user to configure parameters for the SMS client. The user can save and restore parameters as desired and configure default settings, also.

■ MIF Entry is used to fill in MIF forms. The default form, User Information, is displayed when the SMS client is first installed. The systems administrator is able to create additional MIF forms as needed.

■ SMS Client Help is a general help file for the SMS client user. The user is able to obtain help on the Package Command Manager, the SMS MIF Entry program, and Remote Troubleshooting.

Configuring the Help Desk Options

SMS client's Help Desk must be configured for each organization. You can set the following Remote Viewer options with the Help Desk Options program (see Figure 16-3):

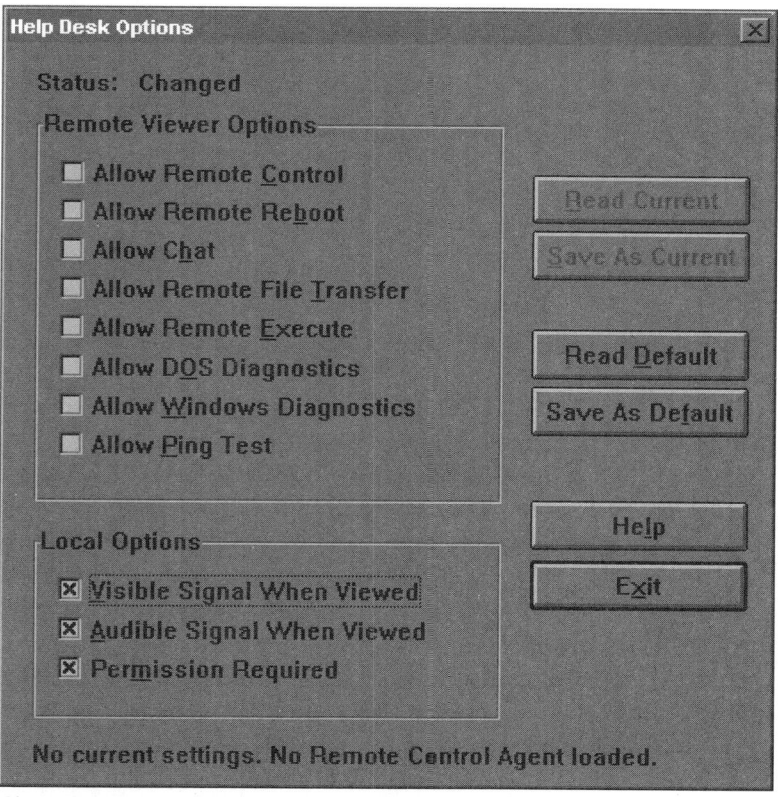

Figure 16-3: Use the Help Desk Options program to set and restore SMS client options.

■ Allow Remote Control lets the client user enable or disable the systems administrator's ability to take control of the client workstation.

■ Allow Remote Reboot lets the client user enable or disable the systems administrator's ability to reboot the workstation. Oftentimes, when correcting problems with a client workstation, it is necessary to reboot to reinitialize Windows or some other low-level component.

■ Allow Chat lets the user enable or disable the chat features.

■ Allow Remote File Transfer lets the user disable the ability to transfer files to and from the client. Note that this feature is different from normal networking file transfers.

■ All Remote Execute lets the user disable the systems administrator's ability to execute a program or application on the client workstation.

■ Allow DOS Diagnostics lets the user disable the systems administrator's ability to run DOS level diagnostic programs. This is necessary because many times DOS diagnostic programs leave the system in an unstable state. (Not usable on Windows NT clients.)

■ Allow Windows Diagnostics lets the user disable the systems administrator's ability to run Windows-level diagnostic programs. This is necessary because many times Windows diagnostic programs leave the system in an unstable state or cause problems with executing Windows applications. (Not usable on Windows NT clients.)

■ Allow PING Test lets the user disable the SMS PING Test. A PING Test sends a message to the client workstation that is returned to the originator. A PING Test may impact system performance. (Not usable on Windows NT clients.)

There are a number of local options that may be set using the Help Desk Options program:

■ Visible Signal When Viewed will display a visible signal when the systems administrator is accessing the client computer.

■ Audible Signal When Viewed will make a warning sound when the systems administrator is accessing the client computer (not usable on Windows NT clients.)

- Permission Required, when checked, specifies that the systems administrator will need the user's explicit permission before remotely accessing the workstation.

    Note: Systems administrators may allay concerns that they will "take over" users' computers by showing the users how to use the Help Desk Options program to configure their client workstations' interaction with the SMS remote control and diagnostic facilities.

Creating MIF Entry Forms

MIF (Management Information Format)-formatted data may include data from custom MIF forms created by systems administrators. Custom MIFs are defined as MIFs created either by a client user or the systems administrator. These custom MIFs are used to expand the database, providing additional information about the SMS client, which is then stored in the SMS database. Any data so stored in the SMS database may then be used by the systems administrator to enhance the system's performance and reliability, for example.

You use the SMS MIF Form Generator program to create MIF forms. This program (see Figure 16-4) allows the administrator to modify an existing form or to create a new form as desired.

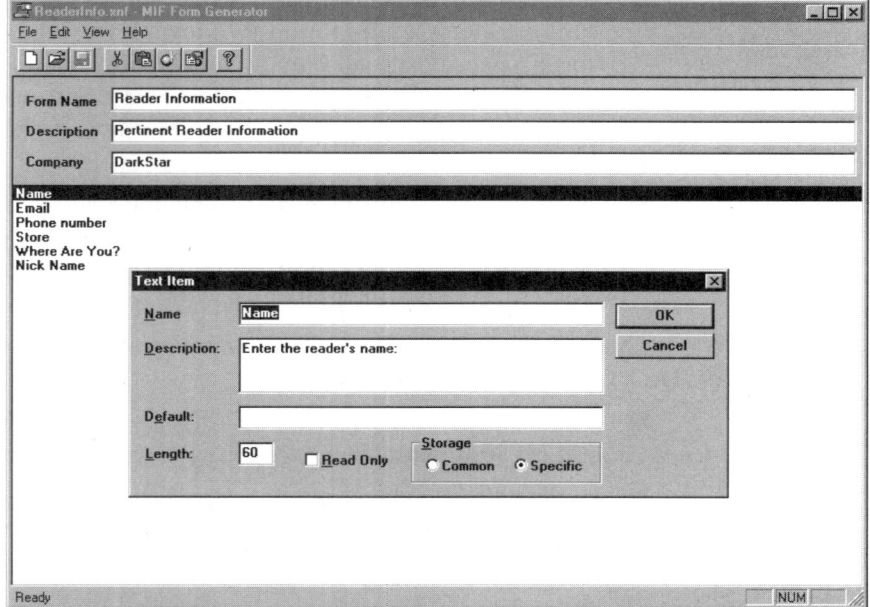

Figure 16-4: The SMS MIF Form Generator, generating the Reader Information form.

Visible in the center of Figure 16-4 is a properties dialog box, the Text Item dialog, which shows the properties for the Name field. Associated with the Name field is a description (not visible to the client user), a default value (which the client user will have as a default), and a read-only flag (it is possible to create a field that has a default and is read-only, to flag the data or to provide data for the user). Additionally, each field may have either common or specific storage. When Common storage is specified, the item will be shared between all group instances. Specify Specific when the data's value will typically be unique for each user.

The steps to create a form (forms are largely intuitive) are:

1. Select File | New from the SMS MIF Form Generator's menu.

2. Fill in the Form Name field. The form name is the name that the client user will see in the MIF Entry program.

    Note: The default form is the first form, based on the form name. Since SMS ships with an initial form called User Information, any form that has a name that sorts before User Information will become the default form. Such is life . . .

3. Fill in the Description field. The description is used by the systems administrator to assist in managing forms. Include a description that is meaningful and descriptive; no use in having a description that when used a few months in the future is indecipherable.

4. Fill in the Company field. You can enter the company name here, or you can enter site, department, or location information.

5. Create the form's fields. Since the SMS MIF Form Generator is a simple program, there is no choice as to field location. Fields will be displayed to the user in the same order as they are in the XNF MIF form template file.

    Note: Fields may be moved using the clipboard's cut-and-paste facility. When pasting, a field is placed above the current selection. To place a field at the end of the list, move the field to above the last item; then move the last item up one place.

6. For each field, you select either number, text, or list.

    ■ For number fields, provide a name (which the user will see as a prompt), a description (used by the systems administrator), and a default value, which will give the client user a default to choose (if applicable). A number field's value is restricted to a short-signed integer (between -32767 and

32767, inclusive). There is an option to make the numeric field read-only (which is used to enter place information into the SMS database or to provide some form of information to the client user) and to specify whether the field is stored in a common or specific location.

■ For character fields, provide a name (which the user will see as a prompt), a description (used by the systems administrator), and a default value, which will give the client user a default to choose (if applicable). The field's maximum length must be specified. There is an option to make the field read only (which is used to enter place information into the SMS database or to provide some form of information to the client user) and to specify whether the field is stored in a common or specific location.

■ For list fields, provide a name (which the user will see as a prompt), and a description (used by the systems administrator). List fields allow the client user to select one entry from a predefined list. This list must be entered by the systems administrator when creating the field. There is an option to specify that the field is stored in a common or specific location.

7. After creating the form's fields, save the form, giving it a meaningful name. If the majority of the client users are using operating systems that support long filenames (such as Windows 95, Windows NT, OS/2, or Apple Macintosh), use a meaningful long filename.

Once a custom MIF form has been created, it must be made visible to the user. A MIF form will be visible when the form is in the client user's \MS\SMS\BIN folder. All form templates (XNF files) that are in the client user's \MS\SMS\BIN folder will be opened whenever the user starts the MIF Entry program. The best distribution method is to create a package that will be sent to the user. This package will copy the form (from a known location) to the user's SMS client folder. For example, place the forms in a folder named MyForms, the SMS server's main folder, and share this folder with the share name of MyForms. Then define a command line that copies the form from this folder to the user's SMS client folder:

```
Copy *.xnf \MS\SMS\BIN\*.*
```

After the package is created, create a Run Command on Workstation job in SMS, which will execute the command on the workstation. (Packages and jobs are the topic of Chapter 18.)

Figure 16-5 shows the newly created Reader Information MIF file being filled in by a client user.

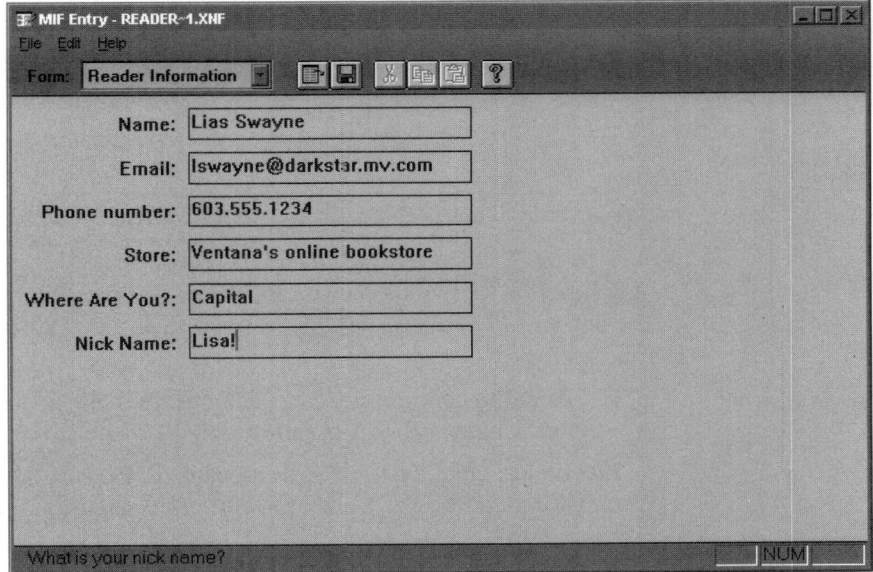

Figure 16-5: A user filling in the newly created Reader Information form.

Automatic Identification of Servers & Clients

The SMS inventory features assist the systems administrator in determining what servers and clients are found on the network. This process is performed using the Sites functionality of the SMS Administrator. In Figure 16-6, two of the workstations on the DarkStar network are visible: Pixel and Long.

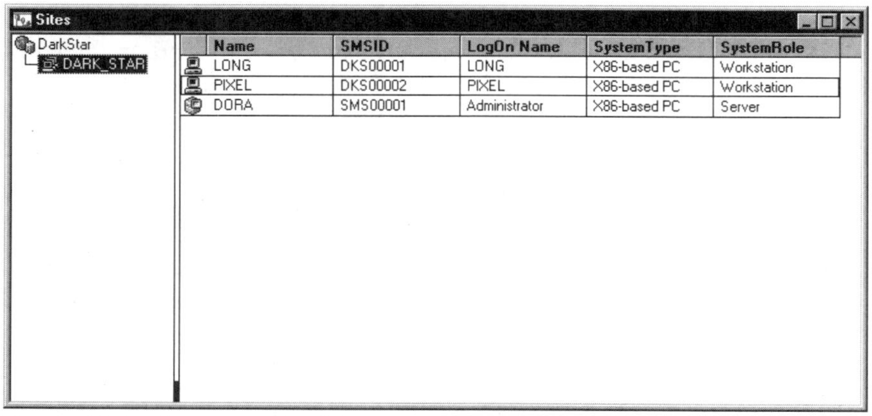

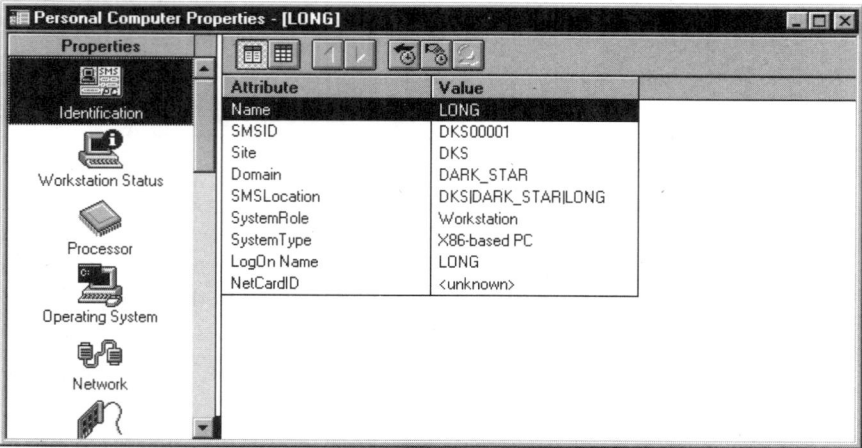

Figure 16-6: Sites on the DarkStar network: the server and two workstations.

It is possible to display a vast amount of information about any client in the Sites list. This information, referred to as a system inventory, is displayed by:

1. Select the client in the Sites list and then either double-click the client site or press Alt+Enter to display the client's properties.

2. The Personal Computer Properties dialog box (shown in Figure 16-7) will display a vast amount of information about the client computer.

Figure 16-7: The Personal Computer Properties list tells all about the client.

Inventories & Queries

SMS is able to provide detailed information about clients on the SMS network. Information about each client's hardware configuration, software installed, and any collected files is available to the systems administrator by using the SMS Administrator program. Generally, the inventory functionalities are performed automatically by SMS.

The results of the inventory of the client (inventories are performed each time the client logs on) are displayed by selecting the client in the Sites list (see Figure 16-6) and either selecting File | Properties, or pressing Alt+Enter.

Inventories

The site's properties will be displayed in the Personal Computer Properties window, which is shown in Figure 16-7. This window allows the systems administrator to view a vast number of properties for the client user. These properties are subdivided into a number of categories, as described in the following sections.

Identification

The Identification property includes general information about the client. This information is useful as a starting point when determining the client's status.

Attributes in Identification include Name, SMSID, Site, Domain, SMSLocation, SystemRole, SystemType, LogOn Name, and NetCardID.

Workstation Status

The Workstation Status property includes status of the client user. This information is useful as a starting point when determining what the client's current status is.

Attributes in Status include Last Hardware Scan, Last Software Scan, Files Not Installed, System Files Not Modified, Failed Hardware Checks, and Standalone Workstation.

Processor

The Processor property includes information about the client's CPU. This information is helpful in determining the client's hardware type. Since Windows NT supports different platforms (such as Alpha, MIPS, and PPC), it is necessary to customize which packages are sent to non-Intel platforms.

Attributes in Processor include Processor Name, Processor Type, and Quantity.

Operating System

The Operating System property includes information about the client's operating system. The operating system displayed will be the client's selected operating system—clients configured as dual boot must select one operating system on which to run the SMS client software. When a client needs to change operating systems, he or she should run upgrade.bat.

Attributes in Operating System include Operating System Name, Version, Country Code, Language ID, Service Pack Version, Installation Date, Registered Owner, Registered Organization, Build Number, Build Type, System Root, and System Start Options. Clients who are not running Windows NT will not return all the attributes.

Network

The Network property includes information about the active network for the client user. Use this property to determine what networking is configured for the client. For Remote Control purposes, it is necessary to run the TCP/IP protocol so using the Network properties can help in determining whether TCP/IP has been installed.

Attributes in Network include Network Active, Network Type, Major Version, Minor Version, IPX Address, IP Address, Subnet Mask, Default Gateway, DNS Machine Name, LogOn Name, Workgroup, Major Shell Version, and Minor Shell Version.

Netcard

The Netcard property includes information about the client's NIC (Network Interface Card). It is common that NICs are upgraded to improve system performance, and the systems administrator can determine the client's NIC and the NIC's configuration using the Netcard property.

Attributes in Netcard include Manufacturer, Port Address, and IRQ. Not all client operating systems will return this information. Some generic NICs, which emulate more commonly known NICs, will return information about the NIC that they emulate.

See "Queries" later in the chapter for an example of using the Netcard property's Manufacturer attribute.

Disk

The Disk property includes information about each locally connected drive, including floppy, hard disk, and CD-ROM drives. This information is useful for determining the client workstation's disk storage status.

Attributes in Disk include Disk Index (the drive letter), Storage Type, File System, Volume Name, Serial Number, Cylinders, Heads, Storage Used (MBytes), Free Storage (MBytes), Storage Size (MBytes), % Disk Full, and Sectors. Not all operating systems and interfaces return Cylinder and Head information.

There will be a record, containing each of these attributes, for each locally attached disk.

PC Memory

The PC Memory property includes information to determine the amount of RAM installed in the client workstation. This information is useful as a starting point when determining whether an application or operating system can be installed without upgrading the system's memory.

Attributes in PC Memory include Base Memory (Byte), Extended Memory (KByte), Total Physical Memory (KByte), Total Paging-File Size (KByte), Page File Name, and Page File Size (MByte). Not all operating systems return all information; however, the Total Physical Memory (KByte) attribute should be available from all clients.

Serial Port

The Serial Port property includes information about each installed serial (communications) port installed on the client workstation.

Attributes in Serial Port include Serial Port Index, Port Address, Current Baud Rate, Parity Enabled, Parity, Byte Size, Stop Bits, Carrier Detect, Data Set Ready, and CTS. Not all operating systems support the Serial Port property.

Parallel Port

The Parallel Port property includes information about each parallel (printer) port installed on the client workstation.

Attributes in Parallel Port include Parallel Port Index and Port Address. Not all operating systems support the Parallel Port property.

Video

The Video property includes information about the client's video system. Most general purpose workstations will report that there is a VGA-type video system installed, perhaps with information about the card's BIOS date.

Attributes in Video include Current Video Mode, Max Rows, Adapter Type, Manufacturer, Display Type, 2nd Adapter Type, and Bios Date.

Mouse

The Mouse property includes information about the pointing device installed on the client user's system.

Attributes in Mouse include Hardware Installed, Mouse Hardware Type, Manufacturer, IRQ, Number of Buttons, Horizontal Mickeys, Vertical Mickeys, and Language.

Services

The Services property includes information about each installed Windows NT service. This information is useful as a starting point when determining which services are installed and running on a Windows NT client.

Attributes in Services include Name, State, Start Type, Start Name, and EXE Path. Only Windows NT clients have the Services property.

Environment

The Environment property includes information about the client's environment strings. This information is useful as a starting point when determining how the client has configured the workstation.

For each environment string, attributes in Environment include Environment String and Value.

IRQ Table

The IRQ Table property includes information about each IRQ on the client user. This information is useful as a starting point when determining how the client system's hardware is configured.

For each entry (IRQ), the attributes in IRQ Table include IRQ Number, IRQ Address, Description, Detected, and Handled By. Not all clients will return IRQ Table properties.

Game Port

The Game Port property includes information about whether a game port has been installed in the client system. This information is useful as a starting point when determining whether to install games. Right, like games are part of the business environment? Well, actually, since game ports are also generally used for MIDI sound interfaces, this property does have a useful purpose.

Attributes in Game Port include Attribute and Value. Typically, Attribute is Game Installed, which when the Value is 1, tells us that the game port has been installed. Not all clients will return Game Port properties.

Queries

All the properties listed above are rather worthless unless the systems administrator is able to make use of them. I made it a point to list each attribute above as these attributes are the basis of the query component of SMS.

The main way to interface with the inventory is to perform a query. The SMS Administrator's Queries window, shown in Figure 16-8, shows that for SMS there are a total of nine built-in queries. The Queries window is opened by either clicking the toolbar's Query button or selecting File | Open from the menu and then clicking Queries in the Open SMS Window's Window Type list.

Figure 16-8 also shows that there is one added query (NIC type is NE2000), which was added to determine which workstations on the network were using an NE2000 type NIC. This added query will be described later in this section.

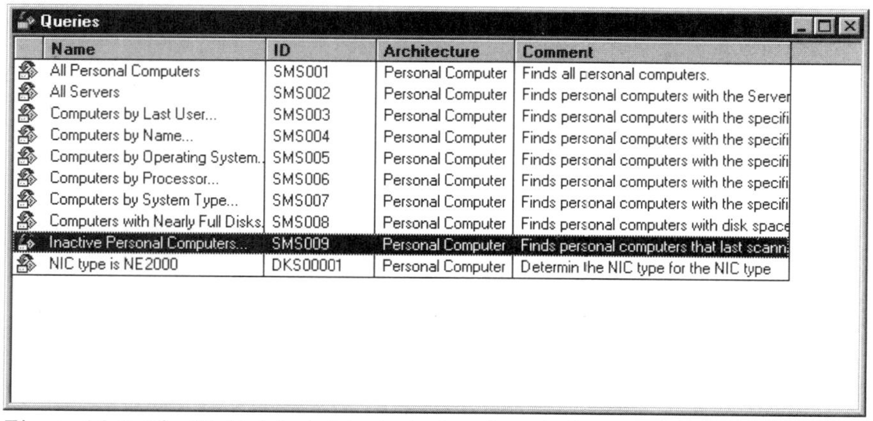

	Name	ID	Architecture	Comment
	All Personal Computers	SMS001	Personal Computer	Finds all personal computers.
	All Servers	SMS002	Personal Computer	Finds personal computers with the Server
	Computers by Last User...	SMS003	Personal Computer	Finds personal computers with the specifi
	Computers by Name...	SMS004	Personal Computer	Finds personal computers with the specifi
	Computers by Operating System.	SMS005	Personal Computer	Finds personal computers with the specifi
	Computers by Processor...	SMS006	Personal Computer	Finds personal computers with the specifi
	Computers by System Type...	SMS007	Personal Computer	Finds personal computers with the specifi
	Computers with Nearly Full Disks.	SMS008	Personal Computer	Finds personal computers with disk space
	Inactive Personal Computers...	SMS009	Personal Computer	Finds personal computers that last scann
	NIC type is NE2000	DKS00001	Personal Computer	Determin the NIC type for the NIC type

Figure 16-8: The SMS Administrator's Queries window.

Built-in Queries

The nine queries that are built into SMS server allow the systems administrator to perform basic management tasks:

- All Personal Computers will return a list of all personal computers on the network.

- All Servers will find all servers on the network. The server's type is not limited (if the Identification property's System Role attribute is Server, then this query will include the client).

- Computers by Last User returns a list of clients, where the username to be searched for must be specified. A username may have a wildcard specified (the % symbol) to broaden the search to a group that shares common attributes in the name field.

- Computers by Name returns a list of clients, where the computer name to be searched for must be specified. A computer name may have a wildcard specified (the % symbol) to broaden the search to a group that shares common attributes in the name field.

- Computers by Operating System returns a list of clients, where the operating system desired will be prompted for.

- Computers by Processor returns a list of clients, where the processor type desired will be prompted for.

- Computers by System Type returns a list of clients, where the system type will be prompted for.

- Computers with Nearly Full Disks returns a list of clients who have disks on which disk space in use exceeds the specified percentage.

- Inactive Personal Computers returns a list of clients who have not had a software or hardware scan since a specified time.

The built-in queries make a starting point for the systems administrator; however, to really use the power of the SMS inventory system, it will be necessary to create new queries.

Creating a Query

Queries are used to gather information about client systems, or to help categorize client systems. Creating a new query is a simple process, as much of the work is done by the SMS Administrator:

1. Open the SMS Administrator's Queries window (see Figure 16-8).

2. Select either the toolbar's New button or File I New from the SMS Administrator's menu. The Query Properties dialog box (Figure 16-9) will be displayed.

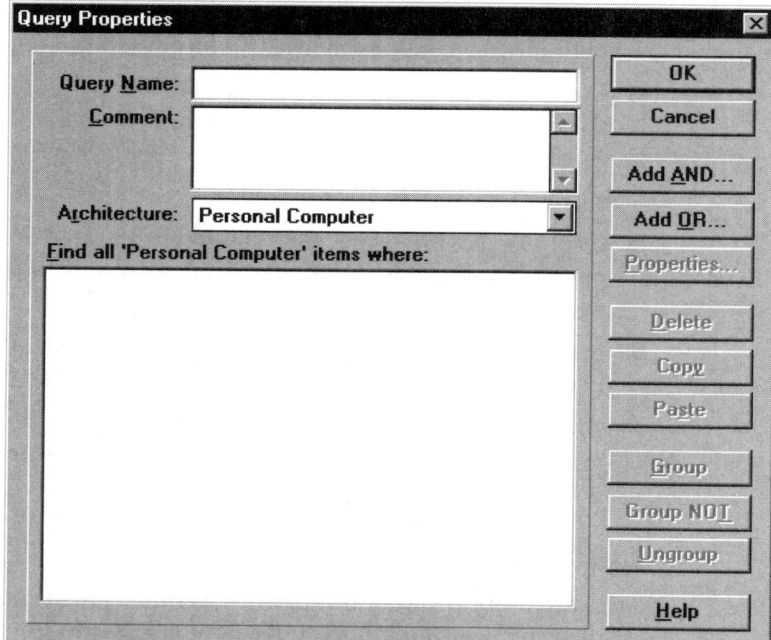

Figure 16-9: The SMS Administrator's Query Properties dialog—ready to create a new query.

3. Enter the Query Name and Comment information. The name should be meaningful, and the comment should describe both how to use the query (such as any parameters that will be prompted for) and the results of the query.

4. Select the architecture for the query from the Architecture drop-down list box. Many times the query will be simply Personal Computer. Other choices include Package Location, User Groups, Job Details, SMSEvent, and SNMP Traps.

5. Click the Add AND (or the Add OR, as appropriate) button to create the initial expression. In the Query Expression Properties dialog box (Figure 16-10), select a property from the column labeled Group and then select the property's attribute from the Attribute column.

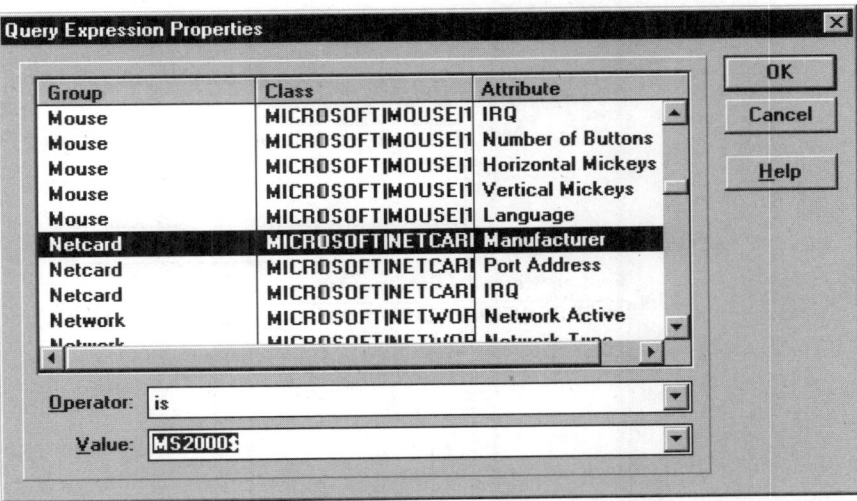

Figure 16-10: The Query Expression Properties dialog—create the query's limiting here.

7. In the Operator drop-down list, select an operator. Typical operators are is, is not, is like, and so on.

8. In the Value drop-down list, select a value. For most attributes, SMS will provide default values. A selection in the Value list allows for providing a prompt that will prompt for the value. For example, we could prompt for what NIC to search for in our example, too, rather than just searching for the Microsoft2000$-type NICs.

9. Click OK when you are done creating the expression.

10. Create any additional expressions by clicking either the Add AND or Add OR buttons. Expressions may have many AND- and OR-joined expressions, but realize that the order of evaluation is simple unless you create a grouping using the Group and Group NOT buttons.

11. When you are done adding expressions, the query should resemble the example shown in Figure 16-11. Click OK to save the query.

Once a query has been saved, the query may be edited by simply double-clicking it. The Query Properties dialog box (Figure 16-11, shown for the query described above) will be displayed.

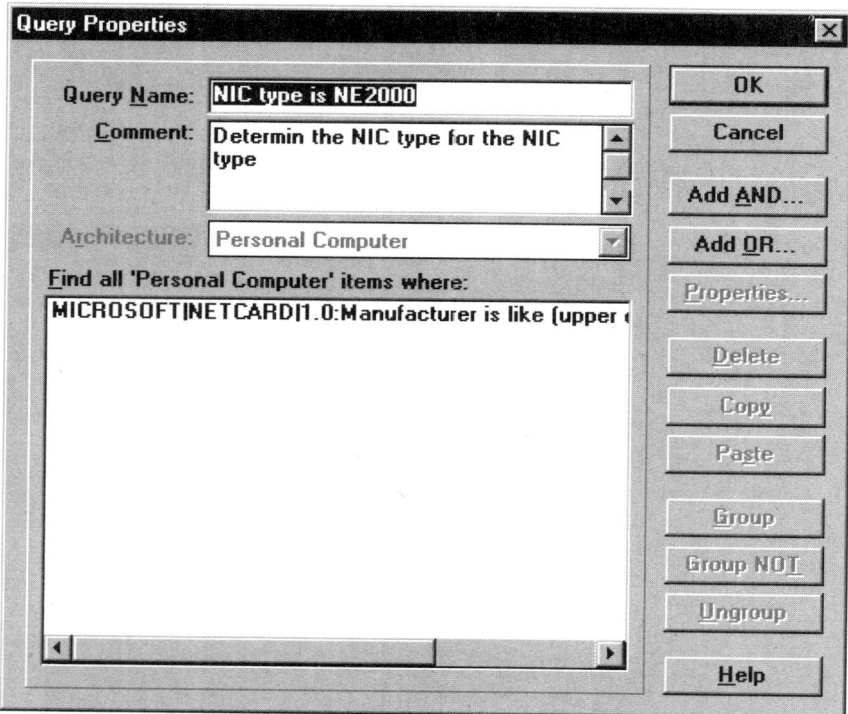

Figure 16-11: The Query Properties dialog box with an existing query loaded.

Any and all queries may be modified, including the queries supplied with SMS. A wise move will be to save the existing query to a new name and modify the copy. This will allow recovery if the modification does not perform as expected.

Using Queries

Once a query has been created, it may be used. There are numerous ways to use a query.

For example, a package (from the Package window) may be dragged and dropped onto the query (in the Query window). In this example, the query will be run, creating a list of client users who match the query's expression. This list of matching client users will then be sent the package as a job. Try it:

1. First, create a package. Open the Packages window and click the toolbar's New button.

2. In the Package Properties dialog, enter a package name and description.

3. Click the Workstations button to create the package's command line(s), the Sharing button to establish whatever sharing resources will be needed for the package's execution, and the Inventory button to configure any inventory rules.

4. Optionally, create a query, as described in the previous section, "Creating a Query."

5. Drag the package created in Step 1 from the Package window to the query (in the Query window). The Job Details dialog box (see Figure 16-12) will appear.

6. After setting the job's details (simply change those parameters who's defaults are not desired), click OK to save the changes. The Job Properties dialog box will appear.

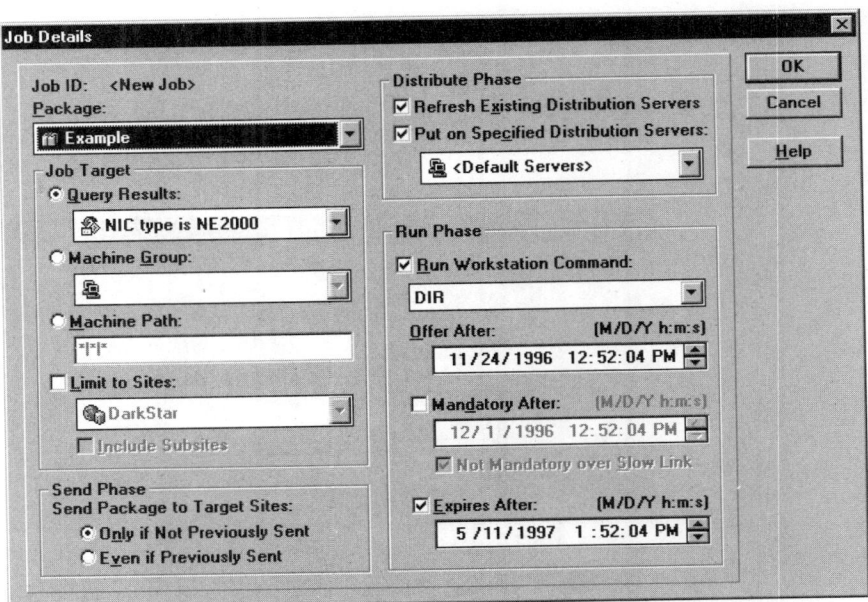

Figure 16-12: The Job Details dialog box: Change any parameters that may be inappropriate.

7. In the Job Properties dialog (Figure 16-13), which is typically hidden under the Job Details dialog box, fill in the job's comments.

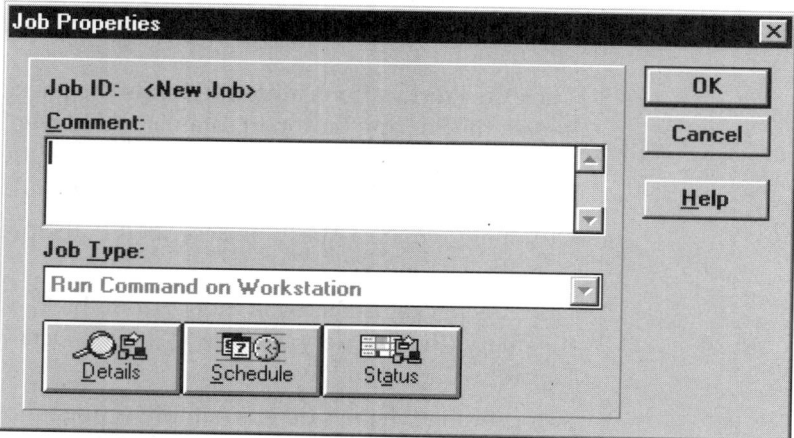

Figure 16-13: The Job Properties dialog box includes a text area to add a comment to describe a job.

■ Clicking the Details button will display the Job Details dialog box (Figure 16-12).

■ Clicking the Schedule button will display the Job Schedule dialog box (Figure 16-14).

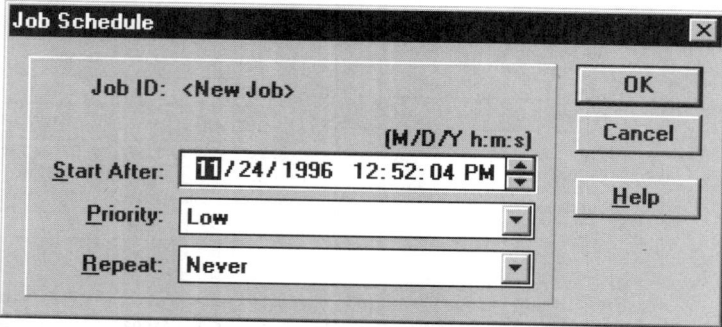

Figure 16-14: The Job Schedule dialog box—don't forget to set the priority if the job is important.

■ Clicking the Status button will display the job's status. For newly created jobs, the Job Status dialog box (Figure 16-15) will not display any details—the job has not yet been created!

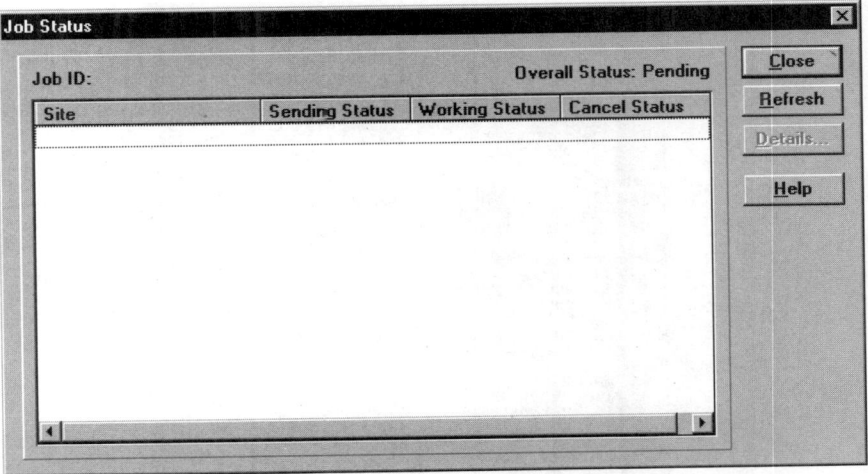

Figure 16-15: The Job Status dialog box—it's blank until the job is saved.

8. In the Jobs window, the newly created job will be displayed. Once a job has been created, the job's properties may be displayed by either selecting File | Properties or by pressing Alt+Enter.

Software Audits

The systems administrator uses software audits to determine what software has been installed on the client workstations. A software audit can be either explicitly defined as a package or by using the audit.cfg file, which is supplied with SMS.

Microsoft provides a file called audit.rul, which is a text-based file from which audit.cfg is created. audit.rul contains a list of over 5,000 software packages that are commonly found on PCs. It is easy to add new (or custom and in-house) applications to the end of the audit.rul file by following the format that exists in the file.

For example, the entry for Microsoft Office 7 is shown below in Figure 16-16.

```
Command 1 - x                                                              _ □ ×
    file "GR_BR.LEX" size 1200319 crc 469087 262145 56164
    file "GRAM.DLL" size 375296 crc 75059 225178 63528
    file "GRAMMAR.DOC" size 206848 crc 41369 124110 16026

package 5038 "Works for Windows 3.0b Australian Win3.x, Microsoft"
    file "WZFRMLTR.DLL" size 158944 crc 31788 95368 64204
    file "WZDBDES.DLL" size 146128 crc 29225 87678 59240
    file "WZLTRHD.DLL" size 100752 crc 20150 60452 64239

package 5039 "Access for Windows 95 7.0 English (USA) Win32 (NT/Win95), Microsof
    file "MSACCESS.EXE" size 2839552 crc 1288704 262145 28346
    file "MSAIN300.DLL" size 1135616 crc 436736 262145 36407
    file "MSACNV30.DLL" size 236800 crc 47360 142081 58456

package 5040 "Project for Windows 95 4.1 English (USA) Win32 (NT/Win95), Microso
    file "WINPROJ.EXE" size 3248912 crc 1493384 262145 52095
    file "PJJRNL32.DLL" size 4608 crc 921 2766 59211
    file "PJ41OLE.DLL" size 161280 crc 32256 96769 59140

package 5041 "Welcome 1.0 English (USA) Win3.x, Acme "
    file "SCOTT.TXT" size 38 crc 7 24 50561

package 5042 "Office for Windows 7.0 English (USA) Win32 (NT/Win95), Microsoft"
    file "MSOFFICE.EXE" size 365056 crc 73011 219034 55021
    file "BINDER.EXE" size 336896 crc 67379 202138 11884
    file "MSOW.EXE" size 46592 crc 9318 27956 22951

package 5043 "Access Developer's Toolkit  7.0 English (USA) Win32 (NT/Win95), Mi
    file "MSADT2.DLL" size 355328 crc 71065 213198 21803
    file "MSADT.EXE" size 40960 crc 8192 24577 64163
    file "MSADT1.DLL" size 37376 crc 7475 22426 41366

package 5044 "Internet Explorer 2.0 English (USA) Win32 (NT/Win95), Microsoft"
    file "IEXPLORE.EXE" size 755712 crc 246784 262145 55969
    file "RATASK.EXE" size 192304 crc 38460 115384 61560
    file "RA.DLL" size 129008 crc 25801 77406 19172

package 5045 "Excel for Windows 95 7.0a English (USA) Win32 (NT/Win95), Microsof
    file "EXCEL.EXE" size 4827648 crc 2282752 262145 66
    file "XLINTL32.DLL" size 595456 crc 166656 262145 24445
    file "XLKEY32.DLL" size 4608 crc 921 2766 31087

package 5046 "PowerPoint for Windows 4.0d English (USA) Win3.x, Microsoft"
    file "POWERPNI.DLL" size 3066240 crc 1402048 262145 4009
    file "POWERPNT.EXE" size 97056 crc 19411 58234 54417
    file "MSROUTE.DLL" size 39936 crc 7987 23962 62850

package 5047 "Visual FoxPro for Windows Professional 3.0b English (USA) Win3.x,
ctrl+end is not assigned to any editor function
g:\sms\primsite.srv\audit\audit.rul (text) Length=19784   Cursor=(19716,0) insert
```

Figure 16-16: Microsoft Office 7's rules.

The first line describes the product (referred to as a package):

- The keyword package specifies that this is the beginning of a new product description.

- The number (5042 in the example) is simply a sequential number. Add new products to the end of the audit.rul file (or create a new audit.rul file if the thousands of products that Microsoft's example audits are not useful to your environment).

- The final item, a quoted string, is the description of the product.

The next three lines describe three files that would always be present when Microsoft Office 7 is installed. Packages that you add may have fewer (or more) file lines; however, there must be one or more file lines to be searched for.

Each file line contains a number of parameters that the audit process uses to determine whether the file is indeed a component of the package. The reason that a number of parameters are needed is that some filenames are used for multiple products—checking a CRC (Cyclic Redundancy Checksum), file length, or another bit of information about the file can help determine whether the file is indeed part of the package to be audited. Possible items (called properties) in the file line include:

- **BYTE**—specifies a byte value that is known. The BYTE property requires a location and a value. The value must be between 0 and 255.

- **CHECKSUM**—specifies a start location, length, and a checksum for the specified area in the file.

- **CRC**—specifies a start location, length, and the CRC for the specified area in the file.

- **DATE**—the file's date.

- **LONG**—specifies a location and the long value (four bytes, 32-bits) for the location.

- **SIZE**—specifies the file's size, in bytes.

- **STRING**—specifies a location and a string that is found at the location. (More than one string may be specified.)

- **TIME**—specifies the file's time.

- **WORD**—specifies a location and the word value (two bytes, 16-bits) for the location.

OK, there are a vast number of ways to determine that a file is the file being searched for. However, each of these properties require that information be provided. For some properties, the value required is easy to obtain. DATE, SIZE, and TIME information is readily available: just use a DIR command to determine this information. Some of the other properties (such as CRC) require complex parameters that are not easily computed. For any file that is accessible to the systems administrator, it is possible to determine property values (easy or complex). Follow these steps:

1. Open the SMS Administrator's Package window.

2. Click either the toolbar's New button or select File I New from the SMS Administrator's menu.

3. In the Package Properties dialog, click the Inventory button. The Inventory dialog will appear. Click either the Add AND or Add OR buttons. The File Properties dialog (Figure 16-17) will appear.

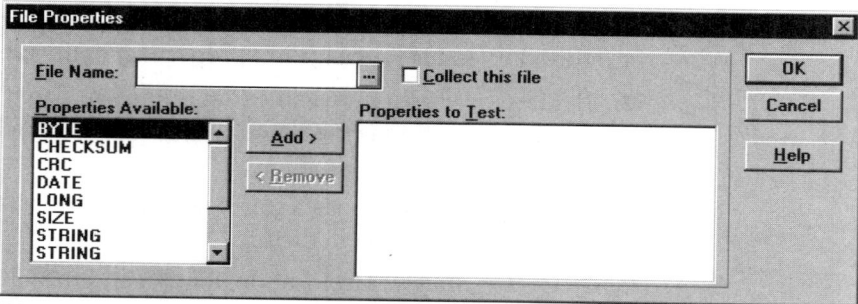

Figure 16-17: The File Properties dialog box—selecting a property to set to determine if this file is the correct one.

4. In the File Name text box, enter the name of the file to be searched for during the audit process. The search button (the button with the ellipsis) may be used to display a file find dialog box.

5. Select each property that will be used in the audit.rul file and click the Add button. A small dialog box will prompt for the property's values. For example, to find the CRC for a file, select CRC in the Properties Available list, click Add, and in the CRC-16 dialog box (Figure 16-18), enter a value in the At Byte text box (pick a meaningful location, one that has data that is unique to this version of the file). In the Length text box, put in a length parameter that will be sufficient to generate a meaningful CRC value. (Note that for a CRC, the longer the length, the more time it may take to perform the audit.) Next click Retrieve to have the SMS Administrator compute the CRC for the starting location and range specified. Jot these values down and then put them into the audit.rul file.

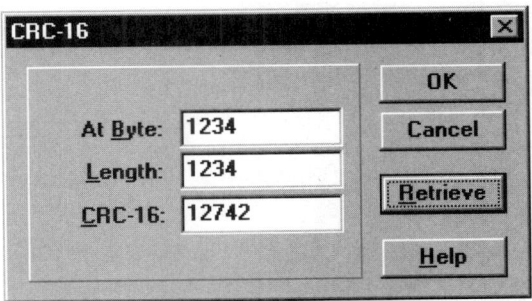

Figure 16-18: Setting the CRC-16 At Byte (starting location) and Length and then clicking Retrieve will fill in the CRC-16.

For many programs and applications, it is sufficient to check one, two, or three files.

Note: Always check the default Microsoft-supplied audit.rul file for the application before adding it again!

Once the audit.rul file is finished, it must be converted to the file audit.cfg. Use the supplied utility RUL2CFG.BAT to generate the audit.cfg file.

The final step to creating a software audit is to create a software audit package. This is done by importing the audit.pdf package definition file. Finally, create a Run Command On Workstation job (drag and drop the newly created audit package to a query in the Query window). Check the job's status in the Job Status window as needed.

Moving On

This chapter discussed the inventory features available with Microsoft SMS, such as automatic identification of server and client hardware and software and software audits.

In the next chapter, we will explain how to distribute and install software using Microsoft SMS.

17

Distributing & Installing Software With Microsoft SMS

This chapter deals primarily with Windows 95 client workstations. The differences between a Windows 95 workstation and a Windows NT workstation are slight, and the processes and procedures to distribute and install software are identical for either platform.

The concept of SMS software distribution and installation is to allow a package to be installed on any of a number of client workstations without the user having to actually have the software's distribution media on hand. In addition, SMS maintains security; were the systems administrator to simply place the application's distribution media online, any user could possibly access and install the application, regardless of whether the user was authorized or not.

There are a number of software distribution and installation tasks performed by SMS, including:

- Distribution and installation on remote workstations and servers. The systems administrator may, for example, drag and drop a package onto the target system.

- Allowing the systems administrator to specify the date and time that the software package will be installed on the client user's system.

■ Allowing a command to be scheduled that will run on a client workstation at the time specified by the systems administrator. Jobs of this type might include disk defragmentation, virus scanning, disk cleanup (deleting TMP files for example), or backup procedures.

Tip

After creating a job, the job may take some time for the SMS system to route to the client users. This delay is introduced by the scheduling used by SMS.

Overview of the Process

SMS manages software distribution and installation using the Packages, Jobs, Queries, and Sites features. Each feature is used when creating a software distribution package.

The first step in creating an installation (or performing virtually any other similar task) is to create a package.

Once a package has been created, the next step is to get the package to the client user. There are two methods to do this: either send it directly to a specific user, using the Sites window, or send it to a group of users based on the results of a search, using the Queries window.

Creating Packages

A package is an object that will be sent to a client workstation. For this chapter, let's define a package as a software installation. (Another type of package is an audit package, as described in Chapter 16.)

When a new package is created, the package's name and a comment describing the package must be specified. Each is found on the Package Properties dialog box (see Figure 17-1).

Note: When a new package is created, the ID field contains the symbol <New Package> rather than an actual package identifier.

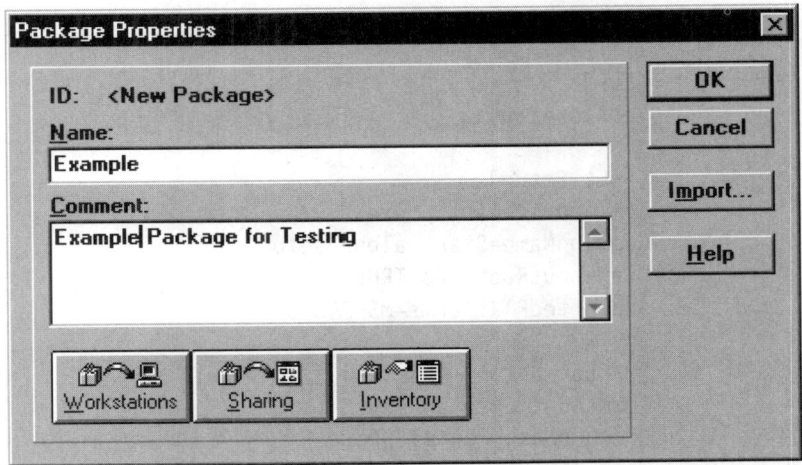

Figure 17-1: The Package Properties dialog box—fill in the Name and Comment text boxes for a new package.

If not importing a PDF file (see the next section), fill in the package's name and description. Imported PDF files contain default name and descriptions, which may be changed as needed.

Importing PDF Files

In the Package Properties dialog box, it is possible to import an existing PDF (Package Description File) file. Importing a package reads the PDF file and uses information in it to initialize the package.

What is a PDF file? Simply stated, a PDF file is a text file that contains information that is necessary to install a package. For example, the folder g:\sms\primsite.srv\import.src\enu contains PDF files for many of Microsoft's products, including the Microsoft Office suite, numerous versions of DOS and Windows, and other miscellaneous applications from Microsoft.

To understand what a PDF file contains, let's take a look at the PDF file (Listing 17-1) to install DOS 6.0. (This PDF file was chosen because it is short and simple!)

Listing 17-1: The dos60.pdf file.

```
[PDF]
Version=1.0

[FULL Setup]
CommandLine=setup.exe /H /G
CommandName=Stand alone setup
UserInputRequired=TRUE
SupportedPlatforms=MS-DOS 5.0

[Manual Setup]
CommandLine=setup.exe
CommandName=Manual Setup
UserInputRequired=TRUE
SupportedPlatforms=MS-DOS 5.0

[Package Definition]
Product=Microsoft DOS
Version=6.0
Comment=Microsoft DOS 6.0
SetupVariations=FULL, Manual
```

As the listing shows, the PDF file to install DOS 6.0 allows the user to select a manual or full setup (the difference is the command line argument; a full setup uses setup.exe with the /H and /G options). The two different setups are specified in the *SetupVariations* variable (see the last line in Listing 17-1). The next section, "Setting Up Packages on Workstations," describes the dos60.pdf.

PDF files are usually made available from the software company and are usually supplied with their products or available online. Do you ever create a PDF file? Sometimes, but not often. PDF files are usually created using tools that are beyond the scope of this book.

Clicking the Import button will display a File Browser dialog box where a PDF file may be selected. Select the applicable PDF file, which will initialize the package's contents.

Setting Up Packages on Workstations

Clicking the Workstations button on the Package Properties dialog box
will display the Setup Package for Workstations dialog box (Figure 17-2).
This step is necessary for all packages; it will be necessary to specify the
installation folder for imported packages.

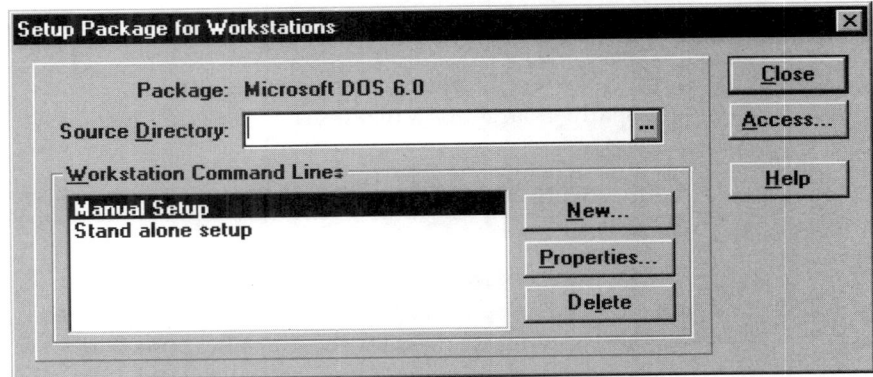

Figure 17-2: The Setup Package for Workstations dialog box.

In the Setup Package for Workstations dialog box, there is a space to
enter the source directory. In this text box, enter the location of the share
from which the installation is to take place. Enter a UNC share name in
the form of \\server\share Entering a local folder will probably cause
problems because the workstation will not have access to folders or
drives that are available on the server.

In the Workstation Command Lines list, it will be necessary to create
one or more commands for the client user. The example shown in Figure
17-2 shows two commands: *Manual Setup*, and *Stand alone setup*. Many
packages, however, will have only one command for the user.

The Program Item Properties dialog box (click Properties in the Setup
Package for Workstations dialog box) is where the Command Line is
defined. The command line that will be executed when the command is
selected and executed should be entered in the Command Line position,
being sure to enter any optional parameters. For those commands that do
not require any user input (the setup program will not be prompting for

any input, for example), check the Automated Command Line box. If in doubt, do not check the Automated Command Line box. For all commands, specify the platforms the command will support by clicking the check box for the platform. For example, if the command will only run under MS-DOS, then only check the MS-DOS check box. Test each command on each platform to make sure that there are no dependencies based on operating platform.

To display the Access dialog box, click the Access button. This dialog box lets you configure whether Users and Guests will have read or write access to the shared folder(s). The default is to grant both read and write access; however, limiting access to read-only may be a wise move, especially in larger organizations.

Configuring Shared Applications

Clicking the Sharing button in the Package Properties dialog box will display the Setup Package for Sharing dialog box (see Figure 17-3). The sharing options are used for those applications that are able to run from a shared network drive (in lieu of a locally installed application that runs from the client user's local drive). For shared applications, the systems administrator will install the application (with whatever applicable options are desired) on a network drive.

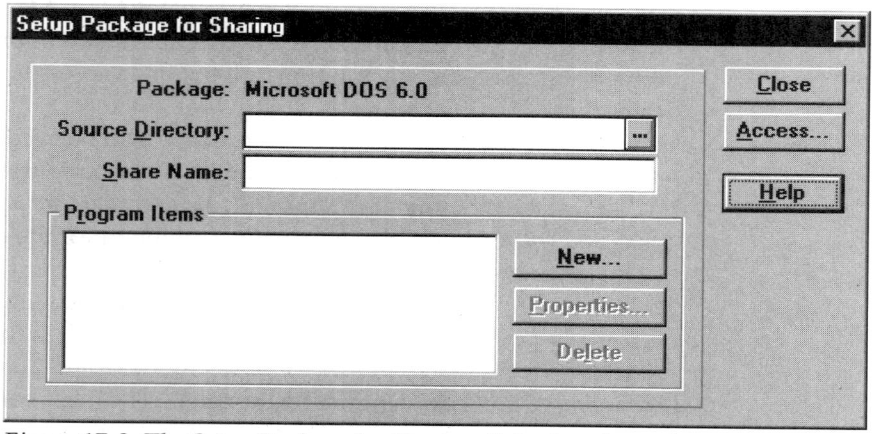

Figure 17-3: The Setup Package for Sharing dialog box for packages that are shared.

If the application is not being configured to run in a shared mode, then it is not necessary to configure the Setup Package for Sharing dialog box.

Tip

Many applications, when installed in a shared mode, require special setup or configuration. Consult the application's documentation for information about setting up the application as a shared program.

In the dialog box, the Source Directory text box will contain the name of the folder that contains the files that make up the package. Typically, this name will be in the form of a UNC share name.

The folder specified in the Source Directory must have been already shared by Windows NT 4 Server.

The Share Name specifies the name of the share that client users will be using to access the package when it is installed. A descriptive name is useful.

In the Program Items section, click Add (or New, if there are no existing Program Items) to add a new program item, using the Program Item Properties dialog box (see Figure 17-4). Each program item may include the application, a setup or configuration program, an icon, and registry information.

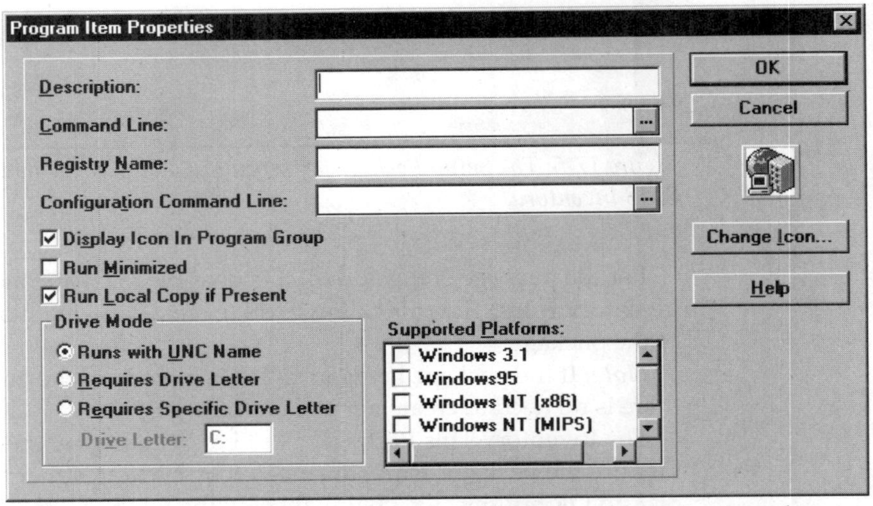

Figure 17-4: The Program Item Properties dialog box—for applications that run from the network.

Checking the Inventory

To configure an optional inventory package (refer back to Chapter 16 for more information about inventory processes), click the Inventory button on the Package Properties dialog box. The Setup Package for Inventory dialog box (see Figure 17-5) will be displayed.

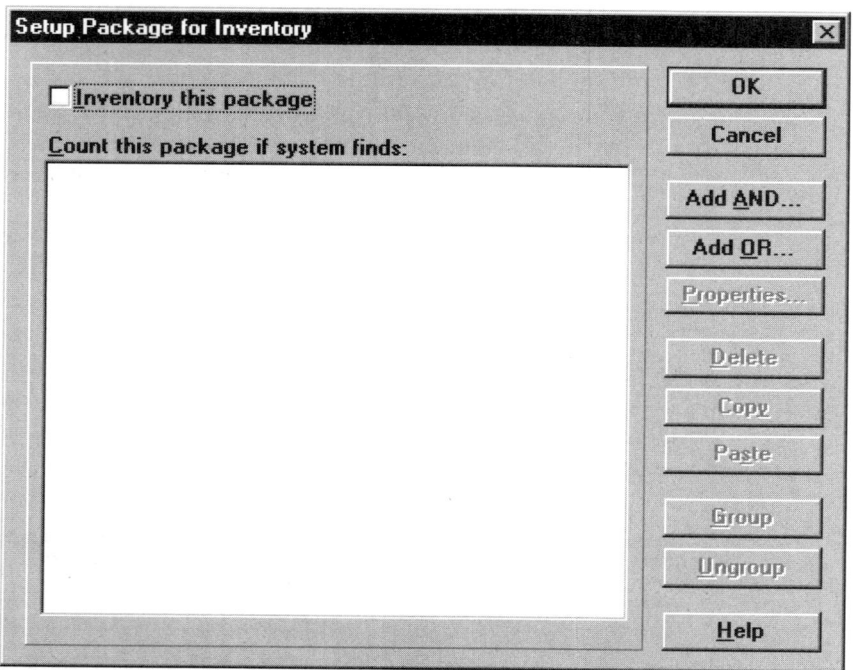

Figure 17-5: The Setup Package for Inventory dialog box adds the package to the SMS inventory.

For the package being added, it is possible to create one or more inventory rules. The rules allow SMS to create and maintain an inventory of the package.

Note: If the package being installed is already in the audit.rul file, then there is no need to create a new inventory rule set.

The Inventory This Package check box will display the rule used to identify the package. Rules are created by clicking either the Add AND or Add OR buttons, which will display the File Properties dialog box (see Figure 17-6).

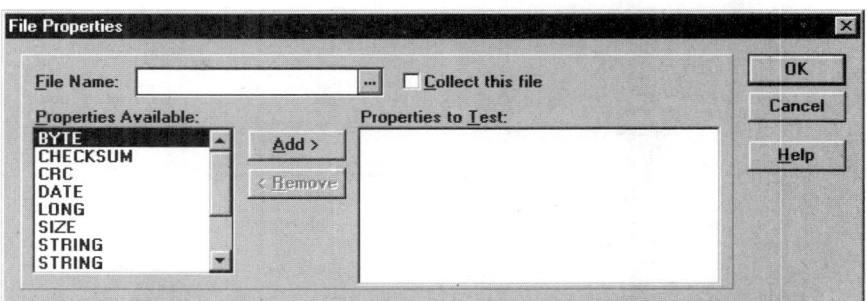

Figure 17-6: Adding properties to an inventory rule with the File Properties dialog box.

Select one or more properties, and provide values for them. Each property will have one or more values that must be filled in. SMS makes it easier to create properties: filling in known information for the location (and optional length) and then clicking the Retrieve button will initialize the necessary value.

Note: For string properties, inventory will want the location of a null-terminated character string. Unfortunately, there is no facility to retrieve a string's location with SMS—it is necessary to use other utilities to locate a string to use as a property.

Sending Packages

Once a package has been created, it may be sent to one or many client users. When sending the package to multiple client users, a query may be used to specify which client users will receive the package. The SMS Manager's Sites window (Figure 17-7) lists all sites that are clients to the specified SMS server.

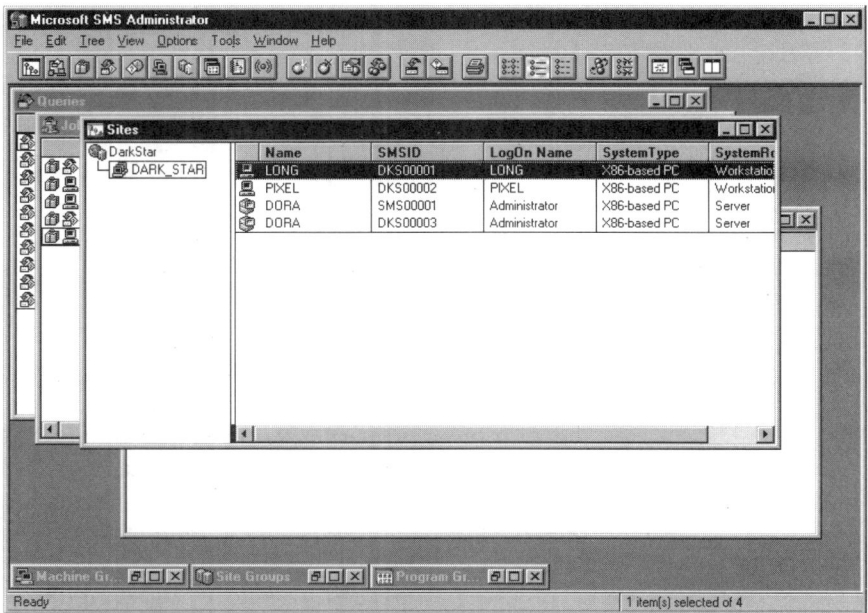

Figure 17-7: The SMS Manager's Sites window—drag and drop packages onto specific sites.

To send a package to a specific site, simply drag the package from the Packages window and drop it onto the site. A package may be dropped onto the domain as well, which will send it to all sites in the target domain.

It's as simple as that—well, almost. When you drop a package on a site or domain, you will have to enter the job's properties and details (or the defaults confirmed). Job properties and details are described in "Specifying Details" later in the chapter.

Sending Packages to Specific Users or Groups

SMS uses queries to limit actions to clients who meet certain specified criteria. For example, it would be unwise to attempt to install Microsoft Office 97 on a Windows 3.x-equipped PC—the program won't run on that platform. It would probably be unwise to attempt to install DOS utilities on Windows NT 4 workstations, too!

Queries are very closely related to inventories (inventories are the main topic of Chapter 16) in that a query is based on the inventory as it exists on the client user's system.

An inventory may consist of both hardware and software components; many queries are based on hardware components (you don't want to install a large, gangly software package on a client system that has only limited hard disk space). Inventory for software is also often a criterion; for example, when upgrading a package, the upgrade should only be sent to those client users that already have the application installed.

For more information about queries, please refer to Chapter 16.

Job Details

Jobs are tasks that must be done. OK, that is a bit harsh as definitions go, but basically it is true. Each job is going to run on one or more client user's machines. For a job, there is status information, time, priority, and other information that may be reviewed as desired.

In SMS, the Jobs window (see Figure 17-8) displays all jobs that exist (regardless of status, the job remains in the Jobs window until it has been deleted).

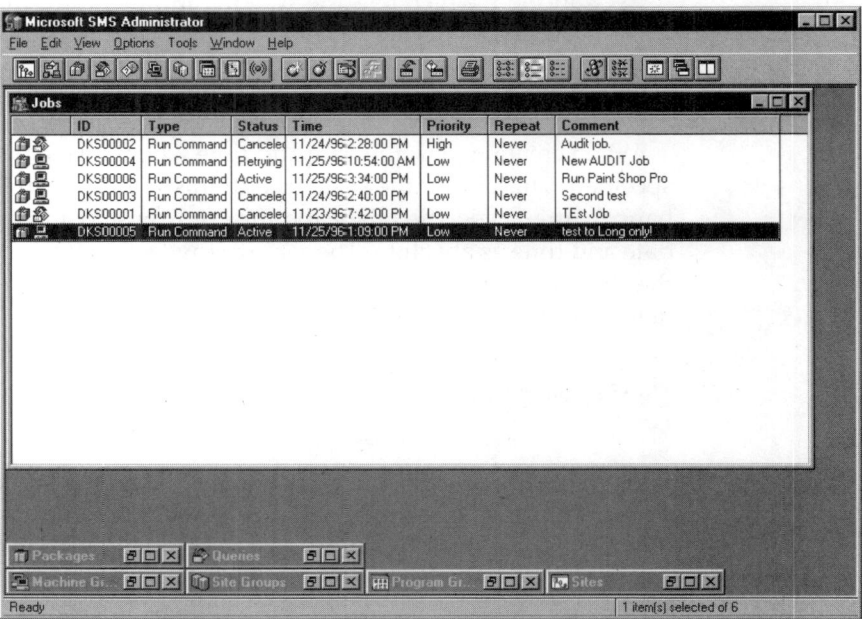

Figure 17-8: The SMS Manager's Jobs window.

As Figure 17-8 shows, details for a job include the job's ID, the type of job, status, time, priority, repeat, and comment information.

Setting the Job's Status

A job's status indicates exactly the state that the job is in at the time it is queried. Once a job has been created, it may not be altered. If an error is discovered in the job, then the job must be canceled, and a new, correct job must be created. The job's status may be:

- Pending, which tells the systems administrator that the client has not received the job at this time.

- Active, which tells the systems administrator that the client has received the job, the job is executing, and that there are currently no errors.

- Retrying, which tells the systems administrator that the job failed and is being retried.

- Complete, which tells the systems administrator that the job has completed successfully.

- Canceled, which tells the systems administrator that the job has been canceled.

- Failed, which tells the systems administrator that the job has failed and there is no attempt to retry the job pending.

When creating jobs, the date and time when the job will be run may be specified. This allows the systems administrator to plan for upgrades to happen after a specified date and time. It is wise not to consider the start date and time as absolute. There are many factors (including the fact that the client may simply not be available at the specified time) that will delay the start of a job.

Configuring Jobs

When created, jobs must be "configured." Dragging and dropping a package on a site or a query will display the Job Properties dialog box (Figure 17-9), and the Job Details dialog box shown in Figure 17-10. The Job Details dialog box must be completed to return to the Job Properties dialog box.

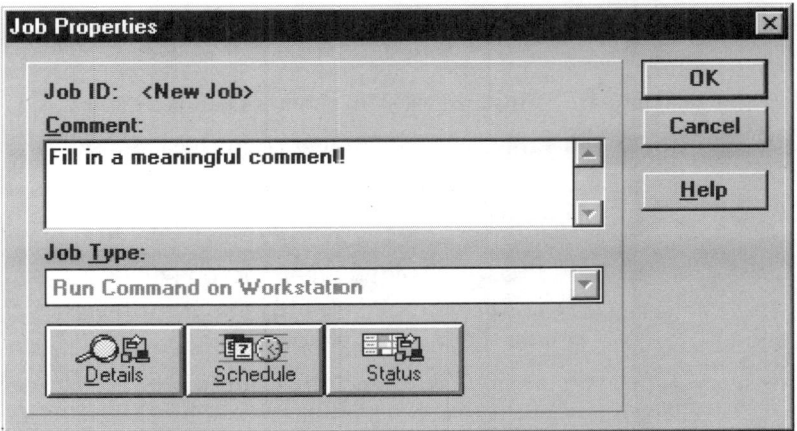

Figure 17-9: The Job Properties dialog box for setting details and schedule.

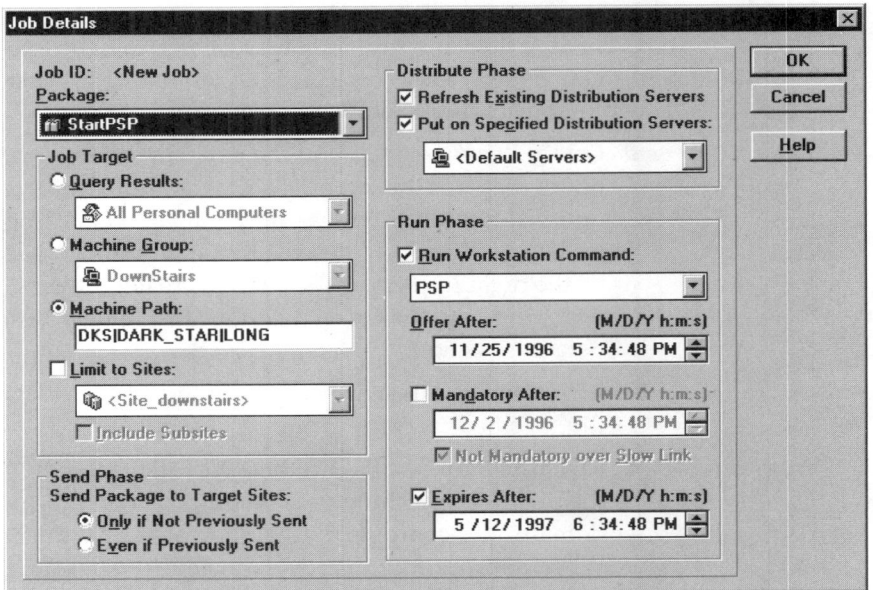

Figure 17-10: The Job Details dialog box for setting the job's details.

The Job Details dialog box is displayed automatically and must be completed before returning to the Job Properties dialog box. However, once the Job Details dialog box has been dismissed, it may be redisplayed by simply clicking the Details button on the Job Properties dialog box at any time before closing Job Properties.

Specifying Job Details

There are four main areas in the Job Details dialog box:

- **Job Target**—specifies where (which client users) the job will be sent.
- **Send Phase**—specifies how the job will be sent to the client user.
- **Distribute Phase**—specifies from where the job will be distributed.
- **Run Phase**—specifies when the job will be run on the client system. (Run Phase is related to scheduling, described in "Scheduling Jobs" later in this chapter.)

Once you are done with the Job Details dialog box, click the OK button. For many packages, the defaults created by SMS will be acceptable.

Job Target

There are four choices in the Job Target section of the Job Details dialog box. The first three are mutually exclusive, while the fourth (Limit to Sites) may be selected in conjunction with one of the first three choices. The four choices in the Job Target section are:

- **Query Results**—will send the job to the clients who match the query that was the target of a drag and drop of a package onto a query. If this job was created by dragging and dropping onto a site in the Sites window, then the first query in the Query window will be the default query. If the job was created by dragging and dropping onto the Query window, then Query Results is the default selection.

- **Machine Group**—will send the job to all sites that are members of the specified machine group.

- **Machine Path**—will send the job to all machines that are located in the path. The machine path is composed of three parts, the site, domain, and computer name, separated by vertical bar characters. When appropriate, an asterisk may be used as a wildcard to specify that all computers, domains, or sites are included. For example, the machine path DKS | * | * will send the job to all computers (clients) in all domains in the DKS site. The machine path dks | dark_star | * will send the job to all computers in the Dark_Star domain. The machine path of * | * | * will send the job to all computers that are part of the SMS system.

■ **Limit to Sites**—may be used with the above options to limit to certain sites based on sites or subsites. Check the Include Subsites check box to include any subsites beneath the site specified.

Regardless of how the job was created, the Job Target may be changed as desired. If you are creating a job for a specific client, and a decision is made that all clients, based on a search, should receive the job, then the job's target may be changed.

Send Phase

The Send Phase section of the Job Details dialog box allows the systems administrator to specify whether or not the job is sent to the recipient client site.

It is possible that the package may already have been sent to the client at some time in the past.

If the Only if Not Previously Sent button is checked, then the job will be sent to those clients that have not already received the package. Any clients who already have the package will not receive it. Select this option if your package has *not* changed.

If the Even if Previously Sent button is checked, then the job will be sent to all clients regardless of whether they may already have a copy of the package. Select this option if your package *has* changed, and must be updated at the client.

Distribute Phase

The two check boxes in the Distribute Phase section of the Job Details dialog box allow the systems administrator to specify how the package will be distributed.

The first check box, Refresh Existing Distribution Servers, determines whether or not the package will be replaced on the distribution servers where it already exists.

The second check box, Put on Specified Distribution Servers, specifies that the package will be added to the specified distribution servers.

The defaults for the Distribution Phase are for both options to be selected, which works well for virtually all jobs. Large jobs or complex SMS sites may require changing these options to minimize the amount of work done by the SMS servers.

Run Phase

The Run Phase section of the Job Details dialog box allow the systems administrator to specify when the package will be "run" on the client computers.

The job will be offered to the client users after the date specified in the Offer After box. Remember, client users may choose to not run this job immediately! The default for Offer After is the current date and time.

A job may be made mandatory after a certain time. Some client users may "procrastinate" and not run a job unless it is forced on them. This option will do just that. Generally, it is wise to give the users a reasonable voluntary time before resorting to mandatory acceptance of the job.

The Not Mandatory Over Slow Link check box allows SMS to defer mandatory jobs for users who are using slow network links (such as users on dial-up RAS links). It is generally a good choice for larger packages that are installing packages or must otherwise transfer large amounts of data over the network.

Expires After is used to specify that the job will expire after a certain period of time. This keeps an old job, which is really no longer desirable, from becoming active on a client system years in the future. The default is six months, though a shorter period before the expiration date may be more appropriate for many SMS sites.

After configuring (or reviewing) the job, click OK to close the Job Details dialog box.

Scheduling Jobs

The Job Schedule dialog box (Figure 17-11) is displayed when the Job Properties dialog box's Schedule button is clicked. Three scheduling options may be set in the Job Schedule dialog box:

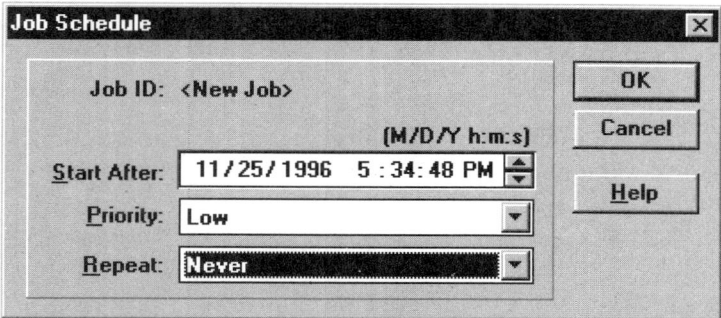

Figure 17-11: Setting a job's schedule with the Job Schedule dialog box.

- **Start After**—lets you specify when the job will be started. Realize that this is start *after*, not start *on*! Client users may choose to defer the execution of the job until a later time.

- **Priority**—lets you set the job's priority as Low, Medium, or High. Setting a high priority may consume more resources, however. The default priority is Low.

- **Repeat**—lets you create a job that will repeat at regular intervals. This allows creating jobs that perform routine tasks such as disk cleanup, virus scans, or backup tasks that will run automatically at the specified date(s) and times. For example, it would be an easy task to create a virus scan that runs every Friday evening. The default repeat rate is Never.

Any job (such as one created with a repeat) may be canceled if the job is no longer needed.

Checking the Status of a Job

The Job Status dialog box is displayed when the Job Status button (in the Job Properties dialog box, Figure 17-9) is clicked. When creating new jobs, there is no information displayed in the Job Status dialog box, and there are no options or actions other than to dismiss the dialog box.

Using the Package

When a client receives a package, the Package Command Manager will automatically display the package for the user (see Figure 17-12). The user may then choose to:

- See details about the job that the user may use to determine if the job should be run at the current time, or perhaps be run later. Jobs are often deferred if the user feels that current work in progress may be affected by running the job.

- Execute the job, which will cause the commands that are defined in the job to be executed

- Archive the job, which will place the job in an archive where the user may, at a later time, retrieve the job for execution.

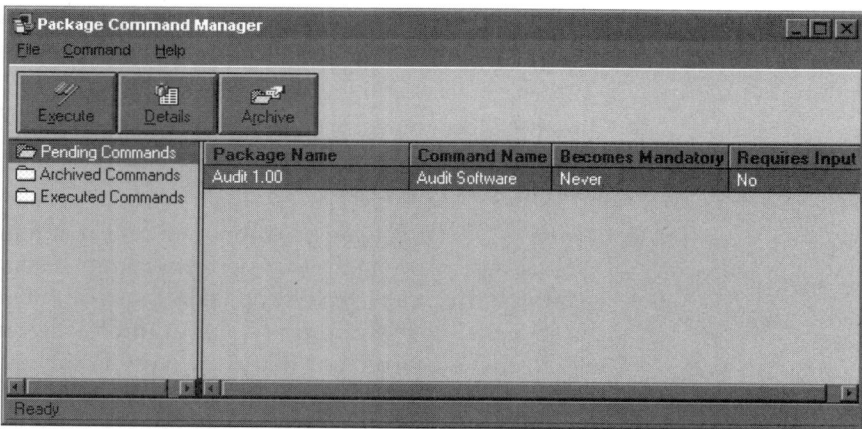

Figure 17-12: The client's Package Command Manager with a pending job called Audit 1.00.

Generally, users have flexibility about when a job is run (after all, it is their computer).

Moving On

This chapter introduced Microsoft SMS's software distribution and installation facilities. These features are very valuable when hundreds or thousands of copies of a software package must be installed. SMS will manage both locally installed (running from the Workstation's local drive) and network-based applications.

Automated installations are made easy when a PDF file is available, either as supplied with SMS (for many Microsoft products) or with the software application.

In the next chapter, we will cover the Microsoft SMS Server's remote control and in-house customer service.

## 18

Controlling Workstations Remotely With Microsoft SMS

In this chapter, we describe Microsoft SMS (Systems Management Server) version 1.2 remote control facilities. With remote control, it is possible for the SMS administrator to perform diagnostic tasks remotely and "take control" of a client workstation, with all of the workstation's input and output being redirected to the systems administrator.

This chapter deals primarily with Windows 95 client workstations. While the differences between a Windows 95 workstation and a Windows NT workstation are slight, and the processes and procedures that utilize remote control are similar, you will find that Windows NT workstations are more consistent when running SMS Remote Control and Remote Diagnostic software.

Most of the remote diagnostic functionality is not available when working with Windows NT clients. Apple Macintosh clients are similarly not supported either for remote diagnostics or for use with remote control.

There are a number of tasks performed by SMS Remote Control and Remote Diagnostics, including:

- Remote control of the input (via a virtual keyboard) and display of the screen's contents on the systems administrator's computer.

- Remote gathering of information useful for diagnosing problems. Information about the hardware and operating system may be obtained using the Help Desk facility.

- Monitoring of client performance and events.

Tip

Well . . . Remote Control and Remote Diagnostics are perhaps the parts of SMS that are the most difficult to use and configure. Additionally, there seem to be many, many problems using Remote Control and Remote Diagnostics with Windows 95 computers. If your client Windows 95 systems do not respond well to Remote Control and Remote Diagnostics, consider local techniques instead.

Installation of the basic SMS client software will install all components that are needed for both Remote Control and Remote Diagnostics. However, each client user who will be the subject of Remote Control or Remote Diagnostics must also run the Remote Control agent, found in the client's Start Menu | Programs | SMS Client | Remote Control.

Diagnosing Possible Problems

If the Remote Control agent does not start, it will be necessary to diagnose the problem locally. I've found that there is a great deal of sensitivity to which NIC is installed in the workstation. In most Windows 95 clients on the Dark_Star domain, there are generic, el cheap-o NE-2000-clone NICs. We are talking some of the cheapest NICs available (they typically cost about $20-$30 each). These cards work fine for all purposes; the sole exception is SMS Remote Control. It took a valuable day's testing and work to determine that the NIC was the problem and 10 minutes to replace the NIC with a more compatible one!

Diagnosing problems with Remote Control can be an exercise in frustration; there is little documentation or other written help that tells what to do when something goes wrong. However, should there be client workstations that are not properly functioning, check the following:

- In the client workstation's SMS installation folder (typically installed on the drive with the most free space) is a subfolder of log files (\MS\SMS\LOGS). Check each log file for errors—all these logs are simple text format files and may be edited with any text editor.

- Uninstall, then reinstall the client software. Before running the runsms.bat file to install the SMS client software, define the environment variable SMSSL=1. To set this environment variable, use the command:

```
set SMSSL=1
```

This environment variable will enable a verbose mode for the SMS client installation routines. Check all messages as they are displayed for errors and problems. It may be a good move to print the screen during various stages of the installation process.

- Remember that Windows 95 does not require the USERTSR or USERIPX TSR programs that are used with MS-DOS and Windows 3.1. Don't try to install these files manually on the Windows 95 platform. If Windows 95 was installed as an upgrade over Windows 3.1x, uninstall the SMS client and reinstall it.

- Sometimes the Remote Control component will not run with Windows 95 clients. Be prepared for the possibility that there may be machines that simply will not work correctly with SMS Remote Control.

Note: Remember, Remote Control will not run if the client Remote Control agent is not running on the client workstation. If there are problems, always check first to ensure that the Remote Control agent is running (and did not fail, producing an error message).

Client Configuration

Prior to using either Remote Control or Remote Diagnostics, it is necessary to configure the client workstation. The configuration process is relatively simple—often doable by the client user.

There are three distinct steps to configuring Remote Control and Remote Diagnostics:

1. The SMS client software must be installed on the workstation. Using runsms.bat will install all necessary components needed to use basic SMS facilities, and runsms.bat will install the core support for Remote Control and Remote Diagnostics. Once runsms.bat has configured the workstation, a call will be added to the workstation's autoexec.bat file, which will call the SMS client batch file, client.bat. The client.bat file will then install the basic SMS client software each time the workstation is booted.

2. The client Remote Control agent program (Start Menu | Programs | SMS Client | Remote Control) must be running on the client. If Remote Control or Remote Diagnostics are to be run often, then the best method to ensure that the client Remote Control agent program is running is to establish a link to it in the client's Start Menu | Programs | StartUp folder. This link will then

run the client Remote Control agent program each time the workstation is started. The client Remote Control agent program does not consume many resources, so the user should not notice any degradation in the way that their workstation performs.

The easiest way to ensure that the client Remote Control agent is always running on the client system is to drag a copy of the client Remote Control agent shortcut from the SMS Client folder to the StartUp folder.

3. The Help Desk Options program (Figure 18-1 is for a Windows 95 client; Figure 18-2 is for a Windows NT client) must be run, and the options to allow Remote Control and Remote Diagnostics to be utilized must be enabled. For security reasons, these options are turned off by default.

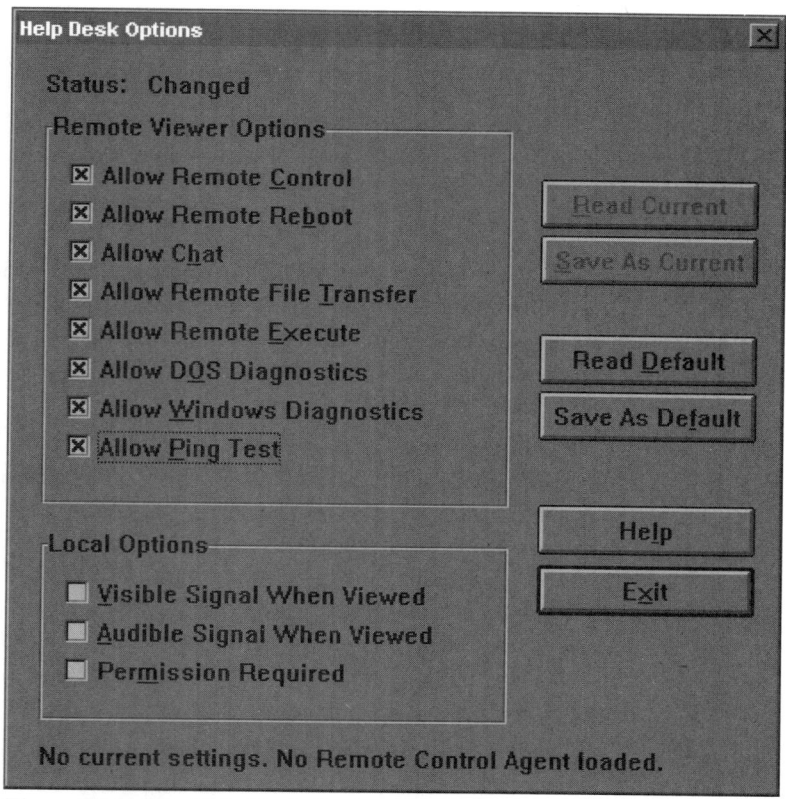

Figure 18-1: The Help Desk Options dialog box for a Windows 95 client.

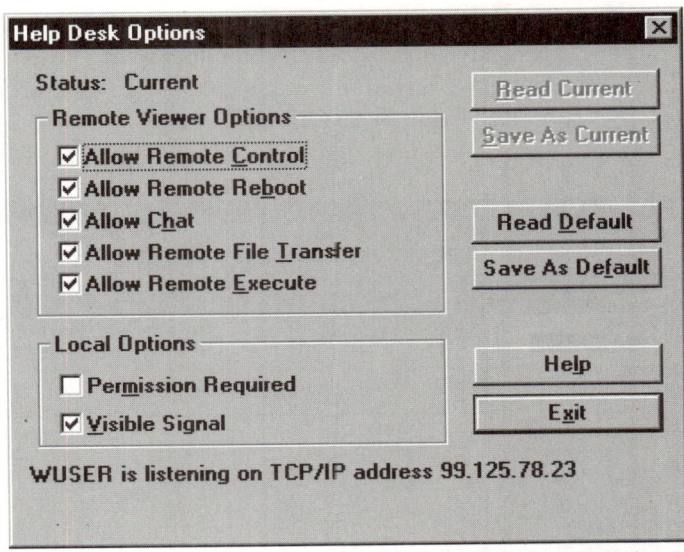

Figure 18-2: The Help Desk Options dialog box for a Windows NT client.

The differences between a Windows 95 client and a Windows NT client is that the Windows NT clients do not support Remote Windows Diagnostics, Remote DOS Diagnostics, and the PING Test, and Windows NT does not support an audible signal when Remote Control is active.

As shown in Figures 18-1 and 18-2, each of the Remote Control and Remote Diagnostics options must be set before the systems administrator will be able to perform the particular task.

Help Desk

The Help Desk options allow the systems administrator to "take control" of the client workstation. There is no magic here; to use the SMS remote control facilities, just:

1. Start the SMS Manager (Start Menu | Programs | Systems Management Server | SMS Administrator).

2. Open the Sites window (File | Open from the menu; then select Sites in the Window Type list or click the Sites button on the toolbar).

3. Expand the site tree, as shown in the example in Figure 18-3. This figure shows the DarkStar site, with four computers. (Our example workstation for this chapter is Pixel, a 75 MHz 486 running Windows 95 OEM-SR2.)

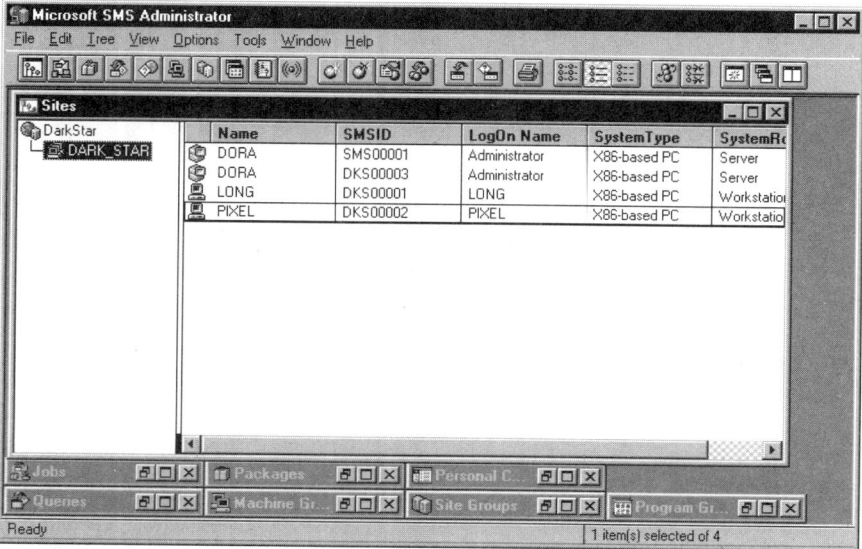

Figure 18-3: The DarkStar site expanded to show all clients.

4. Display the properties for the desired client user by selecting the user in the user list (the right-hand pane of the Sites window) and either double-clicking the client user or pressing Alt+Enter.

5. The user's Properties dialog box will be displayed (as shown in Figure 18-4). Scroll down the Properties list until the Help Desk property icon is visible, and then click Help Desk.

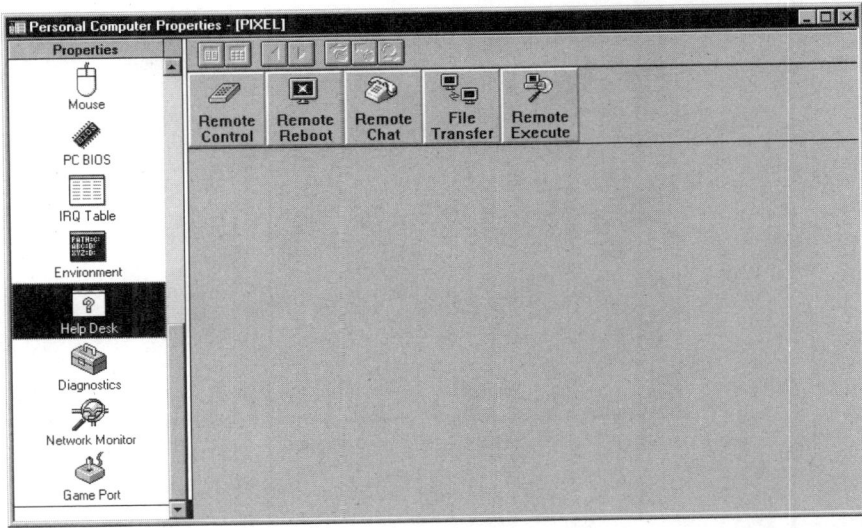

Figure 18-4: A user's properties displayed.

Once the Help Desk properties have been displayed, the systems administrator has five choices that allow him or her to perform a number of different functions.

Remote Control

Remote Control lets the systems administrator "take control" of a client workstation. The process is simple; click on the Remote Control button to display a window showing the screen of the client workstation, as the example in Figure 18-5 shows. The window that shows the remote session is called the Quick Windows Viewer and has a special border (yellow and black), making this window immediately visible on the administrator's system.

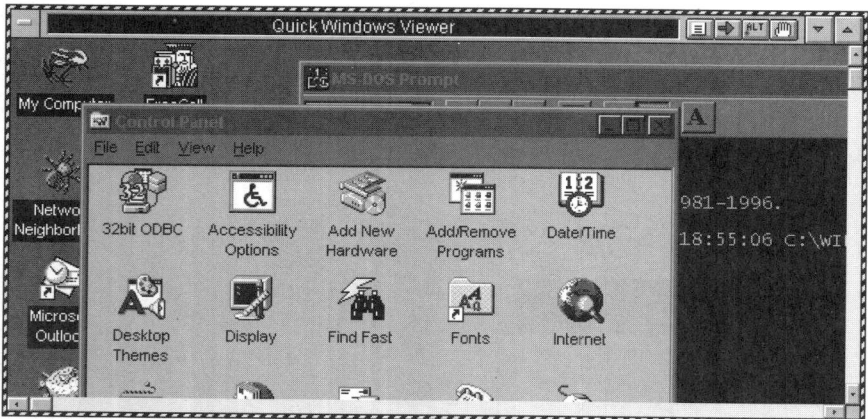

Figure 18-5: Remote Control takes over the client workstation.

Getting Around the Quick Windows Viewer

Whenever the Quick Windows Viewer window has focus, all keyboard input (except for special keys, such as Alt and the Windows key) will be sent to the remote client workstation. In addition, whenever the mouse is over the Quick Windows Viewer, the mouse input will also be sent to the remote client workstation. From the remote client's viewpoint, this input is identical to the input that a local user would provide.

Note: Any time that the remote control session is active, the workstation's user is also able to provide input to the workstation using the locally attached keyboard and mouse. Be careful that the systems administrator who is running the remote control session and the local user don't enter conflicting commands or otherwise interfere with each other!

Figure 18-5 is an example of a remote control session showing a Windows 95 client's screen (with both the Control Panel and a DOS session partially visible). Also visible on the Quick Windows Viewer window is a title bar (very similar to a standard Windows 3.x title bar), a System Menu button on the left, and six buttons on the right:

■ The leftmost button (containing the image of a box with three horizontal lines) in the group of four buttons on the right side of the Quick Windows Viewer displays the client workstation's system menu. Clicking this button simulates the pressing of the Windows key found on keyboards that are compatible with the Microsoft Natural Keyboard. The system menu may then be navigated using the tab and arrow keys.

- The second button from the left (containing the image of a right-pointing arrow) in the group of four buttons on the right side of the Quick Windows Viewer displays the client workstation's Task window. Clicking this button simulates the pressing of Alt+Tab. Once the Task window has been displayed, it may be navigated using the tab and arrow keys.

- The third button from the left (containing the word ALT and a small red dot) in the group of four buttons on the right side of the Quick Windows Viewer toggles the system key pass function. When active, this function allows certain system keystrokes to be passed to the client workstation.

- The last button (containing the drawing of a hand) in the group of four buttons on the right side of the Quick Windows Viewer activates the zoom tool. When active, the Zoom window is displayed, allowing the systems administrator to quickly select the section of the client workstation's display to be shown in the Quick Windows Viewer.

Note: If you are using Microsoft's Intellimouse software, certain strange effects may be seen in the Zoom window, including a tendency for the mouse cursor to try and jump out of the Zoom window. Either disable the Intellimouse drivers or just keep trying to keep the mouse cursor in the Zoom window; it can be done with a bit of practice.

- The final two buttons in the Quick Window Viewer (on the far right) are the Minimize and the Maximize/Normal buttons found in most Windows programs.

Configuring the Quick Windows Viewer

The Configure selection in the Quick Windows Viewer's system menu displays the Control Parameters dialog box, as shown in Figure 18-6.

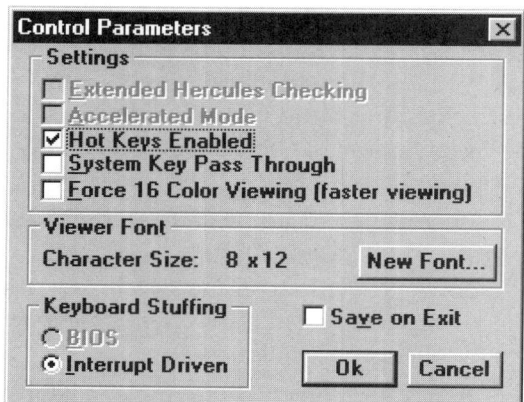

Figure 18-6: The Control Parameters dialog box sets the remote control session's configuration.

There are three sections in the Control Parameters dialog box: Settings, Viewer Font, and Keyboard Stuffing.

The Settings section lets you set options for the session such as:

■ Extended Hercules Checking lets you use workstations that are equipped with Hercules video systems. This option is necessary for Hercules systems and will impact system performance. The Extended Hercules Checking option is disabled (grayed out) if a Hercules video system is not detected.

■ Accelerated Mode supports improved video performance in the Quick Viewer Window for MS-DOS clients. The Accelerated Mode option is disabled (grayed out) if an MS-DOS session is not being controlled.

■ Hot Keys Enabled lets you process hotkeys. See "Using the Quick Windows Viewer" later in the chapter for more information about hotkeys.

■ System Key Pass Through lets you enable and disable the passthrough of system key sequences.

■ Force 16 Color Viewing changes the display of the client in the Quick Windows Viewer window to be in 16 colors (regardless of the number of colors being displayed by either the client workstation, or the systems administrator's computer). This option improves performance by minimizing the amount of video information passed through the network. This option is only available with clients who are running Windows.

The Viewer Font section has a single button, which if clicked will allow the viewer's current font to be changed. This allows the systems administrator to display more information (which may be less legible) by using a smaller font than the default. This option is not available for Windows NT clients.

The Keyboard Stuffing section lets you define how keystrokes are placed into the client workstation's input queue. Using the Interrupt Driven option more closely emulates the actual hardware, while the BIOS selection may provide better performance. The BIOS selection is disabled for both Windows 95 and Windows NT clients.

When done setting the configuration, Save on Exit may be selected to save the settings for future sessions. Click OK (or Cancel) to terminate the Control Parameters dialog box.

Using the Quick Windows Viewer

The Hot Keys selection in the Quick Windows Viewer's system menu displays the Hot Keys dialog box, as shown in Figure 18-7.

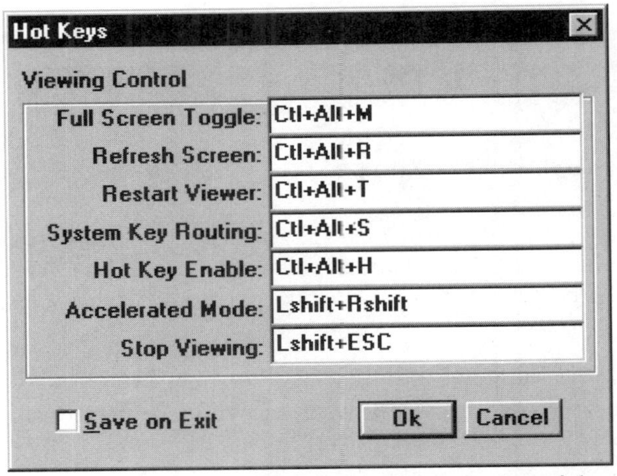

Hot Keys	
Viewing Control	
Full Screen Toggle:	Ctl+Alt+M
Refresh Screen:	Ctl+Alt+R
Restart Viewer:	Ctl+Alt+T
System Key Routing:	Ctl+Alt+S
Hot Key Enable:	Ctl+Alt+H
Accelerated Mode:	Lshift+Rshift
Stop Viewing:	Lshift+ESC

☐ Save on Exit   Ok   Cancel

Figure 18-7: The Hot Keys dialog allows setting of the various hotkeys used in the Quick Windows Viewer.

There are seven Viewing Control settings available to the systems administrator in the Hot Keys dialog box. The settings are self-explanatory. It may be a good idea to write down for future reference the various hotkeys available.

When you are done setting the hotkeys configuration, Save on Exit may be selected to save the settings for future sessions. Click OK (or Cancel) to terminate the Hot Keys dialog box.

The Status History selection in the Quick Windows Viewer's system menu displays a dialog that contains a history list.

To use the Quick Windows Viewer, simply point and click or use the keyboard. Anything that a local user might be able to do may be done from the Quick Windows Viewer.

Ending a Quick Windows Viewer session is as simple as clicking on the Quick Windows Viewer's system menu and selecting Close.

Remote Reboot

The Remote Reboot button allows the systems administrator to reboot the client machine. The reboot is processed after a confirmation message (Figure 18-8) to the systems administrator. The process is simple; click on the Remote Reboot button (in the Help Desk property, see Figure 18-4) to reboot the client workstation.

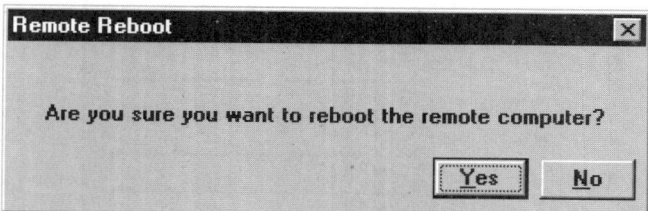

Figure 18-8: A reboot request must be confirmed.

The SMS Manager will then display a confirmation in the Personal Computer Properties window, as shown in Figure 18-9.

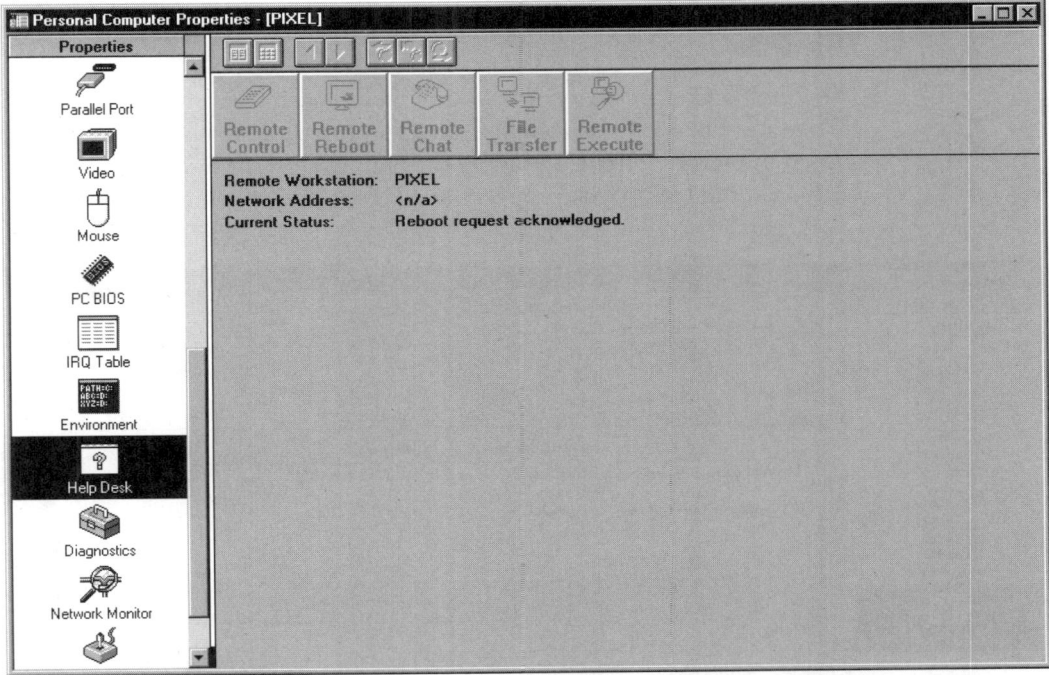

Figure 18-9: The reboot was confirmed by the workstation.

Warning

Danger, Will Robinson, danger!

Do not select Remote Reboot for Windows 95 clients. The remote reboot does not properly shut down the system; rather it forces a reboot. Windows 95 does not always react well to being shut down improperly.

Rather than selecting Remote Reboot for a Windows 95 client, instead open a remote control session and select Shut Down from the Start Menu. Then select Restart the Computer in the Shut Down Windows dialog box, which will be displayed.

Remote Chat

The Remote Chat selection allows a two-way, written conversation to be carried out between the systems administrator and the client user, as shown in Figure 18-10. Chatting is simple; click on the Remote Chat button (in the Help Desk property, see Figure 18-4) to start a chat session.

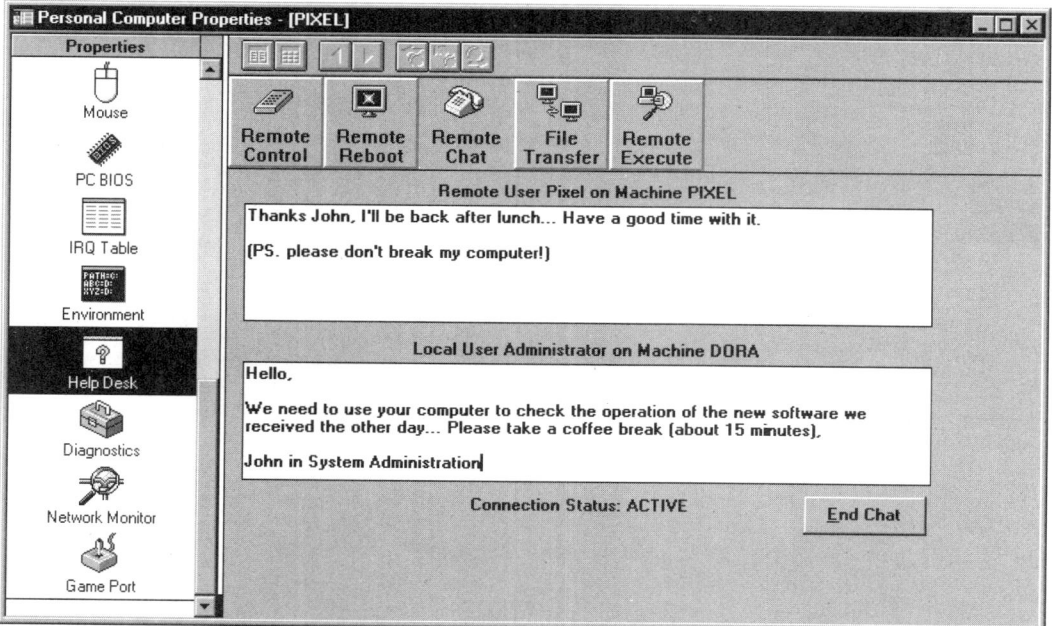

Figure 18-10: Remote chat is useful to tell the client user something—it is real-time and written.

Though Remote Chat is not a replacement for either the telephone or e-mail, a remote chat session is just the trick to getting a quick reply.

Note: Don't forget that with Remote Chat, the Windows clipboard may be used to cut and paste into the chat windows. This might allow the systems administrator to send a complex command sequence that the user may need or allow the user to paste in an error message to send to the systems administrator.

File Transfer

The File Transfer selection allows for files to be copied to and from the client user's drives. Working in a manner similar to FTP, it is necessary to select the file and the file's destination in the file transfer window, as shown in Figure 18-11. The process is simple; click on the File Transfer button (in the Help Desk property, see Figure 18-4) to start the file transfer process.

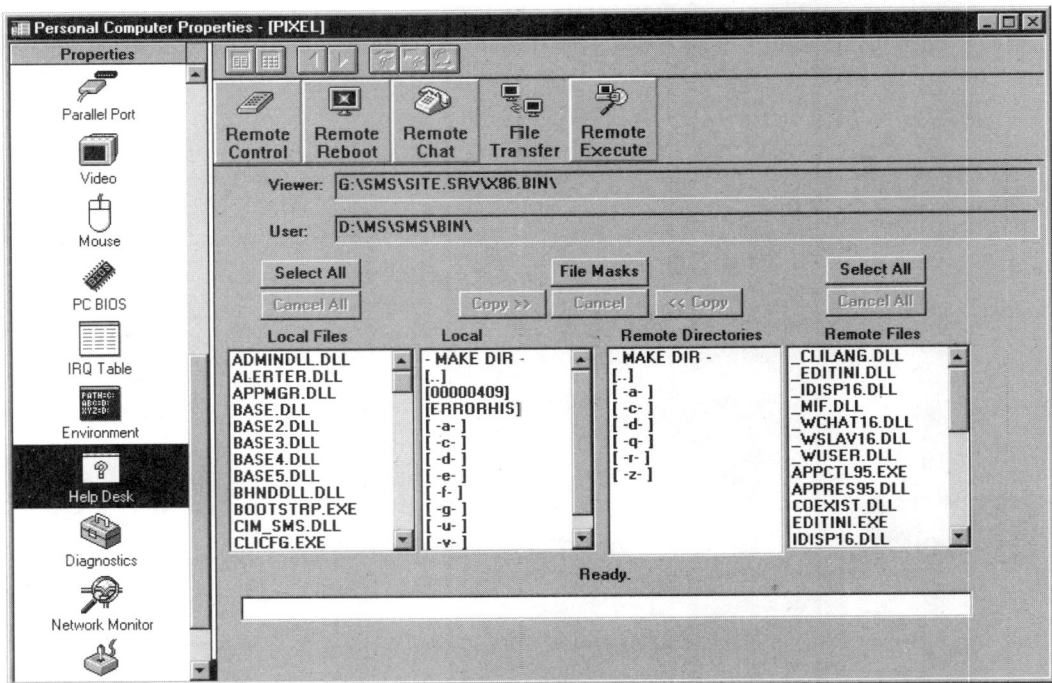

Figure 18-11: File transfer is useful to either send or get files.

Anything that the File Transfer selection is able to do may also be done using shares, if available. The File Transfer selection is very useful when the workstation has not shared the local hard drive.

Remote Execute

If there is a need to execute a single command (or two), then using
Remote Execute is a quick way to do so. Faster and easier to use than
Remote Control, Remote Execute allows a single command (either a DOS
command or a Windows application) to be entered. The effect of running
Remote Execute is the same as if the command was entered in the
Windows Run window. The process is simple; click on the Remote
Execute button (in the Help Desk property, see Figure 18-4) to execute a
command remotely on the client workstation.

Figure 18-12 shows the results of running a command on the client
workstation. When Remote Execute is selected, a dialog box will prompt
for the command to be executed.

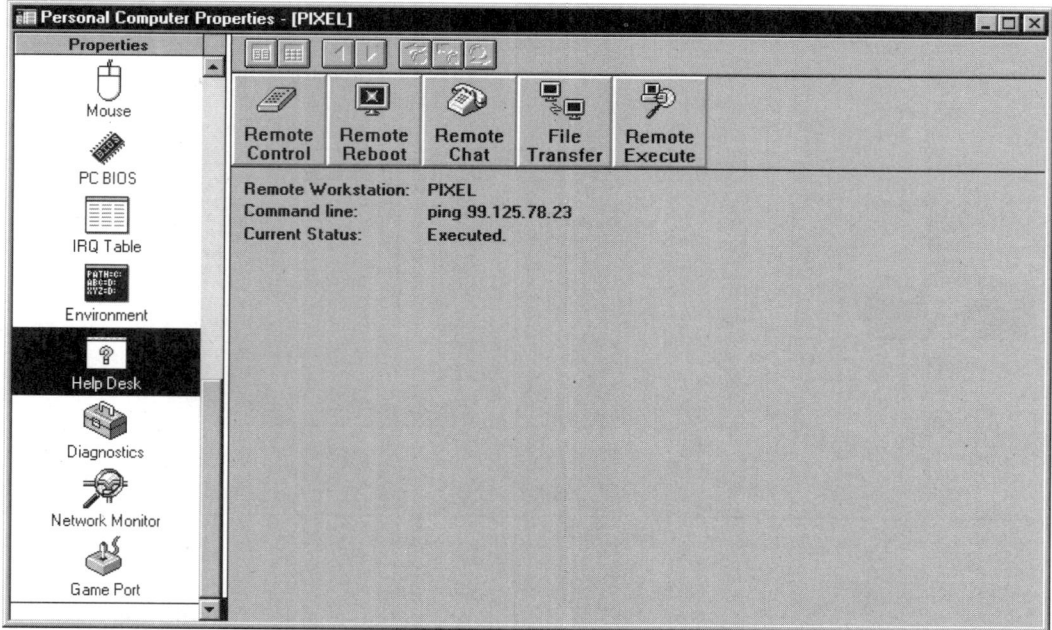

Figure 18-12: Remote Execute runs commands on the client workstation.

With Remote Execute, any output from the command will be lost if it
is not specifically redirected to a file or some other persistent location.

Remote Diagnostics

The Diagnostics selection in the Properties list of the Personal Computer Properties dialog box displays a series of buttons in the right pane, of the Personal Computer Properties window (see Figure 18-13), that allows a number of remote diagnostic functions to be carried out.

This section covers each diagnostic available. We will take a detailed look at those diagnostics that may be more commonly needed.

CMOS Info

The CMOS Info diagnostic provides substantial information about the CMOS configuration for a workstation. CMOS configuration problems can be some of the most difficult to correct.

Figure 18-13 shows a typical CMOS Info display. Shown is information about the basic CMOS configuration, including the date and time, display, memory, CMOS status (such as the battery level), and information about the locally attached drives (including any floppy drives).

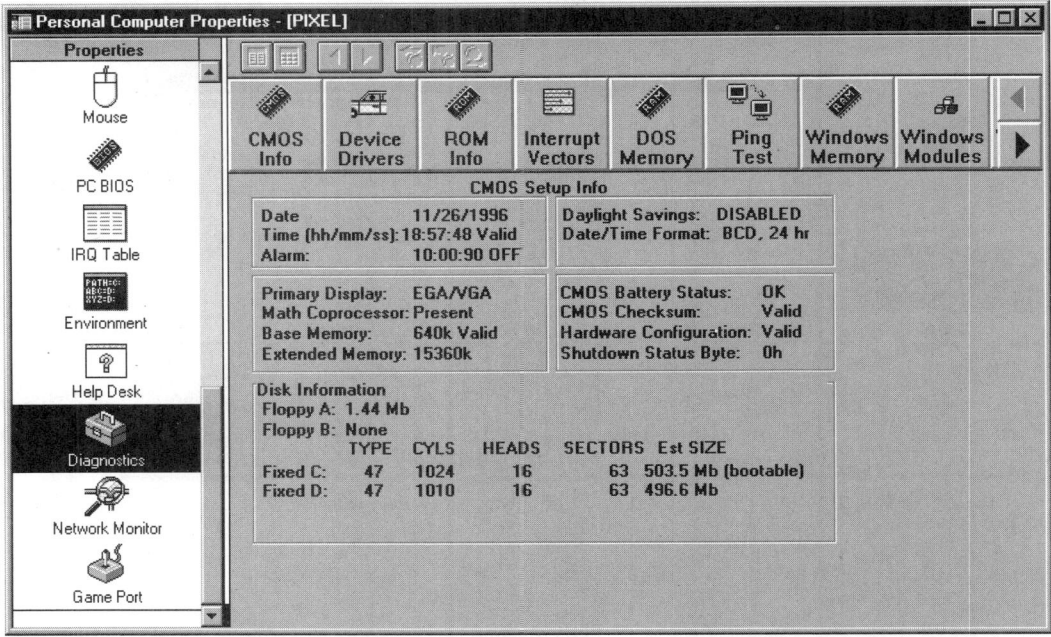

Figure 18-13: The CMOS Info diagnostics screen.

Note: Information about SCSI drives will not be displayed in the Disk Information section as these drives are configured differently than MFM and IDE drives and drive information is not retained in the system BIOS area. Computers with the IBM MCA architecture are also not reported in the CMOS Info display.

Device Drivers

From time to time, workstation users load device drivers, which may cause compatibility problems. The Device Drivers display will list all device drivers on the workstation (similar to the display presented with the DOS command MEM /D).

Figure 18-14 shows a typical Device Drivers display, showing that there are a large number of device drivers loaded on most systems.

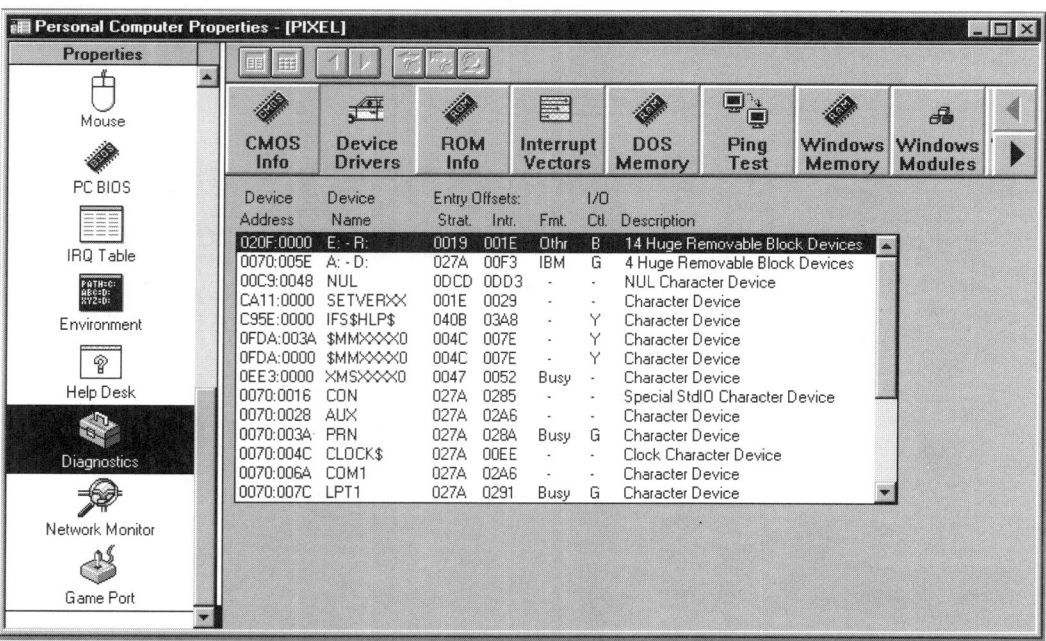

Figure 18-14: Listing device drivers on a Windows 95 client workstation.

ROM Info

The ROM Info window will display information about any accessory cards installed in the client workstation that have on-board ROM BIOS support. Typically, video cards have ROMs, while some network, modem, and other cards may have ROMs, too.

Using ROM Info, it is easy to see which areas of memory above 640K are being used. This allows the systems administrator to determine what areas are free to allocate to high memory use.

Interrupt Vectors

The Interrupt Vectors display provides information about the interrupt vector table that is located in the client workstation's memory.

This display does not necessarily tell which IRQs are in use (use the Properties list's IRQ Table selection to view IRQ assignments), but does tell the systems administrator what the interrupt handler's address is.

DOS Memory

The DOS Memory display (see Figure 18-15) shows the memory allocations for DOS memory. Included in this display are the PSP (Program Segment Prefix) and file handles information for each allocation.

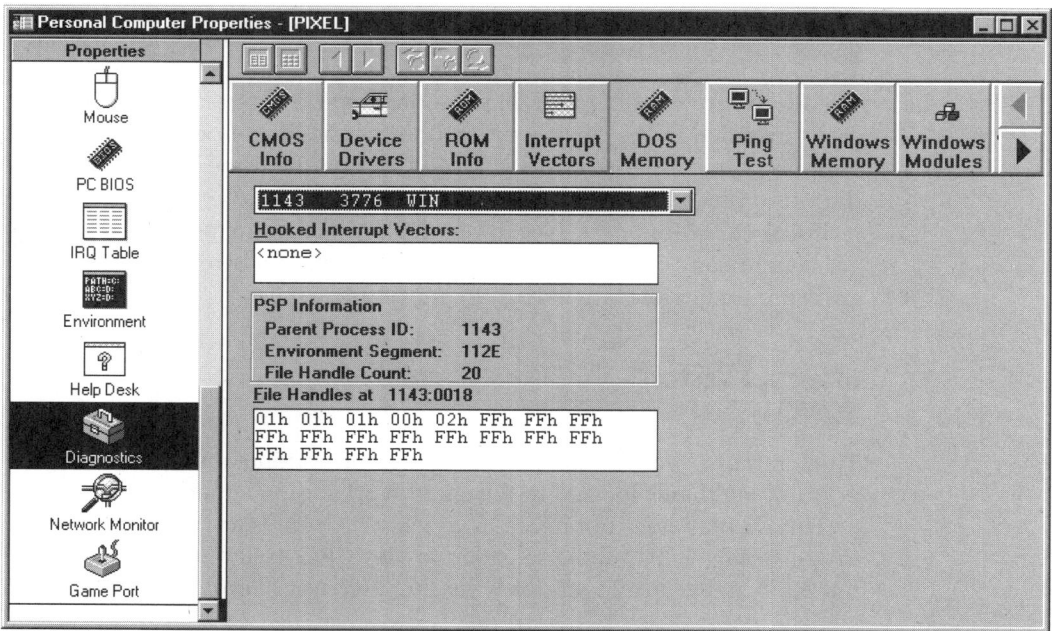

Figure 18-15: The DOS Memory display helps diagnose those pesky out-of-memory errors.

PING Test

The PING Test is used to determine network performance for the client workstation. It is recommended that the PING Test not be run unnecessarily as the amount of network traffic passed by this test may significantly impact network performance for other users.

Windows Memory

The Windows Memory display (see Figure 18-16) shows the memory allocations for Windows memory. This display includes information about the swap file and the system heaps (also see "GDI Heap" and "Global Heap" later in the chapter).

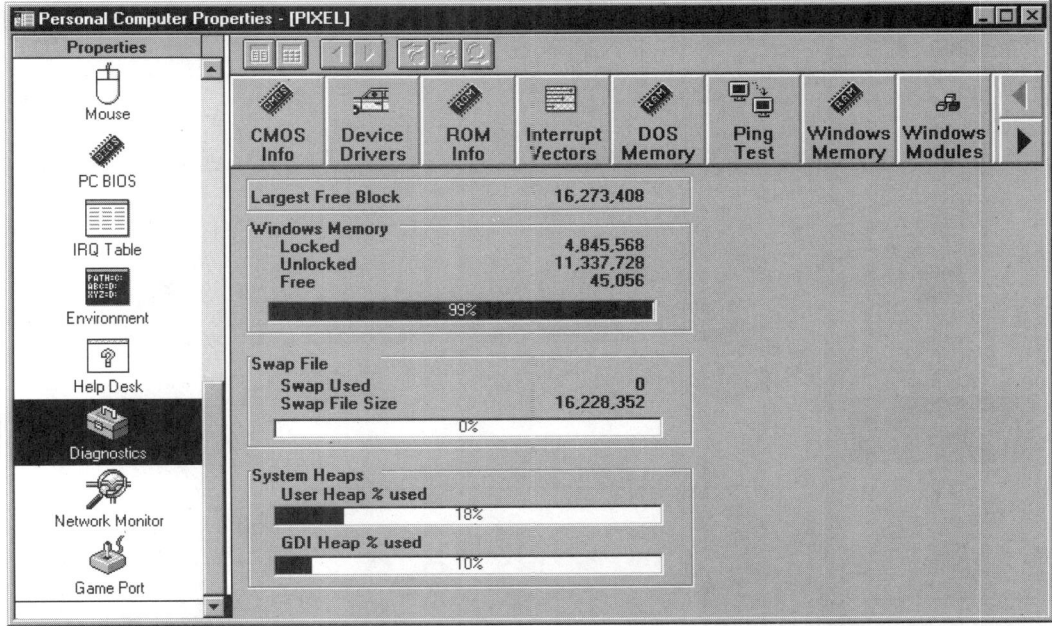

Figure 18-16: The Windows Memory display: How well is Windows using its memory?

Windows Modules

The Windows Modules display (see Figure 18-17) shows each Windows module that is loaded and running. This display includes information about the module's filename, internal name, and the memory objects that are assigned to the module

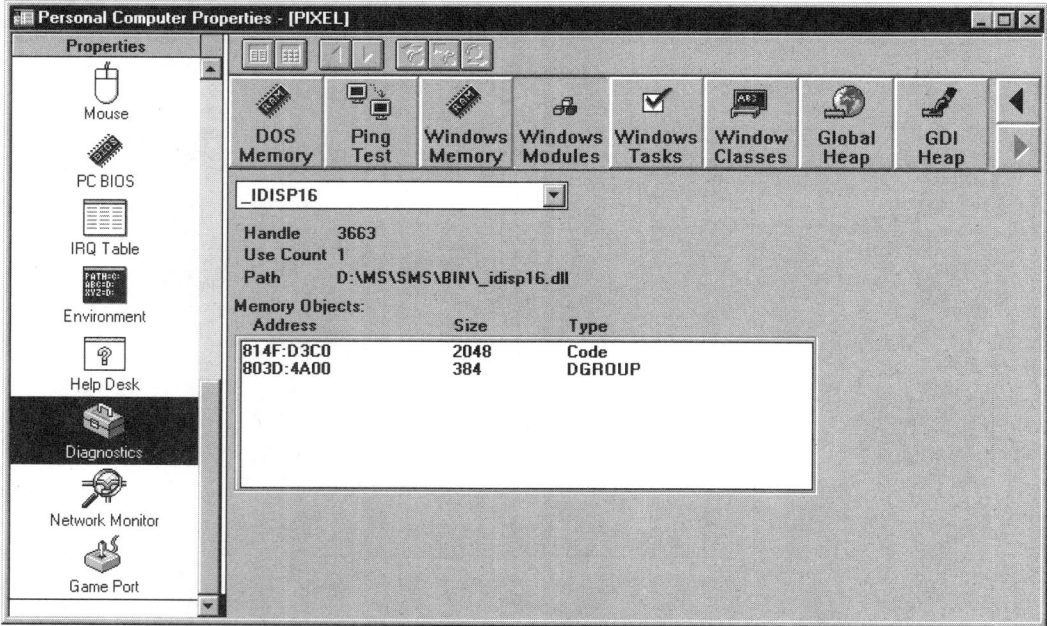

Figure 18-17: The Windows Modules display shows one module at a time.

Windows Tasks

The Windows Tasks display (see Figure 18-18) provides information about each task. The currently executing task is displayed by default, though any loaded task may be displayed by selecting it.

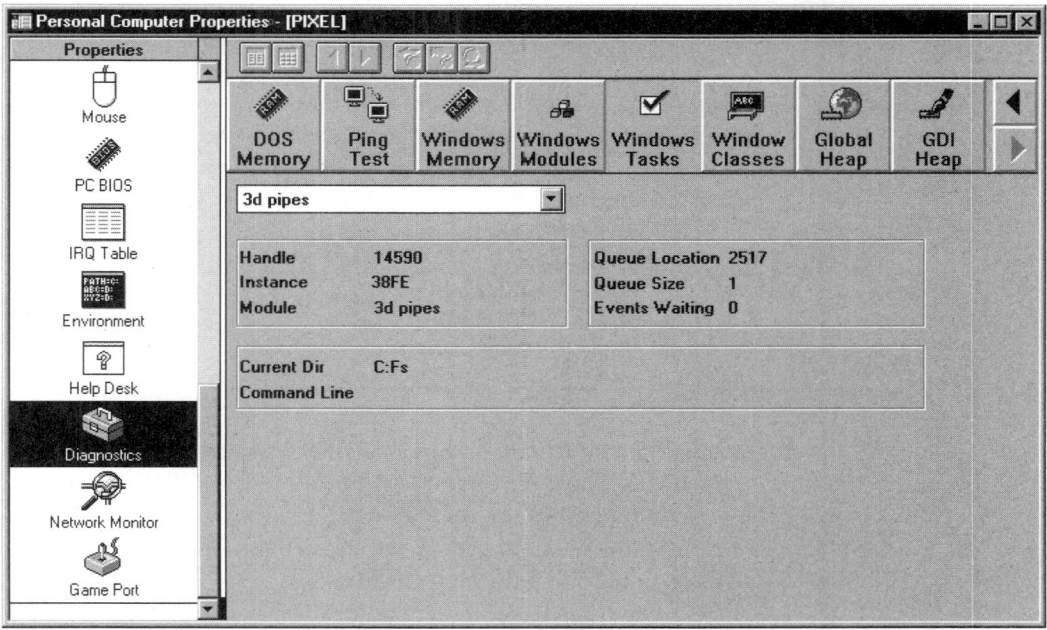

Figure 18-18: Tasks running—3d pipes is the screen saver.

Windows Classes

The Windows Classes display is used to show information about each of the Windows classes that currently exist at the client workstation.

Generally, Windows classes are more significant to programmers while debugging programming issues on the client workstation.

Global Heap

The Global Heap display is used to show information about the Windows global heap as it currently exists at the client workstation. Objects in the global heap are assigned an owner (typically an application that is running), and information about the global heap object is available.

Generally, Global Heap information is more significant to programmers while debugging programming issues on the client workstation.

GDI Heap

The GDI Heap display is used to show information about the Windows GDI (Graphical Device Interface) heap as it currently exists at the client workstation. Objects in the GDI heap are graphical in nature, such as pens, brushes, and bitmaps.

Generally, GDI Heap information is more significant to programmers while debugging programming issues on the client workstation.

Moving On

This chapter introduced Microsoft SMS's Remote Control and Remote Debugging facilities. These features are very valuable when trying to solve problems on workstations that are remotely located from the systems administrator; it is unnecessary to travel to the workstation to perform tasks or to obtain diagnostic information.

This chapter concludes the SMS section of our book. In the next section, we will take a look at Microsoft Proxy Server.

SECTION
IV

Microsoft Proxy Server

19

Installing & Configuring Microsoft Proxy Server

In this chapter we describe Microsoft Proxy Server. The Microsoft Proxy Server is a newly released product (code-named Catapult) that is also new to Microsoft BackOffice 2.5.

To use any of the products included with Microsoft BackOffice, you must first install the Microsoft BackOffice product. Then you may install and configure the individual products included with Microsoft BackOffice.

Microsoft Proxy Server is an important part of Microsoft BackOffice in environments where there are connections to the Internet that must be secured or where there are no IP addresses available for permanent assignment.

Microsoft Proxy Server also includes a Windows NT 4 Server monitor configuration file to allow monitoring of network usage.

Microsoft Proxy Server offers a number of functionalities including:

- A simple, single, and secure gateway to link internal networks with the Internet, without exposing resources on internal networks to the Internet.

- Easy integration into existing networks, including networks using protocols other than TCP/IP. For example, a network client using IPX/SPX is able to interact with the Internet without having to reconfigure the client to use TCP/IP protocol.

- Integration with both Windows NT 4 Server and Microsoft IIS. The main management of Microsoft Proxy Server is done using the Microsoft IIS Internet Service Manager program.

- Support for a wide variety of protocols and applications, including RealAudio, VDOLive, and other advanced Internet applications.

- Support for a dial-in connection to the Internet. By dialing into the ISP on an as-needed basis, Microsoft Proxy Server is able to substantially reduce the costs of maintaining an Internet connection.

- Extensive control over usage of Internet resources, thereby enhancing the ability to limit the misuse of expensive resources.

- Extensive logging of usage, allowing billing and other tracking of usage.

Installing Microsoft Proxy Server

Installing Microsoft Proxy Server is a relatively simple process. Start the BackOffice setup program, and select Microsoft Proxy Server.

Specifying CD Keys & Product ID Numbers

The first screen in the Microsoft Proxy Server setup program is a welcome screen with OK and Cancel buttons. Click OK to display the next screen, where the CD key must be entered. As with most Microsoft products, the setup program will ask for a CD key, which will be found on a small sticker, usually located on the back of the CD case.

Note: Ever lost a CD key? Other than trying to guess a valid key (or trying to use the key from another Microsoft product), it is difficult to recover from a lost CD key!

I've found it very convenient to write the CD key on the CD itself. This minimizes problems that might occur if the CD and the CD's case become separated. But marking on a CD can present a hazard if one is not careful. I use a grease pencil (usually called a China marker) that will not damage the CD. If you use a felt-tipped marker, do so with care; only write on an area that has a printed background or in the very innermost hub area.

After entering the CD key and clicking OK, the product identifying number will be displayed. Be sure to note this number in case it is necessary to contact Microsoft product support—there is no About box for the Microsoft Proxy Server (the About box is where product identifying numbers are usually displayed.)

Specifying Installation Location & Other Options

The next screen in the installation process allows changing the default installation location. The default location for Microsoft Proxy Server is the folder MSP. If there should already be a folder with this name, then change the installation folder to a new name (I would probably use MSProxy for an alternate installation folder).

Once satisfied with the installation folder, click the OK button. The next screen displayed is Installation Options (Figure 19-1). The default installation will install all components that make up Microsoft Proxy Server.

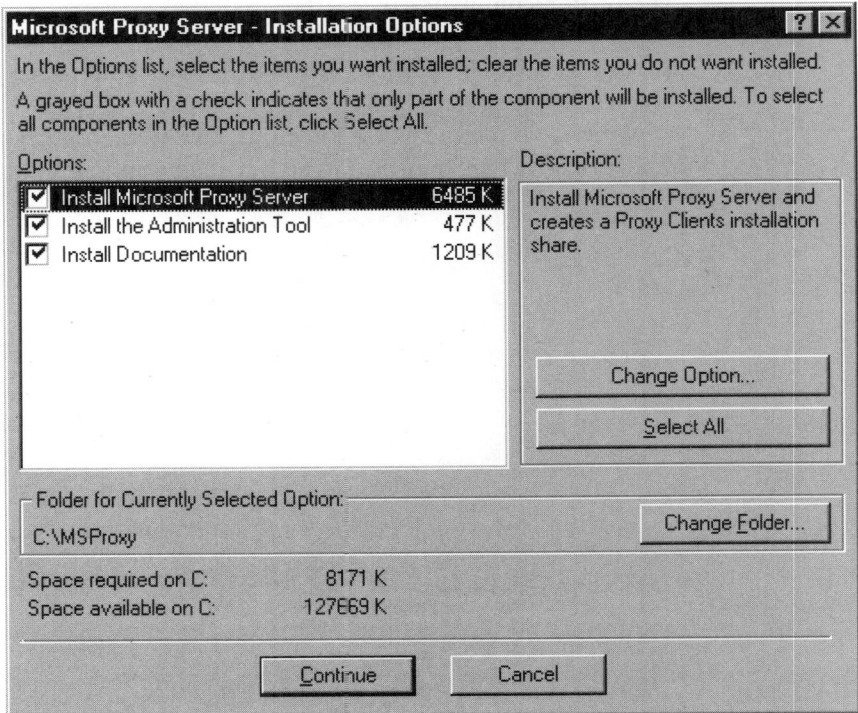

Figure 19-1: The Installation Options dialog box lets you install only a subset of Microsoft Proxy Server.

The Install Microsoft Proxy Server option (the first one listed) is the only option that can be configured. The Install Microsoft Proxy Server dialog box lets you install the server component and client components for Windows NT Intel and Windows 95 clients, Windows NT Alpha clients, Windows NT PPC clients, and Windows 3.x clients. All clients are installed by having the client access the Microsoft Proxy Server Client installation share and running a setup program.

Note: If there are no Alpha, PPC, or Windows 3.x clients, then there is no need to install the client installation components for these platforms. Install client installation software for only those client platforms that are being used on the network. Components may be installed at a later time, if needed, by rerunning the Microsoft Proxy Server setup program.

Configuring the Cache

The next step of the installation process is to configure the cache (see Figure 19-2) that the Microsoft Proxy Server Web Proxy server will use. Microsoft recommends using 100MB of disk space plus a small additional amount of space (about one half MB) for each user. The space allocated should be in 5MB increments—the setup program will round down any allocation to a 5MB boundary.

Note: Keep the cache files on an NTFS volume for best system performance. Cache files may be spread between multiple volumes as needed.

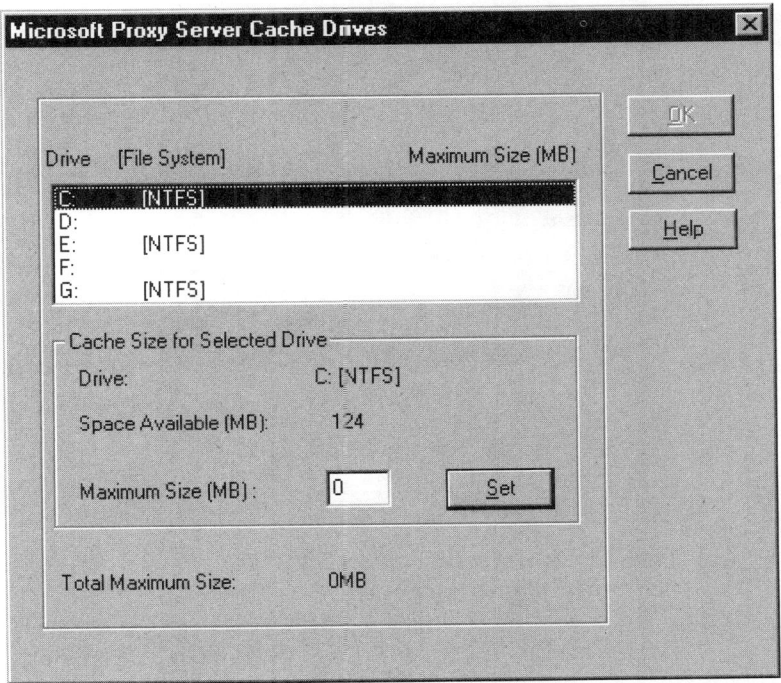

Figure 19-2: Configuring the Cache—it's best to allocate 100 + (Number_clients / 2) MB of space.

Defining the Local Address Table (LAT)

Once the cache has been configured, the LAT (Local Address Table) must be defined (see Figure 19-3). Microsoft Proxy Server makes this process easier by using the Construct Table button.

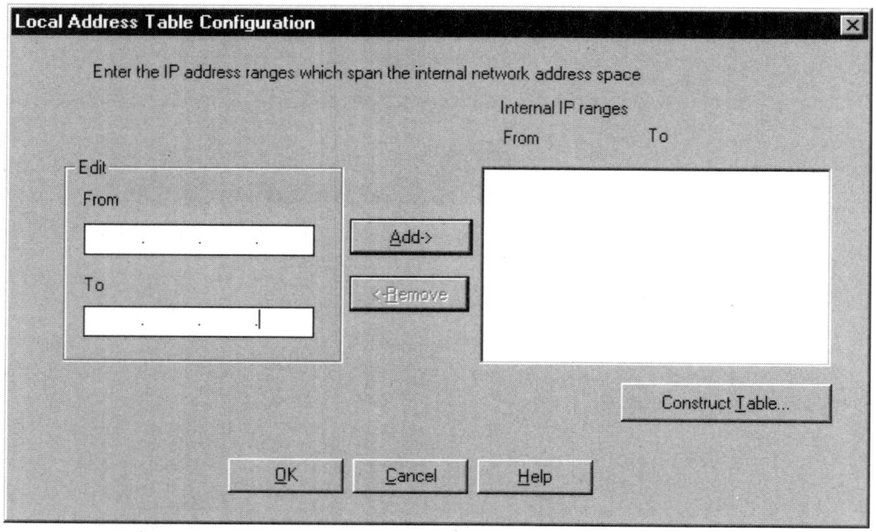

Figure 19-3: The Local Address Table Configuration dialog box—enter all local network IP address ranges here.

Of Numbers & Names

Internet IP address numbers and Internet names are defined in a series of documents on the Internet. The IANA maintains a Web site that has all relevant documents. Search from the address http://www.isi.edu/div7/iana.

For documents regarding assignments, check http://www.isi.edu/div7/iana/assignments.html.

Two RFCs (Request For Comments) document names and IP addresses:

- RFC1591, "Domain Name System Structure and Delegation," describes the concept behind the .COM, .NET, .GOV, .ORG, and .EDU top-level domains. It seems interesting that the .COM top-level domain is becoming unmanageable, yet there does not seem to be any plan to split this domain into subdomains based on true commercial and personal accounts.

- RFC1918, "Address Allocation for Private Internets," describes more fully the addresses that are allocated to private network use.

The Construct Table button will display the Construct Local Address Table dialog box (see Figure 19-4). There are two main choices to be made in the Construct Local Address Table dialog box. The first choice is Add the private ranges 10.x.x.x, 192.168.x.x, and 172.16.x.x-172.31.x.x to the table, and the second choice is Load from NT internal Routing Table.

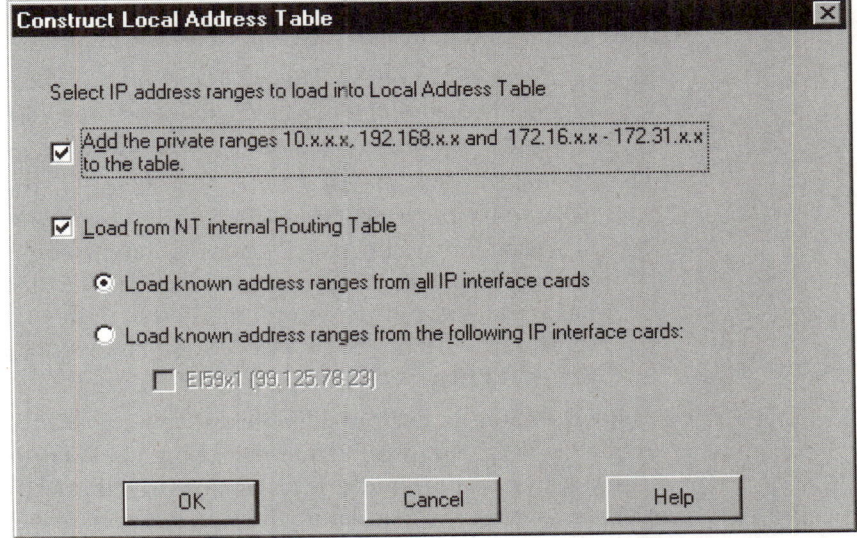

Figure 19-4: Construct Local Address Table makes creating an LAT easy.

When you choose to add the private ranges, the three IP address ranges usable with private TCP/IP networks are included in the LAT. These addresses, established by IANA (Internet Assigned Numbers Authority), should be kept invisible to the Internet; however, there will be no addresses on the Internet in these address ranges:

■ 10.x.x.x represents a single Class A IP address, which will address up to (approximately) 24 million nodes on a private network. Typically, this address will be subnetted to create a number of smaller address spaces that will be assigned to separate private networks in the organization.

■ 172.16.x.x- 172.31.x.x represents a subnetted Class A IP address, which becomes a set of 16 Class B IP addresses. These addresses allow addressing about one million nodes on a private network. Again, this address range would often be subnetted to create a number of smaller address ranges.

- 192.168.x.x represents a single Class B IP address (or a block of 256 Class C addresses) capable of addressing about 65 thousand nodes in a private network. Many Microsoft Proxy Server users will find the 192.168.x.x address range adequate for their needs.

Note: For more information about the private address space described above, consult the document at ftp://ftp.isi.edu/in-notes/rfc1918.txt.

If the internal network uses IP addresses outside the above-mentioned ranges, then the systems administrator has two choices:

- Readdress the internal network to reflect the allocated addresses (as described above). This alternative gives the best results in that all Internet addresses will then be accessible.

- Add the current internal network's addresses to the LAT. This alternative will prevent accessing addresses on the Internet that fall within the local network's address range. For example, if your local network uses the IP address range 196.120.87.x (a single Class C address), then any node on the Internet in the IP address range 196.120.87.x will not be accessible from any workstation using the Microsoft Proxy Server.

Note: No traffic (to or from) the internal network addresses above should ever be routed over the Internet! Using the Microsoft Proxy Server will help insure that these addresses remain private, as Microsoft Proxy Server acts as a firewall—isolating the local network from the Internet.

If the local network's IP addresses are to be added to the LAT (for example, there is a need to add the address range 196.120.87.x), then in the Local Address Table Configuration dialog box (see Figure 19-3), enter 196.120.87.0 in the From location and 196.120.87.255 in the To location, and click the Add button.

When Load from NT internal Routing Table is chosen in the Construct Local Address Table dialog box, any addresses that the Windows NT 4 Server knows about (from the Windows NT internal Routing Table) will also be included in the LAT. This option makes it easy to include address ranges that are outside the three established private IP address ranges.

When in doubt, choose both options (they are not exclusive).

Warning

It is most important that the (local network) address of the Microsoft Proxy Server be included in the LAT. If it is not included, the WinSock Proxy Service will not be able to start, usually returning a 183 error code. It may be necessary to reinstall the Microsoft Proxy Server to correct this error.

Setting Up Client Installation Information

Once the basic LAT has been created, the next step is to configure the clients using the Client Installation/Configuration dialog (Figure 19-5). Selections made on this page will be used when clients install the Microsoft Proxy Server client software, as described below.

The defaults on the Client Installation/Configuration dialog are generally what most users will want. One option (Set Client Setup to Configure Browser Proxy Settings) is particularly important; when it is selected any clients who install the Microsoft Proxy Server client software will have their browser automatically configured to use the correct proxy server settings. This makes installation of the client software and configuration of the client's system very easy.

After the client installation/configuration process is complete, the Microsoft Proxy Server setup program will copy the Microsoft Proxy Server files and configure the system to run Microsoft Proxy Server. Unlike most other network services, Microsoft Proxy Server does not normally require that Windows NT 4 Server be rebooted.

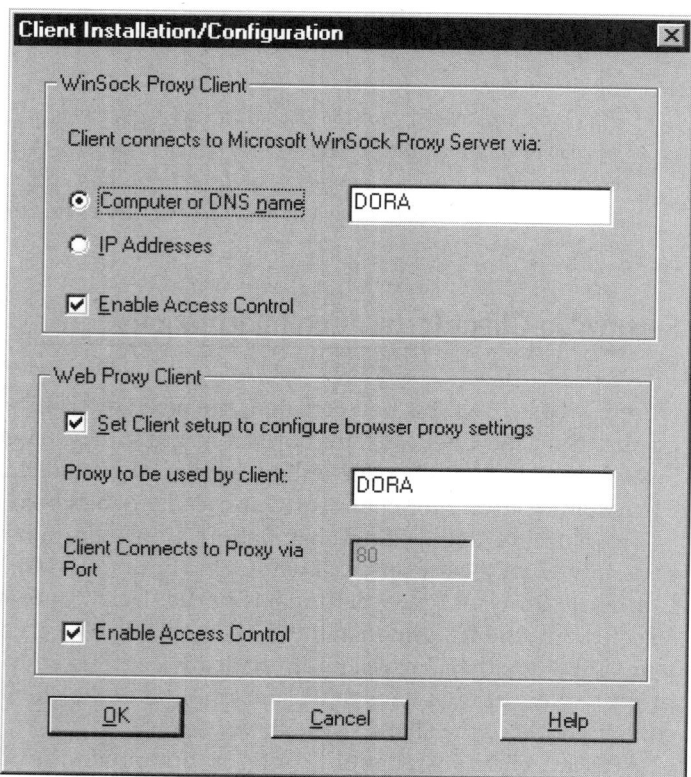

Figure 19-5: The Client Installation/Configuration dialog allows setting options that affect client installations.

Configuring & Using the Microsoft Proxy Server

Both during the installation process and after Microsoft Proxy Server has been installed, the systems administrator is able to fully configure Microsoft Proxy Server. Except for the RAS dial-up connection features Microsoft Proxy Server is configured by executing the Microsoft Internet Service Manager program, either from the Microsoft Proxy Server program group or from the IIS program group.

The Internet Service Manager

The Windows NT 4 Server IIS Internet Service Manager program is used to manage the Microsoft Proxy Server. The Internet Service Manager (take a gander at Figure 19-6) may be started either from Start Menu | Programs | Administrative Tools (Common) | Microsoft Internet Server (Common) | Internet Service Manager or from Start Menu | Programs | Administrative Tools (Common) | Microsoft Proxy Server | Internet Service Manager.

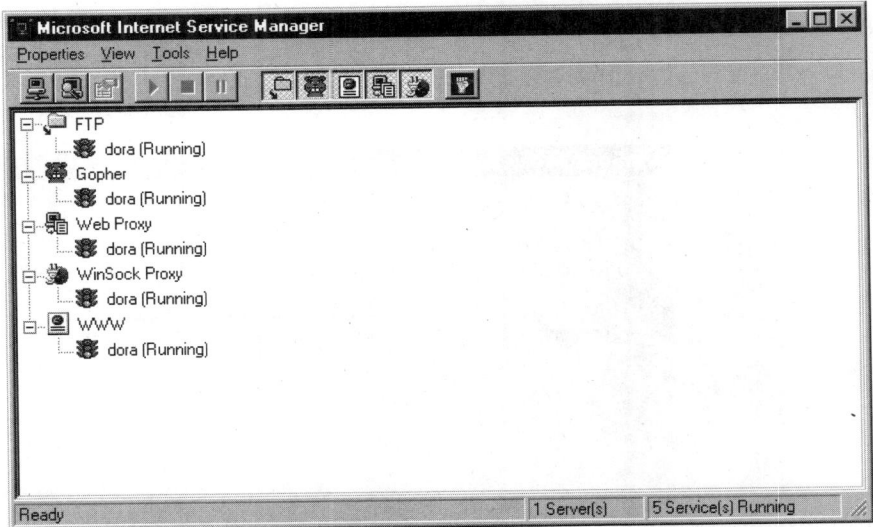

Figure 19-6: The Internet Service Manager—Microsoft Proxy Server has added two new services: Web Proxy and WinSock Proxy.

After installing Microsoft Proxy Server, the Internet Service Manager will show two new services:

■ WinSock Proxy manages the WinSock Proxy agent component of Microsoft Proxy Server. WinSock Proxy is used to specify which Windows Sockets applications will be granted access to the Internet through the WinSock Proxy service. WinSock Proxy also configures ports for both inbound and outbound connections.

■ Web Proxy manages the Web Proxy agent component of Microsoft Proxy Server. Web Proxy is used to manage permissions, caching, logging, and filters, and to view information about current connections.

Selecting the service in the Internet Service Manager and either double-clicking the service or pressing Alt+Enter on the keyboard will display the properties dialog box used to configure each service.

WinSock Proxy

The WinSock Proxy Service Properties dialog is used to configure the WinSock component of Microsoft Proxy Server. The Properties dialog box (see Figure 19-7) has five tabs: Service, Protocols, Permissions, Logging, and Filters:

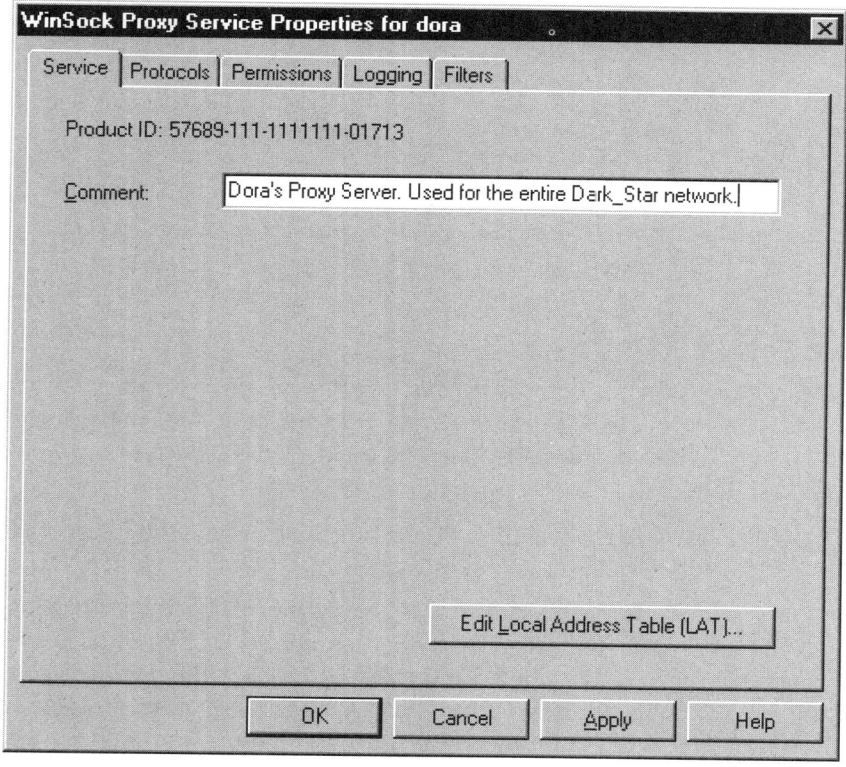

Figure 19-7: The WinSock Proxy Service Properties dialog box.

Service. In the Service tab, enter a comment to describe the WinSock Proxy Service. Any meaningful comment will do, such as the one shown in Figure 19-7.

To modify the Local Address Table, click the Edit Local Address Table (LAT) button. The Local Address Table Configuration dialog (see Figure 19-8) lets you enter new local network addresses. See "Defining the Local Address Table (LAT)" earlier in the chapter for more information.

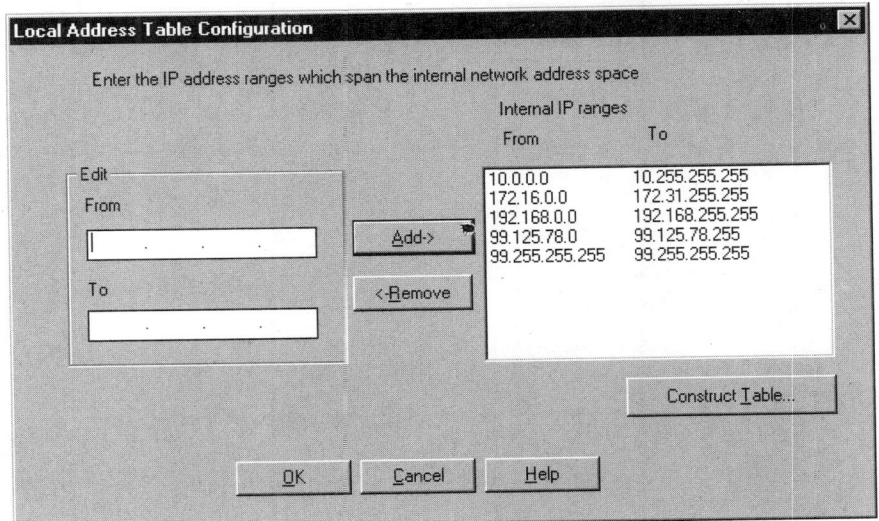

Figure 19-8: The Local Address Table Configuration dialog box—enter your local network's IP address ranges.

Protocols. The Protocols tab (Figure 19-9) lets you add, delete, and configure protocols used by the Microsoft Proxy Server. For each protocol added or modified, the Protocol Definition (Figure 19-10) dialog box is used.

A protocol will have a name. There are many protocols defined, each of which will typically have a port number, a type, a direction (inbound or outbound), and where applicable, a range of ports for subsequent connections.

Generally, the protocols defined in a default installation will be adequate for most installations. Adding new protocols is easy when the protocol's name, port number, type, and direction are known.

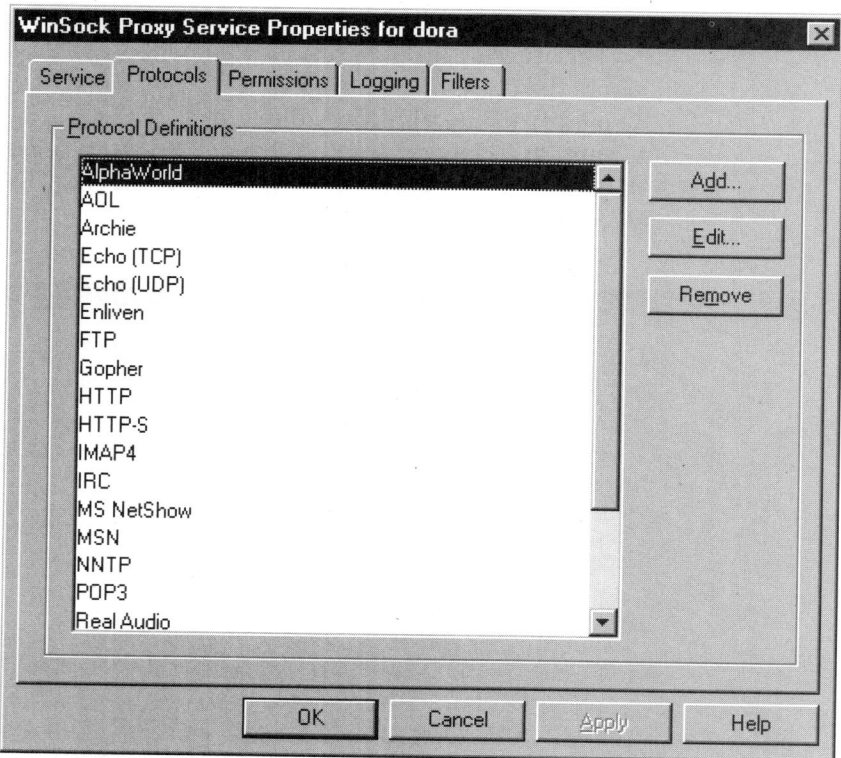

Figure 19-9: The Protocols tab lists each supported protocol so that you can add, delete, and modify them.

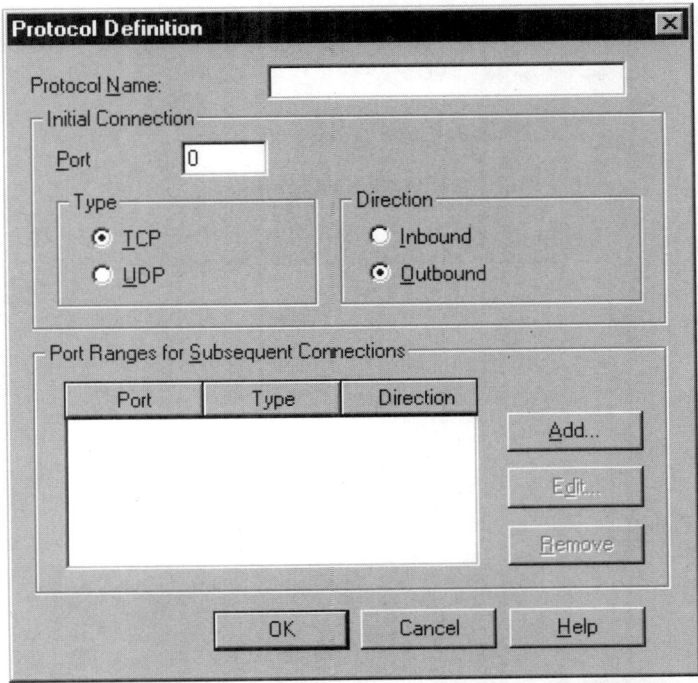

Figure 19-10: Configure each supported protocol using the Protocol Definition dialog box.

Permissions.   Use the Permissions tab (Figure 19-11) to restrict access to any (or all) protocols based on users from the Windows NT 4 Server user list. The User Manager for Domains is used to create the userids that will be referenced in the Permissions tab (see Chapter 2 for more on managing users).

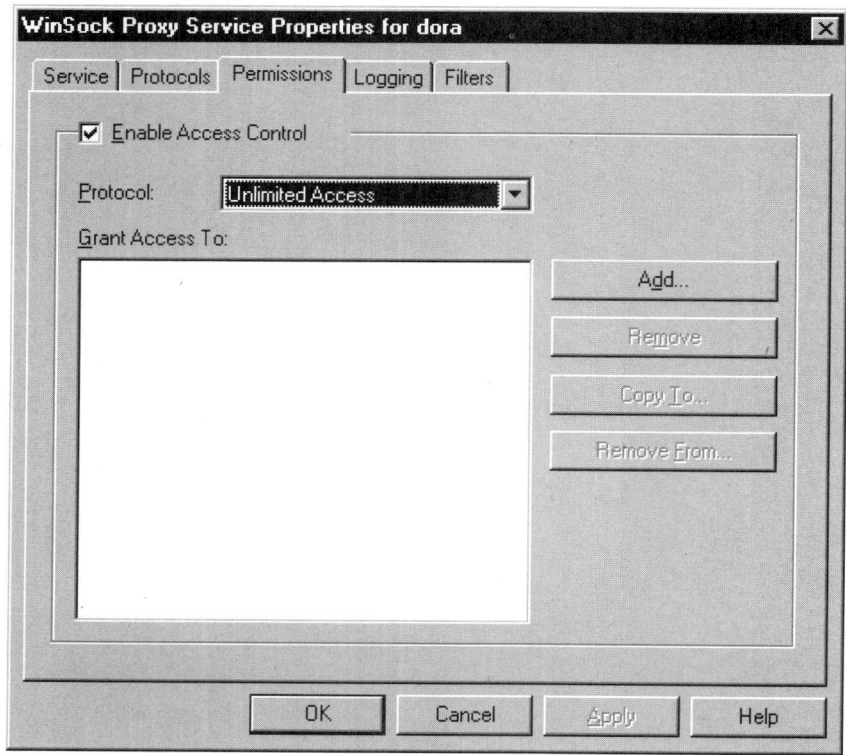

Figure 19-11: Restrict protocols based on accessing userid in the Permissions tab.

Logging.   All Microsoft Proxy Server usage may be logged to either a file or to an ODBC (Open DataBase Connectivity) data source. You configure logging in the Logging tab (Figure 19-12). Maintaining a log is a very wise move, as the logging will enable the systems administrator to determine both who is using the service and how much.

The default location for the log file created by Microsoft Proxy Server is different from the logs created by IIS. The individual user will have to determine whether the IIS logs are combined with the Microsoft Proxy Server logs.

Note: Generally the Microsoft Proxy Server log will contain all information that the IIS logs would contain, therefore it is not necessary to maintain both IIS logging and Microsoft Proxy Server logging at the same time.

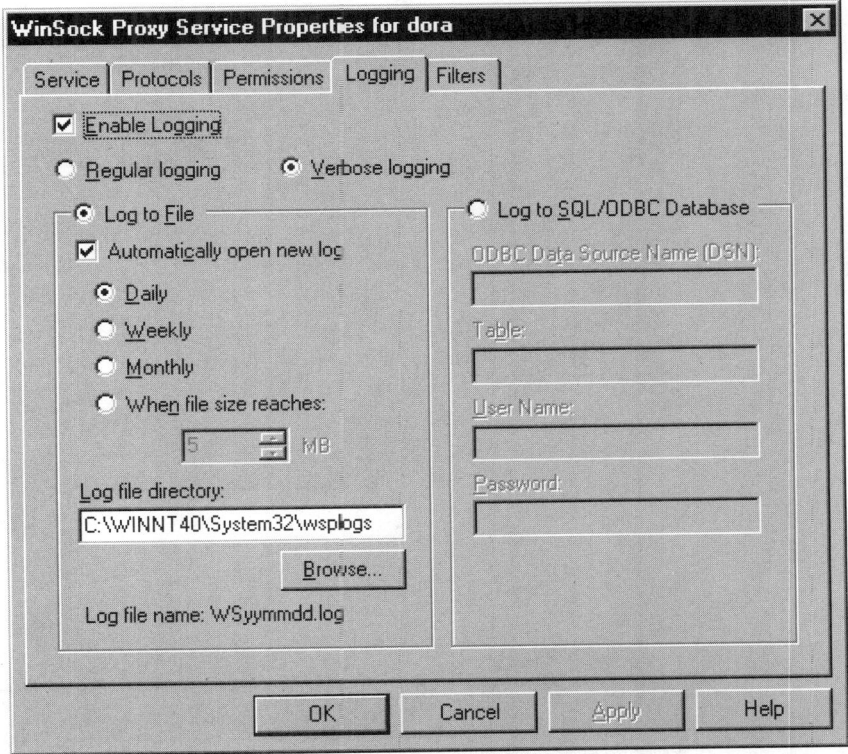

Figure 19-12: Logging is enabled in the Logging tab—log in verbose mode to get the most detail.

Filters.   Use the Filters tab (Figure 19-13) to restrict client access to Internet sites. As with permissions, filters are organized on Windows NT 4 Server userids.

Note: The Filters tab is common to both WinSock Proxy and Web Proxy. Filters set in one service apply equally to either service.

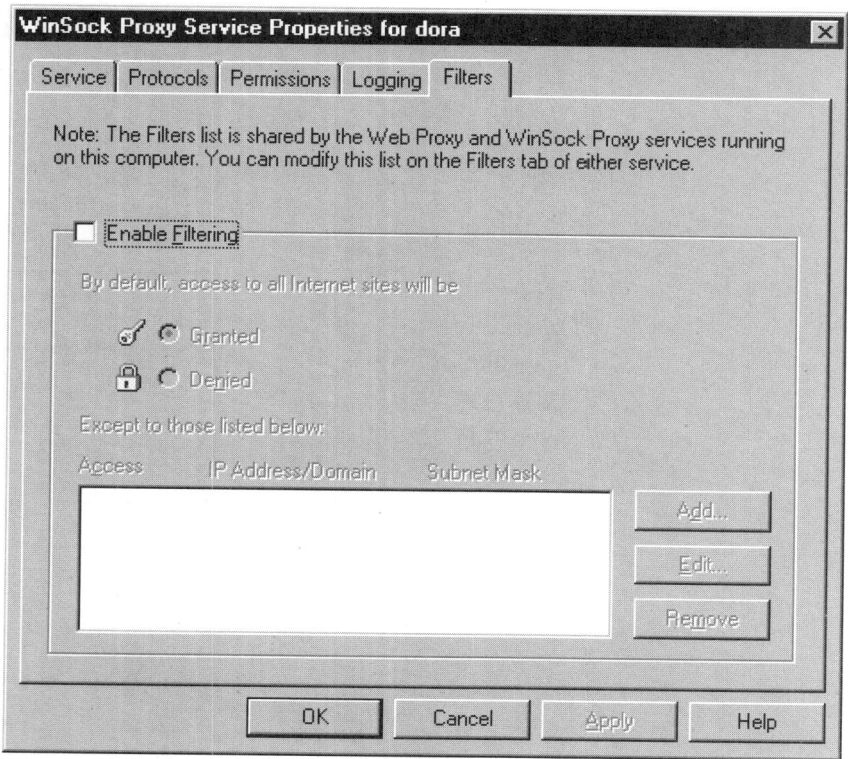

Figure 19-13: Restrict access to the Internet with the Filters tab.

Web Proxy

The Web Proxy Service Properties dialog is used to configure the Web component of Microsoft Proxy Server. The Properties dialog box (see Figure 19-14) has five tabs: Service, Permissions, Caching, Logging, and Filters:

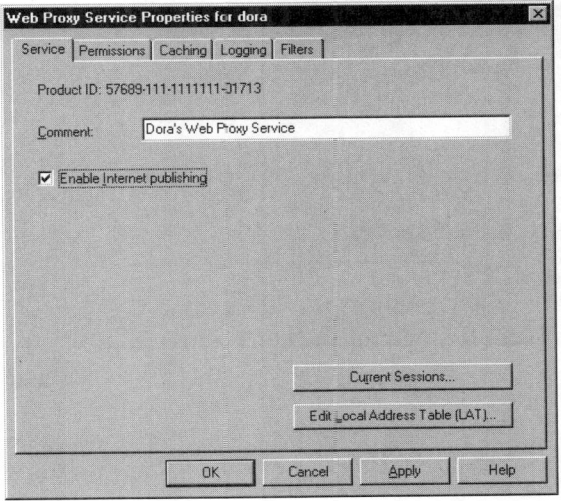

Figure 19-14: The Web Proxy Service Properties dialog box.

Service.   In the Service tab, enter a comment to describe the Web Proxy Service. Any meaningful comment will do, such as the one shown in Figure 19-14.

Whenever Web pages are to be available to Internet users, check the Enable Internet Publishing check box. If the Enable Internet Publishing check box is cleared, then Web pages will only be available to local intranets and not users of the Internet.

To view a list of users currently viewing Web pages on the server, click the Current Sessions button. The list is shown in the Web Proxy Service User Sessions dialog box, which shows some simple statistics as well as the users. There is no interaction on the list of users.

To modify the Local Address Table, click the Edit Local Address Table (LAT) button. The Local Address Table Configuration dialog (see Figure 19-8) lets you enter new local network addresses. See "Defining the Local Address Table (LAT)" earlier in the chapter for more information.

Permissions.   Use the Permissions tab (Figure 19-15) to restrict access to any (or all) protocols based on users from the Windows NT 4 Server user list. The User Manager for Domains (see Chapter 2 for more on managing users) is used to create the userids that will be referenced in the Permissions tab.

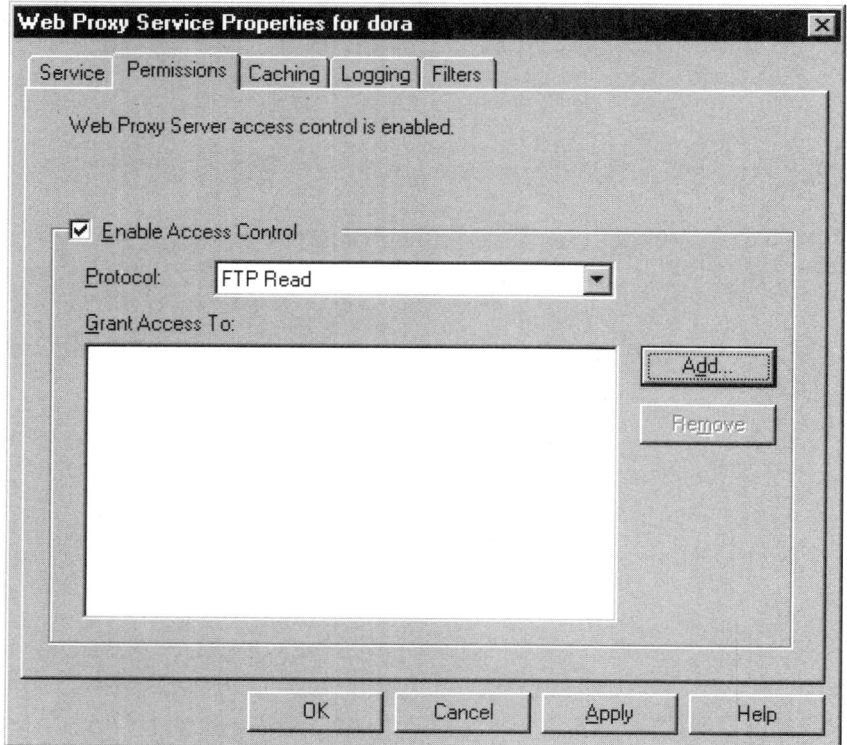

Figure 19-15: Restrict protocols based on accessing userid in the Permissions tab.

Caching. One advantage of Microsoft Proxy Server is that pages that are frequently referenced may be cached on the server. This allows faster access to the pages, as it will not be necessary to fetch them from the originating server.

Caching may be set up on one or more drives, where the system administrator may specify the drive and the maximum amount of space to be used for the cache. The Caching tab (shown in Figure 19-16) allows configuring the cache.

To ensure that the objects in the cache are always the freshest, move the Cache Expiration Policy slider toward the left (Always Request Updates). If performance (that is, minimizing the number of objects requested from the Internet) is most important, move the slider toward the right (Fewest Internet Requests).

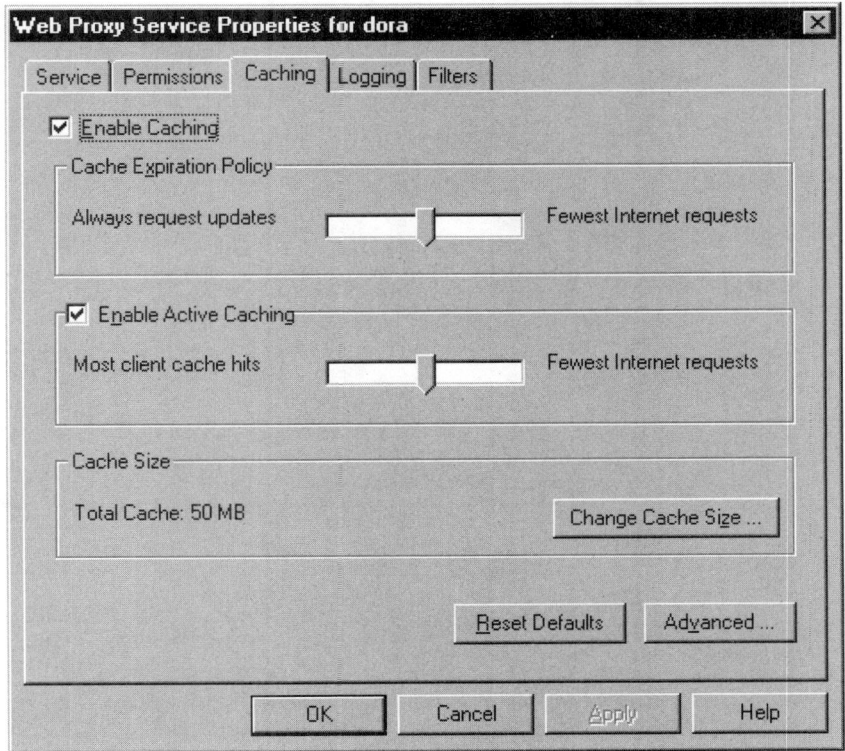

Figure 19-16: The Caching tab is used to configure caching of Web pages to minimize Internet traffic when servicing user's requests.

To use active caching (where the Microsoft Proxy Server updates objects in the cache without necessarily having a pending user request), check the Enable Active Caching check box. To tune active caching, move the slider toward Most Client Cache Hits to cause the updating to be done more actively and toward Fewest Internet Requests to minimize Internet traffic.

The cache is maintained on local hard drives. Much like the Windows NT 4 Server paging file, it is possible to select one or more drives to be used for the cache. Always select NTFS volumes for cache.

Logging.   All Microsoft Proxy Server usage may be logged to either a file or to an ODBC data source. Configure logging in the Logging tab (Figure 19-17). Maintaining a log is a very wise move, as the logging will enable the systems administrator to not only determine who is using the service, but also how much.

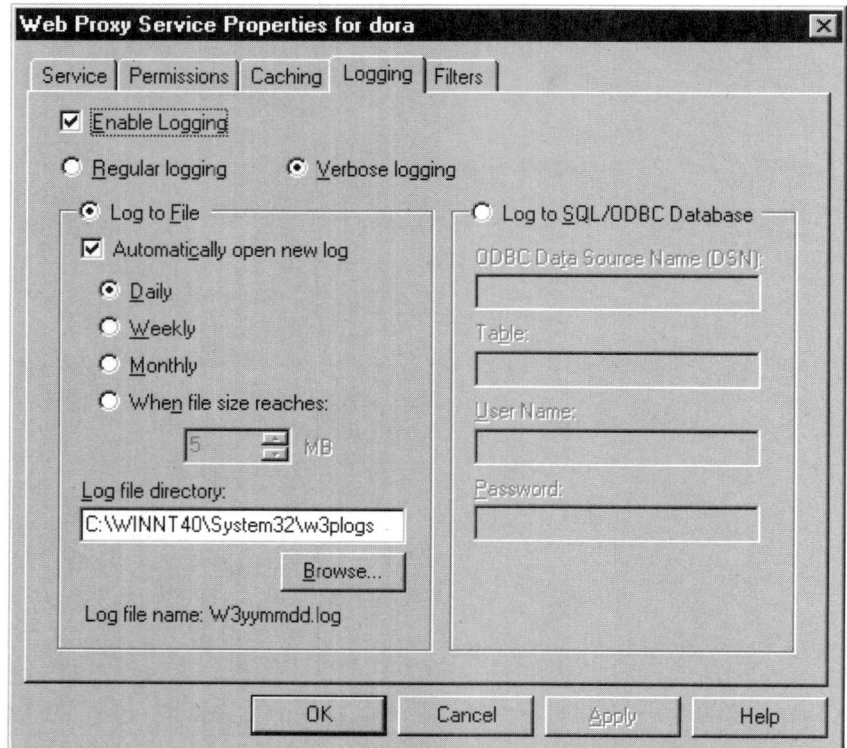

Figure 19-17: Logging is enabled in the Logging tab—log in verbose mode to get the most detail.

The default location for the log file created by Web Proxy Server is different than that of the logs created by IIS. Whether the IIS logs are combined with the Microsoft Proxy Server logs is a choice that the individual user will have to determine.

Note: Generally the Microsoft Proxy Server log will contain all information that the IIS logs would contain; therefore it is not necessary to maintain both IIS logging and Microsoft Proxy Server logging at the same time.

Filters. Use the Filters tab (Figure 19-13) to restrict client access to Internet sites. For more information, see "WinSock Proxy" earlier in the chapter.

Note: The Filters tab is common to both Web Proxy and WinSock Proxy. Filters set in one service apply equally to either service.

Monitoring Microsoft Proxy Server Performance

A shortcut to start the Windows NT 4 Server Performance Monitor, shown in Figure 19-18, can be found in the Microsoft Proxy Server group (Start Menu I Programs I Administrative Tools (Common) I Microsoft Proxy Server).

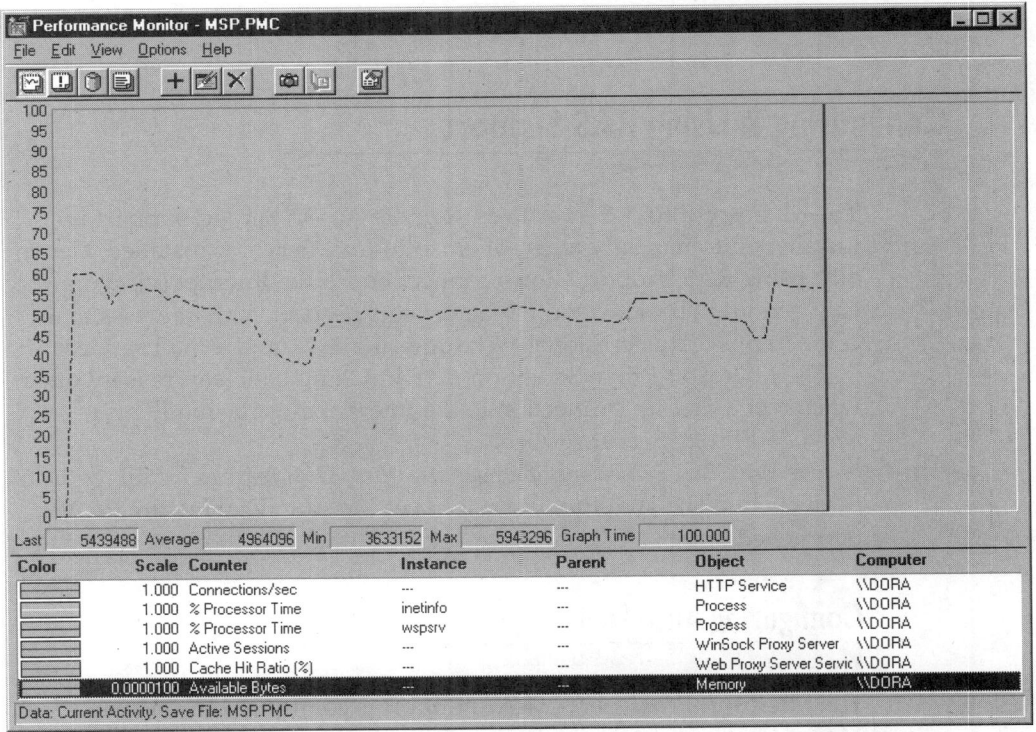

Figure 19-18: Monitoring the Microsoft Proxy Server is important to ensure that the best performance is obtained.

The Windows NT 4 Server Performance Monitor shortcut shows the following performance indicators:

- **Connections/sec**—indicates the number of connections made per second to the HTTP (Web) service.

- **% Processor Time (inetinfo Instance)**—indicates the amount of processor time spent handling the inetinfo thread.

- **% Processor Time (wspsrv Instance)**—indicates the amount of processor time spent handling the wspsrv thread.
- **Active Sessions**—indicates the number of sessions currently active with the WinSock Proxy server.
- **Cache Hit Ratio (%)**—indicates the number of hits to the Web cache (see "Caching" earlier in the chapter).
- **Available Bytes**—indicates the number of bytes of memory currently available to the system.

Configuring & Using RAS Support

The Microsoft Proxy Server RAS (Remote Access Server) support is installed automatically when Microsoft Proxy Server is installed. Generally, using RAS support allows connections to the Internet (via a dial-up connection) to be active only when clients need them. Some uses that come to mind are occasional Web browsing, FTP, and e-mail services.

The Microsoft Proxy Server on-demand Auto Dial feature is invoked whenever a dial-up connection to the Internet must be made by a Microsoft Proxy Server service.

The WinSock Proxy service uses the Auto Dial feature for all requests from clients. The Web Proxy service uses the Auto Dial feature for all noncached objects.

Configuring Auto Dial

The Microsoft Proxy Server RAS support is configured by choosing Start Menu | Programs | Administrative Tools (Common) | Microsoft Proxy Server | Auto Dial Configuration.

Starting the Auto Dial Configuration program will display the window shown in Figure 19-19. Two tabs (Dialing Hours and Credentials) make up the entire user interface for the Auto Dial configuration program.

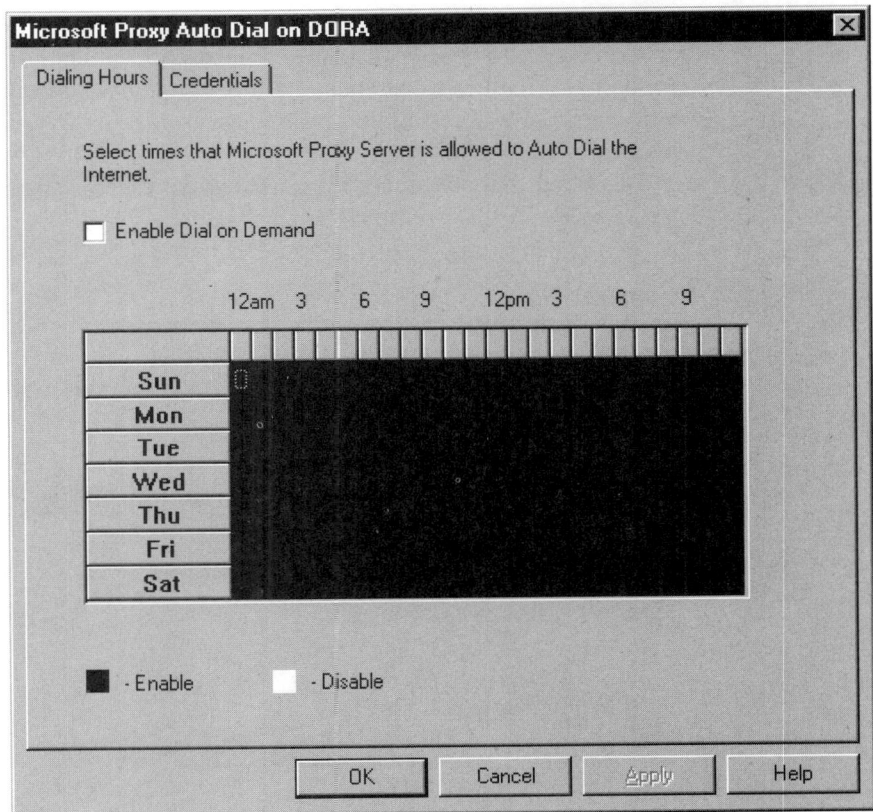

Figure 19-19: The Microsoft Proxy Auto Dial configuration's Dialing Hours tab.

Dialing Hours

By specifying dialing hours, the systems administrator can restrict client users' ability to connect to the Internet using a dial-up connection. For example, there may be a need to prevent client users from using the dial-up connection during the afternoons during business days (perhaps the hardware used for the dial-up connection is also being used for other purposes during this time). Or the call may be a toll call with much higher rates during daytime (or business) hours.

The Dialing Hours tab (Figure 19-19) shows what hours are enabled (the default is to enable all hours). It is also possible to disable the dial-on-demand feature by unchecking the Enable Dial on Demand check box; doing so will require that the systems administrator make the necessary connection manually.

Disabling dial on demand is useful when the ISP imposes an hourly fee or when the call to the ISP is a toll call.

Credentials

The Credentials tab (see Figure 19-20) lets you configure the dial-up connection.

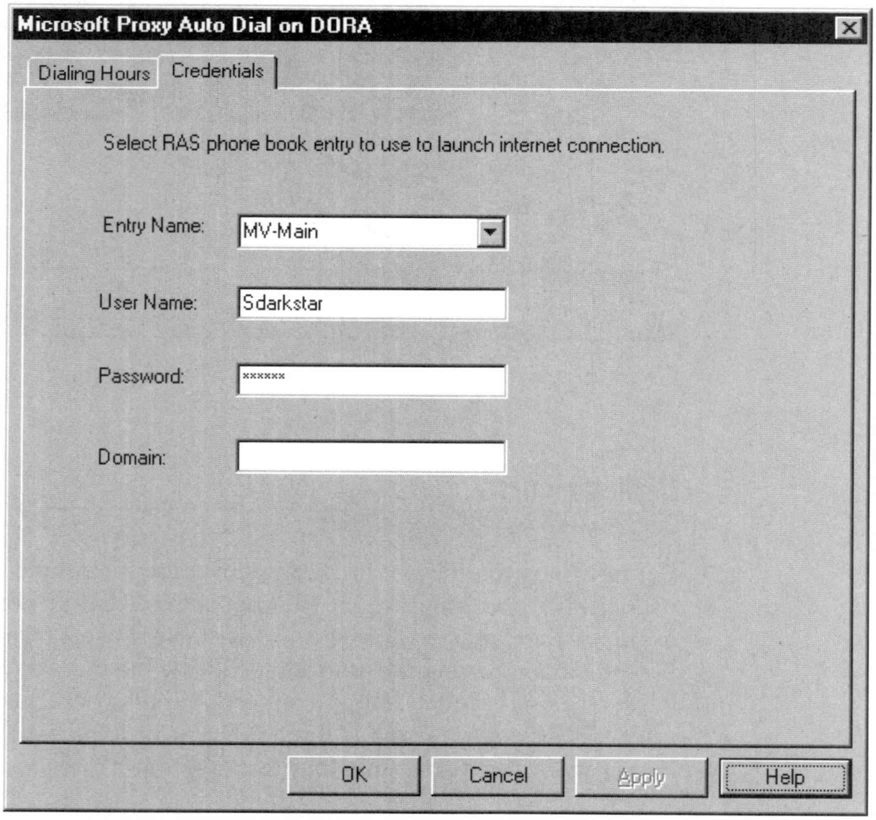

Figure 19-20: The Microsoft Proxy Auto Dial configuration's Credentials tab.

In the Credentials tab, first enter the RAS Phone Book entry name that has been configured to dial into the ISP. If an RAS Phone Book entry has not been created, you'll need to create one (see the next section, "Creating RAS Phone Book Entries").

Note: Doesn't my system know the username and password? When you use a phone book entry, there is a dialog box that is displayed to prompt for the username, password, and domain. Dial-Up Networking displays the RAS connect dialog box, and the information entered in it is not accessible by Microsoft Proxy Server—therefore the information must be reentered for Microsoft Proxy Server.

In the appropriate text boxes, enter the username and password that have been assigned to you by your ISP. Though uncommon, the password field may be unused. If applicable, enter a domain name in the Domain field. If the ISP is not running a Windows NT Server network with domains, leave this field blank; attempting to use a domain name on a non-Windows NT network can result in an abrupt disconnection!

Creating RAS Phone Book Entries

To create an RAS Phone Book entry:

Note: Even though the entries are referred to as RAS Phone Book entries, they are created and managed using the DUN (Dial-Up Networking) manager program.

1. Start the DUN (Dial-Up Networking) manager (Figure 19-21) using Start Menu | Programs | Accessories | Dial-Up Networking.

2. In the Dial-Up Networking manager, click the New button to display the New Phone Book Entry Wizard. The wizard will prompt for all information needed to connect to the ISP. (If you are experienced in creating RAS Phone Book entries, select the I Know All About button and the wizard will allow manual entry of specific information.)

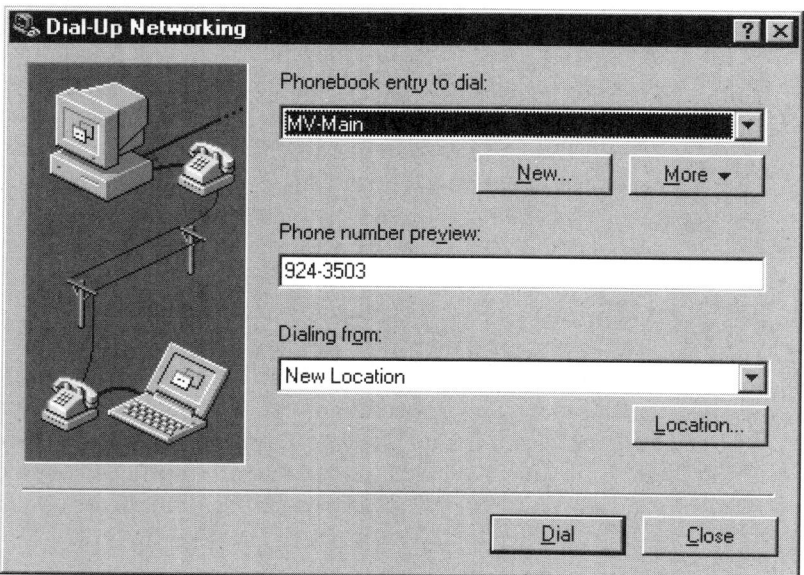

Figure 19-21: The Dial-Up Networking manager—click New to create a new RAS Phone Book entry.

3. Once the new RAS Phone Book entry has been created, test it! Dial into the ISP and establish a connection. Check to ensure that the ISP's name server is functioning correctly (try to PING a remote site, such as www.microsoft.com). If possible also make a Web connection (using Internet Explorer) to double-check the ISP's connection.

4. After completing the configuration, close the Dial-Up Networking manager.

Moving On

This chapter introduced Microsoft Proxy Server; we showed you how to install the Microsoft Proxy Server and some of its basic features. Microsoft Proxy Server works with the Microsoft Internet Information Server (IIS), a component of Windows NT 4 Server.

In the next chapter, we will cover the Microsoft Proxy Server client configuration. Each client user who will be using the Microsoft Proxy Server Facilities will need to have client software installed and configured.

20

Configuring Clients for Microsoft Proxy Server

In this chapter, we describe Microsoft Proxy Server's client configuration. When installed, Microsoft Proxy Server creates a client installation share used by clients to install the necessary support for Microsoft Proxy Server.

The share created by the Microsoft Proxy Server installation is called mspclnt. A user connects to the share (either by mapping a drive to it or by using the UNC share name) and runs the client software installation program called setup. For example, on the Dark_Star network, client users (all are either Windows 95 or Windows NT users) enter the command \\dora\mspclnt\setup to run the setup program.

Installing Client Software

The example client is a Windows 95 workstation connected to the Microsoft Proxy Server via an Ethernet network. The workstation is using both TCP/IP and IPX/SPX protocols. On the Dark_Star network, where the main server is named Dora, the command \\dora\mspclnt\ setup (issued from a DOS command window) was used to run the setup program.

The default location to install Microsoft Proxy Server client software is C:\mspclnt. Generally it's a good idea to use this location name, to retain consistency among clients.

When the client installation starts, a splash screen is presented (simply click Continue). Next the Microsoft Proxy Client Setup window (Figure 20-1) is displayed. In this window, the default location for the Microsoft Proxy Client files may be changed if necessary.

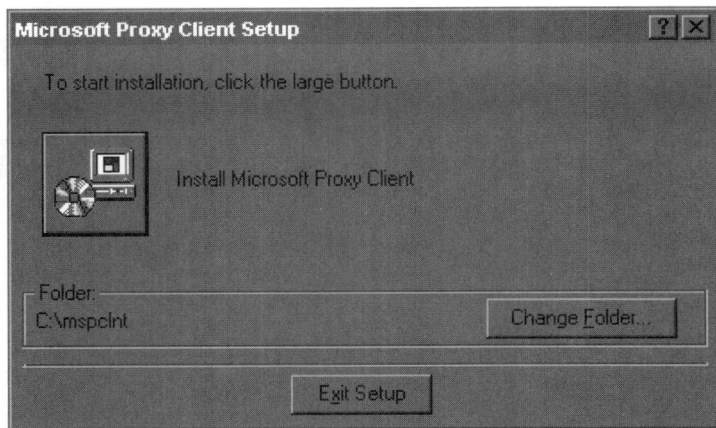

Figure 20-1: The Microsoft Proxy Client Setup window—click the large button to the left of Install Microsoft Proxy Client.

Once the installation of client software has been started, the installation process will continue without further input from the user. At the conclusion of the installation of the Microsoft Proxy Client software, a confirmation dialog will inform the user that the software has been installed.

Configuring the Web Browser

Both Microsoft's Internet Explorer and Netscape's browser may be configured to use a proxy server. It is simple to configure a browser to use Microsoft Proxy Server. (Generally, if the browser is installed after the Microsoft Proxy Client software has been installed, the browser will be configured correctly by the browser's setup program.)

Note: Both Microsoft and Netscape are on a constant revisions schedule for their respective browsers. The average life span for a version of either product is only a few months, so the information presented below may not exactly match the browser version you are using. However, the concepts of using a proxy server are not going to change; once the location for configuring the proxy server has been found, it will not be difficult to do the configuration.

Internet Explorer 3

To configure Microsoft Internet Explorer, follow these steps:

1. Open the Options dialog (Choose View | Options from Internet Explorer's menu).

2. Next click on the Connection tab to display the Connections properties. Different versions of Internet Explorer will have slightly different configurations:

   For Internet Explorer 3.0 (build 1158) on Windows 95, the Connections page will have a button that allows configuration of the connection to the Internet to be made. When you click the Settings button in the Proxy Server section of the Configuration tab, the Proxy Settings dialog box displays (Figure 20-2).

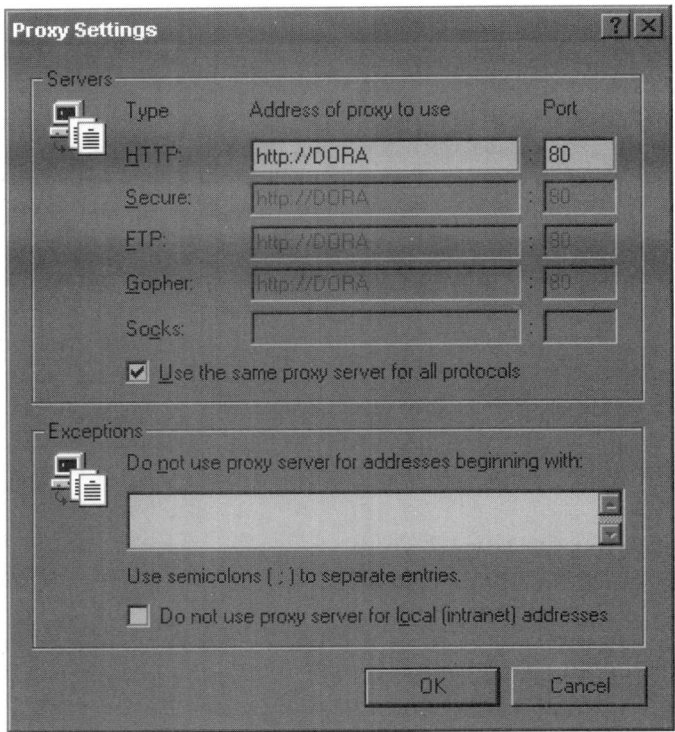

Figure 20-2: The Proxy Settings dialog tells Internet Explorer which proxy server to use.

For Internet Explorer 3.0 (build 1215) on Windows NT, the Connections page will be the settings that are displayed on the Proxy Settings dialog box.

3. To configure one proxy server to use with HTTP, Secure (HTTPS), FTP, Gopher, and Socks protocols, check the Use the Same Proxy Server for All Protocols check box.

4. In the HTTP field, enter the proxy server's name or address. Make sure the name resolves to a single IP address when using TCP/IP protocol. Fill in the port number (typically port 80 is used).

5. In the Exceptions area, enter the server's name or address for those sites that are not to be accessed using the proxy server in the space provided. Wild cards (using an asterisk) are permitted, too. To simply force all systems located on the local intranet to not use the proxy server, click the Do Not Use Proxy Server for Local (Intranet) Addresses control.

6. When you are done configuring Internet Explorer, click the OK button at the bottom of the Options dialog box.

Netscape Navigator

To configure Netscape Navigator, follow these steps:

1. Choose Options | Network Preferences and click on the Proxies tab.

2. In the Proxies property sheet, click the Manual Proxy Configuration radio button and then click View.

3. In the Proxies dialog box, enter the name of the proxy server in the HTTP Proxy field and specify the port to be used (typically port 80).

4. Click OK to save the configuration. Click OK in the Proxies tab in the Preferences dialog box.

Except for the location of the proxy information, configuring Navigator is very similar to configuring Internet Explorer.

Configuring a Browser on the Server

It is not uncommon for a browser to be configured to run on the server. This browser may also use the Microsoft Proxy Server. Configure the browser exactly the same as you would the examples above, with one minor difference: Instead of entering a name for the Microsoft Proxy Server, enter the IP address for the NIC (Network Interface Card) that is connected to the intranet (the internal network). Do *not* enter the IP address of the NIC that is connected to the Internet; this will cause requests from the browser to fail, as the IP address for the NIC, which is connected to the Internet, will not be found in the LAT (Local Address Table).

Configuring Client Software

Microsoft Proxy Server client configuration is simple. After installing the Microsoft Proxy Server client software, a new Control Panel applet, WSP Client, will be in the Control Panel (start the Control Panel from Start Menu | Settings | Control Panel).

Start the WSP Client applet by double-clicking its icon. The Microsoft WinSock Proxy Client window will be shown (see Figure 20-3), which lets you select both the configuration location (the Microsoft Proxy Server's name) and whether the WinSock proxy client is enabled or disabled (it is enabled by default).

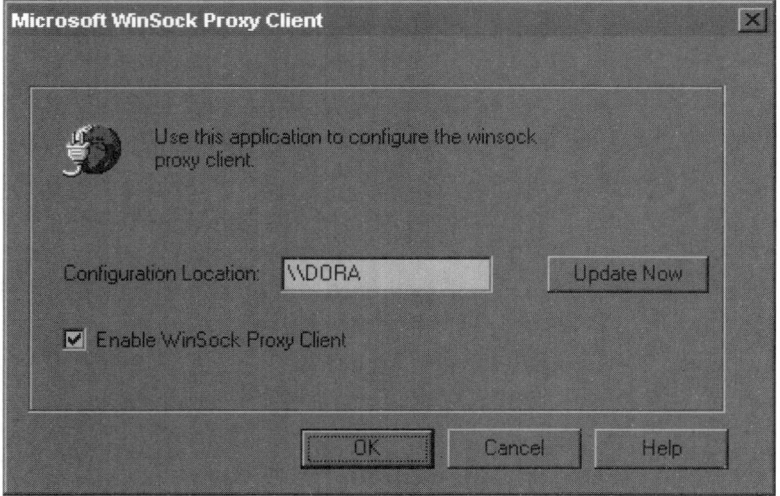

Figure 20-3: Configuring a client user; select the server to obtain configurations from and enable WinSock Proxy.

The configuration location is the server where the particular client will obtain client configuration files. Make sure that the name for the server is a computer name (\\server) and not a name that a DNS might resolve into multiple IP addresses! When you click the Update Now button, the current configuration for the client will be updated.

The Enable WinSock Proxy Client check box lets you disable use of the WinSock proxy client. When selecting this option, it is necessary to reboot the workstation for the option to take effect.

Moving On

This chapter described how to configure the Microsoft Proxy Server clients. Client configuration is easy, and most users will have little difficulty configuring their Web browsers to work with Microsoft Proxy Server.

This chapter concludes Section IV, which covered the Microsoft Proxy Server. In the next section, we will focus on the Microsoft Exchange Server—Microsoft's newest entry into the world of e-mail. Microsoft Exchange Server is a powerful, and configurable, e-mail system that replaced MS Mail in version 2.0 of Microsoft BackOffice. Now, with Microsoft BackOffice version 2.5, we have a new version of Microsoft Exchange Server.

Microsoft Exchange Server

21

Installing Microsoft Exchange Server

Microsoft Exchange Server is Microsoft's replacement for MS Mail, which is part of Microsoft BackOffice 1.5. Microsoft Exchange Server is an advanced, powerful enterprise e-mail server. Microsoft Exchange Server 4.0 is included with Microsoft BackOffice 2.0 and Microsoft BackOffice 2.5.

Microsoft Exchange Client has been a valuable part of Windows 95, Windows NT 4 Server, and Windows NT 4 Workstation. Windows NT 4 comes with basic Microsoft Exchange Client software. Microsoft Exchange Server includes a more advanced version of the Microsoft Exchange Client software that is especially configured to work with it.

Tip

It is beyond the scope of this book to provide a complete reference to Microsoft Exchange Server. If you are working on an implementation of Microsoft Exchange Server, then I recommend that you purchase the printed documentation for it.

Clients for Windows 95, Windows NT, DOS, and 16-bit versions of Windows are included with Microsoft Exchange Server.

Microsoft Exchange Server can be purchased either as a component of Microsoft BackOffice or separately as an individual product. There may be financial advantages to using Microsoft BackOffice: You may find that purchasing Microsoft BackOffice is less expensive than purchasing two or more of the BackOffice products separately.

Warning

The license agreement for Microsoft BackOffice does not allow you to split its various parts between servers. All Microsoft BackOffice components must be installed on a single server, or additional Microsoft BackOffice licenses must be purchased.

In January 1997, Microsoft released Microsoft Office 97. With Microsoft Office 97 is a new client for Exchange, called Outlook. Combining an e-mail client with features such as a calendar, contact management, task lists, journal, and notes, Outlook is a very powerful tool for users. (I speak from experience: I've been an Outlook user for some time, and I'd be hard pressed to do without Outlook now!) In Chapter 23 we will describe Microsoft Outlook more fully.

Note: Microsoft Exchange Server 4.0 has a number of Service Packs available. At the time this book was written, Service Pack 2 was the latest available. First, check to see which Service Packs are already installed. Choose Help I About in the Microsoft Exchange Administrator program to display the About box, which lists the Service Packs installed. If Service Pack 2 has not been installed, obtain it from Microsoft (check Microsoft's Internet Web page) and install it.

Features in Microsoft Exchange Server 4.0

Microsoft Exchange Server offers a number of features that your organization may find valuable. In this section, we'll take a brief look at some of the main features.

Microsoft Exchange Server allows single- and multi-server configurations to be installed easily. A simple installation can take as little as a few hours (plus the time it takes to configure the client users' mail boxes). Exchange Server uses the standard installation program and does not present any difficult choices during installation.

Microsoft Exchange Server allows multiple servers (Microsoft Exchange servers, that is) to be interlinked so that they work together. Services for multiple server installations include replication and management tools.

The various Microsoft Exchange Server clients may use Exchange Client (which is part of Windows NT 4 and Windows 95). As well, Microsoft Outlook 97 works very well with Microsoft Exchange Server. With either Outlook or Exchange Client, a user may send, receive, store, and organize e-mail, voice mail, faxes, forms, and documents. Of course, some of these features may require additional hardware or software support.

Users of Exchange Client can choose how they view their e-mail. Techniques such as filtering, sorting, and grouping can be used to assist in organization and management of e-mail.

Using rules, Exchange clients can perform automatic forwarding, routing, moving, and deleting of messages. This allows messages from mailing lists, for example, to be placed in folders that are reserved for items of different priorities.

Client users who are working with either remote or portable systems are well supported using Windows NT 4 Server's RAS (Remote Access Server). In addition, clients who are using slow networks may choose to not upload all mail, but rather simply retrieve preview headers and later retrieve only those messages they wish to view.

Included with Microsoft Exchange Server is Schedule + client. This client is automatically installed when the client user installs Microsoft Exchange Server Client. Features include scheduling of people and resources (which might include conference rooms and equipment reservations).

Microsoft Exchange Server, like other Microsoft BackOffice products, supports centralized management. Using centralized management allows multiple Microsoft Exchange Server installations to be managed from a single location, significantly reducing the costs of management.

All Internet mail standards (including MIME, SMTP, and UUENCODE) are supported using Microsoft Exchange Server. Users of Microsoft Exchange Server Client may connect to remote Internet mail systems using POP-3 with either dial-up or direct connections to the Internet.

Microsoft Exchange Server supports direct connections to Internet mail systems, using the SMTP protocol. The connections may be either persistent or dial-up (Chapter 22 covers connecting to the Internet).

Microsoft Exchange Server 5.0

On December 9, 1996, Microsoft announced that Microsoft Exchange Server version 5.0 was to be released to broad beta testing. It is expected to be released publicly near the end of the first quarter of 1997. This book describes Microsoft Exchange Server version 4.0; however, I've included some information below about Microsoft Exchange Server 5.0.

Active Server components (HTTP Protocol Support) make access to mailboxes, discussion groups, schedule information, and the directory on a Microsoft Exchange Server possible using a Web browser.

Apple Macintosh Client for Microsoft Schedule + will give Apple Macintosh users access to Schedule +'s group scheduling, task management, and contact management.

HTML (HyperText Markup Language) support allows any information viewed with a Web browser to be viewed as native HTML.

Internet Mail Service Wizard will set up and configure Microsoft Exchange Server as an Internet mail service. This allows Microsoft Exchange Server to exchange e-mail with other Internet mail systems using SMTP (Standard Mail Transfer Protocol).

Netscape Collabra Migration Tools are used to help convert Netscape Collabra Share users to Microsoft Exchange Server.

Newsfeed Configuration Wizard will set up and configure NNTP newsfeeds from other news servers on the Internet.

NNTP (Network News Transfer Protocol) Protocol support allows discussion groups, knowledge bases, and list servers on Microsoft Exchange. They may then be accessed using an Internet newsreader.

Novell GroupWise Migration Tools help convert Novell NetWare GroupWise users to Microsoft Exchange. Items converted include messages, attachments in messages, and scheduling information.

Person to Person Key Exchange sends digitally signed and encrypted e-mail messages over the Internet. Messages may be sent to recipients who are not part of the originating organization.

POP-3 (Post Office Protocol, version 3) support, long missing in Microsoft Exchange Server, uses POP-3 mail protocol to exchange mail between POP-3 clients and Microsoft Exchange Server.

SSL (Secure Sockets Layer) Protocol support ensures secure communication between an Internet mail (POP-3) reader, Internet news (NNTP) reader, or LDAP client and a Microsoft Exchange server.

UNIX Mail Migration Tools help convert users of UNIX SendMail systems to Microsoft Exchange Server.

Installation Requirements

Microsoft Exchange Server is a large product. Minimum system requirements for it include:

- An Intel 486 (or better) or an RISC-based microprocessor (including the MIPS R4000, Digital Alpha AXP, or PowerPC).

- A minimum of 250MB free space on the server's drive(s).

- Additional space for the Windows NT 4 Server paging file. Generally, you will need to add about 50MB of additional paging file space when running Microsoft Exchange Server.

- A minimum of 24MB RAM, with 32MB recommended for Intel platforms. For RISC platforms, 32MB RAM, with 48MB recommended.

These requirements are *minimum* values. To garner maximum performance from Microsoft Exchange Server, configure the Microsoft Exchange Server's computer to have the following:

- An Intel Pentium 90 (or faster) or a Pentium Pro. Alternatively, you can use an RISC computer.

- Hard disk space for all folders and other information, including users' e-mail. Consider the issues of holidays, large e-mail message attachments, and users who do not properly delete their e-mail from the server.

- The use of several physical drives (and multichannel SCSI controllers) to enhance I/O interleaving and performance. (I/O interleaving rearranges I/O to optimize seeks done with hardware.)

- A striped drive set, which also enhances disk I/O performance. Striping (RAID Level 0) is described in Chapter 3.

- Additional paging file space. (Typically, Microsoft recommends 100MB in addition to the amount of RAM installed. I recommend 150MB in addition to the amount of RAM installed, if possible.)

- A minimum of 32MB RAM, preferably 48; 64MB RAM will perform even better. For RISC systems, 48MB minimum, preferably 64MB or even 128MB for better performance.

Virtually all installations will be different. Variations will include number of users, amount and type of e-mail traffic, and other habits. Because of the variations, you should study and follow the recommendations found in the Microsoft Exchange Server Books Online volumes, "Installation Guide" and "Concepts and Planning Guide."

Warning

Only the very brave, or foolish, attempt to run Microsoft Exchange Server, Microsoft SNA Server, and Microsoft SQL Server at the same time on the same Pentium uni-processor server. To do so, you need to have a very fast Pentium (at least a 200 MHz) and a minimum of 128MB of RAM.

Installing Microsoft Exchange

Installing Microsoft Exchange Server is actually a rather easy task that should only take a few hours. After installation, it will be necessary to configure users, mailboxes, and other support—however, configuration, though tedious, is not necessarily difficult.

This chapter covers installation. Configuration is the topic of the next chapter (Chapter 22).

Microsoft Exchange Server must be installable on either a primary domain controller (PDC) or a backup domain controller (BDC). If Windows NT 4 Server is configured as a stand-alone server, then you will need to reinstall Windows NT 4 Server as a PDC.

Note: There is no way to upgrade from a stand-alone server to a PDC/BDC configuration other than to reinstall Windows NT 4 Server.

A typical installation of Microsoft Exchange Server starts with setup from the Microsoft Exchange Server distribution CD-ROM. Insert the CD into the drive and run setup from the correct folder. (There are versions of Microsoft Exchange Server for Intel, MIPS, and Alpha processors.)

When Microsoft Exchange Server is installed, a copy of Microsoft Exchange Client is also installed.

As are other components in Microsoft BackOffice, Exchange Server is available as a separate product. The version supplied with Microsoft BackOffice is virtually identical to the unbundled version—the only difference is that you start the Microsoft BackOffice version of Microsoft Exchange Server's setup program from Microsoft BackOffice Setup.

Figure 21-1 shows the Microsoft Exchange Server Setup program. You must click Typical, Complete/Custom, or Minimum. Be careful: The Change Directory button in the Microsoft Exchange Server Setup window is the only way to modify the folder (directory) where Microsoft Exchange Server will be installed.

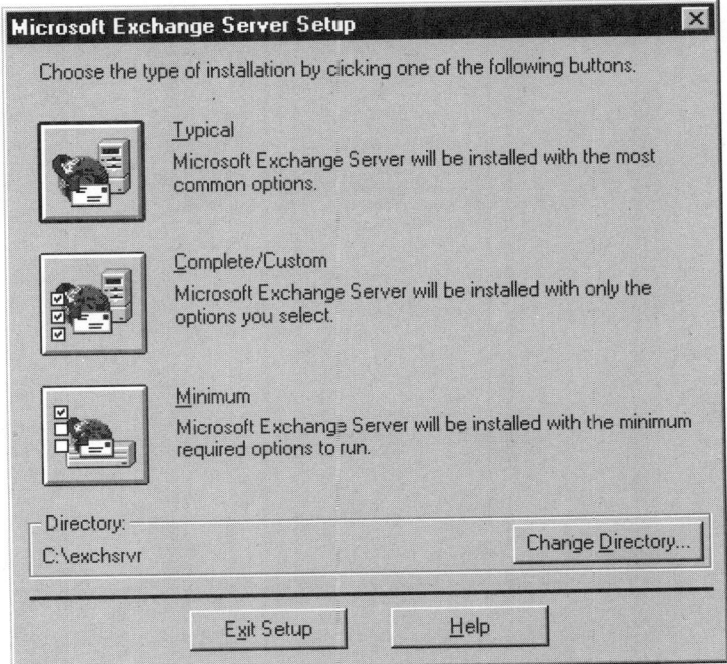

Figure 21-1: The first screen of the Microsoft Exchange Server Setup program—selecting the type of setup.

As shown in Figure 21-2, Microsoft Exchange Server consists of three installable components:

- **Microsoft Exchange Server**—This option installs the actual server portion of Microsoft Exchange Server. The server may be locally or remotely administered, using the Microsoft Exchange Administrator program.

- **Microsoft Exchange Administrator**—This option installs the administrator for Microsoft Exchange Server. The administration of Microsoft Exchange Server may be either at the server or on a remote administration machine.

- **Microsoft Exchange Server Books Online**—This option installs the extended online help system. When installing either Microsoft Exchange Server or Microsoft Exchange Administrator, it is best to install this component.

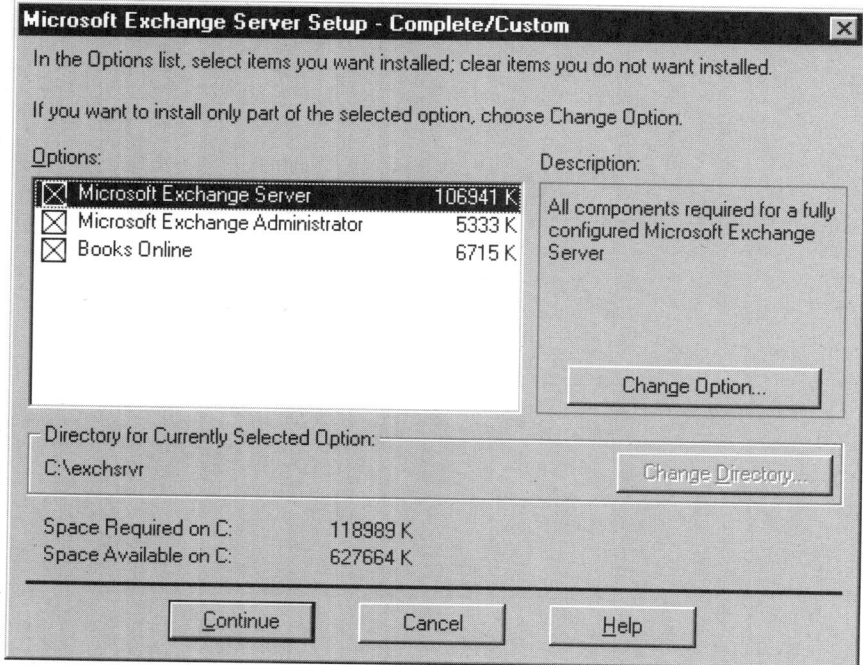

Figure 21-2: Selecting Microsoft Exchange Server options.

On the server, install Microsoft Exchange Server and Microsoft Exchange Administrator. Where Microsoft Exchange Server is being installed on one server and will be administered from another server or workstation, install Microsoft Exchange Administrator on a second system being used for administration.

If you have access to the printed Microsoft Exchange Server documentation, then installing the Books Online may be redundant. However, if the Microsoft Exchange Server printed documentation is unavailable, then installing the Books Online represents a wise choice—Microsoft Exchange Server is a complex and difficult-to-manage system.

Installing Microsoft Exchange Server requires substantial planning, for which Microsoft provides a number of worksheets to assist. These worksheets (for an example, see Figure 21-3) may be printed from the Books Online (search for the topics "Organization Planning Worksheet," "Site Planning Worksheet," and "Server Planning Worksheet").

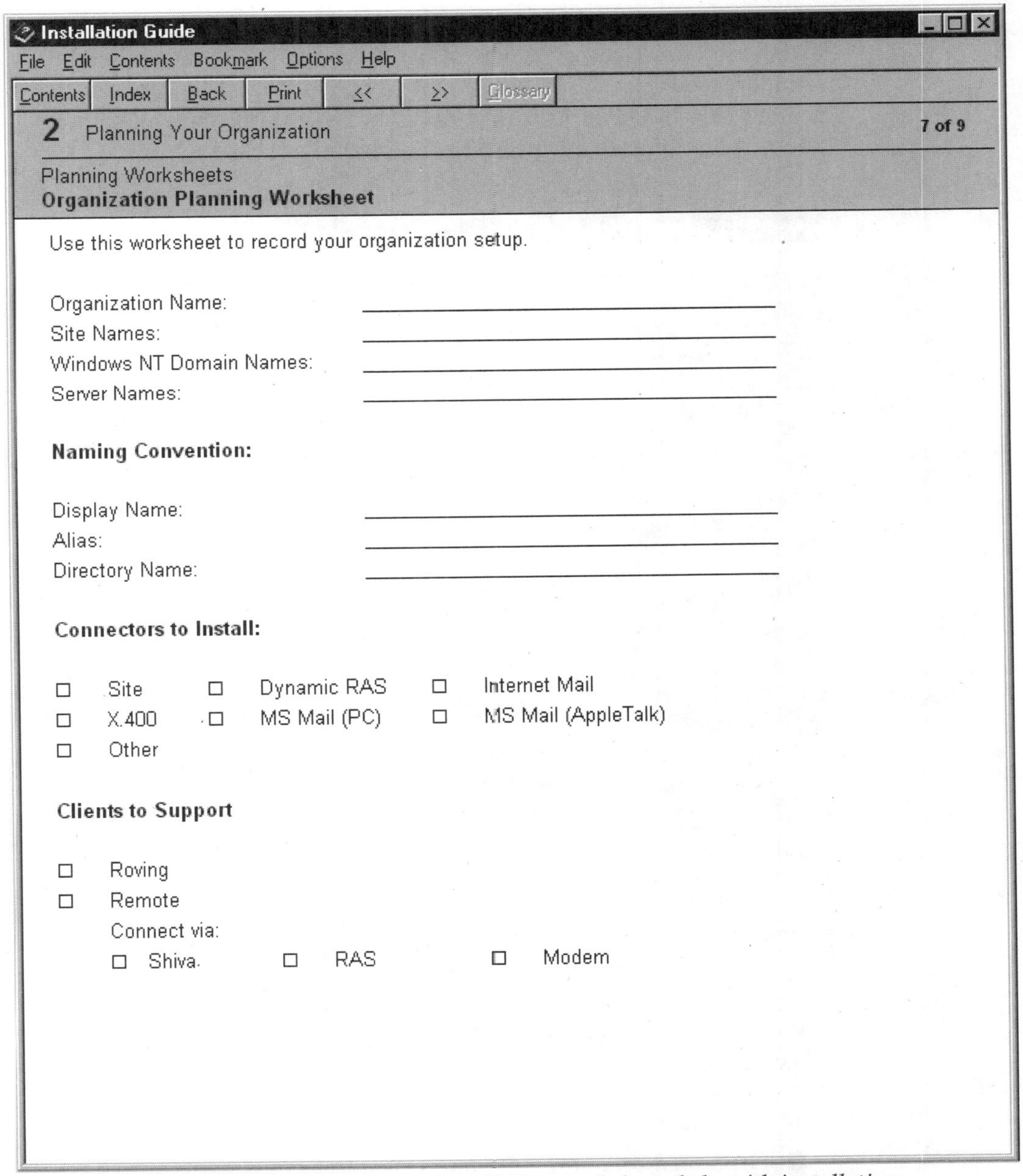

Installation Guide   _ □ ×

File   Edit   Contents   Bookmark   Options   Help

| Contents | Index | Back | Print | << | >> | Glossary |

2   Planning Your Organization   **7 of 9**

Planning Worksheets
Organization Planning Worksheet

Use this worksheet to record your organization setup.

Organization Name: _____
Site Names: _____
Windows NT Domain Names: _____
Server Names: _____

Naming Convention:

Display Name: _____
Alias: _____
Directory Name: _____

Connectors to Install:

☐   Site   ☐   Dynamic RAS   ☐   Internet Mail
☐   X.400   ☐   MS Mail (PC)   ☐   MS Mail (AppleTalk)
☐   Other

Clients to Support

☐   Roving
☐   Remote
    Connect via:
     ☐ Shiva   ☐ RAS   ☐ Modem

Figure 21-3: Microsoft Exchange Server installation worksheets help with installation.

Microsoft server products require that you select a licensing mode at installation time. The two choices, Per Server and Per Seat, should be familiar (see Figure 21-4). If in doubt when installing Microsoft Exchange, select the Per Server licensing mode—your license agreement allows a one-time change from Per Server to Per Seat.

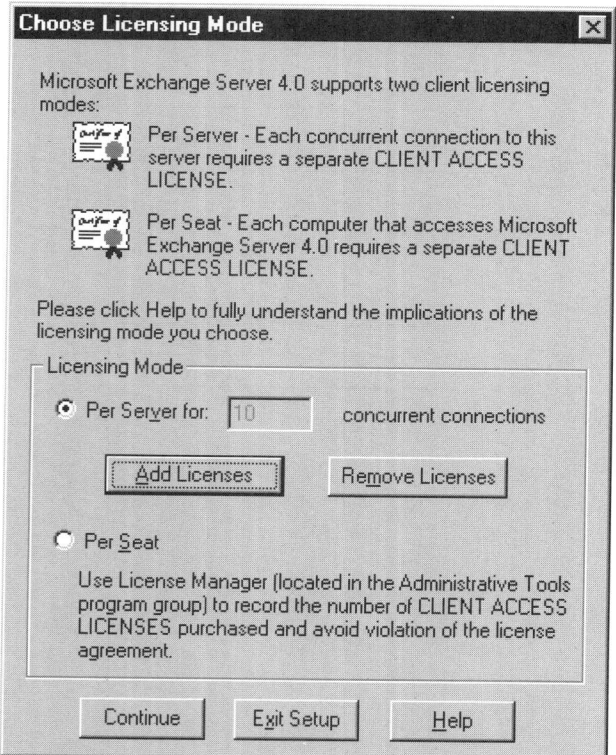

Figure 21-4: Select the licensing mode for Microsoft Exchange Server.

If there is an existing site on another server, Microsoft Exchange Server can be installed as a member of the same site. The alternative is to create a new site (the most popular choice). Creating a new site requires you to provide two pieces of information:

- **Organization name**—the name of your organization, which will be used to form the site's e-mail addresses.

- **Site name**—the name of the site being installed, which will be combined with the organization name to form part of Microsoft Exchange Server's e-mail addresses.

The organization name and the site name form a default e-mail address, such as:

Organization_Name.Site_name.com

where *Organization_Name*, and *Site_name* are the names you entered in the Organization and Site dialog box (see Figure 21-5).

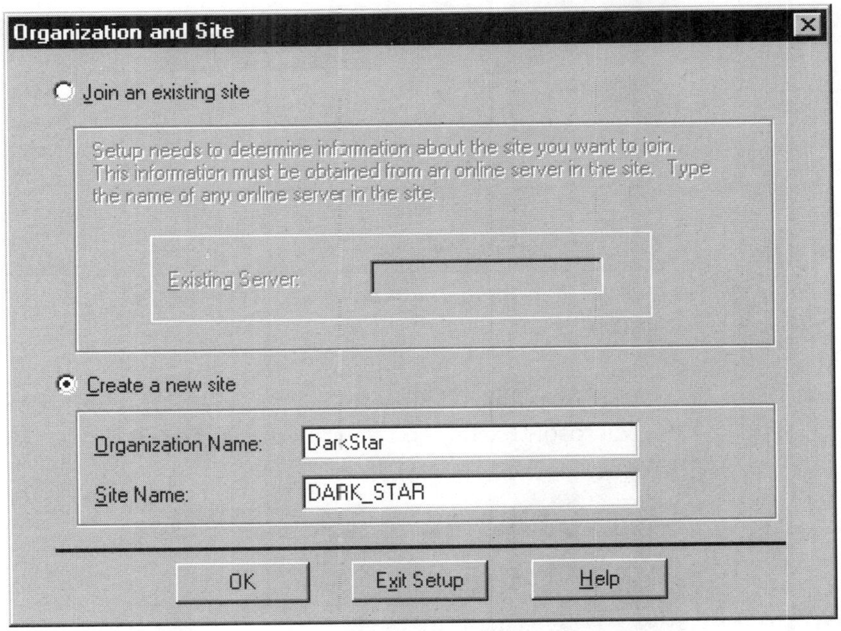

Figure 21-5: Entering the organization name and site name.

Microsoft Exchange Server's setup program will prompt for other needed information, such as the administrator's userid and password (Figure 21-6). If the userid specified does not have the necessary rights to administer Microsoft Exchange Server, then it will be granted the necessary rights. The administrator userid and password can be either one of the Windows NT 4 Server administrators or a new userid created specifically to administer Microsoft Exchange Server.

Figure 21-6: Enter the administrator's Windows NT 4 Server userid and password.

After installing Microsoft Exchange Server, setup will prompt to run the Microsoft Exchange Server Performance Optimizer (see Figure 21-7).

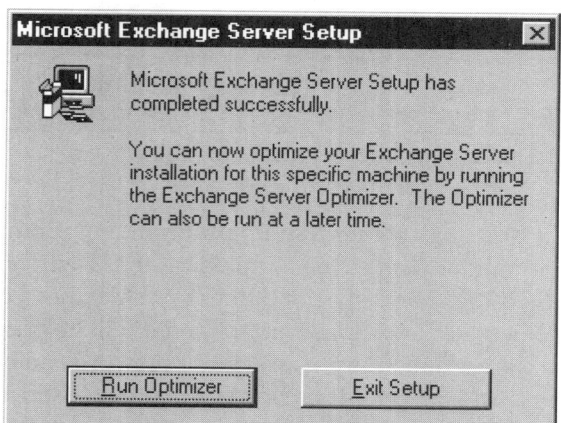

Figure 21-7: Click Run Optimizer to run Microsoft Exchange Server Performance Optimizer for the first time.

If you do not optimize Microsoft Exchange Server during installation, then you should definitely do so before putting the Exchange Server to use.

Optimizing Performance

The Microsoft Exchange Performance Optimizer is a wizard that analyzes the disk resources on the server and determines the optimal placement for Microsoft Exchange Server files. The first screen is shown in Figure 21-8.

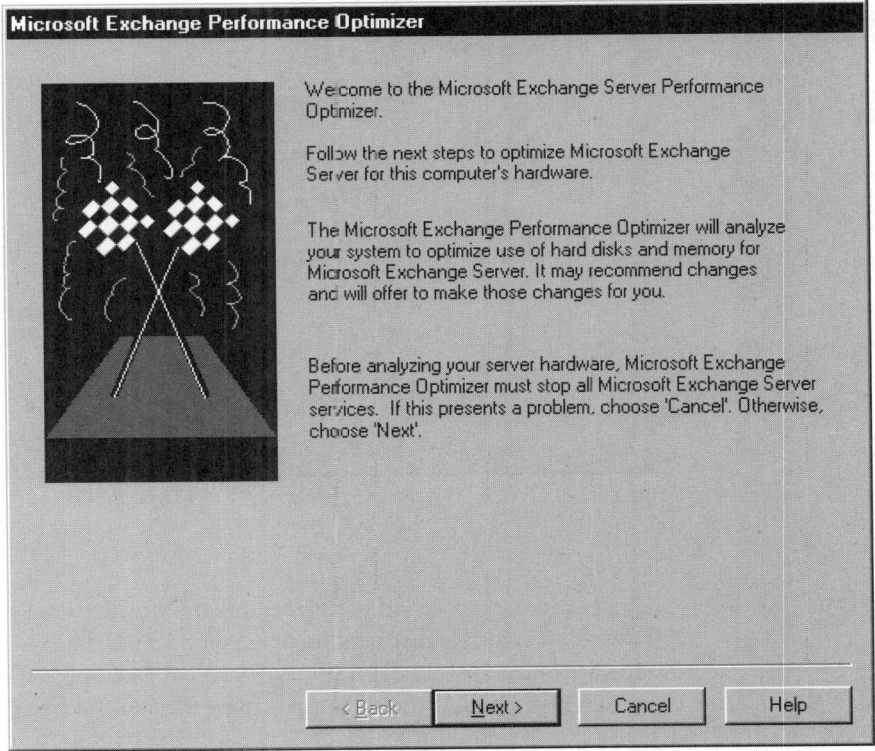

Figure 21-8: Microsoft Exchange Performance Optimizer's first screen.

Microsoft Exchange Performance Optimizer needs information about the size of your Microsoft Exchange Server site. You need to *estimate* the number of users, type of usage, and size of the organization, as Figure 21-9 shows.

For example, the server where Microsoft Exchange Server is installed (DORA) has five hard drives (c:, d:, e:, f:, and g:), each of which has different performance factors and space availability.

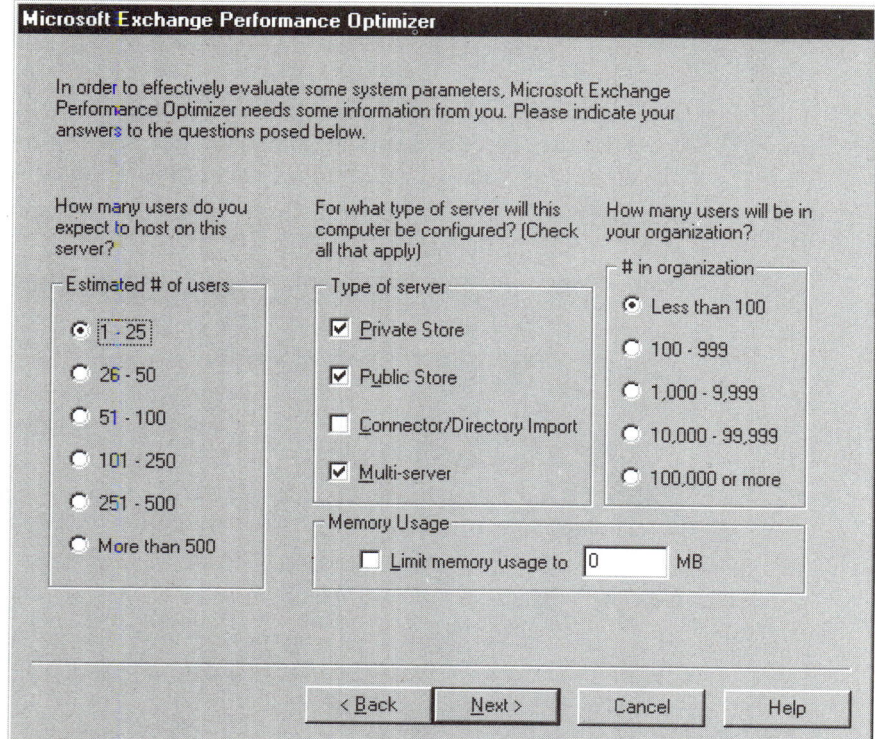

Figure 21-9: Telling Microsoft Exchange Performance Optimizer how big you are.

Once Microsoft Exchange Performance Optimizer has analyzed the hardware, it will suggest new locations for a number of items. Figure 21-10 shows the results of running Microsoft Exchange Performance Optimizer on DORA: the optimizer used four of the five drives on DORA. The ideal outcome would be for Microsoft Exchange Performance Optimizer to spread the load effectively between the different drives.

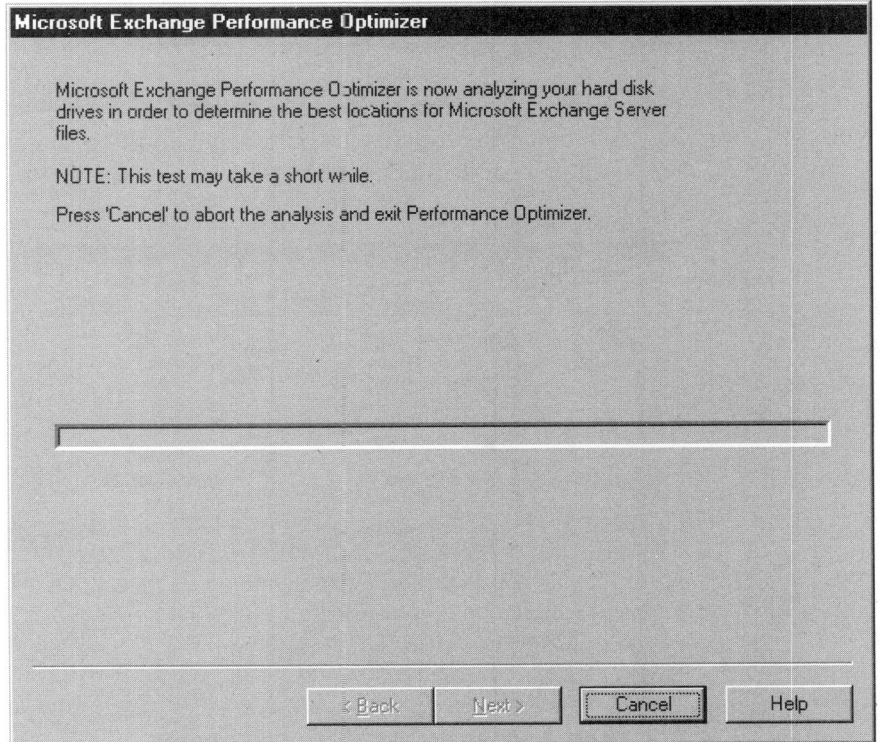

Figure 21-10: Microsoft Exchange Performance Optimizer suggests moving a few files.

If you are running Microsoft Exchange Performance Optimizer as part of a new installation, you do not need to back up these files before moving them. However, if you are running Microsoft Exchange Performance Optimizer on a running Microsoft Exchange Server system, make sure you have adequate backups of all files being moved!

Microsoft Exchange Performance Optimizer is able to move the files automatically (this is recommended).

Components of Microsoft Exchange Server

Once Microsoft Exchange Server is installed, there will be a new Start Menu folder, called Microsoft Exchange. Figure 21-11 shows a typical Microsoft Exchange management folder.

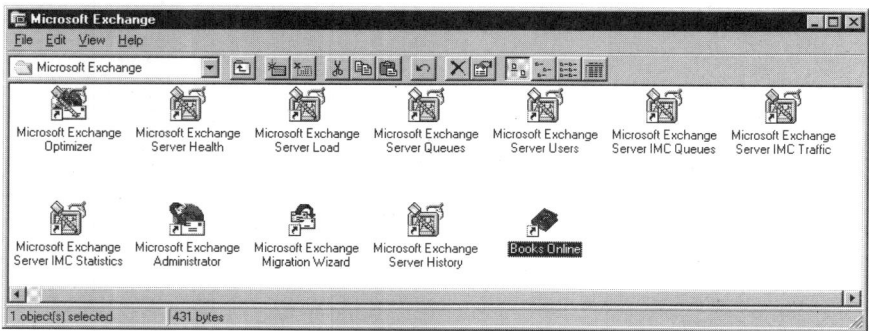

Figure 21-11: The Microsoft Exchange folder—this is where Microsoft Exchange Server is managed.

Microsoft Exchange Server Books Online

The Microsoft Exchange Server Books Online is the main online documentation for Microsoft Exchange Server. Books Online is composed of four books:

- **Installation Guide**—documents the first step in installing Microsoft Exchange Server. Reading through the Installation Guide is an excellent idea, as it is a short volume.

- **Concepts and Planning Guide**—explains how Microsoft Exchange Server works, and includes an overview of the Microsoft Exchange Server product.

- **Administrator's Guide**—provides instructions on how to use the Microsoft Exchange Administrator program, and how to administer a Microsoft Exchange Server installation. This book is the most valuable resource in the Microsoft Exchange Server documentation.

- **Application Designer's Guide**—covers the design of custom Microsoft Exchange applications.

Microsoft Exchange Administrator

The Microsoft Exchange Administrator program manages Microsoft Exchange Server. Start the Microsoft Exchange Administrator program (in Start Menu I Programs I Microsoft Exchange), and log on to a Microsoft Exchange Server to administer.

Microsoft Exchange Administrator has a user interface similar to that of Microsoft SQL Server's Administrator (described in Chapter 12). The main window shows a pair of panes; the left pane shows a tree view of Microsoft Exchange Server, and the right pane shows detail/property information. Microsoft Exchange Administrator is shown in Figure 21-12.

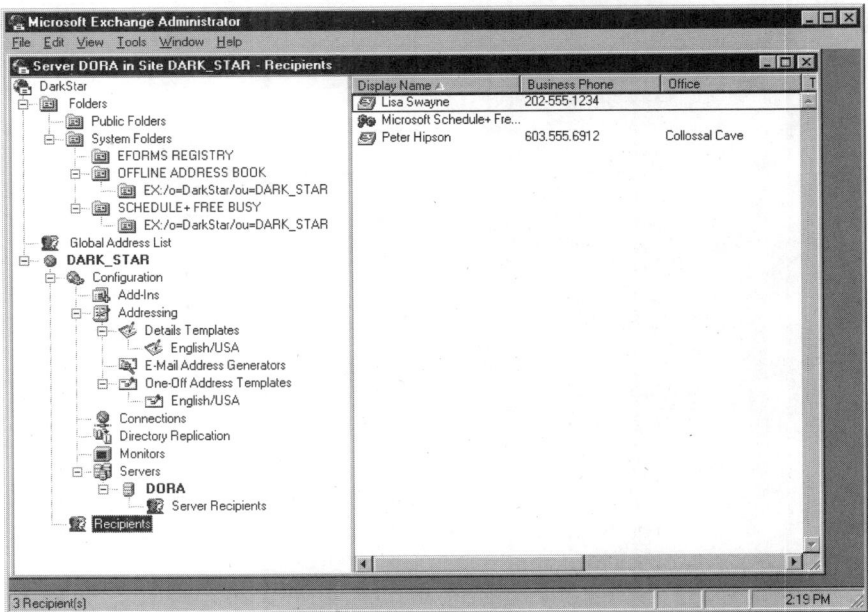

Figure 21-12: Microsoft Exchange Administrator for Dark_Star.

Figure 21-12 shows the relationship between the organization name, site name, and server. You use the Administrator program to create new mailboxes, new distribution lists, and other supporting services.

New Mailboxes

Each Microsoft Exchange client user must have a mailbox. Choosing File I New Mailboxes from Microsoft Exchange Administrator's menu displays the mailbox Properties dialog (Figure 21-13).

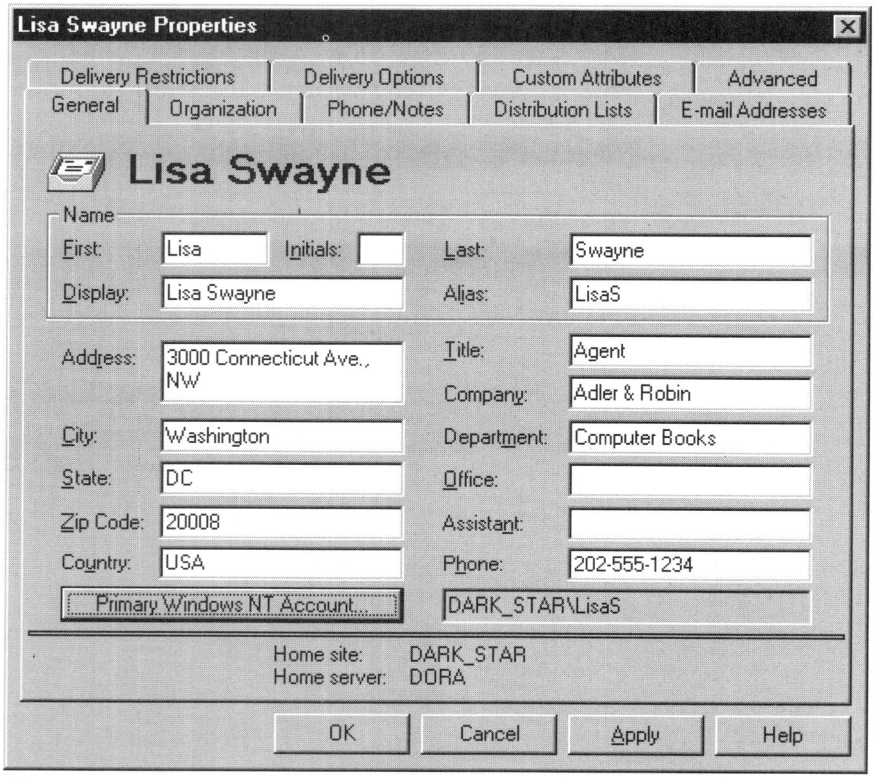

Figure 21-13: The mailbox Properties dialog box for user Lisa Swayne.

The mailbox Properties dialog box has tabs for general information, organization, phone and notes, deliver restrictions, distribution lists, and other information about the user.

After entering the mailbox user's information, click OK to save the information. Chapter 22 will describe configuring user mailboxes in detail.

New Distribution Lists

A distribution list is a method to send a piece of e-mail to more than one user. For example, I have a distribution list called Everyone that can send e-mail to everyone with a mailbox defined on my Microsoft Exchange Server.

If my company were larger, I would create distribution lists for the various departments (such as R&D, Accounting, Marketing, Sales, Administration, and Customer Support). A distribution list can be as flexible as you need it to be.

Figure 21-14 shows the Properties dialog for the distribution list
Authors&Agents. Any message sent to this list will go to all the authors
and all the agents in the mailing list.

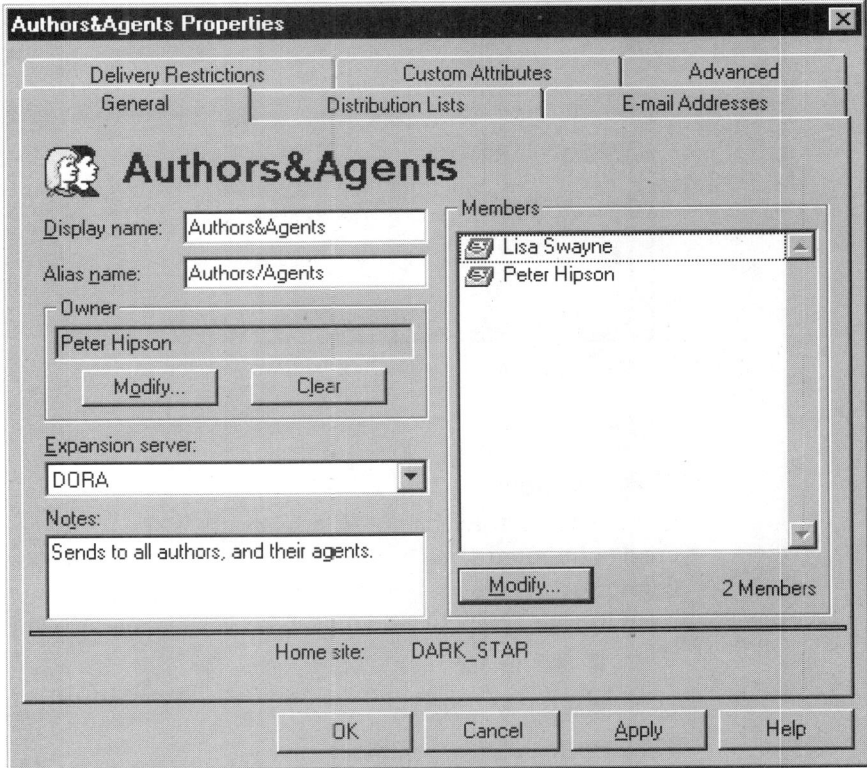

Figure 21-14: The distribution list for Authors&Agents.

The distribution list Properties dialog box has six tabs, including
General (for general information), Distribution Lists, E-mail Addresses,
Custom Attributes, and other information.

Do you see the potential for distribution lists? A simple mail list
configuration can be made with little effort, and each user on the system
can send messages to an entire group using a single name.

New Custom Recipient

The File | New Custom Recipient menu selection allows you to create an
e-mail address for a client user of any supported type. When you create a
custom recipient, a recipient who is not one of the standard (Internet,

Microsoft Mail, and so on) types, there is a prompt to provide the e-mail address type (see Figure 21-15), and then Microsoft Exchange Administrator will display the mailbox Properties dialog box.

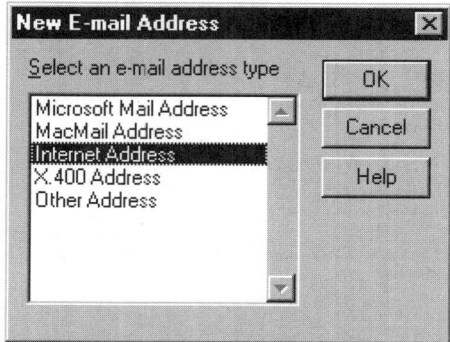

Figure 21-15: Select the custom recipient's e-mail type.

File | New Other

In the Microsoft Exchange Administrator's File menu is a submenu to create other items, such as server monitors, RAS connectors, and site connectors. There are a total of 12 different items that may be created from the File | New Other choice:

- Server Monitor
- Link Monitor
- Recipients Container
- MTA Transport Stack
- X.400 Connector
- Dynamic RAS Connector
- Site Connector
- Directory Replication Connector
- Dirsync Requestor
- Dirsync Server
- Remote Dirsync Requestor
- Information Store

Microsoft Exchange Migration Wizard

The Microsoft Exchange Migration Wizard automates your migration from either MS Mail for PC Networks or Lotus cc:Mail. If you have either of these e-mail systems installed and you wish to convert them to Microsoft Exchange Server, then the Microsoft Exchange Migration Wizard is the tool to use.

Figure 21-16 shows Microsoft Exchange Migration Wizard's first screen, which prompts for the type of system from which to migrate.

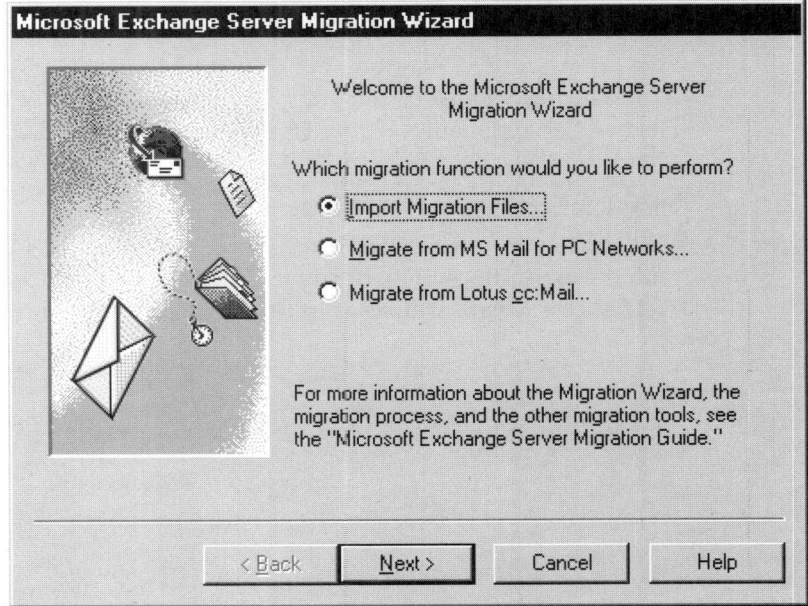

Figure 21-16: Migrating MS Mail and Lotus cc:Mail systems.

Warning

Be sure to back up your files before running Microsoft Exchange Migration Wizard, just in case.

Microsoft Exchange Optimizer

The Microsoft Exchange Optimizer is identical to the Microsoft Exchange Performance Optimizer, described in "Installing Microsoft Exchange" earlier in the chapter.

Use the Microsoft Exchange Optimizer whenever there are changes in the hard drive configuration; otherwise the usage of Microsoft Exchange Server changes significantly.

Monitoring Microsoft Exchange Server

Five preconfigured Windows NT 4 Server Monitor workspace files assist in measuring Microsoft Exchange Server's usage: Server Health, Server History, Server Queues, Server Users, and Server Load.

Microsoft Exchange Server Health

Microsoft Exchange Server Health starts Windows NT 4 Server Monitor with the exhealth.pmw performance monitor workspace file. Figure 21-17 shows Microsoft Exchange Server Health running.

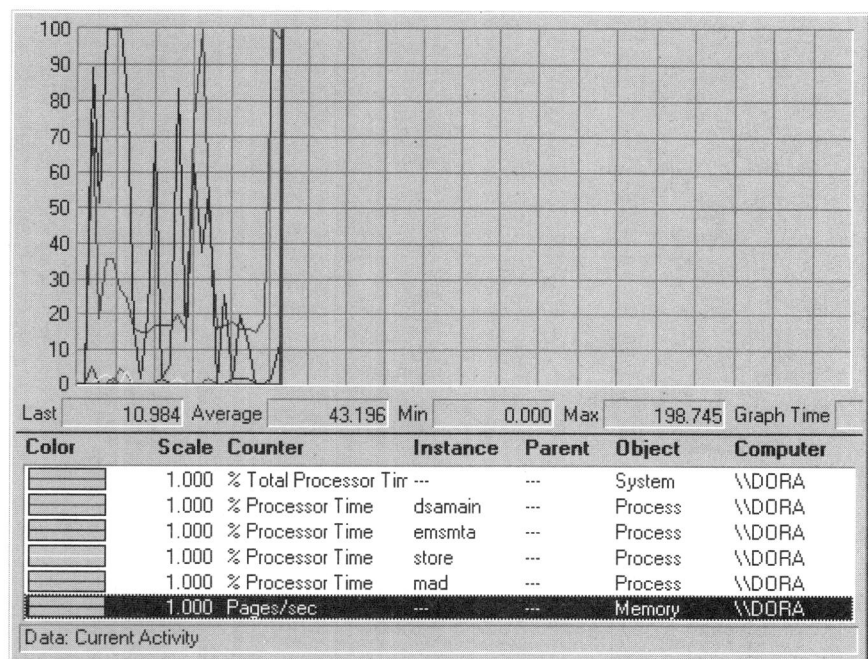

Figure 21-17: Monitoring the health of Microsoft Exchange.

Microsoft Exchange Server History

Microsoft Exchange Server History starts Windows NT 4 Server Monitor with the exhist.pmw performance monitor workspace file. Figure 21-18 shows Microsoft Exchange Server History running.

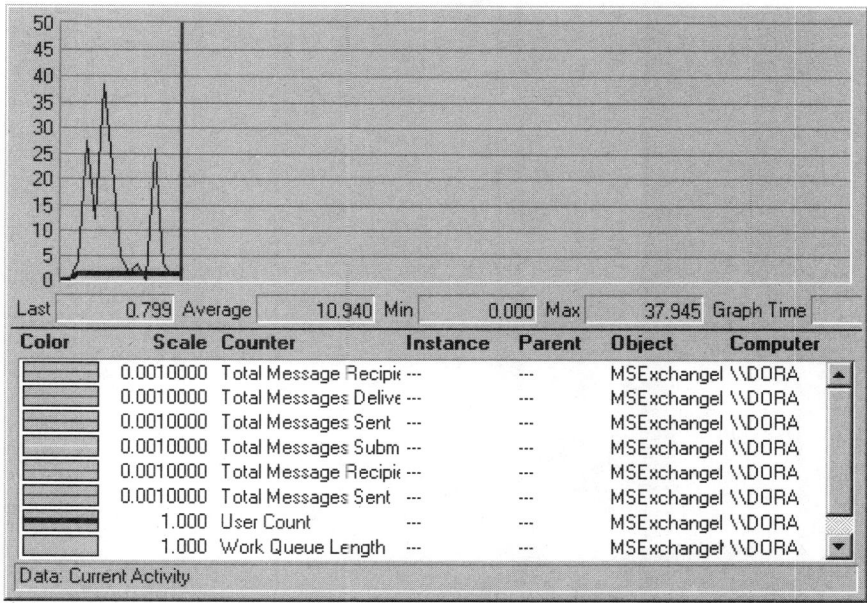

Figure 21-18: Monitoring the history of Microsoft Exchange.

The Microsoft Exchange Server History monitor is very useful when you need to reoptimize Microsoft Exchange Server. With Microsoft Exchange Server History, you can determine Microsoft Exchange Server's usage.

Microsoft Exchange Server Queues

Microsoft Exchange Server Queues starts Windows NT 4 Server Monitor with the exqueue.pmw performance monitor workspace file. Figure 21-19 shows Microsoft Exchange Server backlog.

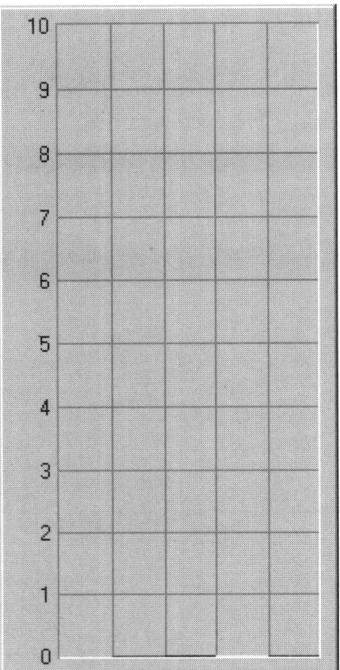

Figure 21-19: Server Queues shows Microsoft Exchange Server backlog.

Bars in the Server Queues performance monitor show:

- Work Queue Length
- Send Queue Length
- Send Queue Size
- Receive Queue Size
- Receive Queue Size

With Microsoft Exchange Server, the Receive Queue Size is monitored twice, while Send Queue Size is not monitored at all. This error can be corrected by adding the Send Queue Size counter (found in the MSExchangeIS Public object) to the chart and deleting the extra Receive Queue Size counter. Chapter 9 explains how to add and remove Windows NT Performance Monitor counters.

Note: Performance Monitor does not prompt to save the workspace—make sure you save any changes you make!

Microsoft Exchange Server Users

Microsoft Exchange Server Users starts Windows NT 4 Server Monitor with the exuser.pmw performance monitor workspace file. Figure 21-20 shows Microsoft Exchange Server with the number of connected users displayed.

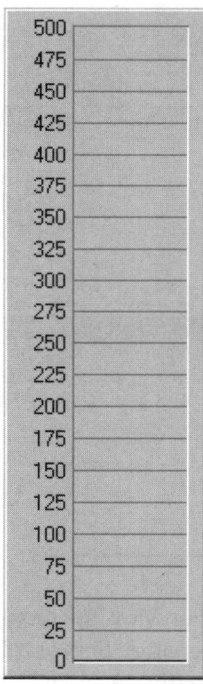

Figure 21-20: Server Users shows the number of users connected to Microsoft Exchange Server.

The one bar in the Server Users performance monitor shows the count of users. Figure 21-20 shows a very lightly loaded Exchange Server—only a few users!

Microsoft Exchange Server Load

Microsoft Exchange Server Load starts Windows NT 4 Server Monitor with the exload.pmw performance monitor workspace file. Figure 21-21 shows Microsoft Exchange Server IMC Traffic running.

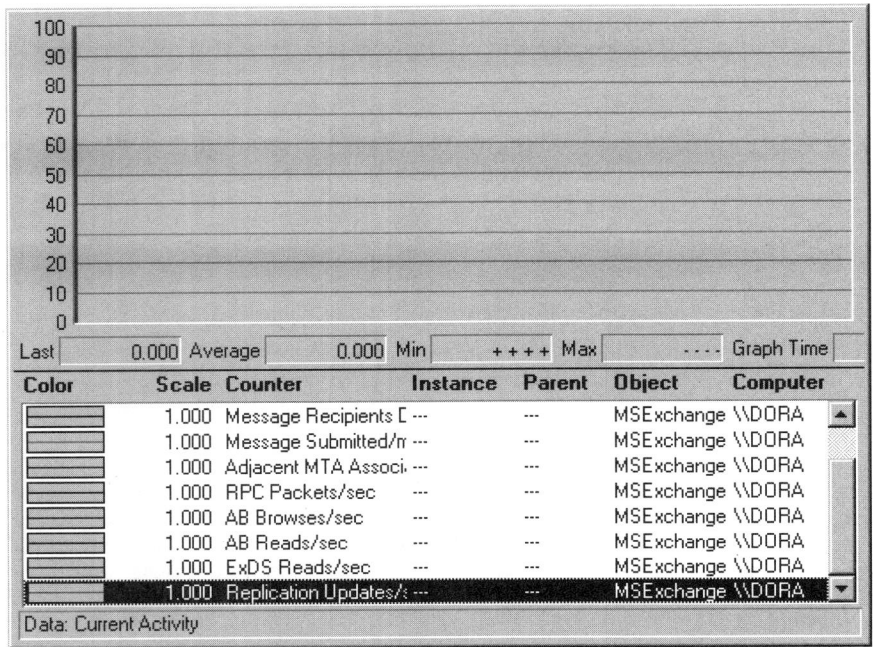

Figure 21-21: Server Load shows Microsoft Exchange Server activity.

Internet Mail Connector Monitoring

Three preconfigured Windows NT 4 Server Monitor workspace files are used to assist in measuring Microsoft Exchange Server's Internet Mail Connector (IMC): IMC Queues, IMC Statistics, and IMC Traffic.

Microsoft Exchange Server IMC Queues

Microsoft Exchange Server IMC Queues starts Windows NT 4 Server Monitor with the imcqueue.pmw performance monitor workspace file. Figure 21-22 shows Microsoft Exchange Server IMC Queues running.

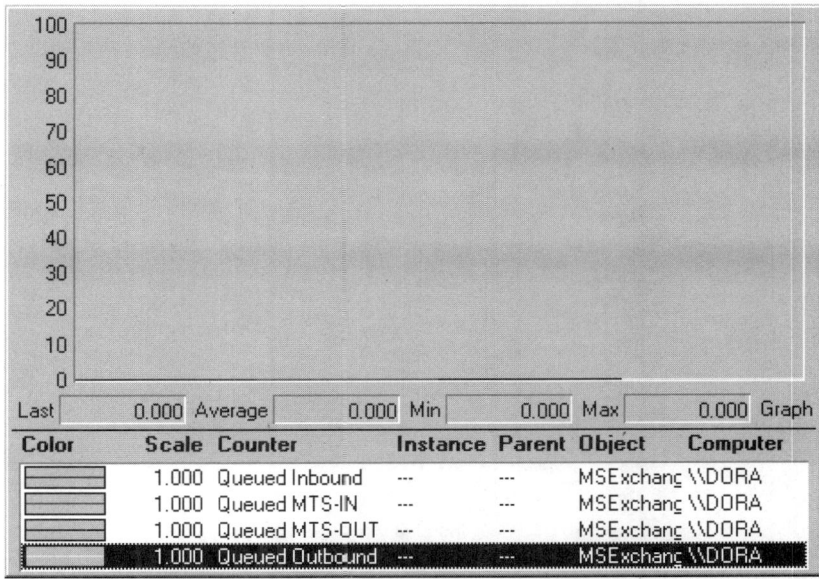

Figure 21-22: Monitoring IMC Queues shows how much Internet mail is being processed.

The Microsoft Exchange Server IMC Queues monitor helps manage Internet e-mail traffic.

Microsoft Exchange Server IMC Statistics

Microsoft Exchange Server IMC Statistics starts Windows NT 4 Server Monitor with the imcstats.pmw performance monitor workspace file. Figure 21-23 shows Microsoft Exchange Server IMC Statistics running.

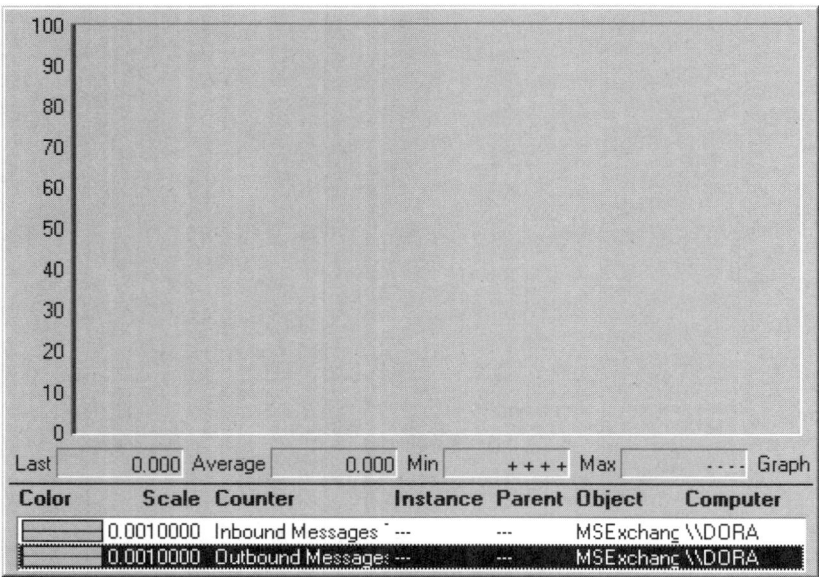

Figure 21-23: Monitoring IMC Statistics shows performance of the Internet Mail Connector.

Both incoming and outgoing e-mail counts are monitored.

Microsoft Exchange Server IMC Traffic

Microsoft Exchange Server IMC Traffic starts Windows NT 4 Server Monitor with the imcflow.pmw performance monitor workspace file. Figure 21-24 shows Microsoft Exchange Server IMC Traffic running.

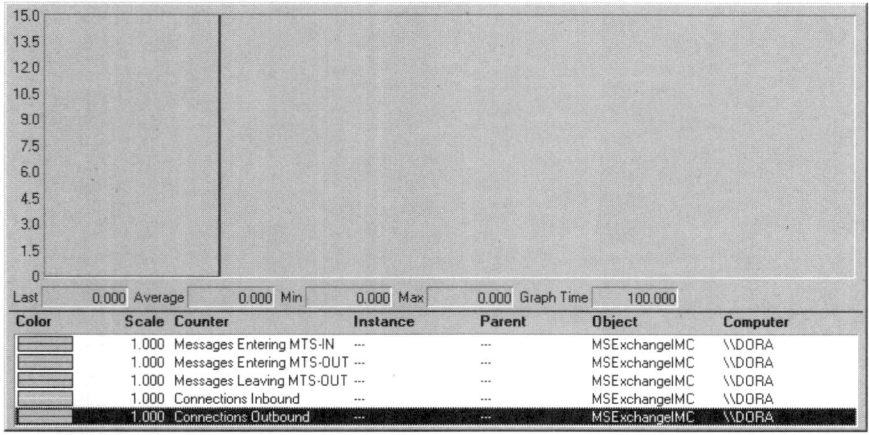

Figure 21-24: Monitoring IMC's traffic.

Moving On

In this chapter we introduced Microsoft Exchange. Microsoft Exchange Server is one of the most complex server components that runs under Windows NT 4 Server. For crganizations that are able to embrace the Microsoft Exchange Clients (which are available for virtually all platforms), Microsoft Exchange Server is a very good choice for e-mail management.

The next chapter introduces how to use Microsoft Exchange Server.

22

Using Microsoft Exchange Server

To use Microsoft Exchange Server, user mailboxes must be configured, and other settings must be modified. Although some of the tasks associated with configuring and using Microsoft Exchange Server are tedious and time consuming, they are not especially difficult to perform.

Briefly, Microsoft Exchange Server configuration consists of adding user mailboxes, distribution lists, and (if applicable) custom recipients. Of course, there are other setups that may be necessary, but a basic, working Microsoft Exchange Server system can be configured by just adding mailboxes.

Setting Options

There are several options that, if set correctly, will make configuring users and mailboxes a bit easier.

First, start Microsoft Exchange Administrator (Start Menu | Programs | Microsoft Exchange | Microsoft Exchange Administrator). The Microsoft Exchange Administrator user interface (see Figure 22-1) consists primarily of a main window, which displays information about each Microsoft Exchange Server being administered.

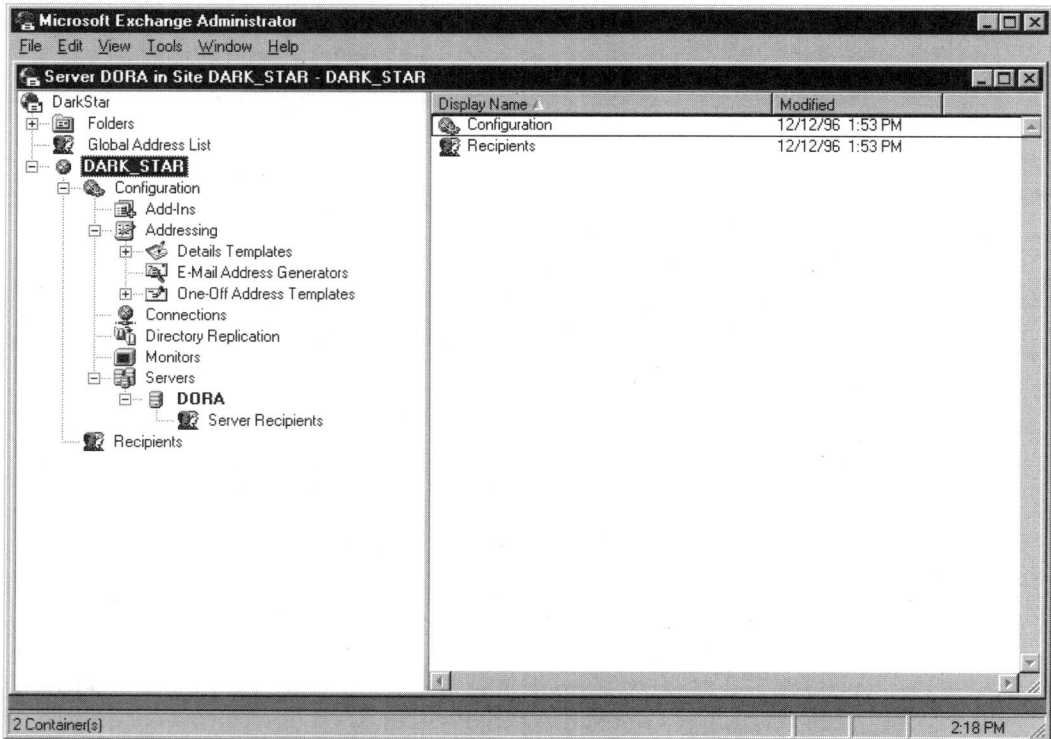

Figure 22-1: The Microsoft Exchange Administrator program's main window shows which server is being managed.

To set options, choose Tools | Options from the Microsoft Exchange Administrator program's main menu. The Options dialog box (see Figure 22-2) will be displayed.

In the first tab, Auto Naming, choose the default display name and alias name formats. For the alias name (the name that is part of the user's e-mail address), most organizations have some form of naming convention for users (often last name first, then first initial). For the display name, using the default convention of first name, then last name, is usually going to be the most acceptable.

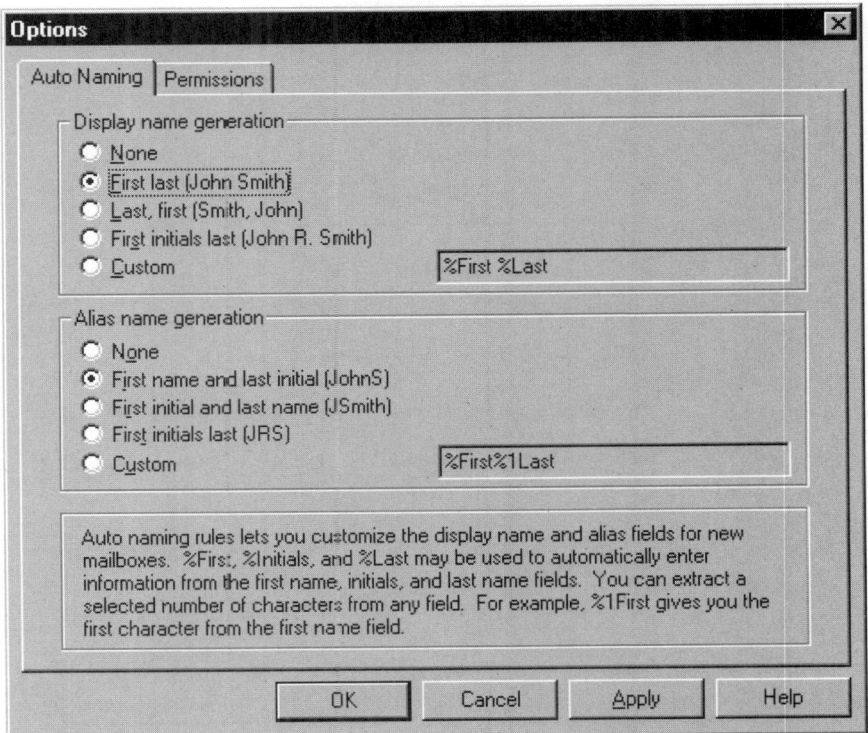

Figure 22-2: The Options dialog box; start with the Auto Naming tab.

The default format for both names can be customized. The substitution keys %First, %Initials, and %Last may be used to specify first name, initials, and last name, respectively. In addition, it is possible to limit the number of characters in a customized name by inserting a number after the % to indicate the maximum number of characters to be used. For example, %3Last would return *Hip* for my last name, which is Hipson.

With the Permissions tab (Figure 22-3), you can configure permissions for Microsoft Exchange Server users. The first entry, Default Windows NT Domain, lets you specify which domain will be used to validate usernames.

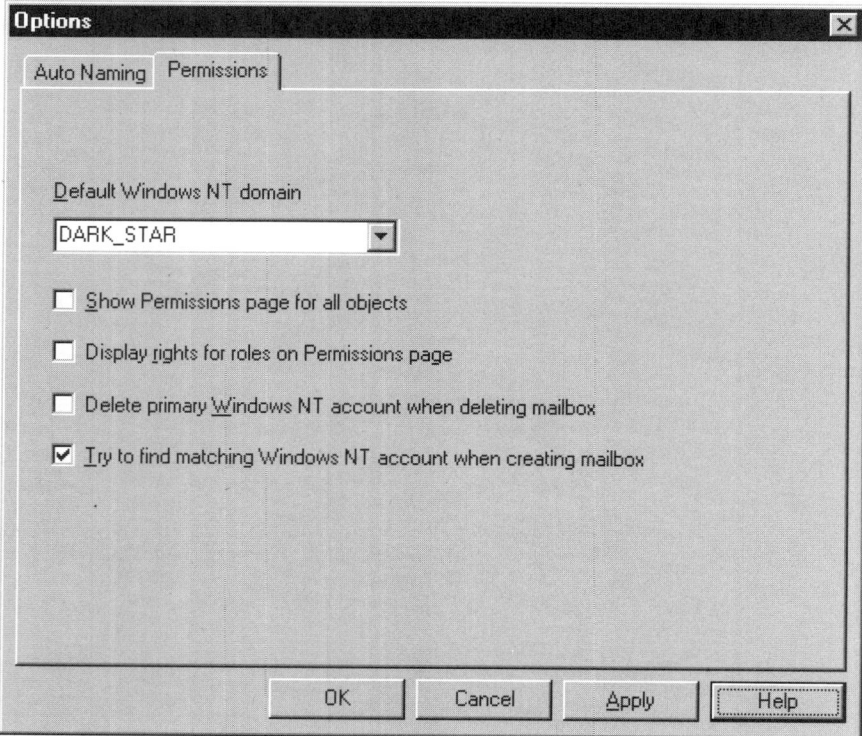

Figure 22-3: The Options dialog's Permissions tab.

The other four options on the Permissions tab are:

- **Show Permissions page for all objects**—forces Microsoft Exchange Administrator to display the Permissions page for any object that has one.

- **Display rights for roles on Permissions page**—causes the rights list to be displayed on the Permissions page.
- **Delete primary Windows NT account when deleting mailbox**—causes the deletion of the main Windows NT 4 Server logon whenever a user mailbox is deleted. This option minimizes the amount of work that must be done when removing users from the system.

- **Try to find matching Windows NT account when creating mailbox**—tries to match a newly created mailbox with a Windows NT 4 Server user. If no user seems to match, the account name has to be manually entered.

Once all the necessary options have been set (the defaults may suffice for many organizations), click the OK button to save the changes.

Adding Mailboxes With Account Lists

The process of adding mailboxes might be tedious were it not for several features that Microsoft Exchange Administrator has. First, it is possible to import the user account information from either a Windows NT Server or a Novell NetWare server. This lets the administrator create default mailboxes for virtually everyone in the organization.

Once user accounts are imported from the server, it may be necessary to edit each mailbox to fill in additional information that is not available from the server's account list. For users who do not (for whatever reason) have an account on the system server, a mailbox must be created manually.

Using Account Lists

There are two methods to add users to Microsoft Exchange Server. The first method is to take the domain's userid list and import the list into Microsoft Exchange Server. The second method is to simply enter userid information manually.

Extracting Account Lists From Servers

Account lists may be extracted from both Windows NT Server and Novell NetWare servers using Microsoft Exchange Server.

To extract the account list from a Windows NT 4 Server, start Microsoft Exchange Administrator (as described in "Setting Options"). From the menu bar, choose Tools | Extract Windows NT Account List. The Windows NT User Extraction dialog box (Figure 22-4) will be displayed.

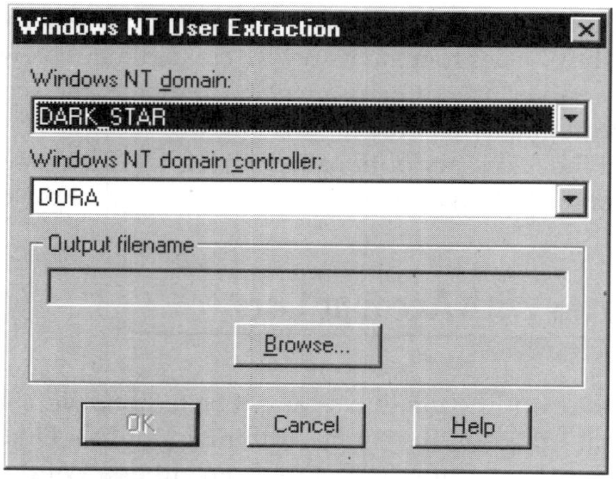

Figure 22-4: The Windows NT User Extraction dialog box—fill in an output filename.

In the Windows NT User Extraction dialog box, you must specify the domain and a domain controller (from which the account information will be obtained). An output filename must be specified also. For the output filename, specify any temporary name desired.

To extract the account list from a Novell NetWare server, start Microsoft Exchange Administrator (as described in "Setting Options"). From the menu, choose Tools | Extract Novell NetWare Account List. The NetWare User Extraction dialog box (Figure 22-5) will be displayed.

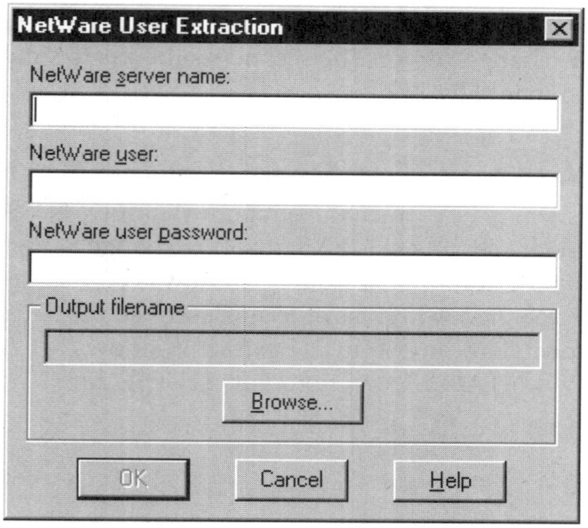

Figure 22-5: The NetWare User Extraction dialog box—fill in an output filename.

In the NetWare User Extraction dialog box, you need to specify the Novell NetWare server's name and your NetWare username and password. An output filename must be specified also. For the output filename, specify any temporary name desired.

The export file consists of a header record and then a record for each userid defined in the login account information. Fields extracted to the export file are:

- **Obj-Class**—the type of object that will be created. This field will typically contain the name Mailbox.
- **Common-Name**—the user's account name (the name used when logging on to the server).
- **Display-Name**—the user's full name.
- **Home-Server**—the user's home server.
- **Comment**—the comment that is in the Novell NetWare server userid account system.

Extracting Account Lists From Exchange Server

To extract the account list from an existing Microsoft Exchange Server installation, start Microsoft Exchange Administrator (as described in "Setting Options"). From the menu, choose Tools | Directory Export. The Directory Export dialog box (Figure 22-6) will be displayed.

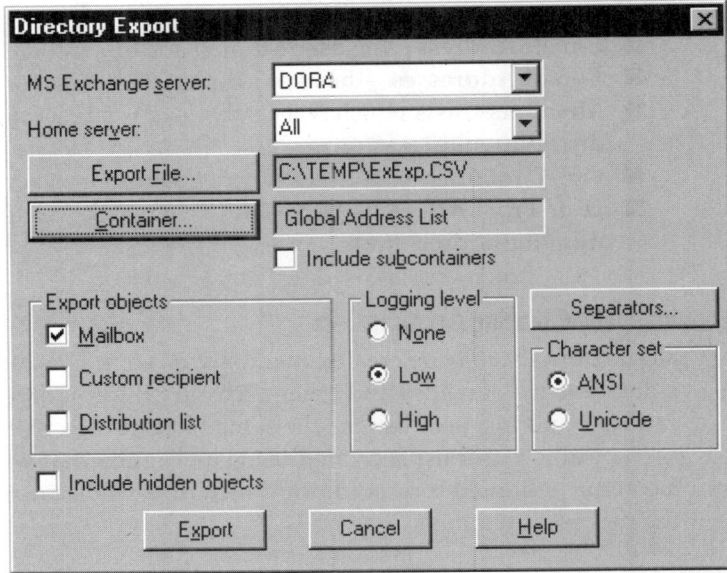

Figure 22-6: The Directory Export dialog box—fill in an output filename, and select options.

In the Directory Export dialog box, specify the Microsoft Exchange Server (or accept the default) and which home servers are to be exported. Other options, such as which objects to export, the logging level, separators, and character sets, should also be set.

An output filename must be specified also. For the output filename, specify any temporary name desired.

The export file consists of a header record and then a record for each object that has been exported. Fields extracted to the export file are:

- **Obj-Class**—the type of object that will be created. This field will typically contain the name Mailbox (a user mailbox), Remote (a custom recipient), or dl (distribution list).

- **Common-Name**—the user's account name (the name used when logging on to the server).
- **Comment**—the comment that is in the Novell NetWare server userid account system.
- **First Name**—the user's first name.
- **Last Name**—the user's last name.
- **Display-Name**—the user's full name.
- **Alias Name**—becomes the user's e-mail name.
- **Directory Name**—typically the same as the user's alias name.
- **Primary Windows NT Account**—the account to which the user logs on.
- **Home-Server**—the user's home server (which may be the same server as the Microsoft Exchange Server).
- **E-mail Address**—the user's e-mail address if there is one defined.
- **E-mail Addresses**—the user's e-mail addresses for each protocol.
- **Members**—lists which objects the user is a member of (including distribution lists).
- **Obj-Container**—describes where this user or object is saved.
- **Hide From AB**—tells Microsoft Exchange Server to hide this entry from the address book.

Manually Creating Account Lists

An account list may be created manually, as well. This can be done using a database list of names and other necessary information. Fields, which can be found in a user list, are the same fields as described above.

Typically, a user list is created using a program that will export data in a comma delimited format (though such files can be created manually, the process is tedious).

Tip

Not all fields need be present when creating an import list file. The fields that are missing will be filled in using defaults obtained from a template userid. If a field is missing, it must be missing from the header and all data records.

Importing Account Lists Into Exchange Server

Once an account list has been created, it may be imported into Microsoft Exchange Server to add mail users to the system. Before importing account lists, there is one task that should be performed: creating a template user.

Creating a Template Userid

The template user entry will be used to "fill in the blanks" when creating new mailboxes using account lists. For example, when extracting names from a Windows NT 4 Server or Novell NetWare server, only a very limited amount of information is available. As Microsoft Exchange Server actually retains a substantial amount of information about user mailboxes, the missing information must either be filled in (manually) or obtained from some other source. This other source is a template user mailbox, which supplies defaults to be used.

Figure 22-7 shows an example of a template userid. The name for this user is not important (I used Template so this mailbox would be easy to recognize), although the address information should be filled in as completely as possible. It is usually not possible to fill in everything: Assistant, Office, and even Department may be difficult to create defaults for (although it is usually sufficient to list the corporate number for the telephone number).

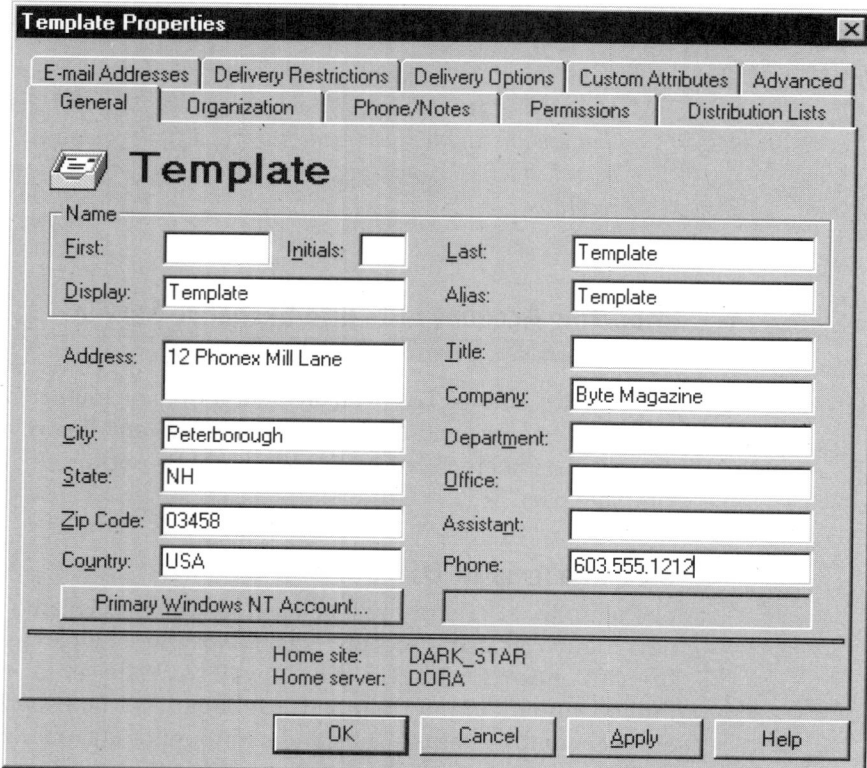

Figure 22-7: A template user can be used to fill in some defaults when importing mailbox information.

Importing Account Lists

To import an account list (from whatever source) into Microsoft Exchange Server, start Microsoft Exchange Administrator (as described in "Setting Options"). From the menu, choose Tools | Directory Import. The Directory Import dialog box (Figure 22-8) will be displayed.

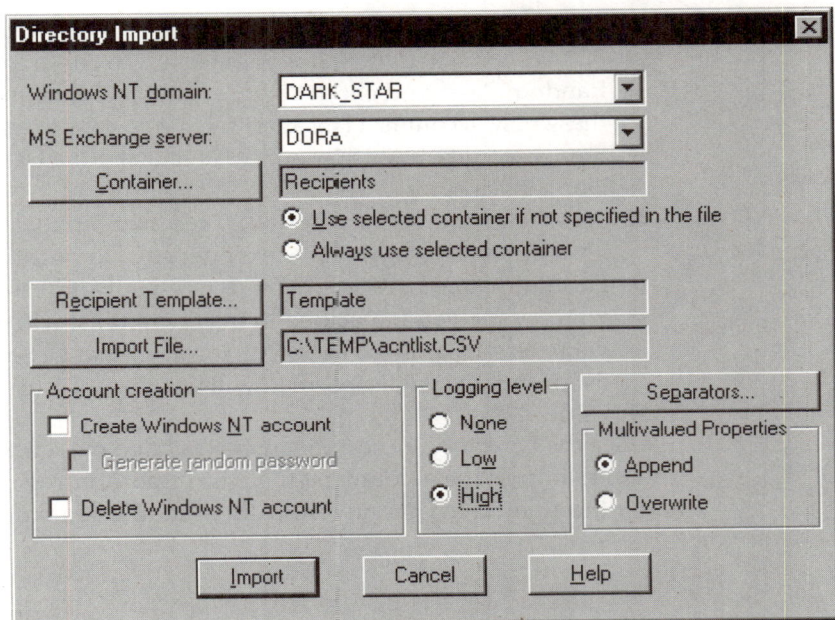

Figure 22-8: The Directory Import dialog box—fill in an import filename, and select options.

Tip

> *It is possible to import not only mailboxes, but also distribution lists and custom recipients.*

In the Directory Export dialog box, you'll need to specify the following items:

■ Recipient Template is the template that will be used to provide default values for those fields that are not contained in the account list file being imported (see Figure 22-7).

■ Import File is the account list file to be imported. The file's format is comma separated, with a header record.

- If the account list is not from the server, check the Create Windows NT Account check box. It would be best to check the Generate Random Password check box to create random passwords for these new accounts. (The alternative is to create passwords for these accounts, after they are created, using the User Manager for Domains program.)
- Set whatever logging is desired (I recommend that High logging level be set unless you have experience in importing account lists).
- For multivalued properties (such as e-mail addresses), choose whether the value specified in the account list will overwrite any value already present in the Microsoft Exchange Server mailbox list or that the value specified will be appended to the existing value, if any.

Once the Directory Import dialog box is filled out, click the Import button to import the account list file. The import process is relatively fast, and if the account list has no errors, there should be no problems.

Tip

It may be a good idea to quickly review each of the newly created objects to ensure that they have been created correctly.

Adding Mailboxes Interactively

Adding a user's mailbox using one of the automated techniques described above may be fast, but only if there is a substantial number of users to be added. For adding only a few user mailboxes at a time, the Microsoft Exchange Administrator program offers an excellent way to add the user mailboxes.

To create a new user mailbox, first start Microsoft Exchange Administrator (as described in "Setting Options"). From the menu, choose File | New Mailbox. The Properties dialog box (Figure 22-9) will be displayed. The mailbox Properties dialog has 10 tabs; they are described in the following sections.

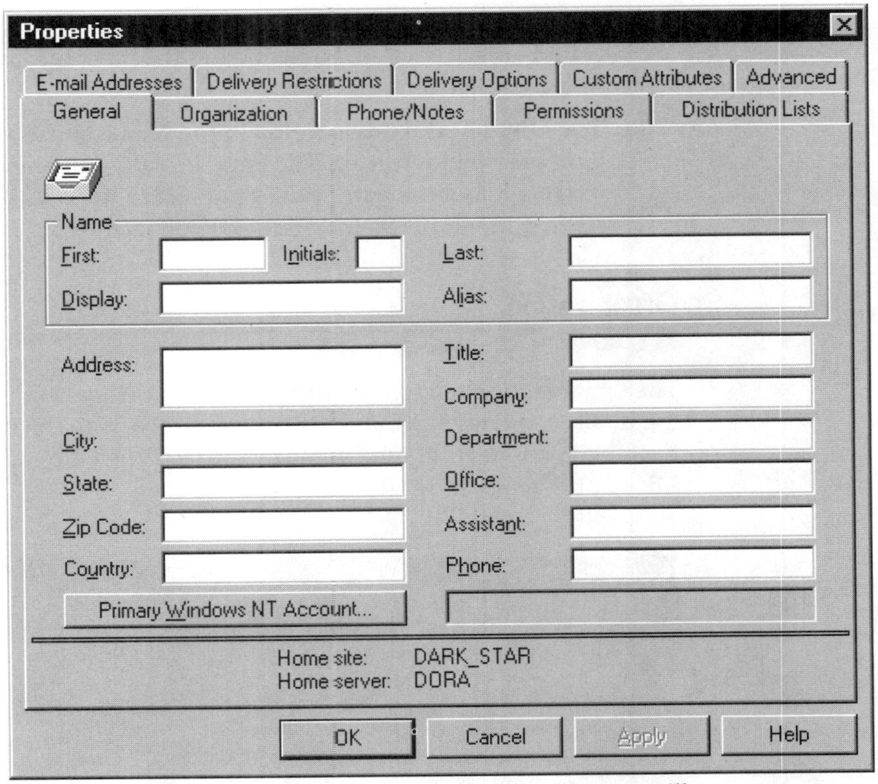

Figure 22-9: The Properties dialog box is used to add new mailboxes; you can edit existing ones, also.

General

The General tab contains information about the user, including physical address, Windows NT 4 Server account name, and other miscellaneous information. Figure 22-9 shows the General tab.

It's important to enter the correct information in some of the fields located on the General tab:

■ **Primary Windows NT Account—the Windows NT logon account (required) for this mailbox user**. There is an option to create a new Windows NT account if this user does not have an account. The user does not have to log on to Windows NT 4 Server to use

Exchange; however, if the user is not logged on to the Windows NT 4 Server, they will have to enter the password to connect to the Microsoft Exchange Server.

■ **The Display and Alias fields in the Name section are required (and may be identical).** The First, Initials, and Last fields may be left blank, but the author does not recommend this as it makes it more difficult to use the address book facility.

Organization

The Organization tab (see Figure 22-10) contains information about who the mailbox owner's manager is and who reports to the mailbox owner. Each person named in the Organization tab is listed by his or her Microsoft Exchange Server username.

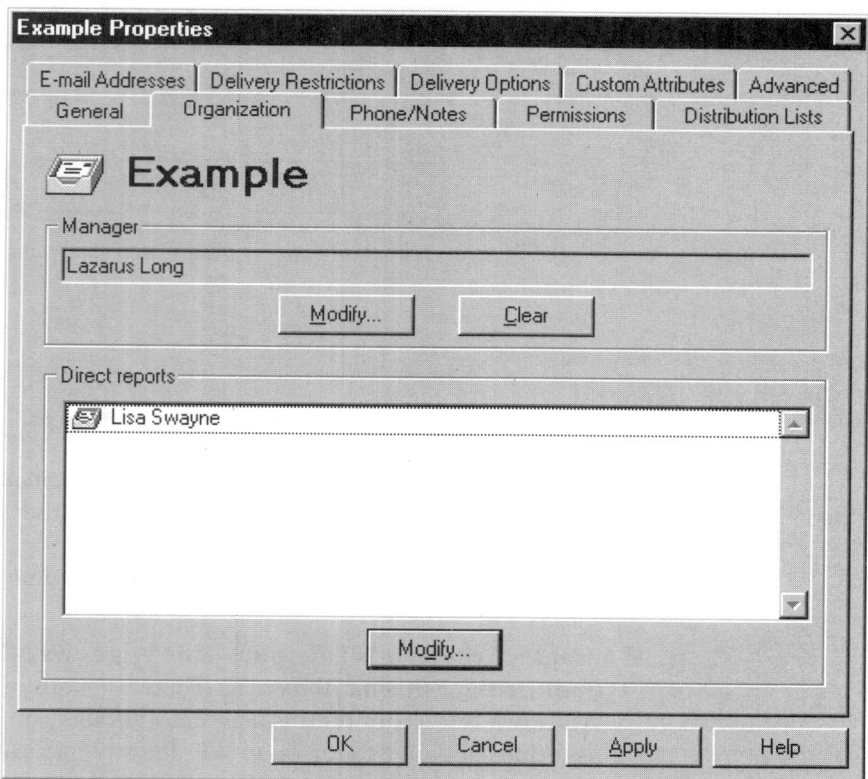

Figure 22-10: In the Organization tab, fill in the user's place in the organization.

The organization information makes it easy to see who reports to whom. This is very useful when a person is not available; it may be possible to contact that person's manager to determine if there is someone else in the organization who can substitute for the missing individual.

Phone/Notes

The Phone/Notes tab (Figure 22-11) lists all phone numbers for the mailbox owner. You can also save a note about this user.

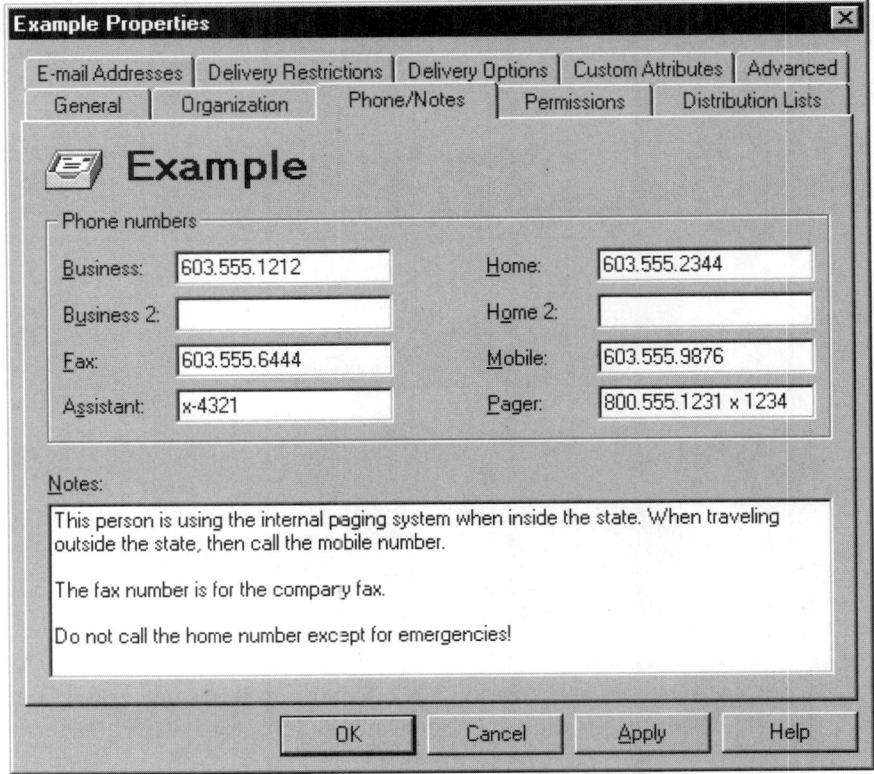

Figure 22-11: On the Phone/Notes tab, you can enter both the user's telephone numbers and lots of notes, too.

Permissions

The Permissions tab is used to set the various permissions that the user will be allowed. Figure 22-12 shows the Permissions tab.

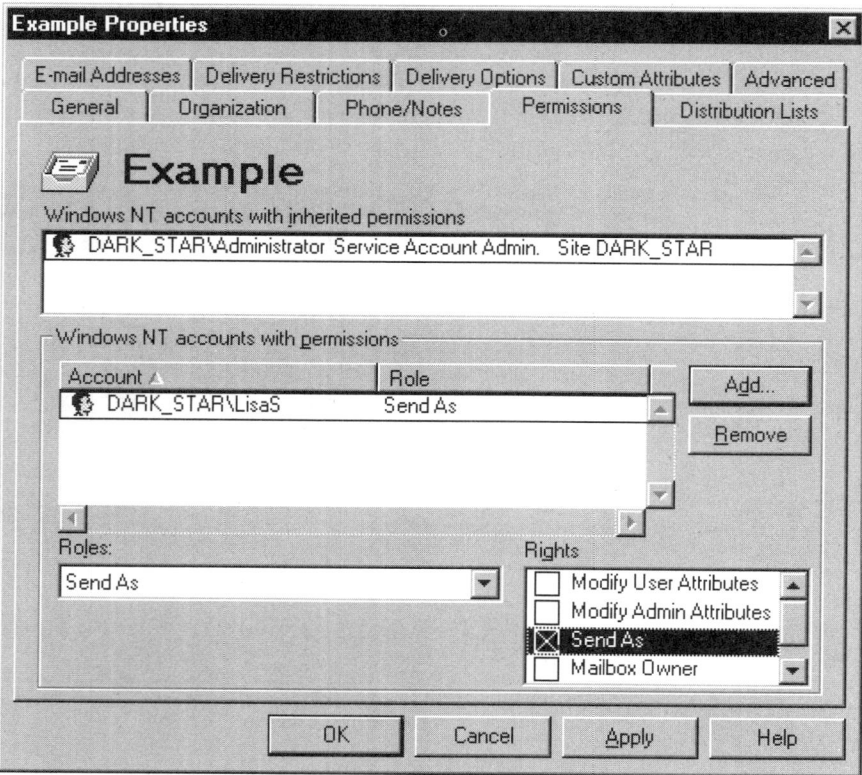

Figure 22-12: Permissions allow other accounts to work with this mailbox.

For each Windows NT account that has been given permissions (or rights, as they are sometimes called), four attributes may be set:

- ■ User allows the specified account to do anything that the mailbox's owner would be able to do.

- ■ Admin. allows the specified account to administer the mailbox.

- Permissions Admin. allows the specified account to administer permissions for this mailbox.
- Send As allows the specified account to send mail as if the specified user were the mailbox's owner.

Distribution Lists

Use the Distribution Lists tab (Figure 22-13) to add this mailbox to distribution lists. Distribution lists are useful when mail must be sent to everyone in a department, for example.

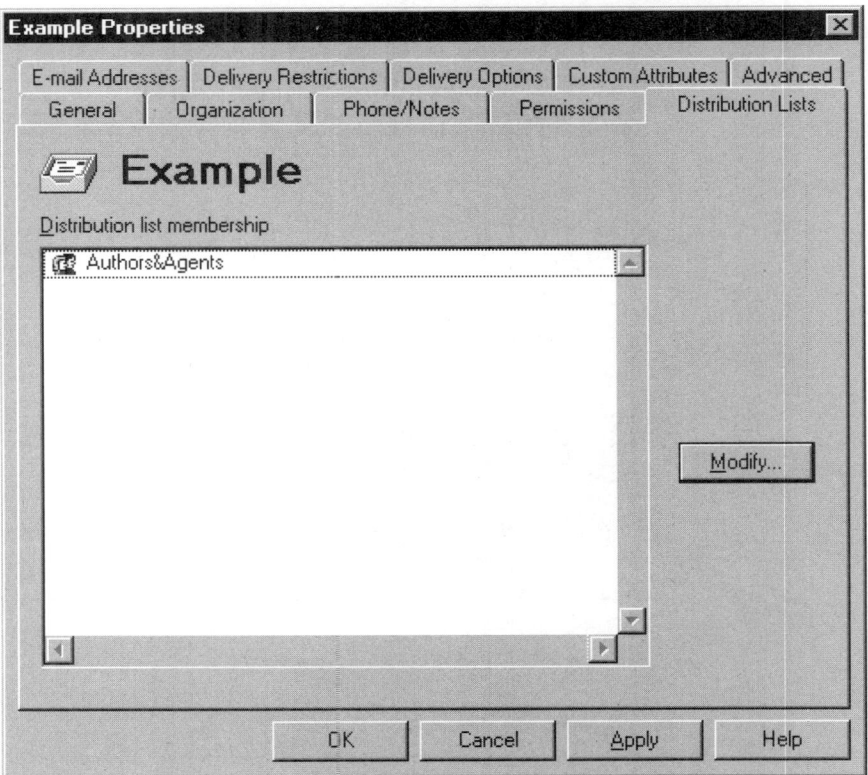

Figure 22-13: Add the user to existing distribution lists.

E-mail Addresses

The E-mail Addresses tab (Figure 22-14) lists the various e-mail addresses assigned to this user. Add, edit, or delete e-mail addresses as necessary.

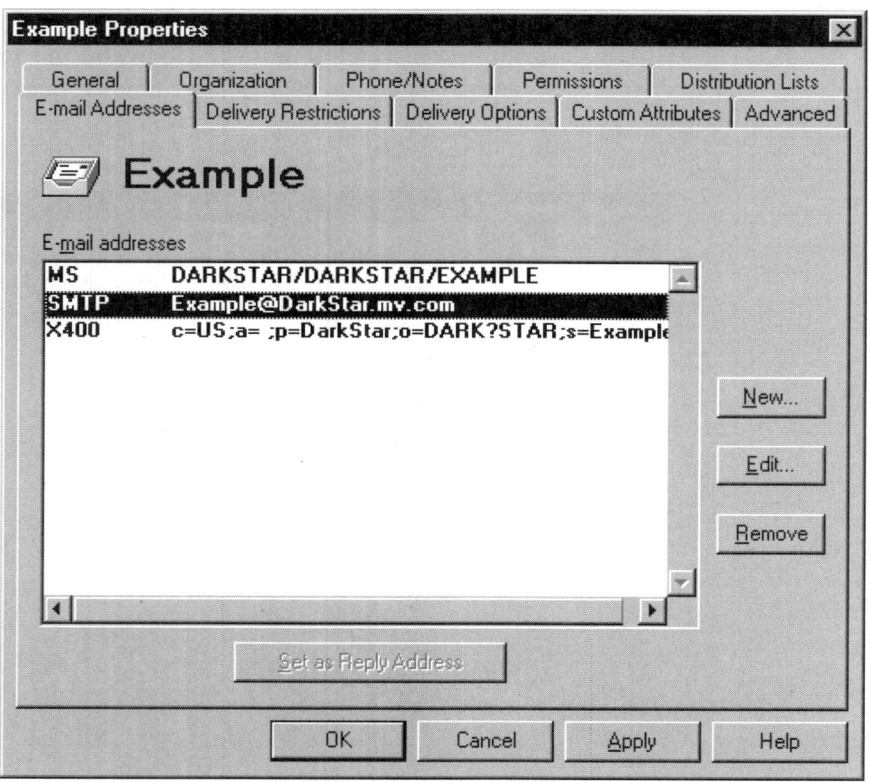

Figure 22-14: Make sure the e-mail addresses are correct.

Delivery Restrictions

The Delivery Restrictions tab (Figure 22-15) allows e-mail delivery to be restricted. You can have both Accept Messages From and Reject Messages From lists. In our example, the user is only able to receive messages from three users.

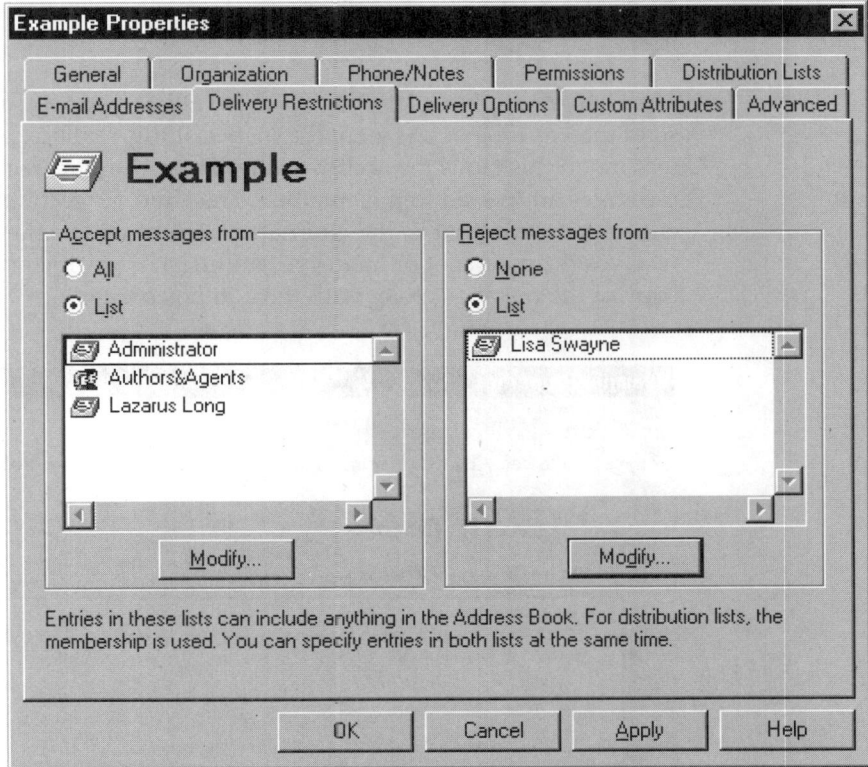

Figure 22-15: Restricting a mailbox helps cut down on undesired e-mail traffic.

When restricting messages, both the Accept Messages From and the Reject Messages From lists may be used at the same time. Using both lists is useful when there is a distribution list in the Accept Messages From list and no messages are to be accepted from a member of the distribution list (put the member who is not allowed to send messages in the Reject Messages From list).

In our example (Figure 22-15), user Lisa Swayne is a member of the Authors&Agents list; however, this mailbox won't accept any messages from user Lisa Swayne.

Delivery Options

The Delivery Options tab (Figure 22-16) allows the specified user(s) to send mail as if he or she were the owner of this mailbox. An additional feature on this tab is the ability to specify an alternate recipient for messages addressed to this mailbox. The alternate recipient may be either exclusive (that is, the alternate recipient will be the only one who receives the message) or inclusive (the alternate recipient will receive a copy of the message along with the mailbox owner).

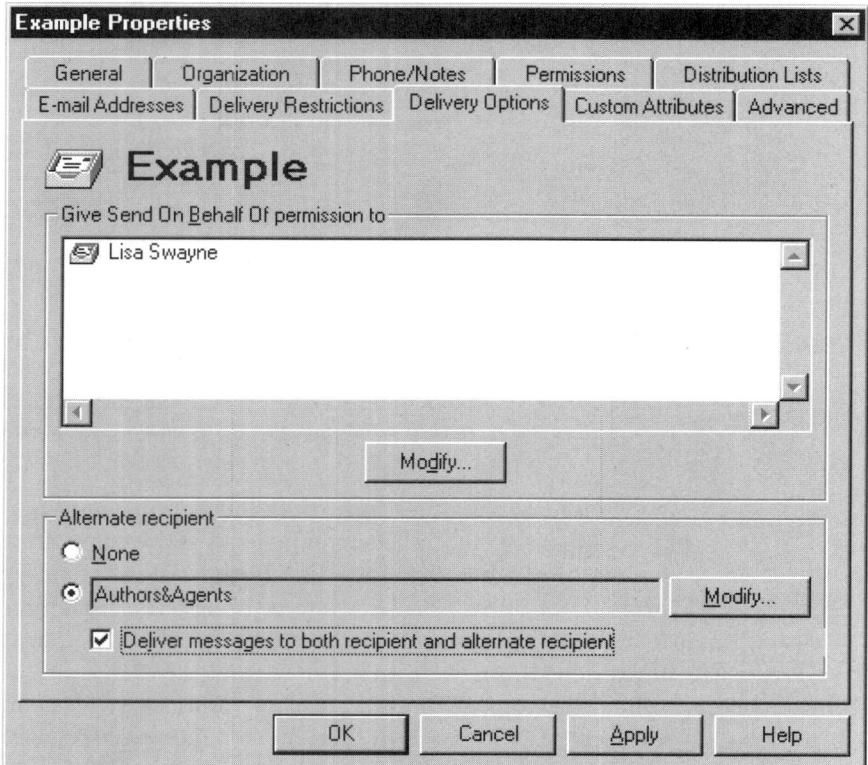

Figure 22-16: Allow other users to send as if they owned this mailbox.

Custom Attributes

Use the Custom Attributes tab (Figure 22-17) to set custom attributes (such as employee number or office number) for each mailbox. In the example shown, the first custom attribute is a description of the languages in which this mailbox recipient is fluent.

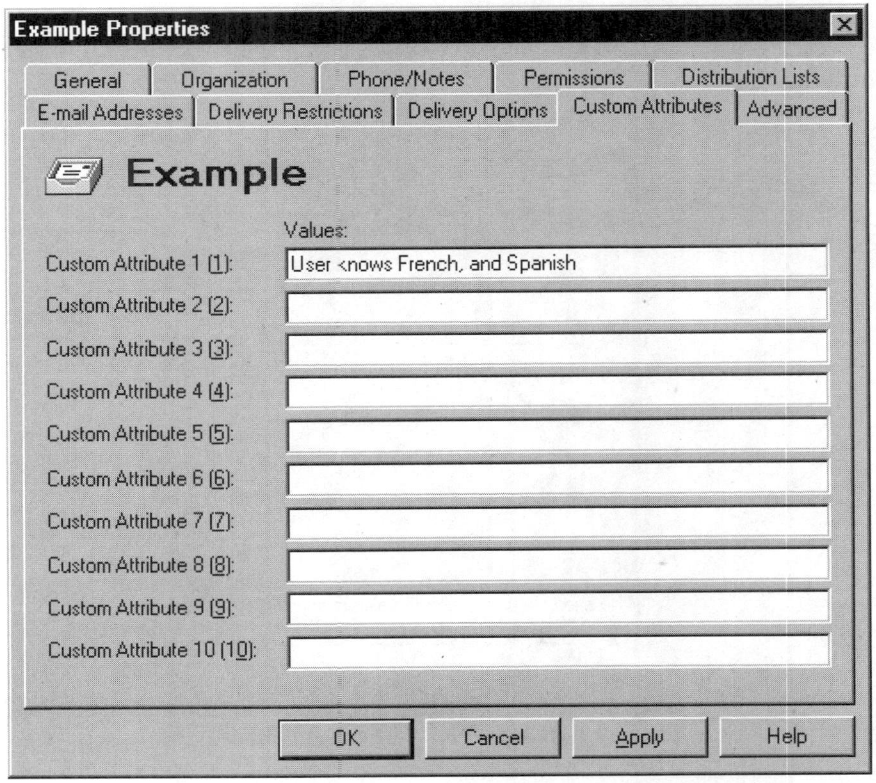

Figure 22-17: Custom attributes may be any information relevant to the organization or perhaps the mailbox user.

Advanced

With the Advanced tab (Figure 22-18), you can set more advanced options:

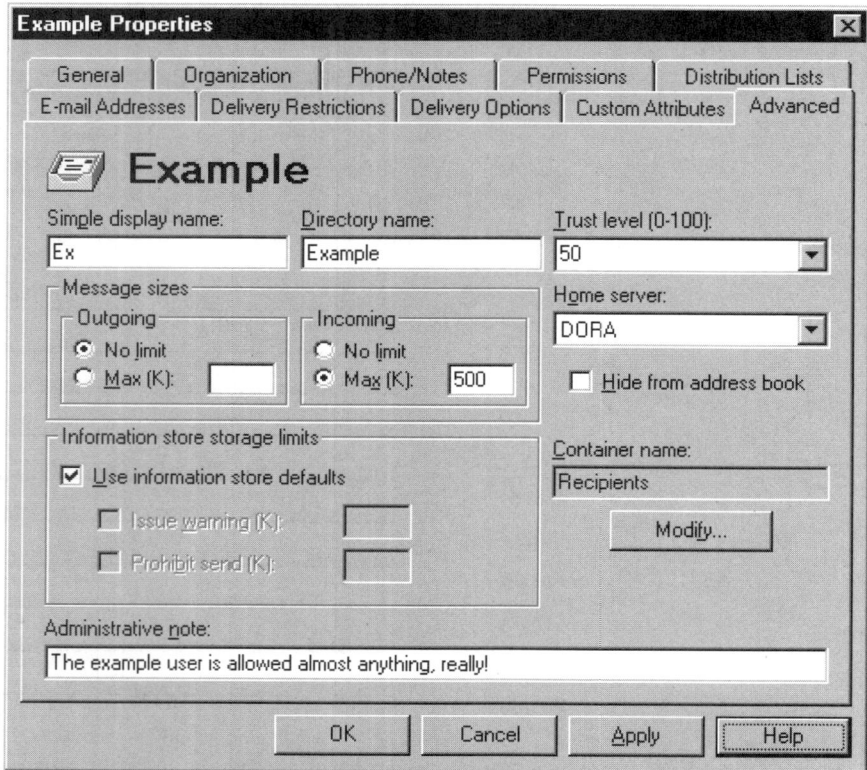

Figure 22-18: Advanced settings are important to many organizations.

- **Simple Display Name**—defaults to the Directory name; used for mail systems that may not support the characters Microsoft Exchange Server allows in a user's display name.
- **Trust Level**—defaults to 20; controls replication. The trust level for the user is compared with the trust level for the container (the target of replication); if the trust level is less than the container, then the name is not replicated.
- **Home Server**—specifies the user's home Windows NT 4 Server.
- **Message Sizes**—controls how much storage is utilized by the mailbox user.

■ **Information Store Storage Limits**—specifies the action taken by Microsoft Exchange Server when storage limits are exceeded.

Once the new mailbox properties are all set, click the OK button to save the mailbox.

Using & Managing Distribution Lists

Distribution lists are very valuable when the same message must be sent to a number of users. For example, you can create distribution lists that include all programmers, everyone in the accounting department, or all your friends who are bicycle riders.

To create a new distribution list, first start Microsoft Exchange Administrator (as described in "Setting Options"). From the menu, choose File I New Distribution List. The Properties dialog box (Figure 22-19) will be displayed.

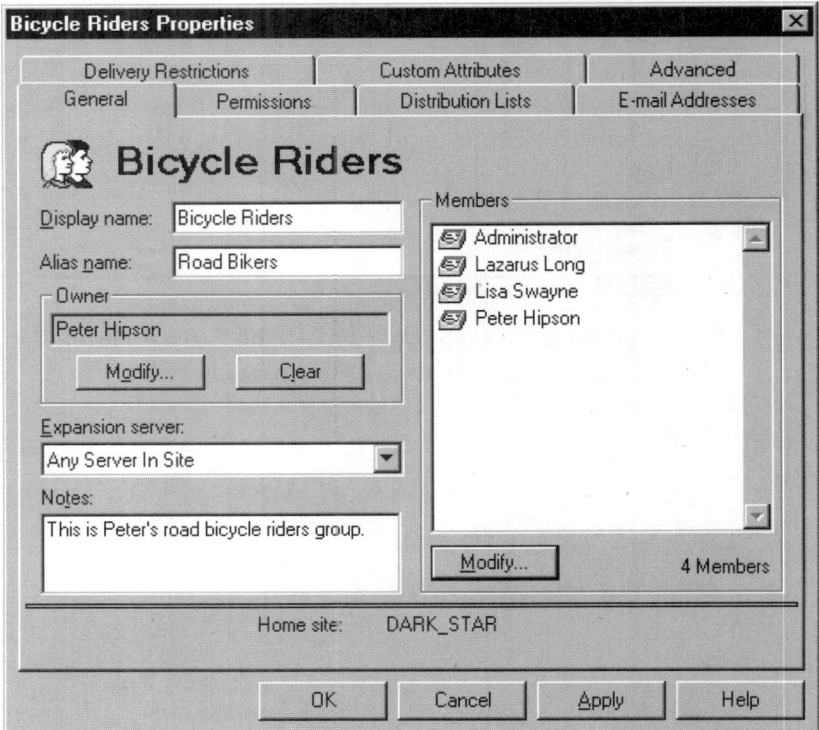

Figure 22-19: The Properties dialog box is used to create (or edit) a distribution list.

The mailbox Properties dialog has seven tabs, each of which is described below.

General

The General tab (see Figure 22-19) is where the distribution list's display name, alias name, owner, and members are listed. Other items that can be set in the General tab include the location of the expansion server (which defaults to any server available) and notes.

New members added to the distribution list might be individual mailbox owners or even other distribution lists.

Warning

Be careful not to create a circular reference, where distribution list A *is a member of distribution list* B, *while distribution list* B *is a member of distribution list* A *also!*

The distribution list owner is able to modify the distribution list's membership using an Exchange Client. If no owner is specified, the administrator must modify the list using Microsoft Exchange Administrator.

Permissions

The Permissions tab is used to set the various permissions the user will have. Figure 22-20 shows the Permissions tab.

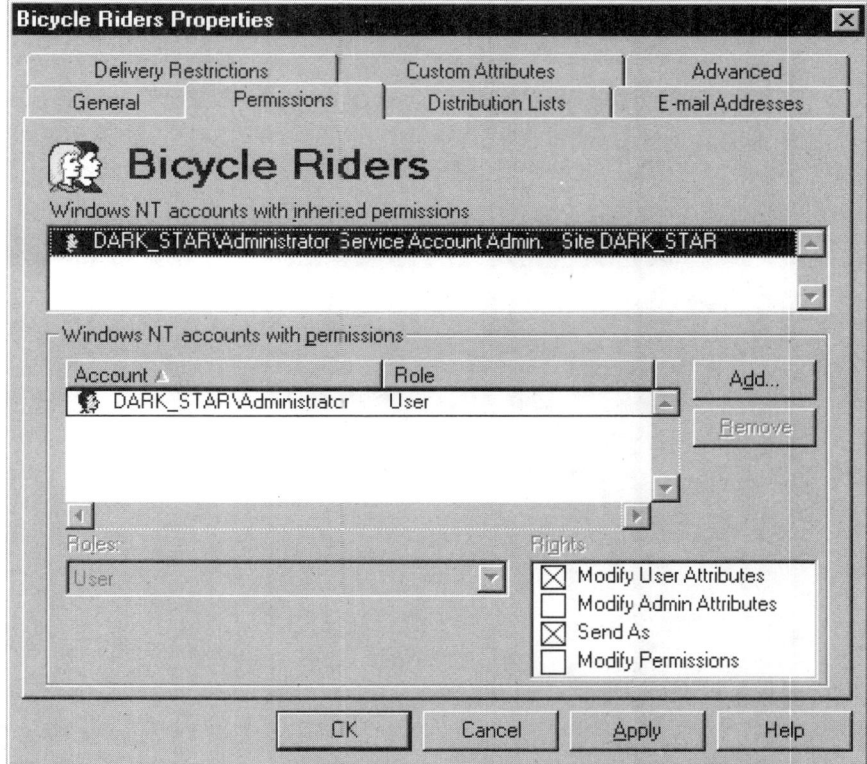

Figure 22-20: Permissions allow other accounts to work with this mailbox.

For each Windows NT account that has been given permissions (or rights, as they are sometimes called), four attributes may be set:

- **User** allows the specified account to do anything that the mailbox's owner would be able to do.
- **Admin.** allows the specified account to administer the mailbox.
- **Permissions Admin.** allows the specified account to administer permissions for this mailbox.
- **Send As** allows the specified account to send mail as if the specified user were the mailbox's owner.

Distribution Lists

Use the Distribution Lists tab (Figure 22-21) to add this mailbox to distribution lists. Distribution lists are very useful when mail must be sent to everyone in a department, for example.

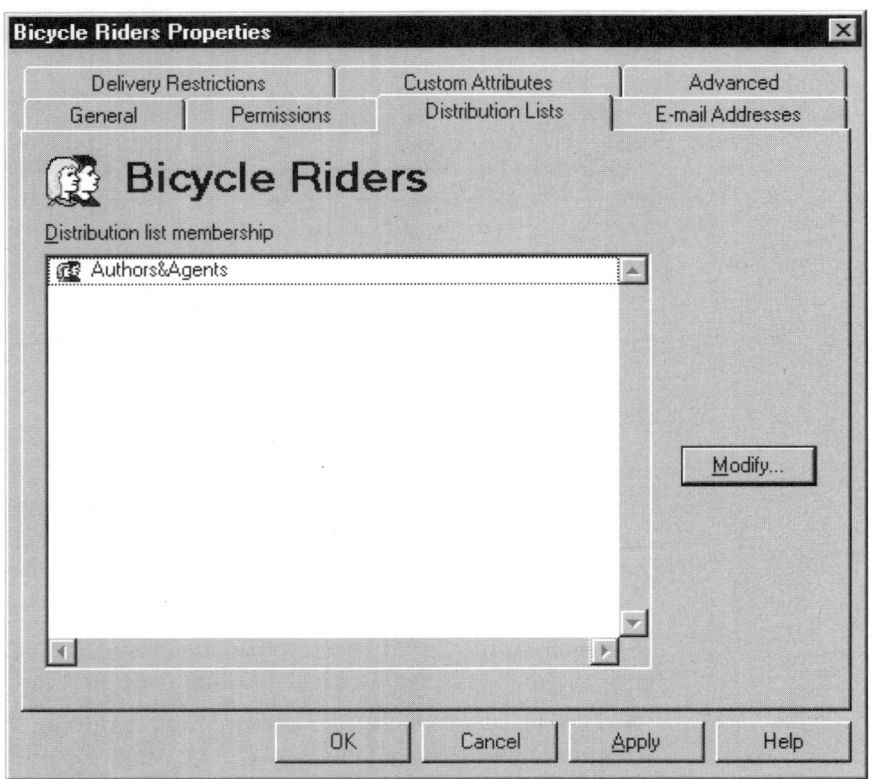

Figure 22-21: Add distribution lists to this distribution list.

E-mail Addresses

The E-mail Addresses tab (Figure 22-22) lists the various e-mail addresses assigned to this user. Add, edit, or delete e-mail addresses as necessary.

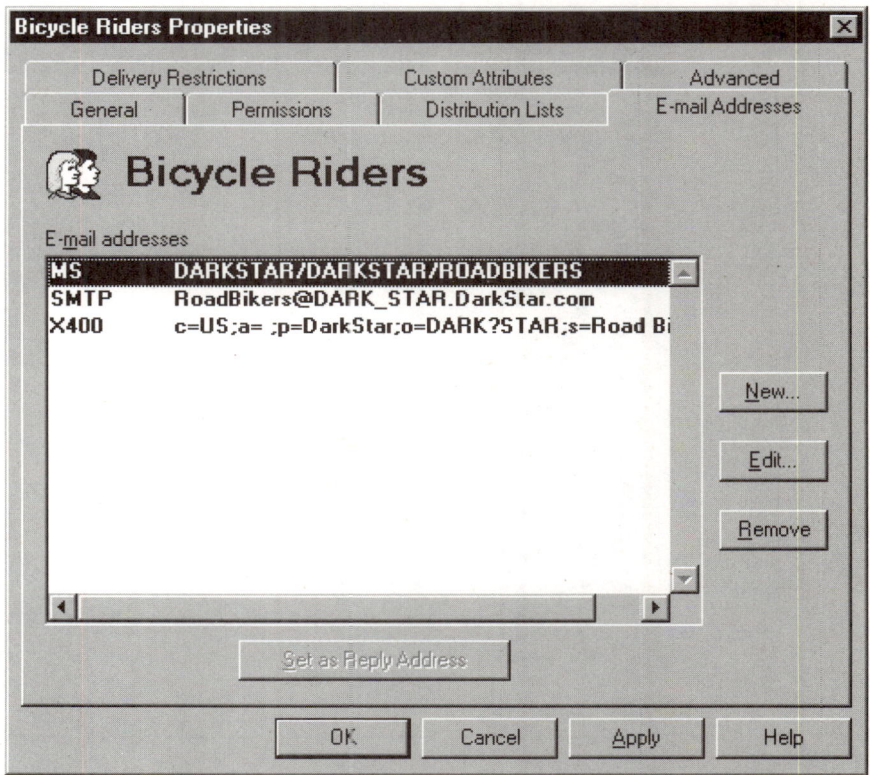

Figure 22-22: Make sure the e-mail addresses are correct to reach the list.

Delivery Restrictions

Use the Delivery Restrictions tab (Figure 22-23) to restrict e-mail delivery to the list. You may have both Accept Messages From and Reject Messages From lists. In our example, the user is only able to receive messages from three users.

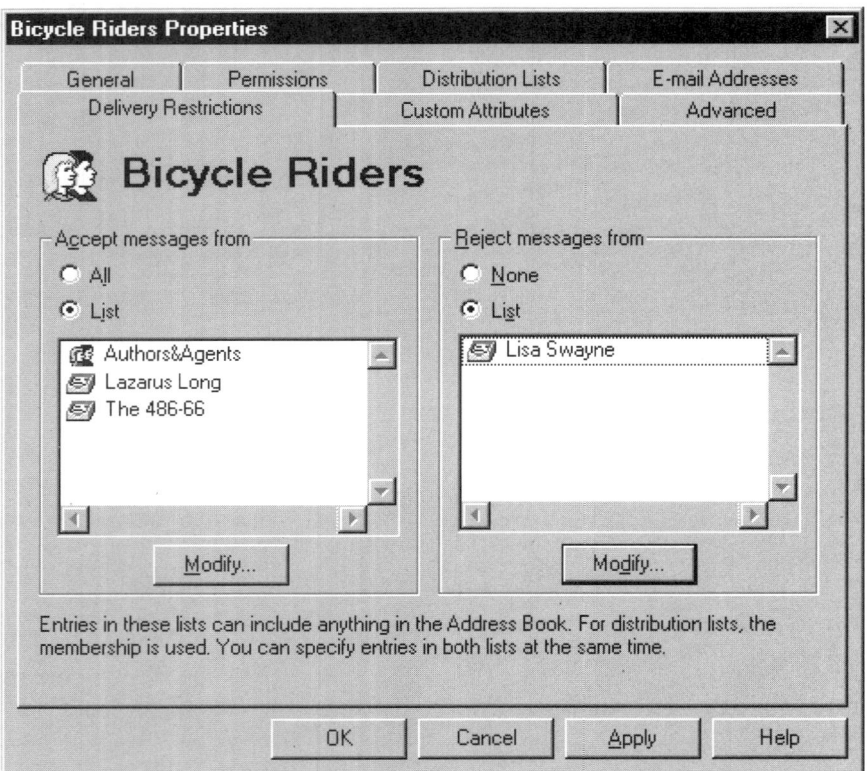

Figure 22-23: Restricting a distribution list helps cut down on undesired e-mail traffic.

When restricting messages, both the Accept Messages From and the Reject Messages From lists may be used at the same time. Using both lists is useful when there is a distribution list in the Accept Messages From list and no messages are to be accepted from a member of the distribution list (put the member who is not allowed to send messages in the Reject Messages From list).

In our example (Figure 22-23), user Lisa Swayne is a member of the Authors&Agents list; however, this mailbox won't accept any messages from user Lisa Swayne.

Custom Attributes

Use the Custom Attributes tab (Figure 22-24) to set custom attributes (such as employee number or office number) for each mailbox. In the example shown, the first custom attribute is a description of the fact that the Bicycle Riders list is personal and is not business related.

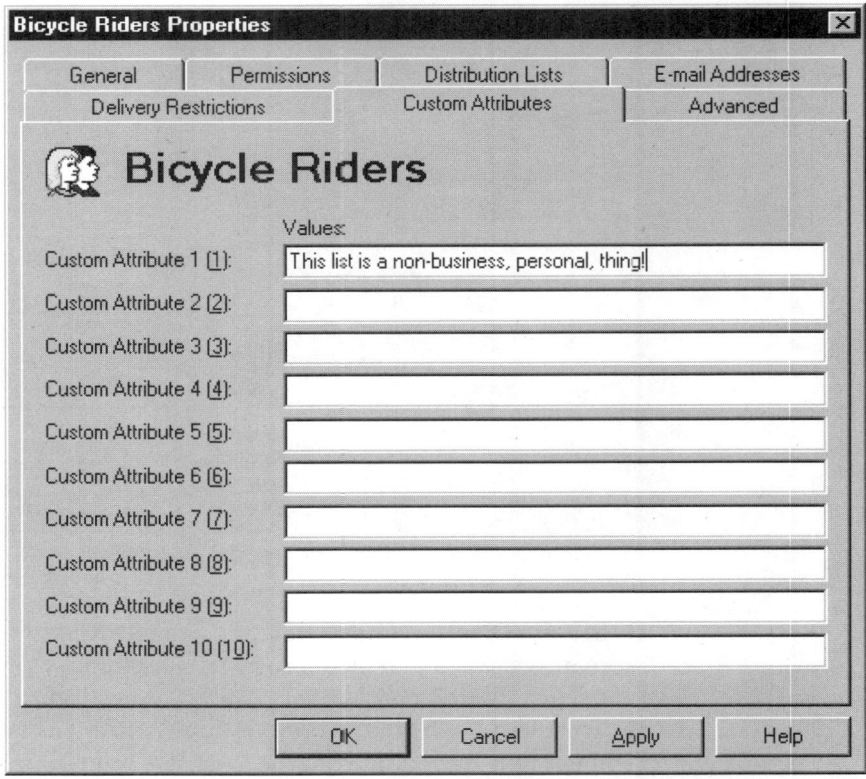

Figure 22-24: Custom attributes may be any information relevant to the distribution list.

Advanced

The Advanced tab (Figure 22-25) lets you set more advanced options:

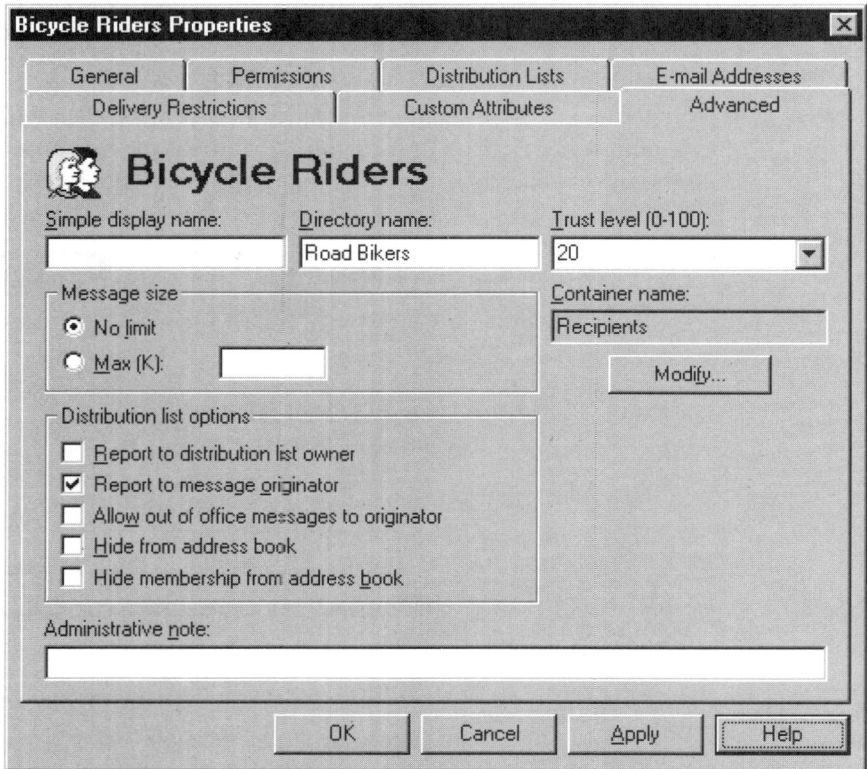

Figure 22-25: Advanced settings are important to many organizations.

- **Simple Display Name**—defaults to the Directory name; used for mail systems that may not support the characters Microsoft Exchange Server allows in a distribution list's display name.
- **Trust Level**—defaults to 20; controls replication. The trust level for the user is compared with the trust level for the container (the target of replication); if the trust level is less than the container, then the distribution list is not replicated.

- **Message Size**—controls how much storage is utilized by the distribution list.
- **Information Store Storage Limits**—specifies the action taken by Microsoft Exchange Server when storage limits are exceeded. This action includes who is notified, whether the distribution list is hidden from the address book, and whether the distribution list's members may be viewed from the address book.

Once the new distribution list properties are all set, click the OK button to save the distribution list.

Moving On

In this chapter we introduced Microsoft Exchange Administrator and covered how to create user mailboxes and distribution lists for Microsoft Exchange Server. Most of the routine maintenance for Microsoft Exchange Server consists of adding, changing, and deleting users. Only occasionally is it necessary to delve more deeply into Microsoft Exchange Server.

The next chapter introduces the Microsoft Exchange Server Clients for Windows 95, Windows NT, DOS, and Windows 3.1x. There is also a Microsoft Exchange Server Client available for the Apple Macintosh platform.

23

Installing & Configuring Microsoft Exchange Server Clients

In Chapter 21 I noted that there are two components of Microsoft Exchange: Microsoft Exchange Server and Microsoft Exchange Client. Some operating systems (Windows NT 4 Server, Windows NT 4 Workstation, and Windows 95) come with default Microsoft Exchange Client software.

Microsoft Exchange comes with new versions of Microsoft Exchange Client. The new versions may be installed on workstations using the installation programs supplied with the various clients.

Tip

There are several issues to consider when installing Microsoft Exchange Server clients: If the currently installed version of the Microsoft Exchange Server client does not have the Microsoft Exchange Service installed, it will be necessary to install new Microsoft Exchange Server client software, regardless of which version is installed.

Be careful that an older version of Microsoft Exchange Client is not installed on a system that already has Microsoft Exchange Client installed. For example, Microsoft will probably release a new version of Windows (most likely called Windows 97) in late 1997, and the new version of Windows may have an updated Microsoft Exchange Client. Check the currently installed version of Microsoft Exchange Client, and if it is later than the version with Microsoft Exchange, don't upgrade it!

Installing Microsoft Exchange Server Clients

The Microsoft Exchange Server client software is found on the BackOffice CD-ROM, which contains Microsoft Exchange Server client software (this CD may or may not be the same CD that has the Microsoft Exchange Server software).

Languages?

If you are not installing English versions of Microsoft Exchange Server client software, the folder to install client software will not be \exchange\clients\eng\.

Non-English versions of Microsoft Exchange Server client software can be found in folders whose names indicate the language. For example:

Arabic is found in the folder \exchange\clients\bidi\ara.

Hebrew is found in the folder \exchange\clients\bidi\hbr.

European (Romantic), Asian, and other languages are found in similar folders, though these languages are typically distributed on special language-specific CDs.

If you are installing a non-English version, instead of using the folder \eng, simply use the path to the folder containing the language that is being installed.

Installing Clients Over the Network

The folder \exchange\clients\eng contains a setup program. This setup program is used to create a share point on a local server drive that network client users can use to install the Microsoft Exchange Server client software.

The setup program presents a few introductory screens and then presents the main installation screen (shown in Figure 23-1). Follow these steps to create a share point for a local server drive:

1. In the main installation screen, select a drive (and folder, if the default folder is not appropriate) on which to install the Microsoft Exchange Server client software. You will also need to create shares to folders within this folder for each client type to be installed (more on that later). Click the OK button.

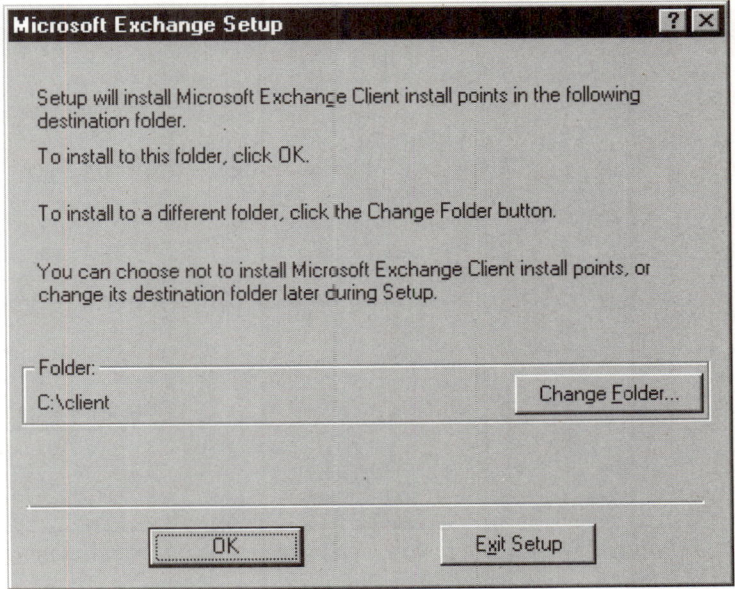

Figure 23-1: Select the drive on which to install Microsoft Exchange Server client software.

2. Next, select whether to do a Complete or Custom installation (see Figure 23-2). To select which Microsoft Exchange Server client software will be supported, choose the Custom option. The Complete option will install all client platforms (including the RISC Windows NT platforms). If there are no RISC computers on the network, then it makes no sense to create installations for these platforms.

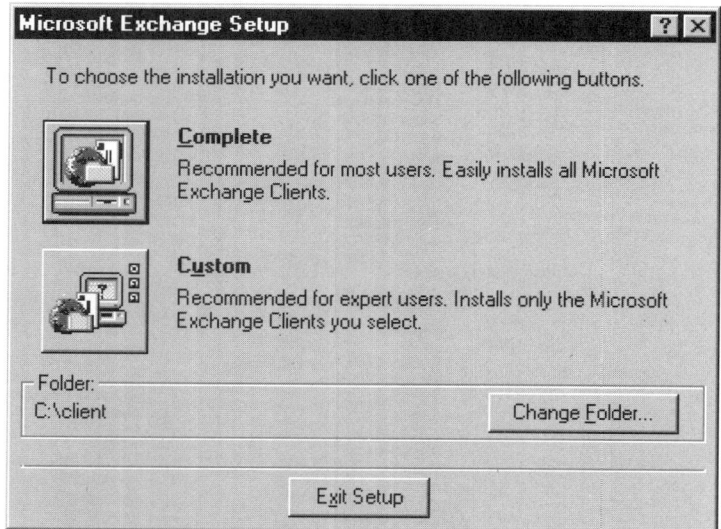

Figure 23-2: Choose to do a Complete or Custom installation (most will want to do the Custom installation).

3. When Custom is selected, the Microsoft Exchange–Custom dialog (Figure 23-3) will be presented. In this dialog, choose which platforms are to be supported. A complete installation will require about 65MB of disk space; if the Windows NT RISC platforms are excluded, the disk space requirements are only about 30MB (a substantial amount of savings, if disk space is a bit tight!).

In my case, I chose not to install the Alpha, MIPS, or PowerPC Microsoft Exchange Server client software, as there are no Windows NT systems on my network running on any of these hardware platforms. If there are no Windows 3.x clients, do not install that option, and if all your users are running Windows, there is no need to have the DOS installation option. (Windows 3.x clients don't need the DOS components.)

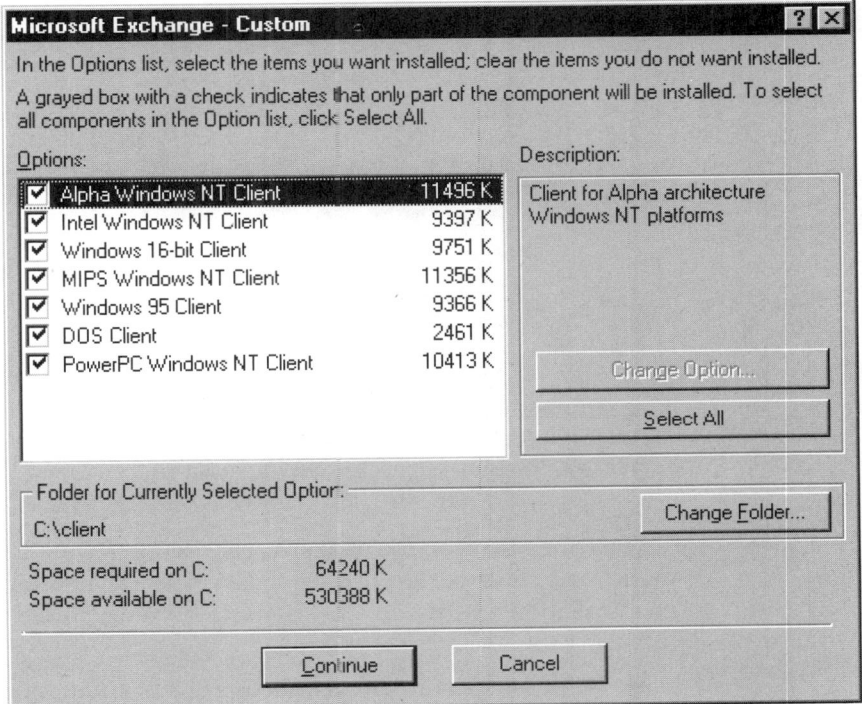

Figure 23-3: Choose which platforms are to be supported by your organization.

Once Microsoft Exchange Server client software has been installed, there is one final step in the installation process for any sites that are not using the same languages for the server as they are for the clients. In this case, you'll need to install language support for Microsoft Exchange Server (see Figure 23-4).

The message shown in Figure 23-4 does not correctly specify which CSV file to load. Search for a file called template.csv. Generally, if there is more than one CSV file in the TPL folder, the other files are for address templates, such as Fax, attachments, Profs, MHS (Novell NetWare Message Handling Service), or SNADS (SNA Distribution Services).

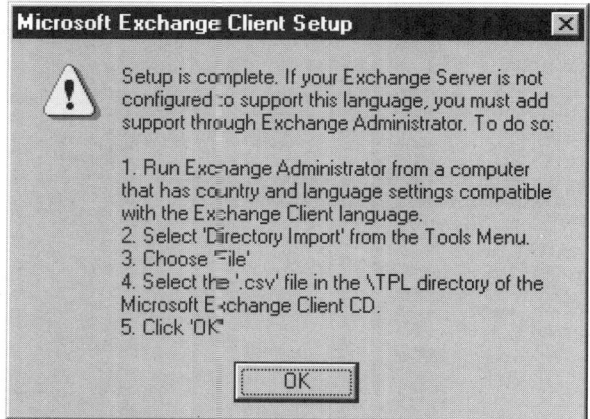

Figure 23-4: Install additional languages support only if Microsoft Exchange Server is not configured for the same language as the clients!

Once the Microsoft Exchange Server client software has been installed to the server's drive, create a set of shares for each folder. For example, an installation where Intel-only platforms are supported would have the following folders:

- **DOS**—installation folder for DOS clients. Windows 3.x clients should not install from this folder.

- **WIN16**—installation folder for Windows 3.x clients. Windows 3.x clients should not install from the DOS folder, even though Windows 3.x is an MS-DOS based application.

- **WIN95**—installation folder for Windows 95 clients.

- **WINNT**—installation folder for Windows NT clients.

Create a share (with a meaningful name, such as EXCHANGE_CLIENT_DOS for the Microsoft Exchange Server DOS client software) for each of the folders that represents each platform that will be supported.

Installing Clients From Diskettes

For client users who are not connected to the network (or perhaps those client users who are connected with slow links, such as dial-up connections), installation of Microsoft Exchange Server client software from diskettes is a logical alternative.

It is not difficult to create software installation diskettes for most of the platforms that need installing.

Creating Diskettes for Windows NT, Windows 95 & Windows 3.x

For Windows NT, Windows 95, and Windows 3.x, the process for creating diskettes is identical (though the number of diskettes required may vary for each platform). First change to the folder that the Microsoft Exchange Server client software was installed into (see Figure 23-1). In this folder will be one or more folders (depending on which Microsoft Exchange Server client software platforms were installed; see Figure 23-3). Change to the folder for the platform for which installation diskettes are needed. For example, if creating Windows 95 diskettes, change into the WIN95 folder.

To create Microsoft Exchange Server client software distribution diskettes, follow these steps:

1. Count the number of CAB files found in the folder. For Windows 95, there are seven CAB files (exchng1.cab, exchng2.cab . . . exchng7.cab). Obtain as many 1.44MB diskettes (sorry, only 3.5-inch, 1.44MB diskettes are supported) as there are CAB files.

2. Format the diskettes. Do not install any system files. Label these diskettes Microsoft Exchange Server Client Software Disk, with the disk number. On the first diskette, add a note that says "Run SETUP to install."

3. On the fist diskette, copy all the files *except* for the CAB files. Then, on the first diskette, copy the exchng1.cab file.

4. On the second diskette, copy the exchng2.cab file.

5. On the third diskette, copy the exchng3.cab file.

6. Continue this process until all the CAB files have been copied onto the remaining diskettes.

Once the diskettes have been created, any client user may use them to install the client software. The client user should insert the first diskette into the diskette drive and enter the command **a:\setup** (where a: is the floppy drive's letter).

Creating Diskettes for DOS Clients

For DOS Microsoft Exchange Server client software, the process for creating a set of installation diskettes is a bit different than for the other versions. Unfortunately, the files for the Microsoft Exchange Server client software for DOS does not fit on a single diskette, and the configuration of the setup program does not lend itself to using two diskettes.

To create Microsoft Exchange Server client software distribution diskettes, follow these steps:

1. Format two diskettes. Do not install any system files. Label these diskettes Microsoft Exchange Server Client Software Disk 1 and Microsoft Exchange Server Client Software Disk 2. On the first diskette, add a note that says "Run install.bat to install."

2. On the first diskette, copy all the files except for exchange.exe.

3. On the first diskette, create the install.bat file containing the code shown in Listing 23-1.

4. On the second diskette, copy the exchange.exe file.

Listing 23-1: A batch file to install Microsoft Exchange Server MS-DOS client software.

```
@echo off
if NOT .%1 == . goto Part2
MD C:\~~EXCL~~
CD C:\~~EXCL~~
Copy a:install.bat C:\~~EXCL~~\*.* >NUL:
C:\~~EXCL~~\Install.bat Part2
goto EndAll
:Part2
goto Prompt
:WrongDisk
Echo    -
Echo Wrong disk inserted in Drive, insert DISK 2 please!
Echo    -
:Prompt
choice /C:CA Insert DISK 2, press C to continue, A to
abort.
if errorlevel 2 goto DestroyAll
if NOT EXIST a:\EXCHANGE.EXE goto WrongDisk
Copy a:*.* C:\~~EXCL~~\*.* >NUL:
C\~~EXCL~~\setup
:DestroyAll
cd c:\
:EndAll
deltree /Y ~~excl~~ >NUL:
```

Installing the Clients Using the Diskettes

Running the install.bat command file will copy both diskettes onto a temporary folder on the c: drive and then execute the Microsoft Exchange Server MS-DOS client software installation program, setup.exe. After the installation has completed, the temporary folder is removed for the user. Also, if there are any errors or the user chooses to abort at the prompt for the second disk, the temporary folder is removed.

Using SMS to Distribute & Install the Clients

For those organizations using Microsoft SMS (Systems Management Server), Microsoft Exchange Server client software may be installed on client workstations using the SMS software distribution facilities (check out Chapter 18 for more information about using SMS to install software).

On the Microsoft Exchange Server client software CD, there is a folder called SMS. There is typically a folder for the installation language in the SMS folder (for the English language, the folder is \exchange\clients\sms\eng).

In this folder are a series of PDF files:

- ■ EXALPHA.PDF is the distribution file for Windows NT Alpha clients.

- ■ EXMIPS.PDF is the distribution file for Windows NT MIPS clients.

- ■ EXWIN16.PDF is the distribution file for Windows 3.x clients.

- ■ EXWIN95.PDF is the distribution file for Windows 95 clients.

- ■ EXWINNT.PDF is the distribution file for Windows NT Intel clients.

Installation of Microsoft Exchange Server client software using SMS can make Microsoft Exchange Server client software installation easier, especially where there will be a substantial number of clients that need to be installed.

The Exchange Client

The Microsoft Exchange Server client software included with Microsoft Exchange Server offers a few features in addition to the features included with the standard Exchange client (a version of Microsoft Exchange Client is included with both Windows 95 and Windows NT 4).

Figure 23-5 shows Microsoft Exchange Server client software running on a Windows 95 workstation. This workstation is currently connected to the Microsoft Exchange Server running on DORA and shows a number of interesting items.

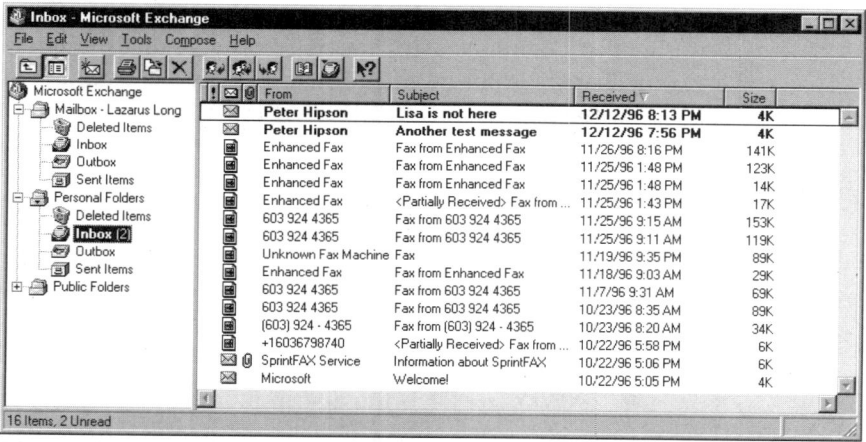

Figure 23-5: Microsoft Exchange Server client software running on Windows 95.

Looking at Figure 23-5, you see that the user's Personal Folders is open, and the contents of the Inbox folder is displayed in the right pane of the window. The number after Inbox, (2), indicates how many messages have not yet been read.

The tree view of the user's folders is shown in the left pane. There are three main folders for this user (other users may have different folder configurations). The first set of folders is named Mailbox–Laxarus Long and represents items that are stored on the Microsoft Exchange Server. The second set of folders is named Personal Folders and consists of locally stored items. These items are stored in the user's PST file(s). There is nothing to prevent a user from having more than one PST file.

Standard objects typically kept in a user's PST file include:

- **Deleted Items**—files that may, or may not, be automatically purged when Microsoft Exchange Client exits. (Automatic purging of the Deleted Items folder is a user option.)

- **Inbox**—receives new messages delivered from the e-mail host or items from other sources (such as incoming faxes).

- **Outbox**—stores outgoing messages until they are sent.

- **Sent Items**—contains a copy of all sent messages.

Other objects kept in a user's PST file might include folders for different topics or interests. (There are several hundred folders in the author's PST.)

Note: Microsoft Outlook has additional items for the user; see "Microsoft Outlook" for more information.

Microsoft Schedule+

Included with Microsoft Exchange Client is a copy of Microsoft Schedule+. The version of Microsoft Schedule+ that is included is configured to work directly with Microsoft Exchange Server.

Note: Outlook has all the functionality of Microsoft Schedule+ built in, so that Microsoft Schedule+ is not included with Microsoft Outlook. There is a conversion utility to allow Outlook users to convert their Microsoft Schedule+ files to Microsoft Outlook.

Figure 23-6 shows Microsoft Schedule+ running on a Windows 95 workstation. The user of Microsoft Schedule+ is able to manage equipment and facilities, such as meeting rooms.

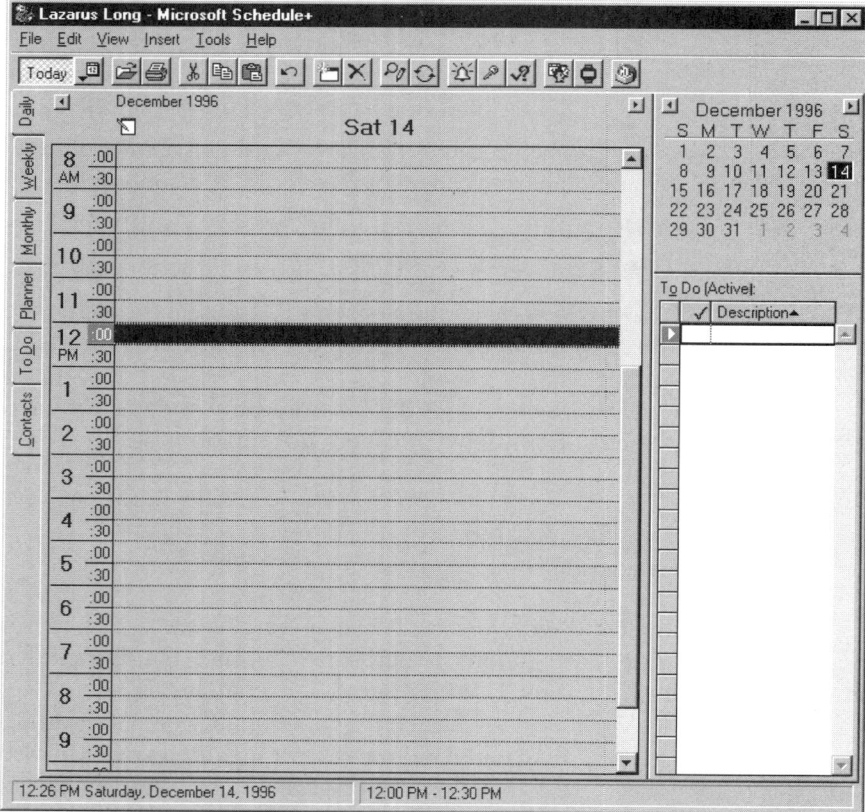

Figure 23-6: Microsoft Schedule+ allows group management. Users can coordinate meetings and events easily.

Some of the features that Microsoft Schedule+ offers include:

■ **Appointments**—allows scheduling, moving, copying, and coordinating of appointments.

■ **To Do Lists**—allows management of lists of items that must be done. Features offered include status management, description and priority, and organization.

■ **Reminders**—displays a reminder for meetings and other events. The lead time for the reminder may be set as desired.

■ **Meeting Wizard**—manages meeting schedules. Often a number of individuals from the same organization will have to be scheduled for a meeting at a time when they are all available.

■ **Contacts**—contains information about individuals and organizations (similar to address book lists). Information contained in the contacts list might include addresses, telephone numbers, e-mail addresses and fax numbers, and miscellaneous information.

■ **Events**—manages typically recurring events, such as holidays and regular meetings (like the ever-present monthly safety meeting).

Microsoft Outlook

A product called Outlook will be included with Microsoft Office 97. Outlook is a powerful, full-featured management and communications tool, which will be well received by users. The Office 97 version of Microsoft Outlook works well with Microsoft Exchange Server.

Figure 23-7 shows Microsoft Outlook running on a Windows NT workstation. The user of Microsoft Outlook is able to communicate (e-mail, fax, and voice mail), perform the functions that Microsoft Schedule+ provides, and use other features that are not part of Microsoft Schedule+.

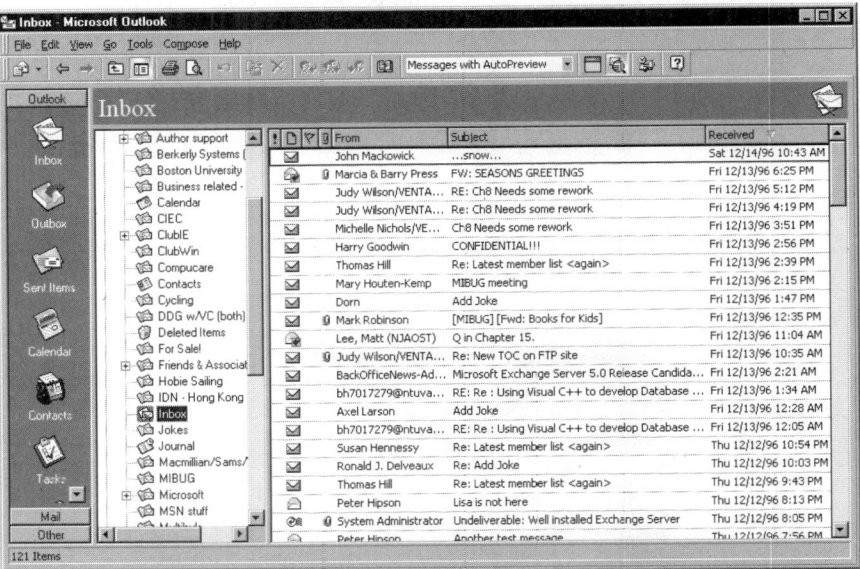

Figure 23-7: Microsoft Outlook allows communications, scheduling, and other functions.

Some of the features that Microsoft Outlook offers include:

- **Calendar**—performs many of the functions that Microsoft Schedule+ does, including Appointments, which allows scheduling, moving, copying, and coordinating of appointments, and Reminders, which is useful to display a reminder for meetings and other events. The lead-time for the reminder may be set as desired. Calendar also includes Meetings, which is managed using the Microsoft Schedule+ Meeting Wizard and helps to schedule meetings for a number of individuals from the same organization. And finally, Calendar includes Events, which manages typically recurring events such as holidays and regular meetings.

- **Contacts**—contains information about individuals and organizations (similar to address book lists). Information contained in the contacts list might include addresses, telephone numbers, e-mail addresses and fax numbers, and miscellaneous information.

- **Tasks**—the Microsoft Outlook equivalent to Microsoft Schedule+'s To Do Lists; allows management of lists of items that must be done. Features offered include status management, description and priority, and organization.

- **Journal**—keeps a record of certain events and actions. For example, each time Word 97 is used to edit a file, a journal entry is created. The same is true for Excel, and PowerPoint journal entries are automatically created to allow the user to determine what was being worked on at any specific point in time.

- **Notes**—holds any bit of information that you might jot down on a piece of paper. It is somewhat the electronic equivalent to sticky paper-type notes. When open, notes are displayed as windows (which can not be minimized, however). Figure 23-8 shows an example note.

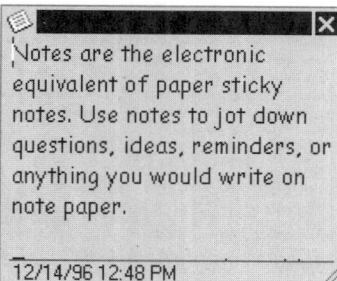

Figure 23-8: Notes are useful to track bits of information.

Moving On

In this chapter we introduced Microsoft Exchange Client and Microsoft Outlook. Whichever client software (either Microsoft Exchange Server client, or Microsoft Outlook) is used, Microsoft Exchange Server offers a powerful tool to allow users in an organization to communicate and work together effectively.

The final chapter in the Microsoft Exchange Server section describes some of the utilities that are included with Microsoft Exchange Server but not well documented by Microsoft.

24

Microsoft Exchange Server Components & Utilities

In addition to the utilities and components of Microsoft Exchange Server covered so far in this section, there are a number of others that are not installed by the default installation process. Many installations will not need to use these components, but knowing about them will help when they are needed.

All items described in this chapter are found on the BackOffice CD-ROM that Microsoft Exchange Server distributed on. The description of each item will include its location.

Note: Utilities come and go more frequently than features. It is possible that some functionality described in this chapter won't be found on future versions of Microsoft Exchange Server. Generally, however, if a functionality or feature is "missing," it is because it is no longer needed!

Microsoft Exchange Server Support Utilities

Each of the utilities described in this section may be found in the \exchange\server\support\utils\ in a folder for the specific platform that your Microsoft Exchange Server is running (I386, Alpha, MIPS, or PPC).

The utilities Authoritative Restore, Error Converter, IMC Queue Dump, IMC Remote Console, Information Store Viewer, Public Folder Replication Verification Tool, and IMC DNS Resolver Test are provided with minimal documentation, and there are no help files available for most of them.

Authoritative Restore

The Authoritative Restore tool (authrest.exe) permits forcing restored directory databases to replicate to other servers after restoring from a backup. This allows all servers to have the newly restored database. It may be used to force Microsoft Exchange Server to replicate the restored directory database to other Microsoft Exchange Servers. This is done after a restore from backup and ensures that the restored version of the directory is used on all Microsoft Exchange Servers.

Typically, when a database is restored, the contents of the database are more out of date than the contents of other servers' versions of the database. If the database is being restored to recover from a failure (hardware for example) and the current replicated databases are generally accurate, then Authoritative Restore would not be run.

However, sometimes the restore is done because of an error in administration (where a change was made, and the change would be difficult or impossible to recover from), and it is undesirable to have other servers update the restored database (in other words, the cost of updating an out-of-date restored backup is less than the costs of repairing the damage done by the error). In that case, forcing the other servers to use the restored version of the database using Authoritative Restore will make the restored version of the database replicate to the other servers.

To use Authoritative Restore, enter the following command from a command prompt:

```
authrest <object version increment> <USN increment>
```

where the options are:

0 *object version increment*—a numeric parameter that specifies the amount to increment the object counter in the restored database so that the objects in the database will appear to be more current than the current database. A good default value for *object version increment* is 1000.

1 *USN increment*—a numeric parameter that specifies the amount to increment the object counters in the restored database so that the objects in the database will appear to be more current than the current database. A good default value for *USN increment* is 1000.

It will be necessary to restart the directory after using the Authoritative Restore tool.

Error Converter

The Error Converter program (error.exe) is an MS-DOS application that will convert an error code into an error identifier. Use the Error Converter when attempting to debug error messages. Knowledge of MAPI (Mail Application Program Interface) will be an advantage in interpreting the results returned by Error Converter. It may be used to convert information store, MAPI, directory, and database error codes to more meaningful error messages. For example, if the error code 0x80040105 were returned, running Error Converter would help determine that a MAPI string was too long to be processed:

```
V:\EXCHANGE\SERVER\SUPPORT\UTILS\I386>error 0x80040105
Error -2147221243 (0x80040105) = ecStringTooLarge-
MAPI_E_STRING_TOO_LONG
```

Note: An error code that is in hexadecimal must be prefixed with 0x to tell Error Converter that the number is not being expressed in decimal (the default number format).

IMC Queue Dump

IMC Queue Dump (imcdump.exe) displays information that describes the contents of the IMC (Internet Mail Connector) queue files. The IMC queue file is located in the IMCDATA folder. Microsoft recommends that IMC Queue Dump not be run unless Microsoft PSS (Product Support Services) requests. It may be used to display information regarding the internal representation of the IMC queues. The IMC queues are stored in queue.dat, located in the IMCDATA directory.

IMC Remote Console

IMC Remote Console (imcremot.exe) obtains detailed information about internal queues and structures of the Internet Mail Connector. This information can then be saved to a file. The IMC Remote Console is an interactive Windows application. It may be used to display (and optionally save to a file) information regarding the internal IMC queues.

Note: IMC Remote Console will create an RPC (Remote Procedure Call) connection to the IMC service, so IMC must be started before running IMC Remote Console.

Information Store Viewer

Information Store Viewer (mdbvu32.exe) allows the administrator to view or set details about a user's message storage files. These files are typically the personal folder file (PST) and the offline folder file (OST). It lets you view or set details regarding users' message storage files. These files are the private information store, the personal folder file (PST) where the user's messages and other information are stored, and the offline folder file (OST).

Figure 24-1 shows the MAPI_FOLDER – Root window, one of the many different views that Information Store Viewer is able to display.

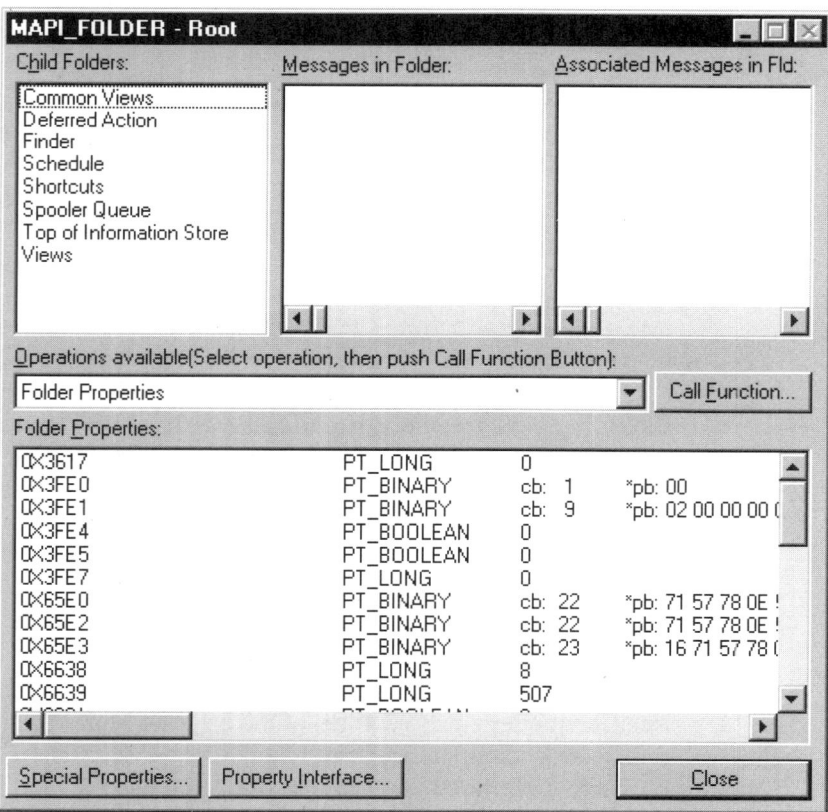

Figure 24-1: MAPI_FOLDER shows information about the selected folder.

With the Information Store Viewer, you can view properties for each message.

Public Folder Replication Verification Tool

The Public Folder Replication Verification tool (replver.exe) compares public folders on Microsoft Exchange servers. This is done to determine if the folder's contents have been successfully replicated. This tool will check the messages in the folders (both contents and flags).

IMC DNS Resolver Test

The IMC DNS Resolver Test (restest.exe) tests the DNS (Domain Name Server) for each name in the IMC's list of servers to ensure that the proper MX (Mail Exchange) records have been implemented. It is used to check the DNS (Domain Name Server) to ensure that the mail exchange (MX) records are correctly set.

Low-level Debugging With WinDbg

WinDbg is a powerful, low-level debugger that Microsoft has supplied to developers for the past few years. Though WinDbg is powerful, it takes experience to use it effectively. Especially important is a thorough understanding of the server's hardware and how the server's CPU works.

WinDbg is found in the folder \EXCHANGE\SERVER\SUPPORT\ WINDBGRM\I386, on the Microsoft Exchange Server distribution CD-ROM.

Typically, WinDbg communications are performed through a terminal attached to one of the communications ports (usually COM1 or COM2). This requires that a terminal be attached to the communications port. WinDbg can work with a window, also, but most developers have found that the act of writing to the window by WinDbg will cause problems with the debugging process.

When running WinDbg from the command line, the following syntax should be used:

```
windbg <options> <filename.ext <options>>
```

The options for the WinDbg command are described in Table 24-1.

Option	Description
[-a]	Tells WinDbg to ignore all bad symbols. A warning message will be displayed regardless, but WinDbg will continue to run even if bad symbols are discovered.
[-g]	Starts the program or application specified in the command line immediately.
[-h]	The child processes will inherit access to all of WinDbg's handles.
[-i]	Causes WinDbg to ignore the workspace. The effect is similar to not loading any ini information or any data from the Registry. Not used with the –w option.
[-k [platform port speed]]	Used to debug in the kernel mode. There are three possible options that may be specified with this option: • platform specifies the CPU type (i386, mips, alpha) • port is the communications port to be used for the debugging terminal (COM1 … COMn) • speed is the communications port speed (9600, 19200, 57600, …)
[-l[text]]	The title of the WinDbg window may be set to text.
[-m]	Start WinDbg minimized.
[-p id [-e event]]	Will cause WinDbg to be attached to the process with the given ID. Signal an event after process is attached. Typically used for JIT (Just In Time) debugging.

Option	Description
[-s[pipe]]	This option will start a remote.exe server, using the named pipe.
[-v]	Initiate the verbose option, where WinDbg will print module load and unload messages.
[-w name]	Used to tell WinDbg to load the named workspace. Not used with the –i option.
[-y path]	Specifies the search path for symbols. More than one search path may be specified, using semicolons to separate each.
[-z crashfile]	Tells WinDbg to debug the specified crash dump file.
[filename[.ext] [arguments]]	To debug a specified program, specify the program's filename (with an extension, if necessary) and any arguments to be passed to the program being debugged.

Table 24-1: Options for the WinDbg command. WinDbg is a powerful machine level debugger.

Warning

It should be clear that WinDbg is generally only useful if the user is very fluent with machine level debugging. It is very easy to cause serious problems (some of which might be difficult, if not impossible, to correct) if WinDbg is used incorrectly. For this reason, it would make sense to not use WinDbg on a working server that has attached clients if at all possible!

Testing Communications With RPC Ping

RPC Ping is a utility used to test RPC (Remote Procedure Call) communications between a server and a workstation. The server component of RPC Ping must be started first on the server from a CMD command prompt.

Once the server component has started (as shown below), the client component may be started on a client workstation. The server component of RPC Ping is rpings.exe. An example of execution of rpings.exe is:

```
V:\EXCHANGE\SERVER\SUPPORT\RPCPING>rpings

+endpoint \pipe\rping on protocol sequence ncacn_np is set for
use.
+endpoint 52 on protocol sequence ncacn_nb_nb is set for use.
+endpoint rping on protocol sequence ncalrpc is set for use.
+endpoint 2256 on protocol sequence ncacn_ip_tcp is set for
use.
+endpoint 53 on protocol sequence ncacn_nb_tcp is set for use.
+endpoint 54 on protocol sequence ncacn_spx is set for use.
+endpoint 2256 on protocol sequence ncadg_ip_udp is set for
use.
+endpoint 55 on protocol sequence ncadg_ipx is set for use.
 -protocol Sequence ncacn_vns_spp not supported on this host

Enter '@q' to exit rpings.
```

The client execution component (for Windows 95 or Windows NT) is shown in Figure 24-2. The client side of RPC Ping may be tested in two modes: Ping Only, which tests the ability to communicate with the RPC facility and server, and Endpoint Search, which searches for UUIDs (Uniform Unique IDs), and endpoints.

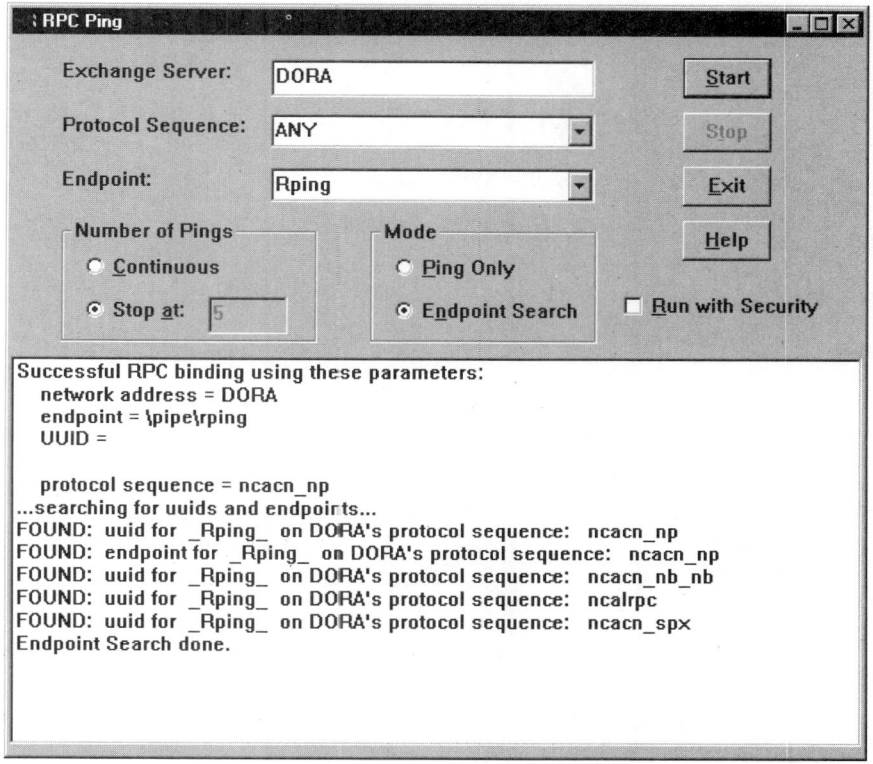

Figure 24-2: Testing RPC communications using RPC Ping.

Moving On

This chapter covered a number of support utilities that are supplied with Microsoft Exchange Server. These utilities are not well documented and may be invaluable in debugging problems discovered in running Microsoft Exchange Server.

The next section introduces Microsoft IIS (Internet Information Server). Microsoft ISS is a powerful yet easy-to-use set of services offering a Web server, Gopher, and FTP servers all rolled into one package that's easy to manage and use. Just the thing for setting up an Internet presence!

Microsoft Internet Information Server (IIS)

25 Overview of IIS

First, a little background information: In keeping with Microsoft's goal to move fully into the world of the Internet, the Microsoft Internet Information Server (IIS) was provided as an optional feature for Windows NT 3.51 Server. IIS is also supplied as part of the Microsoft BackOffice 2.0 product. IIS version 2.0 is now included as a part of Windows NT 4 Server. Microsoft is offering a limited-feature version of IIS for use with Windows NT 4 Workstation and plans a future version of IIS for Windows 95.

Now, what can you do with Microsoft IIS? You can use it to establish a company on the Internet or to set up an intranet. In case you missed our introduction to the Internet and intranets in earlier chapters, an intranet is a network like the Internet, but totally private, usually limited to a single company, corporation, or organization. The Internet, on the other hand, is global (really, worldwide!) and public, and for all intents and purposes, offers unlimited access to its users!

Microsoft IIS consists of three separate server services:

- Gopher
- FTP
- World Wide Web (WWW)

With IIS there are also a few other supporting software applications, files, and sample Web site files that you can install.

First Things First

Don't worry too much about setting up an individual IIS service. Simply load the example files, and start with them. Later, you can customize (or just replace) the Web pages Microsoft provided.

Neither the FTP nor Gopher service has sample files. If you don't provide sample files, the services still work correctly, but users don't get anything. No problem. You can add files to the FTP and Gopher services at any time.

The Microsoft IIS administrator can set a number of options to configure each of the IIS services. Of these three servers, the Web server is probably the most extensively customized by users—Web pages encourage a great deal of Web site individuality and creativity.

Note: If you are planning to install Microsoft Proxy Server, you need to install IIS and Windows NT 4 Server Service Pack 1 first.

This chapter introduces both IIS and the Internet Service Manager. Chapters 26 and 27 cover the other servers.

Tip

Microsoft distributed free beta versions of IIS that worked with Windows NT 3.51 Server (which required a service pack to be installed, also). If you have IIS installed under Windows NT 3.51 Server, be sure to allow setup to install the new version of IIS that comes with Windows NT 4 Server.

Installing Microsoft IIS

Installing IIS is relatively easy. There are a number of ways to do so. Each method, however, will run the same setup program. The only difference between the different installation methods is how the IIS setup program is run.

When Windows NT 4 Server is installed, Setup Wizard prompts you to install IIS. If you do not choose to install IIS at Windows NT 4 Server installation time, the Setup Wizard places, on your Windows NT desktop, an icon for installing IIS. When installing IIS, you must decide on a location for the IIS product (typically IIS is installed in default location, the Windows NT folder: c:\winnt\system32\inetsrv).

It is suggested that you install IIS on an NTFS partition. If Windows NT 4 Server is installed on an NTFS partition, then installing IIS in the default folder is likely the best choice. Using an NTFS partition enhances security for the files IIS uses (NTFS partitions have better security), an important consideration when connected to the Internet.

If you do not install Microsoft IIS when installing Windows NT 4 Server, then you have three choices on how to install IIS:

- ■ You can select the IIS installation icon that Windows NT 4 Server setup has placed on your desktop. This will run the IIS setup program.

- ■ You can run the IIS setup program from the Control Panel (see "Installing IIS From the Control Panel" later in the chapter).

- ■ You can run the IIS setup program from the Windows NT 4 Server distribution CD-ROM. The setup program, inetstp.exe, is found in the inetsrv folder.

Installing IIS From the Desktop

To install Microsoft IIS using the icon placed on the desktop by the Windows NT 4 Server setup program, simply double-click the IIS installation icon. If for any reason you do not have an IIS installation icon (maybe it was deleted), then use one of the two following methods.

Installing IIS From the Control Panel

To install IIS using the Control Panel, follow these steps:

1. Start the Control Panel's Network applet.

2. Select the Services tab.

3. Click the Add button. The Select Network Service dialog box appears.

4. Select Microsoft Internet Information Server 2.0 from the Network Service list, and click OK.

Installing IIS From the Windows NT 4 Server CD-ROM

To install Microsoft IIS from the Windows NT 4 Server distribution CD-ROM, follow these steps:

1. On the CD-ROM, change the current IIS folder to the correct folder for your processor (for Intel, the I386\inetsrv folder).

2. Run the setup program INETSTP (which is the name of the IIS setup program) to install, remove, or modify the current installation of IIS.

3. Follow the prompts to complete the installation of IIS. The setup is identical to setup started from the Control Panel's Network applet, as described in the next section.

The IIS Setup Program

The Microsoft Internet Information Server 2.0 setup program's welcome dialog box appears as shown in Figure 25-1.

The setup program will allow you to select which IIS components are to be installed (you may elect to install Web, FTP, and Gopher services).

None of the Microsoft Internet Information Server components are large. In fact, the entire IIS system occupies less than 5MB, including all of the example HTML pages! The author recommends installing all and then simply stopping those services that are not desired.

Note: When IIS is installed after Windows NT 4 Server has been installed and you use the method described in the steps above (in "Installing Microsoft IIS"), there may be a problem. Installing IIS requires that you start the Control Panel's Network applet. The Microsoft IIS setup program, however, needs to update the Control Panel, which cannot be updated while the Control Panel is open. If you get a somewhat cryptic message saying that a CPL file cannot be copied (yes, this happens often when installing Windows NT 4 Server components), simply close the Control Panel, and click the Retry button (see Figure 25-2).

Figure 25-1: The Microsoft Internet Information Server 2.0 Setup dialog box.

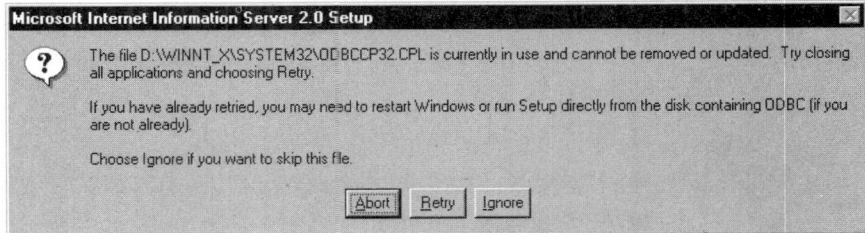

Figure 25-2: IIS setup error: the Control Panel can't be updated.

The installation process is simple and quick. Once completed, you should restart Windows NT 4 Server, which will then start the IIS services.

Setting Up & Configuring IIS

The initial folders used to publish on the Internet are created by the IIS setup program. For the World Wide Web Publishing Directory, the IIS setup program writes (if the help and sample files are installed) several HTML examples. The FTP and Gopher publishing folders do not contain any sample files. If you modify any of the example Web pages that are installed by IIS, and at a later time you reinstall IIS, your modifications will be lost.

When you are using the Internet, you must define a Domain Name Server (DNS). If you have not specified a DNS, the IIS setup program cautions you to configure the DNS entry in the Control Panel's Network applet. The IIS setup program will prompt if the DNS entries are not set correctly.

IIS can use ODBC, SQL Server, or text files (the default) to store the IIS logs. If ODBC Drivers & Administrator was selected, there is a prompt to install the SQL Server ODBC driver.

Note: You are not limited to using SQL Server as your IIS logging device; the default logging device is a comma-delimited text file.

Microsoft IIS is configured using the Microsoft Internet Information Server Manager program—the topic of the next section.

The Microsoft Internet Information Server Manager

After you install Microsoft IIS, there will be a new item in Start Menu | Programs. This item is called Microsoft Internet Server and contains five items:

- Internet Information Server setup
- Microsoft Internet Explorer
- Product documentation
- Internet Service Manager
- Key Manager

The Internet Information Server setup was described in the previous section.

The Microsoft Internet Explorer is version 2, which has been replaced with version 3 of Internet Explorer. The author recommends that the latest version of Internet Explorer be downloaded and used, rather than using the version that comes with Windows NT 4 Server. For the current version of Internet Explorer, check http://www.microsoft.com.

The IIS product documentation consists of a help file that contains the documentation needed to use and manage IIS.

The Key Manager program is used to manage security keys for IIS. With the Key Manager, you can create new key requests and manage keys. More information on keys may be found in Chapter 27.

Microsoft IIS is managed by the Internet Service Manager application. Launch this application using the Start Menu Programs | Microsoft Internet Server | Internet Service Manager selection.

The Internet Service Manager application manages and customizes each of the servers that make up IIS. Management consists of typically starting or shutting down the various servers as needed. For example, if the Gopher server will not be used at your site, simply stop the Gopher server. Each of the IIS servers are independent—and you can start or stop them as needed without affecting the other servers.

Use the Internet Service Manager window (see Figure 25-3) to work with various servers or services. The list below describes the functionality available from the Properties and View menus:

■ From the Properties menu, you can configure each service (locally or remotely), make connections to specific servers, and locate servers and display properties of a service. You can start, stop, and pause services using the service's context menu.

■ From the View menu, you can specify how you want the information presented—by individual service or sorted by field.

■ The Servers view is the default view.

■ Services view and Reports view offer other presentations of the same information.

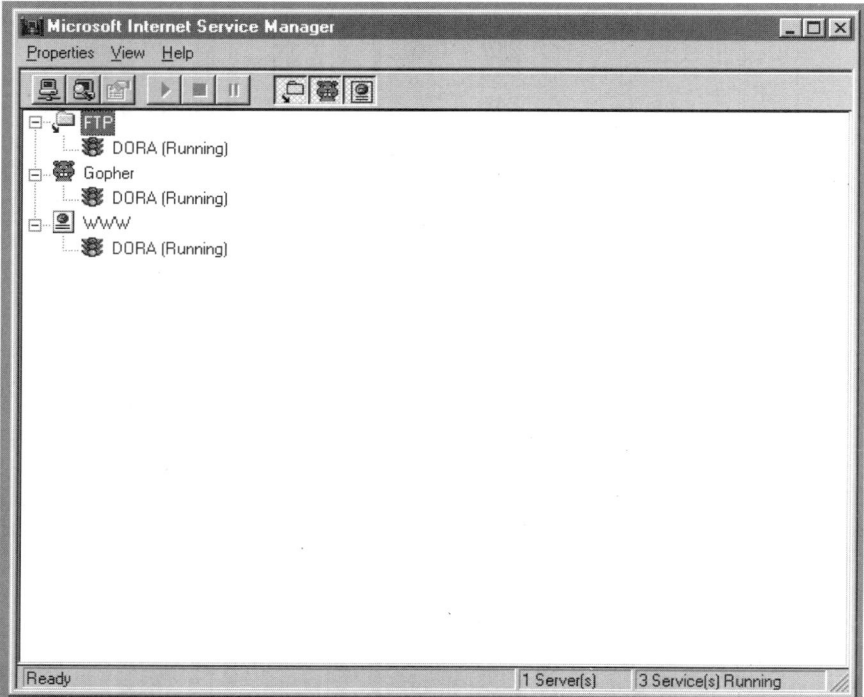

Figure 25-3: The Microsoft Internet Service Manager main window.

Configuring each service is usually simple. Designing the information that the service will publish may be more difficult.

Configuring the FTP, Gopher & Web Servers

You must configure each of the three IIS services before placing them in service. Configuration is not too difficult. Each service uses a similar setup program (minor differences unique to specific service are noted).

The FTP Service Properties dialog box, in Figure 25-4, has five tabs: Service, Messages, Directories, Logging, and Advanced. The Gopher and Web Service Properties dialog boxes have four tabs: Service, Directories, Logging, and Advanced. The Messages tab is only found in the FTP Service Properties dialog box.

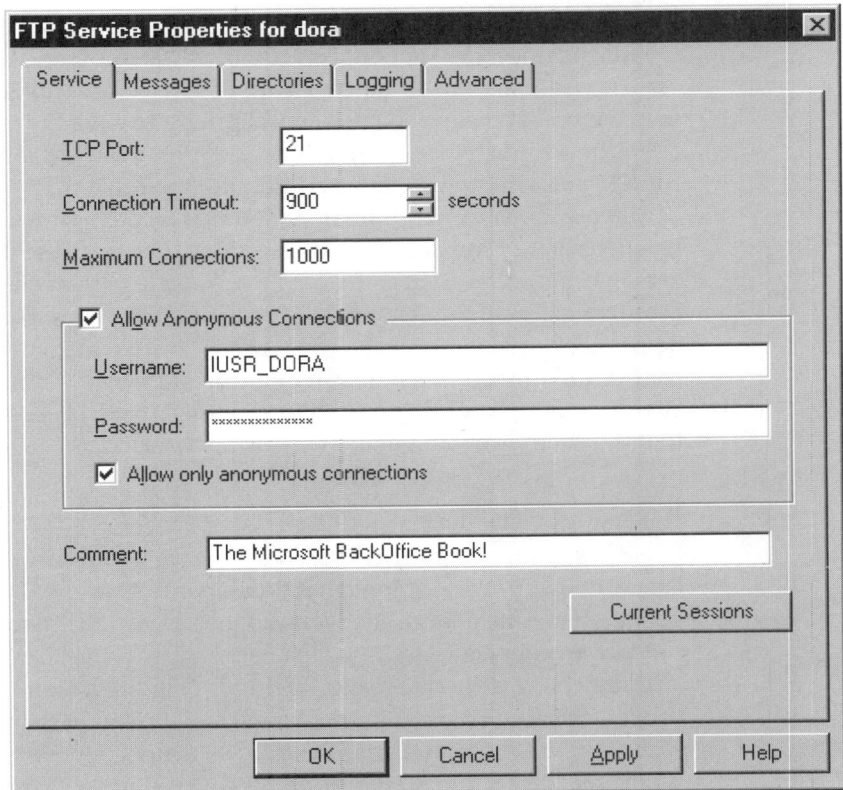

Figure 25-4: The Internet Service Manager FTP Service Properties dialog.

The FTP Service Properties tab functionality is described in detail in the following sections. You can accept many of the defaults for an initial installation of IIS, and later, as you become more comfortable with administrating your site, you can customize more and more of your installation.

Setting Up the Services

The Service tab allows configuration of the service. You can set values for connection timeout and maximum connections, you can choose whether to allow anonymous connections, and you can add the service's comment (which displays in the IIS Manager program).

Connection Timeout

Use the Connection Timeout control to set the number of seconds the service will maintain an inactive connection. Connections become inactive for several reasons—users begin perusing a file or talking on the telephone, for instance—but the most common is the client drops the connection without properly terminating the session.

Having a connection timeout value that is too high will result in resources being consumed by connections that are possibly no longer active. If the connection timeout value is too low, then clients who still are working with the service, but not active, may find themselves disconnected. Therefore, you must use a sensible median value for the connection timeout. The default value of 900 seconds is reasonable—if a client has not responded in 15 minutes, then it can be safely assumed that the client is no longer actively using the service.

Maximum Connections

Use the Maximum Connections control to set the maximum total number of simultaneous connections that this server will allow. Typically, unless you are planning a large site, you will not exceed the default of 1,000 concurrent connections.

It may be worthwhile to consider reducing the maximum connections to a lower value if your Internet connection is slower than a T1 line. If your system uses a fractional T1 or ISDN connection, you may want to set the maximum connections parameter to 50 or 100. For dial-up connections, you may wish to be even more conservative: 5–25 connections are all that most dial-up connections can handle.

Anonymous Connections

Both Gopher and WWW (Web) services use anonymous connections. You can configure the FTP service to allow anonymous connections as well. The IIS setup program does provide a default anonymous userid and password, and you do not need to change this field.

The service uses the anonymous userid and password to access files for the client user. Remember: The service is a system task and does not run using your logon userid.

The FTP service allows three choices for anonymous users:

- **Do not allow anonymous connections.** Set by unchecking the Allow Anonymous Connections check box. Any user who wants to connect to the FTP server must have a userid assigned just as if he or she were a local user. This mode allows the highest degree of security but does not allow anyone who does not have a Windows NT 4 Server userid to connect to the FTP server.

- **Allow only anonymous connections.** Set by checking the Allow Only Anonymous Connections check box. In this configuration, all users must log on as anonymous, and all users will have the same privileges.

- **Allow both anonymous and nonanonymous connections.** Set by checking the Allow Anonymous Connections check box and unchecking the Allow Only Anonymous Connections check box. Allows anyone to connect as anonymous and users who have a userid on the server to connect using their userids. This mode allows the most flexibility: Anonymous users can have limited (read-only perhaps) access, while users with a Windows NT 4 Server userid can be granted more privileges.

The Username field contains the default IIS anonymous userid. You can change this userid if you desire; however, neither Microsoft nor this author recommend using a different username unless you have determined that one is necessary.

The Username field determines permissions of all anonymous connections. Since the great majority of your users will connect with an anonymous connection, the username is important. By default, Internet Information Server setup program creates and uses the account IUSR_computername.

In Figure 25-4, the username is IUSR_DORA, as the computer name is DORA. Note that anonymous users do not know the username, nor do they log on using it.

Figure 25-5 shows the Windows NT 4 Server's User Manager with the properties for the IUSR_DORA displayed. Since a user would never (typically) log on with this userid, the password is not critical. However, to minimize the risks of a security attack on your IIS system, you must use a nontrivial password. IIS setup assigns an initial password, which you do not need to change.

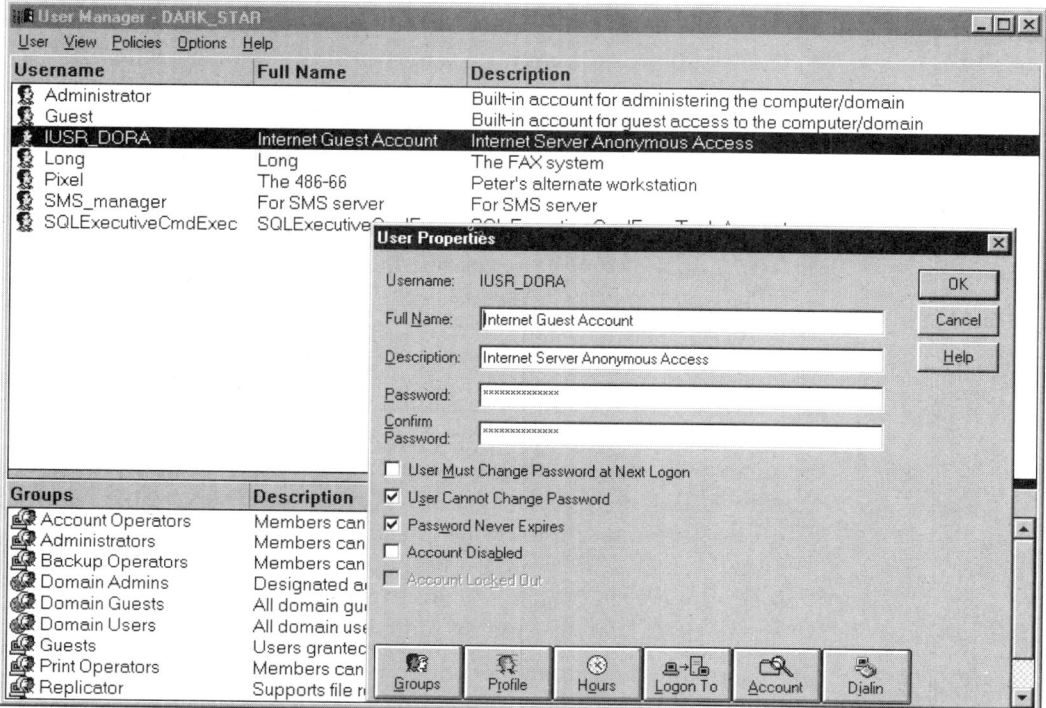

Figure 25-5: The Windows NT 4 Server User Manager.

The Microsoft IIS installation process creates the initial userid (IUSR_computername) for you. If you change the Username field you must manage this userid yourself.

If you change the Username, follow these steps:

1. Start the User Manager for Domains application in the Start Menu | Programs | Administrative Tools (Common) group.

2. Create a new user.

3. Assign the user a password (make sure that the password you select never expires and cannot be changed by the user).

4. Place the new user in the Guests and Domain Users groups, but assign no other group memberships to this userid.

Comment

The Comment text box enables you to specify the text string you want to display in the Internet Service Manager's Report View mode. If you anticipate managing more than one service, then you can use the comment parameter to differentiate between the different servers.

As we said earlier, each service uses a similar setup program. The FTP setup we just described is very much like the Gopher setup. However, now I want to introduce you to fields found on the Gopher Service Properties' Service tab alone, the Service Administrator Name and Email fields.

Gopher's Service Administrator

When configuring the Gopher service, the name and an e-mail address of the administrator must be provided in the Service Administrator box. Some Gopher clients can retrieve this information, allowing the client user to contact the Gopher site's administrator.

In the Name field, enter the administrator's name (that is often your name). This is a "people" readable field, so spell your name as you want people to use it. In Figure 25-6, the Name field contains my name: Peter D. Hipson.

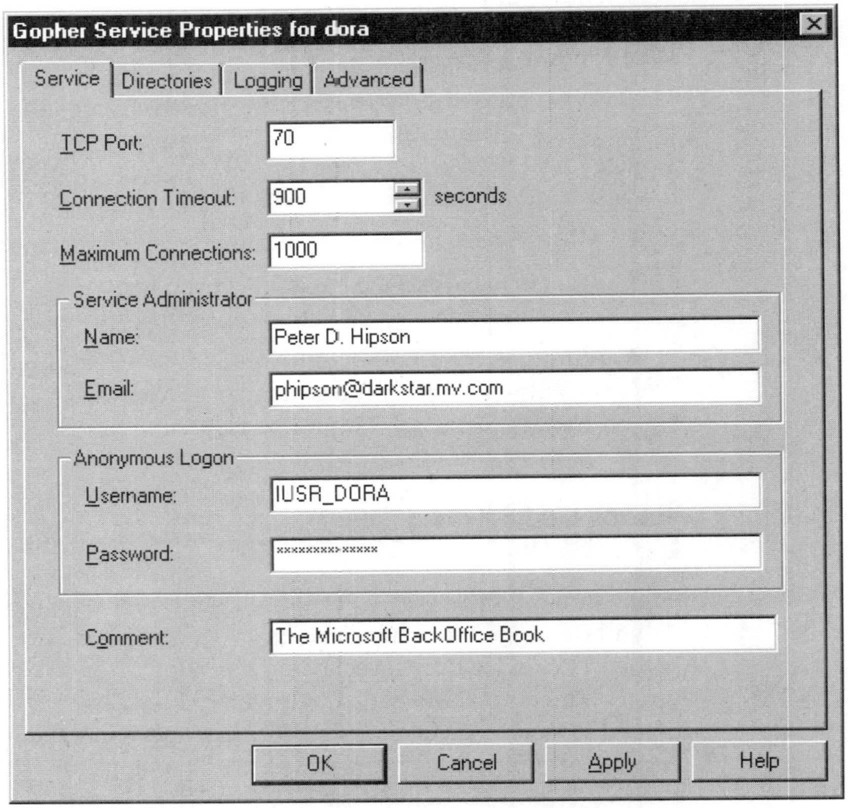

Figure 25-6: The Gopher Service Properties' Service tab.

The Email field holds the administrator's e-mail address. Some administrators create a special e-mail account for each server, such as: gopher_admin@site.organization.com. Be sure that whatever e-mail address you enter exists. No sense in your users sending e-mail to the Internet e-mail black hole! The e-mail address should be in standard Internet format. Try to avoid complex e-mail addresses if possible, because users may have to retype this field when sending you e-mail. In Figure 25-6, the Email field contains the author's e-mail address: phipson@darkstar.mv.com.

Tip

Don't use my name and e-mail address when you set up your Gopher service; I won't know what to do with your e-mail!

WWW's Password Authentication

The WWW setup, similar to FTP and Gopher, has several unique fields that must be filled in. The following are fields found on the WWW Service Properties' Service tab. The WWW service allows you to configure password authentication. Select one or more of the three choices:

- **Allow Anonymous**—permits anyone to connect to the Web server.
- **Basic (Clear Text)**—if a userid is used to connect, the authentication is done using a clear text protocol. This mode is not secure.
- **Windows NT Challenge/Response**—if a userid is used to connect, the authentication is done using the Windows NT Challenge/ Response protocol. This mode is secure.

Setting Up FTP Messages

Of the three services we've been discussing, FTP, Gopher, and WWW, only FTP Service Properties contains a Messages tab. The Messages tab in the FTP Service Properties dialog box allows you to configure the FTP service's messages. Messages are given to users when they first connect to the FTP service, when they disconnect, and when the maximum number of connections has been reached and a user is attempting to connect. Figure 25-7 shows the FTP Service Properties' Messages tab.

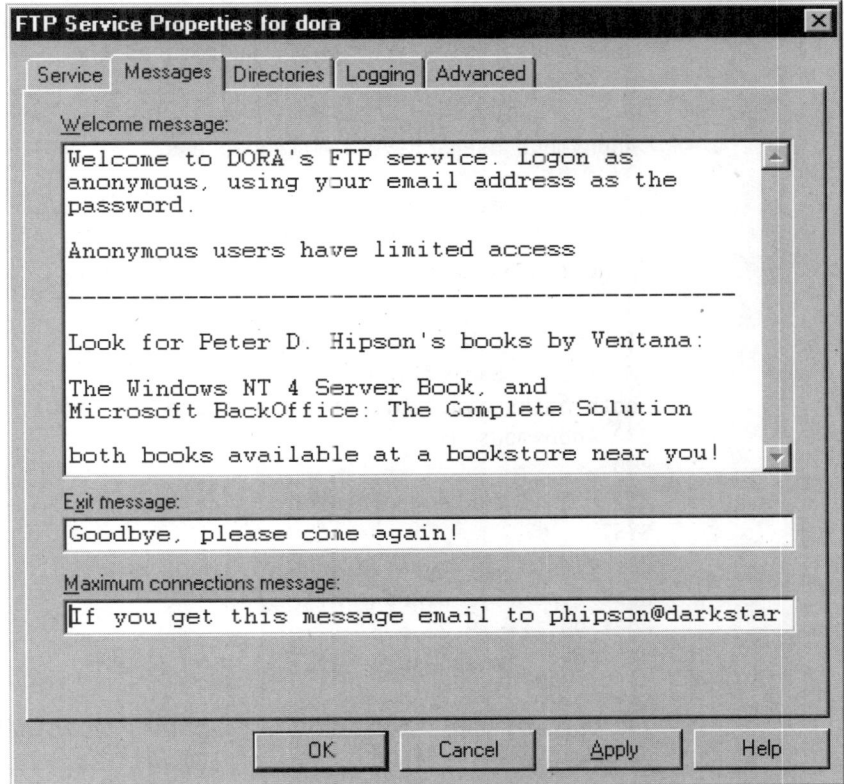

Figure 25-7: The FTP Service Properties' Messages tab.

Below is an example of an FTP session (using Junod's WS_FTP32 program). Notice that an anonymous user cannot create directories (or files, for that matter) in my FTP server:

```
WINSOCK.DLL: WinSock 2.0
WS_FTP32 94.11.28, Copyright © 1994 John A. Junod.
All rights reserved.
- -
connecting to 99.125.78.23 ...
Connected to 99.125.78.23 port 21
220 dora Microsoft FTP Service (Version 2.0).
USER anonymous
331 Anonymous access allowed,
send identity (e-mail name) as password.
PASS xxxxxx
```

```
230-Welcome to DORA's FTP service. Logon as
anonymous, using your email address as the
password.

Anonymous users have limited access

-----------------------------------------------

Look for Peter D. Hipson's books by Ventana:

The Windows NT 4 Server Book, and
Microsoft BackOffice: The Complete Solution
both books available at a bookstore near you!
230 Anonymous user logged in.
PWD
257 "/" is current directory.
SYST
215 Windows_NT version 4.0
Host type (2): Windows NT
PORT 99,125,78,23,6,87
200 PORT command successful.
LIST
150 Opening ASCII mode data connection for /bin/ls.
Received 0 bytes in 0.1 secs, (0.00 bits/sec), transfer
succeeded
226 Transfer complete.
MKD NoDo
550 NoDo: Access is denied.
QUIT
221 Goodbye, please come again!
```

As the example shows, your messages (which are in bold in the
example) should provide useful information for your users. The maximum connections message is more difficult to test—if you feel you really
must test the maximum connections message, set the maximum connections parameter to a number that you can easily exceed (such as one).
Remember, however, even temporarily resetting a parameter such as this
for testing can cause disruptions to legitimate users.

Welcome Message

The welcome message is presented to the user *after* they have successfully logged on to the FTP service. If you have configured your FTP service to accept anonymous logons, then the FTP service automatically sends the following prompt when a user attempts to logon using the Anonymous userid:

```
331 Anonymous access allowed,
send identity (e-mail name) as password.
PASS
```

After logging on the user, the welcome message is then presented.

Many FTP servers have long welcome messages, but it is wise, if possible, to limit the welcome message to one screen (20 or 24 lines of 80 characters each) to avoid having the first part of the message scroll off the user's screen before it has been read.

Exit Message

The exit message is sent to users when they use the FTP quit or bye commands. Limit the exit message text you enter to one or two lines.

Any nice, pleasant message is appropriate here.

Maximum Connections Message

The maximum connections message is sent to users when an attempt is made to log on to the FTP server and the maximum number of users are already connected. The message text should state the problem ("Maximum number of users already connected") and suggest an action for the user to take, such as:

- "Wait and try later" (maybe suggest a time when the FTP server will not be too busy).

- "Other mirror FTP sites are . . . " (if there are mirror FTP sites available).

- Some other reasonable action.

Do be as polite as you can, as the user is going to be disappointed at their inability to connect.

Tip

Consider including an e-mail address where users who receive the maximum connections message can e-mail you or the systems administrator. This will give you an indication that your FTP service is overloaded. Try this for an example: "The maximum number of users are already connected. Try again, and if this error happens again, send me an e-mail at mail@darkstar.mv.com. Thank you!" (Don't use my e-mail address, however!)

Setting Up Directories

The Directories tab allows you to configure a service's directories. With this tab, you configure directory names and properties for the directories. For each service there is typically one home directory and any number of virtual directories.

Warning

Remember security when setting up your directory structure. Be careful not to give access to directories you do not intend to share with clients.

Figure 25-8 shows the Directories tab, with a single home directory configured.

Note: The IIS programs and documentation use the term *directory* when referring to a folder as defined in the Windows NT file structure.

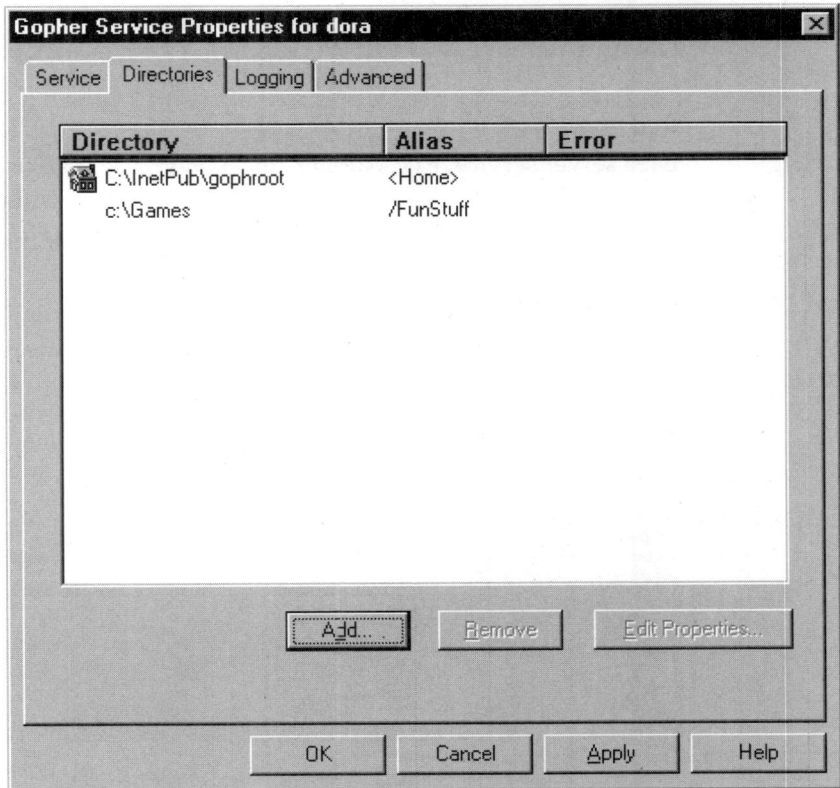

Figure 25-8: The Gopher Service Properties' Directories tab.

The IIS installation program creates a set of folders used by the services. These default folders are:

- **ftproot**—used as the base directory for the FTP service.
- **gophroot**—used as the base directory for the Gopher service.
- **iisadmin**—contains administration files; this folder should not be accessible by FTP, Gopher, or Web users.
- **scripts**—contains script files used by the Web service.
- **wwwroot**—used as the base directory for the Web service.

The folders that end in *root* are the service's root directories. You can then create other folders for your servers, either nested within the service's home folder or in other locations as desired. You can define only one home folder. You must define all other folders as virtual folders.

There are three buttons, which control functionality, in the Directory tab: Add, Remove, and Edit Properties. Let's begin with the Add function.

Add

Each server service, FTP, Gopher, and WWW, uses one or more directories. To add an additional directory to a service, follow these steps:

1. Access the Directory Properties dialog box for the service to which you want to add a directory.

2. You can replace your current home directory or add additional virtual directories as desired. To add a new directory to your server's set of directories, click the Add button. The Internet Service Manager displays the Directory Properties dialog box (Figure 25-9).

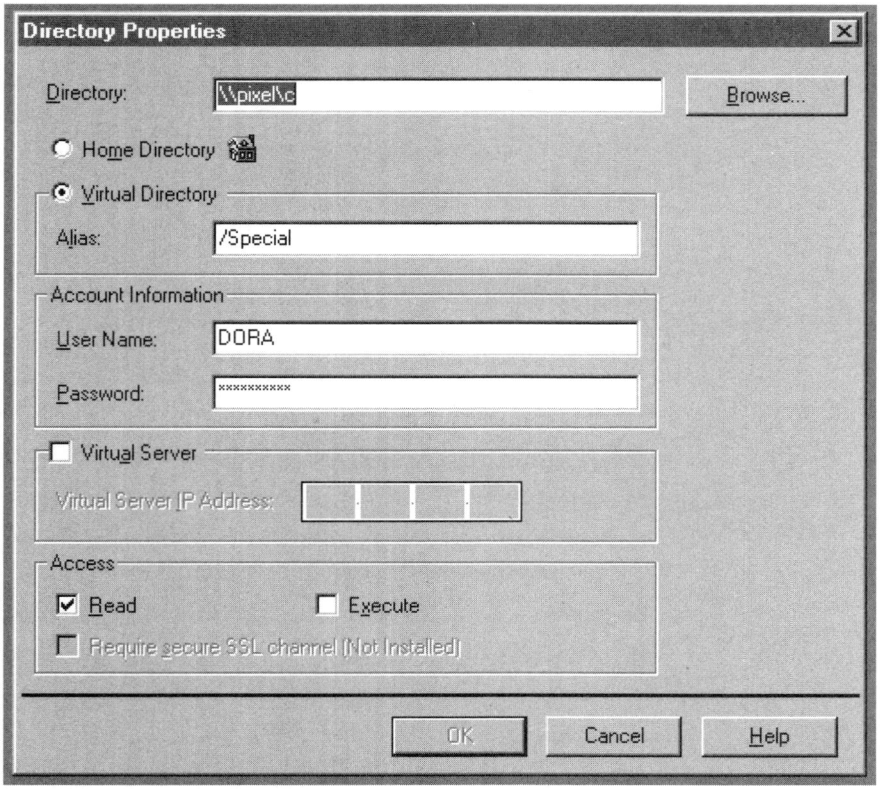

Figure 25-9: The Internet Service Manager Web Directory Properties dialog box.

Each service has a different Directory Properties dialog box. The fields you can configure for each directory are listed in the following sections.

Gopher Directory Properties   You can configure the name of the directory, locate directories to work with, specify a directory as a home directory or a subdirectory under a home directory (as a virtual directory), and provide account information used to access a remote, shared directory.

FTP Directory Properties   Directory name, location, alias, and account information to access networked resources are specified for an FTP directory.
Access to each FTP directory can be read, write, or read/write.

Web Directory Properties   Directory name, location, alias, and account information to access networked resources are specified for a Web directory. Additionally, for a Web directory, you can choose to associate the directory with a virtual server and to limit access to the directory.

Home Directory   In the Directory Properties dialog, you can name the directory (giving the full path name) and assign the directory's attributes. A service can have only *one* home directory; if you select the Home Directory radio button and you already have a home directory defined, this directory will *replace* your current home directory.

Virtual Directories & Their Aliases   For all directories other than the home directory, you can specify an alias for the directory. The alias is a name that the client user uses to access the directory, and it need not match the actual directory name.
If you do not specify an alias, then Internet Service Manager creates an alias for you.
Note: You enter a delimited path name in the Alias field, using UNIX conventions: a *forward* slash between the names. For an example of an alias name, see Figure 25-9. Note the leading forward slash indicating that Special is found under the Web root name.
The use of an alias allows you to create a virtual directory structure for your service. For example, a Gopher user enters gopher://darkstar.mv.com/FunStuff (in Internet Explorer for example), to access the virtual directory funstuff.
This implies that there is a subdirectory under my Gopher home directory called funstuff. Actually, funstuff is an alias to a folder in a different directory tree, and the Gopher server creates the illusion that funstuff is actually a subdirectory under the Gopher root directory, even though it is not.

Virtual directories are always accessed using the alias in the URL as if the alias were a subdirectory of the home directory. That is, the virtual directory will seem to be a subdirectory, even though it may actually be located on a different drive (and perhaps even on a different computer). This allows you to publish using other directories and have these directories be accessible from within the home directory.

When specifying a virtual directory (a subdirectory under a home directory), specify both the directory name and an "alias" that the client users must enter when referring to the directory.

Note: Gopher virtual directories do not appear in directory listings. To make a virtual directory appear in the directory listing, you need to create an explicit link in a tag file for Gopher clients to access virtual directories.

A Gopher user could type in the URL if they know the alias for the virtual directory. To do this, they must prefix the alias name with 11/. For example, to access the virtual directory funstuff from your Gopher server that is named darkstar.mv.com, you use the following URL: **gopher://darkstar.mv.com/11/funstuff.**

You, the administrator, specify the actual location name of the virtual directory (such as c:\users\default) and the virtual name (alias). The alias is the directory name used by Gopher clients; in the example above, the alias is FunStuff.

Directory Account Information   When the directory is located on a different machine than the Gopher server and is accessed using a UNC server and share name, you must provide both a username and password to access the directory. Regardless, all virtual directories on networked drives must be on computers in the same Windows NT domain as the computer that is running Gopher server. An example of a networked virtual directory is shown in Figure 25-9.

The Account Information controls (User Name and Password) are only active if the connection is specified using a Uniform Naming Convention (UNC) server and share name; for example, \\pixel\d\letters. Enter the username and password that have permission to access this directory.

Warning

All accesses to a UNC-named virtual directory are made using the username and password that you specify. Be careful that you do not inadvertently create a security risk by allowing Gopher users to access directories that you do not want them to access.

Directory Virtual Server   The Virtual Server check box allows you to create virtual servers, each of which can has its own unique URL (domain name and IP address). For example, your company is XYZ Corporation, and you have your home Web page at www.xyx.com. XYZ Corporation also has a subsidiary called the AlphaBeta Company, which has a Web home page, also. You set up a domain name for a unique IP address (for example, www.alphabeta.com), and link the www.alphabeta.com IP address to a virtual directory. This sets up two unique URLs (domain names) pointing to a single server. Each URL is separate (unless you point both to the same directory) and unique; users will never know that both URLs are being served by the same computer.

When you have more than one domain name and IP address being serviced by your Web server, and if no IP address is specified for a specific directory, then the directory with no IP address specified is visible to all virtual servers. Default directories created during the IIS installation do not specify an IP address and are therefore visible to all virtual servers.

If you are an Internet Service Provider, or a Web site provider, this feature can be an excellent way to minimize the hardware requirements while creating unique URLs for your customers.

Note: The IP address for the virtual server must be bound to the network card providing the service. Use the Network applet in Control Panel to bind additional IP addresses to your network card. In addition, you need to specify a Class C Internet IP address, which consists of a total of 256 unique addresses in a range. You can route addresses not assigned to virtual Web servers to other machines (users) on the network for their use.

Directory Access   The access level of permissions that users have to the directory is set using the controls in the Access box: Read, Execute, and Requires Secure SSL Channel. The following access levels are valid:

- **Read**—allows a user to view the files.

- **Execute**—allows clients to run programs in this directory. This access level should be selected for program directories. Typically, you would place your scripts and executable files into a directory with execute access.

- **Requires Secure SSL Channel**—selected when using SSL security to encrypt data transmissions.

Tip

Do not select the execute access level for directories containing static content; use the read access level for these directories.

Remove

Click the Remove button on the Gopher Service Properties' Directories tab to remove the currently selected directory in the Gopher Service's directories list (see Figure 25-8). This button is only active when a directory is selected. You can delete the home directory, but the Gopher server does not function without a home directory.

Note: There is no confirmation with the Remove button. If you remove a directory in error, you need to use the Add button to re-add the directory to your Gopher Server's list of directories.

When you remove a directory from the list of directories, you don't actually remove the directory from the disk. If you no longer need the disk folder or directory, explicitly delete the folder or directory using Windows Explorer or a command prompt window.

Edit Properties

Click the Edit Properties button on the Gopher Service Properties' Directories tab to change the properties of a Gopher directory.

You use the Internet Service Manager's Directory Properties dialog when you want to add a directory or when you must change a directory's properties. This dialog box has several items in it. The Internet Service Manager's Directory Properties dialog box is shown previously in Figure 25-9.

FTP's Directory Listing Style

Each FTP directory can have a listing mode: UNIX or MS-DOS. The UNIX mode is more commonly used today; however, MS-DOS file modes are becoming more common as Windows NT 4 Server is used more and more for FTP servers.

Web Default Document

The Web service allows you to specify a default document that displays if the user does not specify a document name. For example, if the default document on my Web service is default.htm, and the user enters:

```
http://darkstar.mv.com/
```

then the user actually receives the document:

```
http://darkstar.mv.com/default.htm
```

A default document allows a user to connect to a site without knowing what the highest level document is. Virtually all Web servers have a default document; the two most commonly used default document names are default.htm and index.htm.

Web Directory Browsing Allowed

Though not often used, directory browsing allows a user to explore the Web site. The author's recommendation is that directory browsing not be allowed unless you have a specific need or requirement for it.

Setting Up Logging

The Logging tab of the Properties dialog box allows you to configure each service's logging of information such as errors and accesses. With this tab, you configure where you want to maintain logging and where you want to place the logging information (either in a file or to an SQL/ODBC database).

Logging can be critical to maintaining statistics for your Internet servers. You should maintain a log, if only to determine who is using your server.

Many sites maintain the log to collect information about which components of their sites are most popular. A frequently active area with lots of return visits indicates an area users are drawn to; an area that is infrequently visited and never generates return visits is an area you can probably remove.

Enable Logging

Click the Enable Logging check box on the Logging tab of the Properties dialog box to have the server log information.

Logging collects information about all clients who connect to your server. A logging entry contains the user's IP address, time of connection, and other information about the transaction (see Table 25-1 for a list of all information that is logged).

It is possible to have separate logging files for each of the IIS services, or you can use a combined logging file. There is sufficient information in the log file entries so that you can determine which service generated the entry.

Log to File

Click Log to File to have the server log information to a file. You must then specify how often to open a new file, where to place the file, and a filename if you want to give it a specific name.

When logging to a text file, the file is written in comma-delimited format. The format of this file is slightly different than the columns written to an SQL/ODBC database. Table 25-1 shows each column and a description of the column's data.

Column Name	Datatype	Description
ClientHost	Character data	Name of the client machine or the client's IP address
username	Character data	The client's username
LogDate	Character data	The date the item was logged
LogTime	Character data	The time the item was logged
service	Character data	The service requested, such as GopherSvc for a Gopher request
machine	Character data	The machine used to process the request
serverip	Character data	The server's IP address
processingtime	Numeric data	Time spent processing this request
bytesrecvd	Numeric data	The number of bytes that were received
bytessent	Numeric data	The number of bytes that were sent to the client
servicestatus	Numeric data	The service status flag
win32status	Numeric data	The Windows Win32 status
operation	Character data	The requested operation, such as GET Dir, File, or Error
target	Character data	The target name or directory
parameters	Character data	Any parameters supplied, or a hyphen (-) if none
blank	Character data	Blank, empty column

Table 25-1: Columns in the Log to File log.

Log to SQL/ODBC Database

Click Log to SQL/ODBC Database on the Logging tab of the Properties dialog box to have the server log information to either an SQL Server database or any other ODBC database. For those users who are not using SQL Server, then logging to an ODBC Access database can be an excellent choice, as Access is capable of producing reports and summary information.

Warning

If IIS is being logged to a local SQL Server and IIS starts prior to SQL Server, then an error condition occurs and no logging is done. This condition can be corrected by telling Windows NT 4 Server that SQL Server must be fully started before starting IIS. This is done by setting the registry key

```
HKEY_LOCAL_MACHINE\System\CurrentControlSet\Services\<service>
```

where <service> is W3SVC for the Web server, MSFTPSVC for the FTP server, and GOPHERSVC for the Gopher server. In this key is a value called "DependOnService" that typically contains two null terminated strings: RPCSS and NTLMSSP. Add the string MSSQLServer to this list, and restart the system.

As always, changes in the Registry are dangerous: Use extreme caution, and back up critical information!

Within the Log to SQL/ODBC Database group box are four text boxes, which become enabled after you select Log to SQL/ODBC Database. Enter the information that applies into each text box:

- **ODBC Data Source Name (DSN)**—the DSN that you have created as a system DSN. For an Access file, the DSN is the name of your database.
- **Table**—the table in the DSN in which the logging information is saved.
- **User Name**—the username for the DSN.
- **Password**—the username's password for the DSN.

The table in the DSN must contain the columns shown in Table 25-2.

Column Name	Datatype	Description
ClientHost	varchar(255)	Name of the client machine or the client's IP address
username	varchar(255)	The client's username
LogTime	datetime	The date and time the item was logged
service	varchar(255)	The service requested, such as GopherSvc for a Gopher request
machine	varchar(255)	The machine used to process the request
serverip	varchar(50)	The server's IP address
processingtime	int	Time spent processing this request
bytesrecvd	int	The number of bytes that were received
bytessent	int	The number of bytes that were sent to the client
servicestatus	int	The service status flag
win32status	int	The Windows Win32 status
operation	varchar(255)	The requested operation, such as GET Dir, File, or Error
target	varchar(255)	The target name or directory
parameters	varchar(255)	Any parameters supplied, or a hyphen (-) if none

Table 25-2: Column names and specifications for ODBC logging.

When you log on to an SQL database, a different set of columns is used. In the iis\server subdirectory there is an SQL file called logtemp.sql. This file generates the necessary SQL table for IIS logging. The following is a listing of a somewhat better version of this SQL script:

```
if exists (select * from sysobjects where id =
        object_id('inetlog') and sysstat & 0xf = 3)
        drop table inetlog
GO
```

```
CREATE TABLE inetlog (
   ClientHost varchar(255),
   username varchar(255),
   LogTime datetime,
   service varchar(255),
   machine varchar(255),
   serverip varchar(50),
   processingtime int,
   bytesrecvd int,
   bytessent int,
   servicestatus int,
   win32status int,
   operation varchar(255),
   target varchar(255),
   parameters varchar(255)
)
GO
```

This script is somewhat better than Microsoft's example; the Microsoft script fails when the table already exists.

Setting Up Access

The Advanced tab of the Properties dialog box allows you to configure access to each service. You can choose to exclude (deny access to) all users except for those you specifically authorize or to include (grant access to) all users except for those you specifically exclude. As well, you can limit the total network throughput for *all* the IIS servers (Gopher, WWW, and FTP) in the Advanced tab (see Figure 25-10).

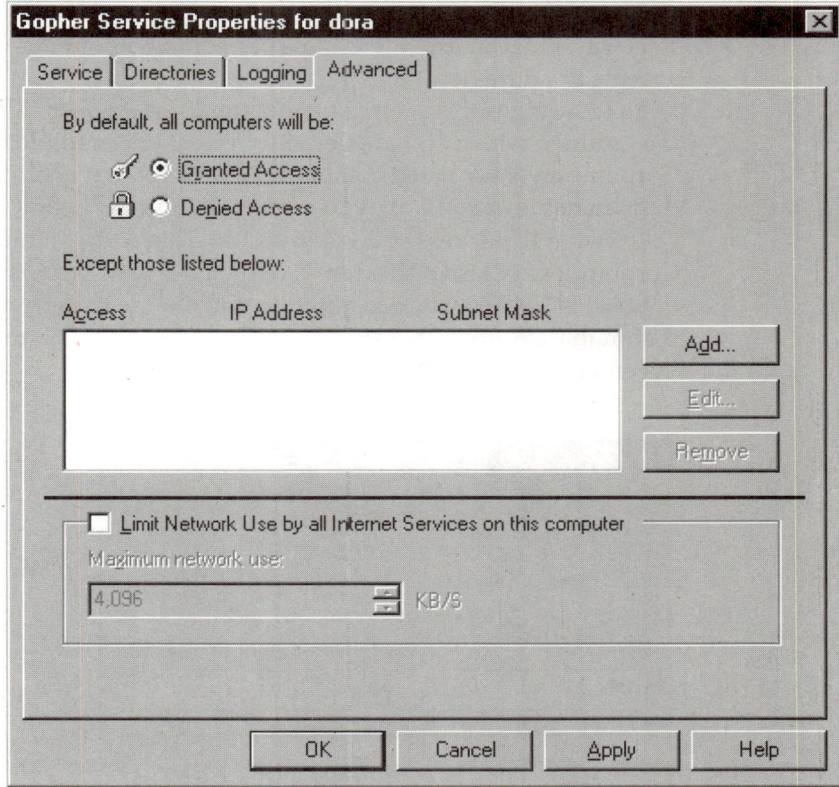

Figure 25-10: The Advanced tab.

Granted Access/Denied Access

Click Granted Access to tell Microsoft IIS to grant access to all users except those who are listed in the Except Those Listed Below list. This is the normal mode of operation for IIS.

Click Denied Access to tell IIS to grant access to no users except those who are listed in the Except Those Listed Below list. This mode of operation is used when the IIS site is *closed* to users other than those specifically authorized.

Except Those Listed Below

The Except Those Listed Below list is a list of users who are to be either denied or granted access. The user's name, IP address, and subnet mask are all shown in this list.

You may choose to grant or deny based on groups of IP addresses, too. This way, you can exclude groups of people without knowing their specific IP addresses.

To deny a group, you must know the Class A, B, or C IP address for the group to which you are denying access. For example, if the XYZ Corporation (your hated competitor) has a Class B IP address and a domain name of xyz.com, you could use PING xyz.com, and you might get back an IP address of 204.146.46.133. This address indicates that XYZ Corporation's Class B IP address (which translates to 65,536 IP addresses) is 204.146.xxx.xxx. You then can choose to deny access to anyone within that group with a single entry—such power! Figure 25-11 shows the entry for our mythical XYZ Corporation.

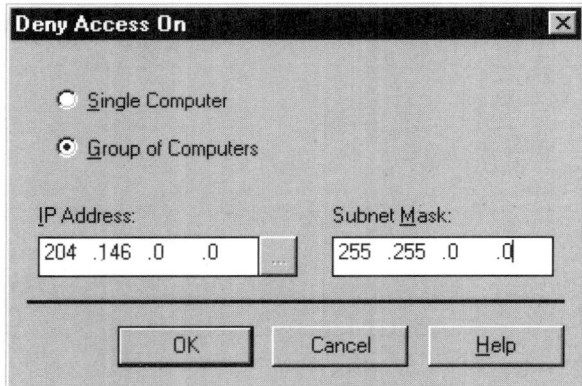

Figure 25-11: The Deny Access On dialog box.

You can add, edit, or remove users from the list using the appropriate buttons.

Limit Network Use by All Internet Services

The Limit Network Use by All Internet Services on This Computer check box (see Figure 25-10) allows you to limit the amount of network I/O performed by the IIS to a value you specify. For example, if your site has a T3 connection to the Internet, and you need to limit the actual I/O to only use a small part of the T3 connection (to leave some bandwidth for other network tasks), set this value to a value that reflects the amount of usage of your T3 connection you wish to assign to the IIS services.

The default value is 4096K. Is this default realistic? You must decide: How important is your Internet presence, how important is your non-IIS bandwidth, and what is the return on the investment for your communications? For example, Table 25-3 shows the communications rate for various methods of communicating with remote networks (such as Internet).

Type of Connection	Speed	Typical Number of Active Users
Dial-up	28,000	1-2
Frame Relay	56,000	5-10
ISDN	128.000	5-15
T1	1,500,000	25-100
Fractional T1	Varies as needed	(Varies)
T3	45,000,000	1000+

Table 25-3: Remote communications speeds.

Reliability

We all strive for reliability. Let's face it—when our system is not reliable, we usually meet with some difficult work. In all, the IIS server is simple. IIS is not a complex program (such as SQL Server is) and should not be prone to failures.

Right—not prone to failures. True, but what most often fails with Internet servers is not the software or the hardware. In all the time that I have been using IIS, I have yet to see it fail. Yes, when it was in beta it had its *glitches*, but IIS has been a very reliable product. The failure is typically the IIS administrator—us. (It was Pogo who said, "We have met the enemy and he is us.") We fail to make our site complete, we have links to *nowhere*, and we have objects (such as FTP and Gopher files) that can't be found. We do all sorts of unexplainable things, most of which tend to convince the user that we are nothing more than a bunch of babbling idiots—when nothing could (we hope!) be further from the truth.

Most failures are caught and fixed quickly when administrators simply check their own work. Nothing is more frustrating to a client user than to click a link and get a message that the link is not valid, the page cannot be found, or that the server doesn't exist.

Performance

If your Internet server is to be useful to client users, it must perform well. Long delays, error transmissions, and cryptic results all detract from the value of the site. Some of the things that can be done to make an Internet site perform better are:

- **Don't run a serious Web site on a dial-up connection.** Even a fast 28.8K modem can only keep up with one user. A minimum connection for a Web server is a 56K ISDN connection, and it's preferable to have a connection with twice that performance. Popular sites have thousands of "visitors" daily. Let's face it—there are not many "home" Internet sites using Windows NT 4 Server!

- **Use the NTFS file system for your data directories if possible.** NTFS offers enhanced security and reliability.

- **Ensure that your server has sufficient RAM to do its job.** Generally IIS does not need large amounts of RAM; however, if you are running a complex server, perhaps with an SQL back end, RAM can be critical.

- **Keep drives on SCSI interfaces and avoid, if possible, IDE drives for Windows NT 4 Server installations.** IDE is fine for desktop applications, but not for servers.

- **Don't serve files from a CD-ROM.** CD-ROMs do not work well when more than one task or user is attempting to access files on the device.

Moving On

In this chapter we covered Microsoft Internet Information Server (IIS). This server consists of three main components—Web, FTP, and Gopher servers—and an administration program to manage each of them.

The next chapter covers the Microsoft IIS Gopher & FTP Services. The Microsoft IIS WWW Server is covered in the chapter that follows.

26

Installing & Configuring the IIS Gopher & FTP Services

In this chapter, both the Gopher and FTP services are described. Gopher is a service that allows users to interact with the server and retrieve information easily. Similar to the WWW, Gopher is a text-based service, but unlike the WWW, it is no longer popular on the Internet. FTP (File Transfer Protocol) is *the* file transfer protocol for the Internet. Virtually all sites support FTP, and recent releases of all browsers support FTP.

Both FTP and Gopher are configured using the Internet Information Service Manager program, as described in Chapter 25.

The IIS Gopher Service

Gopher is a client/server application that has found some popularity on the Internet. Combining some features of Web pages and FTP, Gopher allows users to find and retrieve both information and files. Gopher services require more maintenance than FTP servers, but the management of a Gopher service is usually easier than maintaining a Web site: Gopher is text oriented.

When we talk about the IIS Gopher Service, we usually call it a Gopher service or a Gopher site. You can use the terms interchangeably. Oh, and some people call Gopher services "Gopher holes." I guess Gopher kind of grows on you after a while!

Why a Gopher server? In reality, Gopher servers are infrequently used and are not often implemented as part of new Internet sites. Part of this lack of popularity is the fact that Gopher servers are not well understood by users (not to mention administrators!), and there is a lack of good-quality Gopher client software for the all-important Windows environment. However, many Internet sites support Gopher if only to have a complete set of servers.

Although Microsoft Internet Explorer does access Gopher sites, it is not an optimal client for serious Gopher users.

Many Gopher sites are also poorly maintained, a fact that is somewhat understandable. Students and volunteers at various universities and other noncommercial organizations, a transient population who often have conflicting priorities and excessive responsibilities, run them.

A Gopher server is very similar to an FTP server. Both Gopher and FTP allow you to publish files. There are, however, differences between Gopher and FTP, including:

- The Gopher service allows you to create links to other computers and services—FTP servers typically link to files and directories only.

- The Gopher service allows you to annotate the files and directories that are published—FTP limits file and directory information to their names.

- The Gopher service allows you to create custom menus—FTP menus are simply another word for directories.

The downside of all that Gopher functionality is that you must create the links, configure the folders and directories, and build your menus—manually. Unlike the Web service, there are no automated tools for creating Gopher sites.

The IIS Gopher Service supports all the standard Gopher services and features. Additionally, there is support for Gopher plus selector strings, which permit the Gopher server to provide additional information to the client, including items such as the Gopher Server administrator's name, modification date, and MIME-type information.

Whether or not you decided to implement the IIS Gopher server is a decision you, and your systems administrator, must make. You will find, however, that implementing a Gopher server takes little in the way of resources and is not too complicated if you configure a simple Gopher site. Gopher can provide a better interface to the user, but it does require more effort to configure.

Some examples of the better-known Gopher sites on the Internet include:

- gopher://gopher.nstn.ca/1

- gopher://ukoln.bath.ac.uk/

- gopher://gopher.eff.org/

If you are not a Gopher expert (and many of us are not), then use your Web browser to take a look at each of these sites to get an idea of what is done with a Gopher site. Remember, Gopher does not have the popularity that the WWW has: Web sites can have thousands of visitors each day. A really popular Gopher site may have hundreds of visitors, and although there are no published figures to tell us how much traffic there is to Gopher sites, 10 visitors per day is probably more realistic for most.

Configuring the Gopher Service

Setting up your Gopher service can be as simple as copying your files (and directories) to the Gopher service's root directory. This creates a simple Gopher server. Client users can then browse the Gopher directories using a Gopher client (such as Internet Explorer).

Additionally, you can enhance your site by creating tag files that enable links to other computers or services. Use these tag files to annotate your files and directories and to create custom menus, if desired. All the information that a Gopher client gets from your Gopher service comes from tag files.

A tag file usually contains the following items:

- **Display name**—the name displayed to the Gopher client. The display name is commonly called the "friendly" name.

- **Host name**—the name of the Gopher host.

- **Port number**—the port number (the default is 70) for the item.

Tag files are typically not edited or manipulated by hand. When written to an NTFS formatted drive, the tag file is not available to the user. When a tag file is written to a FAT (File Allocation Table) file system drive, the tag file has the hidden attribute set. Under the FAT file system, a tag file is actually a simple text file:

```
C:\winnt\system32\inetsrv\gophroot>type att01t~1.gtg
0
GdsPriv=Gs1.0;07/25/96;19:20:43
Type=0
Name=Attachment file for Gopher.
AdmN=Peter D. Hipson
AdmE=phipson@darkstar.mv.com

C:\winnt\system32\inetsrv\gophroot>
```

If you are running Gopher Plus, you can add more information to each tag file, such as:

- The name and e-mail address of the server administrator, or the person responsible for the server.

- The creation and last modification dates of the file.

A tag file, under the FAT file system, has the same name as the source file with a GTG extension added. For example, the file hipson.dat has a tag file with the name of hipson.dat.gtg.

On a FAT file system drive, when you are moving Gopher files that have tag files, you must also move the tag file. To move the tag files, follow these steps:

1. First you need to make the tag file visible (as it is hidden). Using Explorer, set the view to include all files.

2. Select the Gopher file you want to move, and the tag file, and move both of the files together (use a drag and drop or cut and paste).

3. Don't forget to rehide the tag file after moving it.

It is not possible to copy or move tag files between drives that are formatted with different file systems.

Some documentation with Microsoft IIS indicates that tag files stored on an NTFS volume can be either directly copied or unhidden. This is not true—the tag information is not directly accessible under NTFS. The tag information is not stored in a file; rather it is stored in an alternate data stream.

Under the NTFS file system, when copying files that have tag information attached, the tag information is automatically copied also.

Warning

When you are short of disk space, be sure to consider the size of the tag files—though not large, tag files do require disk space.

Creating Tag Files

The program GDSSET creates a tag file. This program is run (typically) from a command prompt, and all parameters are entered on the command line. Though it is possible to run GDSSET using the Windows Run command (in the Start menu), it is not convenient to do so. The command syntax for the GDSSET command is:

```
gdsset -c -gn -f "description of file"
-a "administrator's name" -e e-mail filename
```

Table 26-1 lists the options for GDSSET. In all cases, when a parameter is required (such as the AdminName), and the parameter has embedded spaces, then the parameter must be quoted.

Option	Description
-c	Changes the existing tag information. (Default is to create a new tag information.)
-r	Reads and dumps the tag information on console.
-G	Specifies the debug flags to be used.
-D	Specifies the directory for the given file.
-d	Specifies that given file is actually a directory.
-g	Specifies the file's type, as from Table 26-2. This value is a single digit or character. The default, if this option is omitted, is 9, a binary file. (Not valid when the -r option is used.)
-f<FriendlyName>	Specifies friendly name for object. (Valid when -r not used.)
-l	Specifies that link information is to be set for write. (Valid when -r not used.)
-s<Selector>	Specifies the selector for link. (Valid when -l is used.)
-h<HostName>	Specifies the Host for link. (Valid when -l is used.)
-p<PortNumber>	Specifies the Port number for link. (Valid when -l is used.)
-a<AdminName>	The administrator's name (in quotes, if there are embedded spaces). When this option is omitted, the name in the Service tab of the Internet Service Manager is used.
-e<Adminemail>	The administrator's e-mail address. When this option is omitted, the e-mail address in the Service tab of the Internet Service Manager is used.

Table 26-1: GDSSET options.

When you run GDSSET, the tag file is automatically hidden. When the tag file is on a FAT volume, you can unhide and view this file using the ATTRIB command or Explorer. For tag files on NTFS volumes, the tag file is contained in a second data stream. You cannot view or edit tag files on NTFS volumes directly—instead use GDSSET -r to view the tag file's contents.

If you must create a number of tag files, it is possible to use a batch file to do so. For example, the following command creates a series of tag files of the same type:

```
for %1 in (*.txt) do <echo %i&& gdsset -c -gn -f %i %i
```

Table 26-2 lists the allowed Gopher file types. Not all Gopher clients (especially older clients) recognize *all* of the types listed, but most current Gopher clients recognize the types listed in this table.

Type	Description
0	A nonspecific file, typically a flat text file
1	A Gopher directory file
2	A CSO (qi) phonebook server file
3	Error
4	A BinHex'ed Macintosh® file
5	An MS-DOS binary archive
6	A UNIX Uuencoded file
7	An Index-Search server
8	A text-based Telnet session
9	A binary file
c	A calendar or calendar of events
g	A Graphics Interchange Format (GIF) graphics file
h	A WWW HTML hypertext page
I	An image file (generally other than GIF)
m	A BSD format mbox file
P	A PDF document
T	A TN3270 (IBM) mainframe connection session
:	A bitmap image (It is necessary to use Gopher plus information to determine the actual image type.)

Table 26-2: Gopher file type codes.

In short, to set up your Gopher service files, follow these steps:

1. Copy the actual files to the Gopher root directory (and subdirectories, as desired).

2. Then use GDSSET to create tag files for each Gopher file.

Using Tag Files

Once you have created the tag files, a Gopher client can see the friendly name and file type. To see an example, take a look at my Gopher site, shown in Figure 26-1.

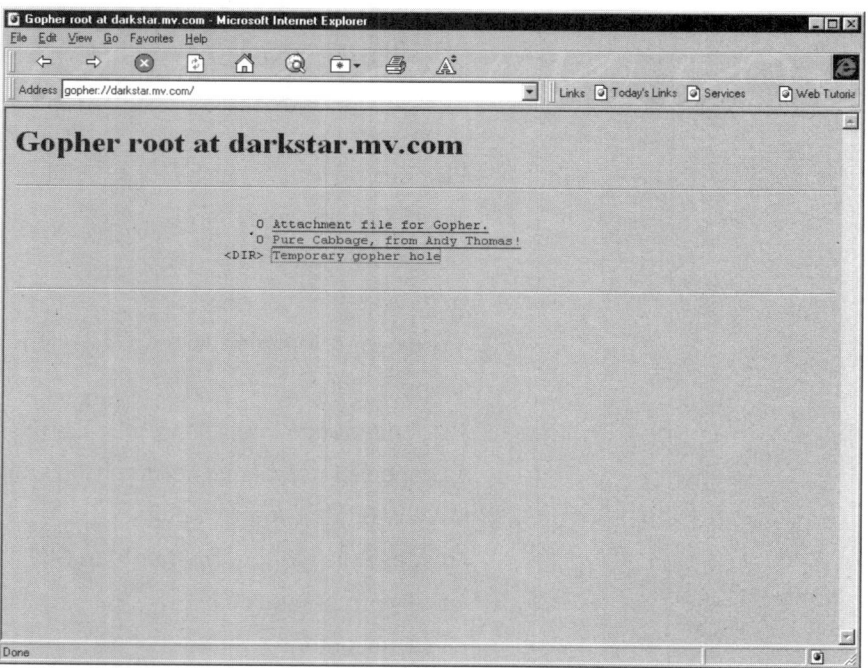

Figure 26-1: Internet Explorer looking at my Gopher site.

Notice how the friendly name displays, and also notice the number beside the two files: the *0* specifies that the file is "A nonspecific file, typically a flat text file" type of file. The <DIR> before *Temporary gopher hole* tells you that this file is actually a directory that the user can open.

Curiosity, having gotten the better of me, made me wonder just what is "Pure Cabbage." I clicked "Pure Cabbage," from Andy Thomas, and saw the contents of the file cabbage.txt, as shown in Figure 26-2.

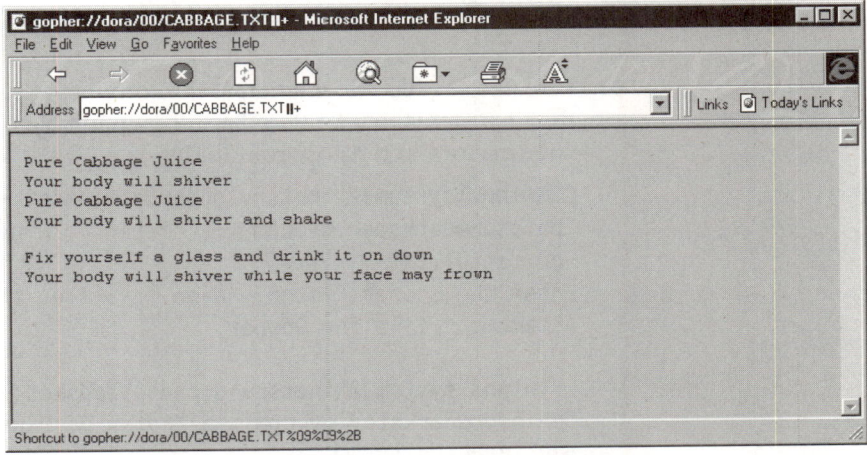

Figure 26-2: Gopher file: "Pure Cabbage," from Andy Thomas.

Andy is a musician and is rightfully proud of his music. He has a style of his own. For an excerpt of the song, take a look at http://www.emmemm.com.

And if you click on Temporary Gopher Hole, you can see the contents of this directory, as shown in Figure 26-3. Notice that the files listed in this figure are formatted differently than those in Figure 26-1, because the files in Temporary Gopher Hole didn't have tag files.

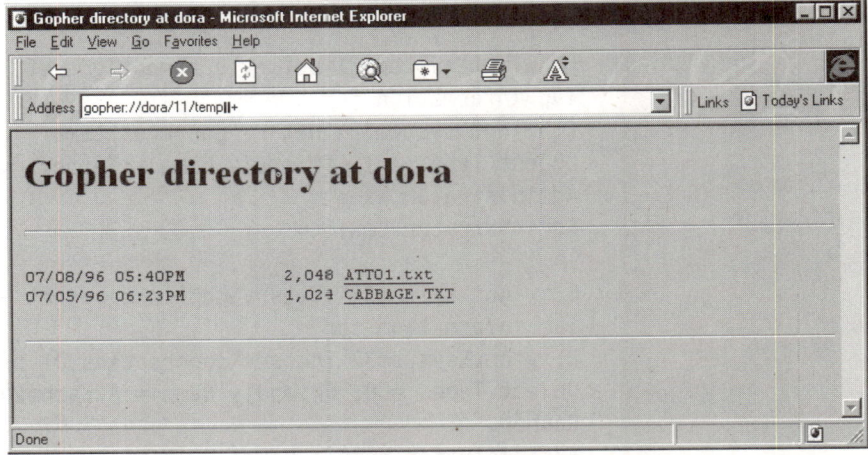

Figure 26-3: The Temporary Gopher Hole directory.

The actual steps I took in creating the tag file information for Figures 26-1, 26-2, and 26-3 are:

1. I created tag file information at the command prompt for each of the files (items that I entered are shown in bold), and for the subdirectory in the gophroot folder:

```
C:\winnt\system32\inetsrv\gophroot>gdsset -e
"phipson@darkstar.mv.com" -a "Peter D. Hipson"
-g0  att01.txt
Enter the Gopher Friendly Name for File( att01.txt)
Attachment file for Gopher.

C:\winnt\system32\inetsrv\gophroot>gdsset -e
"phipson@darkstar.mv.com" -a "Peter D. Hipson"
-g0  cabbage.txt
Enter the Gopher Friendly Name for File( cabbage.txt)
Pure Cabbage, from Andy Thomas!

C:\winnt\system32\inetsrv\gophroot>gdsset -g1  -d temp
Enter the Gopher Friendly Name for File( temp)
Temporary gopher hole
```

2. I started Microsoft Internet Explorer, connected to my Gopher site, and created Figures 26-1, 26-2, and 26-3.

3. After making the figures, I returned to the command prompt and listed the tag file information (items that I entered are shown in bold):

```
C:\winnt\system32\inetsrv\gophroot>gdsset -r temp
Tag information for
C:\winnt\system32\inetsrv\gophroot\temp
Object Type  = 1; Friendly Name = Temporary gopher hole
Administrator Name =
Administrator Email =

C:\winnt\system32\inetsrv\gophroot>gdsset -r att01.txt
Tag information for
C:\winnt\system32\inetsrv\gophroot\att01.txt
Object Type  = 0; Friendly Name = Attachment file for
Gopher.
Administrator Name = Peter D. Hipson
Administrator Email = phipson@darkstar.mv.com
```

```
C:\winnt\system32\inetsrv\gophroot>gdsset -r cabbage.txt
Tag information for
C:\winnt\system32\inetsrv\gophroot\cabbage.txt
Object Type  = 0; Friendly Name = Pure Cabbage, from
Andy Thomas!
Administrator Name = Peter D. Hipson
Administrator Email = phipson@darkstar.mv.com
```

A directory listing for my gophroot folder shows us that there are only a few files there. The gophroot folder is on an NTFS drive, so I told the DIR command to show all files, including the hidden tag files:

```
C:\winnt\system32\inetsrv\gophroot>dir /AD /AH /AA  /s
 Volume in drive C is C - PENTIUM
 Volume Serial Number is 0F44-19DC


 Directory of C:\winnt\system32\inetsrv\gophroot

07/05/96  03:34p       <DIR>          .
07/05/96  03:34p       <DIR>          ..
07/25/96  08:08p       <DIR>          temp
07/08/96  01:40p             2,225    ATT01.txt
07/25/96  08:24p               130    att01.txt.gtg
07/05/96  02:23p               194    CABBAGE.TXT
07/25/96  08:41p               132    cabbage.txt.gtg
07/25/96  08:11p                72    temp.gtg
              5 File(s)        2,753 bytes


 Directory of C:\winnt\system32\inetsrv\gophroot\temp

07/25/96  08:08p       <DIR>          .
07/25/96  08:08p       <DIR>          ..
07/08/96  01:40p             2,225    ATT01.txt
07/05/96  02:23p               194    CABBAGE.TXT
              2 File(s)        2,419 bytes


     Total Files Listed:
              7 File(s)        5,172 bytes
                      235,634,688 bytes free


C:\winnt\system32\inetsrv\gophroot>
```

The IIS FTP Server

FTP (File Transfer Protocol) is the Internet way of moving files between servers and clients. Of the three servers in Microsoft IIS, the FTP server is the easiest to configure; but then, FTP is the most inflexible of the protocols and services on the Internet. Basic configuration of the FTP server is covered in Chapter 25. FTP is strictly text and has a limited user interface that consists of directory listings of filenames and little more. FTP, however, remains popular, mostly by supporting file downloads for Web sites.

Unlike Gopher servers, FTP servers are much more common and more easily understood both by administrators and users. Virtually everyone who is on the Internet has experienced FTP file transfers (that can't be said about Gopher). There are many competent FTP client programs available to users, including Junod's WS_FTP32 program, the Windows NT 4 FTP command, and though limited, Internet Explorer does serve as an FTP client also.

Many WWW sites also host an FTP server to allow clients to download files from the server. FTP sites can be open (allowing anonymous logons) or closed (requiring a preassigned userid and a password to log on). FTP has been around for a very long time and has its roots in UNIX. When using the Windows NT FTP command you will see full well FTP's UNIX parentage.

An FTP server is quite similar to a Gopher server in that both allow the user to access files. However, a Gopher server only transfers files to the client site, where FTP can both send and receive files from clients.

The IIS FTP Service supports all the standard FTP services and features. As the IIS FTP server is Windows NT based, the configuration is slightly different than an FTP server running under UNIX. As well, the IIS FTP server supports long filenames, something that many non-Windows NT servers have difficulty doing.

Whether or not you decided to implement the IIS FTP server is a decision you, and your systems administrator, must make. You will find, however, that implementing an FTP server takes virtually no time to set up and little in the way of resources.

Setting Up an FTP Site

Setting up your FTP server can be as simple as copying your files (and directories) to the FTP root directory. This creates a simple FTP server, which client users can then browse. The client user can use any FTP client (such as Internet Explorer).

As well, you can set up other, virtual, directories as needed. You can use virtual directories to create private areas where users may save files.

Security for an FTP server is based on how a user accesses your FTP server—if anonymous access is used, then allow only read-only access. Users who have a Windows NT 4 Server userid can be granted read/write access as necessary.

Warning

Be very careful about allowing anonymous FTP users write access. There are numerous instances where anonymous users have uploaded "pirated" software to FTP sites for other users to download. This practice can result in civil liability if it happens to your site!

Another problem with allowing anonymous users to upload files is the possibility that an executable file with a virus may be uploaded. If for any reason you allow anonymous users to upload files, use a virus scanner frequently to protect both yourself and your users from viruses.

Moving On

This chapter covered the Microsoft Internet Server (IIS) Gopher and FTP services.

Gopher allows users to interact with the server and retrieve information easily. While Gopher is similar to the WWW, Gopher is a text-based service that is now less popular on the Internet.

FTP (File Transfer Protocol) is *the* file transfer protocol for the Internet. Virtually all sites support FTP, and recent releases of all browsers support FTP.

The next chapter covers using the Microsoft IIS WWW server. The Web has become the most popular feature of the Internet, with a substantial amount of the usage of the Internet being dedicated to WWW transactions.

27

Installing & Configuring the IIS WWW Server

WWW, often called the Web, is the Internet's hypermedia information network. A surprisingly large number of users on the Internet today have Web pages somewhere. Conservative estimates are that over half of the Internet's traffic consists of transfers between Web servers and Web clients (also called Web browsers).

Web usage dwarfs the next most often used Internet service—FTP. The Web browser wars of 1996 pitted Microsoft against Netscape, with each company churning out new releases of their respective products on a two-to-four month basis. The fighting over the browser market has been fierce, with Microsoft essentially giving away Internet Explorer to Windows 95 and Windows NT users. At one point Microsoft was beta testing several consecutive releases of their product at the same time!

This chapter guides you in setting up your IIS (Internet Information Server) WWW Server and configuring an FTP directory structure. I won't try to tell you how to design a specific Web page—heck, I'm not an artist. What I will do is give you some information about tools that can assist you in creating Web pages, but you and your systems administrator will have to take it to the next level.

The IIS WWW Server

A Web server is the most commonly desired Internet server to set up. Management screams for it, users demand it, corporate images live on the Web today. For organizations configuring intranet Web sites, IIS is an excellent choice for the Web server.

Virtually all Internet users with Web sites set up Web servers first. Many Web servers also host an FTP server to allow clients to download files, and some even have Gopher servers. Many Web browsers are capable of working with FTP, newsgroups, and Gopher servers. Web transactions can be secure, though frequently they are not.

A popular Web site can generate thousands (the most popular Web sites, millions) of *hits* or accesses each day. It is now routine for a popular Web site to find that its popularity is its undoing; the server, or the communications link, is unable to keep up with the demand, and system performance fails.

Exotic server systems, including multiple IP addresses (and servers) assigned to a single URL, are being developed to cope with the issues of the high demands placed on popular Web servers. For most of us, communications bandwidth is a problem that we must overcome, a topic covered later in this chapter.

A Web server is a bit different than FTP and Gopher servers: WWW clients do not think in terms of files and directories, although in reality, these elements are as basic to the Web as they are to FTP and Gopher. Rather, a Web client "thinks" in terms of resources, links, objects, and other abstract items. These items are what make the Web work, and you need to understand what HTML (HyperText Markup Language) is.

The IIS WWW Server supports all the standard Web services and features. As the IIS WWW Server is Windows NT based, the configuration is slightly different than a Web server running under UNIX—the differences are not significant enough to warrant discussion (such as differences in file-naming conventions between UNIX and Windows NT). It is important to note, though, that the IIS WWW Server supports long filenames, something that many non-Windows NT servers have difficulty doing. Keep any names the user must type as short as possible. After all, nothing is more disheartening than to type a long URL and have it fail because of a trivial typing error.

Whether or not you decide to implement the IIS WWW Server is a decision you, and your systems administrator, must make. The basic implementation of an IIS WWW Server takes practically no time to set up and little in the way of resources. However, a professional set of Web pages takes planning and work, the amount of effort governed by how much you wish to invest in your Web pages. For a company that is making its presence on the Web known, hiring a professional Web page designer (a webmaster) may be a very good idea.

Setting Up a Web Site

Setting up your Web site can be as simple as modifying the example Web pages that come with the IIS WWW Server. This is perhaps only a temporary solution, however, as Web pages are typically very individualized and customized for each site.

Many Web sites employ a person who is skilled in the creation of Web pages. Such a person has artistic as well as computer skills.

As well as having a single Web page, you can set up other, virtual directories as Web pages. When working with large systems, you can use virtual directories to create areas for products, news, and other information as desired. We discussed virtual directories in Chapter 25.

IIS WWW Server Samples

Microsoft provides a set of Web pages and applications with IIS WWW Server that you can customize and work with to learn how the IIS Web Server works. These examples are found in the inetsrv\wwwroot\samples folder.

The sample applications include an example Web site for a fictitious company, several database examples, some programming examples, and HTML example source.

In addition to these examples, the Microsoft Web site (http://www.microsoft.com) contains many examples. The FrontPage program (included with Windows NT 4 Server) also makes much of the development of your Web page simpler. Also consider FrontPage 97, which offers new capabilities and ease of use.

Sample IIS WWW Server Pages

Microsoft supplies sample Web pages with the IIS WWW Server. These sample pages are divided into four broad categories: sample HTML site, database, programming, and sample HTML styles.

SampSite—An HTML Sample Site

The heart of the SampSite HTML example is a fictitious company called The Volcano Coffee Company (see Figure 27-1). This company's business is coffee over the Internet, and the example pages have a number of interesting features. The user can:

- **Order a sample of coffee.** The user enters data into an HTML form. The data is returned to the Web server for processing. The coffee company ships the sample to the user's name and address.

- **Request specific information.** The user enters his or her name and e-mail address. The Web server adds this name and address to a mailing list. The coffee company sends out the requested information.

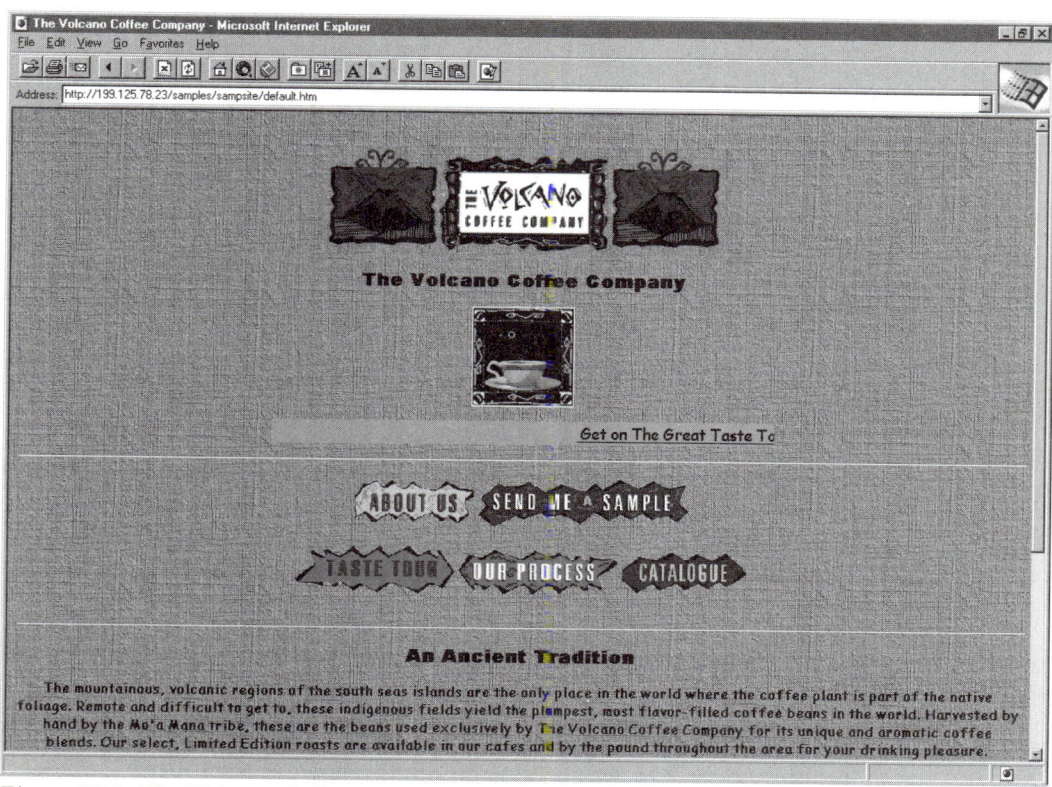

Figure 27-1: The Volcano Coffee Company on the Web.

Database

The database examples are all linked to Microsoft SQL Server. Figure 27-2 shows part of the introduction HTML, which the Web server administrator uses to set up the database examples.

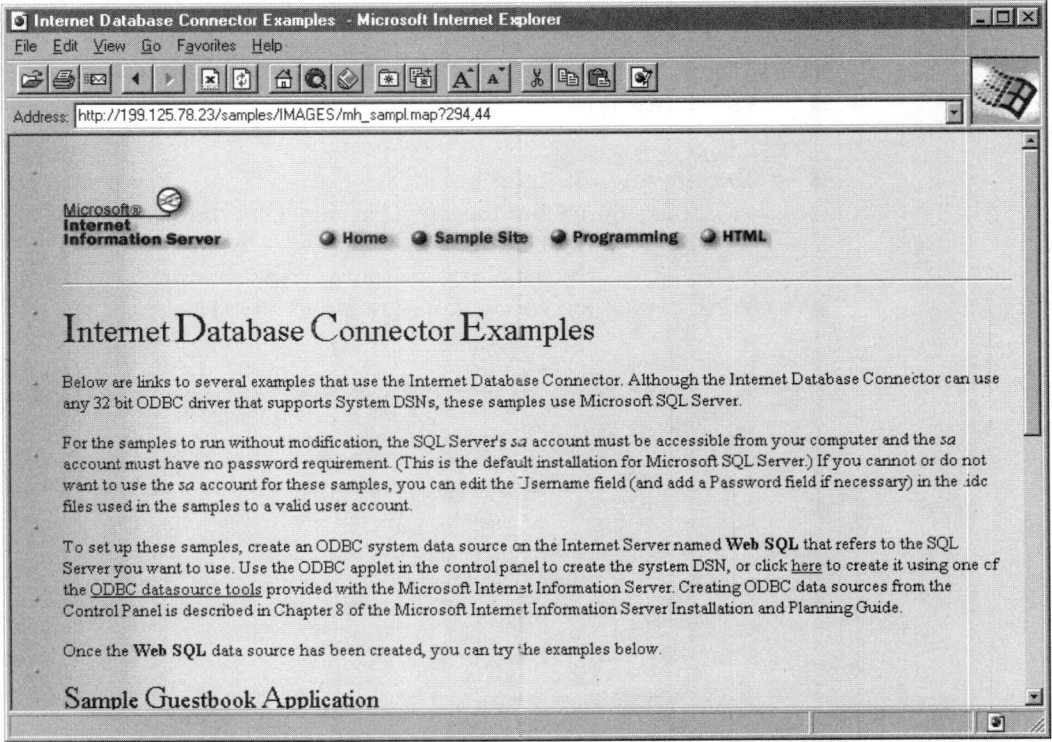

Figure 27-2: The database example—interfacing with SQL Server.

The database examples include:

- **Guestbook**—an application where client users "sign in" using an HTML form. This information is then sent to the SQL Server where it is saved in a table.

- **Query**—an application that allows the client user to make a simple free-format query on the database.

- **FormQuery**—an application that allows the client user to make a simple query on the database. This query is form based.

- **Query, with data returned as hyperlinks**—an application that allows users to make a query and have the results returned as a hyperlink.

All of the database-based HTML examples use Microsoft SQL Server as their database engine. If you are not using SQL Server, use the programming examples as a starting point for accessing other data sources using ODBC (Open Database Connectivity).

Programming

The programming examples offer two different capabilities:

- **A Search function**—allows the client user to search for text in this site.

- **A Favorite Sites Bulletin Board** (see Figure 27-3)—allows users to leave information about their favorite site. One should expect a bit of horn blowing here, touting one's own site, but that's life. All users can access the list of favorite sites. These favorite sites are saved in the file wwwroot\samples\isapi\drop.htm.

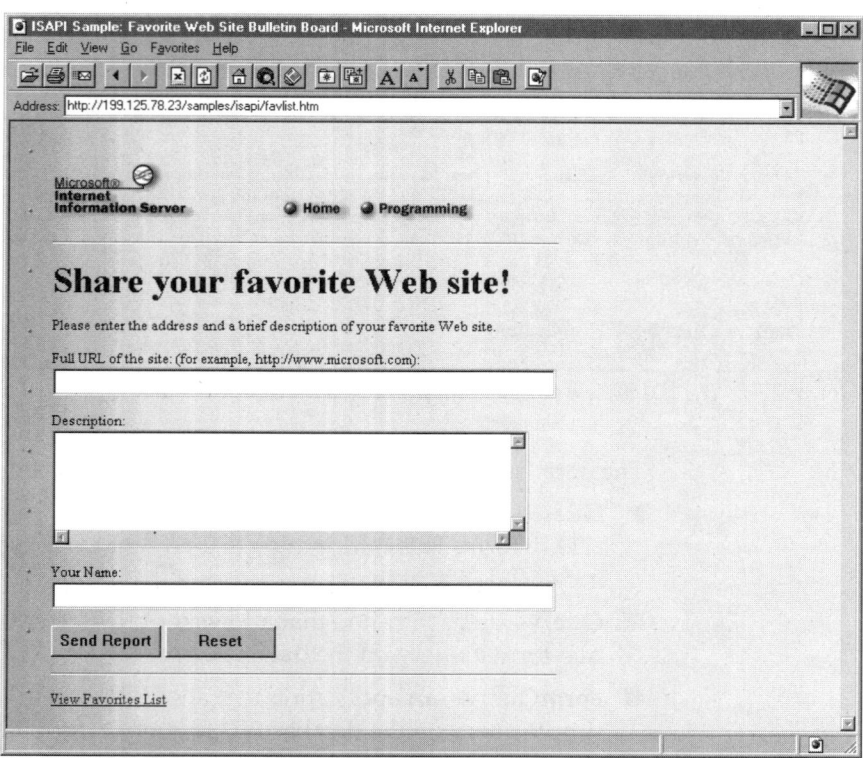

Figure 27-3: The Favorite Sites Bulletin Board form.

As well as these two programming examples, users of Visual C++ 4.1 (and later) will also find other programming examples supplied with Visual C++. Two noteworthy examples are:

- **HTTPSRV**—a simple Web server (no, this program doesn't compete with Microsoft's IIS WWW Server) that runs under both Windows NT 4 and Windows 95. This server is basic, and the code shows how simple it is to create a basic server for the Internet.

- **WWWQUOTE**—a simple stock quote program that queries a database of stock prices and returns information from the query to the client user. The data is canned and in a real application is replaced with an actively updated database.

In Visual C++, there is also an example of a filter, which converts text to uppercase. Filters are an advanced programming topic, well beyond the scope of this book.

HTML Sample Style Sheets

The HTML sample sheets (see Figure 27-4) demonstrate styles for tables, headings, lists, and such. Generally, using Internet Assistant is an easy way to format your HTML documents, where most (if not all) formatting is done using a WYSIWYG (What You See Is What You Get) interface.

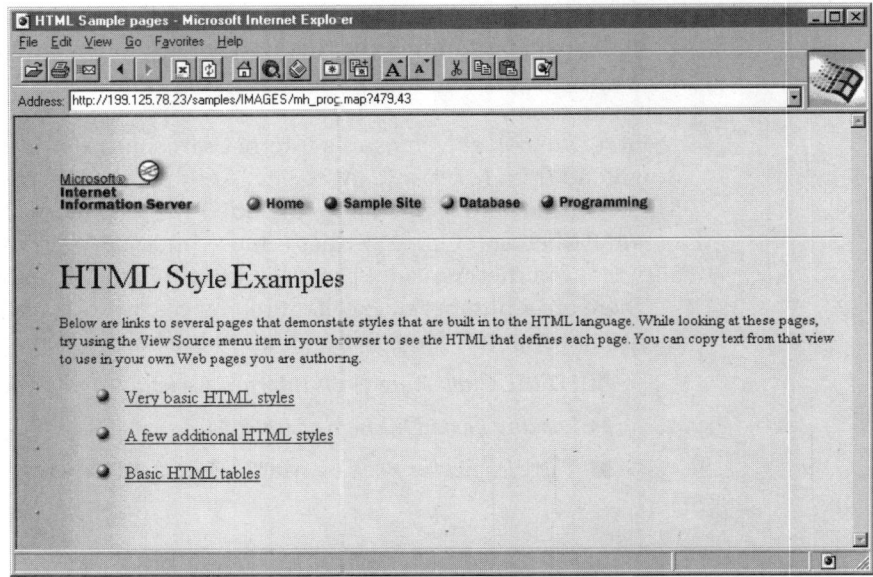

Figure 27-4: The HTML sample style sheets introduction page.

Creating Initial WWW HTML Pages

Web pages are created in a format called HyperText Markup Language (HTML). Although HTML is a text-based format you can edit using simple editors such as Notepad, it is much easier to create and edit your HTML documents using an editor that understands HTML and edits HTML directly and allows you to work using a WYSIWYG format.

The process of creating a Web page is complex. A good Web page must have a number of attributes, including attractiveness, ease of use for the user, and the best mixture of graphics and text.

Tip

Many Web pages have too many large graphic images. Many users are still accessing the Web at speeds of 28K or slower. When a Web page has too many or large graphic images, the time to transfer the page to the user's computer can be excessive. Each image must be separately requested, and large images compound the problem. A Web page should transfer, at 28 kbps modem speeds, in less than five seconds if possible. Large images, if necessary, can be presented in lower resolution, with a link to a higher-resolution version.

In the next part of this chapter, we provide some methods for creating HTML documents and describe some tools you can use to create and maintain them.

First, we look at Microsoft's Internet Assistant, a product you can download from Microsoft's Web site. Another product you can use is Microsoft's FrontPage, which is included with Windows NT 4 Server.

Note: Microsoft Office 97 does not use Internet Assistant: The functionality that Internet Assistant provided is built in to Microsoft Office 97.

There are a number of excellent references on creating Web documents. Several that come to mind (all published by Ventana) are:

- *HTML Publishing With Internet Assistant* by Kidder and Harris
- *Looking Good Online* by Steve Bain
- *The Web Server Book* by Magid, Jones, Matthews, and McConville

Using Microsoft Internet Assistant

Microsoft has created a tool to allow Word for Windows (version 7) to create and edit HTML documents. This tool, called Internet Assistant version 2 (IA for Word 95) is available from Microsoft at http://www.microsoft.com.

Internet Assistant for Microsoft Word for Windows 95 (Word 95 also runs under Windows NT 4) is an add-on available from Microsoft at no charge. Internet Assistant allows users to create and edit HTML documents for the Internet using Microsoft Word for Windows. It is a full-featured Internet authoring tool that can convert a Word file to HTML and provides users with a toolbar (and menu) and an interface for inserting hyperlinks, images, and forms into HTML documents.

Using Internet Assistant, a Web page designer can create a richly formatted HTML document without having to understand the complicated code associated with HTML.

Internet Assistant is available as specified, from the following locations:

- At URL http://198.105.232.4/kb/softlib/mslfiles/WRDInternet Assistant20Z.EXE.
- On the TechNet CD.
- On the Microsoft Network (MSN); use the keyword *Free Stuff*.
- On the CompuServe MSWORD forum.
- Order a disk version from Microsoft, at 1-800-426-9400, for the cost of shipping and handling.

Using Internet Assistant is simple. First, you install it. Next, execute the file that contains Internet Assistant, wrdinternet assistant2z.exe (after you have installed Word for Windows). The installation program then installs the necessary files for Internet Assistant to work.

Some of the features of Internet Assistant include:

- Support for the HTML tags that are most often used.
- Creation of hyperlinks and Internet forms.
- Hyperlinks can be inserted in compound Word documents.
- You can use Internet Assistant to view and edit all your source code.

Figure 27-5 shows a Web page from The Volcano Coffee Shop loaded in Word for Windows with Internet Assistant.

Warning

Your work in creating a set of Web pages isn't finished until you have tested it using as many Web browsers as possible. Always test using at the very least both Microsoft Internet Explorer and Netscape Navigator. You should make sure that features supported by one browser and not by others degrade gracefully. You should view the Web page in a text-only browser, too.

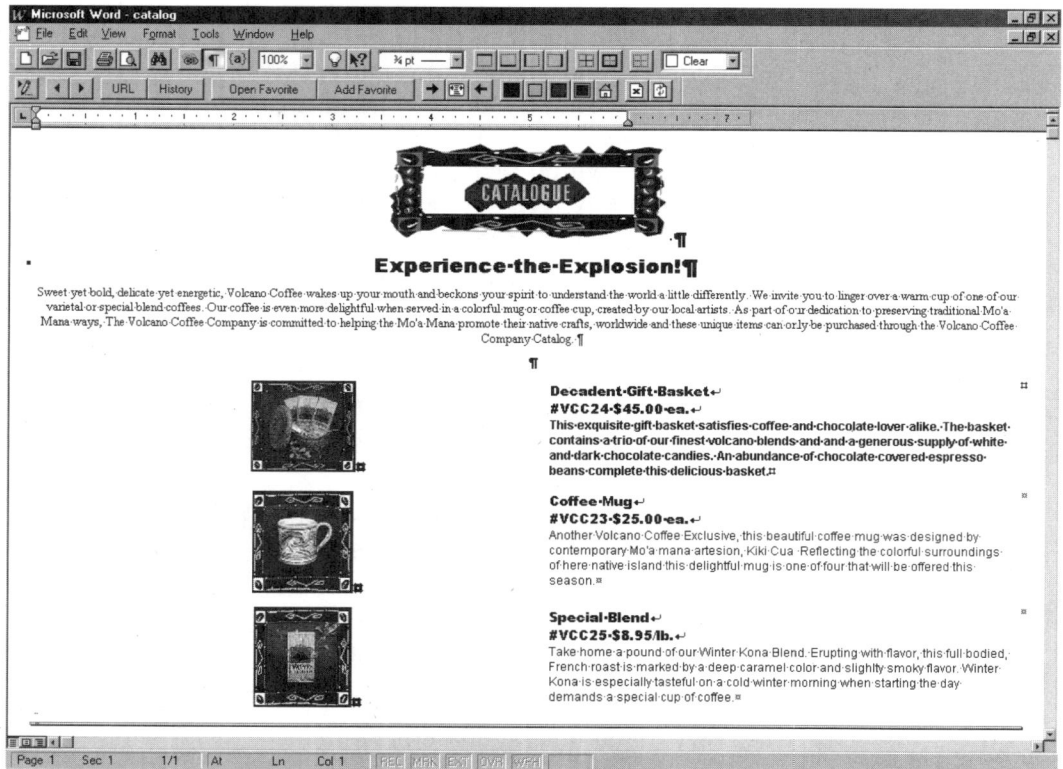

Figure 27-5: Internet Assistant at work editing catalog.html.

Using Microsoft FrontPage

Microsoft, at the eleventh hour, decided to include the Microsoft FrontPage product with Windows NT 4 Server. FrontPage allows creation and management of Web sites and offers the following features:

- **FrontPage Editor**—edits HTML documents. The FrontPage editor is patterned after Microsoft Word for Windows and has a similar user interface.

- **FrontPage Explorer**—browses Web pages both in the normal display mode and in link and outline views.

- **Summary**—provides property information about each page.

- **FrontPage TCP/IP tester**—tests the implementation of WinSock (Windows Sockets, the programming interface to TCP/IP).

- **Server Administrator**—interfaces FrontPage with your Web server. Web servers supported include: FrontPage Personal Web Server, Netscape Commerce Server, Netscape Communication Server, and WebSite.

The main HTML modification tool, the FrontPage Editor, presents a user interface that is similar to Microsoft Word and Internet Assistant.

The Secure Sockets Layer (SSL)

Chapter 25 introduces the subject of securing your Microsoft Information Internet Server from unauthorized access. This section discusses protocols that use cryptography to secure data transmissions to and from your server.

Microsoft IIS provides users with a secure communication channel through support for Secure Sockets Layer (SSL) and encryption from RSA Data Security, Inc.

SSL protocol provides secure data communication through data encryption and decryption. The security provided by SSL is rather good, providing an avenue for commercial transactions on the Web. With SSL you are able to transact business, including credit card transactions, with little risk of a security breach on the network. The IIS WWW Server can send and receive private communications across the Internet to any SSL-enabled client, such as Microsoft Internet Explorer version 2.0 for Windows 95 and Windows NT. Netscape has an SSL-enabled browser available as well.

Defined as a protocol layer between the TCP/IP layer and the application layer (HTTP), SSL provides server authentication, encryption, and data integrity. Server authentication assures the client user that they are indeed connected to the correct server. Encryption ensures both the client and the server that their communications are as confidential as possible. Data integrity ensures that information passed between the server and the client has not been modified, either intentionally or unintentionally.

Enabling SSL Security

To enable SSL security on the IIS WWW Server, follow the steps below:

1. Use the KEYGEN utility to create a key pair file and request file.

2. Request a certificate from a certification authority such as VeriSign for your system. You must pay for the certificate.

3. Install the certificate on your server.

4. Activate SSL security on a Web service directory in the IIS WWW Server configuration dialog. See the "Setting Up Directories" section of Chapter 25 for an example of where SSL is used with the IIS WWW Server.

You must do the following when you enable SSL security on your IIS Web server:

- In either your Web server's root directory, or in one (or more) of the Web server's virtual directories, you must enable SSL security. You do not need to use SSL security for your entire Web site, however.

- After you configure and enable your SSL directories, only clients that have support for SSL security can use them.

- Make references to those directories that have been SSL enabled by using https:// and not http://. Links made using http:// to documents in an SSL-enabled directory do not work!

- You can enable and disable the use of SSL on directories using the Internet Service Manager. The process for enabling and disabling SSL security for a specific directory is described in the "Setting Up Directories" section of Chapter 25.

Obtaining an SSL Certificate

You must obtain an SSL certificate, which is issued from one of the certifying authorities such as VeriSign. Before investing a substantial amount of time going through the complete process to obtain an SSL certificate, contact the certificate issuer. The certificate issuer may have other requirements or information that must be supplied. The following steps will give you a good idea of what you need to do to obtain a certificate:

1. Go to the directory in which you have installed IIS. This directory is usually c:\inetsrv\server. In this directory are two utilities that manage SSL security certificates. The keygen.exe program generates a key request. The setkey.exe program installs the certificate key once it has been returned from the certificate issuer.

2. Use the keygen.exe program to generate the two files described below: The first file is the key file, which contains the key pairs. The second file is the key request file. The key request file is a text file that you can either e-mail or otherwise transmit to the certificate issuer. Display the parameters for the keygen.exe program using the command KEYGEN (without any arguments) from a command prompt.

   The following example shows how to create a set of SSL key files, based on the DORA server. The example shows how to create two files: first the keypair.key file, which contains the key pair, and then the keyreques.txt file, which contains the request for the certificate. When KEYGEN runs, it generates these files in the current directory. (Also see "KEYGEN Reference" later in this chapter.)

   The execution of KEYGEN is shown in Figure 27-6.

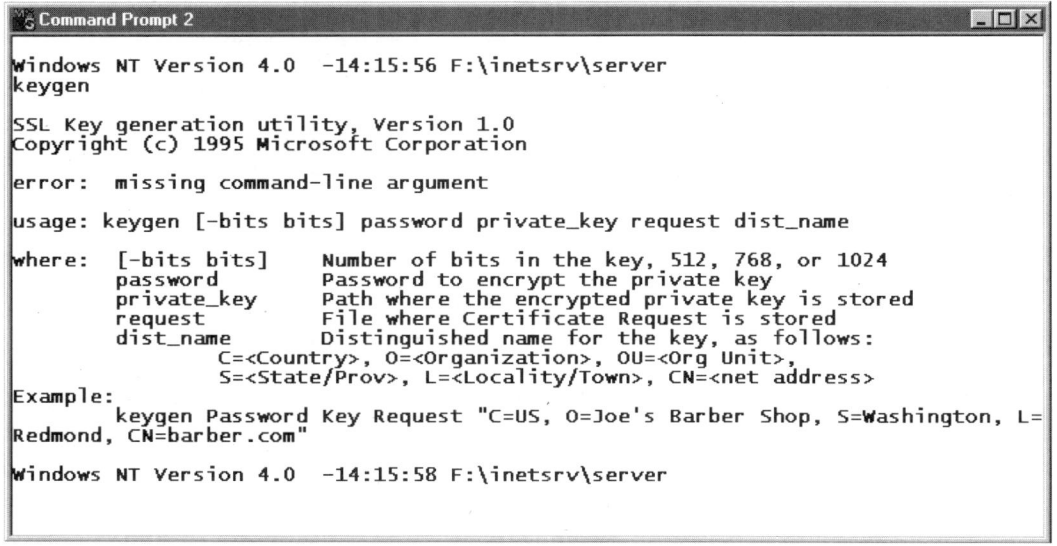

```
Command Prompt 2                                                    _ □ X

Windows NT Version 4.0   -14:15:56 F:\inetsrv\server
keygen

SSL Key generation utility, Version 1.0
Copyright (c) 1995 Microsoft Corporation

error:   missing command-line argument

usage: keygen [-bits bits] password private_key request dist_name

where:   [-bits bits]      Number of bits in the key, 512, 768, or 1024
         password          Password to encrypt the private key
         private_key       Path where the encrypted private key is stored
         request           File where Certificate Request is stored
         dist_name         Distinguished name for the key, as follows:
                     C=<Country>, O=<Organization>, OU=<Org Unit>,
                     S=<State/Prov>, L=<Locality/Town>, CN=<net address>
Example:
         keygen Password Key Request "C=US, O=Joe's Barber Shop, S=Washington, L=
Redmond, CN=barber.com"

Windows NT Version 4.0   -14:15:58 F:\inetsrv\server
```

Figure 27-6: KEYGEN generating key files in a Command window.

2a. To use SSL, you need to obtain a certificate from a certifying authority such as VeriSign for your system. You can find instructions for acquiring a VeriSign certificate on VeriSign's Web site (start at http://www.verisign.com).

2b. You must send your key request to the certificate issuing authority (such as VeriSign). Use e-mail to submit your request. Note, however, you may need to address other issues, including payment for the certificate. You should also provide a copy of the command line instructions that generate the key request file (see Figure 27-6). Don't send your password, however; the password is confidential. The resultant file from the KEYGEN execution is shown in Figure 27-7.

3. It is easy to cut and paste the command line instructions (don't retype it, you may make a typing error!) to the beginning of this file, as shown in Figure 27-8.

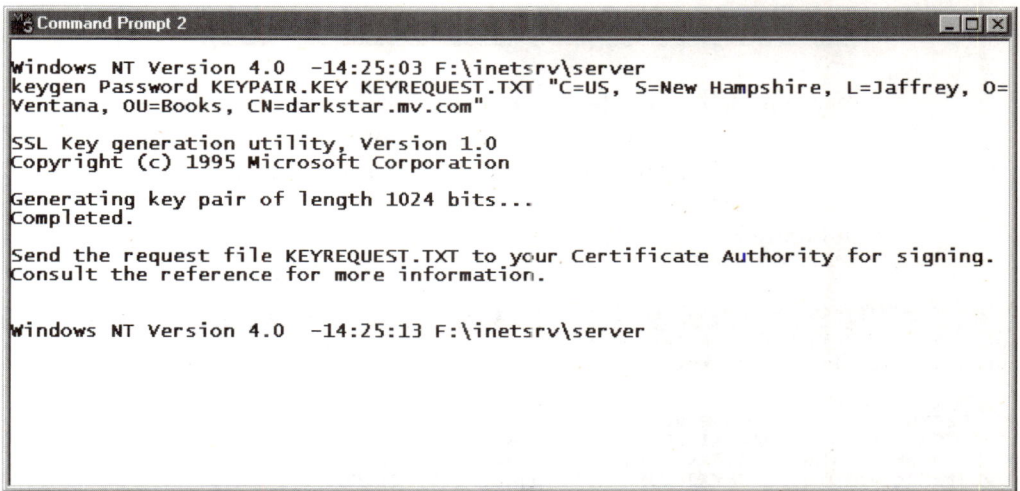

Figure 27-7: The results of running KEYGEN.

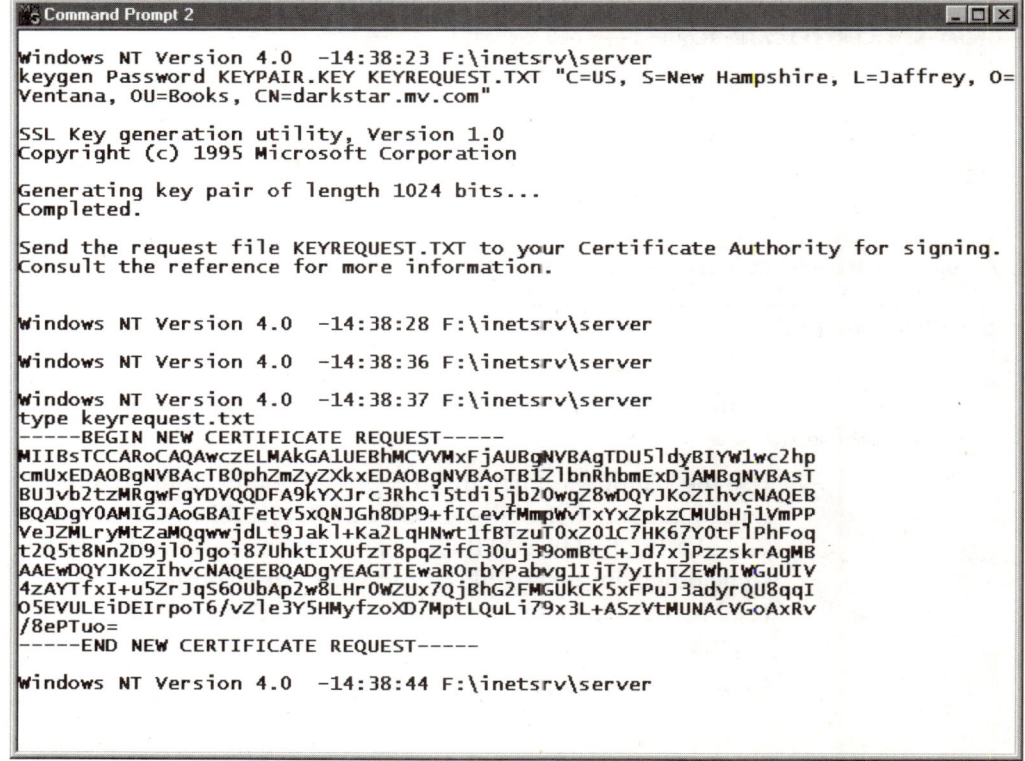

Figure 27-8: The key request file ready to send to the certificate issuer.

Installing the SSL Certificate

Once you have completed these steps, the certificate issuer processes your request and then sends you some form of communication containing information about your actual key. The certificate response you receive (perhaps an e-mail response) may look similar to the one shown in Figure 27-9.

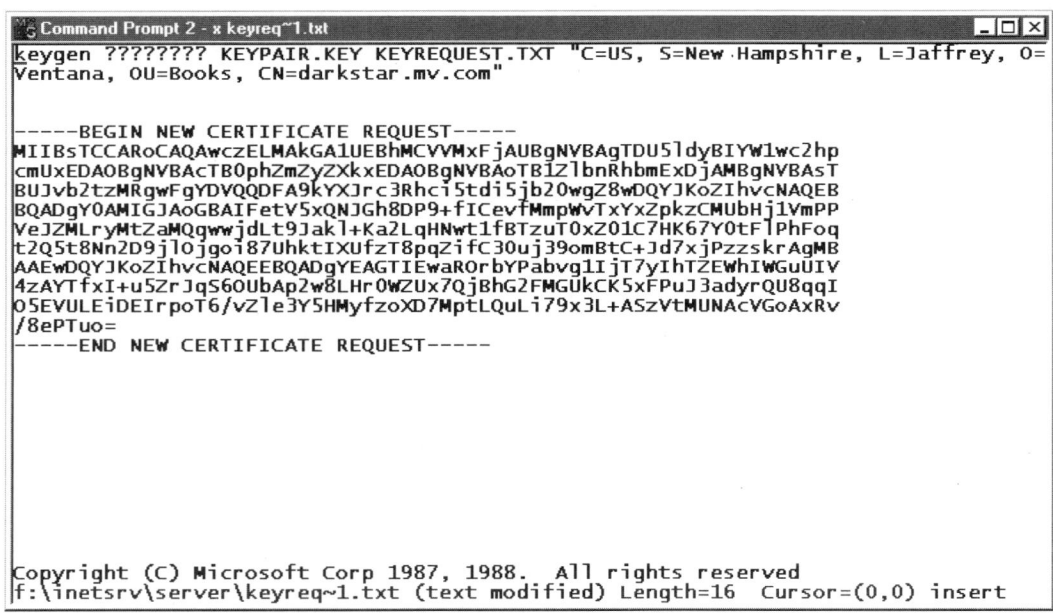

Figure 27-9: Response from the certificate issuing authority.

To copy the key text and install the certificate for your server, follow these steps:

1. Use the Windows clipboard to copy the key text (but not the lines that contain the "——BEGIN CERTIFICATE———" or the "——END CERTIFICATE———" text) into a file. Use Notepad or some other simple text file editor; Word for Windows can be used if you remember to save the file as a text-formatted file with line breaks.

2. Save the file with a meaningful name, such as certificate.txt.

3. Use setkey.exe to install the certificate for your server. (Also see "SETKEY Reference" later in the chapter.) To install an SSL key using SETKEY, enter the command as
SETKEY \\server password key certificate IP_Address

where \\server is the name of your server (for the examples in this book, the server is \\DORA). The password parameter is the password that you use to generate the key. The key parameter is the result of the running of KEYGEN, and IP_Address is the IP address on which the key is used. When all IP addresses are to use the same certificate, you don't need to specify the IP address parameter.

The process just described installs the certificate. Once installed, you can use the Internet Service Manager to configure the Web service to support SSL. There are several important issues when telling Internet Service Manager to use an SSL certificate:

■ To use the same certificate on more than one virtual Web server, do not specify an IP address or domain name when running SETKEY. When no IP address is specified, the certificate is applied to all servers.

■ Use Internet Service Manager to set the Require Secure SSL Channel option for directories that you want to protect by using SSL. See the section titled "Setting Up Directories" in Chapter 25 for information on the Require Secure SSL Channel check box.

■ In their documentation, Microsoft suggests that you use different directories for the secure and nonsecure pages on your Web server.

Warning

As Microsoft states in the IIS documentation, "It is important to avoid having a server directory not protected by SSL as a parent for a secure directory."

■ Do not lose your key pair file (as generated by KEYGEN). Back up this file. Also do not forget the password that you used to generate this file! Backing up to a diskette is a very good idea, and keeping this diskette secure is a wise move.

SETKEY Reference

Usage:

```
setkey [\\server] password private_key certificate
[IP_Address]
```
or
```
setkey -d [\\server]
```

Where:

[\\server]	The Windows NT server the IIS Web server is running on. Server must not be specified when administrating a Web server on the local machine. This parameter is used when remotely administering an IIS server.
Password	Password used to create keys with KEYGEN.
private_key	The filename for the file that contains the key file: keypair.key.
certificate	The filename of the file that contains the returned key certificate from the certificate issuer.
[IP_Address]	The IP address for the virtual server using this SSL certificate. If no IP address is specified, then this key is applied to all virtual servers.
-d	Tells SETKEY to delete all currently installed keys.

Examples:

```
setkey OurUnsecurePassword c:\keys\serverkey
c:\keys\certificate
setkey \\RemoteServer OurUnsecurePassword C:\keys\serverkey
c:\keys\certificate 199.231.22.1
```

Notes:

You must restart the IIS WWW Server when you change the SSL configuration.

KEYGEN Reference

Usage:

```
keygen [-bits bits] password private_key request dist_name
```

Where:

[-bits bits]   KEYGEN can generate keys of 512, 768, or 1024 bits in length. This optional parameter specifies the size of the key, in bits. The default is 1024 bit keys.

password   Your password to encrypt the private key.

private_key   The filename for the file (typically keypair.key) where the encrypted private key is stored.

requestFile   The filename where Certificate Request is stored.

dist_name   Distinguished name for the key, in the following format: C=<Country>, where <country> is the two-letter ISO country designation (for example, US, FR, AU, UK, DE). O=<Organization>, where <Organization> is the organization's name. (Preferably ISO-registered top-level organization or company name.) OU=<Organization Unit> S=<State/Province>, where <State/Province> is the state or province (for example, Washington, Alberta, or California. Do not abbreviate!). L=<Locality/Town> (for example, Redmond, Jaffrey, Calgary, or Redwood City). CN=<net address> (domain name of server; for example, www.darkstar.com).

Example:

```
keygen Password Key Request "C=US, O=Marie's Bike Shop, S=New
Hampshire, L=Pelham, CN=barber.com"
```

Notes:

By default KEYGEN generates keys 1024 bits long.
The argument in quotation marks in the keygen.exe command line
("C=US, S=Washington, L=Redmond, O=Example, OU=Marketing,

CN=www.mycompany.com") specifies several fields for the certificate request related to your organization and server. Do not embed commas in any field.

Note: Do not use commas (such as "Smith, Jones, and Company") in any field. Commas are interpreted as the end of that field and generate a bad request without warning. Simply spell the name without commas: "Smith Jones and Company."

Note: Running KEYGEN two times with the same files results in an error. You must delete the files created by KEYGEN prior to rerunning (if you are rerunning with output to the same files).

Reliability

All Web sites must be constantly maintained and upgraded. The "browser wars" result in new Web browser features every few months, and other parts of the Web change frequently.

To make your Internet site more reliable, consider the following:

- **Test all changes fully.** Don't assume that since a change to a Web page looks good with Internet Explorer, it will look good with Mosaic or Netscape.

- **Keep a list of all external HTTP links, and check them frequently.** Links, names, and addresses change constantly. The Web is a living, evolving, growing entity and links go out of date constantly. To check Web links for validity, a program such as FrontPage can be used.

- **Make sure that links to your own Web pages are valid.** Nothing is more likely to create a bad impression than to have a button that, when used, results in a "not found" message.

- **Use whatever features of HTML you need.** Don't make things more complex, fancy, or whatever, just for the sake of being different. Like any other publishing task, use moderation—limit yourself to one or two fonts, keep the images sensible (in size and complexity), and don't use a riot of color.

- **Don't use a busy background with your Web pages.** Be careful that your background doesn't overpower your message.

- **If you use sounds (such as those supported by Internet Explorer) use MIDI files, not WAV files.** MIDI files are much smaller and take much less time to transfer to the user's system.

- **Be careful of copyright issues.** Don't use clip art, sound clips, or other objects unless you either own them or have permission. A common misconception is that if the sound clip is short, you can use it—not true!

- **Use the NTFS file system if you can for as many of your directories as possible.** NTFS offers enhanced security, performance, and reliability.

In addition to reliability, a Web site must perform well. See the "Performance" section at the end of Chapter 13 for ideas on how to make your Web site perform better.

Moving On

In this chapter we covered the Microsoft Internet Information Server's WWW Server and discussed some of the issues involved in creating Web pages. The sample pages provided with IIS WWW Server and the sample Web applications were covered in this chapter. We also covered SSL, the Secure Sockets Layer.

This chapter concludes our coverage of Windows NT's Internet Information Server.

The next section in the book covers the Microsoft SNA Server. Microsoft SNA server is used to link Windows NT 4 Server networks with IBM-compatible mainframe and minicomputers.

Microsoft SNA Server

28

Overview of Microsoft SNA Server

In this chapter, we describe Microsoft SNA (Systems Network Architecture) Server version 3. The Microsoft SNA Server is used to allow Windows workstations to communicate easily with computers using the IBM mainframe computer protocols.

These large computers (such as the IBM's System/390 and AS/400 systems) are still commonly found in many sites.

Note: IBM is not standing still when it comes to mainframe computers. Common products introduced recently include a System/390 processor, compatible with the IBM MCA (Micro Channel Architecture), and a number of new, full-sized System/390 processors using CMOS technology that require perhaps 10 percent of the resources (physical space, power, and cooling) of earlier products.

If you have no IBM SNA experience and have no requirements to implement Microsoft SNA Server, you may be happier if you skip this section of the book—you may find it filled with confusing mainframe terminology and issues!

Microsoft SNA Server

IBM uses SNA to communicate between minicomputers and mainframe computers (and to communicate with peripherals).

Microsoft SNA Server is an important part of Microsoft BackOffice in environments where an IBM mainframe, AS/400, or other IBM-compatible computers are connected using SNA. In the remainder of this section, I will refer to the IBM mainframe, AS/400, or other SNA-compatible computers simply as the *mainframe*.

Note: Microsoft SNA Server has not appreciably changed in the last few years. However, SNA Server version 3 did introduce a new manager program, new features, and fixes for problems that were apparent in earlier versions of SNA Server.

Microsoft SNA Server is used to connect client workstations running Windows NT 4 Server, Windows NT 4 Workstation, Windows 95, or other supported client operating systems to the mainframe. Additional applications (typically 3270 or 5250 terminal emulator programs) run on client workstations to allow users to interact with the mainframe as if the client user were using a directly connected dedicated terminal.

With Microsoft SNA Server, you are able to emulate a 3270 terminal, a 5250 terminal, APPC, CPI-C, communications that use LUAs, or other IBM-specific communications techniques.

Note: The 3270 interface requires that you install and configure the TN3270 service.

Microsoft SNA Server Configurations

You will be confronted with two typical Microsoft SNA Server configurations. The first configuration is called *centralized servers*, where all the Microsoft SNA Servers are located at one site, typically wherever the mainframe computer is located. The client users may be located locally to the Microsoft SNA Server or remotely, using some form of WAN, SDLC (Synchronous Data Link Control) bridge, router, or perhaps the Internet.

In the second type of configuration, the Microsoft SNA Servers are remotely located near the client sites. Each Microsoft SNA Server connects to the mainframe computer through a communications link that supports SDLC. Each Microsoft SNA Server supports a single, isolated LAN.

When only a single site exists to house both the mainframe and the client users, then configuration is the centralized server method, but without any remotely connected clients.

You must also configure the mainframe to support Microsoft SNA Server. The necessary LUs (Logical Units), terminal definitions, and such must be completed to enable the system to work. Configuring a mainframe computer is beyond the scope of this book; however, the techniques are very similar to adding local terminals.

Using the Microsoft SNA Server Manager

Microsoft SNA Server Manager is the main tool used to manage Microsoft SNA Server. The Microsoft SNA Server Manager program is a major improvement over Microsoft SNA Server 2.11's manager. This version of the Microsoft SNA Server Manager program sports an improved user interface, which allows the user to easily manage and configure the SNA server site.

The Microsoft SNA Server Manager is the main tool for managing the Microsoft SNA Server. The Microsoft SNA Server Manager program allows the administrator to configure:

- Servers and connections
- LU pools
- Users and groups

To provide a smooth user interface, the Microsoft SNA Server Manager program dynamically modifies its menu structure. Generally, when changing tasks, the View menu's items' contents change, and new menu items are added depending on the current task.

Common Administration Functions

Figure 28-1 shows the Microsoft SNA Server Manager program, with the Server view open. The other view that Microsoft SNA Server Manager supports is the Services view, shown in Figure 28-2.

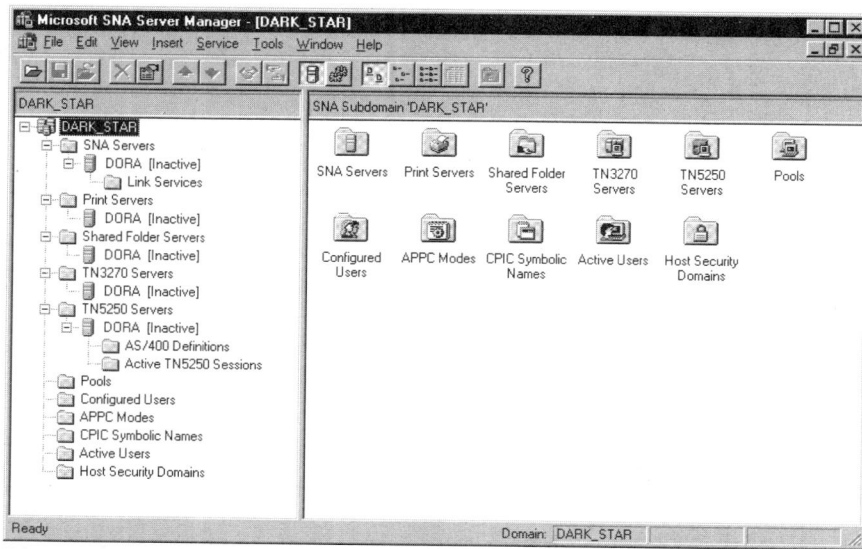

Figure 28-1: The Microsoft SNA Server Manager program with Server view displayed.

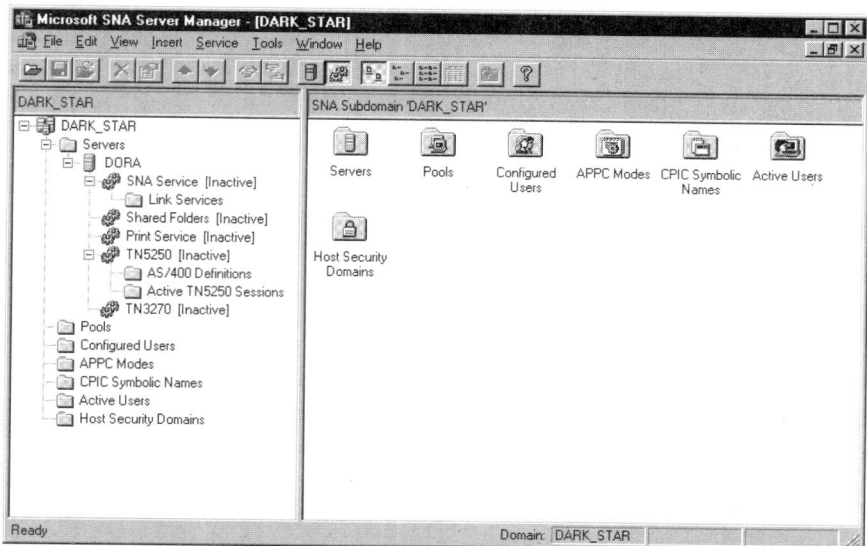

Figure 28-2: The Microsoft SNA Server Manager program with the Services view displayed.

Administering LU Pools

The Microsoft SNA Server Manager program, in the LU Pools mode is shown in Figure 28-3. (Select this mode by clicking on the Pools branch in the left pane in Microsoft SNA Server Manager.)

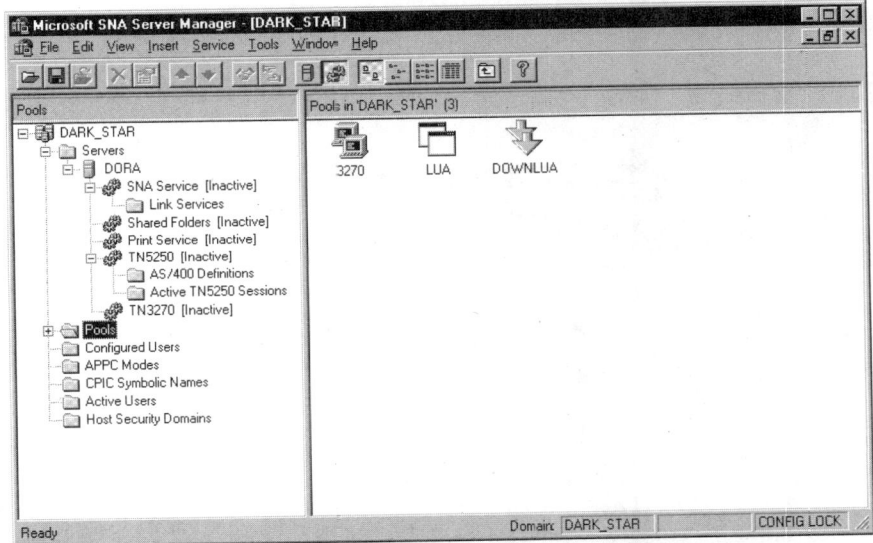

Figure 28-3: The SNA Server Manager program's displaying LU Pools.

You can use the Insert menu to create new pools. The pools may be created by right-(context) clicking the Pools branch in the left pane of Microsoft SNA Server Manager. A context menu will allow creating new pools.

The types of pools supported include:

- **3270 pools**—allow management of 3270 LU resources.
- **LUA pools**—allow management of LUA resources.
- **Down Stream pools**—allow management of LU resources which are located down stream.

Administering Servers & Connections

To administer servers, select the server to be administered in the left pane of the Microsoft SNA Server Manager, as shown in Figure 28-4. In the right pane of the Microsoft SNA Server Manager will be displayed each of the services that the selected server offers. The server DORA has five services configured:

- SNA Service
- Shared Folders
- TN3270
- TN5250
- Print Service

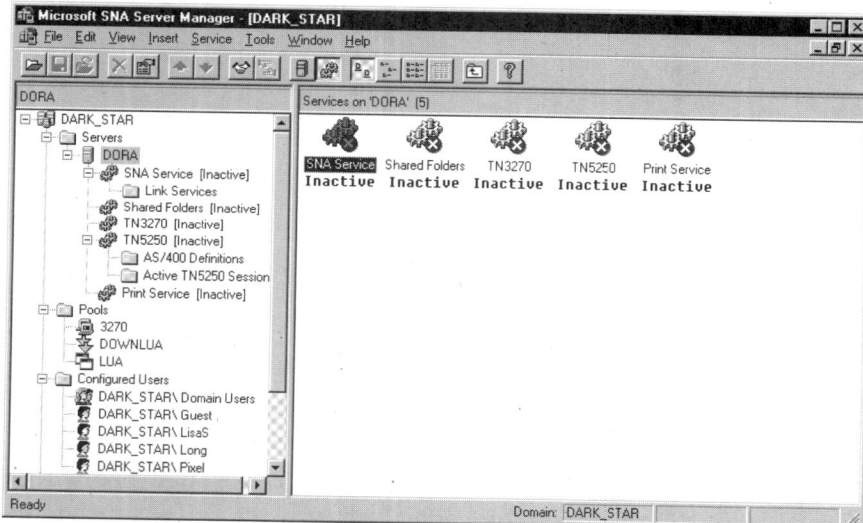

Figure 28-4: The server DORA has five services defined.

You can select any of the services, in either pane, and use the right mouse button to display the context menu. From this menu you may configure, display properties, manage, start, and stop the service.

Administering Users & Groups

When the Microsoft SNA Server Manager program is displaying Configured Users (click on Configured Users in the left pane, as shown in Figure 28-5), all configured users are listed in the right pane. A user's properties may be displayed by selecting the user, and right-clicking to display the context menu. Select Properties in this menu.

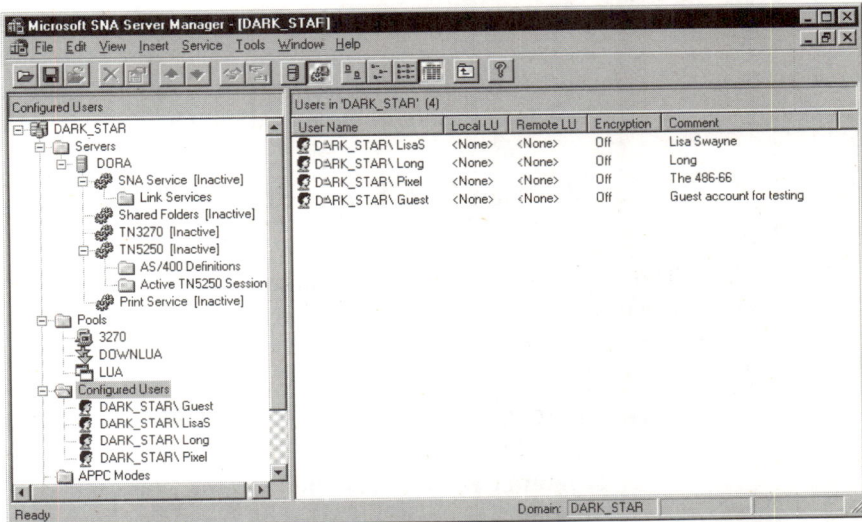

Figure 28-5: There are a total of four SNA users configured for DarkStar.

The properties for user LisaS are shown in Figure 28-6. APPC (Advanced Program-to-Program Communications) Defaults allows setting both a local LU alias, and a remote LU alias.

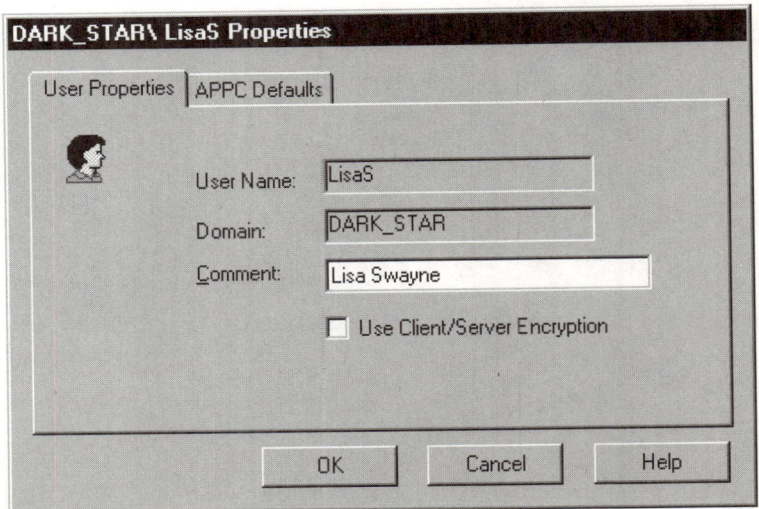

Figure 28-6: User LisaS properties include setting the user's comment, encryption, and APPC Defaults.

To add new users, right-click Configured Users, and select Insert | New User. Then select the user to add from the list presented. Multiple users may be added at one time, if desired. Windows NT 4 Server groups may also be selected as users, allowing easier management of the SNA facilities.

Other Microsoft SNA Server Program Items

The Microsoft SNA Server Manager program allows you to configure Microsoft SNA Server. Additionally, there are a number of other items installed in the Start Menu folder for Microsoft SNA Server when you install it:

- **ODBC Administrator**—manages the StarSQL ODBC driver, which is supplied with Microsoft SNA Server. The ODBC Administrator program (which is also found in the Control Panel) is accessible from the Microsoft SNA Server (Common) group.

- **SNA Server 3270 Applet**—emulates a 3270 display terminal (see Figure 28-7). A 3270 series terminal is typically connected to IBM mainframe computers. The SNA Server 3270 terminal emulator will map those keys that are unique to an IBM 3270 series terminal to the standard PC keyboard.

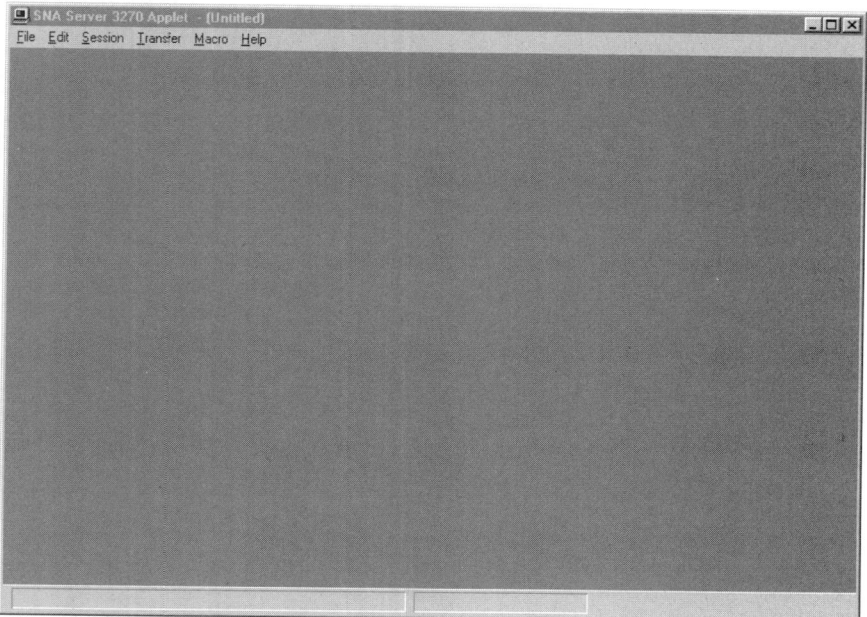

Figure 28-7: The SNA Server 3270 Applet.

- **SNA Server 5250 Applet**—emulates a 5250 display terminal. A 5250 series terminal (see Figure 28-8) is typically connected to IBM minicomputers (such as the AS/400 series).

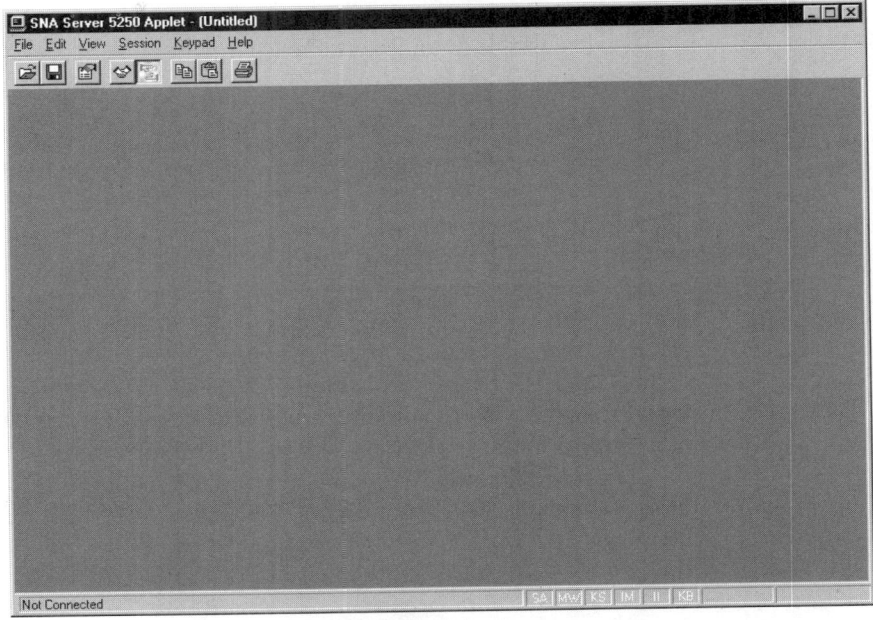

Figure 28-8: The SNA Server 5250 Applet.

- **Host Account Manager**—tool used to manage host user accounts for SNA. This application uses the Windows NT Password Syncronization Service, which must be started before running Host Account Manager.

- **SDK Documentation**—extensive help file containing technical information about the Microsoft SNA Server product. Useful for developers who are working with the Microsoft SNA Server product, though there may be information useful to administrators, also.

- **Release Notes**—read-me file for Microsoft SNA Server. This file contains information that is vital to using Microsoft SNA Server: I recommend that you review this file.

- **SNA Server Setup**—setup program for Microsoft SNA Server.

- **SNA Formats Guide**—help file that contains IBM publication GA27-3136-14, "Systems Network Architecture Formats." If more information about SNA is needed, review this document.

- **SNA Server Trace**—allows you to set trace options. This functionality is also available in the Microsoft SNA Server Manager program.

- **Trace Viewer**—allows you to display trace logs saved using the SNA Server Trace program (described above).

Moving On

This chapter introduced Microsoft SNA Server; we showed you how to install the SNA Server, and some of its basic features. Microsoft SNA Server works with IBM mainframe computers (and any other computer that supports the protocols used by IBM mainframe computers).

In the next chapter, we will cover the Microsoft SNA Server installation and configuration and using the Microsoft SNA Server in a mixed network.

29

Installing & Configuring SNA Server & Its Clients

In this chapter we describe installation of Microsoft SNA (Systems Network Architecture) Server.

The example installation shown in this chapter is for Microsoft SNA Server 3. Microsoft SNA Server 3 setup may have some differences from its predecessor, but the general flow of the installation will be identical.

Note: Many Microsoft products require that a key value be entered whenever the product is installed. The key is usually found on the CD case. Some editions of Microsoft SNA Server have the installation key located on the back inside cover of the *Microsoft SNA Server Installation Guide.*

SNA Configurations

As mentioned in Chapter 28, there are two different ways to configure a Microsoft SNA Server installation. The differences are basically hardware-related (actually, where the hardware is located).

You need to choose how the hardware (and the Microsoft SNA Server) will be configured.

The first configuration is called centralized servers; with this configuration, all the Microsoft SNA Servers will be located at one site, typically in the same location as the mainframe computer. Client users may either be located locally to the Microsoft SNA Server (on the same network or domain) or remotely, using some form of WAN, SDLC (Synchronous Data Link Control) bridge, router, RAS dialup, or perhaps the Internet.

This configuration is shown in Figure 29-1, where the mainframe and the two Microsoft SNA Servers are centrally located. There is a remote network connected to one of the Microsoft SNA Servers using some form of communications link (typically router to router, using TCP/IP protocol).

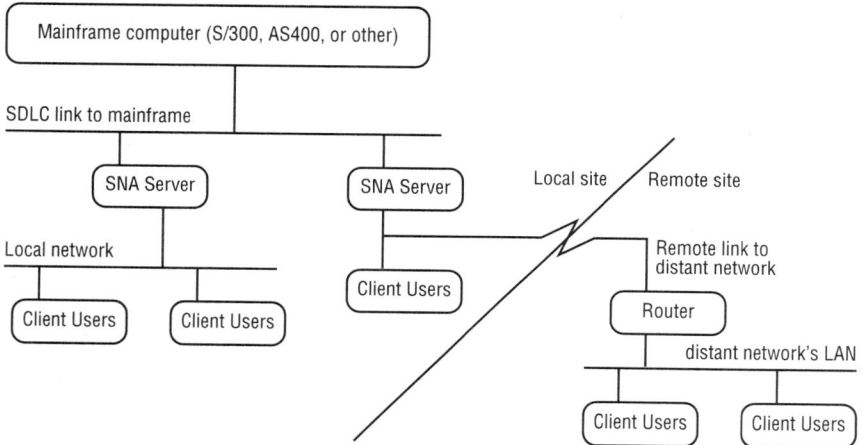

Figure 29-1: Centralized Microsoft SNA Servers are centrally located at the mainframe.

In the second configuration (Figure 29-2), the Microsoft SNA Servers are remotely located to be near the client sites. Each Microsoft SNA Server connects to the mainframe computer through a communications link that supports SDLC. Each Microsoft SNA Server supports a single, isolated LAN.

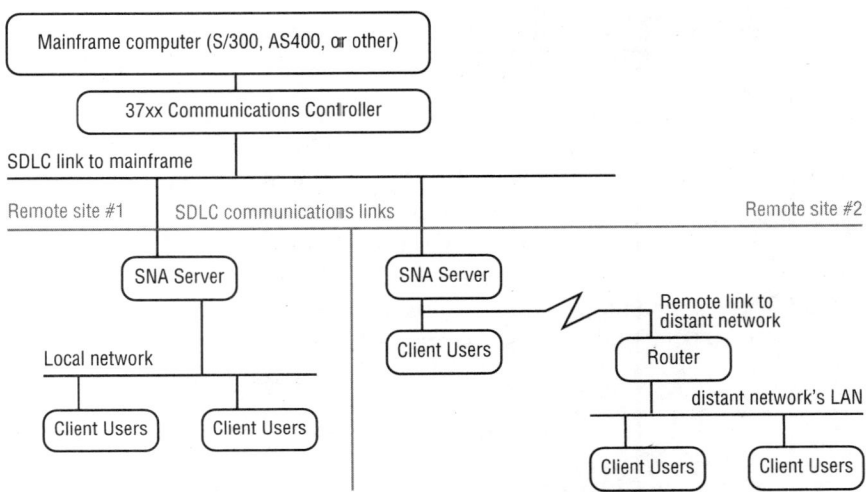

Figure 29-2: Decentralized Microsoft SNA Servers are remotely located at the client users' sites, away from the mainframe.

When only a single site exists to house both the mainframe and the client users, configuration is considered to be a centralized server configuration, but without any remotely connected clients.

Neither installation technique really affects the installation of Microsoft SNA Server; they only affect how the hardware (and communications) is configured.

Note: There is nothing to prevent a hybrid system from being created where there are both centralized and decentralized Microsoft SNA Servers. For a globally spanning organization, a hybrid configuration installation could be the most cost effective, both in terms of management and communications costs.

Warning

Only the very brave, or foolish, attempt to run Microsoft Exchange Server, Microsoft SNA Server, and Microsoft SQL Server at the same time on the same Pentium uni-processor server. To do so, you need to have a very fast Pentium (at least a 200MHz) and a minimum of 128MB of RAM.

A Typical Installation

This section will cover a typical installation of a single Microsoft SNA Server. (Although I'll note the point in the installation where different steps are taken to install additional Microsoft SNA Servers.)

Note: Some versions of Microsoft SNA Server are installed using the Windows NT 4 Server installation system. Check the installation folder on the CD. If there is a file called setup.inf and no program (setup.exe), then follow these steps to install the product (these steps will work for virtually any software package that uses a setup.inf file to install):

1. Start the Windows Explorer program.

2. Right-click the .inf file, and select install from the context menu.

Stopping SNA Server 3 With RAS?

It is sometimes necessary to stop SNA Server. For example, if SNA Server is being upgraded, it will be necessary to stop the SNA service. To do this, open the Windows Control Panel, and select the Services applet. Select each of the installed SNA services (there are typically between four and seven SNA services) and stop each service. If the installed version of SNA Server being replaced is SNA Server 3 (or later), *with RAS support enabled,* additional steps are required. This requirement is due to an interrelationship between the SnaBase service, and the SNA RAS service. To stop the SnaBase service (for any reason) follow these steps:

1. Open the Control Panel's Services applet, and change the startup type for SnaBase to manual.

2. Restart the Windows NT 4 Server.

After SnaBase has been changed to manual startup (and the system has been restarted), it will be possible to properly shutdown the SNA services.

To restart the SNA services, it will be necessary to change the SnaBase service startup type to automatic, and restart the Windows NT 4 Server. If you are re-installing SNA, then the SNA setup program will change SnaBase's startup type to automatic.

Follow these steps to install SNA Server:

1. Start the Microsoft BackOffice Installer program. Enter any necessary user information and the CD-ROM key.

2. Select Microsoft SNA Server 3 from the list of products available. Click the OK button to start the Microsoft SNA Server 3 installation process.

Note: If setup detects that SNA Server is running, setup will attempt to stop SNA Server. Generally setup will be able to stop SNA Server without problems. However, if the version of SNA Server is 3 (or later) and SNA RAS support is installed, setup may not be able to stop the SNA Server. If this happens, setup will end with an error message. See the previous sidebar "Stopping SNA Server 3 With RAS?" for more information.

3. Once started, there will be one or two introductory dialog boxes displayed (providing product version numbers and welcoming you to the installation). The first significant screens to be displayed by setup are the product's Name and Organization Information (see Figure 29-3), and software licensing, Microsoft SNA Server Setup dialog box (see Figure 29-4). Enter the user's name and company name in the Name and Organization Information dialog box. Enter the product ID in the Microsoft SNA Server Setup dialog box.

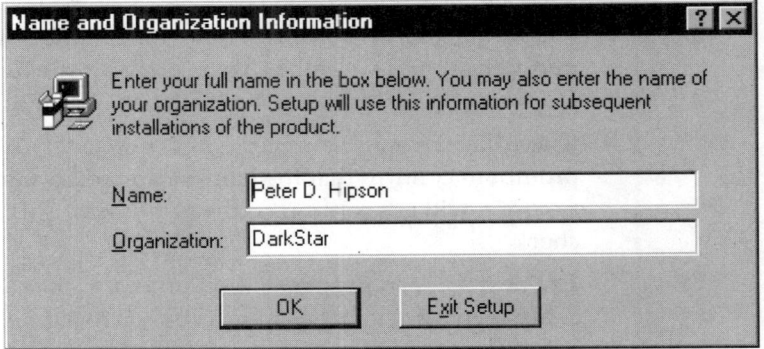

Figure 29-3: Enter your name and company name in the Name and Organization Information dialog box.

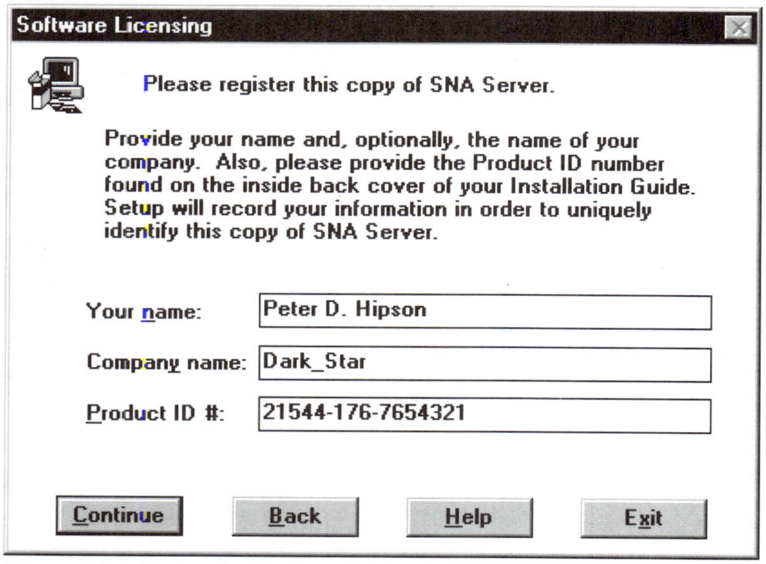

Software Licensing

Please register this copy of SNA Server.

Provide your name and, optionally, the name of your company. Also, please provide the Product ID number found on the inside back cover of your Installation Guide. Setup will record your information in order to uniquely identify this copy of SNA Server.

Your name: `Peter D. Hipson`

Company name: `Dark_Star`

Product ID #: `21544-176-7654321`

[**Continue**] [**Back**] [**Help**] [**Exit**]

Figure 29-4: Enter the Product ID in the Microsoft SNA Server Setup dialog box.

The user's name and company name may be whatever is normally entered for software at this site. Enter the Product ID that is located on the CD case, or for some versions of Microsoft SNA Server, printed on the back cover of the Installation Guide. The Product ID is typically a three-part number, where the middle part of the number (three digits) is the product code: Microsoft SNA Server has a product code of 176.

4. Once the information in Step 2 has been entered, there will be a prompt to confirm that the names entered are correct. The setup program will not continue if the Product ID fails its validation check.

5. The next stage in the installation process is to select which components are to be installed. The Microsoft SNA Server— Select Components dialog box (see Figure 29-5) lists each optional component that may be selected.

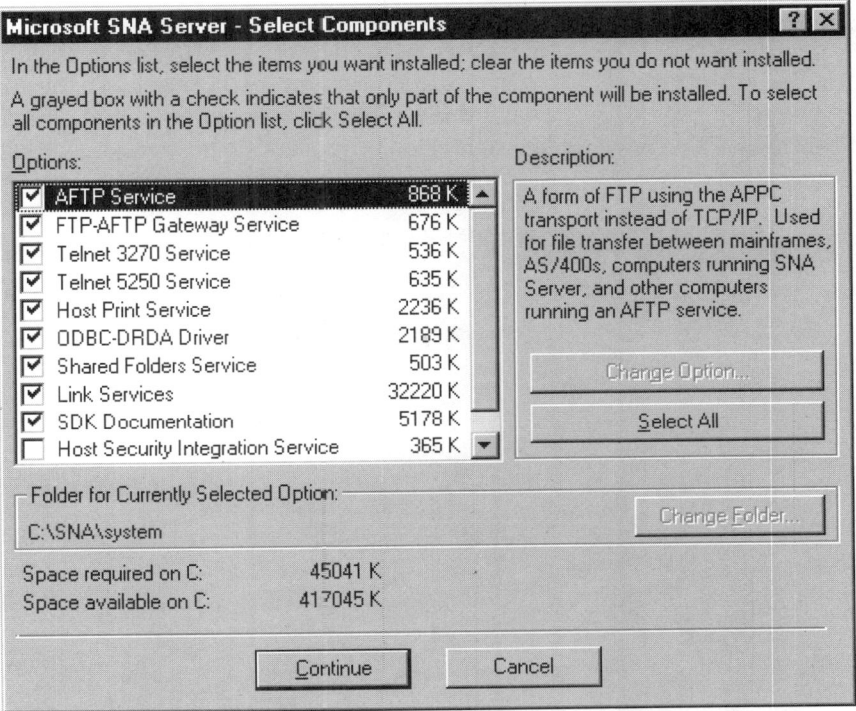

Figure 29-5: Select all optional components to be installed in the Select Components dialog box.

6. Next, if SNA Server RAS service has been selected (in Step 4), a warning dialog box (Figure 29-6) will be displayed to explain the relationships between SNA Server RAS service and SnaBase service. There will be a shortcut to the readme.wri file placed in the Microsoft SNA Server (Common) program group.

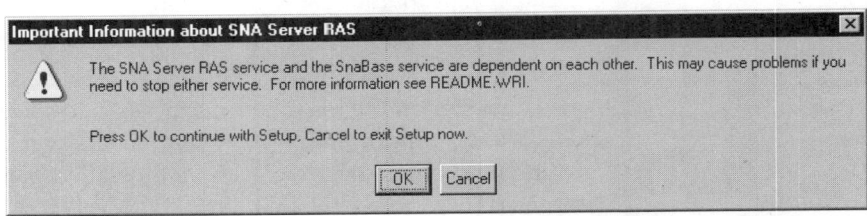

Figure 29-6: Heed the caution about stopping the SnaBase service. The SNA Server's readme.wri file contains much valuable information.

7. It is necessary to provide an account for the SNA Server to use (see Figure 29-7). Though the SNA Server's setup program is able to create an account (to do this, leave the Account and Password fields blank), I recommend that you use an existing account for this purpose.

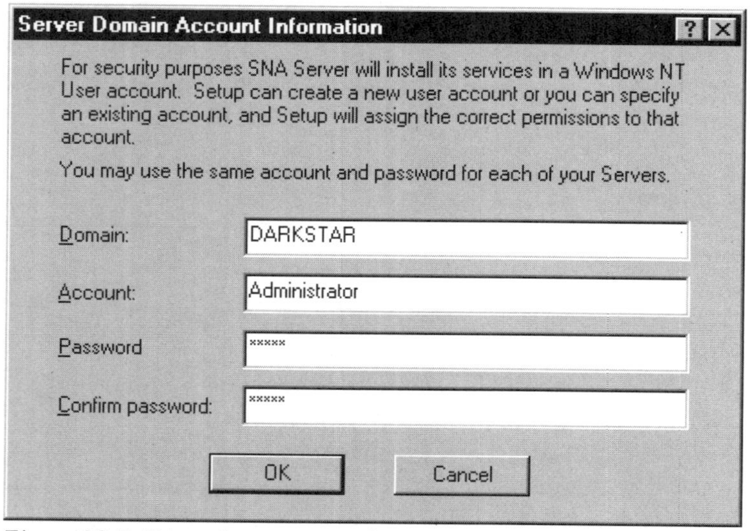

Figure 29-7: Enter the account information for the setup program. SNA Server will use this account also.

8. The SNA Server's role must be defined in the Choose Server Role dialog box (Figure 29-8). If there is only one SNA Server installed, then the default (Primary configuration server) is the correct choice. Otherwise choose either Backup configuration server (if you need to have a backup configuration server installed), or Member server (no configuration). There is more information about roles in the section "SNA Server Roles" following these installation steps.

9. The next step in the installation process is to select which protocols will be supported by Microsoft SNA Server when communicating with client users. Any and all installed protocols may be selected (in Figure 29-9, neither Banyan VINES nor AppleTalk have been installed on the server, so these two protocols may not be selected). Generally, most installers will select all protocols (the default is for TCP/IP to be installed).

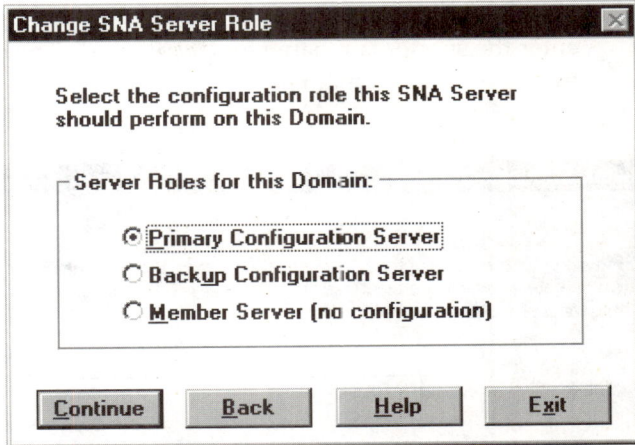

Figure 29-8: Choose this SNA Server's role.

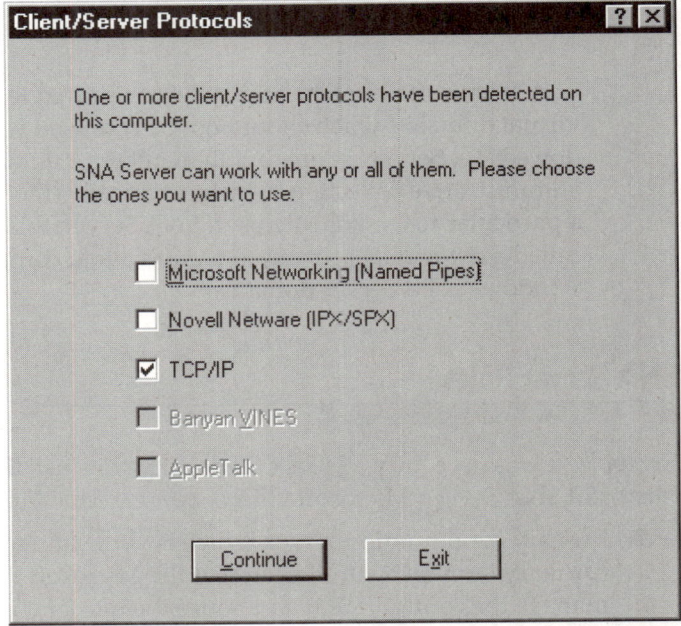

Figure 29-9: Select all protocols used to communicate with clients.

10. In the Network Subdomain Name dialog box (Figure 29-10), enter the subdomain name for the network. The default will be the server's subdomain name.

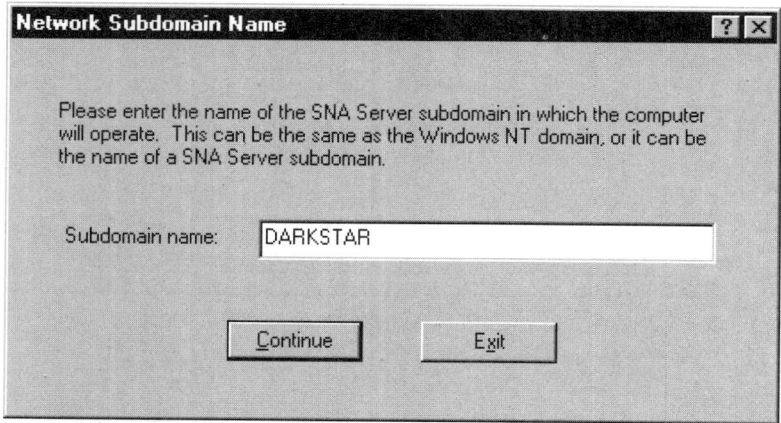

Figure 29-10: Enter the subdomain name (or use the default).

A Microsoft SNA Server may be configured to have its own virtual domain (which should not be confused with the Windows NT 4 Server's domain). Remember: A domain is an administrative collection, which is typically (though not always) a particular LAN. For Microsoft SNA Server, this functionality is called a *configuration server*, to try and avoid confusion over Windows NT 4 Server domains.

SNA Server Roles

In Step 8, it was necessary to select the role for this installation of Microsoft SNA Server. Microsoft SNA Server can be configured as:

■ Primary configuration server, which is very similar to a PDC (primary domain controller) in that the Microsoft SNA Server will manage the configuration and house the master copy of the configuration.

■ Backup configuration server, which is very similar to a BDC (backup domain controller) in that the Microsoft SNA Server will have a backup copy of the configuration, but will use the primary configuration server's configuration database. If the primary configuration server should fail, then a backup configuration server may be "promoted" to become the new primary configuration server.

■ Member servers, the third choice, always obtain configuration from the primary configuration server and do not maintain a backup copy of the configuration.

For sites with only a single Microsoft SNA Server, install Microsoft SNA Server as the primary configuration server. If there are two or more Microsoft SNA Servers, install the second Microsoft SNA Server as a backup configuration server and the remaining Microsoft SNA Servers as member servers. If there are more than, say, five Microsoft SNA Servers, it may be a good move to have two backup configuration servers configured, just in case there are multiple hardware or system failures.

Documentation

Additional documentation may be installed by copying the folder sna30\docs on the Microsoft SNA Server CD-ROM to a local hard drive. A typical location for these additional documentation files would be the SNA Server's installation folder. These documentation files total about 40MB of disk space, so unless the server is so short of disk space that it is not practical to install these help files, I recommend that they be installed with the first installation of Microsoft SNA Server. If at a later time it is determined that they are no longer needed, they can be removed.

Connecting to the Mainframe

The Microsoft SNA Server's hardware must be connected to the IBM-compatible mainframe computer. This is done using a communications adapter (typically connected using SDLC communications).

To configure the link service to be used requires that the Microsoft SNA Server Manager program be started, by selecting Start Menu | Programs | Microsoft SNA Server (Common) | Manager.

In the Microsoft SNA Server Manager program, display the Server View (select View | Server View in the menu). Then expand the SNA Servers tree, until the Link Services folder is visible, as shown in Figure 29-11.

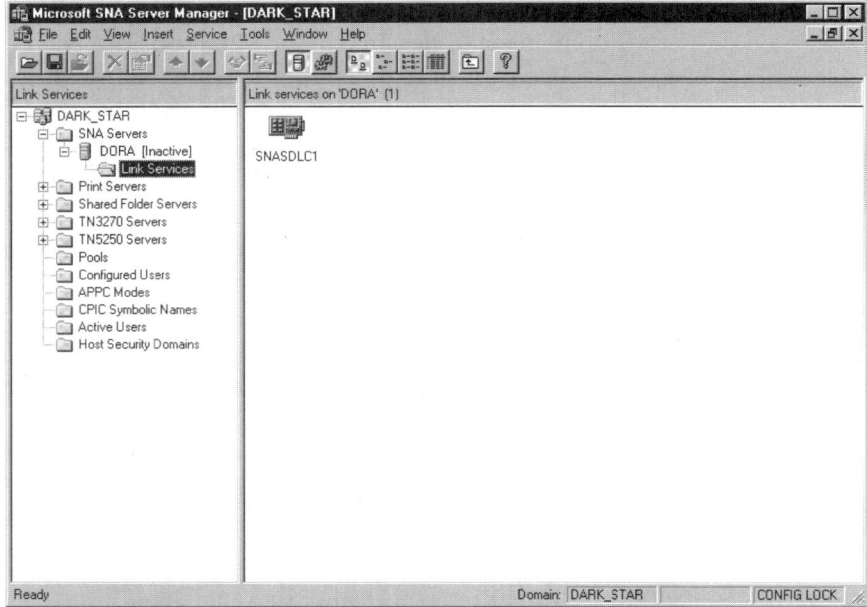

Figure 29-11: Display the Link Services folder in the Microsoft SNA Server Manager.

Choose which adapter is being used in the Insert Link Service dialog box (Figure 29-12). Display the Insert Link Service.

Note: The link service is, essentially, the equivalent to an NIC. And like NICs, there may be more than one link service connecting to more than one mainframe computer.

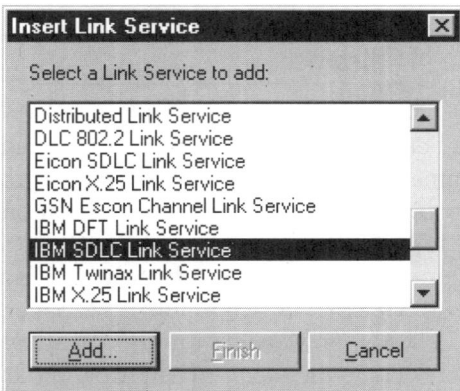

Figure 29-12: In the Insert Link Service dialog box, select a link service to install and click Add.

After you click the Add button, a dialog box (see Figure 29-13) specific to the adapter selected will be displayed. For many adapters, you'll need to enter information such as the base I/O address (using the Card Configuration tab) and the type of communications line used to connect the adapter to the mainframe computer.

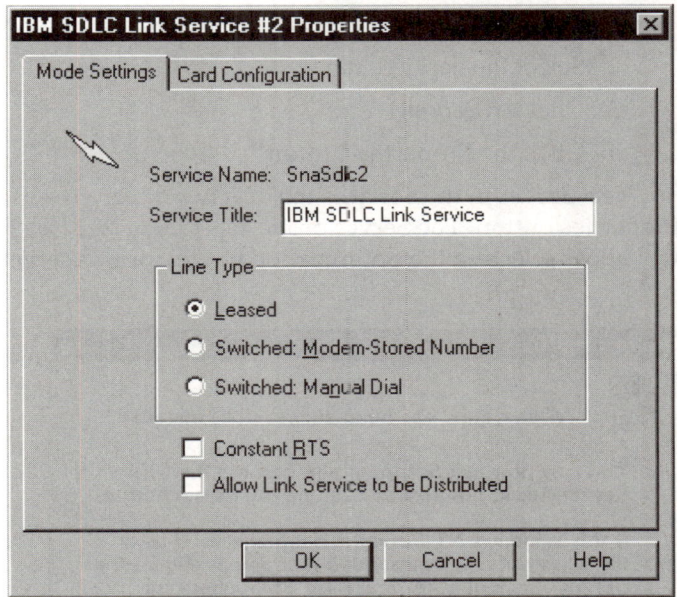

Figure 29-13: Configure the link service adapter.

Once the link service adapter has been installed, the Insert Link Service dialog box is redisplayed (see Figure 29-12), and a second link service adapter may be installed, if necessary. Once all the installed link service adapters have been configured, click the Continue button to continue with the installation.

At this point, the installation of Microsoft SNA Server is complete. There may be additional information dialog boxes; however, these dialog boxes should require no user input other than to dismiss them by clicking either OK, Exit, or Continue.

Optimizing the Server

Microsoft recommends that if the server on which Microsoft SNA Server is being run is not being used as a file server, you configure the server to "Maximize Throughput for Network Applications" (see Figure 29-14). To do so:

1. Start the Control Panel and then open the Network applet.

2. Select the Services tab.

3. Click on Server.

4. Click the Properties button.

Select Server in the Services tab's Network Services list; then click the Properties button. The Server properties dialog box (see Figure 29-14) will allow selecting the optimization model for this server.

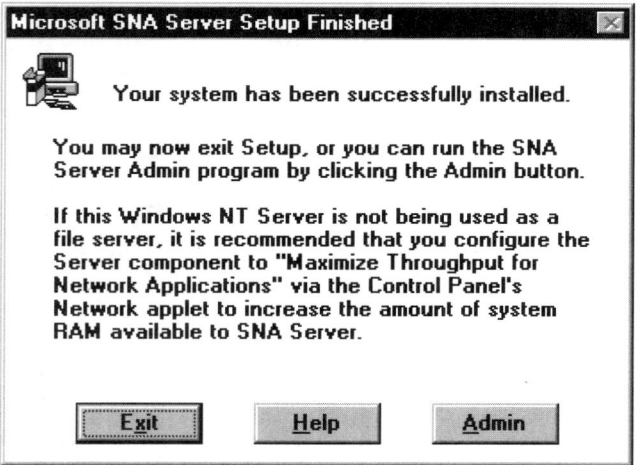

Figure 29-14: Optimize to "Maximize Throughput for Network Applications" if the server is not serving files, too.

Microsoft SNA Server Clients

Microsoft SNA Server clients may be installed either from a shared folder or from diskettes. It is probably easier, and faster, to install Microsoft SNA Server from a networked share, so we'll cover that method first.

Creating Microsoft SNA Server Client Installation Shares

The technique for setting up client shares is basically manual. Follow these steps to create your client installation shares:

1. Create a folder on any drive from which you can share it and call it smsclients.

2. Insert the Microsoft SNA Server CD in the CD drive, and change to the clients folder (the clients folder will be located in sna30\clients if you are installing Microsoft SNA Server version 3).

3. Verify that the clients that are to be installed are in the Microsoft SNA Server clients folder. Clients available should include:

■ **MAC**—the Apple Macintosh version of the Microsoft SNA Server client software. Support for Apple Macintosh is new to Microsoft SNA Server 3.

■ **MSDOS**—the MS-DOS version of the Microsoft SNA Server client software. Is there anyone who is still running just MS-DOS?

■ **OS2**—the OS/2 version of the Microsoft SNA Server client software. The versions of OS/2 supported are not specified, and a test installation of the OS/2 client software should be performed using the version of OS/2 currently in service before releasing the client to users.

■ **WIN3X**—the Microsoft Windows 3.x version of the Microsoft SNA Server client software. Users should consider upgrading to Windows 95 if possible, rather than installing the Windows 3.x client (Windows 95 will provide somewhat better performance).

■ **WIN95**—the Windows 95 version of the Microsoft SNA Server client software.

■ **WINNT**—the Windows NT version of the Microsoft SNA Server client software. This version should run under both Windows NT Server and Windows NT Workstation.

4. Use either Explorer or a command prompt XCOPY to copy these folders (and all subfolders, too) to the folder created in Step 1.

5. Verify the folder structure matches the folders on the Microsoft SNA Server distribution CD.

Note: It is possible to use the Microsoft SNA Server distribution CD to install client software too. However, there are several problems when sharing CD-ROM drives, especially with performance: CD-ROM drives are typically designed as single-user devices and do not perform well when accessed concurrently by more than one user.

6. Create a share for each folder (as listed in Step 3). Give the shares meaningful names (such as SNACDOS, etc.). If you are sharing the MS-DOS or Windows 3.x clients, remember that many network clients may not support share names longer than eight characters. Assign passwords for the shares as necessary.

Once the shares have been created, client users are able to use the share to create an installation. The process is very easy:

1. At the client workstation, establish a link to the Microsoft SNA Server client share (created in Step 6, in the previous set of instructions). This link does not need to be persistent, as once the Microsoft SNA Server client software has been installed, the share will not be needed.

2. From the link established in Step 1, run setup.exe.

Note: Windows NT clients will have to take the additional step of changing into the folder that matches their hardware platform. For example, Windows NT users with Intel systems would have to change into the I386 folder and then run setup.exe.

Conclusion

In this chapter, you learned how to install Microsoft SNA Server. We showed the two different models that are used for configuring Microsoft SNA Server hardware and a typical installation of Microsoft SNA Server.

This chapter showed you how to create and install the SNA Server client software for the different platforms that Microsoft SNA Server supports.

This is the final chapter in the book. If you started at the front cover and have read this far, you are to be congratulated! (OK, most of us skip around a bit!) The appendices include an introduction to this book's Companion CD-ROM and a listing of the TCP/IP ports.

appendix A

About the CD-ROM

The CD-ROM included with your copy of *Microsoft Backoffice 2.5: The Complete Solution* contains software programs that complement the book.

Navigating the CD-ROM

Installation: Each software program resides in its own directory on the CD-ROM. To use the software on the CD-ROM, first go to Windows Explorer and copy the desired directory from the CD-ROM to the hard drive. Then follow the instructions in the README that comes with each program on how to install.

Most of the programs are trial versions that require registration and payment of a fee after the trial period. Please consult each program's README file for more information about this.

For the Microsoft Internet Assistant products below, please follow the steps below for installation:

1. Open the Microsoft application that uses the Add-in.

2. On the Tools menu, point to Add-ins, and then click Internet Assistant.

3. Follow the instructions in the Internet Assistant dialog boxes.

Software Descriptions

Program	Description
Free Agent v 1.1	Free Agent is a newsreader and is your guide to news, fun, and information in the Usenet newsgroups. Its features include: flexible article purging; database compaction; substantial speed improvements in threading/purging; send an e-mail carbon copy (cc) when posting articles; and editing of all header fields for messages and articles, to name a few. Free Agent copyright © 1997 Forte Advanced Management Software, Inc. All rights reserved. For more information, visit http://www.forteinc.com on the World Wide Web.
Internet Assistant for Microsoft Word for Windows 95	It's a no-charge add-in that makes it easy to create and edit great looking documents for the Internet and intranets right from within Microsoft Word. For more information, visit http://www.microsoft.com on the World Wide Web. Portions © Microsoft Corporation 1997. All rights reserved.
Internet Assistant for Microsoft Excel for Windows 95	Microsoft Excel Internet Assistant is a no-charge add-in that makes it easy to leverage existing Microsoft Excel spreadsheet data to create, edit, and convert information for publishing on an intranet, or the Internet. For more information, visit http://www.microsoft.com on the World Wide Web. Portions © Microsoft Corporation 1997. All rights reserved. Note: Once installed, this software can be accessed under the Tools pull-down menu in the Internet Assistant Wizard.
Internet Assistant for Microsoft PowerPoint for Windows 95	Transform your PowerPoint slides into rich HTML pages for publishing to the Web. For more information, visit http://www.microsoft.com on the World Wide Web. Portions © Microsoft Corporation 1997. All rights reserved.

Program	Description
Internet Assistant for Microsoft Access for Windows 95	It's an add-in that will allow any user to create meaningful output from their structured data and share it on their intranet, or on the Internet. For more information, visit http://www.microsoft.com on the World Wide Web. Portions © Microsoft Corporation 1997. All rights reserved.
Internet Assistant for Microsoft Schedule+ for Windows 95	Internet Assistant for Schedule+ not only makes publishing to the Web easier, but provides the good-looking Schedule+ calendar interface. For more information, visit http://www.microsoft.com on the World Wide Web. Portions © Microsoft Corporation 1997. All rights reserved.
Microsoft PowerPoint Animation Player for Windows 95	Add animation to your PowerPoint presentations for viewing over the World Wide Web. For more information, visit http://www.microsoft.com on the World Wide Web. Portions © Microsoft Corporation 1997. All rights reserved.
Microsoft Index Server	Microsoft Index Server works with Windows NT Server 4.0 and Internet Information Server 2.0 to provide your organization access to all of the documents stored on your intranet or Internet site. It allows you to perform full-text searches and retrieve all types of information from any Web browser, in just about any format, with just the click of a mouse or button. For more information, visit http://www.microsoft.com on the World Wide Web. Portions © Microsoft Corporation 1997. All rights reserved.

Table A-1: Programs on the Companion CD-ROM.

Technical Support

Technical support is available for installation-related problems only. The technical support office is open from 8:00 A.M. to 6:00 P.M. Monday through Friday and can be reached via the following methods:

Phone: (919) 544-9404 extension 81

Faxback Answer System: (919) 544-9404 extension 85

E-mail: help@vmedia.com

FAX: (919) 544-9472

World Wide Web: http://www.vmedia.com/support

America Online: keyword *Ventana*

Limits of Liability & Disclaimer of Warranty

The authors and publisher of this book have used their best efforts in preparing the CD-ROM and the programs contained in it. These efforts include the development, research, and testing of the theories and programs to determine their effectiveness. The authors and publisher make no warranty of any kind expressed or implied, with regard to these programs or the documentation contained in this book.

The authors and publisher shall not be liable in the event of incidental or consequential damages in connection with, or arising out of, the furnishing, performance, or use of the programs, associated instructions, and/or claims of productivity gains.

Some of the software on this CD-ROM is shareware; there may be additional charges (owed to the software authors/makers) incurred for their registration and continued use. See individual program's README or VREADME.TXT files for more information.

appendix B

TCP/IP Port Assignments

This appendix contains a list of the most recognizable TCP/IP port assignments. It does not include all port assignments (no such list exists).

For more information on TCP/IP port numbers, check out URL http://www.con.wesleyan.edu/~triemer/network/docservs.html.

It is sometimes necessary to add new ports (such as when installing SNA Server). To add a new port definition, in the file %SystemRoot%\system32\drivers\etc\services, add a new record for the new port. In Listing B-1 is a segment of the services file, with port 24 added for SNA Server's tn3270 port.

Listing B-1: Adding port 24, the SNA Server's tn3270 port.

```
qotd           17/tcp      quote
qotd           17/udp      quote
chargen        19/tcp      ttytst source
chargen        19/udp      ttytst source
ftp-data       20/tcp
ftp            21/tcp
telnet         23/tcp
tn3270         24/tcp      #Added for SNA
smtp           25/tcp      mail
time           37/tcp      timserver
```

For port numbers that do not have a short name, there is no standard name defined. Not all port numbers have a definition, even though the port number may be assigned. In the services file, any characters following the pound (#) sign are comments and will be ignored by Windows NT 4 Server.

For additional information also see RFC768, "User Datagram Protocol," and RFC793 "Transmission Control Protocol—DARPA Internet Program Protocol Specification."

Port Name	Port Number	TCP Port?	UDP Port?	Description (if known)
	0	TCP	UDP	Reserved
tcpmux	1	TCP		TCP Port Service Multiplexer
compressnet	2	TCP		Management Utility
compressnet	3	TCP		Compression Process
rje	5	TCP		Remote Job Entry
echo	7	TCP	UDP	The ECHO protocol simply returns the data that are passed back to the sender. Both PING and TRACERT use this port.
discard	9	TCP	UDP	Discard
discard	9		UDP	Discard
systat	11	TCP		Active Users
daytime	13	TCP	UDP	The time-of-day service. Connecting to this service returns the current date and time to the requester.
qotd	17	TCP	UDP	Quote of the Day. Returns sayings back to the requester.
rwrite	18	TCP	UDP	RWP rwrite

Port Name	Port Number	TCP Port?	UDP Port?	Description (if known)
msp	18	TCP	UDP	Message Send Protocol
chargen	19	TCP	UDP	Character Generator
ftp-data	20	TCP		FTP File Transfer [Default Data]
ftp	21	TCP		FTP File Transfer [Control]
telnet	23	TCP		Telnet
	24	TCP	UDP	Any private mail system
tn3270	24	TCP		SNA Server's 3270 port
smtp	25	TCP		Simple Mail Transfer (SMTP)
nsw-fe	27	TCP	UDP	NSW User System FE
msg-icp	29	TCP	UDP	MSG ICP
msg-icp	29		UDP	MSG ICP
msg-auth	31	TCP	UDP	MSG Authentication
msg-auth	31		UDP	MSG Authentication
dsp	33	TCP	UDP	Display Support Protocol
	35	TCP	UDP	Any private printer server
	35		UDP	Any private printer server
time	37	TCP	UDP	Time
rap	38	TCP	UDP	Route Access Protocol
rlp	39		UDP	Resource Location Protocol
graphics	41	TCP	UDP	Graphics
nameserver	42		UDP	Host Name Server

Port Name	Port Number	TCP Port?	UDP Port?	Description (if known)
nicname	43	TCP		Who Is
mpm-flags	44	TCP		MPM FLAGS Protocol
mpm	45	TCP		Message Processing Module [recv]
mpm-snd	46	TCP		MPM [default send]
ni-ftp	47	TCP	UDP	NI FTP
auditd	48	TCP	UDP	Digital Audit Daemon
login	49	TCP		Login Host Protocol
re-mail-ck	50	TCP	UDP	Remote Mail Checking Protocol
la-maint	51		UDP	IMP Logical Address Maintenance
xns-time	52	TCP	UDP	XNS Time Protocol
domain	53	TCP	UDP	Domain Name Server
xns-ch	54	TCP	UDP	XNS Clearinghouse
isi-gl	55	TCP	UDP	ISI Graphics Language
xns-auth	56	TCP	UDP	XNS Authentication
	57	TCP	UDP	Any private terminal access
xns-mail	58	TCP	UDP	XNS Mail
	59	TCP	UDP	Any private file service
	60	TCP	UDP	Unassigned
ni-mail	61	TCP	UDP	NI MAIL
acas	62	TCP		ACA Services
covia	64	TCP		Communications Integrator (CI)
tacacs-ds	65	TCP		TACACS-Database Service
sql*net	66	TCP		Oracle SQL*NET

Port Name	Port Number	TCP Port?	UDP Port?	Description (if known)
bootps	67		UDP	Bootstrap Protocol Server used in conjunction with DHCP to initialize a DHCP client at boot time
bootpc	68		UDP	Bootstrap Protocol Client
tftp	69		UDP	Trivial File Transfer
gopher	70	TCP		Gopher
netrjs-1	71	TCP	UDP	Remote Job Service
netrjs-2	72	TCP	UDP	Remote Job Service
netrjs-3	73	TCP	UDP	Remote Job Service
netrjs-4	74	TCP	UDP	Remote Job Service
	75	TCP	UDP	Any private dial-out service
deos	76	TCP	UDP	Distributed External Object Store
	77	TCP	UDP	Any private RJE service
vettcp	78	TCP	UDP	vettcp
finger	79	TCP		Request for information on the system or users on the system
http	80	TCP		World Wide Web HTTP
hosts2-ns	81	TCP	UDP	HOSTS2 Name Server
xfer	82	TCP	UDP	XFER Utility
mit-ml-dev	83	TCP	UDP	MIT ML Device
ctf	84	TCP	UDP	Common Trace Facility
mit-ml-dev	85	TCP	UDP	MIT ML Device
mfcobol	86	TCP		Micro Focus Cobol
	87	TCP	UDP	Any private terminal link

Port Name	Port Number	TCP Port?	UDP Port?	Description (if known)
kerberos	88	TCP		Kerberos
su-mit-tg	89	TCP		SU/MIT Telnet Gateway
dnsix	90	TCP		DNSIX Security Attribute Token Map
mit-dov	91	TCP		MIT Dover Spooler
npp	92	TCP	UDP	Network Printing Protocol
dcp	93	TCP	UDP	Device Control Protocol
objcall	94	TCP	UDP	Tivoli Object Dispatcher
supdup	95	TCP	UDP	SUPDUP
dixie	96	TCP		DIXIE Protocol Specification
swift-rvf	97	TCP	UDP	Swift Remote Virtual File Protocol
tacnews	98	TCP	UDP	TAC News
metagram	99	TCP	UDP	Metagram Relay
newacct	100	TCP		[unauthorized use]
hostname	101	TCP	UDP	NIC Host Name Server
iso-tsap	102	TCP	UDP	ISO-TSAP Class 0
gppitnp	103	TCP	UDP	Genesis Point-to-Point Trans Net
acr-nema	104	TCP		ACR-NEMA Digital Imag. & Comm. 300
csnet-ns	105	TCP	UDP	Mailbox Name Nameserver
3com-tsmux	106	TCP	UDP	3COM-TSMUX
poppassd	106	TCP		Password Server
rtelnet	107	TCP		Remote Telnet Service

Port Name	Port Number	TCP Port?	UDP Port?	Description (if known)
snagas	108	TCP		SNA Gateway Access Server
pop2	109	TCP		Post Office Protocol—Version 2
pop3	110	TCP		Post Office Protocol—Version 3
sunrpc	111	TCP	UDP	SUN Remote Procedure Call
mcidas	112	TCP		McIDAS Data Transmission Protocol
auth	113	TCP		Authentication Service
audionews	114	TCP	UDP	Audio News Multicast
sftp	115	TCP	UDP	Simple File Transfer Protocol
ansanotify	116	TCP	UDP	ANSA REX Notify
uucp-path	117	TCP		UUCP Path Service
sqlserv	118	TCP	UDP	SQL Services
nntp	119	TCP		Network News Transfer Protocol
cfdptkt	120	TCP	UDP	CFDPTKT
erpc	121	TCP	UDP	Encore Expedited Remote Pro.Call
smakynet	122	TCP	UDP	SMAKYNET
ntp	123	TCP	UDP	Network Time Protocol
ansatrader	124	TCP	UDP	ANSA REX Trader
locus-map	125	TCP		Locus PC-Interface Net Map Ser
unitary	126	TCP	UDP	Unisys Unitary Login
locus-con	127	TCP		Locus PC-Interface Conn Server
gss-xlicen	128	TCP	UDP	GSS X License Verification

Port Name	Port Number	TCP Port?	UDP Port?	Description (if known)
pwdgen	129	TCP	UDP	Password Generator Protocol
cisco-fna	130	TCP	UDP	cisco FNATIVE
cisco-tna	131	TCP	UDP	cisco TNATIVE
cisco-sys	132	TCP	UDP	cisco SYSMAINT
statsrv	133	TCP	UDP	Statistics Service
ingres-net	134	TCP		INGRES-NET Service
loc-srv	135	TCP	UDP	Location Service
profile	136	TCP		PROFILE Naming System
netbios-ns	137	TCP	UDP	NetBIOS Name Service
netbios-dgm	138	TCP	UDP	NETBIOS Datagram Service
netbios-ssn	139	TCP	UDP	NETBIOS Session Service
emfis-data	140	TCP	UDP	EMFIS Data Service
emfis-cntl	141	TCP	UDP	EMFIS Control Service
bl-idm	142	TCP	UDP	Britton-Lee IDM
imap2	143	TCP		Interactive Mail Access Protocol v2
news	144		UDP	NewS
uaac	145	TCP	UDP	UAAC Protocol
iso-tp0	146	TCP	UDP	ISO-IP0
iso-ip	147	TCP	UDP	ISO-IP
cronus	148	TCP	UDP	CRONUS-SUPPORT
aed-512	149	TCP	UDP	AED 512 Emulation Service
sql-net	150	TCP	UDP	SQL-NET
hems	151	TCP		HEMS
bftp	152	TCP	UDP	Background File Transfer Program

Port Name	Port Number	TCP Port?	UDP Port?	Description (if known)
sgmp	153	TCP	UDP	SGMP
netsc-prod	154	TCP	UDP	NETSC
netsc-dev	155	TCP	UDP	NETSC
sqlsrv	156	TCP		SQL Service
pcmail-srv	158	TCP		PCMail Server
nss-routing	159	TCP	UDP	NSS-Routing
sgmp-traps	160	TCP	UDP	SGMP-TRAPS
snmp	161		UDP	SNMP
snmptrap	162		UDP	SNMPTRAP
cmip-man	163	TCP	UDP	CMIP TCP Manager
cmip-agent	164	TCP	UDP	CMIP TCP Agent
xns-courier	165	TCP	UDP	Xerox
s-net	166	TCP	UDP	Sirius Systems
namp	167	TCP	UDP	NAMP
rsvd	168	TCP	UDP	RSVD
send	169	TCP	UDP	SEND
print-srv	170	TCP	UDP	Network PostScript
multiplex	171	TCP	UDP	Network Innovations Multiplex
cl/1	172	TCP	UDP	Network Innovations CL/1
xyplex-mux	173	TCP	UDP	Xyplex
mailq	174	TCP	UDP	MAILQ
vmnet	175	TCP	UDP	VMNET
genrad-mux	176	TCP	UDP	GENRAD-MUX
xdmcp	177		UDP	X Display Manager Control Protocol
nextstep	178	TCP	UDP	NextStep Window Server
bgp	179	TCP		Border Gateway Protocol

Port Name	Port Number	TCP Port?	UDP Port?	Description (if known)
ris	180	TCP	UDP	Intergraph
unify	181	TCP	UDP	Unify
audit	182	TCP	UDP	Unisys Audit SITP
ocbinder	183	TCP	UDP	OCBinder
ocserver	184	TCP	UDP	OCServer
remote-kis	185	TCP	UDP	Remote-KIS
kis	186	TCP	UDP	KIS Protocol
aci	187	TCP	UDP	Application Communication Interface
mumps	188	TCP	UDP	Plus Five's MUMPS
qft	189	TCP		Queued File Transport
gacp	190	TCP	UDP	Gateway Access Control Protocol
prospero	191	TCP		Prospero Directory Service
osu-nms	192	TCP	UDP	OSU Network Monitoring System
srmp	193	TCP	UDP	Spider Remote Monitoring Protocol
irc	194		UDP	Internet Relay Chat Protocol
dn6-nlm-aud	195	TCP		DNSIX Network Level Module Audit
dn6-smm-red	196	TCP		DNSIX Session Mgt Module Audit Redir
dls	197	TCP	UDP	Directory Location Service
dls-mon	198	TCP	UDP	Directory Location Service Monitor
smux	199	TCP	UDP	SMUX
src	200	TCP	UDP	IBM System Resource Controller

Port Name	Port Number	TCP Port?	UDP Port?	Description (if known)
at-rtmp	201	TCP	UDP	AppleTalk Routing Maintenance
at-nbp	202	TCP	UDP	AppleTalk Name Binding
at-3	203	TCP	UDP	AppleTalk Unused
at-echo	204	TCP	UDP	AppleTalk Echo
at-5	205	TCP	UDP	AppleTalk Unused
at-zis	206	TCP	UDP	AppleTalk Zone Information
at-7	207	TCP	UDP	AppleTalk Unused
at-8	208	TCP	UDP	AppleTalk Unused
tam	209	TCP	UDP	Trivial Authenticated Mail Protocol
z39.50	210	TCP	UDP	ANSI Z39.50
914c/g	211	TCP	UDP	Texas Instruments 914C/G Terminal
anet	212	TCP	UDP	ATEXSSTR
ipx	213	TCP	UDP	IPX
vmpwscs	214	TCP	UDP	VM PWSCS
softpc	215	TCP	UDP	Insignia Solutions
atls	216	TCP		Access Technology License Server
dbase	217		UDP	dBASEUNIX
mpp	218	TCP	UDP	Netix Message Posting Protocol
uarps	219	TCP	UDP	Unisys ARPs
imap3	220	TCP		Interactive Mail Access Protocol v3
fln-spx	221	TCP	UDP	Berkeley rlogind with SPX auth
rsh-spx	222	TCP	UDP	Berkeley rshd with SPX auth

Port Name	Port Number	TCP Port?	UDP Port?	Description (if known)
cdc	223	TCP	UDP	Certificate Distribution Center
sur-meas	243	TCP	UDP	Survey Measurement
link	245	TCP	UDP	LINK
dsp3270	246	TCP	UDP	Display Systems Protocol
pdap	344	TCP		Prospero Data Access Protocol
pawserv	345	TCP	UDP	Perf Analysis Work-bench
zserv	346	TCP		Zebra server
fatserv	347	TCP		Fatmen Server
csi-sgwp	348	TCP	UDP	Cabletron Manage-ment Protocol
clearcase	371	TCP	UDP	Clearcase
ulistserv	372	TCP	UDP	Unix Listserv
legent-1	373	TCP	UDP	Legent Corporation
legent-2	374	TCP	UDP	Legent Corporation
hassle	375	TCP	UDP	Hassle
nip	376	TCP	UDP	Amiga Envoy Network Inquiry Proto
tnETOS	377	TCP	UDP	NEC Corporation
dsETOS	378	TCP	UDP	NEC Corporation
is99c	379	TCP		TIA/EIA/IS-99 modem client
is99s	380	TCP		TIA/EIA/IS-99 modem server
hp-collector	381	TCP	UDP	hp performance data collector
hp-managed-node	382	TCP	UDP	hp performance data managed node

Port Name	Port Number	TCP Port?	UDP Port?	Description (if known)
hp-alarm-mgr	383	TCP	UDP	hp performance data alarm manager
arns	384	TCP	UDP	A Remote Network Server System
ibm-app	385	TCP		IBM Application
asa	386	TCP	UDP	ASA Message Router Object Def.
aurp	387	TCP	UDP	AppleTalk Update-Based Routing Pro.
unidata-ldm	388	TCP	UDP	Unidata LDM Version 4
ldap	389	TCP		Lightweight Directory Access Protocol
uis	390	TCP	UDP	UIS
synotics-relay	391	TCP	UDP	SynOptics SNMP Relay Port
synotics-broker	392	TCP	UDP	SynOptics Port Broker Port
dis	393	TCP	UDP	Data Interpretation System
embl-ndt	394	TCP	UDP	EMBL Nucleic Data Transfer
netcp	395	TCP	UDP	NETscout Control Protocol
netware-ip	396	TCP	UDP	Novell NetWare over IP
mptn	397	TCP	UDP	Multi Protocol Trans. Net.
kryptolan	398	TCP	UDP	Kryptolan
iso-tsap-c2	399	TCP	UDP	ISO-TSAP Class 2
work-sol	400	TCP	UDP	Workstation Solutions
ups	401		UDP	Uninterruptible Power Supply
genie	402	TCP	UDP	Genie Protocol

Port Name	Port Number	TCP Port?	UDP Port?	Description (if known)
decap	403	TCP	UDP	decap
nced	404	TCP	UDP	nced
ncld	405	TCP	UDP	ncld
imsp	406	TCP	UDP	Interactive Mail Support Protocol
timbuktu	407	TCP		Timbuktu
prm-sm	408	TCP		Prospero Resource Manager Sys. Man.
prm-nm	409	TCP		Prospero Resource Manager Node Man.
decladebug	410		UDP	DECLadebug Remote Debug Protocol
rmt	411	TCP	UDP	Remote MT Protocol
synoptics-trap	412	TCP	UDP	Trap Convention Port
smsp	413	TCP	UDP	SMSP
infoseek	414	TCP	UDP	InfoSeek
bnet	415	TCP	UDP	BNet
silverplatter	416	TCP	UDP	Silverplatter
onmux	417	TCP	UDP	Onmux
hyper-g	418	TCP		Hyper-G
ariel 1	419	TCP		Ariel
smpte	420		UDP	SMPTE
ariel 2	421	TCP		Ariel
ariel 3	422	TCP		Ariel
opc-job-start	423	TCP		IBM Operations Planning and Control Start
opc-job-track	424	TCP		IBM Operations Planning and Control Track
icad-el	425	TCP		ICAD

Port Name	Port Number	TCP Port?	UDP Port?	Description (if known)
smartsdp	426	TCP	UDP	smartsdp
svrloc	427	TCP	UDP	Server Location
ocs_cmu	428	TCP	UDP	OCS_CMU
ocs_amu	429	TCP	UDP	OCS_AMU
utmpsd	430	TCP	UDP	UTMPSD
utmpcd	431	TCP	UDP	UTMPCD
iasd	432	TCP	UDP	IASD
nnsp	433	TCP	UDP	NNSP
mobileip-agent	434	TCP		MobileIP-Agent
mobilip-mn	435	TCP		MobilIP-MN
dna-cml	436	TCP	UDP	DNA-CML
comscm	437	TCP	UDP	comscm
dsfgw	438	TCP	UDP	dsfgw
dasp	439	TCP	UDP	dasp Thomas Obermair
sgcp	440	TCP	UDP	sgcp
decvms-sysmgt	441	TCP		decvms-sysmgt
cvc_hostd	442	TCP	UDP	cvc_hostd
https	443	TCP		https MCom
snpp	444	TCP	UDP	Simple Network Paging Protocol
microsoft-ds	445		UDP	Microsoft-DS
ddm-rdb	446	TCP	UDP	DDM-RDB
ddm-dfm	447	TCP	UDP	DDM-RFM
ddm-byte	448	TCP	UDP	DDM-BYTE
as-servermap	449	TCP	UDP	AS Server Mapper
tserver	450	TCP		TServer
sfs-smp-net	451	TCP	UDP	Cray Network Semaphore server
sfs-config	452	TCP	UDP	Cray SFS config server

Port Name	Port Number	TCP Port?	UDP Port?	Description (if known)
creativeserver	453	TCP	UDP	CreativeServer
contentserver	454	TCP	UDP	ContentServer
creativepartnr	455	TCP	UDP	CreativePartnr
macon-tcp	456	TCP	UDP	macon-tcp
scohelp	457	TCP	UDP	scohelp
appleqtc	458	TCP	UDP	Apple QuickTime
ampr-rcmd	459	TCP	UDP	ampr-rcmd
skronk	460	TCP	UDP	skronk
exec	512	TCP	UDP	Remote process execution
login	513	TCP	UDP	Remote login a la Telnet
who	513		UDP	Maintains data bases showing who's who
cmd	514	TCP	UDP	Like exec, but automatic
syslog	514		UDP	
printer	515	TCP	UDP	spooler
talk	517		UDP	
ntalk	518	TCP		
utime	519	TCP	UDP	unixtime
efs	520	TCP	UDP	Extended file name server
router	520		UDP	Local routing process (on site)
timed	525	TCP	UDP	Timeserver
tempo	526	TCP	UDP	Newdate
courier	530	TCP	UDP	rpc
conference	531	TCP	UDP	chat
netnews	532	TCP	UDP	readnews

Port Name	Port Number	TCP Port?	UDP Port?	Description (if known)
netwall	533	TCP	UDP	For emergency broadcasts
apertus-ldp	539	TCP	UDP	Apertus Technologies Load Determination
uucp	540	TCP		uucpd
uucp-rlogin	541	TCP	UDP	uucp-rlogin
klogin	543	TCP	UDP	
kshell	544	TCP	UDP	krcmd
appleqtcsrvr	545	TCP	UDP	appleqtcsrvr
new-rwho	550	TCP	UDP	new-who
dsf	555	TCP	UDP	
remotefs	556	TCP	UDP	rfs server
openvms-sysipc	557	TCP	UDP	openvms-sysipc
sdnskmp	558	TCP	UDP	SDNSKMP
teedtap	559	TCP	UDP	TEEDTAP
rmonitor	560	TCP	UDP	rmonitord
monitor	561	TCP	UDP	
chshell	562	TCP	UDP	chcmd
9pfs	564	TCP	UDP	plan 9 file service
whoami	565	TCP	UDP	whoami
meter	570	TCP	UDP	demon
meter	571	TCP	UDP	udemon
ipcserver	600	TCP	UDP	Sun IPC server
nqs	607	TCP	UDP	nqs
urm	606	TCP	UDP	Cray Unified Resource Manager
sift-uft	608	TCP		Sender-Initiated/ Unsolicited File Transfer
npmp-trap	609	TCP	UDP	npmp-trap
npmp-local	610	TCP	UDP	npmp-local

➡

Port Name	Port Number	TCP Port?	UDP Port?	Description (if known)
npmp-gui	611	TCP	UDP	npmp-gui
ginad	634	TCP	UDP	ginad
mdqs	666	TCP	UDP	
doom	666	TCP		doom Id Software
elcsd	704	TCP	UDP	errlog copy/server daemon
flexlm	744	TCP	UDP	Flexible License Manager
fujitsu-dev	747	TCP	UDP	Fujitsu Device Control
ris-cm	748	TCP	UDP	Russell Info Sci Calendar Manager
kerberos-adm	749	TCP		kerberos administration
rfile	750	TCP	UDP	
loadav	750		UDP	
pump	751	TCP	UDP	
qrh	752	TCP	UDP	
rrh	753	TCP	UDP	
tell	754	TCP	UDP	send
nlogin	758	TCP	UDP	
con	759	TCP	UDP	
ns	760	TCP	UDP	
rxe	761	TCP	UDP	
quotad	762	TCP	UDP	
cycleserv	763	TCP	UDP	
omserv	764	TCP	UDP	
webster	765	TCP	UDP	
phonebook	767	TCP	UDP	phone
vid	769	TCP	UDP	
cadlock	770	TCP	UDP	
rtip	771	TCP	UDP	

Port Name	Port Number	TCP Port?	UDP Port?	Description (if known)
cycleserv	772	TCP	UDP	
submit	773	TCP	UDP	
notify	773		UDP	
rpasswd	774	TCP	UDP	
acmaint_dbd	774		UDP	
entomb	775	TCP	UDP	
acmaint_transd	775		UDP	
wpages	776	TCP	UDP	
wpgs	780	TCP	UDP	
concert	786	TCP	UDP	Concert
mdbs_daemon	800	TCP	UDP	
device	801	TCP	UDP	
accessbuilder	888	TCP	UDP	AccessBuilder
xtreelic	996	TCP	UDP	Central Point Software
maitrd	997	TCP	UDP	
busboy	998	TCP	UDP	
puparp	998		UDP	
garcon	999	TCP	UDP	
applix	999		UDP	Applix ac
puprouter	999	TCP	UDP	
cadlock	1000	TCP	UDP	
ock	1000		UDP	
	1023	TCP		Reserved
	1024		UDP	Reserved

Index

V

W

X

Z

The Comprehensive Guide to VBScript
$39.99, 864 pages, illustrated, part #: 470-7

The only complete reference to VBScript and HTML commands and features. Plain-English explanations; A-to-Z listings; real-world, practical examples for plugging directly into programs; ActiveX tutorial. The CD-ROM features a hypertext version of the book, along with all code examples.

The Microsoft Merchant Server Book
$49.99, 600 pages, illustrated, part #: 610-6

Open the door to your online store! Now the long-awaited promise of retail sales is closer to fulfillment. From basic hardware considerations to complex technical and management issues, you'll find everything you need to create your site. Features case studies highlighting Microsoft Banner sites and a step-by-step guide to creating a working retail site. The CD-ROM features convenient customizing tools, Internet Information Server, Wallet, ActiveX SDK, Java SDK and more.

Build a Microsoft Intranet
$49.99, 624 pages, illustrated, part #: 498-7

Streamline your Intranet design using Microsoft's uniquely integrated tools. Plan, install, configure and manage your Intranet. And use other Microsoft products to author and browse web pages. Includes CD-ROM supporting and reference documents, pointers to Internet resources.

VENTANA

Java Programming for the Internet

$49.95, 816 pages, illustrated, part #: 355-7

Master the programming language of choice for
Internet applications. Expand the scope of your
online development with this comprehensive, step-
by-step guide to creating Java applets. The CD-ROM
features Java Developers Kit, source code for all the
applets, samples and programs from the book, and
much more.

The Visual Basic Programmer's Guide to Java

$39.99, 450 pages, part #: 527-4

At last—a Java book that speaks your language!
Use your understanding of Visual Basic as a
foundation for learning Java and object-oriented
programming. This unique guide not only relates
Java features to what you already know—it also
highlights the areas in which Java excels over
Visual Basic, to build an understanding of its
appropriate use. The CD-ROM features compara-
tive examples written in Java & Visual Basic, code
for projects created in the book and more

Net Security: Your Digital Doberman

$29.99, 400 pages, illustrated, part #: 506-1

Doing business on the Internet can be safe . . . if you know the risks and take appropriate steps. This thorough overview helps you put a virtual Web watchdog on the job—to protect both your company and your customers from hackers, electronic shoplifters and disgruntled employees. Easy-to-follow explanations help you understand complex security technologies, with proven technologies for safe Net transactions. Tips, checklists and action plans cover digital dollars, pilfer-proof "storefronts," protecting privacy and handling breaches.

Intranet Firewalls

$34.99, 282 pages, illustrated, part #: 506-1

Protect your network by controlling access—inside and outside your company—to proprietary files. This practical, hands-on guide takes you from intranet and firewall basics through creating and launching your firewall. Professional advice helps you assess your security needs and choose the best system for you. Includes tips for avoiding costly mistakes, firewall technologies, in-depth reviews and uses for popular firewall software, advanced theory of firewall design strategies and implementation, and more.

The Comprehensive Guide to Visual Basic 5

$49.99, 600 pages, illustrated, part #: 484-7

From the author of Ventana's bestselling *Visual Guide to Visual Basic for Windows*! Command and syntax descriptions feature real-world examples. Thoroughly covers new features, uses, backward compatibility and much more. The CD-ROM features a complete, searchable text version of the book including all code.

Visual C++ X Power Toolkit, Second Edition

$49.99, 800 pages, part #: 528-2

Completely updated to cover all new features in the latest version of Visual C++ — including graphics, animation, sound, connectivity and more. Class libraries, tutorials and techniques offer programmers a professional edge. The CD-ROM features fully compiled class libraries, demo programs and complete standards files for all major picture formats.

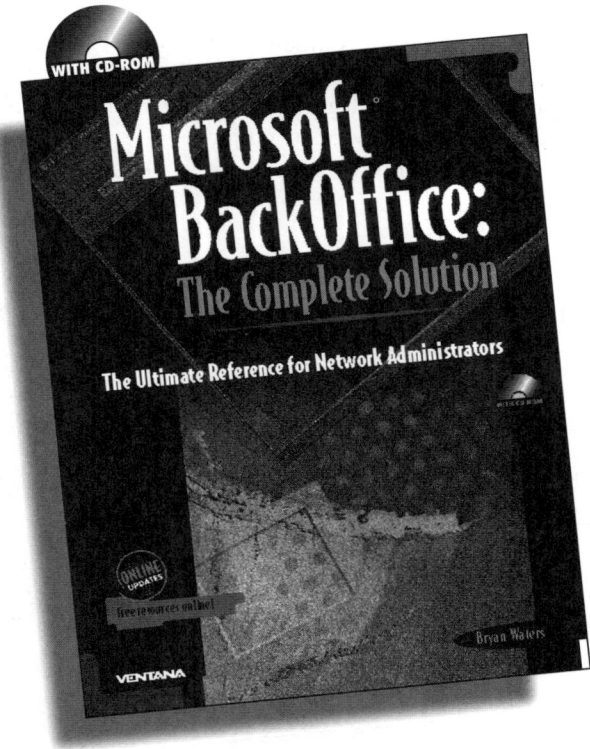

VENTANA

TO ORDER ANY VENTANA TITLE, COMPLETE THIS ORDER FORM AND MAIL OR FAX IT TO US, WITH PAYMENT, FOR QUICK SHIPMENT.

TITLE	PART #	QTY	PRICE	TOTAL

SHIPPING

For orders shipping within the United States, please add $4.95 for the first book, $1.50 for each additional book.
For "two-day air" add $7.95 for the first book, $3.00 for each additional book.
For orders shipping to Canada, please contact our Nelson Canada at 800/268-2222 to place your order:
For orders shipping outside the United States and Canada, phone 800/332-7450 or
Email: vorders@kdc.com for exact shipping charges.
Note: Please include your local sales tax.

SUBTOTAL = $ _____

SHIPPING = $ _____

TAX = $ _____

TOTAL = $ _____

Mail to: Media Group Customer Service • International Thomson Publishing • 7625 Empire Drive • Florence, KY 41042
☎ **800/332-7450 • fax 606/283-0718**

Name _____

E-mail _____ Daytime phone _____

Company _____

Address (No PO Box) _____

City_____ State_____ Zip_____

Payment enclosed ____VISA ____MC ____ Acc't # _____ Exp. date_____

Signature _____ Exact name on card _____

Check your local bookstore or software retailer for these and other bestselling titles, or call toll free:

800/332-7450

8:00 am - 6:00 pm EST